Africa
in
World History

From Prehistory to the Present

Second Edition

Erik Gilbert
Arkansas State University

Jonathan T. Reynolds
Northern Kentucky University

PEARSON
Prentice
Hall

Upper Saddle River, New Jersey 07458

Library of Congress Cataloging-in-Publication Data

Gilbert, Erik.
  Africa in world history : from prehistory to the present / Erik Gilbert,
Jonathan T. Reynolds.—2nd ed.
    p. cm.
  Rev. ed. of: Africa in world history / Jonathan T. Reynolds, Erik Gilbert.
  Includes bibliographical references and index.
  ISBN-13: 978-0-13-615438-9
  ISBN-10: 0-13-615438-7
  1. Africa—History. 2. Civilization, Western—African influences. I.
Reynolds, Jonathan T. II. Reynolds, Jonathan T. Africa in world history.
III. Title.
  DT20.R49 2008
  960—dc22
                                                    2007022591

Publisher: Charlyce Jones Owen
Executive Editor: Charles Cavaliere
Senior Assistant: Maureen Diana
Senior Managing Editor: Mary Carnis
Production Liaison: Louise Rothman
Operations Supervisor:
  Mary Ann Gloriande
Operations Specialist: Maura Zaldivar
Director of Marketing: Brandy Dawson
Marketing Manager: Kate Mitchell
Director, Image Resource Center: Melinda Reo
Manager, Visual Research: Beth Brenzel
Manager, Cover Visual Research & Permissions:
  Karen Sanatar

Image Permission Coordinator: Craig Jones
Cover Design: Bruce Kenselaar
Cover Illustration: Corrin Skidds
Inside Front Cover Map: How Big Is Africa's home
  site is www.bu.edu/africa/outreach where the
  map can be purchased and many other
  teaching resources on Africa can also be
  found. © Boston University.
Composition and Full Service Project Management:
  Patty Donovan/Pine Tree Composition, Inc.
Insert Printer: Phoenix Color Corporation
Printer/Binder: RR Donnelley/Harrisonburg
Cover Printer: RR Donnelley/Harrisonburg

Credits and acknowledgments borrowed from other sources and reproduced, with permission, in this textbook appear on appropriate page within text or on pages 437–438.

Pearson Education LTD.
Pearson Education Australia PTY, Limited
Pearson Education Singapore, Pte. Ltd
Pearson Education North Asia Ltd

Pearson Education, Canada, Ltd
Pearson Educaión de Mexico, S.A. de C.V.
Pearson Education–Japan
Pearson Education Malaysia, Pte. Ltd

10 9 8 7 6 5 4 3 2

ISBN-13: 978-0-13-615438-9
ISBN-10:   0-13-615438-7

*To Donna and Victoria, again,
with love and thanks.*

Contents

PART 2   AFRICA SINCE 1500 C.E.   137

Chapter 8   Slavery and the Creation of the Atlantic World   141

Chapter 9   West and West-Central Africa: 1500–1880   175

List of Maps

Special Features

Controversies in African History

Voices from African History

Foreword

Here is a fine volume that conveys the excitement and complexity of the African continent and the importance of its societies in the world. The book begins with a reminder that Africa is the ancestral home of us all, as shown by the geneticists and paleontologists who have now confirmed that societies of Homo sapiens emerged in Eastern Africa roughly 200,000 years ago. The long-term interplay of people—very much like ourselves—in the African homeland and the rest of the world remains as central to human history today as it was at the beginning.

Erik Gilbert and Jonathan Reynolds, two energetic and knowledgeable scholars, convey the results of their study and their experience in African life and history. When the first edition of this book appeared in 2004, crowds of scholars appeared at meetings of the African Studies Association in the United States, to welcome the book and debate its implications. Indeed, Gilbert and Reynolds summarize effectively the achievements of research in African Studies during the past fifty years.

Our understanding of world history has also expanded and changed greatly. In previous times, "the world" was thought to focus on the Classical Mediterranean and on European empires. Gilbert and Reynolds present a wider version, showing the global significance of African commerce, religious traditions, government, and artistic creativity. This volume goes beyond "filling in the gaps" in knowledge about Africa—it shows how Africans have reflected the full range of human patterns in land and society. It documents African connections and debates with each other and their contributions to the peopling and culture of Eurasia and the Americas.

The authors portray the African present as well as the past. Africans, after undergoing conquest by invading Europeans a century ago, began to regain political independence in the mid-twentieth century. At last count, over 50 nations of Africa and nearby islands hold seats at the United Nations.

Overall, Gilbert and Reynolds balance and link the eras, regions, and issues of the African past: from the early formation and developments of African societies through the eras of enslavement, racial discrimination, and colonial rule to the conflicts and achievements of the contemporary world of national states. This book, with its clear prose and good humor, will enable its readers to see African experience as representative of the world.

Patrick Manning
University of Pittsburgh

Preface

Notions of Africa

Always something new out of Africa (Greek Proverb Quoted by Pliny the Elder, first century C.E.)

[Africa] is no historical part of the world; it has no movement or development to exhibit. (George Hegel, *Lectures on the Philosophy of History*, early nineteenth century)

Africa has, for generations now, been viewed through a web of myth . . . only when the myth is stripped away can the reality of Africa emerge. (Paul Bohannan, *Africa and Africans*, 1964)

Perhaps, in the future, there will be some African history to teach. But at present there is none, or very little: there is only the history of the Europeans in Africa. The rest is largely darkness, like the history of pre-European, pre-Columbian America. . . . (Hugh Trevor-Roper, *The Rise of Christian Europe*, 1965)

[There is a] desire—one might say the need—in Western psychology to set Africa up as a foil to Europe, as a place of negations at once remote and vaguely familiar, in comparison with which Europe's own state of spiritual grace will be manifest. (Chinua Achebe, *Hopes and Impediments. Selected Essays 1965–1987*, 1988)

Far from being a kind of Museum of Barbarism whose populations had stayed outside the laws of human growth and change through some natural failing or inferiority, Africa is now seen to possess a history which demands as serious an approach as that of any other continent. (Basil Davidson, *Africa in History*, 1991)

For many students, *Africa in World History* and the course for which it was purchased will be your very first introduction to the *study* of Africa and Africans. We hope that the material presented in this text will be both surprising and challenging. Why? A simple glance at the preceding quotes should give you some insight into the answer to this question. The meaning of both Africa and African History is deeply contested—even more so than that of most world regions. This is in no small part a result of the historical agendas and biases that have influenced the way Africa has been represented. As typified in the quotes by Hegel and Trevor-Roper, for hundreds of years Western scholars openly discounted the idea that Africa even had a history that could be recorded and studied. Since the 1950s these views have been challenged by Africanists as typified by Bohannan, Achebe, and Davidson. These more modern views of African History have adamantly argued that Africans have a very real and dynamic history.

Perhaps you might not even be familiar with the various academic views listed above. Nonetheless, you have certainly been influenced by the way they have been manifested in more popular media. Most of us grow up unwittingly observing and accepting myriad myths about Africa. Many of the blatantly negative representations of Africa and Africans can be found in popular novels, magazines, films, and even television commercials. On the opposite end of the spectrum can be found notions of Africa that present a much more idealized perspective of the continent and its inhabitants. Indeed, there are many notions of Africa—sometimes mutually reinforcing and sometimes completely contradictory. Here are some that might be familiar.

Primitive Africa —As evidenced by some of the earlier quotes, there is a popular idea that Africa has somehow failed to "develop" along with the rest of the world. This might also be thought of as a "Static Africa," a place without change. In this view, simply by going to Africa one can travel back in time and view how people once lived in the "deep dark past." Have you ever heard of African societies described as "Ancient Tribes?" Ever thought of Africa as "Stone Age?" As a land without writing? All these elements are hallmarks of the "Primitive Africa" perspective.

Wild and Dangerous Africa —These are among the most common images of Africa presented by the media. This Africa seems to be either an impenetrable jungle or a vast and trackless desert. The inhabitants are either wild animals or wild people—both untamed and dangerous. When you think of Africa, do you see images of charging rhinos? Of lions? As a place where at every turn vicious animals or mysterious diseases wait to attack? Do you think of Africa as a land constantly at war and where everyone seems to own an assault rifle or grenade launcher? If so, then you have been influenced by this particular notion of Africa.

Exotic Africa —Another popular favorite. This notion of Africa stresses the differences between Africans and other human societies—especially Western civilization. In this Africa, people are either naked, covered in fanciful designs, or clothed in bizarre and outlandish outfits. Further, in Exotic Africa everyone seems to spend their time in the practice of lavish ceremonies, and people have superstitions instead of religion. For an example of Exotic Africa, just leaf through a few copies of *National Geographic*. Notably, this version of Africa seems to be dominated by a group known as the Masai. Because the Masai do actually wear some pretty impressive outfits and still occasionally carry spears (something the vast majority of modern Africans would feel very silly doing), they seem to fit the notion of Africans as exotic. As such, they find their way into television commercials, travel pamphlets, and coffee table books of African photography. The 1998 *Sports Illustrated* swimsuit edition even featured the Masai as a backdrop for supermodels in bikinis. You can't get much more exotic than that.

Unspoiled Africa —This perspective represents a very different interpretation of the core aspects of both "Primitive" and "Wild and Dangerous Africa." Here, the idea is that Africa has avoided progress and, as a result, has remained pure and untainted by the evils of the modern world. Here is an Africa that is undamaged by human exploitation of natural resources and where people are free of greed and conflict. Here Africa is still seen as being outside history, but from this perspective that is a good thing. The portrayal of the KhoiSan ("Bushmen") in the movie *The Gods Must Be Crazy* or any number of nature shows set in Africa are examples of this perspective.

Utopian Africa —This is a notion of Africa that stands somewhat apart, although it shares some elements with Unspoiled Africa. Quite opposed (consciously or unconsciously) to the largely negative images that dominate popular ideas of Africa, this perspective presents an idealized Africa. Here Africa was (if not is) the abode of egalitarian societies living in harmony. This Africa is often defined as a homeland for members of the African diaspora, and as a place in which they can be free of the racism and oppression that all too often defines the world of those whose ancestors were forcibly removed from the continent. In such an Africa, any conflict or suffering is the result of the destruction of African culture and unity—usually by outside forces.

Broken Africa —This is perhaps the most contemporary version of Africa. Here is an Africa in which nothing works. "Broken Africa" is a land of decay, sickness, and starvation. Attempts at economic, social, or political development are doomed to failure. The causes of this decay are legion. They could be attributed to African culture, to the slave trade, to Neo-Colonialism, or to the African environment. This "Broken Africa" can either be presented as a source of amusement, such as in travelogues like the book *Malaria Dreams,* or as a source of resignation. For example, in September of 1994 the *Washington Post* ran a special section entitled, "Is Africa Falling Apart?" This story featured a full-page image of buildings being destroyed by encroaching vines, a non-too-subtle representation of civilization defeated by "Wild and Savage Africa." Many Africanists refer to the "Broken Africa" model as "Afro-Pessimism"— the idea that there is no hope for Africa.

Notably, not everything about these various notions of Africa is completely wrong. Indeed, anyone who wanted to find some sort of evidence for each perspective could do so. There are, after all, rhinos and lions in Africa, though most Africans have never seen either. Similarly, there are Masai in Africa (even if they make up far less than 1 percent of the continent's population). Further, contemporary Africa faces very real challenges—there is no denying that poverty and conflict are a reality for all too many modern Africans. Yet, it does a disservice to Africa and

Africans to represent the entire continent via any single characteristic. Indeed, these various notions did not simply materialize out of thin air. Most are the products of very real agendas—whether social or political, past or present.

Where then, does *Africa in World History* fit? We the authors do indeed have agendas of our own (if your instructors haven't already told you, everyone who writes has an agenda). First, as Africanists, we very much believe that there is a very real history to Africa. As historians, we believe that the key to better and more accurately understanding modern Africa is to better understand that history. Sources for the reconstruction and study of a textured and multi-faceted African history abound, and they reveal a continent that has been and is ever changing and vibrant. In terms of the tone of this text, we hope to neither unwarrantedly acclaim nor condemn the history of Africa. Like all regions of the world, Africa's past and present are full of goodness and evil, of great achievements and great failures. Our goal is to present the history of Africa in all its diversity and dynamism. Indeed, we hope to present no single image of Africa—the job of the historian is often to show that things are complex, rather than simple. In so doing, we seek to undermine each of the notions of Africa discussed earlier. More so, we will continuously stress the fact that history is about controversy. As such, we will often discuss the opposing viewpoints of different historians of how to interpret historical evidence and how to explain historical events that took place in Africa.

Finally, we hope to show that not only is there a vibrant and fascinating history that is unique to Africa, but also that Africa has played an important role in world history as well. One of the remarkable aspects of the extremes of anti- and pro-African scholarship is how they have both stressed the isolation of Africa from the rest of the world. It is our hope to show that Africa and Africans have long played a role in world history, both influencing and being influenced by other regions and peoples of the world. Indeed, it is one of our central goals to show that modern Africa is very much a creation of long-running global forces and themes. We are earnest in our belief that to better understand African history is to better understand world history. Though far from complete in its presentation of African history, we hope this text will provide enough ideas and information to do both.

Erik Gilbert and Jonathan Reynolds

Changes to the Second Edition

The Nigerian novelist Chinua Achebe once said that one's books are like one's children, and he therefore refused to indicate which of his books was his favorite. Books are different than children, however, in that they are subject to modification and revision. As much as we loved *Africa in World History*, soon after its parturition we noticed its flaws. Some of these were minor. We had, for example, transposed a prominent nationalist politician from one side of the continent to the other. Others had to do with more fundamental questions of organization and interpretation.

Responding to our own concerns about the book, and the criticism of others, we have reorganized the first half of the book. The former chapters 2 and 4 have been modified into two new chapters 2 and 3. This was partly a response to concerns about continuity but also allowed us to incorporate lots of new evidence, some linguistic and some genetic, about African pre-history. Chapter 1 has also been substantially rewritten both to take into account new evidence about human evolution and to focus more squarely on the debates concerning the details of human evolution in Africa. Other chapters have been rewritten in less dramatic ways, mostly to correct minor errors or to change their emphasis or tone.

Perhaps the most visible change in the second editon is that we have dramatically increased the number, and we hope the quality, of the maps and images in the book. We have added a second color section and included more commentary on each of the images. The result is that we now have two photo essays, one of which offers a graphic extension of the "Notions of Africa" section that begins the book. This first photo essay, "Imagining Africa," looks at the way various ideas about Africa are represented visually. The second photo essay, "Crossing the Borders of African and World History," offers visual examples of the type of world historical connections that are a major theme of the text. We have also increased the number of special features in the text, so that each chapter now has either a "Controversies in African History" or "Voices from African History" selection.

Despite the shortcomings of the first edition, we still view it with parental pride. It came out just as the question of Africa's place in the global history narrative was becoming a hot topic. Since its publication, the African Studies Association has considered the topic at its annual meeting. The World History Association has done likewise. There have been journal issues dedicated to the topic, workshops for teachers, and debates on H-Africa and H-World (the African and World history listservs). We are not under the illusion that *Africa in Would History* triggered this debate, but we do think that it made a contribution to that debate. Above all, we hope that it helped draw the attention of teachers of both African and World history to the existence of this debate and gave them the means to globalize their teaching of Africa and to Africanize their teaching of the world.

We would like to thank the reviewers of this second edition: Katherine Sadler, Clark College; John David Leaver, Armstrong Atlantic State University; Arthur Abraham, Virginia State University; and Maxim Matusevich, Seton Hall University. Tim Carmichael at the College of Charleston, provided a helpful critique of the project in its late stages and Katie Janssen provided very helpful editorial assistance. We also wish to thank our editor, Charles Cavaliere, who has been supportive and patient, stoic even, throughout the process of revising the book.

Jonathan extends his thanks to his department chair, Professor Jeffrey Williams, for unflagging support and tolerance. Also, a special thanks goes to Dr. Kristin Stapleton at SUNY Buffalo and Yufeng Mao at George Washington University. Erik would like to thank his department chair, Pam Hronek, for allowing the time needed to finish the project. Additional thanks to James Quirin of Fisk University and Emmanuel Mbah of CUNY college of Staten Island.

About the Authors

ERIK GILBERT

Erik Gilbert is Professor of History at Arkansas State University, where he teaches African history and world history, and other things as needed. He holds a B.A. from the College of William and Mary, an M.A. from the University of Vermont, and a Ph.D. from Boston University. His research has focused on nineteenth and twentieth century Zanzibar and its relationship to the western Indian Ocean world. He is the author of *Dhows and the Colonial Economy of Zanzibar* (2004) and, with Jonathan Reynolds, *Trading Tastes: Commodity and Cultural Exchange to 1750* (2006). His interest in African history was triggered by a childhood spent in the West African countries of Ghana, Nigeria, and Cameroun. He has since done research in Tanzania, Kenya, Yemen, Oman, and Massachusetts.

JONATHAN T. REYNOLDS

A hopeless generalist as an undergraduate, Jonathan graduated from the University of Tennessee in 1988 with majors in Honors History, Anthropology, and Ancient Mediterranean Civilizations. He also worked as Site Anthropologist and Camp Manager for the Kavousi Excavations on Crete during the summer excavation seasons from 1987–1989. He completed his Ph.D. in African History at Boston University in 1995. A specialist in West Africa and Islam, he has traveled and researched extensively in the region—including an ill-fated attempt at driving across the Sahara Desert in a British Rally Car in 1994. His research has been supported by the Fulbright Foundation, the West African Research Association, and Northern Kentucky University. In addition to publications on West African History, he has written extensively on the subject of Africa in World History, and has published *Trading Tastes: Commodity and Cultural Exchange to 1750* (Prentice Hall 2006) with perennial co-author Erik Gilbert. He has taught at Bayero University (Nigeria), The University of Tennessee, Livingstone College (where he received the Abna Aggrey Lancaster Award of Excellence in Teaching in 1998), and Northern Kentucky University (where he was named Outstanding Junior Faculty) in 2001. In 2005, he was elected to the Executive Board of the World History Association. Dr. Reynolds currently holds the rank of Associate Professor of History.

Part 1

Africa up to 1500 C.E.

One of the historian's most challenging jobs is to break history up into manageable units of analysis. Because it would be impossible to simply write the history of the continent from start to finish as a single narrative, a survey of African history necessitates a system of organization by which the authors break the material down into bite-size pieces, which the reader can digest without getting a bad case of intellectual indigestion. Typically, the units utilized are those of time (periodization), space (geographical units), or frameworks of historical causation (thematic). *Africa in World History* is no exception. On the macroscale, this text is organized into two parts. Part 1 covers the history of the continent up to about 1500 C.E. Part 2 covers the history of Africa since that time. Here we will discuss our rationale for organizing Part 1 the way we did.

If you glance through the first seven chapters of *Africa in World History*, you will see that the first section of the book follows a thematic approach, and also one that is often further subdivided by geographical units and periods of time. This organization reflects what we see as the complexity of the early African historical experience. That is, prior to 1500 C.E., African history is characterized by diversity. Very different things were occurring in different parts of the continent at different times and with different outcomes. For example, due to environmental factors, sedentary agriculture and state-level societies developed thousands of years earlier in the Nile Valley than they did in southern Africa, leading to divergent cultural and societal developments at these two geographical extremes of the continent. Similarly, northern and eastern Africa's relative ease of interaction with other world regions (via seaborne transport and overland routes) led to much greater cultural and economic exchange than that experienced by the forest regions of west and west-central Africa or southern Africa. Indeed, rather than speak of a single "African history" during the period prior to 1500, perhaps it is much more logical to speak of many shifting African histories.

In recognizing the diversity of early African history, however, it is important to keep an open mind on what very different parts of Africa, nonetheless, maintained in common. No intellectual border of time, space, or theme is absolute, and though we have tried very hard to choose chapter topics that illustrate important grand narratives of early African history, keep in mind that they are in many ways artificial—they are modern frameworks created by historians. Thus, although northern and eastern Africa might have had considerable interaction with other parts of the world, they were still very much in contact with both near and distant regions of Africa via trade and migration. Therefore, there is very much an internal dynamic to African history—one that places an African stamp even on those cultural elements and forces that come from without. All borders are permeable to history, whether they be those constructed by historians or the very outline of a continent.

MASTER TIMELINE: AFRICA TO 1500 C.E.

25,000–10,000 B.C.E.—Rock paintings in North Africa, Sahara, and southern Africa

10,000 B.C.E.—Beginnings of agriculture

5000 B.C.E.—Sedentary farming communities along Nile Valley and in Ethiopia

4000 B.C.E.—Earliest possible date for beginnings of Bantu migrations

3600 B.C.E.—Complex settlements at Nagada and Hierakonpolis in Upper Nile region

3100 B.C.E.—Narmer/Menes unifies Nile Valley in Egypt via conquest

3100–2575 B.C.E.—Archaic Period of Ancient Egypt

2700 B.C.E.—Origins of complex settlements in Nubia (Gash Culture)

2575–2180 B.C.E.—Old Kingdom of Ancient Egypt (time of pyramid building)

2400 B.C.E.—Rise of state of Kerma in Nubia

2180–2040 B.C.E.—First Intermediate Period (collapse of centralized authority in Egypt)

2040–mid-seventeenth century B.C.E.—Middle Kingdom period of Ancient Egypt

2000 B.C.E.—Origins of Nok culture in central Nigeria

1530–1070 B.C.E.—New Kingdom period of Ancient Egypt

1070–332 B.C.E.—Late Period of Ancient Egypt

1000 B.C.E.—Rise of state of Kush in Nubia

1000 B.C.E.—Possible innovation of iron-smelting technology in East African lakes region

1000–500 B.C.E.—Origins of ironworking in West Africa

1000 B.C.E.—Carthage founded as Phoenician Colony

730 B.C.E.—Kushan conquest of Egypt

700 B.C.E.—Ethio–Sabean states in Horn of Africa and Ethiopia

663 B.C.E.—Assyrian conquest of Egypt

591 B.C.E.—Rise of state of Meroë in Nubia

332 B.C.E.—Alexander the Great's army invades Egypt

264–146 B.C.E.—"Punic Wars" between Carthage and Rome

21 B.C.E.—Roman conquest of Egypt

0 C.E.—Arrival of bananas in East Africa

41 C.E.—Apostle Mark arrives in Egypt

100 C.E.—Rise of state of Aksum in Ethiopian highlands

300 C.E.—Rise of state of Ghana in West African Savannah

330 C.E.—Conversion of King Ezana of Axum to Christianity

350 C.E.—Advent of Arian Christianity in Egypt

429 C.E.—Vandal invasion of North Africa

639–642 C.E.—Islamic conquest of Egypt

651 C.E.—Islamic army defeated by Christian Nubians at Dongala

700 C.E.—Beginnings of Swahili "Stone Towns"

900 C.E.—Bronze castings at Igbo–Ukwu in southern Nigeria

969 C.E.—Fatimid conquest of Egypt

1076 C.E.—War between Ghana and Almoravids

1100 C.E.—Rise of Kingdom of Benin in West African forest region

1137 C.E.—Zagwe Dynasty established in Ethiopia

1171 C.E.—Salah al–Din overthrows Fatimids and establishes Ayyubid Dynasty in Egypt

1200 C.E.—Rise of state of Great Zimbabwe

Thirteenth century—Building of Lalibela churches in Ethiopia

1230 C.E.—Sundiata defeats Soumaro at battle of Krina; birth of Ancient Mali

1250 C.E.—Mamluks seize power in Egypt

1270 C.E.—Solomnids overthrow Zagwe Dynasty in Ethiopia

1324–1325 C.E.—Hajj of Mansa Musa

1331 C.E.—Ibn Battuta visits Swahili Coast

1352 C.E.—Ibn Battuta travels to West African Savannah

1434 C.E.—"Doubling" of Cape Bojador

1453 C.E.—Ottomans capture Constantinople

1460–1470s C.E.—Expansion of Songhai Empire

1471 C.E.—Portuguese establish trading center at El Mina

1484 C.E.—Congo and Portugal exchange embassies

1485 C.E.—Diaz rounds Cape of Good Hope

1491 C.E.—King Njinga of Congo converts to Christianity

1492 C.E.—Columbus reaches Carribean Islands

1497 C.E.—Da Gama visits Swahili Coast and India

CHAPTER 1

Africa and Human Origins

When, exactly, does history begin? Put another way, when does it become the business of historians to talk about the past? For a long time, historians only dealt with societies that left a written record. Times and places without a written record were left to archaeologists—scholars who specialize in retrieving and analyzing the physical record left behind by human groups and societies. Another group of scholars, paleontologists, examines the actual remains of living organisms in the form of fossils. African historians take pride in their interdisciplinary approach to history. That is, we are willing to use any form of evidence that tells us about what happened in the African past. For the subject of this chapter—human origins, evolution, and diffusion—the work of archaeologists and paleontologists is critical, for we are dealing with a historical scope that covers millions of years, long, long before anything was written down. As you will see, Africa is almost certainly the part of the world where most or even all of the critical stages of human evolution took place. In this chapter we will examine how the human species evolved, both in terms of physical changes and also the development of culture—for it is as much what humans do as what we are that makes us different from other living things. However, we will also examine how our understanding of such things has changed over time, and how different characterizations of Africa's place in human evolution have reflected widely divergent perspectives on humanity in general and Africans in particular. As we shall see, how people have understood human history has all too often been deeply influenced by the conception of "race."

Early Perspectives on Human Origins and the Notion of Race

The fact that people living in different places varied in physical appearance was no secret to most pre-modern societies. Particularly in regions where long-distance trade played an important role in people's economic lives, there was considerable awareness of the degree to which different communities varied in terms of skin color or other physical features. However, it is important to note that awareness of such variations did not necessarily mean that these differences were given any sort of special "meaning." Rather, physical differences were often simply recognized as being no more or less significant than any other differences, such as those of language, dress, or religion. Certainly, these various categories could be used to distinguish and even denigrate other peoples. It is, after all, hardly uncommon for human societies to think of their own way of living as somehow better than everybody else's. But there is no clear indication that most, if any, pre-modern peoples thought that physical differences were what *determined* other characteristics. That is, none seemed to believe that certain physical or intellectual characteristics were not only fixed, but in turn determined the culture and behavior of the people who possessed them.

The belief that certain sets of physical characteristics, what are now often categorized as "races," were linked to certain systems of cultural behavior or even intelligence and morality seems to have developed fairly recently in world history. Not until perhaps the eighteenth century did such ideas become influential, apparently taking shape first in Western Europe. This situation may well reflect the growing influence of the Atlantic slave trade on European economies during this time, a topic which we will address in greater detail in Chapter 8. Initially, explanations of race in Europe were built largely upon religious foundations. Such explanations of race had to deal with the description of human creation in Genesis, which stated that all humans were descended from Adam and Eve, and which made the presence of different "races" rather mysterious. In answer to this quandary, some scholars suggested that different races were the descendants of Noah's various sons, with the associated argument that the descendants of Ham (who was cursed by his father) were destined to be slaves. Not surprisingly, the group identified as "Hamitic" tended to change, depending on who was likely to be enslaved at the time. Others argued that sin led to physical deformity, and that racial differences (that is, those not associated with Europeans) were thus a result of spiritual distance from God. Still others argued for *polygenesis*, the idea that there actually had been many creations of different peoples in many Edens (and perhaps as a result God frowned upon their intermixing). All of these explanations contained a degree of *racism*—a suggestion that certain races were naturally more or less better than the others. The Western Europeans who held such ideas increasingly tended to see themselves as the "best" of the races not only in terms of sanctity, but also in terms of morality and even physical beauty.

Evolutionary Perspectives on Human Origins

During the Scientific Revolution of the seventeenth and eighteenth centuries, at the same time that the notion of race seems to have been taking shape, scholars in Western Europe were also beginning to establish systems of taxonomy that grouped all living things into categories based upon shared physical characteristics. Foremost among these scholars was Carl Linnaeus, a Swedish biologist for whom the system of Linnaean Taxonomy now used by almost all biologists is named. Linnaeus was one of the first scholars to suggest that human beings were actually related to

the great apes and other primates. Interestingly, Linnaeus was both aware of the
theological implications of his conclusions and troubled by them himself, as he
wrote in 1747:

> It is not pleasing to me that I must place humans among the primates, but . . . it will
> be the same to me whatever name is applied. But I desperately seek from you and
> from the whole world a general difference between men and simians from the prin-
> ciples of Natural History. I certainly know of none. If only someone might tell me
> one! If I called man a simian or vice versa I would bring together all the theologians
> against me.

Such questions as those raised by Linnaeus remained largely a private matter
among scholars and theologians for a little over 100 years. In 1856, however, workers in a German quarry uncovered the remains of a skeleton that they could not
identify. Eventually named "Neanderthal," the remains became the focus of a major
scientific and theological debate, with some early scholars arguing that the skeleton
represented an "intermediate" link between humans and apes. With the discovery
of an increasingly vast number of fossils of other extinct species during the late
1800s, the scientific community began to debate the possibility that the nature of
life on Earth had changed considerably over time. Likely, it was the publication of
Charles Darwin's *On the Origin of Species* in 1859 that best represented the changing
perspective of many scholars toward the history of life on Earth. Rather than a fixed
number of creatures created at some single point in time, there seemed instead to
be increasing evidence that the earth had been home to a whole host of species that
had changed, diverged, and developed over a time span measured in millions,
rather than thousands, of years. These ideas were later applied to human origins by
Thomas Huxley in his book *Evidence as to Man's Place in Nature* (1863) and by Darwin in *The Descent of Man* (1871).

The advent of a more scientific perspective on human origins did little, if anything, to lessen the degree of racism that seemed inherent to discussions of human
origins and diversity. Indeed, it may well have made things worse. Over the course
of the second half of the nineteenth century and into the early twentieth century, a
number of scientists devoted their careers to establishing a clear hierarchy of racial
superiority. Using techniques ranging from measuring the size and shape of skulls
("Craniometrics") to the weighing of brains, these scholars sought to provide
"objective" scientific evidence of the superiority of European populations over all
others. These ideas were often used to justify racial segregation, the denial of rights,
and even the extension of European (and later Japanese) colonial rule over "inferior" races. Some even went so far as to argue that Europeans ("whites") and
Africans ("blacks") were distinct species, not just physical variants within a common
human population. Significantly, these ideas also had historical implications, as
some scholars sought to prove that only "whites" were capable of creating civilized
societies. Thus, by implication, groups such as the ancient Egyptians had to have
been "white." Often now dismissed as "pseudo-scientific racism," these works were
nonetheless once considered cutting-edge research. Perhaps the most notorious
evil wrought by these beliefs was the rise of Fascism and the Nazi Holocaust, but it is

important to recognize that these ideas played a significant role even in otherwise democratic societies, resulting in the denial of many peoples' basic humanity and the oppression of millions.

Evolutionary Perspectives to the 1980s

Despite the evils of scientific racism, over the course of the early twentieth century an increasingly complex picture of the development of the human species began to take shape—giving birth to the field of Paleoanthropology in the process. New finds, such the "Taung Child" discovered in South Africa in 1924, suggested that the evolution of modern humans could be traced back over millions of years, with the earliest human ancestors originating in Africa. Over the twentieth century a number of fossils were found that apparently belonged to human ancestors, and by the late 1980s, paleontologists believed they had a fairly clear sequence of human evolutionary development worked out, with each stage looking more and more like modern humans.

The earliest of these apparent human ancestors were specimens called *Australopithecus afarensis,* which were found in southern and eastern Africa. While *A. afrarensis* did not appear to have brains significantly larger than those of the great apes, they were nonetheless upright bipeds, and, in combination with certain dental characteristics, were seen as likely human ancestors. "Lucy," discovered in 1974 at Hadar, Ethiopia, is probably among the most famous examples of this set of fossils. *A. Afarensis* was followed by *Australopithecus africanus,* of which the Taung Child was an example. *A. africanus* was notable in that these specimens had somewhat larger brains, with some fossils revealing cranial capacities as large as 600 cubic centimeters. Both species were thought to have existed largely in southern and eastern Africa, and to have predominated from roughly 4.3 million to 2.3 million years ago. Notably, there were significant variations in size and shape for the *A. africanus* fossil, and paleoanthropologists have debated extensively as to whether these represented a different genus altogether, or perhaps reflected a difference between males and females of the species. Others suggested that the diversity of *A. africanus* was a matter of adaptation to different diets.

The next stage in human evolution identified by latter-twentieth-century paleoanthropologists was that of *Homo habilis* (handy man), which is significant in that it was the earliest human ancestor first to be termed **Homo,** meaning "Human." *H. habilis* fossils date from roughly 2.5 to 1.5 million years ago, and have been found largely in eastern and southern Africa. The species itself was characterized by an increased cranial capacity of 600 to 700 cc—a significant increase over previous human ancestors. *H. habilis* likely also looked much more like modern humans, with a shorter and flatter face, and jaws less adapted to heavy chewing. Finally, as the name implies, *H. habilis* is also associated with tool use (though some scholars believe that Australopithecines also used basic tools) in the form of what are known as "Oldowan" choppers and flake tools. Such tools could have been used to dismember game and perhaps fight off predators. It is likely that the expanded brain capacity of *H. habilis* led to changes in social behavior, allowing groups of *H. habilis* to coordinate various activities in new and sophisticated ways.

The next stage in human evolution identified by scholars in the mid- to late twentieth century was known as *Homo erectus,* or "Upright Man." The dates for *H. erectus* have long been debated, but this new variety of human likely emerged about 1.6 million years ago, and may have survived in some regions of Asia until as recently as 27,000 years ago. *H. erectus* was different from *H. habilis* in significant ways. Indeed, from the neck down, *H. erectus* had almost exactly the same physique as modern humans, with an upright posture completely adapted to life on the ground. Some fossil specimens are estimated to have been as much as six feet tall. While *H. erectus'* cranial morphology exhibited some nonmodern features (such as very heavy brow ridges), they had a brain size of around 1,000 cc. While still roughly one-third smaller than the average cranial capacity of modern humans, this was a significant increase over *H. habilis,* which suggests that early humans were gaining the intelligence necessary to more successfully control their environment via tool use and culture. The unstable climate of the Pleistocene era, during which time *H. erectus* lived, was likely a driving force behind the selection of traits that would allow an organism to adapt to many (or changing) climates.

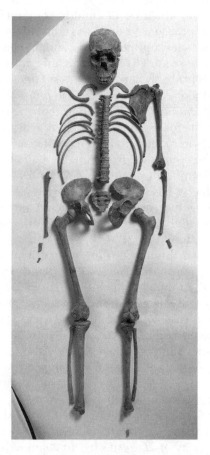

Homo erectus fossil from Turkana, Ethiopia.

The material artifacts found at *H. erectus* archaeological sites certainly show that *H. erectus* was capable of some very significant innovations. In the area of stone tools, for example, *H. erectus* is associated with the development of "**Acheulean**" hand axes. These tools were not only more effective at cutting and chopping game, but they also made more effective use of raw materials, showing that *H. erectus* was capable of doing more with the resources available. The presence of charcoal at some *H. erectus* sites suggests that perhaps as early two million years ago these human ancestors had learned how to use (if not make) fire. Some paleontologists believe that *H. erectus* was also capable of some degree of complex language, allowing for much more sophisticated forms of social interaction and group cooperation.

Paleontologists of the 1980s also agreed that *H. erectus* did something quite remarkable. *Homo erectus* expanded out of their native environment in eastern and southern Africa, and ventured outward into other regions—not just other parts of Africa, but into Asia and eventually Europe. Very few living creatures are capable of moving to different environments. Species generally evolve and adapt to exploit a very particular set of resources. A polar bear, for example, would not willingly set off for Mexico. *H. erectus* was the first human ancestor to show the unique human ability to handle radically new environments via technology and culture. Humans could thus adapt to a new environment in only a few generations, rather than waiting for natural selection to provide suitable physical adaptations (which can take thousands or even millions of years).

Why would *H. erectus* leave their place of origin in Africa? Scholars debate whether the motivation was one of necessity (brought on by forces such as climatic change or population pressure) or an early manifestation of the human desire to explore. Whatever the case, by one million years ago, it is clear that *H. erectus* had successfully expanded their range into much of Asia. The earliest dates for *H. erectus* in Europe are estimated at around 800,000 years ago. The spread of *H. erectus* over such a large area led to some interesting variations, as well. Acheulean hand-axe technology, for example, is found frequently in Africa and Europe, but is not well represented in Asia. Conversely, *H. erectus* in Asia seemed to have a much better knack for using fire.

Prior to the 1990s it was widely believed by paleontologists that after the migration of *H. erectus* out of Africa, populations in Africa, Asia, Australasia, and Europe evolved in relative isolation from one another, each eventually developing into modern humans, but also evidencing the sort of variations in skin color and physical appearance that are generally referred to as "racial characteristics." This theory is often referred to as the "Multiregional Model." From this perspective, modern racial differences can be traced back nearly one million years. Further, this particular perspective on evolution argued that human populations in Europe passed through an additional stage, that of Neanderthals, before the eventual development of "modern" humans. Neanderthals were notable in that they were different from modern humans in some fairly obvious ways (having very heavy brow ridges and heavier dentition, for example), but their brain sizes were comparable to those of modern humans. This early development of a large-brained variety of early humans in Europe and around the Mediterranean (where Neanderthal fossils have been found) led some scholars to attribute such early developments to what they saw as the "racial superiority" of European populations. Not surprisingly, many of the old charts showing stages of human evolution ended with a decidedly European-looking representative of "modern humanity."

New Perspectives and Debates since the 1980s

Beginning in the 1980s, a host of new fossil finds, the refinement of dating techniques, and the development of new forms of genetic analysis resulted in extensive debates and broad reappraisals of the nature of human evolution. Indeed, the rate of new discoveries and the flood of new information has been so great that most scholars now admit that they are incapable of providing a "clear progression" of human evolution. Many specialists now joke that the human family tree has turned out to be a "family bush," as new finds such as that of *Sahelanthropus tchadensis* (found in Chad in 2001) and *Homo floriensis* (found in Indonesia in 2003) have thrown considerable doubt upon the previous linear model of human development. Rather, it is increasingly apparent that there were perhaps times when there were several possible species of human ancestors living in different parts of Africa. Specialists point out that such discoveries do not disprove the evolutionary model, but rather show just how active the process of selection and adaptation was for our human ancestors.

Perhaps the most significant reappraisal in human evolution has come as a result of new genetic and archaeological discoveries. In 1987, a group of biochemists undertook an analysis of Mitochondrial DNA (mtDNA) from a selection of women from all over the world. MtDNA is unusual in that it is passed down from mothers to children without any alteration, thus allowing a unique insight into

A stereotypical perspective of human evolution, with a European male at the peak of genetic progress.

human ancestry. The analysis of these mtDNA samples showed that all human populations share an incredibly close genetic relationship—among the closest of all mammalian populations. Further, the study showed the greatest variation in mtDNA among African populations, suggesting that humans have lived longest in that part of the world. Indeed, in what is often called the "African Eve" thesis, these biochemists theorized that all modern humans could trace their ancestry to a single African female, who lived perhaps 150,000 years ago.

Since the original mtDNA analysis, a number of genetic studies, including some examining the male Y chromosome, have reinforced the notion of a fairly recent (in evolutionary terms) development of modern humans in Africa. Further, analysis of Neanderthal DNA has suggested that Neanderthals were so genetically different from other human populations that they cannot be considered human ancestors, but must rather be seen as an evolutionary "dead end." Finally, and perhaps most significant, was the discovery of anatomically modern humans dating to around 160,000 years ago in Ethiopia. Known as *Homo sapiens idaltu*, these fossils represent the first known appearance of modern humans anywhere in the world. Similarly, the discovery of what are considered "modern" tool types (including polished spear points and artwork in the form of incised ochre blocks) dated to 70,000 years ago in Blombos Cave, South Africa, have further reinforced the notion of a first appearance of modern humans in Africa.

The combined weight of these new discoveries has led many scholars to question the Multiregional Hypothesis and embrace what is often called the "Out of Africa" model, which posits that modern humans developed first in Africa, perhaps around 180,000 years ago. Then, perhaps as early as 100,000 years ago, human populations first moved out of Africa across the *Bab el-Mandeb* (the narrow gap at the mouth of the Red Sea) and generally worked their way eastwards—likely first moving along the tropical coastline of southern Eurasia. It was not until some 40,000 years later that human populations first moved into Western Eurasia (Europe). Notably, some academics argue that these two movements represent two different waves of migration out of Africa, a factor that may account for some genetic differences found in the populations. In either case, however, these populations are believed to have largely displaced existing populations of Neanderthals and *H. erectus*—a feat not necessarily achieved through violence, but rather through the ability of modern humans to more effectively compete for resources via their more sophisticated use of culture and technology.

Questioning Race

One of the outcomes of the new information about human evolution, particularly the growing acceptance of the "Out of Africa" model, is that it forces us to radically reconsider our understanding of what is meant by "race." Indeed, while the Multiregional model argues that the various races had roots millions of years deep, the Out of Africa model suggests that the physical variations often identified as "race" are much more recent developments than previously thought. From such a perspective, all modern humans are really "Africans"— even if we aren't all "black." Indeed, more and more scholars today are questioning whether there is really any biological basis

Controversies in African History: **Race and Human Origins**

"As stated in the preface, everyone who writes has an agenda. As a corollary to this point, consider the statement 'All history is political'— that is, every historical argument has important political implications for the present. This is true even for prehistory, as the debate between the proponents of the Out of Africa and Multiregional theories of human evolution shows. The following excerpts originated in none other than the editorial page of the *New York Times*—showing that these scholars knew very well the public implications of their scholarly debate.

Neanderthals on the Run

The people who replaced the Neanderthals 40 millennia ago, the Cro-Magnons, began to emerge from Africa less than 100,000 years ago. The African emigrants eventually replaced all other hominid species—Neanderthals in Europe, Solo Man in Java, and the descendants of Peking Man in China.

The implications for the idea of race are profound. If modern humanity is made up of people who are all recent descendants of a few African pioneers, it is equally clear that Homo sapiens must be a startlingly homogeneous species. We simply have not had time to diverge genetically in any meaningful manner. . . . In the past, the races were assumed to be the vestiges of million-year-old cleavages in the human family tree. Race had a profound biological meaning by that reckoning. But now it has become apparent that our differentiation into Eskimos, Bushmen, Australians, Scandinavians and so on occurred only in the last 50,000 years, and that race is a short, and superficial coda to the long song of evolution.

Nevertheless, some scientists and those with narrow political agendas have put forward arguments to sustain the idea that races exist with fundamental biological differences.

Instead of concocting divisive theories, we would be better served to recognize the importance of recent data. . . . Our DNA lineage points unmistakably to a common ancestor whose offspring evolved into Homo sapiens shortly before the African exodus. Though modern humans may not look exactly alike, we are indeed all Africans under the skin. (Christopher Stringer and Robin McKie, *The New York Times*, July 27, 1997.)

Don't Bring Politics into Neanderthal Debate; Lack of DNA Evidence

With the analysis of a small piece of Neanderthal mitochondrial DNA, we look forward to an exciting time of competing ideas. But Chris Stringer and Robin McKie, in their July 27 Op-Ed article arguing that our DNA can be traced to a relatively recent African ancestor, stifle this process by trying to discredit their opposition and playing the race card.

Their opposition, they say, is motivated by 'narrow political agendas,' to 'sustain the idea that races exist with fundamental biological differences.' They accuse the opposition of concocting theories to back this agenda. Opposing scientists do not have political agendas. The differences live on because the new DNA results are not complete or unambiguous enough to resolve the main questions about human origins.

Nor can the new data resuscitate the writers' failed Eve theory: that if we are relatively recent descendants of African origin, we are 'a startlingly homogeneous species' and haven't 'had time to diverge genetically in any meaningful manner.'

Only the maternally inherited mitochondrial DNA is homogeneous today. Human nuclear DNA has normal variation for a primate. What the Neanderthal DNA shows is that there was normal mitochondrial DNA variation earlier as well.

Having only a few African ancestors would have reduced nuclear and mitochondrial DNA variation, but mitochondrial DNA would recover variation faster than nuclear DNA because it mutates faster. In modern humans, however, it is the nuclear, not the mitochondrial, DNA variation which is normal. Clearly another scenario must have occurred."

Milford Wolpoff, Alan Mann, and Rachel Caspari,
New York Times, August 2, 1997

for what was once dubbed "race." Certainly, there are instances when being the wrong race in the wrong place at the wrong time can get you into trouble, but that is more a reflection of social and political, rather than biological, reality. Thus, race may seem real in that some human beings have attributed meaning to certain physical characteristics and acted in response to their beliefs—often in what are considered "racist" ways. Yet, these actions don't mean that those people were (or are) right. The tensions over race perhaps are only an example of the power human beings have to create systems of identity, and just how real those created systems of identity can be once they become entangled with systems of political, social, and economic power. Certainly, the divergent interpretations of the place of Africa in world history highlight the power of race in influencing how people understand the world.

Africa and Human Origins in Global Perspective

Not too long ago, it was common for European and American scholars to marginalize Africa's role in world history—even from the standpoint of human origins. The evolutionary perspective of human paleontology presents a very different story. Both an ever-increasing body of fossil evidence and more recent genetic studies have greatly improved our understanding of human evolution. Although scholars currently debate whether the first human ancestors left Africa as *Homo erectus* or as Homo sapiens, all are in agreement that the great bulk of human evolution took place in the continent of Africa itself. From either point of view, Africa is the very source of human history. There can be little doubt that Africa represents the cradle of humanity. Such a reality not only highlights the crucial role of Africans in early world history, but also the importance of scientific evidence in informing our understanding of that history. And yet, the vociferous debate over the origins of the modern human physical variations that we call "race" points up exactly how deeply our notions of the present inform our perspectives on the past. Debates aside, as we shall see in the next chapter, Africa not only helped give rise to human evolution, but its environment also gave rise to some of the most significant early human technological and cultural adaptations.

Useful Works on This Chapter Topic

There are a number of excellent surveys of physical anthropology available for students who are interested in a more in-depth perspective on early human evolution. Bernard Wood's *Human Evolution, a Very Short Introduction* (2006) provides not only an overview of recent discoveries and research, but also an excellent summary of changing perspectives on evolution over the past 150 years. Frank E. Pouirier and Jeffrey K. McKee's *Understanding Human Evolution* (2004) offers a somewhat more detailed evaluation of each "stage" of human evolution. Alan J. Almquist's *Contemporary Readings in Physical Anthropology* (2000) has the advantage of allowing students to see the debates between scholars in the field as they unfolded in such venues as the *New York Times* editorial page. Students are, of course, encouraged to examine the core texts of the debate between the Multiregionalist and the Out of Africa camps. These include Milford Wolpoff and Rachel Caspari's *Race and Human Evolution: A Fatal Attraction* (1997) and Christopher Stringer and Robin McKie's *African Exodus: The Origins of Modern Humans* (1998). Both offer persuasive arguments for their very different conclusions. For an excellent discussion of how our definitions of race have changed over time, see Stephen Jay Gould's *Mismeasure of Man* (1996), and also G. Frederickson, *Racism, A Short History* (2002). For a detailed (and controversial) examination of how genetic evidence is reshaping our understanding of evolution, see Nicholas Wade's *Before the Dawn: Recovering the Lost History of Our Ancestors* (2006).

CHAPTER 2

Physical Context of African History: Geography and Environment

History and geography are inextricably intertwined. African history, like any other history, unfolds in the context of a physical setting that constrains and shapes the decisions and options faced by the human actors who make history. Although we would hesitate to argue that geography determined the trajectory of African history, we will argue that Africa's past—and present, too—have been profoundly shaped by geography and environment. Africa's relationship to the non-African world has also been shaped by geography and environment. In some places, coastal East Africa, for instance, placid seas and favorable wind patterns encouraged maritime trade. As a result, coastal East Africa has enjoyed the benefits of long-distance trade but also suffered invasion from the sea. By contrast, some other parts of the continent were isolated from outside contact by sheer distance and a disease environment that killed visitors but spared locals.

As we saw in the previous chapter, Africa was almost certainly the home of the first modern humans. And part of the evolutionary process that created those first humans was a response to a changing environment. The physical environment is never static. Forests grow and shrink, as do deserts and grasslands. Rainfall comes and goes. Sometimes humans help to trigger these changes; other times they are forced to react to a changing environment. So where do we begin our account of the ever-changing African environment? Probably the best starting point would be the Upper **Paleolithic** (the later part of the old stone age), a time when human culture began to change rapidly and human creativity blossomed in dramatic new ways that allowed humans to begin to shape and manage the world around them in equally new ways. Although this chapter is about the physical world, it is also about humans and their interactions with their environment.

Physical Features of the Continent

The most prominent feature of the African continent is its size. It is large beyond most of our imagining. A single African country—the Democratic Republic of the Congo—is nearly the size of Western Europe. It is possible to fit a map of the continental

United States on the map of Africa three times, with only a few bits sticking out here and there. Because the continent is so large, its terrain and climate are widely variable. In fact, one can find just about any imaginable type of terrain or climate somewhere on the continent. There are glaciers on Mt. Kilimanjaro, Mt. Kenya boasts world-class ice climbing, and Morocco's Atlas range has ski areas. One can also find vast tropical forests, the largest desert in the world, grasslands, mangrove swamps, hot coastal towns, chilly highland areas, and places with California-like weather that support a surf culture and viticulture. The southern tip of the continent supports a population of penguins. The point of this little digression is to show that there is no such thing as an "African environment." The continent is much too varied to lend itself to broad generalizations about terrain and environment, to say nothing of human culture.

The northern edge of the continent is bounded by the Mediterranean Sea. From Algeria to Morocco the coastal strip enjoys what is called a Mediterranean climate. That is to say, the climate is mild; there is good, predictable rainfall in the winter months; and the summers are usually dry. Iberia, southern France, Italy, and Greece all have similar climates. Farther east, Libya and Egypt have much drier coastal climates. The climate in North Africa allows the cultivation of grapes (usually made into wine), olives, wheat, and barley.

South of this coastal strip lies the Sahara. "Sahara" is the Arabic word for desert. The desert here is such a perfect example of the genre that it needs no other name. It

If there exists a typical African environment it would be the mixed grass and trees of the Savannah.

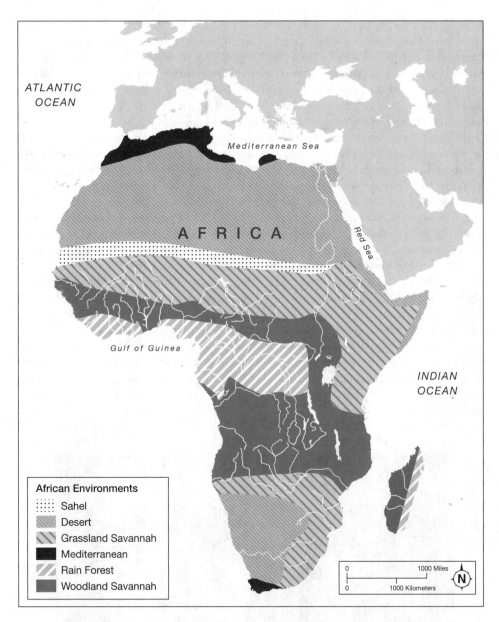

Map 2-1: African environments

is simply the desert. It may not be the world's driest or most forbidding, but it is huge. From the Niger River north to the cultivated parts of Algeria it is more than 1,000 miles. From Mauritania on the desert's western edge to the Nile River in the east is more than 2,000 miles. Currently, the desert is very dry, and although there are places that support permanent human habitation, they are few. If we were to look back to the Upper Paleolithic, we would find a rather different situation. The desert was going through a wet period from about 30,000 to 10,000 years ago. A band of lakes and swamps stretched across the southern edge of the desert—Lake Chad is a remnant of these lakes—and the center of the desert was wet enough to support grass and some trees. During this wet phase, the Sahara was the site of some of the first steps in the process that led to the invention of agriculture.

South of the Sahara is a vast savannah. Here the rainfall is sufficient to support a mixture of grass and trees. Closer to the desert, there is less rainfall and hence more grass and fewer trees. Farther south and closer to the equator there is more rainfall, and the mix tends more toward trees. If there is a "typical" sub-Saharan environment it is the savannah. Not only is this the most common terrain type on the continent, it is also one of the most human-friendly and so has been the site of much of the continent's human history. The savannah stretches from the Sahara's edge in the north to the edge of two other deserts—the Kalahari and the Namib in the south. (Purists will object that the Kalahari is actually a steppe rather than a desert, but everyone agrees that the Kalahari's neighbor, the Namib is the real thing.) As the savannah extends to the south it replicates the pattern found north of the equator. The closer one is to the equator, the wetter and more forested it is, and the farther from the equator one is, the drier and grassier it is.

Enfolded in this vast savannah is an equatorial forest zone. Historically, rain forests covered much of the coast of West Africa from modern-day Sierra Leone to the Volta River in modern Ghana. Around the Volta there is a gap in the forest, and the savannah reaches to the sea. The forest resumes again in Nigeria and extends into the Congo basin. These forests are true triple-canopy tropical forests (like those of the Amazon basin) and are home to giant trees. Rainfall in the forest zones is high; they are called

Pygmy men in the process of felling a rainforest tree. Note the steel axe.
Pygmies do not live in isolation and obtain metal tools through trade.

rain forests for a reason. Where in most places farmers worry about not getting enough rain, farmers in the forest zone worry about getting too much. The forest zone has proven a difficult environment for humans to exploit; clearing land is difficult, farming is difficult, and finding livestock that can survive there is difficult. But people have risen to the challenge and as new crops and technologies have been discovered, they have colonized more and more of the forest. Today much of the western part of the forest is gone, having been logged or cleared for farmland. The Congo basin is still heavily forested, but that too is changing. However, change is nothing new. It appears that the rain forests of West Africa have gone through several cycles of expansion and contraction in the last 10,000 years. It also seems that humans may have played a role in creating some rain forest environments. There are places in West Africa in which the islands of rain forest are surrounded by savannah. Until recently, scientists assumed that people had created the savannah by cutting down the forests. They are less sure of this now, and some scholars have proposed that human activity created islands of rain forest in an existing savannah. Scientists are now proposing that parts of the Amazon basin are anthropogenic, that is, shaped or created by humans. There are pockets there of highly fertile soil that apear to have been created intentionally by humans and the distribution of certain types of fruit trees may also be the work of humans. So it would not be surprising if a similar process had occurred in Africa and it may be that more than just rain forest islands are the result of human manipulation of the environment.

At the very southern tip of the continent, south of the Kalahari and the Namib deserts, is a small pocket of Mediterranean climate. The Cape region of South Africa has the same winter rains and mild climate that are found on the continent's north coast. Grapes, wheat, apples, and other Mediterranean crops have all been introduced and thrive in the Cape. There is a pattern here. Because the continent straddles the equator, the climatic zones are arranged more or less symmetrically around the equator. From north to south one finds in order: Mediterranean-desert-savannah-rain forest-savannah-desert-Mediterranean.

Challenges of the African Environment

Despite all the myths about the fertility of tropical soils, most African soils are actually rather poor. There are several reasons why this is so. First, the continent is geologically inactive. As a result the soils are ancient, highly leached, and weathered so that plant nutrients are less abundant in the soil than a farmer might like. There is also less organic material in the soils because most of the continent is hot year-round, and so organic materials in the soils decompose all year. By contrast, in more temperate climates the breakdown of organic material stops in the winter, so the levels of organic materials in the soils tend to be higher. Thus, the productivity of the land is lower than one would find in a more geologically active and cooler place—North America, for instance—and farmers are forced to go to great, labor-intensive lengths to add nutrients and organic matter to the soil.

That said, it is worth noting that there are many areas of the continent that defy this broader pattern. These are the volcanic highlands, which are cooler and have richer soils. Ethiopia has a large highland area, as do Kenya, Tanzania, Rwanda, Burundi, Uganda, and Cameroon. These areas are noteworthy in that they tend to have high population densities and so are often loci for state formation, empire building, and other examples of human ambition. These areas are often well suited to growing crops such as coffee (coffee is native to the Ethiopian highlands) and tea with high export values, and so were of particular interest to European imperialists in the nineteenth and twentieth centuries.

Another limitation on agricultural productivity is rainfall. Although rainfall is adequate in most of the continent—indeed in some places it is prodigious—it is also cyclical. Unlike North America, where rainfall is distributed relatively evenly throughout the year, in sub-Saharan Africa rainfall is an all-or-nothing thing. At some times of the year it rains every day; at others it does not rain at all. Thus, in some places where average rainfall amounts are reasonably high, the fact that all the rain comes in two or three months limits the agricultural utility of the rain. The oft-cited example of this is the comparison of the Nigerian city of Kano and the American city of Chicago. Both receive roughly the same amount of rain each year. Whereas Chicago's rain is evenly distributed, Kano gets all its rain in the course of a couple of months. The result is that Chicago sits in the midst of some of the finest agricultural land in the world, and Kano is home to a camel market. This is not to say that the presence of a camel market precludes agriculture. In fact, the area around Kano produces a variety of food and fiber crops, but not the staggeringly huge amounts of food that are produced in the American Midwest.

The reason for this cyclical rain pattern has to do with something called the Intertropical Convergence Zone (**ITCZ**). The ITCZ, sometimes called the "rain belt," is the boundary between the dry continental air over the desert and the wet air that comes from the sea. The ITCZ moves north and south each year as wind patterns change. It is usually at its most southerly in January and at its most northerly in July and August. As it moves north, it brings rain to those areas it passes over. The farther north a place is, the less time it spends south of the ITCZ, and hence the shorter the rainy season. Because, like all natural phenomena, the ITZC's movements are variable, the timing of the rains each year is variable, and more northern locations are susceptible to complete failure of the rains when the ITCZ retreats early. Farming in areas with a cyclical rainfall pattern requires that farmers carefully time their planting to coincide with the rains and that they be prepared for the rains to fail completely every now and then.

The final challenge that the African environment poses is that of disease. Humans and other creatures very much like humans have lived in Africa longer than they have lived anywhere else on the planet. In the millions of years available to them, the microbes of Africa have evolved an astonishing variety of ways to prey on humans. The result is a disease environment that poses a serious, but certainly not insurmountable, challenge to humans living there. In the long run, the disease environment also protected sub-Saharan Africans from invasion. Until the nineteenth century, when new medical technologies entered the equation, outsiders fared poorly in the tropical parts of the continent, whereas people who had grown up there fared much better.

Two diseases were primarily responsible for this situation: **malaria** and **yellow fever**. Malaria is found almost worldwide. The word we use for the disease comes from the Italian for "bad air," reflecting the early European belief that noxious vapors from swamps were the cause of this disease. Of course, it was not swamp vapors but the mosquitoes that bred in the swamps that caused the problem. Certain species of mosquitoes are capable of carrying with them the plasmodium—a multicellular, microscopic creature—that causes malaria and of delivering it while biting someone. Malaria was once endemic in Europe and North America, but has been mostly eliminated in the past century. So malaria is by no means unique to Africa or the tropics. However, there are particularly virulent strains of malaria that occur only in the tropics and that are much more common in Africa than in other tropical places.

Foremost of these is the *Plasmodium falciparum* strain that attacks the central nervous system, causing a life-threatening form of the disease called cerebral malaria. Unlike other forms of malaria, which usually cause severe, but generally not fatal, illness, cerebral malaria is frequently fatal, especially to young children. In those parts of Africa where cerebral malaria is endemic, most children suffer several bouts with the disease, and many of them die in the process. By most estimates, malaria kills more African children than any other disease, and it causes more deaths worldwide than any other disease except tuberculosis. Unlike some diseases—the mumps or chicken pox, for example—a person who has had malaria and lived does not gain immunity to the disease. One can be reinfected over and over again; however, if a person survives four or five bouts with the disease as a child, that person gains a degree of resistance to it. That is to say that the person's subsequent bouts with the disease are much less likely to be fatal. If a person survives into adulthood in an area in which cerebral malaria is common, the disease becomes more of a source of annual annoyance than a life-threatening danger. On the other hand, if a person arrives in the same area as an adult, the chances of contracting a fatal case of cerebral malaria within a year are quite high.

The implications of this are profound. First, malaria exacts a tremendous human toll in Africa. By some estimates, the cost of treating those afflicted with the disease and the work lost because of the temporary debilitation caused by the disease is close to 5 percent of GDP (gross domestic product) in many African nations. Presumably the disease has exacted a similar toll in the past, although there is some evidence to suggest that malaria was not widespread until the rise of agriculture. The other historically important effect of malaria was that it served to limit the movement of outsiders into tropical Africa. Although the children of immigrants might acquire resistance to the disease through repeated exposure, the first to arrive died with reckless abandon. Malaria was one of several factors—human and natural—that served to limit large-scale settlement by outsiders before the middle of the nineteenth century. Malaria has exerted so great a selective pressure on people who live in these regions that a number of genetic mutations that offer protection against malaria are found in sub-Saharan Africans. The best known of these is the sickleing trait that when inherited from only one parent offers protection from malaria, but when inherited from two parents causes the debilitating disease sickle cell anaemia. Obviously, this is a stiff price to pay for protection from a disease, so the selective pressure exerted by malaria must be powerful indeed.

Yellow fever, the second of Africa's two major diseases, was (and is) far kinder to Africans but just as hard on outsiders as malaria. It, too, is mosquito borne, but unlike malaria, a virus rather than a plasmodium causes it. Most people who grow up in places in which yellow fever is endemic get the disease as children and are then immune to it for life. As is the case with many viral diseases that are well adapted to preying on humans—chicken pox is a familiar example—children experience few symptoms when they have the disease. But when people contract yellow fever for the first time as adults, the symptoms are much more severe and are often fatal. Yellow fever's effects on sub-Saharan Africa's relations with the outside world were much like that of malaria. Outsiders, who usually arrived as adults, dropped like flies, whereas Africans, whose childhood experience of the disease meant they were immune to it, were unaffected. The other crucial difference between malaria and yellow fever, at least in our times, is that there is an effective vaccine for yellow fever, so it now rarely affects travelers to the tropics. By contrast, malaria remains difficult to prevent and challenging to treat and continues to pose a threat to visitors and to people born in the tropical regions of Africa.

Finally, it is worth noting that diseases that primarily affect animals can still exert a powerful effect on human history. **Trypanosomiasis**, or sleeping sickness, is the best example of such a disease. A protozoan that is transmitted by the bite of the tsetse fly causes trypanosomiasis. Some forms of the disease affect humans, and in some areas the disease is a real killer, but its effect on livestock is much larger and historically far more important. The trypanosome that causes the disease infects a variety of wild animals, which act as a reservoir for the disease. The flies that transmit the disease can carry it from a wild animal to a domestic animal or from one domestic animal to another. Infected animals usually die, and some species and varieties of livestock are more susceptible than others. Horses are highly susceptible and usually die shortly after entering a tsetse fly belt. Cows are more susceptible than goats or sheep, but a few varieties of cattle found in West Africa are resistant to the disease.

Trypanosomiasis is historically important because it prevented people in large swaths of the continent from keeping cattle. At first glance this may not seem like that big a deal, but cattle produce meat, milk, blood, hides, and manure. And they do all this while eating grass—a food that humans cannot eat themselves. For people in tsetse belts, not keeping cattle is a real economic loss. The other historically important effect of trypanosomiasis is its deadly effect on horses. Horses are militarily useful, and they can pull carts and plows or carry loads. That the range of the horse was limited to North Africa and the northern reaches of the savannah, where they survive but rarely breed succesfully, was yet another economic loss to people forced to live without them.

Tsetse flies require certain types of brush to survive. Places with large numbers of people tend to have less brush—people clear the brush for their farms and dwellings—and hence fewer flies. Social disruption may lead to the regrowth of brush and hence the colonization of an area by tsetse flies, which of course then makes it unsuitable to cattle. Many people believe that the widespread presence of tsetse flies and the trypanosomiasis they carry is a recent development. They contend that the disruptions caused by the colonization of Africa in the late nineteenth century resulted in human depopulation and thus in the expansion of the fly belts. So although archaeological evidence indicates that tsetse flies are more ancient than humans, their widespread presence in sub-Saharan Africa may be a relatively recent development.

Clearly, the African environment poses challenges to its human inhabitants. Some economists interested in the question of why some parts of the world are more economically developed than others have gone so far as to conclude that Africa's environment accounts for a 2 to 4 percent drag on GDP growth. But bear in mind that any environment poses challenges to human habitation and development. A similar description of North America might include references to vast areas of desert, large and economically marginal Arctic wastelands, and a continent divided by large and difficult-to-cross chains of mountains. So remember that for every desert there is a cool and fertile highland zone and for every thicket buzzing with tsetse flies there is a prosperous farmstead.

Controversies in African History: Joseph Greenberg and Historical Linguistics

For the most part, historical scholarship is shaped by the steady accumulation of small insights from many different people, each of whom makes a small contribution to the larger process. But occasionally someone comes along who fundamentally reshapes the way some aspect of the past is understood. Our understanding of African historical linguistics has been profoundly affected by one such giant: Joseph Greenberg (1915–2001).

Greenberg, who taught at Stanford, was a sort of rogue linguist whose work fascinates nonlinguists and often troubles professional linguists. His book *The Languages of Africa* (1963) proposed the now standard division of Africa's languages into the four phyla we used in this chapter: Khoisan, Nilo-Saharan, Afro-Asiatic, and Niger-Congo. Historians and others with little training in linguistics have enthusiastically embraced Greenburg's classification because his proposed language families mesh so nicely with what we know about African cultural history. He created these classifications using a system of language classification he called mass lexical comparison, which is quite different from the standard comparative method used by most linguists of showing a relationship between two languages.

The comparative method used by most mainstream linguists requires that any proposed relationship between languages be proven through the demonstration of systematic and regular shifts in sound patterns between the two languages. Thus, one might demonstrate that words that contain the letter "v" in language X routinely appear in language Y with a "b" replacing the "v". What this method tries to do is show that there are consistent and predictable patterns in how languages differ, which indicate that both had a common ancestor and thus are related.

Greenberg contended that this method was fine for looking at small numbers of languages, but when looking at thousands of languages one needed a different approach. Mass lexical comparison involves looking at huge lists of words and trying to find structural similarities. On some level, his method seems to be as much about his personal ability to perceive relationships between languages at the gut level as it is about scientific rigor. Naturally, the majority of historical linguists, even if they accept the basic outlines of the language families he saw in Africa, reject the method he used in proposing the continent's language groups.

Greenberg, who was a tireless worker and had an uncanny ability with languages, did not stop at proposing a revolutionary classification of African languages. He went on to devise a radically simplified system of classification for the languages of the Americas in 1987. Most specialists in American Indian languages considered the languages of the Americas to be quite diverse, with many hundreds of language families. Greenberg concluded that there were just three such families; languages that had long been considered totally unrelated were, in his mind, relatives. In a field of splitters, Greenberg was the ultimate lumper. Historical linguists have almost universally rejected his classification of American languages, but DNA studies do show genetic relationships among the people he said were linguistic relatives.

Undeterred by the criticism of his work on the Americas, Greenberg went on to propose a super-family of languages called Eurasiatic, which lumps together several phyla of Eurasian and North American languages. In perhaps the ultimate feat of language lumping, in the last years of his life Greenberg proposed that Eurasiatic and Amerind (one of his three American Indian language families) were sister language families and that both came into existence as modern humans first moved into areas from which ice was retreating as the last ice age ended.

Humans and the Environment: Foraging for Food

African environments are challenging environments. It was in these various African environments that some of the critical steps in human historical development occurred. The first anatomically modern humans lived exclusively in Africa. Their range was originally restricted to the northeastern parts of the continent and it was there that our ancestors went through a profound cognitive change that added modern behaviors to their modern anatomy. Perhaps the most revolutionary change associated with this transformation, and one that almost certainly took place while humans were still confined to the African continent, was the development of language. During this period, humans developed a range of skills and technologies that allowed them to move out of this restricted area and engage in an epic journey that involved both the colonization of other regions of the African continent and the rest of the world.

For most of human history, and for all of the early period we are concerned with here, people foraged for their food. Agriculture and stock-keeping are relatively recent and profoundly revolutionary developments. Agriculture is probably no more than 10,000 years old, whereas modern humans have been around for roughly 100,000 years. So foraging is a big part of the human story in general, and because foragers shaped their environment and laid the foundations for the development of agriculture—which involves direct human manipulation of the environment—their story is also crucial to an understanding of the human relationship to the African continent.

Reconstructing the world of foragers is difficult. We have only three sources of information about their lives, and none is completely satisfactory. The first, of course, is archaeology. Archaeology offers direct evidence about the tools foragers used and allows for relatively certain dating. As such, it would seem like an ideal source of information, but like any type of historical evidence, it has limitations. Compared to urban civilizations, or even simple farming societies, foragers' mobile camps left a small archaeological footprint. Furthermore, what did survive to be studied is only the hard stuff that resists decomposition. Occasionally, when conditions are just right, a basket or a sandal is preserved, but in general it is stone and bone tools and carbonized (i.e., burned) wood that survives. As a result, archaeology can tell only part of the story. Among other things, this tends to make tools used for hunting—spear points and arrowheads, for instance—archaeologically visible, whereas tools used for gathering— baskets and wooden digging sticks—are archaeologically invisible.

So what makes anyone think that foragers had baskets and digging sticks anyway, if there is no archaeological evidence for them? For one thing, there is sometimes indirect archaeological evidence for soft things; baskets can leave impressions on clay, for instance. But scholars who study the world of ancient foragers also make inferences about ancient foragers based on the behaviors of modern foragers. This has the virtue of allowing scholars to look at a living, functioning foraging society. They can study their diets, social structures, technologies, health, and population density, most of which is unknowable through archaeology alone. But there are problems with using this type of ethnographic data. Most troubling, it assumes that surviving foraging societies are static. Given that most foragers have been coexisting with nearby food producers for at least a couple of thousand years, it seems unlikely that any modern foraging society is totally unaffected by the changes that have happened in the surrounding world. Even if a surviving foraging society were completely unaffected by its neighbors, it would have had thousands of years to develop and refine techniques that might have been totally unknown to Paleolithic foragers.

A third source of information on these early societies comes from the analysis of genetic material. This comes in two forms, the genetic material of modern people, which carries information about their ancestors, and the genetic material of ancient people, which is occasionally extracted from ancient bones or teeth. The information that comes from the analysis of human genes is intriguing. It is often able to indicate relationships between different groups of people and give at least a relative sense of when various groups split off from each other. Genetic analysis has given researchers a powerful new tool to corroborate other types of evidence, or occasionally, to reconsider the findings of archaelogists when they seem to be at odds with the evidence offered by the analysis of genes. The problem with this approach is its novelty. Genetic analysis is a very new science and geneticists themselves often have bitter disagreements as to what the genetic evidence means. At present it serves primarily as a useful adjunct to more traditional types of evidence, though it has occasionally forced the reconsideration of conventional wisdom about population movements.

It is worth noting that there is a fourth possible source of information about the lives of our ancestors, and this is linguisitc evidence. As we shall see when we get to our discussion of the languages of Africa, some scholars contend that the genealogy of language families may reach into the deep past.

Despite the shortcomings of these sources, historically judicious use of the three has allowed researchers to create a reasonably full picture of foragers' lives. We can do this best beginning with the Upper Paleolithic period, that time about 50,000 years ago when anatomically modern humans first began to act modern. Before that, humans seem to have behaved in fundamentally different ways that make inferences from modern societies particularly problematic. They made a surprisingly limited range of tools and used a limited number of materials to make those tools. The tools they made lacked standardized shapes, and there is little evidence of regional styles in toolmaking. They made no art and seem not to have engaged in trade. Prior to 50,000 years ago, people may have looked like us, but they did not behave like us.

But then for reasons that remain uncertain, humans underwent a dramatic cultural change that seems to be unrelated to any observable change in their skeletons. Their brains stayed the same size, their skulls looked the same, but the detritus they left around their camps changed dramatically. Their stone tools became smaller, were more varied in their uses, and were based on standardized regional patterns. They began to use new materials. Tools made from animal bones entered the archaeological record. Bone was used to make harpoon points, fishhooks, and needles. The bow and arrow and the spear thrower were invented. Ropes and nets, made from plant fibers, enabled people to capture new types of prey. Perhaps most interesting, art was invented in this age. Prior to the Upper Paleolithic there were no cave paintings, no statues, no carvings (with the exception of a few recent finds at Blombos Cave in South Africa) and no jewelry. But after 50,000 B.P. (Before Present) there was an explosion of art making. It is also after 40,000 B.P. that we see the first evidence of ritualized burials of the dead, suggesting that religion may also have begun about this time. Humans also seem to have first used boats to move across fairly large expanses of water at this time. In doing so, they were able to colonize Australia and New Guinea—the first human migration outside Africa and Eurasia.

The earliest evidence of this profound change in human behavior comes from South and East Africa. At Blombos Cave in South Africa (mentioned in Chapter 1), modern tools and carved ochre blocks have been dated to around 70,000 B.P. These and a few bone harpoons that appear to date from about 100,000 B.P. suggest to some archaeologists that this revolution in human behavior may have begun earlier than 50,000 B.P., but there is little other evidence for this and most scholars prefer the more recent date. Numerous sites that show modern tools and also jewelry—necklaces made from ostrich eggshells—date from about 50,000 B.P. A few thousands of years later these modern behaviors show up in archaeological evidence throughout the Old World. How to explain these developments is one of the great debates in the study of early human history.

Some scientists contend that there was a slow accumulation of new behaviors and techniques that eventually led to modern behaviors. Others believe that there was an abrupt change driven not by accumulated cultural innovation, but by a fundamental rewiring of the human brain, something that would have to have been caused by a genetic change. They believe that this change was linked to the development of what may be the most critical of all modern human behaviors: language. Other creatures use language to a degree. Birds, whales, and dolphins all communicate through the sounds they make. Other primates, particularly the vervets, use sounds to communicate too. Vervets make a variety of warning calls that distinguish between different types of dangers. But it is a long way from "Ahh! A leopard!" something a vervet parent could say to a child, to "Be careful near big trees like that, there are often leopards in them," something a human parent can say to a child. Humans seem to be the only animals that have moved beyond vocabulary to grammar. In doing so they acquired a powerful tool. Hunters who could use language to plan a hunt in advance and then communicate while hunting must have had a huge advantage over those who could not. The invention of language seems to have been the critical trigger that led to the innovations associated with the Upper Paleolithic in creating most of the behaviors we associate with behaviorally modern humans. Although some of these traits reached their fullest fruition in other places (rock painting, for instance, began first in Australia and Western Europe almost simultaneously around 37,000 B.P.), the transition to language and modern behavior happened when modern humans only lived in Africa. These are, so to speak, African innovations.

So what were these societies like, how did they acquire the food that is the most basic of human economic needs, what was their relationship to their environment, and how was their social life organized? Most foraging societies seem to have been small. They formed bands of 50 to 150 members. One hundred and fifty seems to be the maximun number of people that humans are able to know and keep track of as social intimates. Few environments can support a dense population of foragers, forcing the bands to remain small and to move regularly, but those movements would have occurred within a territory which the group defended vigorously against outsiders. Typically, modern foraging bands are highly egalitarian, with no formal leaders, though of course some individuals' opinions and suggestions usually carry more weight than others. That they must move regularly adds to this egalitarianism, because it means that no one can accumulate much in the way of property. Furthermore, in modern foraging groups there is great social pressure placed on people who have temporarily acquired a surplus of goods, perhaps through a successful hunt, to share that surplus and never to brag about it. Ancient foraging bands were probably equally egalitarian. Foraging bands like these are so egalitarian that they often have real difficulty with the resolution of disputes within the group. Often the aggrieved party simply packs up and strikes off on his own.

If one were to look only at the archaeological evidence, one would assume that ancient foragers were primarily hunters. Most of the stone and bone tools they made seem to have been intended for killing animals or fish or for butchering their carcasses. The cave shelters and encampments they used are often littered with the bones of wild animals. Until the 1960s this "Man the Hunter" view held sway in most circles. Many museum dioramas still present foragers in this way—a group of hairy and usually slightly perplexed-looking fiberglass humans huddle around a fire as one of their number trudges into the camp with a dead animal draped over his shoulder. And to be sure, ancient foragers were hunters, some quite expert. The bones found in their cave shelters were a by-product of their hunting (and sometimes scavenging), and their favorite subjects when it came to rock painting were the animals on which they preyed. And as humans moved into new environments in which animals had not had previous experience with bipedal predators, they exterminated most of the larger animal species. The arrival of humans in Australia and the Americas was followed closely by the disappearance of many species of large, slow-moving animals.

But hunting is hardly the whole story. More careful analysis of the trash left behind by ancient foragers and studies of their modern counterparts suggest that hunting was less central to their economy than the bone piles suggest. In modern foraging societies hunting usually furnishes fewer than 20 percent of the calories consumed by the band. The rest comes from foods that are gathered. These might include anything from fruits, nuts, grubs, insects, fish, eggs, grass seeds, roots and tubers, to the pith of certain trees and honey. Knowledgeable gatherers can find a huge variety of foods, and gathered foods tend to have a fairly predictable return in calories per hour expended looking for them. By contrast, hunting sometimes requires hours and hours of work with no payoff at all and at others times can yield a tremendous number of calories with little effort. As anyone who has spent time hunting with modern weapons will verify, there is a reason it is called hunting as opposed to killing.

The implications of this are interesting. Part of the "Man the Hunter" interpretation of forager life was the idea that hunting was related to male dominance. Women, it was argued, tended children and lurked around the camp while their husbands went off to hunt, bringing back meat that they shared with their wives and children. It was a neat picture that provided an anthropological justification for mid-twentieth-century gender roles and social ideals about the nuclear family.

But here, too, a look at surviving foraging societies is illuminating. First, in most foraging societies the gender division of labor (the social rules about what is men's work and what is women's work) is far more fluid than is the case in farming societies. To the extent that there are such gender divisions, women gather and men hunt. But men do lots of gathering and women rarely hesitate to kill game they encounter while gathering. Indeed, one gets the impression that men in these societies hunt for much the same reason that men in industrial societies hunt; a successful hunt does much for the social status of the man who makes the kill. So rather than being passive recipients of the bounty of men's hunting, women in modern foraging societies actually produce more of the food than men do. In all likelihood, the same was true in ancient foraging societies.

Another myth about foraging life has to do with our perception of foragers as "savages." Their lives may at first glance seem to embody the Hobbesian state of nature, "nasty, brutish, and short." Closer examination of the evidence partly discredits this belief. Viewed through a lens that sees leisure time rather than material goods as wealth, foragers are rich. Depending on the environments they inhabit, modern foragers usually work two to five hours a day. When we consider that modern foragers usually live in marginal areas that farmers have not seen fit to take from them, it seems possible that ancient foragers, who had access to more productive land, might have worked even less. Furthermore, because their material wants were so limited, everybody had all the possessions they could imagine having. One anthropologist has gone so far as to dub them the "original affluent society." And there seems to be something to this. When anthropologists compare the bones of ancient foragers with those of ancient farmers, it is the foragers who appear to have been physically larger and healthier, which suggests that they ate better than early farmers. Because they lived in small groups and moved frequently, they were not forced to live with their own filth the way sedentary peoples do. Thus, they were less often exposed to disease and parasites and so probably would have been healthier than farmers, even if their diets were not richer and more varied. Clearly, some foragers saw their way of life as superior to that of farmers. The archaeological evidence, both in Africa and the Middle East, suggests that in many cases foragers lived near farmers for centuries, even millennia, without abandoning foraging in favor of food production. Among modern foraging groups, these sentiments are especially strong. In the 1970s and 1980s the government of the East African nation of Tanzania made several attempts to get the Hadza, a nomadic group of foragers, to settle and become farmers. In each case, few Hadza remained more than a year or two in the villages constructed for them before reverting to their foraging ways.

To be sure, a foraging life hardly qualifies as the average Western person's dream retirement. Foragers rarely live past 40 years of age, they often endure long periods of time when they are not able to eat as much as they would like to eat, and their lives are often filled with physical dangers that few of us would like to risk. Part of this risk comes from the real threat of violent death that was part and parcel of foraging life. Hunting large animals, or even small animals, is a risky occupation. But foragers also have to worry about their fellow humans. Modern foraging groups, as well as groups that live off a mixed economy of farming and foraging, live appallingly violent lives. While they rarely fight pitched battles with neighboring groups, they are usually engaged in chronic tit-for-tat raiding with them. When modern foragers do engage in pitched battles the result is often carnage, with casualty rates in the 30 to 40 percent range. By contrast the bloodiest battles of the American Civil War saw casualty rates in the 20 percent range. The more common raids may have been less dramatic, but they took a serious long-term toll on population levels. Estimates derived from modern foraging groups

Map 2-2: Probable homeland of the first behaviorally modern humans

indicate the average ancient foraging groups lost 0.5 percent of their population each year to violent death. If those numbers were applied to the twentieth-century populations over two billion people would have lost their lives to warfare.

Violence aside, the lives of ancient foragers appear to have been reasonably comfortable, especially when compared to those of early farmers. Foragers ate a more varied diet and ate as much as, if not more than, farmers. They obtained their daily food requirements in fewer hours of work than farmers. That left lots of free time for things like conversation, storytelling, game playing, and other things people like to do with each other when they have time. Consider also that they probably lived in societies that were more egalitarian than farming societies, both with respect to class hierarchies and gender relations.

So what happened? Why, if on balance it appears that foraging was at least a slightly more desirable way of life, did foragers stop foraging and start producing their own food? The short answer is that no one knows for sure, and archaeologists continue to debate the question. But the simplest answer is that foragers never made a conscious decision to begin producing food; instead, food production was a gradual development that evolved slowly, over thousands of years, out of the gathering habits of foragers. No one woke up one morning and decided to plant a garden instead of going out to look for food. What is often called the agricultural revolution took place so gradually that in all likelihood none of the revolutionaries noticed that change was afoot. That said, the development of food production changed human life more than any other event in human history.

Regional Foraging Strategies

One of the central themes of this book is the regional variety of the African continent. Africa's vast size and geographical diversity virtually demand that humans adapt to the continent's many environments in different ways. Furthermore, humans seem to thrive on cultural creation and variety so it should not surprise us that there is huge variety in the social worlds that people made for themselves in Africa. Africans of the Upper Paleolithic seem to have fallen into four broad groups defined by language and foraging habits. Indeed, because the Upper Paleolithic began in Africa, and because the creation of discrete social groups seems to have been a feature of this transformation in human behavior, it may be that social groups are, in effect, an African creation. We know about these groups primarily through two types of evidence—archaeological and linguistic.

The Evidence

By now you are probably quite familiar with the nature of archaeological evidence. Archaeologists recover physical evidence left behind by people in the past. Archaeological evidence includes the physical remains of people, buildings, the detritus that people left behind, and other things like pollen from the plants they grew. These things are dated either directly if they are organic, and hence can be carbon dated, or indirectly, if they are inorganic. The basic premise used for indirect dating is that the older things are found at lower levels and more recent things at higher levels. Things found together are considered contemporaneous.

Linguistic evidence is a bit trickier to understand. It assumes that closely related languages will have more common and related words than more distantly related languages. Furthermore, it assumes that related languages descend from a common ancestor and become different languages when speakers of the common ancestral tongue become separated from each other. Thus, by studying a group of related languages, linguists can reconstruct the history that led from a single ancestral tongue, Latin, for instance, to a group of related languages, like Spanish, French, Italian, Romanian, and Portuguese, which all descend from Latin. Linguists can also determine a fair amount about the cultures of the people in the distant past by studying their languages. For example, if all the Romance languages have a common or closely related word for something—cow, for instance—then we can assume that the people who spoke the ancestral language, Latin, had cows. If a group of otherwise closely related languages have wildly different words for something, we can then assume that the speakers of the ancestral language did not have a word for that thing and hence did not have that thing. Of course, this is a gross oversimplification. Languages borrow from other languages and influence each other in complex ways, which can confuse things. One critic of linguistic evidence has argued that judging from the fact that the Romance languages all use closely related words for coffee and cigars, presumably the anceint Romans drank coffee and smoked cigars, which, of course, they did not. However, most historians accept that linguistic evidence is capable of loose reconstruction of the lives of ancient peoples.

What is more controversial is the claim that the date at which the splitting of an ancestral language occurred can be determined by linguistic evidence alone through what is called **glottochronology**. The premise of glottochronology is that languages change at a predictable rate. Thus, not only can linguists determine the order in which languages hived off from each other; they can assign approximate dates to those separations. This idea, which was once widely accepted, has lately been subject to intense criticism. Most historians are no longer willing to accept glottochronological dates without supporting evidence from archaeology. We will try to avoid using dates obtained only through glottochronology, and when we do we will indicate that we are doing so.

Many linguists think that languages change too rapidly for linguistic evidence to be of much use for periods earlier than 10,000 years ago. But recently, scholars have begun to challenge this notion and have been trying to use language history to reconstruct the very early history of modern humans and to trace their movements within the African continent. Going a step further, some are trying to reconstruct the original movement of modern humans out of Africa and into other parts of the world.

Scholars divide languages into families that are roughly comparable to biological phyla. These groupings are seen as the most basic divisions in the world's languages and range in size from families like Austronesian and Niger-Congo that include over 1,000 languages each to smaller families like East Bird's Head that has but three members (all spoken in New Guinea, one of the world's great centers of linguistic diversity). To give a sense of the scale of these groupings, English is a member of the Germanic subgroup of the Indo-European language family that includes most of the languages of Europe as well as Persian, Hindi, and Hittite, to name but a few of its non-European members. In the last twenty years or so, scholars have tried to group these languages into super-groups of related families. By way of example, the Dene-Caucasian super-group lumps together the Sino-Tibetan family (the various languages of China and Tibet) with Navajo and Basque (spoken in the mountains between Spain and France). If there is any validity to these super-groups, they must reflect very ancient movements of people, possibly offering a window on the earliest movement of modern humans into the various regions of the world.

Africa is home to four of the world's language families and has come to host a fifth. The original four are Khoisan, Niger-Congo, Nilo-Saharan, and Afro-Asiatic. The recently arrived fifth is Austronesian. The Khoisan languages were probably once spoken in most of the continent south of the equator. Khoisan comprises twenty-nine

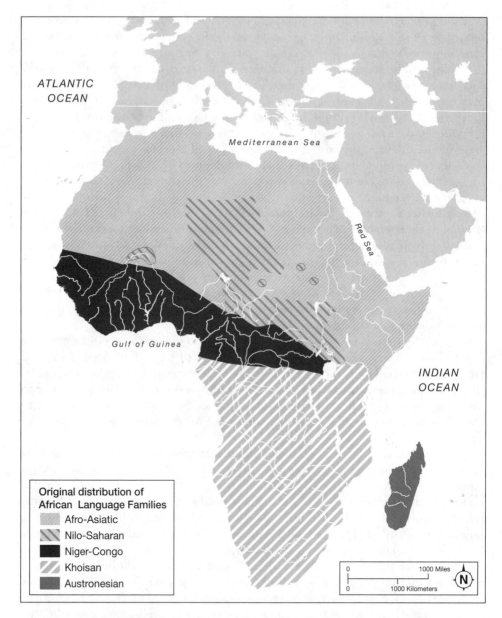

Map 2-3: Original distribution of African language families

modern languages and uses clicking sounds that are absent (with a couple of exceptions where clicks seem to have been borrowed recently) in all other languages used anywhere else in the world.[1] Current linguistic theory suggests that this may be the

---

[1]Of course, there is one exception. A language used only for ceremonial purposes by a small group of Australian Aborigines also contains clicks. No one has a good explanation for this.

most ancient family of languages on the planet and that all human languages fall into two broad groups: Khoisan and everything else.

Most Khoisan speakers are currently found only in a few areas of southern Africa, but their language may have originated farther north. There are a few isolated languages, spoken in Tanzania, thousands of miles from the majority of Khoisan speakers, that use clicks. Linguists believe that northeast Africa may have been the original home of the Khoisan languages and that they spread southward from there into their current southern African home. This makes sense, especially if we remember that at one point all behaviorally modern Africans lived in this region. The vast majority of modern Khoisan speakers are found in the Kalahari desert, but Khoisan speakers are thought to have dominated the southern third of the continent until some time in the last 2,000 years. Khoisan speakers developed a set of foraging strategies that were adapted to life in the arid regions of southern Africa. Indeed their languages may be in part an adaptation to hunting. Some modern foragers tell anthropologists that when they hunt they communicate with their fellow hunters exclusively through clicks, which they say disturbs game animals less than other forms of speech. The most widely used of the Khoisan languages, Nama, is used by only 250,000 people and some Khoisan languages like Hadza are spoken by fewer than 1,000 people. It seems that Khoisan speakers may have always been thin on the ground as is customary among foragers.

The other three language families of Africa seem, like Khoisan, to have originated in northeast Africa. Speakers of Niger-Congo, Afro-Asiatic, and Nilo-Saharan languages each developed a distinct approach to foraging and ultimately settled new regions of the continent. One or more of these groups probably pioneered the occupation of the tropical regions of Asia by modern humans. The unique foraging styles of these groups also led to different agricultural traditions as each would develop a unique crop repertoire that derived from their foraging habits.

Niger-Congo speakers are currently found in much of West and southern Africa. Their foraging style emphasized the gathering of wild yams and the nuts of the oil palm.

Afro-Asiatic speakers ended up occupying much of the Sahara at a time when it was significantly wetter than it is now. They learned to gather the seeds of wild grasses in the region at least 20,000 years ago, developing a form of intensive foraging that allowed them to break through some of the usual limits that come with foraging. Grass seeds store well and offer a dense calorie source and so encouraged a degree of sedentary living, something that not all foragers can achieve. Grass seed gathering spread out of the Sahara and into Southwest Asia, possibly bringing with it the Afro-Asiatic language group—though some scholars contend that the Afro-Asiatic languages reached Southwest Asia before the development of intensive grass seed gathering. The Semitic languages, of which Arabic and Hebrew are the best known, are part of the Afro-Asiatic group and are presumed to have developed out of the spread of this language family into the region. (It is also only fair to note that some scholars believe that the Afro-Asiatic family originated in the Middle East and spread into Africa rather than the other way around.)

The modern distribution of Nilo-Saharan languages is intriguing. Nilo-Saharan speakers live along the middle Nile River, around the inland delta of the

Niger River, and in a big part of the central Sahara. There is currently very little ecological coherence to the distribution of these languages. Some are spoken in places
that are so wet that they are virtually swamps while others are found in places that are
as dry as any environment that humans are able to occupy. By contrast, Niger-Congo
and Afro-Asiatic languages are typically spoken in coherent types of environments,
the former in places where root crops thrive and the later in places where grains
thrive. How are we to explain the variety of climates where Nilo-Saharan languages
are spoken?

As it turns out, Nilo-Saharan languages do relate to a coherent type of ancient
environment. Nilo-Saharan speakers all live in places that were once so wet that
they were full of large, shallow lakes and swamps. Until about 10,000 years ago the
Sahara was much wetter than it is now. In what is now the dry center of the desert
where there is hardly any plant life, Afro-Asiatic speakers were able to live off abundant wild grasses. At what is now the desert's southern edge there was a system of
swamps and lakes that stretched for thousands of miles. Lake Chad is a small, and
shrinking, remnant of one of these lakes. The Sudd, a vast swampy area along the
Nile River, is most likely also a remnant of this formerly watery region. Thus, Nilo-
Saharan languages correlate nicely with areas that are or were once very wet. Linguistic and archaeological evidence both suggest that Nilo-Saharan speakers
developed an "aquatic tradition" that took advantage of this environment. They
lived off fish and from hunting aquatic animals like hippos and crocodiles, neither
of which is a form of hunting that should be undertaken by the faint of heart.

One crucial piece of technology for people engaged either in fishing or the
hunting of crocodiles or hippos is the boat. These were probably first made from
bundles of reeds or other buoyant plant material. And it is their presumed familiarity with boats and watery environments in general that make Nilo-Saharans the
leading (though unconfirmed) candidates for the first modern humans to leave
Africa and begin the long-term occupation of tropical Asia. A previous wave of modern humans seems to have left Africa as early 100,000 years ago and settled lands of
the eastern Mediterranean, but their numbers were few and they were forced to
compete with Neanderthals over whom they had few advantages at the time. This
was a tentative and ultimately inconsequential move out of the African continent.
By contrast, the people who left the eastern part of the African continent and settled the coastal regions of the Indian Ocean, a process that occurred between
80,000 and 50,000 years ago, established a permanent modern human presence
outside of Africa. That they were able to do this suggests that something about the
changes that occurred in human behavior in the Upper Paleolithic gave them new
advantages that they did not have before.

To do this they would have had to cross the Bab al-Mandab, the straits between
the Horn of Africa and Yemen in the Arabian Peninsula, a feat that would have
required at least simple boats. They could then have occupied coastal areas along
the southern edge of Asia all the way into Southeast Asia. Approximately 50,000
years ago, people first crossed into Australia and New Guinea, which were then connected as a single landmass because of low sea levels. The descendants of these pioneers ultimately settled the temperate regions of the Old World, gradually displacing
its other human inhabitants—*Homo erectus* in Asia and Neanderthals in Europe.

Roughly 10,000 years later, the descendants of these African pioneers began to move into the temperate regions of Eurasia and the Americas. If this scenario is accurate, then most of the world's language would be the distant offspring of the Nilo-Saharan language group.

In 10,000 B.P., most of the habitable parts of the African continent were occupied by one of four groups of Africans. In much of the north, there were Afro-Asiatic speakers who lived off wild grains. In the swampy areas along the southern edge of the then-wet Sahara lived the Nilo-Saharans with their aquatic tradition of foraging, hunting, and fishing. South of them in the west were Niger-Congo speakers, who lived off grass seeds in some areas and tubers and palm nuts in others. Occupying the southern subcontinent were Khoisan speakers who lived off a diverse mix of foraging techniques. Of the four only the Khoisan remained fully mobile. All the other groups were using intensive foraging techniques that allowed them to live in semipermanent settlements. It was these settled populations that would in the next 5,000 years make the transition to farming, each following a different path as they adapted their foraging patterns to food production.

The African Environment and the First Modern Humans in Global Perspective

For much of the twentieth century Africa was treated as if it were at the margins of world history. Even after the African origins of humans came to be commonly accepted in the second half of the century, Africa was still seen as a passive recipient of most subsequent innovation. It is now clear that the first behaviorally modern humans, the first people like us, lived in Africa and gave us some of the fundamental social and mental habits that distinguish us from our other primate relatives.

Most critically they gave us language. It is almost certain that the first language was spoken in Africa, and it is quite possible that there was only a single first language and that all others descend from it. Some linguists think that the clicks of the Khoisan languages are a survival of the original language. Thus, all modern languages are African languages, however distantly.

The new sociability and increased potential for organization that came with language made the first behaviorally modern humans a formidible force. It enabled them to spread out of their original home in eastern Africa to occupy the diverse environments of the African continent. Some new intellectual inventiveness allowed the first modern humans to move into environments as diverse as steamy tropical rain forests, cool highlands, and arid lands from the more familiar East African Savannahs. That same inventiveness let them adapt to changes in these environments as the Sahara began to dry and the vast system of swamps and lakes on its southern edge disappeared. Their newly inventive minds let them adapt to and occupy new areas and then remain there as their new homes changed.

That same inventiveness, and no small amount of courage, let a small group of pioneers take their simple boats across the straits at the southern end of the Red Sea to the Arabian peninsula. That voyage, though it was only twenty miles or so, was the most pivotal voyage in human history. By comparison, the seafaring exploits of Columbus, Da Gama, and Zheng He pale in comparison. That small group of settlers, probably fewer than 150 in number, set in motion the occupation of the habitable continents of the planet by modern humans.

They spread rapidly across the Indian Ocean coast of Asia. By 50,000 B.P., their decendants had made another sea voyage and reached the Australian continent. Asia was already inhabited by a competing species of human, the *Homo erectus*. *Homo erectus* lacked the skills to make boats and so had never reached Australia. This was untouched, virgin territory, and it took inventiveness and mental adaptability to get there and then to figure out how to deal with its novel environment and surreal fauna. By 45,000 B.P. humans had reached the southern edge of the Australian continent.

By 40,000 B.P. the descendants of the original 150 African pioneers were in the process of occupying the temperate regions of Asia and Europe. This required not just the flexibility to adapt to fundamentally different enviroments; it also meant coming into competition with *Homo erectus* in Asia and Neanderthals in Europe. Neanderthals in particular must have been formidable competitors. They were bigger and stronger than modern humans and well adapted physically to the cold conditions in Europe. After a 15,000-year war of attrition, modern humans had eliminated the Neanderthals from Europe. In Asia it is clear the modern humans and *Homo erectus* overlapped with each other, but the role of moderns in the demise of *Homo erectus* is less clear. Some erectus-like humans, the recently discovered *Homo florensis*, survived on an isolated island in Southeast Asia as late as 13,000 B.P. At some time, possibly as early 35,000 B.P., modern humans, probably equipped with a new style of skin-covered boat, began to cross into the Americas. By 15,000 B.P. virtually every climate zone that could support human habitation had been occupied by descendants of the original African pioneers.

All of the inventiveness, adaptability, and sociability that makes us what we are now traces back to the African origins of modern behavior.

Useful Works on This Chapter Topic

There are several accessible works on human and more specifically African prehistory. One of the best and most far-reaching in its conclusions is *Guns, Germs, and Steel: The Fates of Human Societies,* by Jared Diamond (1998). More recently, Nicholas Wade's *Before the Dawn* (2006) covers some of the same ground as Diamond, but makes use of genetic and linguistic studies published since Diamond's book came out. On the relationship between African languages and the rest of the world's languages, see Patrick Manning, "*Homo Sapiens* Populates the World," *Journal of World History,* 17:2 (2006). For more specifically African subjects, see *Archaeology of Africa: Foods, Metals and Towns,* edited by Thurston Shaw et al. (1993) and *Gender in African Prehistory,* by Susan Kent (1998).

CHAPTER 3

Settled Life: Food Production, Technology, and Migrations

By 10,000 B.P. humans had occupied the entire African continent. In various parts of the continent, language and cultural groups pursued different foraging strategies to prise a living from the environments in which they found themselves. During the next ten millenia Africans would invent fundamentally new ways of producing their own foods, discover how to make metals, and create a number of social institutions that helped them to deal with the unique challenges of farming. These new developments occurred unevenly. Some Africans learned to farm and herd, and others did not. In some cases this resulted in farmers moving, over very long time scales, into the territories of foragers in processes called migrations or expansions.

The Origins of Food Production

Humans never have a passive relationship with the physical world. The environment shapes human societies and they shape it right back. Although this is truer of farming and industrial societies, it is also true of foraging societies. Foragers burned the land to improve the hunting; much of the East African savannah may derive from millennia of burning. But foragers also manipulate the environment in subtler ways that are often referred to as **tending**. Tending involves nurturing individual plants or stands of plants that produce food. For example, gatherers might remove competing nonfood plants from a stand of edible plants. Gatherers are often careful not to harvest an entire stand of plants to allow the stand to reseed itself. One of the most interesting examples of tending comes from Australia, where foragers would harvest the roots of yams but replant the inedible tops, which would grow an edible yam the next year. This is not farming; they did not prepare the soil, store seed for part of the year, or weed the yam stands, but it is clearly a step along the way. The gathering of plant foods also used much of the same technology that farming would. Digging sticks, often with a stone weight attached, got their start as foragers' tools but later became farmers' tools. (Eventually they evolved into the shovel.) Sickles made from a stick with small flakes of stone set into it served equally well for harvesting wild grass seeds and domestic grains. The baskets that gatherers carried could also be used to thresh and store domesticated grains. Thus, the change from foraging to farming did not require a huge leap in technology or in knowledge. Foragers already had most of the tools they needed to farm and had much of the knowledge about plants and how to manage their reproduction that would eventually allow them to farm.

There are two basic schools of thought about why foragers started to produce food. One school suggests that climate change may have compelled foragers to find new ways of supporting themselves, even if those changes meant working longer for less food than had previously been possible. Another, and currently "hot," school contends that the transition was triggered by social demand. According to this theory, emerging elites in foraging society engaged in food production not so much because they desperately needed the foods, but rather because they wanted to use the food, or more often the intoxicating drinks that could be made from starches and sugars, for feasting. The feasts enhanced their social status, enabling them to recruit more people to help produce the next crop, which led to a bigger feast the next time around. This second school of thought neatly accounts for much of what we know about early farming: that it spread slowly from the places where it first began (not what you would expect if there were a food crisis), that it seems to have happened first in richer environments rather than marginal ones, that many of the first plant domesticates can be used to make beer, and that there seems to be a link between farming and the emergence of social hierarchy. What it does not explain is why people in so many parts of the world suddenly (and several thousand years is "suddenly" from some perspectives) decided that it was time for some competitive feasting. Farming seems to have been independently discovered in at least three and possibly as many as seven or eight different places, all within a 5,000-year period. Unless there is something worked into our genes that suddenly kicks in 35,000 years after the invention of art compelling us to start producing food (paving the way for the catered art gallery opening), the synchronized timing of these inventions of food production suggests that some environmental force was at work in addition to whatever social forces had a hand in this transition.

Although it is almost certain that the first food producers lived in the Middle East, Africa may have played a leading, or at least participatory, role in creating the conditions that led to the transition to food production in the Middle East. The first farmers in the Middle East grew wheat and barley. These first food crops were the domesticated descendants of wild grasses whose range extends from the Middle East into North Africa and, 10,000 years ago when the first farmers appeared, into what is now the Sahara. This particular discovery of agriculture derived from intensive gathering of wild grass seeds. The earliest evidence for this style of foraging suggests that it began somewhere between the Nile and Red Sea about 20,000 B.P. Grain gatherers were able to collect enough food from these wild stands of grain that in some instances they became sedentary. The remains of permanently occupied villages have been found in the Middle East that apparently lived mostly off stored wild grass seeds. The area in which people practiced this form of intensive gathering corresponds with the area in which people speak languages of the

Afro-Asiatic family, a family that includes the Semitic languages among others. Linguistic reconstruction of the early history of the Afro-Asiatic family suggests that it originated in northeast Africa and spread from there across North Africa and into the Middle East. The best explanation for this is that its spread was associated with the spread of grass seed gathering. As grass seed gatherers moved into new areas, they either pushed out the prior inhabitants or incorporated them into their own societies, bringing Afro-Asiatic languages to new areas as they did so. It appears that the foraging style that led to the development of food production and the spread of the Afro-Asiatic languages in the Middle East, and ultimately to the first urban civilizations, has its roots in Africa. By 5000 B.P. farming communities were established in the Nile Valley and in other parts of North Africa and possibly in Ethiopia, too. These farmers used the same basic crop repertoire that was found in the Middle East—wheat, barley, lentils, and flax.

Agriculture soon emerged in other parts of the continent, and it is not clear whether farming in the rest of the continent derived from the North African farming tradition or not. One possibility is that farming in other regions of the continent is the result of contact diffusion. Contact diffusion occurs when people learn of the existence of a new technology or technique, writing or agriculture, for instance, and then try to devise their own version of it. The classic example of this occurred in the nineteenth century when various nonliterate people first encountered literate people. After observing that it was possible for people to record words and sounds with written symbols, they quickly devised writing systems for their own languages. The Cherokee script is the best-known example of this, but similar developments occurred in Africa. It is possible that the general idea of farming, but not the specifics of how to do it, spread from the northern part of the continent to the south. Even if this were the case, techniques that worked in the Mediterranean climate of the north would be ill suited to farming south of the Sahara. Furthermore, both the crops used south of the Sahara and the techniques used to grow them are so different that most scholars believe that they probably developed independently of North African farming.

Indeed the number of different areas of crop domestication in sub-Saharan Africa is remarkable, especially when compared to Eurasia. In Eurasia the wheat- and barley-based approach to agriculture that developed in the Middle East was able to spread across a broad swath of that continent and North Africa. As new people accepted this approach to agriculture, they often added a few local domesticates to the crop repertoire, but the fundamentals remained the same. A second center of agricultural innovation occurred in East Asia involving rice farming, and there may have been an independent development of root crop farming in Southeast Asia. Because Eurasia has an East–West axis, huge areas of the continent had roughly similar climates and could support similar crops. Africa is arranged on a North–South axis, which means it has many more types of climates. This restricts the spread of domesticated crops. The result is that Africa, like the similarly configured American continents, had many areas of agricultural innovation, and some parts of the continent, notably southern Africa, acquired their first farmers in recent times. The continent's geography was not the only hindrance to the rapid spread of agriculture. The number of wild plants that make good candidates for domestication is few south of the Sahara, especially when

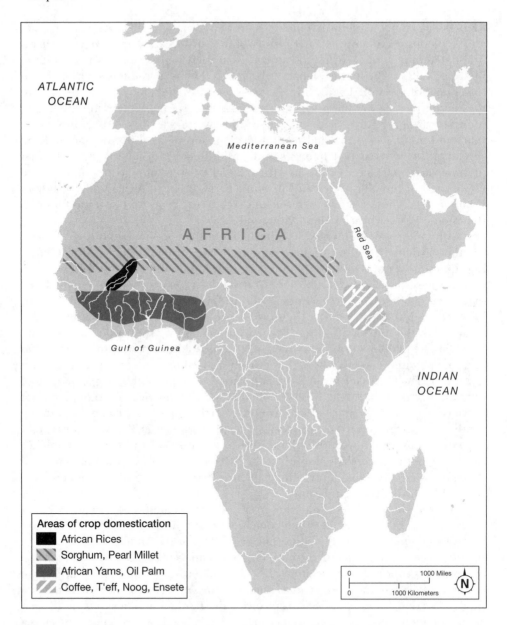

Map 3-1: Areas of crop domestication

compared with the Middle East, where such plants abound. The result was a more deliberate pace to the spread of agriculture and the use of crops that have in some cases been abandoned as other more productive crops have become available.

There are at least three different loci of crop domestication in sub-Saharan Africa. One is in the West Africa Sahel where **sorghum** and pearl **millet** were domesticated. Another is Ethiopia where such crops as t'eff, noog, qat, finger millet,

A man harvesting sorghum, one of the crops originally
domesticated in West Africa.

ensete, and—most critically—coffee were domesticated. The final major center
of domestication is in the West African forest belt where yams and the oil palm
were grown. It is also possible that in both Ethiopia and the Sahel there were
actually two different centers of domestication, giving us a total of five centers
of domestication in sub-Saharan Africa.

Let us look first at the Sahel. Here local wild grasses were domesticated as
early as 5000 B.C.E. Two varieties of sorghum—guinea sorghum and bicolor
sorghum—were complemented by pearl millet. Other varieties of millet were domesticated in other parts of Africa and Asia, but pearl millet appears to be a uniquely
Sahelian crop, which spread from there to other parts of the world, including the
Middle East and India. Sorghum is also a uniquely African crop that has achieved a
worldwide distribution. (Millet should be familiar to you as the small yellow seeds
found in bird food and seven-grain bread; sorghum is grown in North America and
Europe as feed for cattle, but unless you live in farm country you may never have
seen it.) These two grains were well adapted to the climate of the Sahel. Both are
much better suited to the rainfall pattern of the Sahel than are wheat and barley.
Wheat and barley thrive where there is dependable rainfall in the winter. In the
Sahel the rain comes in the summer months and is anything but dependable. In the
northernmost reaches of the Sahel, where the rainfall is minimal and unpre-
dictable, millet is the crop of choice. Some varieties of pearl millet can be harvested
within 60 days of planting and can scrape by with tiny amounts of moisture.
Sorghum is more productive than millet, but also requires more moisture. It is
grown in wetter climates, its range reaching almost to the edge of the forest zone.

Another crop was domesticated in this region, and it is sufficiently different
from millet and sorghum that it may constitute a separate instance of agricultural

innovation. **Glaberrima rice** (*o. glaberrima*) is a type of rice grown in only a few regions of West Africa. Though it is currently being replaced by Asian rice (*o. sativa*), it has an ancient history. Elaborate terracing and special tools are often used in its cultivation, and these are sufficiently different from the dry land farming techniques used for growing millet and sorghum that some historians believe that the inland delta of the Niger, where glaberrima rice was first domesticated, may represent an independent locus of domestication.

The first concrete evidence of crop domestication in the West African forest zone appears in 3000 B.C.E. However, the nature of the crops grown in the forest makes dating difficult. The two crops that formed the core of the forest farming crop repertoire were the guinea **yam** and the oil palm. Guinea yams are root crops. Unlike grains, which can leave behind archaeological evidence, root crops are basically archaeologically invisible. They are soft and prone to rot rapidly compared to grains and so tend to turn to mush rather than survive to be studied by archaeologists. As a result, the dating of their domestication is based on indirect evidence, mostly the presence of tools that appear to be intended for their cultivation. The oil palm is also difficult to date because it is only semidomesticated—there are no real differences between the plants that grow wild and those that are cultivated. Thus, it is difficult to know whether the palm nuts that appear in the archaeological record are farmed or gathered. Given these conditions, it is not surprising that the dating of these events is contentious. Based on the presence of what appear to be hoe blades, some scholars have suggested that some type of farming of root crops might have occurred as early as 20,000 B.P., which if it were true would be the earliest known farming on the planet. Linguistic evidence, however, supports the more recent date of 3000 B.C.E.

Farming in the forest zone has always been a challenge. The high rainfall amounts make it almost impossible to grow grain, so the cultivation of millet and sorghum could not spread into the forest, just as wheat and barley could not be grown in the Sahel. Thus, early West African farmers were "stuck" with guinea yams. Guinea yams are tasty, but they are not very productive. Their low productivity, coupled with the dangers of living on a single crop, probably served to keep the population density of the forests fairly low. It has also meant that forest zone farmers have typically been on the lookout for new crops; and crops introduced from other parts of the world, notably the banana, manioc, and maize, gained rapid acceptance in the forest zone.

Probably the most prolific and historically problematic center of plant domestication is Ethiopia. Ethiopia is unusual in that its climate can support Mediterranean crops such as wheat and barley, but it is also the locus of an amazing number of local domestications. Some of these crops have enjoyed worldwide popularity, whereas others have remained primarily local. Some of the Ethiopian crops that have gained acceptance outside of Ethiopia are finger millet and, of course, coffee. Finger millet was probably once used as a primary food crop, but it is now used mostly for making beer. It is found all over East Africa and is cultivated as far away as India.

But the majority of Ethiopian crops are cultivated exclusively in Ethiopia. The "king" of Ethiopia's grains is **t'eff**. T'eff is a tiny seeded grain that thrives at high altitudes. It is used for making enjera, which is the spongy, flat bread that is the backbone of Ethiopian cuisine. Small amounts of t'eff are grown in South Arabia, which has strong cultural ties to Ethiopia, but otherwise it is found only in the highlands of Ethiopia. Noog, an oil seed, is also an exclusively Ethiopian crop. These crops thrive only in the higher regions of Ethiopia. Also at home in the highlands are coffee and qat, a tree whose leaves are chewed for their stimulating effect.

In the lower and warmer regions, a completely different crop is grown. This is ensete, also called the "false banana," which looks a bit like a banana tree. However, it is not the fruit of the tree that is eaten, but its starchy pith. Ensete is grown only in the Ethiopian lowlands, despite its impressive productivity. Under good conditions it can support high population densities. As is the case with glaberrima rice in West Africa, ensete is so different from the crops grown in the adjacent areas that some scholars consider that its domestication may have occurred independently of the grains domesticated in the area. Thus, Ethiopia may be home to two separate, distinct developments of agriculture.

The dating of Ethiopian agriculture is difficult. Linguists see evidence for farming as far back as 7000 B.C.E., which would put ancient Ethiopians among the world's first farmers. Archaeologists are unconvinced by the linguistic evidence and put the date closer to 3000 B.C.E. Whatever the antiquity of Ethiopian agriculture, it is clear that the area was a hotbed of domestication and agricultural innovation. Ethiopia is also unique in that it is the only area of sub-Saharan Africa where the use of the plow and animal traction is ancient.

Animal Domestication

For the most part Africa's first farmers used locally domesticated crops. Over time, some of the crops they domesticated spread to other areas of the globe, and they in turn acquired new crops from Asia and the Americas. Interestingly, only one animal was without a doubt domesticated in Africa, and that is the guinea fowl. Other probable domestications include the domestic cat and the onager—a type of donkey. But all of the really essential domestic animals were introduced from outside. These include cattle, sheep, goats, camels, and chickens. Some, like cattle and camels, were introduced more than once at different times and from different sources. Why this should be the case is puzzling. If Africans were capable of domesticating so broad a range of plants, why did they not domesticate any of the many large animal species that roamed the continent?

The answer seems to have to do with the luck of the draw. For whatever reason, despite the abundance of large animals in Africa, none of them seem to be temperamentally suited to domestication. It is clear from wall paintings that the Egyptians tried without success to domesticate gazelles. Gazelles are simply too nervous and prone to flight to make good domesticates. In the last couple of hundred years, several different people have tried to domesticate zebras. They seem to be so much like donkeys and horses that one would think they would be excellent candidates for domestication. However, no one has succeeded—in part because zebras are ill tempered and prone to biting and not letting go. Elephants were occasionally tamed; we know this because several armies left the continent bent on conquest in Europe and Arabia equipped with elephants, but even Asian elephants are never really domesticated. They refuse to breed in captivity and have to be captured in the wild.

Through no fault of their own, Africans did not domesticate any of the large animals (except possibly the onager) available to them. However, they did make early and extensive use of sheep, cattle, and goats. In many instances it appears that herding preceded farming in Africa, and there are some regions of the continent, the Cape region of South Africa for instance, that were suited to agriculture but held only herders until recent times. In most of the rest of the world the pattern is the opposite; agriculture nearly always preceded herding.

By 6000 B.C.E. domestic cattle were found throughout North Africa. These were probably introduced from Southwest Asia. This strain of cattle eventually made its way across the Sahara into West and East Africa. One surviving variety of this type of cattle is the West African N'Dama breed. The **N'Dama** is a small cow that has the unique property of being sufficiently resistant to trypanosomiasis that it is able to survive in the tsetse belts of West Africa. This broad category of cattle breeds was joined by another type of cow around 1500 B.C.E., when humped cattle were introduced from India. These cattle spread from east to west across the continent, giving rise to a number of new breeds that are noted for their hardiness.

The evidence for the spread of goats and sheep is less detailed than it is for cattle, but it is clear that it did not substantially precede the arrival of cattle and that all African goat and sheep varieties derive from species originally domesticated in the Middle East. Camels, first domesticated in Arabia, appeared in the Nile Valley by 700 B.C.E., and horses appear to have been introduced to the Nile by 1600 B.C.E. The chicken (from India) was common in North Africa by Roman times and appears south of the Sahara by 600 C.E.

Controversies in African History: African Food Crops in the Non-African World

The story of the transfer of American food crops like maize, potatoes, cassava, and tomatoes to the Old World after Columbus opened a sea route between Europe and the Americas has become a fairly common theme in the world history narrative. This exchange of crops was a crucial part of a larger process which was dubbed the Columbian Exchange by the historian Alfred Crosby. Crosby was one of the first scholars to point out the revolutionary effect that these new food crops had on Old World diets. In cold, damp northern Europe the potato proved an invaluable addition to the crop repertoire. In the Punjab region of South Aisa, no meal is complete without tomatoes, potatoes, and chilies, all of which derive from the Americas and were unknown to Indian cooks before 1500. For Africans, maize and cassava, both immensely

productive plants, were probably the most significant additions to their diets. But other American crops were also added to African cuisines. How West Africans got along without the chilies that are now essential to many of their dishes is difficult to imagine. There is no doubt that food crops brought to Africa from other regions, both before and since Columbus, have played a major role in shaping African diets and economies.

But the transfer of crops from the Americas and elsewhere to Africa is hardly the whole story. There is long history of African food crops leaving the continent and being adopted in other regions of the world. Before the Columbian Exchange the most important of these was sorghum. Sorghum was first domesticated in the West African Sahel possibly as early 4000 or 5000 B.C.E. It and pearl millet ultimately spread worldwide, and now both are staples in the Middle East, and South and East Asia. In fact, sorghum ranks fourth in global consumption after rice, wheat, and maize.

The global spread of sorghum happened thousands of years before Columbus, but Africa was more than just a passive recipient of food crops during the Columbian Exchange. According to Judith Carney, author of the book *Black Rice* (2001), African crops and African farmers played a central role in the spread of rice to the Americas. There are two centers of rice domestication in the world, one in East Asia and the other in West Africa. Currently, most of the rice grown in West Africa and all of the rice grown in the Americas is the sativa variety that derives from East Asia. But a close reading of the early accounts of rice growing in the Americas suggests that in both Brazil and South Carolina the varieties used by the first rice farmers were West African glaberrima rices rather than sativa rices.

Furthermore, most of the early rice growing was done by African slaves or by communities of escaped slaves, usually for their own consumption. In South Carolina, which has been more thoroughly studied than the Brazilian case, it is also clear that it was Africans who adapted West African tidal irrigation systems to South Carolina's tidal estuaries. In West Africa several different sets of techniques were used to grow rice in different environments. The most distinctive of these was called mangrove rice. In mangrove rice cultivation, mangrove trees were cleared from tidal creeks and the fertile but salt-filled soil was enclosed by earthen levees. When the tide went out and fresh water filled the creeks, the fresh water was admitted to the fields to rinse the salt out. When the tide came in the hollowed-out logs that allowed water into the fields were blocked to keep the salt water out. Eventually the salt washed out of the soil and rice was planted in the fertile soil. Men did the work of preparing these fields with a long-handled shovel called a *kayendo*. Women handled the harvest and the processing of the rice.

As much work went into processing rice as went into growing it. The rice had to be pounded sufficiently hard to remove the husk but not so hard as to break the grains. Removing the husk was relatively easy. The real challenge was to get the bran off, and thus make the rice white rather than reddish brown. This was done by lengthy but careful pounding. A skilled rice miller could finish having broken only 10 percent of the grains; a less competent one might easily break half of them. Thus, the preparation of rice was as much a skilled task as growing it. One of the techniques used by West Africans to prepare rice was parboiling. This involved briefly boiling the rice soon after it was harvested and before it was pounded. The effect was to drive nutrients in the bran into the grain and to make cooked rice less sticky. All over West Africa rice is cooked without fat in it and the cook's goal is to produce grains that do not stick to each other. By contrast, East Asians prefer varieties of rice and cooking techniques that cause their rice grains to stick to each other. In India, the Middle East, and southern Europe rice is always cooked with fat.

South Carolina plantations used field preparation techniques devised by West Africans to harness their tidal estuaries for irrigation. They used tools, like the hollow log sluices and *kayendo,* that also came from West Africa. Their plantations also had many, though not all, of the elements of the gender division of labor that prevailed in West African rice growing. Techniques invented in Africa for the processing of rice also came to the Americas where pounding rice was the standard processing technique until the advent of mechanical rice milling in the eighteenth century. African rice preparation techniques also came to the Americas. How do North Americans prefer their rice? They eat it parboiled, prefer grain separation, and cook it without fat. Although sativa rice has replaced glaberrima rice because it is better suited to mechanical milling, every other aspect of rice culture in North America is African.

The Social, Political, and Economic Impact of Food Production

The change to food production involved changing plants and animals to suit human needs. It also required significant changes in human behavior. Without a doubt, the advent of food production is the single biggest change that has happened in human history. Although it is fairly certain that sedentary living preceded the origins of agriculture, agriculture allowed for settled groups to become significantly bigger and allowed the creation of social hierarchies, the accumulation of wealth, and the creation of government. Agriculture also required more disciplined work, different ways of perceiving the passage of time, more long-range planning, and the capacity to ration the harvested crop so that it would last through the year.

Perhaps the single most important change was that food production supported much denser human populations. Where a foraging band might number 150 people, a farming village might have as many as a couple of thousand people in it. The implications of this are many. First, it means that any conflict between a group of farmers and a group of foragers was likely to be decided in the farmers' favor. The force of numbers alone would be sufficient to give them a significant advantage. Numbers, however, were not their only advantage. When people lived in small, mobile bands, they probably had little experience of infectious disease. If an outbreak of disease occurred, it would usually kill the whole band, and the spread of the disease would stop there. As a result, foragers lacked immunity to many of the diseases that are a familiar part of life for those of us who live in settled communities. As farming communities got bigger, infectious diseases took hold in these communities. Farming communities were large enough that despite what must have been horrific early experiences with disease, they were able to reach a sort of equilibrium with the microbes that preyed on them. There were enough survivors of epidemics for the communities to survive and over time for the diseases to become childhood diseases. Most children would be exposed to the diseases, and if they survived the experience they would then be immune. Thus, farming communities became breeding grounds for diseases and humans who were immune to those diseases. Contact between such communities and small foraging communities, even if it were friendly contact, could have lethal results for the foragers.

These traits—high population density and the accompanying diseases—give farming communities what Jared Diamond has termed "farmer power." Farmer power is responsible for the steady replacement of foragers by farmers, not just in Africa but worldwide. Although there are foraging societies in modern Africa, they are few and usually occupy land that is unsuitable for farming. Over the millennia farmers and herders have taken over all the land suited to food production. While some of these groups, notably the Pygmies of Central Africa and the San in parts of southern Africa, may represent a continuous foraging tradition, it is by no means certain that all the foraging groups left in Africa are "survivors" of an older way of life. It appears that some of them may have been forced by adversity into foraging within historic times.

As farming became established in Africa, several different styles of food production appeared. These variations were caused by the crops that were used and by the nature of the environment. In North Africa and Ethiopia the plow was used to grow grain. In the rest of the continent the plow was not used, either because the tsetse fly precluded the use of large animals for traction or the soils were not well suited to the use of plows. In the southern tip of the continent, where there were good soils and no tsetse flies, isolation meant that there was no farming. In those regions where the plow was not used, the hoe was the standard agricultural implement. Hoe-wielding farmers grew a wide range of crops from yams in the forest to sorghum and millet in the savannahs.

In much of the continent, especially those areas where hoe-based farming was employed, the environment posed challenges for farmers. The responses that African farmers devised to those challenges shaped African societies in interesting ways. In most of the continent, soils are too poor to be farmed continuously. Instead, farmers practice what is called **shifting cultivation**. They clear the trees and brush from a field and then burn the brush. The burning serves several purposes. It gets the trees out of the way; it releases the nutrients stored in the trees, increasing the fertility of the soil; and the heat of the fire kills most of the weed seeds that would otherwise compete with the crop. After a few years—two or three where the soils are really poor or as many as ten where the soils are better—the field is abandoned and the process is repeated in a new field while the old field is allowed to recover. This is a labor-intensive way to farm. The human labor requirements of farming with hoes and clearing new land on a regular basis created unique social structures.

For most of African history land has been abundant and labor scarce. The challenge faced by farming societies and ambitious individuals was usually that of getting access to labor rather than to land. A wealthy people or a wealthy person controlled the labor needed to clear and farm land. There were several ways different African societies went about organizing labor. The most common of these was the kinship group. Various types of familial groups, from the simple extended family to larger groups such as clans, could be called on to do agricultural labor. Women were central to these kinship groups. Because most (though certainly not all) farm work is done by women in hoe-farming societies, the number of women in a family or kinship group was critical to its success. The number of women in a kinship group is also a critical determinant of the group's reproductive potential. The more women, the more potential children, and the bigger and stronger the group. Thus, polygyny, which is the practice of men having multiple wives, became widespread in Africa. Obviously, this is not practicable for all men—there are never enough women in a society for all men to have multiple wives. Polygyny was and is a social ideal in most of Africa, and it is widely practiced and valued by elites. Obviously, no one knows for certain how African societies were structured 3,000 years ago, but many recent African groups have followed the pattern just outlined.

If women perform much of the agricultural labor in Africa, the clearing of new land has traditionally been men's work. Social institutions that mobilize men's labor for this purpose are many, but a notable one is the age set. In many African societies groups of young men of approximately the same age are initiated into groups, called *age sets* or **age grades** by anthropologists, to which they will belong for life. The age sets serve several purposes, one of which is to provide social solidarity across kinship lines. But another purpose they serve is that they allow the mobilization of labor for really big jobs. Some tasks, notably war and the clearing of land, often require more labor than kinship groups can muster. The age set can be called on for these purposes. As the members of an age set get older and new age sets are initiated, their rights and duties change. Younger age sets are typically expected to do more vigorous work whereas older age sets do things that require experience and judgment, such as governance and attending to judicial matters.

Food production changed African life in profound ways. It allowed for higher population densities, opening the door to social hierarchy and to the creation of states. It shaped social institutions, especially those related to labor. The rest of this book deals with the results of this change. All the migrations, wars, cities, states, empires, colonies, and struggles that are African history depend on food production.

The Bantu Expansion

In the late nineteenth century, as colonial governments and missionary organizations began the systematic study of African languages, European scholars noticed something interesting. If one were to draw a line from the Cameroun Highlands (on the border between Cameroun and Nigeria) to where the equator crosses the East African coast, one would find that with a few exceptions, all of the languages spoken in this large area are closely related. Obviously, most geographically linked languages are related, but the similarity of these widely dispersed languages was such that it caught the attention of early observers. In an area much larger than Western Europe people spoke languages almost as closely related as the Romance languages (French, Italian, Spanish, Portuguese, and Romanian). These languages cover only a fraction of Europe, whereas in southern Africa languages of a roughly comparable degree of similarity cover an area much larger than Europe.

This language family is referred to as **Bantu**, which is a combination of -ntu— the common root for person—and ba, which is a common plural prefix. The Bantu languages are a subgroup of the larger Niger-Congo group that is spoken from modern Senegal to South Africa, but more than half of this geographical area is covered by just one minor branch (Bantu) of the **Niger-Congo family** tree. Early scholars also observed that there were tiny pockets of isolated languages, which is to say languages totally unrelated to their neighbors, dotted throughout the area otherwise covered by the Bantu languages. In Tanzania there is a language called Sandawe, which has some interesting similarities to the **Khoisan** languages that are spoken in parts of southern Africa. Specifically, Sandwe and the Khoisan languages have clicking sounds that are found in almost no other languages. Scholars also noticed that, like the few surviving Khoisan speakers in southern Africa, the speakers of the Khoisan isolates in Kenya and Tanzania were almost all foragers rather than farmers. They concluded that most of the area where Bantu languages are spoken now was once inhabited by speakers of Khoisan languages. These people would have been foragers and were probably, like the Khoisan, physically small. The Pygmies of the central African rain forest may be descendants of these original inhabitants or they may represent a lost language tradition, because they now speak Bantu languages. Up to this point most modern scholars would agree with their predecessors. But they do not agree with the earlier position about how Bantu speakers replaced the Khoisan speakers.

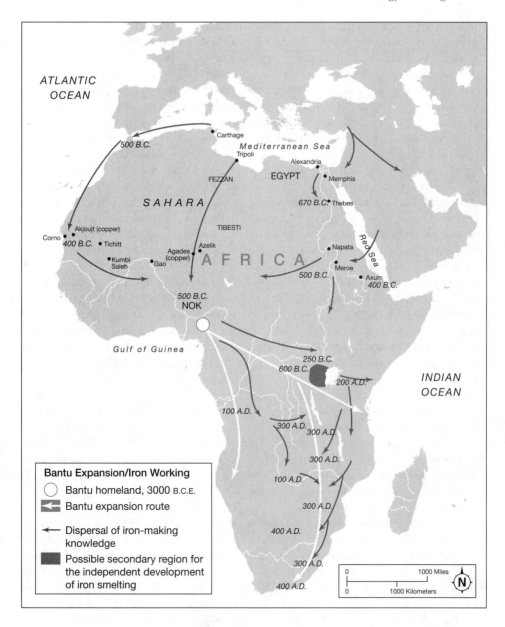

Map 3-2: Bantu expansion and iron working

Early scholars, reflecting prejudices and notions of their time—as historians always do—concluded that a great folk migration had occurred in southern Africa. They belived that the Bantu people, who were iron-wielding farmers, displaced the smaller foragers who inhabited the southern subcontinent. They drove the Pygmies into the most isolated parts of the forest and the San into the unfarmable parts of the Kalahari. According to this interpretation, these events took place over a fairly short period of time, comparable perhaps to the Germanic invasions of Western Europe. Moreover, like the Germanic invasions of ancient Western Europe, this Bantu migration was a deliberate, conscious, and military affair.

Few modern scholars take this last part of the story seriously. First of all, this version of the story seems awfully convenient from an imperialist's perspective. When these ideas were cooked up in the early part of the twentieth century, Europeans were in the final stages of conquering the areas of the continent inhabited by Bantu speakers. How convenient that the Bantu speakers' claim to the land came not as aboriginal inhabitants, but as recent conquerors, just like the Europeans! Furthermore, this was a time when racial hierarchy fascinated European scholars. To them, it seemed only natural that taller "Negroid" Africans should subjugate smaller "pygmy" peoples and that this process should take place through military conquest. Again, it is easy to see how this scenario might serve European interests, consciously or unconsciously. If a superior race could occupy vast territories at the expense of an inferior one once, surely the same thing might legitimately occur again.

To be fair, early scholars were basically right about the Bantu expansion. What they got wrong were the timing and the causes. Instead of being a brief conquest, it took place over millennia. The first stages, especially, took place at a glacial pace—sometimes as slowly as 3 or 4 kilometers a decade. Later the pace of the expansion picked up, but it was always a gradual affair. Second, it was not a conquest in the classic military sense. Rather, it was a case of farmers occupying land that from their perspective was unused. There must at times have been real conflict with the aboriginal inhabitants, but in general it seems that the Pygmies and others were more often absorbed, subordinated, or just slowly squeezed out. Finally, the Bantu speakers did not supplant the indigenes because they had iron and the Pygmies and Khoisan did not. In fact, the expansion began long before anyone in Africa (or anywhere else in the world) had iron, though iron may have been a factor in the later stages of the expansion. Instead the root cause of the expansion was probably "farmer power," Jared Diamond's term for the advantage that farmers enjoyed over foragers.

By looking for words that are common to almost all Bantu languages, linguists have been able to reconstruct the world of the early Bantu speakers. They had words for **yam** and *oil palm* and terms related to pottery, but none for metalworking nor any for grain. Thus, it appears that they came not from the savannah where grains are grown but from the forest. They made pottery but not metal. Instead they would have used stone tools, probably of the smooth, polished kind we mentioned earlier in this chapter, as the archeological marker that indicates Stone Age farmers. The modern distribution of the Bantu languages, the environment that is indicated by proto-Bantu vocabulary, and some archaeological evidence all suggest that the proto-Bantu probably lived on the border between Cameroun and Nigeria. Sometime around 3000 B.C.E. they began to move into new territory.

This probably occurred for a number of reasons. Farmers need to open up new fields periodically, either because old ones are exhausted or because of population growth. Because their world was sparsely populated, they would not always have gone simply to the nearest bits of land, but rather to the most desirable. In so doing, they would have leapfrogged over the mediocre bits of land to get to the best. Farmers probably would have pushed their way down rivers, which often had good land nearby. As the newly established communities grew and good land became scarcer, settlers would have filled in some of the land that was initially skipped over. Farming communities probably also spread as people with political ambitions struck out on their own, forming new communities where they could get out of the shadow of powerful elders and others who might thwart their ambitions.

Farming communities spread for other reasons, too. According to Diamond, part of "farmer power" has to do with superior numbers. Farming supports more people in a smaller area than does foraging. This means that farmers had a military advantage over foragers. It also means that they might have hosted parasitic and infectious disease that helped to eliminate the foragers they did come into contact with as they moved farther south and east. For example, the rise of farming in West Africa seems to have coincided with the rise of malaria. Indeed, it is yam farming—the very crop grown by the proto-Bantu—that is thought to have created the conditions that allowed the right kind of mosquitoes to begin to live near people in the forest. Thus, as the early Bantu-speaking farmers moved into new territories, they may have brought diseases—among them malaria—that weakened or killed the foraging peoples who had less experience with these diseases.

Whatever allowed the Bantu speakers to supplant the aboriginal foragers, it did not result in their complete removal. Foragers survive into the present in the forests and to a lesser extent in other regions. Some modern Pygmies still exchange meat and honey for other foodstuffs or manufactured goods, just as their ancestors likely traded for bananas and metals. Many Pygmies also seek work on the farms of their farming neighbors. Furthermore, Pygmies enjoy an odd status in many Bantu societies. They are recognized as the original inhabitants, and as such they often are needed to symbolically confer legitimacy on those in political authority. Oral tradition often credits Pygmies with teaching the first farmers how to live in the forest environments that were new to them (not unlike the stories every American schoolchild learns about Native Americans rescuing the Pilgrims from starvation). At the same time, Pygmies are also looked down on as a type of savage. In southern Africa the Khoisan often survive as political subordinates of Bantu herders or farmers. Here, too, it is clear that the situation is more complex than a quick look at the patron–client relationship suggests. Many of the Bantu languages of southern Africa include clicks, apparently borrowed from the Khoisan tongues. So Bantu farmers did not simply kill off the foragers or even just move into areas where disease had eliminated the foragers. Instead, they lived in close enough contact with them to absorb elements of the language.

The initial phase of the Bantu expansion occurred in the forests of central Africa. By the first century C.E., Bantu speakers mostly occupied the forests. For further expansion to take place, Bantu speakers had to move into the savannahs of eastern Africa, to them an unfamiliar territory. There, where rainfall was less intense and less predictable, their standard crop repertoire of root crops and oil palm would not work. They had to master a new type of farming, often done in conjunction with hunting, or in some cases they adopted cattle keeping as a way of life. As Bantu speakers moved into these new territories, they encountered **Cushitic** speakers, from whom they seem to have learned a great deal about grain farming. Much of the agricultural vocabulary in eastern Bantu languages derives from Cushitic, which is part of the Afro-Asiatic family.

By the first century C.E., some Bantu farming communities were probably present on the East African coast. From there the expansion turned southward, where farmers began to augment their food production with systematic hunting. As they moved into the southern reaches of the continent some groups became cattle keepers. By 1100 C.E., Bantu speakers were present from Cameroun to southern Somalia to South Africa. They made their livings in a variety of ways, from fishing to farming to keeping cattle. Some lived in major states, some in stateless societies, and others in the emerging city-states of the East African coast.

Metallurgy and the Banana

Two major technologies appeared during the course of this expansion, iron working and the banana (food crops are technologies of a sort). The histories of both these technologies are relevant to more than just the Bantu expansion. Both were used by Africans all over the continent, but they both played a particular role in the Bantu expansion and so fit nicely in this chapter. Iron was almost certainly discovered first in Anatolia (modern-day Turkey) and diffused from there to the rest of the Old World. The Hittites of Anatolia figured out how to make iron around 1400 B.C.E. They managed to keep their new technology to themselves for almost 200 years, but by 1200 B.C.E. the cat was out of the bag. Iron was too useful a technology to keep under wraps. People all over the world made use of copper and its alloys (bronze and brass) long before they had iron. And unlike iron, copper smelting and the making of copper alloys was discovered independently many times in the Old World. Copper, however, is soft and does not make good cutting tools. Bronze and brass are harder, but are soft compared with iron, and the ores needed to make them are rare compared to iron ore. The process of smelting iron requires more of a creative leap than making copper. Copper ores look metallic, and the melting point of copper is so low that you can melt copper with a really hot wood fire. Thus, the smelting of copper was a reasonably intuitive process. By contrast, iron ore looks like dirt and rocks more than it looks like metal. Further, iron smelting requires tremendous heat, well beyond what a normal fire can produce, and a successful smelt requires a chemical flux (usually lime or crushed seashells) in addition to heat and ore.

In short, we should be amazed that the Hittites ever figured out the process, rather than wondering why anybody else did not figure it out themselves. Regions such as Europe and North and West Africa likely learned ironworking via a diffusion of the technology along lines of trade or migration. Only Native Americans and Austronesians appear to have been so isolated as to have been beyond the spread of this important technology.

Iron is wonderfully useful compared to copper or bronze. Iron ore is common, and many parts of the African continent have high-grade ore. Dala Hill, the historic center of the ancient city of Kano in northern Nigeria, is basically a huge mound of high-grade iron ore. One of the most common soil types in Africa—laterite—is a low-grade iron ore. By contrast, copper is a rather rare metal, so much so that on modern construction sites copper wire scraps are saved and given to apprentice electricians to recycle as a sort of bonus. Copper is too expensive to use for agricultural tools and too soft to really be useful anyway. Copper was used mostly to make luxury items, and copper alloys were used to make weapons, but agriculture remained Neolithic. Iron, because it is harder and its ores are more common, is a more egalitarian metal. Once the techniques needed to make it are understood, it can be used to make tools for farmers and weapons for the common person. Metal tools served to make farmers more productive, and metal weapons made soldiers more deadly.

Knowledge of the techniques needed to make iron initially entered Africa from Southwest Asia. Egyptians were aware of iron as early as 1000 B.C.E., but apparently did not make it. Iron making requires tremendous amounts of heat produced by charcoal. It takes the charcoal of 10 to 15 trees to make a single kilo of iron. A successful smelt producing 10 to 20 kilos of iron can easily consume 20,000 pounds of wood. Throughout the world, the development of ironworking technology resulted in substantial deforestation. Egypt has long been poor in trees and so was not an easy place to make iron. In the middle of the seventh century B.C.E., iron-wielding Assyrians invaded Egypt and forced Egypt's Nubian rulers to retreat down the Nile to their Nubian homeland. With them came knowledge of ironmaking. The kingdom of Meroë, which flourished from 591 B.C.E. to 300 C.E., turned this knowledge into a major industry. Meroë had trees in abundance (at least in comparison to Egypt) and was able to become an iron exporter. Even now, huge heaps of slag, the by-product of iron making, can be seen around the ruins of Meroë. One theory about the fall of Meroë is that the iron industry there consumed so many trees that the area was deforested and lost its ability to sustain agriculture.

From Meroë the knowledge of ironmaking continued to spread southward, likely following existing trade networks. By 250 B.C.E., the technology had reached the Great Lakes region and by 400 C.E. the southern tip of the continent. The chronology of the Iron Age archaeological sites in this chain of diffusion is straightforward—the farther south you go the later evidence of ironmaking appears, which suggests diffusion from the north. There is, however, an important anomaly. In the interlacustrine region (i.e., the area between lakes Victoria and Tanganyika) there are ironmaking sites that appear to date from the early sixth century. If these dates are right, then ironmaking appeared in this region at roughly the same time it appeared in Meroë, a thousand miles to the north. This anomaly suggested to some archaeologists that there may have been an independent discovery of ironmaking in this region.

Foremost among the advocates of "African Innovation" in ironworking is the ethnoarchaeologist Peter Schmidt. Schmidt combined traditional excavations of iron-smelting sites in East Africa with oral interviews of inhabitants who had smelted and worked iron in the early twentieth century (prior to being driven out of business by imports of cheap scrap iron from Europe). Based on this research, and with the help of his aged informants, Schmidt was able to re-create working examples of East African–style iron smelters. His resulting analysis is that the East African technology was distinct from that introduced into North and West Africa from Anatolia—and thus an innovation rather than a transfer of knowledge. In particular, the East African smelters seem to have achieved significantly higher temperatures than those elsewhere in the world, because their furnaces utilized a system of pipes and bellows that both preheated and forced air into the smelting chamber. This design apparently produced steel rather than iron because the temperature was high enough to bond carbon atoms to the iron. Thus, argue Schmidt and his supporters, the East African furnaces were not only different, but actually superior.

The second major route by which iron was introduced to Africa was across the Sahara. By 500 B.C.E., iron was being produced at **Nok** in modern Nigeria. From there it spread south and east into the rain forests of Central Africa. By 100 C.E. it had reached the lower reaches of the Congo near the Atlantic coast, and by 300 C.E. it had spread upriver to the headwater regions deep inside central Africa.

Iron was revolutionary everywhere it appeared. There is probably no more significant difference between the societies of the Old World and those of the New World than the presence of iron in the former and its absence in the latter. But the changes wrought by iron in the forest regions of Africa were especially profound. Felling large trees is difficult even with iron tools; it must have been virtually impossible with stone tools. Iron tools allowed the Bantu speakers who had occupied the forest regions to exploit their environment much more intensely, and their populations increased proportionately.

At roughly the same time that iron entered the scene, another equally transformative technology appeared—the banana. To most Americans the banana is a sweet, yellow fruit, but the fruit we know from our grocery stores is but one of almost 200 varieties of banana. Many are starchy rather than sweet, and many are green or reddish in color rather than yellow. In Africa and other parts of the world bananas are roasted, fried, or boiled and mashed. Indeed, bananas serve more or less the same dietary role as do potatoes in the United States. Instead of being served only as a sweet fruit, bananas are a staple. There are even beers and wines made from bananas, and these are tastier than one might think.

In addition to being incredibly versatile, bananas produce lots of food. A relatively small banana garden can supply the needs of a household. But perhaps the banana's best quality is that it can do all this in the wet conditions of the rain forest. One of the problems facing early settlers in the rain forests was that they had only two crops that could survive there—yams and oil palm. Grains, such as millet and sorghum, could not tolerate the high humidity. Bananas were thus a boon to the farmers of the rain forest, and in combination with iron this led to an intensification of the settlement of the forests.

The origins of the banana are poorly understood. The major center of banana domestication is Southeast Asia. However, a possible wild ancestor of the banana was discovered on the island of Pemba off the coast of East Africa, and a fossil banana was discovered in West Africa in 2001 that appears to date from 500 B.C.E. It appears that bananas arrived in Africa not once but in several waves. The earliest of these occurred 3,000 years ago, early enough to have played a role in the Bantu expansion. No strong candidates have been proposed as the human agents in this transfer, but the huge variety of plantains (a type of banana) that are cultivated in

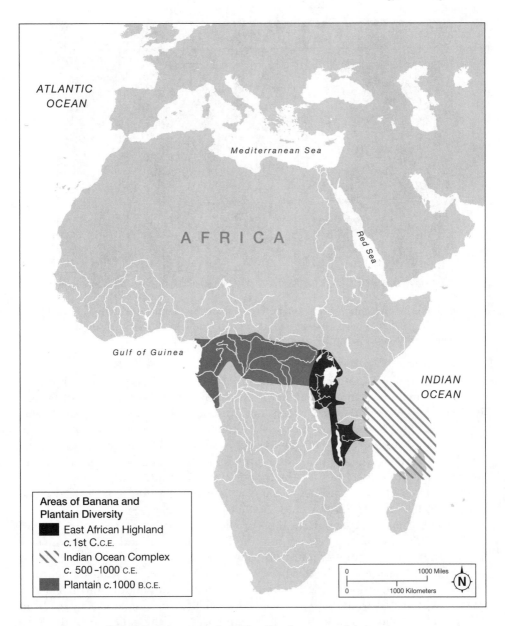

Map 3-3: Asian crops in Africa: The banana and Asian rice

tropical central Africa suggests that the plantian must have arrived in the distant past. A second wave of bananas seems to have arrived around 500 C.E. and these varieties are cultivated around the Great Lakes region of east-central Africa. A third wave of banana varieties arrived relatively recently and these are cultivated on the East African coast and islands. These varieties are part of a broader diffusion of crops associated with Arab trade in the Indian Ocean.

An offering of scrap metal to Gu, god of iron and blacksmiths. Iron making is usually treated as more than just a mundane technology. There is usually a whiff of the supernatural to both smiths and their work.

The second of these waves of banana introductions is associated with one of the great human migrations of all time—the Austroneisan expansion. **Austronesian** is a language group of the same order of magnitude as Indo-European, Afro-Asiatic, or Niger-Congo. Austronesian speakers are found from Hawaii to New Zealand to the island of Madagascar just off the coast of East Africa. That is a remarkably large area for a language family to cover. Until the global spread of English, French, Spanish, and Portuguese pushed the Indo-European family of languages to the far corners of the globe, Austronesian languages had a greater geographical reach than any other language family on the planet.

The earliest Austronesian speakers probably lived in southern China. Around 3000 B.C.E. they began to move out into the Pacific to the island of Formosa (now known as Taiwan). From there Austronesian speakers moved south into the islands of Southeast Asia and into the northern edge of New Guinea. As seafaring ventures most of these migrations were rather minor affairs. The amount of open water these early travelers would have crossed was small, and they could usually see from one island to another. But by the first millennium B.C.E. the ancestors of the Polynesian branch of the Austronesian family were venturing far into the Pacific, settling the islands of Fiji, Tonga, and Samoa. By the first millennium C.E. they had reached Hawaii, New Zealand, and Easter Island, voyages that required extraordinary seamanship, navigation skills, and boats.

It is also clear that one branch of this great migration went west across the Indian Ocean toward Africa, rather than east into the Pacific, and that it ultimately fetched up on the island of Madagascar. The people of Madagascar speak a language (or family of languages) called Malagasy. Malagasy's closest linguistic relative is spoken on the island of Borneo, many thousands of miles away across the Indian Ocean. Further confirming the link between the Malagasy and other Austronesian speakers are such cultural habits as reburial of the dead. With these migrants came, or so it seems at first glance, crops such as the banana, rice, and new varieties of yams and at least one new technology, the outrigger canoe.

The timing of these events is, to say the least, murky. Linguists studying the Malagasy language have concluded, using glottochronology, that Malagasy split off from its Austronesian sibling languages about 2,000 years ago. Further, they assert that there is linguistic evidence for several waves of settlement and for some sustained contact between Madagascar and Southeast Asia. This fits neatly with the standard date for one of the arrivals of the banana, which is about 2,000 years ago. The difficulty comes when archaeology is factored in. Archaeologists can find no evidence that anybody at all lived in Madagascar before 800 c.e., and then they cannot link the cultural materials they have found to any particular Southeast Asian group. That is to say that the tools and pottery they have found at these early sites are not clearly linked to either mainland African sites or to any recognizable tradition in the Austronesian world.

How and when the Malagasy reached Madagascar remains a mystery. But there is no doubt that Madagascar was settled by the westernmost thrust of the Austronesian expansion. Whether they entered an uninhabited island world or moved into a place already settled by mainlanders who had crossed the Mozambique channel is not certain. But over time the people of the mainland coast influenced the Malagasy. They seem to have learned about cattle from the people of the mainland, and their words for cattle and terms related to animal husbandry derive from the Bantu languages of the coast. There are also records of raids carried out by the Sakalava people of northwestern Madagascar as far north as modern Tanzania. By the twelfth century the northern coasts of Madagascar were partly Islamized, and there was trade between Madagascar and the mainland. The Malagasy are different in many respects from other eastern and southern Africans. Their origins and language are different, and their island home allowed them to remain culturally distinct. However, their migration brought new crops and technologies to the continent, and ultimately the Malagasy ended up as participants in the history of eastern Africa.

The arrival of bananas in the forest zone of Central Africa changed the relationship of the Bantu-speaking farmers to their environment. Where once farmers had been forced to rely on the relatively unproductive yam and oil palm combination, they could now add bananas to their crop repertoire. The result was a more intensive style of agriculture and an increase in the population of the forest zone. Ultimately, the histories of these two expansions—Bantu and Austronesian—are intertwined.

Political and Religious Culture in Early African History

In Chapter 2 we discussed the social organization of early African societies—particularly those aspects relating to the division of labor. The question remains to be answered, however, of how these early communities organized themselves politically and how they created a spiritual, as well as physical, landscape. Political and religious frameworks might themselves be seen as forms of human technology because they help groups form identities and operate as communities rather than as individuals.

The challenge of re-creating ancient African societies is often considerable. In the absence of an indigenous written tradition and given the poor archaeological preservation that was often the case in the regions affected by the Bantu expansion, scholars have sought to reconstruct information on these societies by extrapolating backward from existing communities, examining their oral traditions, utilizing linguistic analyses, and examining records left by travelers. Further complicating the issue, however, is the reality that there are a great variety of specific political and religious systems to be found in Africa—a fact that we hope will become increasingly apparent as you work your way through this text. Almost every ethnic group had its own political and religious system. Nonetheless, there are enough factors in common that we can at least speak in general terms about the sort of systems that many, if not most, African societies developed.

In antiquity, many African peoples formed what are now often referred to as "stateless societies," although such systems became increasingly rare over time. These communities were remarkable in that they had no professional political class. That is, nobody spent all their time telling other people what to do. In part, the absence of such a class of political leaders might have existed because forest environments made it difficult to produce a consistent enough surplus of food for a ruling class to live off—especially prior to the introduction of bananas or New World crops such as maize and cassava. Also, the low population density, decentralized nature, and mobility of pastoralist communities made centralized government all but impossible. It is also possible that many of the populations simply preferred not to have professional politicians around. The Igbo-speaking populations of southeastern Nigeria maintained a generally stateless political system into the early twentieth century. The Igbo even have a saying, "The Igbo have no kings." Implicit in such a statement is that the Igbo knew perfectly well what kings were (their neighbors in Benin, as we shall see later, had them), but simply didn't want them.

It is important to keep in mind that not having a state does not mean that these societies were chaotic or anarchic. The absence of a state does not necessarily mean the absence of authority. Kinship, age, knowledge, and personal achievement all provided standards by which relative authority could be established. Further, without a political class, communities tended to solve problems and pass judgments as a unit through discussion (often referred to as palaver in West Africa) and consensus, a process facilitated by the generally small size of forest settlements or pastoralist groups. One might even see these societies as being very democratic in nature in that they allowed the wider population a relatively equitable degree of political influence and provided for a high degree of social mobility based on one's own merit rather than inherited status. Indeed, some political scientists believe that it was via contact with stateless societies in Africa and the Americas that European thinkers began to question the notion that absolute authority invested in an aristocracy was essential to the maintenance of order—a crucial step to developing the idea of popular sovereignty (the idea that "we the people" should be in charge, not an elite minority), which was one of the critical intellectual breakthroughs of the Enlightenment in Europe.

Though individual forest or pastoralist communities tended to be relatively small, the wider spheres of identity could be quite large. Even if separated into villages that contained only a few extended-family units, wider notions of ethnic, linguistic, and religious identity could bring groups together to act as larger units in times of need—such as if threatened by a larger state. Institutions often known as age grades were crucial to such transregional bonds. Children of a recognized generation were deemed to belong to a single age grade and would have the opportunity to interact and grow to know one another during regional festivals that occurred at various times and places. Such bonds could serve as forces of cohesion in times of need. Thus, although outsiders might see no visible institutions of governance for groups such as the Igbo, Dinka, or Masai, in reality there were complex social systems that allowed these "stateless" societies to act as a larger unit when necessary, while otherwise dispensing with the disadvantages of having an elite class in charge of things the rest of the time.

There are hundreds, if not thousands, of indigenous African religions. Despite their diversity, however, these systems share some root commonalities. First, unlike certain religious traditions that originated in the Middle East, African religions tend to be pantheistic rather than monotheistic. Thus, rather than imagining a single god who is all powerful, African religions tend to see the power of the divine as diffuse. There may be only one "true" god, but that god's power is too distant and too powerful to even conceive. As such, it was manifested through a variety of lesser deities who specialized in specific tasks. Within Yoruba religion, for example, there is a high god, Olodumare, who is usually given credit for the creation of the world, humanity, and lesser divinities. For the Yoruba these lesser gods are known as the Orisa, and each has its own special areas of power. For example, Ogun, the god of iron, was first the Orisa of blacksmiths and soldiers, but has in recent decades emerged as the patron of auto mechanics and taxi drivers.

Such a system should be familiar to many readers because certain aspects of pantheism can be seen in the Christian trinity (where Jesus Christ, who lived both as God and Man, serves as the understanding intermediary between humans and the distant and stern "God the Father") and especially in Catholic tradition (with its many saints who serve as "specialized" intermediaries between humans and God). Sufi Islam also allows for the intercession of saints between the believer and God. However, an important distinction between most African religions and Christianity or Islam is the fact that African religions tend not to see the past and future as a conflict between good and evil. Rather, the divine is capable of bringing both good and bad fortune to people, depending on human behavior. Few African religions have an evil devil who is the enemy of the high god or who specializes in leading people astray.

It is also important to distinguish pantheism from polytheism. An example of polytheism would be the religion practiced by the ancient Greeks, who saw the individual gods as "free agents" who often fought among themselves and even occasionally overthrew the high god—as in the case of Zeus overthrowing (and castrating) his father, Chronos. Such a chaotic image of the divine would be inconceivable from the perspective of most African religious systems.

Notably, within traditional African religious systems, humans are capable of both interacting with and eventually becoming part of the spirit world. Many African religions incorporate a belief in spirit possession, wherein individuals can be temporarily inhabited by deities (not unlike being possessed by the Holy Spirit in Pentecostal Christianity). Such individuals are often considered to be imbued with religious power and authority and might be consulted as healers or diviners who could recommend courses of action to avoid or forestall trouble. The power of the world of spirits could also be utilized by the immoral to harm others, and the belief in witchcraft has played an important role in African religious systems. Thus, for many Africans, the divine was and is a very real element in daily life and could be experienced and utilized by all people for both good or ill. Further, an important component of many African religions is the belief that after death, one's ancestors become an important component of the divine. Thus, you may pray to your dead grandmother for aid, just as you might to a specialized deity. All of these factors helped to blur the line between the living and spirit worlds.

Finally, within most African cultural systems, religion was not a separate or unique part of life to be restricted to certain times and places, but rather something that was part and parcel of all activities. Although there might be occasions that demanded religious activity, on a day-to-day basis there was no notion of the secular. Every single element of life could demand spiritual attention. Thus, family relationships, political issues, work, artistic expression, or anything else could easily be seen as spiritual.

Early African Migrations, Technology, and Culture in Global Perspective

Does the African environment pose challenges that other environments do not? Were African responses to the environmental challenges they faced comparable to those of other human societies in other places?

Other tropical environments are challenging for their inhabitants. The tropical parts of Asia and the Americas have similar problems associated with poor soils, seasonal rainfall patterns, and heat that causes the rapid decomposition of humus in the soil. They, too, suffer from the diseases that thrive in hot places. The Americas, like Africa, are north-south oriented and saw the spread of agriculture slowed by the need to adapt crops to new environments. Maize (or corn), which was domesticated in Mexico, took more than 3,000 years to get to northern New England.

Compared with temperate climates, however, the African environment seems more problematic. It hosts any number of debilitating diseases that are not found in cooler places. Its soils are rarely as good as those of more temperate places. In temperate places the winter stops the process of humus decomposition for at least a couple of months a year; furthermore, most of Eurasia has geologically newer soils with more available plant nutrients. In short, the African environment is not significantly more inhospitable to humans than most of the tropical world, but it is a tougher place to make a living than the cooler, temperate parts of Eurasia. It is also worth noting that food production—probably the biggest change humans have been through yet—came later to most of Africa than it did to most of Eurasia. Farming was widespread in Africa before it was widespread in the Americas, but still it lagged millennia behind Eurasian farming.

It is not clear exactly what the implications of this are, but recently Jared Diamond has suggested that it takes at least a couple of millennia of farmer power before a people will create an urban civilization and the social and political institutions that accompany it. Typically, urban civilizations enjoy the same sort of advantages compared to village-level farming societies that villagers enjoy compared to foragers. This is not to say that there is anything inherently better about urban civilization compared to village-level farming, or foraging for that matter. But it does seem that urban states can usually easily dominate other types of societies. Obviously, one can think of numerous counterexamples: the Mongols who crushed many an urban civilization under the hooves of their horses and the Igbo people of Nigeria who lived for centuries next to the state of Benin without coming under its sway. But in general, the pattern seems to favor the urban state.

If and when a society gets its first state is predicated on when it gets its first farmers; getting its first farmers later rather than earlier may be a problem. It is worth noting that in most respects Africa's encounters with Eurasians were much more equal than the American encounter with Eurasia. This may be attributable in part to the earlier rise of agriculture in Africa than in America. By the same token, the late arrival of farming in Africa compared with Eurasia may have meant a long-term, though probably slight, disadvantage for Africans compared with Eurasians.

Africans' responses to their environment are not unlike the responses of other people in tropical places. Shifting cultivation is almost universal in the tropics. In most places where shifting cultivation is practiced and hoes are used instead of the plow, women play a critical farming role. Polygyny is widespread, though not universal, in such places. (Nor, it should be noted, is polygyny exclusively associated with tropical places or hoe farming.) The use of kinship networks to mobilize labor is also common worldwide, though the age grade system seems to be an exclusively African institution.

In the end the important thing is that Africans faced one of the most daunting sets of environmental challenges faced by people anywhere on the planet. They rose to the challenge and devised ways of foraging successfully. Later they domesticated local plant species and produced new breeds of introduced animals that let them exploit the environment even more intensely than they had as foragers. It was and is a remarkable achievement.

The transition to agriculture in Africa caused the expansion of language families and cultural complexes just as it did in some other regions of the world. By way of example, Indo-European languages are spoken from Ireland to India, Afro-Asiatic languages are spoken from Iraq to Nigeria, and the Sino-Tibetan family is spoken from China to Tibet. In each of these cases the expansion of these languages out of a core area into their current distribution is thought to be the result of the discovery of some particularly useful way of making a living that allowed speakers of these languages to rapidly (relatively speaking, of course) occupy new areas. Thus, the rapid expansion of the Chinese into what is now China was probably the result of the spread of early agricultural innovators in its early stages, and the result of imperial policy in its later stages. By contrast, highland New Guinea is home to almost one-fifth of the world's languages. And many of these languages seem to be fundamentally unrelated. The Americas also display a confusing dog's breakfast of linguistic diversity. North American languages are so diverse that linguists have great difficulty classifying them. That North America's languages display such diversity is thought to be the result of a past in which no decisively superior means of farming emerged, allowing its practitioners to rapidly occupy new territory. Instead, many local agricultural innovations occurred as people domesticated a broad variety of food crops.

Unlike the Americas or New Guinea, Africa has several large language families indicating that in terms of its agricultural history, it has more in common with Eurasia than with the Americas. Four major language groups arose on the African continent. One of these—Afro-Asiatic—spread out of Africa and into the Middle East. Speakers of Hebrew and Arabic, both members of the Afro-Asiatic family, are in a loose sense speakers of "African" languages. The arrival of Austronesian speakers would seem a relatively minor matter were it not for the useful crops they brought. Thus, these types of expansions worked both to send African languages and crops out into the world and to bring non-African crops to the continent. Again, unlike the Americas or Australasia, Africa was sufficently connected to Eurasia that innovations of rare importance—ironmaking for example—difused into Africa, affecting the daily lives of farmers and soldiers all over the continent.

During this period Africans developed a critical economic and technological foundation for their world. The technologies and social habits they developed served them well over the last two millennia and ensured that when Europeans appeared on their shores in the fifteenth century, the encounter was between two groups of iron-using farming societies, and hence far more equal than the encounters between Europeans and the stone tool–using farmers and foragers of Australasia and the Americas that happened at roughly the same time.

Useful Works on This Chapter Topic

The standard work on human geography of Africa is James Newman, *The Peopling of Africa: A Geographic Interpretation,* (1995). For an account of the origins of agriculture in Africa and elsewhere and the long-term historical impact of food production on people, see Jared Diamond's *Guns, Germs, and Steel* (1998). On iron, see Peter Schmidt, *Iron Technology in East Africa: Symbolism, Science, and Archaeology* (1997), and Thurston Hall, *Archaeology of Africa: Foods, Metals, asnd Towns* (1998). There are few texts that deal specifically with the issue of stateless societies, but there are a few ethnographic and historical works that offer insights into the working of such groups. These include M. M. Green's *Ibo Village Affairs* (1964), Joseph Calder Miller's *Kings and Kinsmen: Early Mbundu States in Angola* (1992), and Jan Vansina's *Paths in the Rainforest: Towards a Political Tradition in Equatorial Africa* (1990). Benjamin C. Ray's *African Religions: Symbol, Ritual and Community* (1999), John S. Mbiti's *African Religions and Philosophy* (1992), and E. Thomas Lawson's *Religions of Africa: Traditions in Transformation* (1998) offer useful introductions to the complex topic of African traditional religions.

Chapter 4

North and Northeast Africa in Early World History

Many African societies, rather than being isolated from other world regions, have long interacted with other parts of the world in a number of important and complex ways. In this chapter, we will examine the ways that northern African societies, including Egypt and Carthage, and northeast African societies, such as Nubia and Ethiopia, have played important roles in early world history—indeed, interactions that go back to the very beginnings of sedentary agriculture and urban settlement. Via the Mediterranean Sea, Red Sea, and Indian Ocean, these early African communities influenced and were in turn influenced by other societies in the Middle East and southern Europe. There is, however, little scholarly consensus on the nature of these exchanges, for the politics of race and identity have long clouded our interpretation of the role of Africa in early world history. In this chapter, we will examine the history of Ancient Egypt, Nubia, and Carthage and their interactions with other early civilizations. Further, we will look at how the politics of race and identity have "colored" our interpretation of these interactions.

Egypt in Early World History

Although all too many history texts tend to overlook the history of Africa in general, that tendency does not extend to Ancient Egypt. Indeed, if you have studied any African history before, there is a good chance that it was the history of Egypt. Yet, Ancient Egypt is something of a historical enigma. Where it belongs in history is viciously contested. To some Afrocentric scholars, Egypt is the very essence of African history. For many others Egypt is often characterized as more a part of Mediterranean, Middle Eastern, or even European history, but it just happens to sit on the edge of Africa. Perhaps, for example, you have studied Egypt as part of a Western civilization course. As we shall discuss later, these arguments are also tied into the difficult racial politics of exactly who the Ancient Egyptians were.

The origins of Ancient Egypt represent some of the first instances of complex human societies. Indeed, the Nile Valley is the perfect place to start a state-level society. The annual flood brings fertile silts from the Ethiopian highlands to the plains along the Nile River Valley, allowing agriculture to continue indefinitely without overtaxing the soil. Evidence suggests that the inhabitants of the upper Nile region (that is, the "upstream" or southern regions of Egypt) were harvesting wild barley as early as 10,000 B.C.E. Perhaps as early as 5000 B.C.E. permanent agricultural settlements had been established both in the upper and lower Nile regions. These settlements were similar in some ways to other sites found in what is now known as Egypt's Western Desert. Pottery found at the early Nile sites is of a style also found across the West African Sahel and North African region. This evidence suggests that the early Nile settlers may have come to the river valley to escape a savannah that was beginning to make the transition to desert. Still, during the period up to the third millennium B.C.E., the region around the Nile Valley was well enough watered by rain to support some degree of agriculture, so it is probably more accurate to think of the drying of the Sahara as a series of "nudges" rather than as a "shove."

During the period from 3600 to 3300 B.C.E., the settlements along the upper Nile appear to have begun the process of creating what anthropologists call complex societies by developing a specialization of labor and moving toward more hierarchical political and economic systems. Two of these early Nile states have been excavated and examined in some detail: Nagada and Hierakonpolis. Nagada was

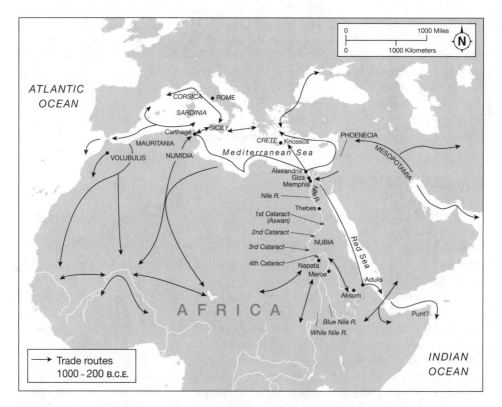

Map 4-1: Regions, cities, and trade in Ancient North & Northeast Africa

located just south of where the city of **Thebes** would later be established, and Hierakonpolis lay just to the north. The inhabitants of both protostates undertook a process of environmental modification. They cleared trees and heavy growth to expand the area of arable land and also built dykes and canals to control the flow of water. These efforts were successful enough that by around 3500 B.C.E. they had expanded the amount of arable land fourfold and led to a population explosion of up to 1,000 percent—perhaps reaching a population density of 1,000 persons per square kilometer. Such an increase is a testimony both to their ingenuity and to the bounty of the Nile. Further, the major towns of Nagada and Hierakonpolis were walled, suggesting that the inhabitants were sometimes forced to defend their newly created wealth from their neighbors.

Both towns show increasing economic activity by the middle of the fourth millennium B.C.E. Hierakonpolis seems to have developed an economic specialization in the manufacture of a fineware pottery known to archaeologists as "Plum Red," and examples of this pottery were exported throughout the Nile Valley. The town was also the home of one of the world's first large-scale breweries, producing an estimated 1,200 liters of beer a day. Such economic specialization led to social differentiation. Rather than a relatively egalitarian society with very few differences in wealth from individual to individual or family to family, now some people were rich and others were not. Within the towns, a wide variation in the size of homes suggests growing social distance between the rich and poor. Cemeteries found in the Nagada region during this period show an increasing social stratification. Some tombs include luxury items such as gold jewelry, gems, and finely decorated pottery. The wealthy tombs tended to be clustered together in a certain part of the cemetery, maybe as family groups or maybe just to be separate from the poor, even in death.

Even in this period before the unification of the Nile, there was considerable contact with other regions. Although the archaeological record for the lower Nile is less complete, it is clear that there was some degree of exchange along the Nile Valley, no doubt aided by the fact that whereas the current runs north, the prevailing winds blow south, allowing for relatively easy round trips. Contacts and trade were not limited to the north, though. The presence of valuable goods and female "goddess" figurines in many of the burials in Nagada, for example, is a practice shared with the Nubian region to the south, practices not found in Lower Egypt until after unification. The presence in Nagada and Hierakonpolis of gold (mined near the coast of the Red Sea) and such items as cylinder seals from Mesopotamia also show the links of Upper Egypt far to the east, even during this early period.

Unification and the Rise of the Old Kingdom

The unification of the Nile Valley and the creation of the ancient Egyptian state is perhaps one of the most remarkable events in early world history. Like other early states in Mesopotamia and the Indus Valley, Ancient Egypt would be one of the first parts of the world to develop a highly bureaucratic state apparatus to regulate the economy and extract taxes from the population. Unlike other regions, though, Egypt would develop an amazingly durable political ideology built around the concept of "divine kingship." Combined with the agricultural wealth and ease of communication brought by the Nile, this political system would make Ancient Egypt the longest-lived state in world history.

The impetus for the unification of the Nile Valley came from the Upper Nile, likely from Hierakonpolis itself. It was here that the famed Narmer Palette was found. Each side of this carved slab of stone has images of King Narmer (some argue that the unifier was named Menes) of Hierakonpolis executing his enemies. On one side, he wears the white crown of Upper Egypt and is accompanied by the god Horus (in the form of a falcon). On the reverse side, he wears the red crown of Lower Egypt. Narmer's conquest probably took place around 3100 B.C.E., and was probably not the first attempt to unify the Nile. The successful unification of Upper and Lower Egypt (from the first cataract to the delta), though, was to set the stage for the development of a powerful centralized state. The unification came to be symbolized by a cosmology that gave legitimacy to both the southern god Seth and the northern god **Osiris**. The pharaoh, as the embodiment of the god **Horus** (the son of Isis and Osiris), was responsible for balancing the power of these two rival gods. Narmer established a new capital at Memphis in the Lower Nile, perhaps as a symbol of his conquest of the region.

The period from 3100 to 2575 B.C.E. is referred to as the Archaic period and represents an era in which the ruling class established their complete authority over the whole of the Nile Valley and established their right to regulate the economy and society. Aiding the rulers in this endeavor was not only military power, but also writing. First developed in Egypt around 3200 B.C.E., the hieroglyphic system of writing helped the pharaohs in creating a relatively stable religious doctrine that legitimized their rule and also facilitated the building of a professional bureaucracy that could keep track of taxes owed and collected. The first few hundred years of unification were not easy ones. A continued drying trend in the Sahara led to encroachment by nomadic groups from the west, and there were also conflicts with Nubia to the south. At the same time, the reduction in rainfall led to a general decrease in the level of the Nile floods, which necessitated careful regulation of taxation and redistribution of resources. Not too surprisingly, early pharaohs' divinity was manifested (or perhaps tested) by their ability to keep chaos at bay and ensure the fertility of the Nile. At several points in time, the unity and independence of Archaic Egypt nearly collapsed, but the state persevered and gradually grew in power. It is during this early period of Ancient Egypt that the stage was set for the remarkable centralization of power that was to characterize the Old Kingdom.

The difference between the Old Kingdom and the Archaic period is mostly scale. During the period from 2575 to 2180 B.C.E., the ruling class of Ancient Egypt experienced a remarkable increase in power and wealth, none-too-subtly symbolized by the construction of the great pyramids near the capital of Memphis. These structures, built as tombs for individual pharaohs (the largest, at Giza, being built for Pharaoh Khufu in the late twenty-fifth century B.C.E.), are remarkable testimonies to the ability of the pharaohs to command the labor of their subjects and the resources of the region. Some scholars see this fact as evidence of the brutal and oppressive self-glorification of the ruling class of the Old Kingdom, whereas others prefer to see it in terms of the dedication of the subjects to their rulers and religion (the same debate exists over the building of cathedrals in medieval Europe). Recent excavations of what are believed to be the "Workers' Villages" near the sites of the great pyramids seem to show a relatively free and well-cared-for-workforce, with little overt evidence of coercion or oppression. This is a fine example of what can be learned when researchers move away from looking at only the elites (the pharaohs and their tombs) and examining the dwellings and property of "common folk."

The pyramids also represent a change in the religious identity of the pharaohs. Rather than serving as a symbolic mediator between Seth and Osiris, during the Old Kingdom the pharaohs increasingly came to be associated with Ra, the sun god. The pyramids served not only as tombs, but also as physical representations of the sun's rays and spiritual ladders to help the dead pharaohs ascend to the heavens and take their place among the divine. Despite the changes in the divine identity of the pharaohs, some scholars have argued that Ancient Egypt's system of succession was still matrilineal, that is, traced through the female side of the family rather than the male. This theory explains the practice of many pharaohs marrying their own sisters, which served as a means of keeping the position of pharaoh within the royal family (rather than having it pass to an outsider in the form of the daughter's husband). For example, Pharaoh Menkavie, who ruled from 2548 to 2530 B.C.E., married his sister.

Overseeing such projects as the building of the pyramids required not only the authority of the pharaohs, but also a skilled bureaucracy and a remarkable knowledge of engineering and mathematics. The Old Kingdom's rulers were supported by a cadre of educated scribes who possessed high status and remarkable authority over the peasantry.

Trained specialists managed the allocation of floodwaters, assessment and collection of taxes, a small army, and the priesthood. A small population of skilled craftspeople manufactured luxury goods and more common items. Traders were involved in commerce not only along the Nile, but also into the Mediterranean, Middle East, Nubia, and to southern Arabia and Ethiopia via the Red Sea. The great mass of the population served as agricultural laborers under the command of the central government. If they did not benefit materially from the grandeur of the Old Kingdom, they did at least benefit from a long period of relative peace, for the Old Kingdom of Egypt saw a remarkable absence of war or internal conflict. Notably, Egyptian women seemed to enjoy considerably more rights and freedom than many of their counterparts elsewhere in the ancient world. For example, they could own property and had the ability to bring cases or present evidence before the courts. Visiting Egypt around 450 B.C.E., the Greek historian Herodotus was more than a little surprised to note that Egyptian women were free to carry out business and make purchases in the markets, while men stayed at home and did the weaving.

First Intermediate Period and the Middle Kingdom

Several factors led to the decline of the Old Kingdom. Perhaps paramount was a period of extended drought. Droughts probably led both to a decline in agricultural productivity and an increase in migration from the surrounding (and increasingly dry) territories. Such a double blow no doubt taxed the ability of the state to

An Egyptian family from the Middle Kingdom congratulates their son on his marriage, while their daughter-in-law looks on. (*Source:* The Art Archive/Egyptian Museum Cairo/Dagli Orti)

regulate the production and redistribution of wealth. Further, the pharaoh's legitimacy was connected to the fertility of the Nile, and repeated failure of the floods could not help but undermine central authority. Beginning around 2250 B.C.E., Egypt saw the first of a series of famines that were to strike over the next three centuries. Under such a burden, central authority first weakened and later collapsed. By 2180 B.C.E., the Nile Valley was divided up between dozens of small states, each under the authority of local rulers. The rulers of Memphis still referred to themselves as pharaoh, but their power was a mere shadow of their predecessors'.

Just as in the initial unification of Egypt, the conquest that led to the reunification of the Nile and the formation of the Middle Kingdom came from the upper Nile region. In 2040 B.C.E., Pharaoh Mentohotep succeeded in completing a reconquest of the Nile that had begun in Thebes roughly a century before. It was during the Middle Kingdom that the power of Ancient Egypt reached a new high. The pharaohs of the period extended the boundaries of the state to include much of Lebanon in the northeast and Nubia in the south. These conquests greatly expanded the raw materials available to the kingdom. Trade was also expanded during the period, and there is considerable evidence that Egyptian traders ranged far into the Mediterranean. In particular, there seems to have been considerable exchange between Minoan Crete and Egypt.

The Middle Kingdom also saw fewer grandiose state structures and greater investment in productive endeavors. Perhaps most impressive was the agricultural development of the Fayum depression, which lies to the west of the Nile in Lower Egypt. Extensive irrigation works turned this marshy area into highly productive land, allowing for greatly increased agricultural output. Like the pyramids before it, this undertaking was a marvel of engineering and state organization.

Voices from African History: Be a Scribe!

The following document was written by an anonymous Egyptian teacher as a lesson to his recalcitrant student sometime during the Middle Kingdom. It seems that even in the third millennium B.C.E., students tried to get out of doing their readings! Aside from reminding us of the universality of human nature and the value of education, it also provides a valuable insight into the everyday lives of common Egyptians.

"The royal scribe and chief overseer of the cattle of Amun-Re, King of the Gods, Neb-mare-nakht, speaks to the scribe Wenemdia-mun, as follows: You are busy coming and going, and don't think of writing. You resist listening to me. You neglect my teachings.

You are worse than the desert antelope that lives by running. It spends no day in plowing. Never at all does it tread on the threshing floor. It lives on the oxen's labor, without entering among them. But though I spend the day telling you 'Write,' it seems like a plague to you. Writing is very pleasant!

See for yourself with your own eye. The occupations that lie before you.

The washerman's day is going up, going down. All his limbs are weak, from whitening his neighbors' clothes every day, from washing their linen.

The maker of pots is smeared with soil, like one whose relations have died. His hands, his feet are full of clay; he is like one who lives in the bog.

The cobbler works in vats to tan leather. His smell is penetrating. His hands are red with madder [dye], as if he is smeared with blood.

The watchman prepares garlands and polishes vase-stands. He spends a night of toil just as one on whom the sun shines.

The merchants travel downstream and upstream. They are as busy as can be, carrying goods from one town to another. They supply him who has wants. But the tax collectors carry off the gold, that most precious of metals.

The ships' crews are from every house. They receive their loads. They depart from Egypt for Syria, and each man's god is with him. But not one of them says 'We shall see Egypt again!'

The carpenter who is in the shipyard carries the timber and stacks it. If he gives today the output of yesterday, woe to his limbs! The shipwright stands behind him to tell him evil things. The worker who is in the fields, his is the toughest of all jobs. He spends the day loaded with his tools, tied to his toolbox. When he returns at night, he is loaded with the toolbox and the timbers, his drinking mug, and his whetstones.

The scribe, he alone, records the output of all of them. Take note of it!

Let me also expound to you the situation of the peasant, that other tough occupation. The flood comes and soaks him. He attends to his equipment. By day he cuts his farming tools; by night he twists rope. Even his midday hour he spends on farm labor. He equips himself to go to the field as if he were a warrior. When he reaches his field he finds it broken up. He spends time cultivating, and the snake is after him. It finishes off the seed as it is cast to the ground. He does not see a green blade. He does three plowings with borrowed grain. His wife has gone down to the merchants and found nothing for barter. Now the scribe lands on the shore. He surveys the harvest. Attendants are behind him with staffs, Nubians with clubs. One says 'Give grain.' The farmer replies 'There is none.' He is beaten savagely. He is bound, thrown in the well, submerged head down. His wife is bound in his presence. His children are in fetters. His neighbors abandon them and flee. When it's over, there is no grain.

If you have any sense, be a scribe. If you have learned about the peasant, you will not be able to be one. Take note of it! . . .

I spend the day instructing you. You do not listen! Your heart is like an empty room. My teachings are not in it. Take note of it!

Furthermore, I instruct you to make you sound; to make you hold the palette freely. To make you become one whom the king trusts; to make you gain entrance to treasury and granary. To make you receive the ship-load at the gate of the granary. To make you issue the offerings on feast days. You are dressed in fine clothes; you own horses. Your boat is on the river; you are supplied with attendants. You stride about inspecting. A mansion is built in your town. You have a powerful office, given to you by the king. Male and female slaves are about you. Those who are in the fields grasp your hand, on plots that you have made. Look, I make you into a staff of life! Put the writings in your heart, and you will be protected from all kinds of toil. You will become a worthy official.

Do you not recall the life of the unskilled man? His name is not known. He is ever burdened in front of the scribe who knows what he is about."

The Second Intermediate Period and the New Kingdom

The Middle Kingdom was not immune to the forces of entropy that all states face. By the seventeenth century B.C.E., a series of disputes over succession had significantly weakened the administration in Thebes. When Lower Egypt was invaded by a people known as the **Hyksos** from the Middle East, the Middle Kingdom government was unable to maintain the unity of the Nile. In seizing the delta region, the Hyksos were aided by their use of bronze weapons and chariots, both of which gave them a significant advantage over the Egyptian troops of the time. Further, the kingdom of **Kerma** in **Nubia** took advantage of the situation and attacked northward to Aswan. Thebes thus lost control over lands both to the north and south and was forced to pay tribute to retain a fragile independence from outside control. For over 100 years, the Hyksos controlled the Nile Delta from their new capital at Avaris. Notably, there had been a significant "Middle Eastern" population in the delta for some time. Over the years, the wealth of Egypt had attracted many skilled laborers from the region. Perhaps more interesting, however, is the fact that even though victorious militarily, the Hyksos themselves assimilated to Egyptian culture. The rulers called themselves pharaohs and followed Egyptian religious practices. Within a few generations, they were hard to distinguish from other Egyptians. Such a practice of "stooping to conquer," the ability to assimilate even one's conquerors, would later become a source of strength for ancient China as well.

The unity of the Nile Valley was restored in 1530 B.C.E. by Ahmose the Liberator, who defeated the Hyksos. Ahmose and his successors, however, were not content with reuniting the Nile Valley. Having adopted the chariot-based military technology that had so well served the Hyksos, they established a large standing army and expanded the borders of Ancient Egypt to their greatest historical extent. By 1500 B.C.E. the Egyptians had invaded the Middle East, coming close to conquering the Levant. In the south, they expanded deep into Nubia by invading Kerma as far as the fourth cataract, giving them access to such critical goods as gold, animals, and lumber (all of which were in short supply in Egypt itself) and leading to a considerable Egyptianization of Nubian culture during the period and a spread of chariot technology into Saharan Africa. Cultural exchange, however, is a two-way street, and many Nubian cultural elements spread to Egypt. For example, the golden fly amulet of Nubia became a common Egyptian military symbol. During this period, Egypt also expanded its trade links deeper into Africa. **Hatshepsut** (one of the few female pharaohs) sent a large trading expedition down the Red Sea to Punt, in the horn of Africa. The expedition, launched in the early fifteenth century B.C.E., was a remarkable success, as the ships returned with large quantities of trade goods such as spices and myrrh.

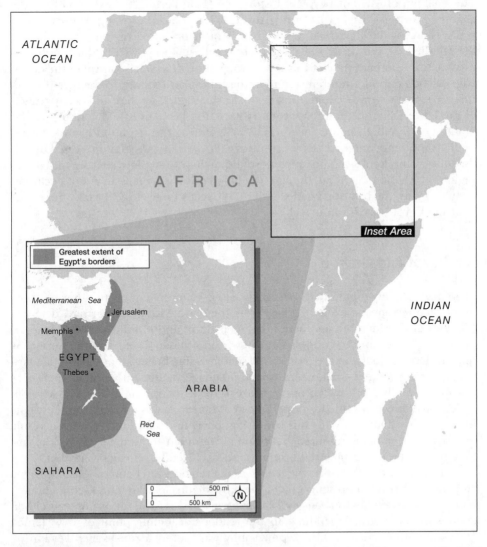

Map 4-2: Imperial Egypt—this map gives a rough approximation of the greatest limits of Egyptian imperial power.

The New Kingdom also saw shifts in the religious symbolism of power in Egypt. The Valley of the Kings, just across the Nile from Thebes, became the funerary center for the burial of rulers. It is here that Tutankhamun's tomb was found intact in 1922. Tutankhamun was not a terribly important ruler as pharaohs go, but the discovery of his intact tomb has helped make him one of the world's best-known ancient rulers.

The Late Period (1070 to 332 B.C.E.)

The final era of Ancient Egyptian history, the "Late Period," was a time of rapidly changing fortunes for Egypt. During this era, Egypt faced growing power from its rivals. Not only did Egypt see the breakaway of its occupied regions in Nubia and the Middle East, but it also saw these regions eclipse it in power. In the eighth century B.C.E. the Nubian state of **Kush** was strong enough to seize control of the entire Nile Valley, a period often referred to as the Ethiopian Dynasty. In the seventh century B.C.E. the Assyrians would displace the Kushans, sack Thebes, and occupy much of the Lower Nile. In the fourth century B.C.E. the Persians would conquer Egypt. Still, there were high points for Egypt as well. During the reign of Pharaoh Necho in the late seventh and early sixth centuries B.C.E., work was begun on a canal to link the Nile to the Red Sea, and ships were dispatched to explore the distant coastal regions of Africa. In general, though, the Late Period is seen as an era of declining fortunes. With the invasion of Alexander the Great's forces in 332 B.C.E., the era of "Ancient Egypt" was drawn to a close.

Ancient Egypt and Greece

As we have already mentioned, Egypt had active economic ties with other societies in the Mediterranean Sea, particularly from the Middle Kingdom forward. There is evidence of considerable interaction between Egypt and Middle Minoan Crete, in particular. For example, goddess figurines from Minoan Crete and the period of the XIII Dynasty in Egypt are remarkably similar. Some believe that the Minoan language itself belonged to the Afro-Asiatic language family, rather than the Indo-European family from which ancient Greek developed. Similarly, some scholars believe that the early Minoan script, known as Linear A, was derived from Egyptian hieroglyphics. Sadly, to date this script has been undeciphered, and as a result scholars lack a valuable resource that could tell us much about the extent of the cultural links between Egypt and this important early Mediterranean civilization.

The argument regarding the nature of the relationship between Ancient Egypt and ancient Greece represents one of the most vicious in academia. George James' book *Stolen Legacy: Greek Philosophy Is Stolen Egyptian Philosophy,* for example, is either famous or infamous, depending on the reader's academic point of view. James makes the argument that Greek philosophy was merely a repackaged version of Egyptian thought, and that true credit for the source of Western philosophy belongs to Africa, not Greece. More recently, Martin Bernal's multivolume series, *Black Athena,* has pushed the debate over the Egyptian legacy to the academic forefront. Bernal argues that linguistic evidence shows a strong Egyptian influence on early Greek culture. His books take their title from his assertion that Athena (the patron goddess of Athens) was actually a transplanted version of the Nile Delta goddess Neith. Also, Bernal has maintained that more scholars should take the work of the Greek historian Herodotus seriously. At many points, Herodotus (who traveled in Egypt around 450 B.C.E.) stated that many Greek gods had their origins in Egypt and that the Egyptians were the inventors of mathematics. Bernal's work has been lauded by some and attacked by others. In particular, classicists such as Mary Lefkowitz, who published the book *Not Out of Africa,* have invested considerable effort in disproving Bernal's thesis. With Bernal's recent publication of a new volume presenting new linguistic evidence for his argument, the debate will likely continue for some time.

Whichever side they take in the debate over Ancient Egypt and Greece, most scholars would agree that by the latter first millennium B.C.E. there were extensive contacts between Egypt and Greece. Trade in wine and olive oil from Greece and grain from Egypt led to extensive exchange. By around 600 B.C.E. there were large numbers of Greek traders and mercenaries living in Egypt. Given this Greek awareness of Egypt's wealth, there should be little surprise that when Alexander the Great set off to conquer the Greek known world (and pretty much whoever else he happened to meet on the way), he included Egypt in his plans for conquest. In 332 B.C.E., Alexander's army was reputedly welcomed by the Egyptians, who perhaps hoped that his rule would be less onerous than that of the Persians, who had conquered Egypt only some eleven years before. While in Egypt, Alexander visited the temple of Zeus Ammon (which some scholars see as further evidence of a link between Egyptian and Greek religion) and there was informed (perhaps accidentally) that he was "the child of Zeus"—which further inflated his already considerable ego. Alexander ordered the building of a new city, Alexandria (one of several dozen of the same name that he founded during his conquests), on the western edge of the delta coast and handed rule of the region over to his general **Ptolemy.** The building of Alexandria shows not only the advent of overt Greek influence in Egypt, but also the increasing shift in the economic focus of Ptolemaic Egypt toward the Mediterranean and away from the regions toward the south.

Ptolemaic rule was to bring considerable change to Egypt. The language of government became Greek, a first step in the eventual demise of the Egyptian language. The blending of Egyptian and Greek linguistic elements and scripts gave rise to Coptic, which is the closest surviving language to Ancient Egyptian, and is still the liturgical language of the Christian Church in Egypt. Further, the administrators implemented a harsh system of taxation that allotted lands based on the amount of taxes paid. This system tended to concentrate land in large estates and deny the Egyptian peasants ownership of land they had worked for generations. Notably, however, the new rulers of Egypt did not attempt to change everything. Rather, they called themselves pharaohs and relied on the same system of religious and political legitimacy as had previous Egyptian rulers. Thus, the era of the Ptolemaic rulers should be seen not so much as an imposition of Greek culture on Egypt but as a blending of the two cultures.

Carthage and Rome in Early Northern Africa

Egypt was not the only part of northern Africa to play a substantial role in early world history. **Carthage,** located roughly in the same area as modern-day Tunisia, was one of the most important western Mediterranean states, and its economic influence also extended to the kingdoms in the West African Savannah. Carthage was originally founded as a colony by the Phoenicians around 1000 B.C.E. From a power base along the coastline of the southeastern Mediterranean (what is now Israel, Lebanon, and Syria), the Phoenicians established colonies not only in Carthage, but also in Spain and the islands of Corsica, Sardinia, and Sicily. Of these, Carthage grew to become the most powerful, eventually becoming independent of Phoenicia and overseeing affairs in the other western Mediterranean colonies. Emphasizing trade by sea, the Carthaginians did not seek to expand their authority far beyond the coastal plains surrounding their city. They did, though, interact and intermarry with the local **Berber**-speaking populations, creating a hybrid language and culture known as **Punic.** The nearby Berber states of **Numidia** and **Mauritania** were sometimes allies and sometimes adversaries of the Carthaginians. In the fifth century B.C.E., a Carthaginian explorer, Hanno, is reputed to have led an expedition around the coast to western Africa—perhaps the earliest seafarer to successfully make such a trip. Though they emphasized sea trade, the Carthaginians also engaged in a rapidly expanding trans-Saharan exchange, trading goods for gold and ivory from the Savannah to the south.

By the latter part of the first millennium B.C.E., Carthage was the greatest power in the western Mediterranean, with a population of several hundred thousand in the city of Carthage alone. In the fifth and fourth centuries B.C.E., the Greeks unsuccessfully challenged Carthage for dominance of the region. The island of Sicily was a major focus of the conflict. Sicily was also to be the flashpoint for the first of three Punic Wars between Carthage and Rome. In this first conflict, Carthage expected its navies to win the day, but was defeated when Rome implemented a strategy of naval warfare that emphasized using troops to board their enemies' ships. Sicily was gained by Rome, but the power of Carthage itself was little reduced. The second conflict with Rome began in 218 B.C.E., when Rome declared war as a result of Carthage's expanding influence in the Iberian Peninsula (modern Spain). This war lasted seventeen years and is famous for Hannibal's invasion of Roman Italy after crossing the Alps (complete with war elephants) and for Scipio Africanus' counterinvasion of Carthage. Aided by the Berber-speaking Numidians, Scipio was able to defeat Hannibal in 202 B.C.E. and force harsh terms on the Carthaginians. In 146 B.C.E., Rome again declared war on Carthage. Though weakened by blockade, Carthage refused to surrender and was defeated only after brutal fighting. In revenge, Rome not only razed the city, but also sold the inhabitants into slavery. It was a harsh end for a remarkable society.

Following the defeat of Carthage, Rome set about developing the North African region as a colony of its own. Indeed, the Roman name for the region, **"Ifrikia,"** is the source of the continent's modern name. Rome developed the North African coast mainly for agriculture, developing estates for the growth of wheat and olives largely through the imposition of slave labor. Rome took advantage of the expansion of the trans-Saharan trade brought about by the introduction of the camel. Gold traded across the Sahara (possibly through ancient Ghana) became an important trade good for the Romans, who established a mint in Carthage to take advantage of the commodity.

Egypt itself was one of the last regions of the circum-Mediterranean to be added to Rome's territories. This occurred after Cleopatra VII became embroiled in the Roman civil war and sided with Mark Antony against Octavian. They were defeated, however, at the battle of Actium in 31 B.C.E. Rome treated Egypt harshly, demanding heavy taxes to extract the maximum amount of wheat from Egypt's fertile river plains to feed Rome's burgeoning urban populations. Ultimately, the greatest challenge to Roman rule in Egypt and North Africa was to come from Christianity. This topic will be taken up in Chapter 5.

Ancient Nubia and the Horn of Africa in the Ancient World

We have already discussed Nubia and the Horn in our coverage of Ancient Egypt. Both regions had considerable, but varying, degrees of economic, cultural, and political exchange with Ancient Egypt. It would be misleading, though, to think that Egypt was the only source of influence or interaction for these regions—a common misconception that often portrays Nubia (or even the rest of Africa) as merely a "shadow of Egypt." As we shall see, both Nubia and the Horn developed on their own and also interacted with other parts of the world as well.

Nubia is a generic term for the region of the Nile Valley south of the first cataract. It was home to a number of societies over the period of history discussed in this chapter. Archaeologists identify the early human settlers of the region as the "Gash culture"—a social complex that lasted from 2700 B.C.E. to roughly 1400 B.C.E. These early inhabitants of the region are recognized by their distinct ceramic styles and an economy that relied on a mixture of pastoralism (sheep, goats, and cattle) and the cultivation of barley. Later Gash culture is also notable for the marking of burials with large stone monoliths, particularly around the permanent settlement of Mahal Teglinos—a possible link to the stelae later found in Aksum. Even in the period of the third millennium the Gash culture shows links not only with Egypt, but also with the Horn of Africa and southern Arabia.

Around 2400 B.C.E. there is clear evidence not only for permanent settlement, but also the formation of a state-level society in the region between the third and fourth cataracts of the Nile. Named Kerma for the presumed capital city, this state may be the second oldest in Africa, second only to Egypt itself. Kerma appears to have been a wealthy and complex society. The city had significant mud-brick walls, perhaps to defend it from Egyptian invasions, and very large temples. Even common burials included numerous high-quality bronze items, which reflect not only a relative degree of wealth for the society, but also Kerma's ability to produce its own

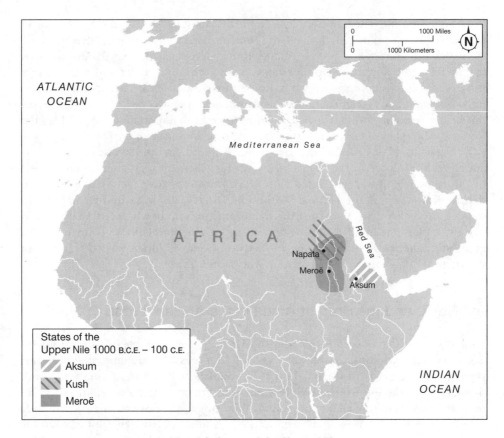

Map 4-3: States of the Upper Nile

metals. The rulers appear to have enjoyed even greater wealth and were buried in large mounds, often surrounded by sacrificial victims. Interestingly, the wealth of Kerma seems to have been greatest when Egypt was facing hard times. The state thrived during Egypt's First and Second "Intermediate Periods" when the unity of the Nile Valley collapsed. Indeed, it was Kerma that allied with the Hyksos and invaded Upper Egypt to bring about the Second Intermediate Period. This may be a result of reduced trade along the Red Sea during the intermediate periods, which would have forced trade from the Horn (the Land of Punt) to flow directly through Kerma. As we have seen, with the reunification of the Nile and the formation of the New Kingdom around 1500 B.C.E., Egypt was eager to both subjugate Kerma and reestablish sea trade with Punt. Indeed, Egypt's invasion to the fourth cataract of the Nile spelled the end of Kerma as a civilization.

The region of Nubia did not see another independent state develop until the waning of the New Kingdom's power around 1000 B.C.E. It was Kush that was to rise up to fill this growing power vacuum. Based near Karima, the state of Kush reflected many elements of Egyptian culture that had been reinforced during Nubia's rule by the New Kingdom. Egyptian was the dominant language, Egyptian gods were worshiped (along with local deities), pyramids were built at the religious center of Napata, and the rulers called themselves pharaohs. Kush grew in power to such a point that in 730 B.C.E., Pharaoh Piye invaded the upper Nile and captured the city of Thebes. He and his descendants ruled the entire Nile Valley as the twenty-fifth (or "Ethiopian") dynasty for over half a century, until they themselves were driven out by an Assyrian invasion in 663 B.C.E.

In 591 B.C.E., after recovering from the Assyrian invasion, the Egyptians launched an invasion of Kush and sacked Napata. Perhaps in response, the center of Nubian civilization was moved south to Meroë, between the White and Blue Niles. Farther south, this region was relatively well watered by seasonal rains. As a result, agriculture was possible without reliance on the Nile flood or irrigation, and Meroë could support a more diversified and less densely settled population than that found to the north. Meroë grew to become a society of notable wealth. Queen Shanadakhete, who ruled up to 160 B.C.E., was one of Meroë's great rulers and builders, overseeing the construction of many public works. Ironwork developed as a center of the local economy—fed by wood from the surrounding forests. To this day, huge heaps of slag, a by-product of the iron industry, still dot the landscape. Iron weapons made the Merotic military a force to be reckoned with. Meroë also gained wealth by trading iron and other goods such as gold and ivory over great distances, not only north along the Nile but also overland to the west and east to the Horn of Africa—a trade facilitated by the relatively recent introduction of the camel to the region. Meroë even traded and occasionally fought with Rome after that state seized control of Egypt. Indeed, during one excavation in Meroë, archaeologists were surprised to find the head of a statue of the Roman emperor Augustus—likely captured by Merotic troops during raids on Roman Egypt around 25 B.C.E.

Over time, Merotic culture diverged from the quasi-Egyptian roots that had so characterized the kingdom of Kush. The local lion god, **Apedemek,** for example, grew in importance over Egyptian gods such as Isis and Osiris. Hieroglyphics and demotic script also fell into disuse, and a linear script unique to Meroë was developed. This language is as of yet undeciphered, and if it can be translated, a great wealth of knowledge about Meroë and one of Africa's earliest civilizations will be revealed. Currently, excavations in the Sudan are revealing that the scope of the Merotic state was much greater than previously believed. At Dangeil, north of the modern Sudanese capital of Khartoum, an entire city has recently been discovered.

Meroë remained a powerful state into the third century B.C.E. By around 300 B.C.E., however, its power was waning—perhaps in part due to environmental decay brought about by the deforestation required to provide wood to make charcoal for the iron industry. The end of Meroë came at the hands of Aksum, itself a state located in the highlands of Ethiopia in the Horn of Africa. The Horn had long been a region of significant economic and cultural exchange. As early as the second millennium B.C.E. the region was home to an "Afro-Arabian" cultural complex evidenced by similar styles of pottery and tool technologies found on both sides of the Red Sea. This exchange foreshadowed the creation of Swahili culture that will be discussed in Chapter 7. During the second millennium B.C.E., the Horn of Africa was home to the mysterious Land of Punt, which played an important role as trading partner for Egypt. Very little is known about Punt itself, except that it was on the coast, perhaps that of modern Somalia, and that it was reputedly ruled by a queen, at least at the time of Hatshepsut's expedition at around 1493 B.C.E.

By the first quarter of the first millennium B.C.E. there was evidently growing exchange with southern Arabia, a process that was perhaps made possible by the decline of Egypt. Around 700 B.C.E. there is evidence along the coasts and highlands of Ethiopia and Yemen for the presence of two Ethio-**Sabean** states, Saba and Daamat. Rock inscriptions and religious materials, for example, suggest the presence of settlers from southern Arabia, whereas more day-to-day artifacts such as ceramics and foods suggest considerable local cultural continuity. Likely, the combination reflects a melding of populations from the two regions. Still, the eventual dominance of Ge'ez, a local language, over the Sabean introduced by southern Arabian immigrants testifies to the dominant role of local African culture in the region.

By about 100 C.E., the region of the Horn saw the rise of the state of **Aksum.** Perhaps beginning as a confederation of trading towns, the power of Aksum grew quickly because it benefitted from its ability to tap into trade not only with Nubia and Roman Egypt, but also with the Middle East, Arabia, East Africa, and the subcontinent via the Indian Ocean. It was under Aksum that Adulis grew to become one of Africa's great port cities. Aksum became a wealthy and powerful state. As early as the third century C.E. it commanded tribute from states in southern Arabia (modern Yemen). It was also one of the first states in the region to establish its own currency in coin. The graves of rich Aksumites are notable for their stelae—stone towers of up to 100 feet tall carved out of single pieces of rock. As the power of Aksum expanded, it came into conflict with Meroë. It was under King **Ezana** of Aksum that Meroë was invaded and destroyed in the early to mid-fourth century C.E. Ezana is also famous for being the first ruler in the region to convert to Christianity and in so doing set the stage for the Christianization of Ethiopia, about which we will learn more in Chapter 5.

Ancient Africa United: The Afrocentric Argument

This chapter has touched on the Afrocentric perspective at several points. Indeed, it would be bad scholarship to discuss the history of Ancient Egypt and Nubia without taking into account Afrocentric perspectives on the history of these regions, because Afrocentrism argues that the Nile Valley played a central role in the history of Africa, and indeed much of the Western world. Central to the Afrocentric idea is the belief that Africa represents not so much a great diversity of human cultures, but rather a single cultural unit within which there are many expressions of commonly held beliefs. Thus, although some Africanists may stress African cultural diversity, Afrocentric scholars argue that similarities are what define the continent. These "African commonalities" have been identified as matriarchy, traditional African religious systems, and divine kingship. Specific elements range from styles of crowns to the design of fish traps.

Obviously, to argue for a common African culture is to identify a common origin or root. And for Afrocentrists, this root is the Nile Valley. Thus, the "home" of African culture was the Nile, and the core elements of African culture spread outward to other parts of the continent. Similarly, as argued by James and Bernal, some Nilotic cultural elements also spread to Europe. Thus, Cheikh Anta Diop's *The African Origin of Civilization, Myth or Reality* (1955) is seen as one of the first

Afrocentric works, though it should be noted that some Western academics voiced similar ideas decades before, such as in the case of Charles Seligman's 1932 essay, "Egyptian Influence in Negro Africa."

Although few Africanists would see themselves as minimizing the influence or importance of the Nile Valley civilizations, there is nonetheless a sense among many that the Afrocentrists are overstating the case. Indeed, some have responded by dubbing Afrocentrism "Nilocentrism" and arguing that an overemphasis on the Nile denies the creativity and agency of other African regions and societies. As you might guess, such assertions have been met with condemnation by Afrocentrists. Witness the following comment made by Molefe Asante.

> I want to see studies of Africa that take Africa seriously as (sic) agent in human history. But this is not possible so long as [Africanists] continue [to write] papers with no connectedness to the source of African culture or civilization. . . . How is it possible that [Africanists] do not see the relevance of Ancient Egypt, Nubia, Axum, and Ghana to the rest of African studies? It is only possible because the definition of African studies advanced by Eurocentrists . . . is essentially Africa as seen through the eyes of Europeans.
>
> Molefi Asante, "More Thoughts on the Africanists' Agenda," *Issue, A Journal of Opinion* 23, no. 1 (1995)

As stated in the preface, there is no shortage of controversy in the history of Africa.

Ancient North and Northeastern Africa in Global Perspective

The study of the region of North and northeastern Africa clearly shows the richness and the complexity of the history of early human societies in Africa. Egypt, Carthage, and the states of Nubia and the Horn all developed complex societies that influenced the lives of their citizens and their neighbors. Perhaps most importantly, the study of these early African societies highlights the degree to which they existed not in isolation, but rather in complex economic, political, cultural, and even genetic systems of interaction with their neighbors in the Mediterranean and Middle East. Even in the earliest eras of settlement and state formation, African societies were far from isolated.

Each of the states examined in this chapter highlights important themes in early human history. The early Egyptians struggled with the interaction between technology and nature, particularly in terms of how to utilize the bounty of the Nile floods to maximize production. In this way, the Egyptians are a prime example of what some historians have dubbed "hydraulic civilizations"—those that rise to power via the necessity of controlling water. Other hydraulic civilizations include Mesopotamia, Harappa, and early China. The ancient Egyptians also dealt with the question of how to legitimize rule by a small elite class. Their creation of a system of "divine kingship" perhaps represents one of the longest-lasting systems of political ideology ever seen in the world. Further, with its huge population, considerable wealth, and stable government, Egypt exerted economic, political, and cultural influence not only on its neighbors in Africa, but on the wider world as well. Sometimes Egypt was the conqueror, sometimes the vanquished—yet the contributions of Egyptian culture, preserved in philosophy, science, mathematics, and monuments, continue to influence and intrigue the world today. Perhaps as we learn more about other African states they, too, will inspire us in similar ways.

Carthage, too, teaches us much about early human history. The very founding of Carthage by Phoenician settlers shows us just how mobile early human populations were. Similarly, the creation of a new "Punic" society that blended Phoenician and African/Berber elements highlights the cultural flexibility of human populations. Were the Carthaginians invaders of Africa or were they Africans? Perhaps the answer to both is "yes." Much the same paradox faces us today in defining the identity of human populations who have settled new lands.

Finally, the study of the states of Nubia and the Horn, such as Kerma, Kush, Meroë, and Aksum, offers us many insights into early African and world history. Each of these societies was at times subjugated by more powerful states. Yet, they were not merely "shadows" of the dominant societies. Although they certainly were influenced by the dominant culture, they also exerted powerful economic, political, and cultural influences of their own and often rose to positions of dominance themselves—as when both Kerma and Kush invaded Egypt. It is important not to see the forces of history as flowing only from the strong to the weak. Humans, as individuals and as societies, always influence one another when they come into contact.

 Controversies in African History: **Who Were the Ancient Egyptians?**

The racial identity of the ancient Egyptians is a subject that has been contested for some time. Hollywood portrayals of Egyptian rulers have often used white movie stars to play Egyptians. Conversely, African-American representations of Egyptians generally appear overtly black. Academics, too, have been involved in this debate. Some scholars argued that the Egyptians were white. For example, the "Egyptologist" James Breasted, whose 1924 text *The Conquest of Civilization* was an early classic of world history, stated emphatically that the Egyptians were part of the "Great White Race." Others, such as Cheikh Anta Diop, have argued that the ancient Egyptians were black. As he emphatically stated, "The ancient Egyptians were Negroes. The moral fruit of their civilization is to be counted among the assets of the Black world." Why do we even ask? In part we do so because notions of race and civilization have so permeated much of historical writing in recent centuries. Thus, many scholars have tried to lay claim to the ancient Egyptians as proof of the achievements of what they saw as their race. Yet, it is not easy to answer the question of the ancient Egyptians' identity by viewing the historical record. Herodotus, the Greek "father of history," made reference to the Egyptians as having "black skin and wooly hair," though some scholars say that this description was only relative to that of the fair-skinned Greeks. Given that Thebes, the real power center of ancient Egypt, lay far to the south near Nubia, it would be natural to expect that many ancient Egyptians would today be considered "black" or that at least a fair degree of genetic exchange went on. Indeed, many pharaohs had Nubian names or Nubian mothers. Images and sculptures created by the ancient Egyptians themselves cover a fairly wide range of what would today be considered races. Perhaps the true answer lies in the fact that there is no such thing as a "pure" race or perhaps even race itself. This is in no small part true because Egypt, as one of the world's great crossroads, has for so long sat astride so many historical systems of cultural, political, and economic exchange. The Nile River ties Egypt both to the Mediterranean and deep into sub-Saharan Africa. The Red Sea links Egypt both to the Middle East and eastern Africa. Perhaps the reality is that Egypt was both unique to itself and a component of a wider system of human interaction. Further, the debate over the identity of the ancient Egyptians is especially remarkable if you think that the ancient Egyptians themselves seem to have had little notion of "blackness" or "whiteness." Race, as we understand it, is a far more modern construction. Indeed, the fact that we ask the question, "Who were the Egyptians?" reveals more about ourselves than the answer reveals about the Egyptians.

Useful Works on This Chapter Topic

Any student seeking information on ancient Egypt will find an overwhelming amount of material. Ian Shaw's edited volume, *The Oxford History of Ancient Egypt* (2000), will likely provide a useful introduction to just about any topic a student might imagine. John Baines and Jaromir Malek's *Cultural Atlas of Ancient Egypt* (2000) might also provide useful general information. An excellent in-depth discussion of connections between ancient North Africa, the Mediterranean, and the Middle East is available in the form of W. V. Davies and L. Schofield (eds.), *Egypt, the Aegean and the Levant, Interconnections in the Second Millennium* (1995). For both ancient Egypt and the states of Nubia, Joseph O. Vogel's edited collection, *Encyclopedia of Precolonial Africa: Archaeology, History, Languages, Cultures, and Environments* (1997), provides an excellent resource for nuts-and-bolts discussions of specific times and places—particularly from an archaeological perspective. For a work on Carthage that does not rely too heavily on Roman sources, students may examine Serge Lancel's *Carthage: A History* (1997). Important Afrocentric works include Cheikh Anta Diop's *The African Origins of Civilization, Myth or Reality* (1955); Molefe Asante's *The Egyptian Philosophers: Ancient African Voices from Imhotep to Akhenaten* (2000); and Re Monges' Kush, *The Jewel of Nubia: Reconnecting the Root System of African Civilization* (1997).

Chapter 5

Africa and the Early Christian World

Many students assume that Christianity was not introduced to Africa until the nineteenth century. This is an unfortunate yet understandable mistake. American and European images of Africa from the era of colonialism sought to portray Africa as a "heathen" land in need of salvation—salvation that could only be provided by Western missionaries. Explorer/missionaries like David Livingstone, for example, are widely known. It is true that in the nineteenth century far more Africans practiced traditional African religions and Islam than practiced Christianity. Yet, the student of history must be very careful not to make assumptions on the past based on the nature of the present or recent past. As we will see in this chapter, Africans played a central role in early Christianity. Populations in North Africa, the Nile Valley, and the Horn of Africa were among the first people in the world to embrace Christianity, and many of their descendants long maintained their beliefs in the face of great spiritual hardship. In so doing, these African Christians played a substantial role in influencing the development of their religion. Indeed, many of the foremost thinkers of the early church were Africans, and many of the early doctrinal disputes over the nature of Christianity had their origin in Africa. Eventually, conflicts between Christian groups would lead to the oppression of Donatist Christians in North Africa and the creation of the **Coptic** church in Egypt. To illuminate the history of early Christianity in Africa, first we will discuss the expansion of Christianity into Africa, and then we will examine the contributions of Africans to early Christian thought.

The Spread of Christianity in Africa

Why did Christianity spread into Africa? No doubt, for many Africans, the reasons were the same as for converts in the Middle East, Inner Eurasia, and Europe. Jesus' message of salvation and redemption, combined with the strong communal focus of early Christianity, held a powerful appeal to many whose lives were filled with struggle. The very nature of Christ as both human and God (more on this later), rather than as a distant and incomprehensible deity, served to bridge the gap between the faithful and the divine. Here was a powerful yet benevolent deity who sacrificed himself for the good of all people.

From a different perspective, Christianity offered a means of resistance to the often repressive rule of the Roman Empire. Egypt and North Africa had resisted Roman conquest for hundreds of years. Once incorporated into the empire they suffered higher taxes, especially in the form of foodstuffs, than those elsewhere in the empire. Those who resented high taxes and oppressive laws (particularly those that targeted noncitizens) could express their dissatisfaction by converting to a religion that refused to recognize the divinity of the Roman emperor. Indeed, the refusal to offer sacrifice to the emperor was a key reason for the Roman persecution of early Christian communities. At the same time, Christian missionaries were able to take advantage of Roman trade and transportation networks to spread their message throughout the empire. Ironically, although Christianity in much of North Africa would begin as a form of resistance to Roman rule, it would later serve as a locus of resistance to the domination of the Roman church.

There were other factors that made African converts receptive to Christianity. Geographical proximity as well as strong cultural and trade links tied Palestine to Africa and facilitated the spread of the "good news" of the new religion. Alexandria, which was easily the most important port in the eastern Mediterranean, was to become one of the first homes of a Christian community. The tradition of the Coptic church (the origins of which we will discuss shortly) tells us that Jesus fled from Herod's persecution and found refuge in Egypt. Coptic Christians also believe that St. Mark was the first apostle of Egypt, coming to Egypt to establish a church as early as 41 C.E. Mark was later martyred in Alexandria, but his first convert, Anianus, succeeded him as patriarch of the Christian church in Egypt. Indeed, early Christian writings from Egypt, written in Coptic script, likely predate early Greek versions of the Bible. For many African Christians, Egypt was just as much a part of the holy land as was Palestine.

Another element was the presence of a significant minority of Jews living in North Africa, the Nile Valley, and Ethiopia. Jewish communities were present in urban centers throughout North Africa. As far back as the eighth century B.C.E., Isaiah listed the Nile Valley and Kush as having significant populations of Jews. To those familiar with the story of the exodus, such a Jewish presence in Africa should be easy to grasp. In the first century C.E., as much as 15 percent of the population of Egypt was Jewish. The **Beta Israel** Jews of Ethiopia (also sometimes identified by the somewhat pejorative term *Falasha*) have been present in the highlands of Ethiopia for thousands of years, though the population likely represents a series of movements by Jewish populations into the region, rather than a single migration at some point in time. The Beta Israel in Ethiopia localized to the point that they developed their own liturgy utilizing Ge'ez (a language shared with the Aksumites and the Coptic church of Ethiopia). The presence of these Jewish populations in Africa helped the spread of Christianity in several ways. First, many of the earliest converts to Christianity were themselves Jewish (Jesus' disciples often called him "Rabbi"). Also, the fact that Christians accepted Jewish scripture (renamed the Old Testament by Christians) as valid meant that the new religion was not entirely unfamiliar to populations in regions where Jews had long resided.

Some scholars have argued that Christianity incorporated many spiritual elements from ancient Egyptian religion. In particular, these scholars point to the story of the god Horus, the child of the goddess Isis, who died and was resurrected. Horus became a powerful symbol of rebirth and renewal for the ancient Egyptians. Further, many see strong similarities between the imagery of Isis and Horus and later representations of Jesus and Mary. Similarly, the Egyptian symbol for eternal life, the ankh, is very similar in form to the cross. Indeed, the Coptic cross even incorporates the ankh's circular elements. Whether or not Christianity built on or borrowed such Egyptian religious concepts is, of course, difficult to ascertain. It is easy to see, though, that such similarities could easily have made Christianity seem familiar and appealing to potential converts in Egypt and the Nile Valley.

The spread of Christianity into Egypt and North Africa was relatively rapid, and by the second and third centuries C.E. there were numerous Christian communities in the region—particularly in urban areas. Notably, Christianity seemed to spread most quickly among the poor and politically oppressed. Perhaps these populations were most in need of a religion that stressed the spiritual purity of the meek and poor. Thus, Egyptian peasants saw Christianity as a source of empowerment that would distinguish them from Roman or Jewish elites. Alexandria was not only home to a large Christian community, but also to such important early Christian theologians as Clement and Origen. In Scillia, near Carthage, there are references to the martyrdom of numerous Christians as early as 180 C.E. In Carthage itself, a wealthy Roman landowner, Cyprian, converted to Christianity and gave all his wealth to the poor. Cyprian later was named Bishop of Carthage. To the sick of Carthage during an outbreak of plague, the ministry of Cyprian and his Christian followers was said to be a major factor in encouraging others in the area to convert. Cyprian himself was martyred in 258 C.E. Christians in North Africa were remarkable for their defiance in the face of the Roman persecutions. Often, rather than worship in secret (as in the catacombs of Rome), North African Christians chose to worship in public and accept persecution and even martyrdom as the duty of true Christians.

Clearly, the expansion of Christianity was a political issue for the Roman state. It was, however, also an important issue for the wider society. Because devout Christians were expected to avoid any professional or social setting that celebrated pagan gods, they could easily draw the ire of those who found such avoidance insulting or even treasonous. Tensions could even exist on the family level. Tertullian, a prolific early Christian writer, described the difficulties faced by a woman who had converted to Christianity while her husband continued to practice his traditional religion.

She is engaged in a fast; her husband has arranged a banquet. It is her Christian duty to visit the streets and the homes of the poor; her husband insists on family business. She celebrates the Easter Vigil throughout the entire night; her husband expects her in his bed. She steals into prison to kiss the chains of a martyr and to offer a loaf of bread; her husband resents the depletion of his cupboard. She who has taken a cup at the Eucharist will be required to take a cup with her husband in the tavern. She who

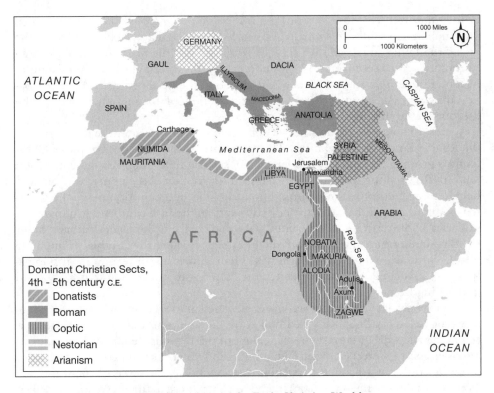

Map 5-1: Africa in the Early Christian World

has foresworn idolatry must inhale the smoke arising from the incense on the altars of the idols in her husband's home.

> Robert Sider, "Early Christians in North Africa: The Witness of Tertullian," *Coptic Church Review* 19, no. 3 (1998): p. 2.

In the late second century C.E. in Alexandria, African Christians established one of the first catechetical schools, the **Didascalia.** Given Alexandria's long-standing role as a center of learning, it is not too surprising that it would be chosen to play such a role for the new religion of Christianity. The Didascalia grew to become a focus of early Christian learning. Many early church bishops traveled to the school to study—with discussions being held in both Coptic and Greek. Saint Jerome, known for the first translation of the Bible into Latin, is believed to have studied at the Didascalia, for example.

Christianity spread into the upper Nile Valley and the highlands of Ethiopia somewhat more slowly than in Lower Egypt and North Africa. Likely, this relative slowness is due in part to the fact that the upper Nile and Ethiopia lay beyond the borders of the Roman Empire. Nonetheless, ancient trade links along the Nile and by way of the Red Sea and Indian Ocean facilitated the movement of Christianity deeper into Africa. Between 320 and 350 C.E., King Ezana of Aksum converted to Christianity. The story told is that he was converted by two shipwrecked Christians,

Frumentius and Aedisius. This process is recorded in the coins he minted, which offer homage to southern Arabian gods early in his reign and to the cross near the end. Frumentius and Aedisius, though Syrians, were members of the church in Alexandria. After returning to Egypt and calling for a formal Christian mission to Aksum, Frumentius was named the first bishop of the upper Nile region. The Coptic church in Alexandria carried on the tradition of naming the head of the Ethiopian church into the twentieth century.

It is notable that Ezana's conversion came very shortly after the conversion of the Roman Emperor Constantine. This fact represents a parallel example of Christianity's growing acceptance by political elites at the time. King Ezana's conversion not only fostered the spread of Christianity in the region of the upper Nile, but also helped forge cultural, economic, and political links between Aksum and the Christian communities of the eastern Mediterranean. In the fifth century, a group of missionaries known as the "Nine Saints," who hailed from Syria and perhaps other eastern Mediterranean regions, arrived in Ethiopia, where they translated the Bible into Ge'ez and established monasteries. Their efforts at converting local populations to Christianity helped to balance the "top down" conversion that had begun under King Ezana.

So deeply did Christianity become entrenched in the region that in the sixth century King Kaleb of Ethiopia invaded Yemen (in the southern Arabian Peninsula). This action was allegedly undertaken at the behest of the Byzantine emperor Justinian and was ostensibly to protect Christian communities in Yemen from repression at the hands of the region's non-Christian population. Some scholars, however, discount the religious motivations of the two monarchs and stress that perhaps their goal was to weaken the Persian empire and gain greater control over the lucrative trade that flowed

Illuminated page from an Ethiopian Bible, written in Ge'ez.

through Arabia. Either way, the cooperation of the Byzantine and Aksum monarchs says much about the transregional nature of early Christianity. King Kaleb is also notable for his building of the Aksum Seyon Cathedral and for resigning his kingship in 540 C.E. in order to become a monk. Indeed, when he stepped down from the throne, his crown was sent to Jerusalem, where it was hung in the Church of the Holy Sepulchre.

Christianity would continue to grow and thrive in Ethiopia. As in Rome, religion and politics in Aksum were closely related. By the ninth century, the ruling Aksumite dynasty was bolstering its legitimacy by claiming to be descended from King Solomon and the Queen of Sheba. Around 945 C.E., however, a succession dispute weakened the Aksumite dynasty, and in the ensuing power struggle, a daughter of the family emerged victorious. Known as the "Queen of Habasha," she is reputed to have driven her own father into exile, laid waste to the capital of Aksum, and even destroyed many churches—though this final charge may have been a fabrication intended to damage her legacy. In any case she either founded or cleared a path for the rise of the **Zagwe** dynasty, which succeeded the Aksumites. The Zagwe rulers established a new capital at Adafa. They also launched a period of aggressive expansion, with the Coptic church and monasteries playing a central role in the expansion of state power. By converting newly subjected peoples to Christianity, the Zagwe kings hoped to forge a state that drew its unity from both political and religious legitimacy—a remarkable similarity to the role of the Roman church in the politics of medieval Europe. The Zagwe king, Lalibela, even sponsored the building of churches that were hewn out of solid rock. Indeed, Lalibela apparently commissioned the churches in hopes of reclaiming the splendor of old Jerusalem. The Lalibela churches are a unique feat within the Christian tradition and stand today as a testimonial to the longevity and vitality of Ethiopian Christianity.

A stone-cut church from Ethiopia.

Voices from African History: **The Kebra Negast**

"And the King answered and said unto her [Sheba], 'Verily, it is right that they (i.e., men) should worship God, Who created the universe. . . . It is meant that Him alone we should worship, in fear and trembling, with joy and with gladness. For He is the Lord of the Universe, the Creator of angels and men. And it is He Who killeth and maketh to live, it is He Who inflicteth punishment and showeth compassion, Who raiseth up from the ground him that is in misery, Who exalteth the poor from the dust. . . . Who raiseth up and Who bringeth down. No one can chide Him, for He is the Lord of the Universe, and there is no one who can say unto Him, 'What hast Thou done?' And unto Him it is meant that there should be praise and thanksgiving from angels and men. And as concerning what thou sayest, that 'He hath given unto you the Tabernacle of the Law,' verily there hath been given unto us the Tabernacle of the God of ISRAEL, which was created before all creation by His glorious counsel. And He hath made to come down to us His commandments, done into writing, so that we may know His decree and the judgment that He hath ordained in the mountain of His holiness.'

And the Queen said, 'From this moment I will not worship the sun, but will worship the Creator of the sun, the God of ISRAEL.

And that Tabernacle of the God of ISRAEL shall be unto me my Lady, and unto my seed after me, and unto all my kingdoms that are under my dominion. And because of this I have found favour before thee, and before the God of ISRAEL my Creator, Who hath brought me unto thee, and hath made me to hear thy voice, and hath shown me thy face, and hath made me to understand thy commandment.'

And the Queen used to go [to SOLOMON] and return continually, and hearken unto his wisdom, and keep it in her heart. And SOLOMON used to go and visit her, and answer all the questions which she put to him, and the Queen used to visit him and ask him questions, and he informed her concerning every matter that she wished to enquire about. And after she had dwelt [there] six months the Queen wished to return to her own country, and she sent a message to SOLOMON, saying, 'I desire greatly to dwell with thee, but now, for the sake of all my people, I wish to return to my own country. And as for that which I have heard, may God make it to bear fruit in my heart, and in the hearts of all those who have heard it with me. For the ear could never be filled with the hearing of thy wisdom, and the eye could never be filled with the sight of the same.'"

Translation by E. A. Wallis Budge, 1932.

In 1270 C.E., the **Solomonid** dynasty overthrew the Zagwe. The Solomonids claimed to belong to the same Aksumite dynasty that had sought to legitimize their authority by claiming descent from Solomon and Sheba. The Solomonids, under King Amda Seyon (1314–1344) however, reinforced this claim through the authorship of a text called the *Kebra Negast* (The Glory of Kings). In this story (unique to Ethiopia), the Ethiopian Queen, Sheba, journeyed to Jerusalem to learn the art of governance from Solomon. During her stay, Solomon converted her to monotheism. She returned to Ethiopia pregnant with a son fathered by her tutor. Named Menelik, he would later return to Jerusalem to meet his father, be crowned King of Ethiopia, and return to Ethiopia with the Ark of the Covenant. To this day, the Coptic church in Ethiopia claims to be the keeper of the Ark, one of the holiest relics of Judaism, Christianity, and Islam. By possessing both the blood of Solomon and the artifact of the Ark, the Solomonids legitimized themselves as Christian rulers and Ethiopia as the new Zion. Like the Zagwe kings, the Solomonids continued to use the church and monastaries to incorporate newly subjected peoples into the Ethiopian state. It is worth noting that over the next several hundred years, the Solomonid dynasty endured conflicts both with neighboring Islamic states and with Beta Israel kingdoms in the highlands to survive until the Ethiopian revolution of 1974 forced King Haile Selassie, the last of the Solomonid rulers, into exile.

Aksum and Ethiopia were not the only regions of the Upper Nile to embrace Christianity. During the sixth century, Nubia became the focus of considerable missionary attention. At this time, Nubia was divided into three kingdoms: Nobadia in the north, Makuria in the central region, and Alodia in the south. In 543 C.E., Theodora, the wife of the Roman emperor Justinian, sent a Monophysite mission, which converted the court of Nobadia. Makuria was converted by Roman Catholic missionaries in 569 and Alodia by Longinus, the Bishop of Philae (a Monophysite), in 580. Such competition for African converts among the various Christian sects of the day highlights the importance of African populations and states in the early missionary activities of the church. Further, the strong links between the Nubians and other Christian communities was evidenced by the fact that early Nubian Christians wrote texts in Greek, Nubian, Ge'ez, and Arabic.

Perhaps as early as the seventh century, Nobadia merged with Makuria, creating a much larger and more powerful Christian state. This unity may have played a role in Christian Nubia's successful resistance to Islamic invasions in 641 and 651 (see Chapter 6). However, some scholars argue the unification did not take place until the rule of King Mukurios (c 697–720). The political unity of the region was soon mirrored by a growing theological unity. The rulers of Makuria embraced the authority of the Coptic church, which continued to be based in Alexandria despite Egypt's incorporation into the expanding Islamic state. Though the creation of Lake Aswan in Egypt from 1964 to 1976 flooded much of the region once occupied by Makuria, extensive archaeological operations prior to the filling of the lake revealed a wealth of information about Christian Nubia. In particular, a very well-preserved cathedral at Faras yielded frescos of great variety and artistry, many of which depict early Christian events, saints, and also Nubian church and political leaders.

African Contributions to Early Christian Thought

Early Christianity faced a number of theological challenges. Central among these were the need to deal with classical philosophy (particularly Neoplatonism), to define the nature of Christ and the Trinity, and to work out a system of authority that would define the nature of orthodoxy and the church itself. Each of these debates was hard-fought and led to schisms and conflict within the Christian community. Here we will seek to examine the central role of African Christians in these debates and what this role meant for the development of Christianity in Africa and elsewhere.

Neoplatonism provided a particular challenge to early Christian thinkers. Fundamental to Neoplatonism was the concept that ideas (logos) existed on a higher level than did the material world. Ideas were perfect and permanent, whereas the material world was imperfect and temporary. Indeed, the physical world was an illusion compared to the absolute reality of ideas. The human soul struggled to attain the realm of ideas, while the human body, itself a part of the physical world, resisted such striving. The similarity of these ideas to the Christian soul's struggle for eternal salvation and the need to put aside the temptations of the physical world were apparent to many early Christian thinkers. Justin Martyr, an early Christian theologian living in Rome in the early second century, sought to establish certain Greek texts as early forms of revelation and to identify Jesus as a personification of logos—wisdom himself. Building on Justin's work were Clement of Alexandria and his student Origen (sometimes referred to as "the Father of Theology"), who lived in the late second and early third centuries. Indeed, both Clement and Origen were on the staff of the Didascalia, mentioned earlier. In particular, these early scholars helped to refute the writings of Tertullian, a Carthaginian author who had argued that classical learning was not relevant to Christian thought. Clement and Origen did much to help legitimize classical thought as relevant to Christian theology and to define early Christianity as not only a religion of faith, but one of reason as well.

Gnosticism was perhaps the earliest challenge to "orthodox" Christian thought. Of growing influence in the second century C.E., Gnostic Christianity drew heavily on Neoplatonism, being based on the Greek term *gnosis,* meaning "knowledge." To the Gnostics, many of whom lived in Egypt and North Africa, there was no original sin. Rather, it was matter (this world) that was evil, and only "secret knowledge," which they believed to have been passed down from Paul, could ensure salvation. The Gnostic position that matter was evil created difficulties for the church, because it meant that Jesus' human form was itself evil and was only a vessel used by Jesus. In so doing, the Gnostics were contradicting the growing church orthodoxy that Christ was a perfect union of God and humanity and foreshadowed future debates over **Arianism** and **Monophysitism.** Further, the Gnostics rejected the church hierarchy and stressed the importance of individual knowledge and experience as a means to salvation. Finally, the Gnostics recognized a feminine component within the Divine and also allowed women to preach and even baptize, a source of no small scandal in the otherwise patriarchal early Christian church. The church worked hard to eradicate Gnostic beliefs. Indeed, these early attempts to refute Gnosticism helped create a growing body of theological commentary that formed the basis of "orthodox" Christian thought.

Though Gnosticism was eventually to be displaced by less-mystical forms of Christianity, it may in part be responsible for the development of one of the most enduring of Christian institutions, the monastic movement. In the third century C.E., in the desert along the Nile, a devout Christian later known as "St. Anthony of the Desert" foreswore all worldly goods and pleasures and moved to live a life of absolute poverty and religious contemplation. Whether his denial of worldly things was influenced by the Gnostic belief that matter was evil or was motivated by a desire to follow Christ's example of poverty is hard to discern, but it is clear that his emphasis on the spiritual over the worldly met with great respect. Many followed his example, and a community of desert monks (male and female) grew quickly. In the early fourth century, Anthony organized the first formal monastic order. This order was reputed to have greatly assisted the poor and prison populations of Alexandria and as such to have attracted many converts to Christianity. In nearby Caesarea, influenced by St. Anthony's example, Pachomius and Basil drew up the first rules of chastity, obedience, and poverty—rules that were to become the basis of all future monastic orders. Pachomius, who went on to found nine monasteries and two covenants, greatly influenced John Cassian, who later founded the first monasteries in Gaul. For his example, St. Anthony is known as "the Father of Monasticism."

Perhaps the greatest debates in the early Church focused on the nature of Jesus himself—to what degree was he divine and to what degree was he human? In attacking Neoplatonism, Tertullian had been one of the first to argue that Jesus was both—completely human and completely divine. Not all early Christians were in agreement. Indeed, two of the most significant schisms in the early church took place over this issue, and each time the challenge was based in Egypt.

Beginning in the late third century C.E., a priest in Alexandria named Arius began to preach that Jesus was not himself divine. Rather, said Arius, Jesus was a perfect creation of the Father, but was a creation that was not eternal. That is, Jesus was created by God rather than being God himself. Further, Jesus had no direct contact with God, but acted only on the basis of his divinely created perfection. Finally, the term "son of God" was a general reference that could apply to all humanity and did not relate specifically to Jesus. The fact that the Emperor Constantine had recently legalized Christianity further complicated what was already a difficult theological dispute. Constantine hoped that Christianity could be used as a force to unify the disparate social groups of the far-flung Roman Empire and was concerned that such controversies might undermine that goal. As a result, Constantine called the Council of Nicea in 325 C.E. This council declared Arianism to be a heresy and established the Nicean Creed as a central component of orthodox Christianity. Not only did these events lead to an increasingly rigid Christian orthodoxy, but they also showed how the growing union of church and state in the Roman Empire was shifting the balance of power in the Christian community toward the Roman church. Though declared a heresy, Arianism was to last for some time and expand far beyond Egypt. For example, in the fourth century, an Arian missionary, Ulfilas, was to convert many of the German tribes north of Rome to Arian Christianity. Thus, in the fourth century, African Christianity was sending missionaries to pagan Europe—quite a contrast to our modern notions of Africans being converted to Christianity by Europeans!

In the early fourth and fifth centuries, a conflict raged between two camps within the church. One group, known as diophysites, argued that Christ's human and divine natures were distinct, while the monophysites advocated a single nature. In 431 C.E. the Council of Ephesus resulted in the schism of the Nestorian Church in the Middle East. The conflict continued, however, and in 451 the Emperor Theodocious II called the Council of Chalcedon to once again establish an orthodoxy and declare those who disagreed as "heretics." As a result, the Alexandrian pope Dioscorus was tried and eventually exiled. Most Egyptian bishops, in turn, rejected the actions of the council. The result was yet another schism, this time resulting in the creation of the Coptic church, which, as we have already seen, grew to dominate Christian belief and practice in the lower and upper Nile valley. Notably, Egypt was still under the control of the Eastern Roman (later called Byzantine) Empire, which considered the Coptic church a heresy. As a result, the political power of the empire was often used to persecute Coptic Christians.

The growing power of the Roman church did not only meet with resistance in Egypt. In North Africa, a group of bishops called the Donatists (who took their name from the Numidian bishop Donatus) increasingly came into conflict with the Roman church. During the Diocletian persecution, the Donatists had differed with the Roman church over how Christians who had recanted their faith in order to escape persecution or martyrdom should be treated. The Roman church argued for leniency and for allowing these lapsed Christians to return to the fold. The Donatists, who tended to see the Christian community as a small group of elect rather than as a large group of less-than-perfect seekers, took a harder line, saying such people had forfeited their membership in the church. Also, the Donatists argued that baptisms by less-than-perfect priests were not valid, whereas the Roman church argued that the priest, however flawed, was merely the means for transmitting divine grace.

The debate between the Roman and Donatist Christians raged throughout the fourth century. A vociferous opponent of the Donatists, Augustine (who himself later became Bishop of Hippo in Africa) wrote his famous work, *City of God,* in part to refute Donatist thought, which tended to argue the importance of actions over faith. Following the conversion of Constantine, Christian emperors used Roman troops to suppress the Donatists. Thus, the legalizing of Christianity did not bring to an end official Roman repression of Christians—it simply meant that the Roman church could seek to use the power of the state to impose its will in matters of doctrine. Indeed, the Donatists argued that the Roman church had sold out by aligning itself with the Roman state. The Donatist primate of Carthage chided the Roman Christians with the statement, "You come with edicts of Emperors, but we hold nothing in our hands but volumes of the Scriptures." True to their beliefs, however, the Donatists only saw the continued persecution as a means of weeding out those whose faith was lacking. The Donatists also developed a strong identity that stressed the African nature of their religious roots, and the role of Africans, such as Simeon of Cyrene, in establishing the Christian church. Some evidence also suggests that they utilized local languages such as Punic to seek converts from beyond the Roman strongholds of the urban coast.

The Donatists, however, were not always at a political disadvantage. When the Emperor Julian quarreled with the Catholic church, he backed Donatist bishops as a balance against the Roman church's power. By the latter fourth century, the Donatists had grown to become the dominant religious force in North Africa. Indeed, they became large enough to suffer their own internal schisms, as in 390 C.E. when Bishop Rogatus of Carenna and followers broke with the Donatists to form a pacifist sect. In 429, the invasion of North Africa by Gaiseric the Vandal greatly weakened the Donatist church. Notably, the Vandals were predominantly Arians—bringing this variant of Christianity back to North Africa some 200 years after its advent. The Vandals were eventually overthrown in 533 by the Byzantine emperor Justinian, and state-supported Christianity was reasserted in the region.

The Decline of African Christianity

The expansion of the Islamic state throughout the Middle East and across North Africa (and even into southern Europe) in the seventh century did not spell a sudden end for African Christianity. Indeed, North African Christians in many cases welcomed the advancing Islamic armies as liberators from the political and spiritual oppression of Byzantium. The exception was Christian Nubia, which twice defeated the Muslim armies at **Dongola** and was recognized as a sovereign state by the Islamic leaders in a treaty known as a baqt—the only Christian government so legitimized. In the North, Christians were encouraged, but not forced, to convert. Contrary to popular belief, the Muslims did not demand conversion on threat of death, but rather granted spiritual freedom to those Christian (and Jewish) communities that recognized Islamic suzerainty and paid a special tax. Indeed, the tax burden imposed by the new Islamic state was far less than that demanded previously by Byzantium. Under such a system, the numbers of Christians in North Africa and the Nile Valley would slowly dwindle over the next several hundred years. As late as the tenth century, Christians were still a majority in Egypt. Though Christians would make up only about 10 percent of the Egyptian population by the nineteenth century, Christianity has remained the dominant religion in Ethiopia to the current day.

Despite the slow decline of African Christianity, it is interesting to note that until the advent of the transatlantic slave trade, most Europeans tended to assume that Africans were Christians. Largely cut off from Africa by Muslim conquest, Europeans assumed that African Christianity survived. During the era of the crusades, Christians in the invading armies hoped that "**Prester John,**" a mythical Christian African king, would attack the Muslims from the south and help reunite the wider Christian world. When the Ethiopian king Wadem Arad sent a mission of Coptic priests to Rome in 1306, European images of a Christian Africa were reinforced. Sadly, the advent of the transatlantic slave trade necessitated the creation of a negative image of Africa—of heathen Africans whose need for salvation was seen as a legitimate justification for generations of slavery. So successful was this redefinition of Africa that when the Scottish traveler James Bruce returned from Ethiopia in 1783 with tales of a wealthy Christian kingdom, he was branded a charlatan. Of course, the transatlantic slave trade did little to introduce Christianity into Africa. Beginning in the 1800s, the era of European conquest and colonization would bring a second round of Christian expansion into Africa, though on very different terms from the ancient spread of Christianity in the continent.

Early African Christianity in Global Perspective

Clearly, the common Western belief that Christianity was unknown in Africa before the coming of European missionaries in the nineteenth century is a myth. Rather, North Africans and inhabitants of the Nile Valley played a central role in the development of early Christianity, both as some of the new religion's first converts and as theologians who helped guide the development of the faith in its crucial first centuries. Indeed, long before there were substantial communities of Christians in much of what we now define as Europe, there were large numbers of Christians in North African towns such as Alexandria and Carthage. Because of doctrinal conflicts and schisms, Christianity in North Africa and the Nile Valley developed along a somewhat different trajectory than Christianity elsewhere, creating in the Coptic church a form of the religion different from that found under the domain of the Roman Catholic or Eastern Orthodox churches.

Such a reality highlights two important points for consideration. First, Christianity is not a "foreign" religion to Africa, as is occasionally argued by some Eurocentrists, cultural nationalists, or Afrocentrists. Africa was as much a home to early Christianity as was the Middle East or Europe. Indeed, as seen in this chapter, Africa was very much a part of the early "Christian World." Christianity may have originated in a small region known as Palestine, but the religion itself developed even as it expanded, and much of that early expansion and development took place in parts of Africa. This brings us to the second point. Christianity is often today considered a "Western" religion—a perspective that privileges the Catholic and Protestant variants of Christianity that developed in southern and Western Europe. However, the examination of the early Christian history of Africa (and, for that matter Central Asia), provides us with a much richer, multifaceted, and more complex understanding of the religion's early forms and development.

Finally, it should be noted that the expansion of what are often called "Salvation Religions" (which include Buddhism and Islam, in addition to Christianity) is one of the most important "Grand Narratives" of world history. Over the course of the past 2,500 years, these three religions have come to dominate the world's religious communities, often displacing (and also syncretizing with) local pantheistic religions. Thus, the expansion of Christianity (and later, as we shall see in the next two chapters, Islam) in Africa, is very much a part of this critical theme in the human story.

Useful Works on This Chapter Topic

Likely the single most comprehensive work on this chapter's topic is Elizabeth Isichei's *The History of Christianity in Africa: From Antiquity to the Present* (1995). Maureen A. Tilley's *The Bible in North Africa: The Donatist World* (1997) offers an even more detailed discussion of the Donatists and their opponents. Tilley also offers primary documents on the subject in her edited collection, *Donatist Martyr Stories: The Church in Conflict in Roman North Africa* (1998). In *Christianity in Africa: The Renewal of Non-Western Religion* (1996), the Ghanaian scholar Kwame Bediako argues that Christianity as practiced in Africa (in antiquity and the present) represents the purest form of the Christian message. More specific works on the subject of early African Christianity include Joseph Trigg's *Origen* (1998), Christian Cannuyer's *Coptic Egypt: The Christians of the Nile* (2001), Robert Sider's *Christian and Pagan in the Roman Empire: The Witness of Tertullian* (2001), and James E. Goehring's *Ascetics, Society and the Desert: Studies in Early Egyptian Monasticism* (1999). On the subject of Ethiopian Judaism, see James Quirin's, *The Evolution of the Ethiopian Jews* (1992).

CHAPTER 6

North and West Africa and the Spread of Islam

For many students, Islam is a mysterious religion that conjures up images of exotic desert landscapes and negative stereotypes of bomb-planting terrorists. This is terribly unfortunate. Islam represents one of the world's richest religious traditions—and also one of its most varied. In part because Islam was so successful in expanding beyond the lands of its origin in the Arabian Peninsula, it has interacted with peoples and cultures in every part of the world—from Southeast Asia to the Americas. As you probably guessed from the title of this chapter, Islam also expanded into Africa. Much of Africa is part of what Muslims call the **Dar al-Islam**—the "abode of peace," or the part of the world in which Islam guides people's lives. Over the centuries, Islam has greatly influenced the history of much of Africa—and in turn Africans have deeply influenced the development of Islam in Africa and beyond. This chapter will seek to show how expansion of Islam into Africa can be seen as a blending of religions, cultures, and human populations that has helped create cultural and economic links between Muslim Africans and a wider Islamic world.

This chapter will focus on Islam's expansion into North and West Africa, and the next chapter will focus on Islam in East Africa. Because Islam expanded and developed differently in these two regions, we have chosen to divide the discussion into two sections, though in some ways this division may still be artificial. Remember that one of the key challenges facing the historian is how to divide history in terms of geographical, chronological, and thematic units. No such division is ever easy or perfect.

The Origins of Islam

Islam shares the same core religious traditions that gave rise to Judaism and Christianity. Indeed, many parts of the Qur'an would be familiar to Jews and Christians. For example, Islam considers Abraham, Moses, and Jesus to be among the most important prophets of the religion. The key difference, though, is that Muslims do not recognize Jesus as divine and believe that Muhammad was the final Prophet of God (Allah). For the purposes of this brief introduction to Islam, we will begin with Muhammad.

Muhammad was born in the Arabian Peninsula sometime around 570 C.E. During this time, Arabia was a zone of contention between three powerful states— the Byzantines to the north, the Sassanids to the east, and Aksum to the south. Rival Arab trading families vied for power and influence within this fluid political setting. Muhammad was orphaned at an early age and was never formally educated. Through his marriage to a wealthy widow, he became moderately successful as a car- avan trader. In Mecca, the region's dominant trading city and his home, Muham- mad gained a reputation as a wise arbitrator of disputes and as someone who was deeply concerned with issues of justice. Indeed, he was given to periods of intro- spection when he would isolate himself in the hills outside Mecca and reflect on the nature of the world. During one such period of reflection, Muhammad experi- enced the "Night of Power," when he was visited by the Archangel Gabriel and informed that he was to be Allah's last prophet. After this visit, Muhammad found that he could recite flawless religious poetry—no less than the Word of God. These verses and others that followed became the Sura (chapters) of the Qur'an. These verses and the Sunna (sayings and actions) of the Prophet became the basis for Islam—a religion that stresses absolute monotheism and absolute submission "Islam" to the will of Allah.

As is so often the case with prophets, Muhammad soon found himself at odds with the religious authorities of the region, which was the center of worship for pan- theistic local religions. In 622 C.E. he and his expanding group of followers were forced to flee from Mecca to Medina, several hundred miles to the northeast. In 632 C.E. the Muslim community had grown strong enough to defeat the authorities in Mecca, which became the destination of Islam's annual pilgrimage, called the Hajj. Though Muhammad died that year, the religion and the new Islamic state (generally, Islam does not seek a division between the religion and politics) contin- ued to grow rapidly (initially via military conquest) and soon expanded beyond the Arabian Peninsula into Asia and Africa.

Islam in North Africa

The expanding Islamic state quickly set its sights on Egypt and North Africa. Egypt was one of the world's most populous and economically productive regions. Simi- larly, the North African coastline was fertile and wealthy. Much of this wealth was because North Africa sat astride trade routes that linked sub-Saharan Africa with Europe. Further, Egypt and North Africa's populations provided the potential for millions of converts to Islam. Contrary to Western stereotypes, Muslims almost never try to force people to convert through threat of violence. It is the duty of Muslims to try to convert nonbelievers, but voluntary conversion is seen as the only legitimate acceptance of Islam. As we shall see, though, the establishment by force of an Islamic government over non-Muslims was certainly fair game for the expanding religion.

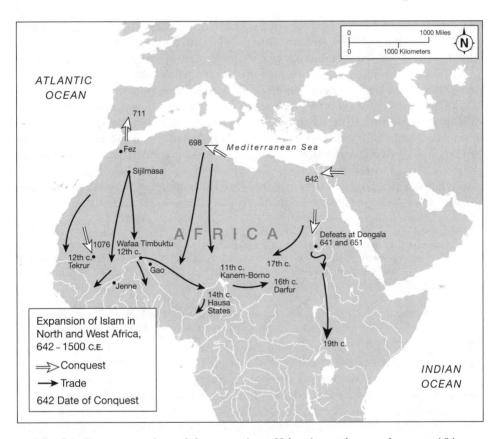

Map 6-1: Conquest, trade, and the expansion of Islam in northern and western Africa

So, when we talk about the early expansion of Islam in North Africa, we are really talking about the expansion of a political system that was then followed by a slow process of conversion over the next several hundred years.

The Islamic conquest of Egypt occurred over a three-year period from 639 to 642 C.E. Although the Byzantine army in Egypt was defeated, their navy proved to be much too powerful for the young (and not terribly sea-savvy) Islamic state. Because the Byzantines controlled the Mediterranean, the Muslims were forced to shy away from Alexandria and build a new city just inland—the origin of the modern Egyptian capital of Cairo. In general, though, the conquest of Egypt was remarkably easy. This is likely in no small part because the Byzantine rulers of Egypt were unpopular with the region's population. This was partly due to religious differences between the local Coptic church and the Eastern Orthodox rulers of Byzantium (see Chapter 5), but was also a result of the high tax burden placed on Egypt by Byzantium. Indeed, the Christians of Egypt largely viewed the Muslims as liberators because the distinctions between Islam and Christianity were not yet so clear (in fact, a large component of the early Muslim armies were Christians of the Nestorian and Coptic sects). By and large, the new Muslim government of Egypt allowed greater religious freedom than had the Byzantines, and Coptic Christians continued to make up the majority of Egypt's population into the eleventh century. Non-Muslim subjects, called *Dhimmi*, were required to pay a special tax, the Jiziya, in return for the right to practice their own religion and manage the internal affairs of their communities. In general these tax burdens were considerably reduced from Byzantine levels.

The expansion beyond Egypt proved to be much more problematic for the Muslim armies that sought to expand into Africa. Attempting to expand up the Nile River into Nubia, the Muslims were, in 641 and 651 C.E., dealt defeats at the hands of Christian Nubians at Dongola, near the first cataract of the Nile. As a result of these Nubian victories, the Muslims agreed to recognize the legitimacy and independence of Christian Nubia—a rare thing for the expanding Islamic state. Witness the following description of one battle by the Muslim scholar al-Baladhuri:

> One day they arrayed themselves against us and we were desirous to carry on the conflict with the sword. But they were too quick for us and shot their arrows, putting out our eyes. The eyes they put out numbered 150. We at last thought the best thing to do with such a people was to make peace.

> Al-Baladhuri: *The Origins of the Islamic State.* Translated by Philip K. Hitti (New York: Columbia University Press, 1924), pp. 379–381.

Although the treaty included provisions for trade (including a trade in slaves) along the Nile between the two regions, the victory of the Nubians over the Muslim forces was to long delay the spread of Islam into the region of the upper Nile.

To the west, which the Muslims call the Maghreb (which actually just means "west" in Arabic), the expanding Islamic state also encountered great resistance. The Christians of North Africa met the expanding Muslims with the same independence with which they had faced attempted Roman and Byzantine domination. Similarly, the Berbers of the desert fringe and interior were little inclined to accept Islam (just as they had largely spurned Christianity). In particular, a woman known by the Muslims as **al-Kahina** ("the Soothsayer") offered fierce resistance to the Muslim forces in the region of modern Tunisia until she and her supporters were finally defeated in 698 C.E. Her leadership may in part be understood as a rejection not to Islam's strict monotheism, but as a resistance of the region's matrilineal system to that of Islam's strict patriliny.

The expansion of the Islamic state was largely facilitated by the Muslims' building of fortified towns known as **ribats.** These fortresses both established a frontier for the Dar-al-Islam and helped isolate Arab Muslim migrants from the very real possibility that they would be slowly assimilated to local culture via interaction and intermarriage with local non-Muslim populations. One of the most important of these towns, Qayrawan, was to become crucial not only to the expansion of Islam in the Maghreb, but also as an important center for Islamic learning in the region for centuries to come. With the establishment of ribats all along the North African coast and with the building of an Islamic navy that could at last defeat the Byzantines, the forces of Islam were by the turn of the eighth century able to lay claim to all of the North African coast and even begin the conquest of the Iberian Peninsula.

It is at this point very important to stress that even in the early era of Islam, there was no single Islamic orthodoxy. Just as we saw with Christianity in Chapter 5, early Muslims faced a number of difficult disputes over what the true practice of Islam was to be and over what constituted a legitimate Islamic government. North Africa was to play a crucial role in the development of Islamic orthodoxy and in the future of the Islamic state itself. Of particular importance was the fact that during the early era of Islam, North Africa played a role as a haven for those Muslims who found themselves at odds with the growing Sunni orthodoxy of the central Islamic state. Two of Islam's early sects, the **Shi'i** and the **Kharijites,** settled in the **Maghreb** in relatively large numbers. The Shi'i were a group that believed that the only legitimate leadership for the Islamic state could come from the family of the Prophet Muhammad—specifically from those descended from his daughter Fatimah and son-in-law Ali. Ali was the fourth and last of the Rashidun, or "Rightly Guided Caliphs," of Islam. He was challenged and overthrown by Mu'awiya, who founded the Umayyad Caliphate. Following this defeat, many of the Shi'i (both of the Ibadi and Isma'ili sects) fled to North Africa. As we shall later see, some also fled to East Africa. The Kharijites had originally supported Ali, but abandoned him when at one point Ali agreed to halt a battle and settle the dispute with Mu'awiya through arbitration. Though the Kharijites ceased to support Ali, they continued to oppose the Umayyads and were also forced to flee to North Africa. The Maghreb's relatively sparse population and the limited nature of Umayyad authority (still largely restricted to the ribats) meant that both the Shi'i and the Kharijites could hope to exist and organize without too much fear of Umayyad oppression.

In particular, the Kharijites found haven in the small oases of the northern Sahara and in the hills of the Kabylia and Atlas Mountains. To a limited extent, the Kharijites also found a certain kinship with the Berbers, with whom they shared a dislike for centralized authority and a rejection of the Umayyad emphasis on Arab identity in early Islam. Indeed, early Berber converts to Islam were notable for their rejection of what might be considered "Arabization" in terms of language and culture. Nonetheless, it is likely that the Kharijites were the first group to make progress toward converting the Berbers to Islam. Also, the Kharijites of the oases became involved in the trans-Saharan trade, allowing for the first penetration of Islamic influence into the southern regions of the Sahara. Like the Kharijites, the Shi'i found refuge in the more remote regions of North Africa. Some sources even state that the Ibadi had established a settlement at Zawiya (near Lake Chad) in the eighth century. The Shi'i, too, made some converts among the Berbers. The Shi'i gained particular influence among the Kutama in the Kabylia Mountains in eastern Algeria. Here, the Shi'i grew in power until in the early tenth century, when they felt strong enough to challenge the power of the now-dominant Abbasid Caliphate. Beginning their revolt in Tunisia, they overthrew the Abbasid governor and defeated the Berber Kharijites led by Abu Yazid. The victorious Shi'i established the **Fatimid Caliphate** under the leadership of Ubayd Allah. In 969 C.E. the Fatimids had grown so powerful that they were able to continue their conquest into Egypt (where they relocated their capital) and even expanded into Syria and western Arabia. Thus, it was in Africa that this particular Islamic state was nurtured and very nearly rose to seize the heartland of Islam. Though the Fatimids failed to overthrow the Abbasid Caliphate, they were to remain in power in Egypt for nearly two centuries. Notably, in the mid-eleventh century, the Fatimids lost power over the Maghreb to the pro-Abbasid Zirids based in Qayrawan. The Fatimids attempted to destroy the Zirids by inviting Arab nomads from Arabia, the Banu Hilal, to invade the Maghreb. Though these invasions did cause considerable trouble to the Zirids (and perhaps kept them from threatening Fatimid Egypt), in the end these Arab invaders settled down to live in relative peace with the local Berbers. They are in part responsible for the spread of Arabic language, culture, and Islam into rural North Africa and the blurring of the ethnic lines between the rural and urban populations in the region—an interesting example of the porosity of North African and Middle Eastern populations.

Aside from the limited influence of the Shi'i and Kharijites, there was really little Islamic penetration of the region beyond the coastal plains of North Africa before the eleventh century. Some elements of Islam had indeed spread among the Saharan Berber populations, but the practice of the religion was often far from orthodox. The first real step toward the establishment of Islam was to take place in the region of modern Mauritania in the early eleventh century. In 1035, an unnamed chief of the Lamtuna Berbers, from the region near the important trading town of Awdaghost, undertook the Hajj. This event is important in that it highlights that some of those in the region were influenced by a desire to fulfill their obligations as Muslims. It also is a fine example of the importance of the pilgrimage in the history of Islam in Africa. In the course of his journey, this chief realized the disparity between his own people's practice of Islam and that elsewhere in the Dar al-Islam. During his return home, he convinced the Moroccan scholar, Abdallah Ibn Yasin, to accompany him to his homeland to educate his people in the proper practice of the religion. Yasin first attempted a "Jihad of the Mouth," wherein he preached the nature of "true" Islam to the Sanhaja. Finding few converts, he later declared himself Mahdi and instigated a "Jihad of the Sword," wherein he sought to establish an Islamic state that would foster a more orthodox practice of Islam. In this he was successful. The result was the **Almoravid** state that expanded to include much of the modern regions of Mauritania, Morocco, western Algeria, and southern Spain (another example of African influence in Europe). The Almoravids remained in power for over a century, until they were displaced in the Maghreb and Spain by the Almohads during the early twelfth century.

Like the Almoravids before them, the Almohads began as a movement to "purify" the practice of Islam in their homelands. And, like the Almoravids, they expanded into southern Spain, where they unified the region's fractured Muslim states. These conquests also added a new chapter to the long-standing process of cultural, economic, and political exchange between northwestern Africa and the Iberian Peninsula. However, the Almohads differed from the Almoravids in that they were more influenced by the teachings of the Middle Eastern scholar al-Ghazali, an important example of the close intellectual ties between the Maghreb and the heartland of Islam. Further, al-Ghazali was important in helping to legitimize Sufism, which was a more mystical path to holiness than the predominantly acts-based legalism of previous Sunni orthodoxy. The Almohads also gained fame for their investment in the building of huge and ornate mosques.

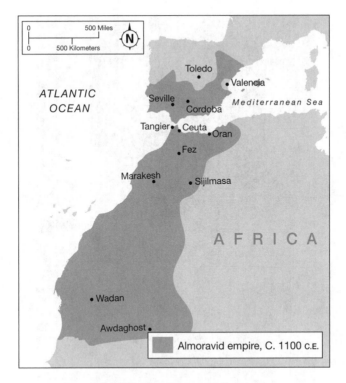

Map 6-2: The Almoravid Empire

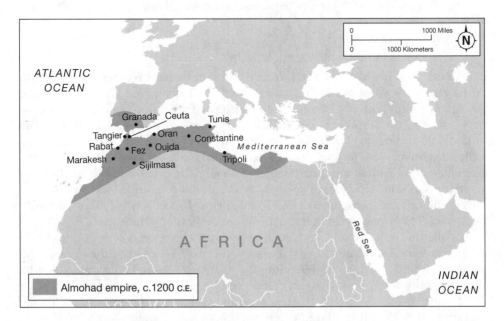

Map 6-3: The Almohad Empire

The "Unfinished Mosque," located in the Moroccan capital of Rabat, gives a sense of Almohad architectural skills.

Both Sufism and al-Ghazali's thought were to become further established in Africa with Salah al-Din's (Saladin's) overthrow of the Fatimids in 1171. It is important to see the twelfth century as a time when North and Saharan Africa came to increasingly embrace the Sunni and Sufi traditions of Islam. In particular, the more scriptural Sunni orthodoxy dominated the towns in which centers of Islamic learning, called Madrasas, were located. The more mystical Sufi tradition that came to predominate in rural areas was spread largely through long-distance trade and by independent Sufi scholars. Not surprisingly, it was this rural Sufism that was to most successfully spread into sub-Saharan West Africa. Indeed, as we shall later see, Sufism was to become a particularly African expression of Islamic piety.

Salah al-Din is famous for much more than the spread of Sunni and Sufi Islam, however. Of Kurdish origin, he is famous for his defeat of the second crusade. It was in the process of defending the Nile Valley from the crusaders that he also overthrew the Fatimid dynasty, ending centuries of Shi'i influence in Egypt. In 1187, Salah al-Din captured Jerusalem from the crusaders, who had controlled the city since 1099. His battles and interactions with Richard Lionheart (whom he eventually defeated) became legend in Europe.

From a base in Egypt Salah al-Din established the **Ayyubid** dynasty. Like the Fatimids he utilized Coptic Christians as the basis of the region's civil service. Interestingly, Salah al-Din and his descendants built the military power of Ayyubid state on a group called the **Mamluks.** The Mamluks, who were slaves from the shores of the Black Sea and from the Turkish region of Anatolia, developed a reputation for discipline and bravery. This raises the question of how someone could build an army of slaves and not worry about them taking power. Indeed, the idea is that slaves make excellent soldiers (and even generals), in part because they cannot become legitimate rulers. Under such a system, it makes sense to give power to slaves rather than to free persons. Indeed, over the course of world history, slave militaries have actually been fairly common.

The strategy seems to have worked for the Ayyubids for a little more than half a century. In 1250, however, the Mamluks took advantage of the death of the Ayyubid Sultan al-Malik al-Salih to seize power. When another Ayyubid claimant returned to Egypt, he was quickly dispatched by the Mamluks. Despite their slave origins, however, the Mamluks legitimized themselves as Muslims by defending the Dar al-Islam from two sets of invaders. First, in 1250, they defeated yet another host of crusaders, capturing the French King Louis IX in the process. Then, far more importantly, the Mamluks halted the Mongol invasion of the Middle East in 1260, first stopping the Mongols near Egypt and then driving them from the Abbasid capital of Baghdad. For some time, the Mamluks were the most powerful Islamic authority in the region of North Africa and the Middle East. They also expanded their authority up the Nile at the expense of Christian Nubia. Not until the expansion of the Ottomans in the sixteenth century was their power truly challenged—a topic to which we will return in Chapter 10.

Empires, Trade, and Islam in the West African Savannah

As we have seen in previous chapters, the West African savannah was an area of considerable innovation in the early centuries of the first millennium. Domestication of millet and sorghum, ironworking technology, and a fishing and hunting economy along the Niger River helped make for a thriving local economy. Further, the savannah's position as a "border" region between the distinct environments of the forests of the south and the Sahel and desert to the north allowed the population to mediate not only between the gold-producing regions of the forests and the salt mines of the Sahara, but also between North Africa and sub-Saharan Africa in a trade that included ivory, grains, hides, kola, copper, and dates. The introduction of camels to the region around 300 C.E., for example, fostered an expansion in trans-Saharan trade, which itself helped lead to the development of state-level societies in Ghana, Bornu, and a number of urban centers along the Niger River, including **Jenne-Jeno** and **Gao.** Thus, well before the advent of Islam in North Africa, the West African Savannah was already a region of vibrant economic, political, and cultural life. Indeed, the West African savannah was the only "grassland" region of the world to so successfully urbanize prior to the advent of modern transportation. This is a powerful testimony to both the unique setting of the savannah and the creativity of its inhabitants

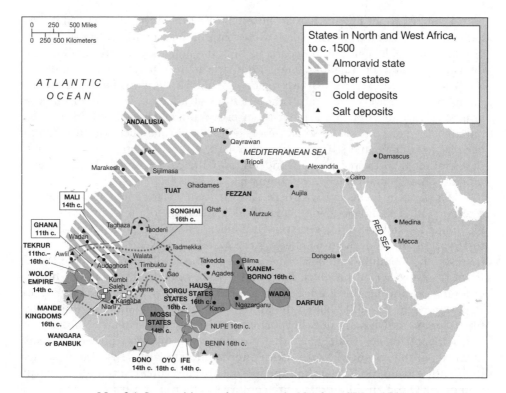

Map 6-4: States, cities, and resources in North and West Africa

Nonetheless, the expansion of Islam was to have an increasingly profound effect on the Savannah region from the ninth century onward. Islam was to change the nature of government and increasingly orient the region's perspective to the north and east as the region slowly became part of the Dar al-Islam. The coming of Islam to this area is also significant for historians in that it helps bring the savannah into the written historical record, giving us an additional source beyond archaeological, oral, and linguistic evidence with which to reconstruct the history of the region.

The savannah region of West Africa was known to early Muslim authors as the Bilad al-Sudan (Land of the Blacks). Some sources suggest that contact and trade with the inhabitants of the Savannah was discouraged by authorities in the north. For example, in the latter tenth century, Ibn Abi Zayd, a scholar in Qayrawan, wrote that "trade to the territory of the enemy and to the land of the Sudan is reprehensible." It is clear, though, that many Muslims, particularly merchants, did not share Zayd's rather isolationist viewpoint. The trans-Saharan trade had tied North and West Africa together long before the advent of Islam, and there is no evidence to suggest that Islam slowed this trade. Quite to the contrary, the expanding Islamic state seems only to have fostered the demand for goods from the south. Given the size, wealth, and influence of ancient Ghana, it is no surprise that it was of interest to Muslim traders and scholars. As early as the eighth century, the geographer al-Fazari, living in Baghdad, made reference to ancient Ghana's wealth in gold. In the tenth century, Ibn Hawqal declared that the ruler of Ghana was "the richest king on

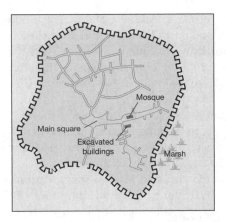

Map 6-5: Kumbi Saleh based on archaeological excavations

the face of the earth by reason of the wealth and treasure of [gold]." Active trade in salt, copper, and a variety of textiles was also noted by many early authors.

The trans-Saharan trade was driven in part by the desire of North African and European rulers to mint gold coins. Minting one's own coins was a crucial symbol of sovereignty and the waning power of the Abbasids and the rise of various successor states in North Africa after 900 led to a growing demand for gold. West Africa was well-endowed with gold, but lacked other resources, most notably salt. People who subsist primarily on grain, as West Africans did, require supplementary salt in their diets. West Africans obtained salt locally from a variety of sources. These included: animal sources (meat and dairy products contain dietarily significant amounts of salt), extracting it from the ashes of plants that naturally concentrate salt, evaporating seawater to obtain the residual salt, and mining it from dried-out lake beds. All of these methods can work well, but the salt obtained from burning salt-concentrating plants is expensive because of the labor involved. However, many parts of West Africa are far from the sea, and much of the mineral salt mined in West Africa contains various forms of natron. Some of these natrons were useful for industrial applications such as tanning hides and others were used as medicines. But these varieties were poorly suited to meeting the critical dietary demands that only sodium chloride will provide.

During the ninth century, Berber merchants started bringing increasingly large quantities of salt from mines in the northern Sahara to Ghana to exchange for gold. There are Arab geographers' accounts that mention gold being exchanged equal weight for equal weight with salt, though its difficult to imagine that market forces did not quickly bring about a more favorable rate of exchange for the gold sellers. West Africa became a leading source of gold for the Mediterranean world and Ghana dervied much of its income from its control over the gold trade. Gold was important enough to the fortunes of the Savannah states, but gold and salt were never the whole story. Beads, textiles, leather goods, slaves, and even books crossed the desert on these caravan routes, linking the two shores of the Sahara's sea of sand.

Most of the North African merchants who participated in this trade were Muslims. The Berbers, who controlled the trade routes, were late, but enthusiastic, converts to Islam. Trade brought more than salt to the West African Savannah; it also brought Islam. Early sources in Arabic make it clear that by the eleventh century, Muslims were an accepted part of the cultural landscape of the Savannah. Al-Bakri (a Muslim geographer living in Spain) wrote in 1068 that the capital of ancient Ghana, Kumbi Saleh, had a separate town where the city's population of Muslims lived (perhaps a parallel to the ribats in North Africa). His description suggests that although both groups saw the others as culturally different, they made every effort to respect one another's values. For example, although citizens of Ghana were required to show respect to the king by dropping to their knees and sprinkling dust on their heads (a practice common in West Africa), Muslims were only required to clap their hands as a form of greeting to the king.

Relations between Ghana and Muslim states were not always peaceful. Given the scarcity of resources in the Sahel and importance of the trans-Saharan trade, there should be little surprise that the inhabitants of the region occasionally found themselves at odds with one another. Perhaps the most serious of these conflicts was that between Ghana and the newly formed Almoravid state over the trading city of Awdaghust. Ghana had seized the town in the late tenth or early eleventh century and thus expanded the scope of its control over the trans-Saharan trade. In the latter part of the century, the Almoravids sought to reclaim the town. Al-Bakri wrote that the Almoravids took harsh retribution against many inhabitants of Awdaghust because of their acceptance of rule by Ghana. Whether the Almoravids were driven by religious fervor or simply the desire to expand their economic influence to the south is hard to gauge, though there is no reason to believe that both motivations were not of influence. In the past, some scholars have claimed that the Almoravid expansion led to the destruction of ancient Ghana. This does not appear to be the case, though the loss of Awdaghust and the disruption of the trans-Saharan trade during the conflict certainly did not aid the power of ancient Ghana.

The conflict between Ghana and the Almoravids does not seem to have seriously damaged relations between the inhabitants of the Savannah and the Muslim populations to the north. By the eleventh or twelfth centuries, some rulers of the Savannah states appear to have converted to Islam. Al-Bakri states that rulers in Takrur (in modern Senegal) and Gao (in modern Mali) had converted to Islam. Another geographer, al-Zuhri, wrote in 1137 that the king of Ghana had converted to Islam in 1076 (though as mentioned earlier, some suggest that this was a sign of Almoravid victory). Another source, al-Idrisi, corroborates this fact in a work from 1154.

The Rise of Mali

The epic tale of **Sundiata** provides an excellent example of the tension between the traditional religious role of West African kings and the growing influence of Islam in the Savannah. After the decline of Ghana in the thirteenth century, something of a political vacuum developed in the Savannah. All of the building blocks for a state were still present—population, agriculture, technology, and trade—and the only question was who was going to put them together. One candidate for the position was **Soumaoro,** king of the Soso. Another was Sundiata, a chief of the Malinke. The oral epic of their contest for power was handed down by generations of griots (oral historians) before being transcribed and translated for readers everywhere. Throughout the epic, Sundiata is represented as the "good" king and Soumaoro as the "evil" king. Clearly, the epic is biased in that it was authored by the winner's side, sometime after Sundiata's forces defeated Soumaoro at the battle of Krina in 1230. Likely, it also reflects the changing views of the regional audience. As the region became more Muslim, so did the portrayal of Sundiata.

In the epic, Soumaoro is portrayed as evil because he relied on "witchcraft" for his power. Sundiata is portrayed as good in part because he embraced Islam, at least when it was appropriate to do so. In particular, this is when he was in an urban setting—reflecting the increasing Islamic atmosphere of the cities of the Savannah during the thirteenth and fourteenth centuries. When in rural areas or when leading his army, Sundiata was depicted as the "hunter king." Indeed, Sundiata clearly represents the unique blend of traditional and Islamic religious traditions that was essential to kingship in the region at the time. For example, Sundiata's mother was possessed by the "wraith" of a wild buffalo, which his father, King Nare Maghan, had to overcome with magic and cunning to consummate their marriage. This fact evidences both the spiritual power of women in many traditional African religions and the role of kings as religious practitioners. Sundiata, however, is also portrayed as a Muslim. For example, after defeating Soumaoro, he received homage from the local rulers of Mali while wearing "robes such as were worn by a great Muslim king"—perhaps an indication that the wealth and power of Mali flowed not only from the land itself, but also from trade and contacts with the wider world.

In defeating Soumaoro, Sundiata helped build one of the world's great empires. Ancient Mali stretched from the Atlantic coast of the Senegambia and extended far eastward along the Niger River to the towns of **Timbuktu** and Gao. The capital was at Niani near the gold fields of Bure. Because ancient Mali's territory covered a wide range of environmental zones, the state's economy was richly diversified. The Niger flood plain provided cereal crops, particularly millet and sorghum. The river itself yielded fish and also supported an industry based on the hunting of hippopotami. From the drier regions to the north came a wide range of animal products produced by pastoralists such as the Fulani. The Atlantic coast to the west produced fish.

Ancient Mali's wealth was not only produced internally, though. Like Ghana before it, Mali sat astride the important south–north trade routes that ran across the Sahara desert. From the north came salt and from the south came gold and forest products. Because Mali extended farther to the west and east than Ghana, the new state was even better positioned to control this trade. By taxing the flow of goods out of, into, and across its borders, Mali became one of the wealthiest states in the world.

More trade also meant more contact with Muslims to the north. Thus, as the wealth of Mali grew, so did the influence of Islam. Perhaps no event better represents this growing Islamic influence than the pilgrimage of **Mansa Musa** in 1324 and 1325. Seeking to fulfill the "Fifth Pillar" of Islam (to make the pilgrimage if one is healthy and wealthy enough to do so), Mansa Musa set out for Mecca with thousands of retainers and 100 camel loads of gold. The story of Mansa Musa's spending and generosity while enroute is legendary. The caravan spent so much gold in Alexandria that prices reportedly skyrocketed and took years to recover from the surge of inflation. Also importantly, Mansa Musa's time in Alexandria brought him

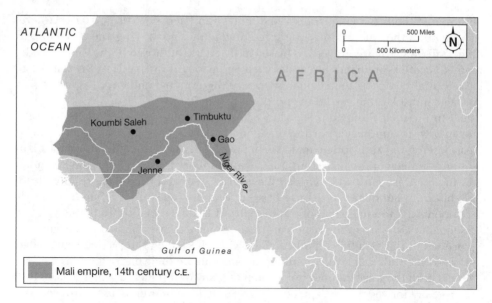

Map 6-6: The Empire of Mali

to the attention of Venetian merchants (Alexandria was the only Islamic port in which Europeans were allowed), who returned to Europe to spread tales of the great wealth of this Muslim African king. These tales clashed with the predominant European belief that black Africans were Christians (remember Prester John?), but also fueled a growing European interest in the wealth of sub-Saharan Africa.

Mansa Musa's pilgrimage also helps to undermine one of the most pervasive myths about Africa—that Africans had neither interest nor influence beyond the borders of the continent. His journey shows not only the links between Islam in West Africa and the Hijaz in the thirteenth century, but also that the "known world" for African rulers could be large indeed. Interestingly, the Egyptian scholar al-Umari reported that during Mansa Musa's visit, he spoke of sending an expedition of ships (probably large fishing canoes) to the west to explore the Atlantic Ocean. Although few scholars believe these open vessels reached the Americas intact, it is important to realize that the desire to "explore" the world is not a uniquely European characteristic.

Mansa Musa did not only travel to Egypt and Arabia for his own spiritual needs. It is clear that he had the spiritual well-being of his subjects in mind as well. The king brought with him from Arabia the Andalusian architect Abu Ishaq Ibrahim al-Sahili to design and oversee the building of new mosques. The Mansa also began to invest heavily in scholarship and education. Scholars from Mali were sent to Fez to study before returning to help spread Islamic education in their homeland. Many scholars settled in Timbuktu, which was to become home of Sankore University, one of the greatest learning centers of its time. Visiting Mali during the reign of Mansa Musa's successor, Mansa Sulayman, the traveler and geographer **Ibn Battuta** reported that young men in the towns of Mali were kept in irons until they had memorized the entire Qur'an. The Mansa's campaign to foster

The Minaret of the Agadez Mosque rises above the surrounding town.

Islamic education was so successful that books were reported to have become one of the most valuable products to trade into the region. Scholars from North Africa and the Middle East who visited Mali often found themselves outclassed by those of Timbuktu. No doubt, the efforts of Mansa Musa and of his brother Mansa Sulayman after him greatly fostered the spread of Islam in Mali, at least in the urban areas where trade and government provided the basis of the economy.

Despite its wealth and power, Mali was not immune to the forces of entropy. Beginning in the fifteenth century, Mali suffered from a series of weak rulers and internal conflict. Outside forces, particularly the Mossi to the south and the Tuareg to the north, took advantage of these opportunities to raid Mali for booty and even seize territory from the once-powerful state. Timbuktu fell to the **Tuareg** in 1433, for example. Mali did not suffer a single catastrophic defeat or sudden political collapse. Rather, the state slowly withered as it lost control over resources and trade. By the 1600s, little was left of the once-massive empire. Trade and education continued to flourish, though, and a new state was rising to fill the political vacuum left by Mali's decline.

The Rise of Songhai

Songhai was not a new state. As early as the ninth century the inhabitants of the river city of Gao had expanded to control the area of the Niger bend. Eventually, the city and surrounding area were incorporated by Mali, but as Mali weakened,

Voices from African History: Ibn Battuta on Women and Matriliny in West Africa

"My stay at Iwalatan lasted about fifty days; and I was shown honour and entertained by its inhabitants. It is an excessively hot place, and boasts a few small date-palms, in the shade of which they sow watermelons. Its water comes from underground waterbeds at that point, and there is plenty of mutton to be had. The garments of its inhabitants, most of whom belong to the Massufa tribe, are of fine Egyptian fabrics.

Their women are of surpassing beauty, and are shown more respect than the men. The state of affairs amongst these people is indeed extraordinary. Their men show no signs of jealousy whatever; no one claims descent from his father, but on the contrary from his mother's brother. A person's heirs are his sister's sons, not his own sons. This is a thing which I have seen nowhere in the world except among the Indians of Malabar. But those are heathens; these people are Muslims, punctilious in observing the hours of prayer, studying books of law, and memorizing the Koran. Yet their women show no bashfulness before men and do not veil themselves, though they are assiduous in attending the prayers. Any man who wishes to marry one of

them may do so, but they do not travel with their husbands, and even if one desired to do so her family would not allow her to go.

The women there have 'friends' and 'companions' amongst the men outside their own families, and the men in the same way have 'companions' amongst the women of other families. A man may go into his house and find his wife entertaining her 'companion' but he takes no objection to it. One day at Iwalatan I went into the qadi's house, after asking his permission to enter, and found with him a young woman of remarkable beauty. When I saw her I was shocked and turned to go out, but she laughed at me, instead of being overcome by shame, and the qadi said to me 'Why are you going out? She is my companion.' I was amazed at their conduct, for he was a theologian and a pilgrim [to Mecca] to boot. I was told that he had asked the sultan's permission to make the pilgrimage that year with his 'companion'—whether this one or not I cannot say—but the sultan would not grant it."

Ibn Battuta, *Travels in Asia and Africa 1325–1354,*
translated and edited by H. A. R. Gibb (London:
Broadway House, 1929)

Songhai was able to reassert its independence. With a powerful cavalry and also a fleet of war canoes, the leaders of Songhai, known as the Sonni dynasty, expanded aggressively during the fifteenth century. The most successful of these leaders was **Sonni Ali.** Ali defeated and drove back both the Tuareg and the Mossi, who previously had been so successful in hastening the decline of Mali. He extended the boundaries of the new state to include Timbuktu in 1468 and Jenne in 1473.

Despite his military successes, Sonni Ali was unpopular with some of his most important subjects—particularly the traders and scholars of the urban areas he now controlled. Much like Sundiata before him, Sonni Ali attempted to represent both the traditional and Islamic populations of his empire. But, in the centuries between, the economic and political influence of the urban Muslim populations had grown considerably. Sonni Ali found himself criticized for his lack of attention to Islam (for example, his critics reported that he did not pray in public and often drank alcohol). His attempts to use force to quash this dissent only resulted in growing opposition. Eventually, Sonni Ali found himself faced with an outright

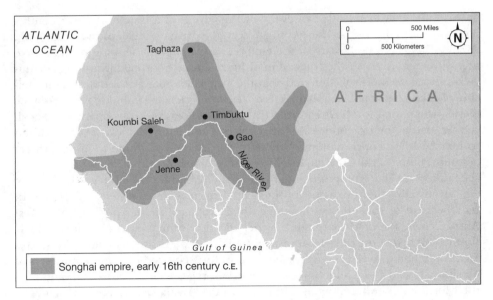

Map 6-7: The Empire of Songhai

challenge to his legitimacy. The ulama, the Islamic scholars, announced a takfir—a decision that Sonni Ali was not a Muslim and thus not a rightful ruler. Shortly afterward, in 1492, Sonni Ali drowned in the Niger (which some of the Muslim faithful attributed to the power of Allah) and was replaced by his son, Sonni Baru. Baru, though, was faced with a military challenge by one of his father's generals, Muhammad Ture (later known as **Askiya Muhammad**), who had entered into alliance with the ulama. A skilled commander, Ture handily defeated Sonni Baru at the battle of Anfao in 1493 and established the Askiya dynasty.

The overthrow of the Sonni dynasty represents an important watershed in the history of Islam in sub-Saharan Africa. It is one of the first recorded instances of Muslims in the Savannah region demanding a government that met Islamic standards of piety. In a reflection of the growing Islamic focus of the state, Ture allowed greater privileges to Islamic scholars, led a **jihad** of the sword against the Mossi, and even made the pilgrimage to Mecca in 1495. There Ture met the Sharif of Mecca and was reportedly named "Caliph of the Sudan." Clearly, a critical power shift had taken place, and the precedent of the newfound authority of the Islamic community would be a significant one for the future.

The era of the Askiya dynasty was not to be untroubled, though. Despite his newfound religious legitimacy and economic and military successes (including the seizure of the Saharan salt mine of Taghaza), Muhammad Ture was overthrown by his son, Askiya Musa, in 1528. Like Sonni Ali, Musa found himself at odds with the ulama and was eventually overthrown by his brother, Isma'il, in 1537. Isma'il freed his elderly father from captivity, but remained on the throne himself. Another of Ture's sons, Dawud, ruled from 1549 to 1582 and oversaw a period of relative peace and prosperity. During this period, the reputation of the region for Islamic scholarship continued to grow, and there were over 150 Islamic schools in Timbuktu alone at this time. Dawud's death, however, saw the advent of a time of dynastic conflict and civil war in the 1580s. These conflicts served to weaken the empire considerably. Aware of the vulnerable state of the empire, the Moroccans sent an invasion force across the desert under the leadership of Judar Pasha. Equipped with firearms, this relatively small force was able to defeat the larger Songhai army under the leadership of Askiya Ishaq II. The inhabitants of key towns such as Timbuktu, led by Islamic clerics, responded to Moroccan rule through a process of noncooperation. Harsh reprisals led to the execution of some scholars and the deportation of several dozen to Marakesh for imprisonment. Although Morocco was not able to impose direct administration over the region, the descendants of the Moroccan invaders, known as the arma, were able to continue their rule of the region for over 100 years.

Ironically, the Moroccans profited little from their conquest of Songhai. In part because of the growing influence of European trading posts on the West African coast, the gold that had so enriched the Savannah states was increasingly flowing not across the desert but instead south and to Europe via sailing ships. This fact, combined with the reduced state support for Islam, led increasing numbers of Muslim scholars and traders to leave the urban regions of the Savannah and seek their fortunes elsewhere. Often referred to as the "**Dyula** Diaspora," this migration helped Islam expand into rural areas of the Savannah and even for the first time into the forest regions of West Africa.

Islam in Kanem-Bornu and Hausaland

Although many texts have rightfully focused on the power and wealth of the Savannah empires of Ghana, Mali, and Songhai, these were not the only political systems in the Savannah and not the only ones to be influenced by, and eventually to embrace, Islam. Kanem-Bornu and the city-states of Hausaland, located roughly in the region to the east and west of Lake Chad, also played a part in the expansion of Islam in Africa. Kanem-Bornu was one of the first states in the Savannah region to turn to Islam, with evidence suggesting that the Mai (kings of Kanem) converted to Islam during the rule of the Saifawa dynasty in the twelfth century. To bolster their Islamic legitimacy, these rulers claimed descent from an Arab hero, Sayf bin Dhi Yazan. By the thirteenth century, the rulers were devout enough to undertake the Hajj and establish a hostel in Cairo for students from Kanem-Bornu who traveled there to study at Al-Ahzar University. As was the case of Timbuktu for Mali, the capital of Bornu, N'gazargamu, became an important center of Islamic scholarship. Kanem-Bornu was very much a part of the Dar al-Islam.

To the west of Lake Chad, in the Hausa-speaking region that now makes up much of northern Nigeria and southern Niger, a number of city-states were growing in economic and political influence. The rulers and merchants of such important cities such as Katsina, Kano, Gobir, and Zinder had begun to accept Islam as early as the fourteenth century. It was at this time that Yaji, the **sarki** (king) of Kano, was converted by Wangara (Muslim traders) from Mali. The link between trade and the expansion of Islam is well illuminated by the following excerpt from the *Kano Chronicle*, a nineteenth-century history from the city of the same name.

The whole of the products of the West were brought to Hausaland [and] roads from Bornu to Gwanja [were opened]. In [King] Yakabu's time [1452–1463] the Fulani came to Hausaland from Melle, bringing with them books on Divinity and Entymology. . . . At this time, too, the [Berber Taruegs] came to Gobir, and salt became common in Hausaland.

Similar to the case of Mali, the early Hausa rulers combined their local religious beliefs with Islam. In Kano, this took the form of the city's first mosque being built under a sacred tree. Over the next few centuries, the practice of Islam in the Hausa states would become increasingly orthodox. An influx of pastoralist **Fulani** (who had been quick to accept Islam) from the west helped bring the religion into the rural areas of Hausaland. In the cities, economic and political contact with Songhai via the trade in kola and salt and the payment of annual tribute meant that the Hausa states shared in the growing Islamic consciousness of the region. The fifteenth-century scholar **al-Maghili** visited Kano. During his visit, he provided the sarki with a text entitled "The Obligations of Princes," which outlined the proper behavior of an Islamic ruler. Similarly, al-Maghili reportedly convinced the sarki to cut down the city's sacred tree. Such a step is a powerful symbol of the increasing level of Islamic orthodoxy in the region—at least among the urban ruling class. Elsewhere, particularly in rural areas, local religious practices continued. As we shall see in Chapter 10, Hausaland was, in the nineteenth century, to become the locus of Islamic renewal in the form of the Sokoto Jihad. Further, to this day in rural areas of Hausaland, many people still practice **Bori,** a local religion that both incorporates and rejects elements of Islam.

African Traditional Religions and Conversion

For the thoughtful, the question of why Africans would choose to convert to Islam might have arisen. There is an unfortunate tendency to simply assume that "primitive" local religions were automatically replaced by "more advanced" religions such as Islam (and Christianity). As we saw in Chapter 3, Africans in the West African Savannah and elsewhere were not without complex religious systems of their own prior to the introduction of Islam. Why, then, did so many Africans convert to Islam from their traditional religions? As we have already seen, this growing move to Islam generally occurred first at the upper levels of society, with rulers and successful traders being the most likely to convert to Islam. Only much later did poorer and rural groups convert. As a result, scholars have long made reference to early Islam in the West African Savannah as "the religion of court and commerce," because the religion tended to spread first to those in political and economic power.

Some scholars, particularly Robin Horton, have suggested that the tendency of rulers and traders to convert to world religions is a reflection of the fact that such positions fostered worldviews that extended beyond the scope of local deities. This worldview demanded a religion that provided a similar global outlook. Thus, the very fact that rulers and traders dealt with people and issues that extended beyond their local religious systems necessitated systems of belief that explained the presence of widely divergent places and cultures. Trans-Saharan trade, for example, would have played a critical role in showing Savannah rulers and traders the breadth of the wider world. Similarly, according to Horton's argument, the pilgrimage to Mecca was not so much about going to Mecca as it was showing Muslims just how large and varied the world was.

Despite the reality of Islam's growing influence in the Savannah, it would be a mistake to think that Islam simply replaced African religions. As we have already seen, Islam did not immediately replace local religions, but rather these systems often blended with Islam—a process known as "syncretism," wherein each system adapts to the other, creating a new and unique system of religious ideology. And because many African religions do not have a system of orthodoxy that draws a hard-and-fast distinction between "our" religion and "their" religion, elements of Islam that were seen as useful or desirable were quickly expropriated for local needs. The balance of Islamic and local religion utilized by Savannah rulers such as Sundiata or the building of the first Kano mosque under a sacred tree are both cases in point. Local rulers who converted to Islam could not afford to turn their backs on the religions of their subjects without the danger of losing their legitimacy. As such, one important theme of political Islam in the Savannah is the degree to which rulers played dual roles—representing themselves as Muslims at certain times and as traditional religious leaders at others. The power of writing, both for practical or spiritual ends, was quickly utilized. To this day in many Islamic parts of Africa, charms that contain passages of the Qur'an are seen as sources of good luck or protection from harm. It is a common practice in many parts of Africa, for example, for verses of the Qur'an to be written in water-soluble ink, then washed off, and the resulting mixture drunk as a powerful form of religious "medicine." In light of such realities, there is a long-standing academic debate over just how "African" Islam in Africa has become. In some places, the influence of African culture has been extensive; in others, Islam is practiced much as it is in the Middle East. Remember, Africa is a big and varied place.

The Africanization of Islam

A common theme regarding the study of Islam in Africa, particularly sub-Saharan Africa, has been to suggest that the practice of Islam in the region has somehow been imperfect, leading some scholars to distinguish between "Islam in Africa" and "African Islam." In French scholarship, it was common to hear reference to *L'Islam Noire* or "Black Islam." Such a perspective, however, fails to recognize that the religon of Islam (just like other religions) has always been in a process of change as it has moved through time and space. Africans in different parts of the continent certainly influenced the religion as they made it their own, but in doing so they were not behaving any differently than were converts in regions such as Persia, Southeast Asia, or southern Europe.

By "Africanizing" Islam, as David Robinson has characterized the process, what African converts were doing was making the religion less "foreign" and more familiar. The creation of "fictive" kinships with the heartland of Islam was certainly one way in which African converts, particularly those with political aspirations, could attain this end. We have already seen that the Saifawa dynasty of Kanem-Bornu claimed descent from the Arab hero Sayf bin Dhi Yazan. Similarly, the ruling dynasty of Mali eventually characterized themselves as being the descendants of **Bilali Bunama,** one of the first converts to Islam and a close companion of the Prophet Muhammad. Bunama was originally a slave from Abyssynia, but after his conversion served as the first *muezzin* of Medina and Mecca and was a commander of early Islamic armies, eventually helping to conquer much of Syria. Thus, by claiming descent from Bunama, the heads of the Malian dynasty were linking themselves not only to early Islam and a successful military tradition, but also tying themselves to perhaps the first Muslim African.

In the Hausa-speaking region of what is now northern Nigeria and southern Niger, the story of **Bayajidda** tells of how a "prince from Baghdad" traveled to the region. Arriving at the town of Daura, he found the well guarded by an evil snake named *Sarki* (king) which was tormenting the people by allowing them to draw water only one day a week. Bayajidda killed the snake and married the queen. Their children became the rulers of the various Hausa city states. Such a story is rich in symbolism, in that it likely relates not only the desire of the Hausa ruling class to link themselves to the Middle East, but also relates to the shift from matrilineal to patrilineal descent that likely came with the introduction of Islam to the region. The snake may be just a bit Freudian.

Another powerful influence in the "Africanization" of Islam was (and is) Sufism. As mentioned previously, Sufism takes a more mystical approach to Islam than the somewhat legalist and "works based" approach of orthodox Sunni Islam. Sufi's believe that it is possible for individuals to experience God's love in this life. Such enlightenment is generally attained through extensive study and prayer, but can also be encouraged through physical deprivation or working oneself into a trance-like state via dance. Whatever the "path" to enlightenment, those who achieve union with God become special. They are known as *Walis* (friends of God), and are believed to be imbued with *Baraka*, a spiritual power that allows them to perform miracles and intercede on behalf of others with God. Not surpisingly, these Walis are often referred to as Sufi "saints." All Sufi orders (known as Brotherhoods or *Tariqa*, meaning "path" in Arabic) trace their origins back to a founding Wali. Contemporary leaders in each Brotherhood must trace their spiritual authority through a line of teachers back to this founder. These links, known as a *Silsila*, serve to bind together the Sufi community across both time and space. African Sufis are no less a part of the community than anyone else, in that they are participants in, rather than recipients of, a process of belief and worship. Further, the fact that many African Sufis are themselves believed to have attained the status of Wali has further "indigenized" African Sufism. Indeed, the tombs of many Sufi leaders have become places of pilgrimage and prayer, helping to create Islamic holy "space" in Africa, just as it exists elsewhere in the Muslim world.

Islam in North and West Africa in Global Perspective

The expansion of Islam into North and West Africa reflects a number of important global comparisons and themes. First, just as with Christianity, Africa's interaction with Islam is a key part of the story of one of the world's most influential religions.

From the very beginning, Africans have both embraced, and influenced the development of, Islam. By and large, this interaction unfolded in two stages. First was the rapid expansion of the Islamic state into North Africa. Then came the more gradual expansion of Islam into the West African Savannah. The military conquest of the Maghreb was in many ways similar to initial expansion of Islam in the Middle East, with the imposition of the Islamic state being followed by a gradual conversion of existing populations to Islam over several centuries. One point on which this comparison breaks down, however, is in terms of human migration and cultural change. The influx of Arabic-speaking peoples into the Egyptian-, Greek-, and Berber-speaking regions of North Africa brought not only religious change, but cultural change as well. In Egypt, Arabic would eventually become the dominant language and lead to the gradual demise of spoken Egyptian. In other parts of North Africa there remains today a divide between Arabic- and Berber-speaking populations that share a religion but not a spoken language or single culture.

As we have seen, Islam spread in the West African Savannah in a very different way than it did in North Africa. Islam diffused across the Sahara via economic, political, and intellectual exchange in a process that developed over hundreds of years. Indeed, the expansion of Islam into West Africa is much more like the expansion of the religion elsewhere in the world, such as was the case across much of the Indian Ocean and into Indonesia. Indonesia, like the Savannah, shows evidence of the presence of Islamic traders as early as the eighth century C.E. No doubt, the location of Indonesia along the busy trade route of the Malacca Strait helped bring Islamic traders to the region. Evidence of the conversion of local rulers to Islam begins in the latter thirteenth century, an example being the ruler of Samudra, Sultan Malik al-Saleh, only shortly after the rise to power of Sundiata in Mali. Interestingly, Sufi Islam was to play a significant role in expanding Islam into the wider population of Indonesia, just as it did in West Africa. Thus, in most of the Savannah, the religious expression of Islam preceded the religion's political influnce in the form of the Islamic State.

Useful Works on This Chapter Topic

Recent years have seen a considerable expansion in the scholarly material available for the study of Islam in Africa. Perhaps the most accessible new additions have been Nehemia Levtzion and Randall L. Pouwels' substantial edited volume, *The History of Islam in Africa* (2000), and David Robinson's *Muslim Societies in African History* (2004). Peter B. Clarke's *West Africa and Islam* (1982) and Mervyn Hiskett's *Development of Islam in West Africa* (1984) provide somewhat more general overviews of the topic. J. Spencer Trimmingham's earlier works, such as *A History of Islam in West Africa* (1962), are useful, if somewhat heavy on detail. Some excellent primary documents are available in the form of N. Levtzion and J. F. P. Hopkins (eds.), *Corpus of Early Arabic Sources for West African History* (1981); Said Hamdun and Noel King (eds.), *Ibn Battuta in Black Africa* (1994); and D. T. Niane (ed.), *Sundiata: An Epic of Old Mali* (1995).

CHAPTER 7

East Africa and the Advent of Islam

The vast empires of the West African Savannah and Mediterranean North Africa were connected to each other through trade across the Sahara. Trade also linked East Africa to the heartland of the Islamic world, in this instance across the Indian Ocean. But sea trade is a different thing from an overland caravan trade, and the societies that engaged in the trade were different from those we saw in the previous chapter. The end result was also different. The **Swahili** civilization that emerged in East Africa was a merchant's civilization characterized by Muslim city-states ruled sometimes by kings and sometimes by oligarchies. The city-states were militarily weak, putting more social store in wealth than warfare, and they vied with each other endlessly over the seaborne trade that supported them. Although it is possible to imagine that the empires of the Savannah might have grown up in the absence of the trans-Saharan trade, the Swahili world would have been fundamentally different without the oceanic trade that came to be a defining element of the Swahili civilization. It was the sea and the monsoon wind system characteristic of the western Indian Ocean that made possible the long-distance trade that indelibly shaped the Swahili world.

The Monsoons

More than any other, the Indian Ocean is a sailor's ocean. It is warm, has few storms except in its southern reaches, and it has a wind system that seems tailor-made for sailors. As a result, humans were making long-distance sea voyages across its waters long before they dared to venture out into the more challenging waters of the Atlantic or Pacific. As early as the first century C.E., Austronesian seafarers somehow managed to get from Indonesia to East Africa. There is even evidence suggesting there may have been a Bronze Age sea trade between Mesopotamia and East Africa that ended with the great political upheavals at the beginning of the last millennium B.C.E. What made all this possible was the **monsoon** wind system.

The monsoons are seasonal winds that blow one way for part of the year, then turn around and blow the other way at other times of the year. From November to April the northeast monsoon blows out of the northeast (winds are named for the direction they come from) toward the southwest. It is a steady, hot, dry wind that makes it easy to sail from South Arabia, the Persian Gulf, or India to East Africa. By way of example, a sailing ship can go from Muscat in Oman to **Zanzibar** in about three to four weeks during the northeast monsoon. Then in late May or early June, the winds reverse, and the southwest monsoon begins. It blows out of the southwest toward the northeast. Unlike the northeast monsoon, the southwest monsoon brings rain and rough seas, but it also provides a tailwind to ships trying to make the return journey from East Africa to Arabia or India. The southeast monsoon ends in late September or early October.

The effects of this are many and interesting. The monsoons allow sailors to travel both legs of a journey on the Indian Ocean with a tailwind, something that is more or less essential in sail-powered craft. The monsoons facilitate movement, but they also enforce long stay-overs for ships' crews. Although it would be theoretically possible for a ship to ride the last month of one monsoon on its outward voyage and the first month of the next on its homeward voyage, in practice no one did this. The beginning and ending of the monsoons are a bit fickle, and no ship captain would want to risk being caught halfway to his destination when the wind died. So sailors erred on the side of caution. Ships setting out to ride the northeast monsoon usually left in December and arrived at their destinations in January or February. They would usually leave on the southeast monsoon in June or September to avoid the rough seas that occur at the height of the monsoon in July and August. As a result, ships regularly spent four to six months at either end of this trade route. During this time, the ships' crews lived ashore, mingling with the people in the port cities. Thus, oceanic trade left its mark on Indian Ocean ports, whether in Africa or Arabia, in a way that the trans-Saharan trade could not mark the cities of the Sahel.

Swahili Origins

"Swahili" means people of the coast and derives from the same Arabic root as "Sahel," which of course refers to the southern "coast" of the Sahara. The ancestors of the Swahili first appeared in both the archaeological and written records in the first centuries C.E., and although they lived on the coast, it is evident that they were much less engaged in trade than their descendants would be. Archaeologists have found evidence that small farming and fishing communities inhabited much of the East African coast in the first century C.E., living on islands just off the coast as well as on the mainland. Until recently it was thought that the inhabitants of the first coastal communities were probably Cushitic speakers and herders rather than farmers, but now recalibrated carbon dating of early farming communities suggests that Bantu-speaking farmers were present on the coast quite early and lived in close proximity to pastoralists and foraging peoples. All three groups would continue to occupy the coast into historical times and to play a role in the making of Swahili civilization, but because Swahili is a member of the Bantu language family, it was the Bantu farmers who played the critical role in this process.

These communities were very much like farming communities elsewhere in East Africa. The farmers lived in small villages, grew sorghum and millet, and ate both game and domestic animals; they even produced pottery that was stylistically similar to what their inland neighbors made. They had access to the resources of the sea, which their inland neighbors did not, so their diets included fish, shellfish, and turtles, which of course were not on the menu for inland communities. But the sea offered more to these communities than just culinary pleasures; it also offered trade. We know this because archaeologists have found evidence of trade goods in these sites, though never in huge quantities. Archaeological sites on the coast have produced glass beads and glassware that appear to come from the Mediterranean. Culturally similar sites away from the coast lack these trade goods. We also know of this because we have a written document that describes the coast in the first century.

That document is the *Periplus of the Erythrean Sea,* a sort of ancient Fodor's Guide to the western Indian Ocean. It was written by a Greek resident of the Egyptian city of Alexandria in the first century C.E. It was meant to be a merchant's guide to the trading ports of the western Indian Ocean. The author described the trading conditions and commodities of Arabia and western India and also included a section on a trading voyage he made to East Africa. From his account, it is evident that trade to East Africa was a regular part of the commercial life of south Arabian merchants and an occasional part of the commercial life of Roman and Greek merchants. His description of the physical features of the coast and the sailing distances between various points is astonishingly accurate.

After describing the coast of Somalia and a group of islands that is probably the Lamu archipelago, he described an island called Menouthias, which is probably the island of Pemba. The inhabitants of Menouthias, we are told, made dugout canoes and "small sewn boats" and "fish in a peculiar way with wicker baskets, which they fasten across where the tide goes out." Interestingly, dugouts and fish weirs are still in use on the Swahili coast, and sewn boats—boats stitched together with cord rather than fastened with nails—were made in East Africa until the 1930s. Thus, in light of continuity of technology and the now-revised estimates of when the first Bantu-speaking farmers arrived, it appears that the author of the *Periplus* encountered the people whose descendants would be the Swahili.

Just south of Menouthias was a place called **Rhapta** that was the southern terminus of the trade. Here the Arab merchants who carried out the long-distance trade sold iron tools and glassware in exchange for ivory and tortoise shell. They also brought wheat and wine with them, "not for trade, but to gain the good will of the barbarians." Archaeologists have not located Rhapta, and it may not have been a permanent settlement. Instead, it might have been an annual trade fair where people gathered to buy and sell with the monsoon voyagers, or it might have been a permanent settlement that has been covered over by the shifting of a river mouth.

Rhapta is also mentioned in Ptolemy's *Geography,* which was written about 100 years after the *Periplus.* So it is clear that the booming Indian Ocean trade of the late classical period reached to East Africa and that the ancestors of the Swahili were participants in that trade. Given the goods that the proto-Swahili traded to the Arabs (i.e., ivory and tortoise shell), it seems likely that they were acting as middlemen for hunters who killed the elephants, much as they would later in their history. Thus, early in the first century C.E., the stage was partly set for the emergence of the full-blown Swahili civilization. But then the trading system of the western Indian Ocean contracted in the wake of the turmoil associated with the collapse of the western Roman Empire in the fourth and fifth centuries C.E. It was not until the eighth century that Indian Ocean trade would revive and the Swahili emerge as full-fledged participants in that trade.

Islam and the Emergence of the Swahili as a Distinctive Group

Although the original coastal communities differed only slightly from their neighbors in the near interior, the Swahili towns that emerged in the eighth and ninth centuries were profoundly different. They were towns, not villages. The towns contained buildings made of cut coral stone. Their inhabitants were deeply involved in trade. And above all, the people of these towns were Muslims. Islam came earlier to the East African coast than to any other part of sub-Saharan Africa; indeed the first evidence of Islam here is almost contemporary with the arrival of Islam in the western reaches of North Africa. Interestingly, it also predates the Christianization of parts of northern Europe.

The Swahili people who inhabited these towns were not immigrants or colonists from Arabia, but the descendants of the Bantu-speaking farmers who first settled the coast and traded with the Arabs in the time of the *Periplus*. Scholars in the first half of the twentieth century believed that these Swahili towns and cities were the work of Arab settlers. They were imperialist historians, who were usually apologists for colonialism, and they found it difficult to accept the idea that Africans might have created an urban civilization themselves. After all, one of the justifications for European imperialism was that it brought civilization to those who could not create it themselves. Thus, when confronted with the ruins of large, stone-built cities and towns, they reflexively attributed them to prior invaders and colonists (often imaginary), whom they saw as early precursors of their own civilizing mission.

More recently, historians have taken a diametrically opposed, but no less political, position and sought to deny any outside contribution to the creation of urban civilization in East Africa. They have done so for the entirely laudable purpose of counteracting the earlier excesses of the imperialist historians. However, in denying any outside role in the rise of the Swahili civilization, they have missed the essential contribution made by the arrival of Islam.

One reason for this is that until recently, most scholars relied on documentary evidence to date the arrival of Islam. Most of the Arabic sources that discuss the Swahili coast even as late as 1100 tend to dismiss the inhabitants as non-Muslims. It is not until the great Ibn Battuta visited in the fourteenth century that an Arab visitor described all the people he encountered as Muslim.

Photo Essay I: Imagining Africa

As discussed in the Preface, the representation of African history is often highly controversial and politically charged. This is true not only in terms of scholarship, but also in the way the image of the African landscape and Africans themselves have been represented. It is (too often perhaps) said that "a picture is worth a thousand words," but the problem is that the thousand words in question may be the wrong words. As a result, images of African subjects, especially those found in popular media, are often every bit as politically charged and potentially misleading as other sources.

In this brief photo essay, we will strive to present a variety of visual representations of things African. Some of these photos have been chosen precisely because they represent particular "Notions of Africa." Others have been chosen because they represent a very different and perhaps less familiar aspect of African reality. Mind you, this contrast does not mean that any of the images presented are necessarily "wrong." Indeed, to the best of our knowledge, all of the photographs are of real events and real people (though some may well have been staged by the photographer to create a certain impression). The more important question, however, is why do certain images of Africa and Africans predominate, and why are certain other images far less common in popular Western media? As you examine the following images, ask yourself where you might have seen a similar photograph. In what sort of context (book, documentary, archive, and so on) might you find such an image? What sort of feeling does the image evoke for you?

The Notion of Primitive Africa

In this image, two Hadza foragers dress out and process the haunches of a large game animal, perhaps a waterbuck or eland. Despite numerous attempts by the government of Tanzania to "settle" the Hadza (who number perhaps 1,000) on farmland, many have chosen to continue in what anthropologists would call a "hunter-gatherer lifeway."

Photo by James F. O'Connell, University of Utah

While it is probably true that most Africans are more likely to take their meals at home than are Westerners, it is certainly also the case that far more Africans eat in restaurants every day than forage for their meals as do the Hadza. This photo shows one of many "Mr. Bigg's," a Nigerian-based fast-food chain. On the menu one will find American-style hamburgers, hot dogs, and chicken; British-style meat pies; Indian-style samosas, fried rice; and a variety of Nigerian dishes. In just about every African city or town, one can find a variety of restaurants, ranging from low-cost establishments selling basic foods to laborers to expensive establishments specializing in international cuisine.

Photo by Jonathan T. Reynolds

A key element of the "primitive" Africa notion is the implication that Africa is a continent without "change" or "progress." For example, the leatherworks and dye pits of Fez, Morocco, are a common image featured in textbooks or photo collections. Such images are often accompanied by a discussion of the "traditional" economy of North Africa. Certainly, the Fez dye pits are remarkable in that they have been producing high-quality leather goods in the same location for hundreds of years.

Photo by Jonathan T. Reynolds

Photo by Jonathan T. Reynolds

A different perspective on the Fez leatherworks, however, is quite revealing. When the wider location is presented, it becomes apparent that the dye pits are actually located in a densely developed neighborhood of multistory apartment buildings—almost every one of which is festooned with multiple satellite antennas.

More so, it is worth noting that the main reason for the Fez leatherworks' survival in the current era is that the old city of Fez is a major tourist destination, and hundreds or even thousands of visitors pass through on a daily basis. The presence of the leatherworks provides a major selling point for the shops that line the walls above the pits. Thus, the pits may indeed be "traditional" in terms of the technology utilized in the production of leather, but their location, like the market that they serve, is both very modern and very global.

Closely related to the notion that Africa was, or is, largely without change is the notion that all major forces for change on the continent are a result of "outside forces." This perspective often suggests that any sort of technological or social development in Africa must be a result of contact with "superior" outsiders.

Very much in this vein is the popular belief that it was Western missionaries who brought Christianity and other elements of "civilization" to an otherwise backward and "barbaric" African population.

Photo by Friedrich Stark, DAS PHOTOARCHIV/Peter Arnold, Inc.

Copyright Danita Delimont Photography

As this twelfth-century Ethiopian fresco highlights, Christianity has long been a part of many Africans' religious world. Indeed, populations in northern Africa and the Nile Valley were among the first to convert to this new salvation religion.

Critical to understanding the nature of global exchange is to learn to question the popular historical notion that certain cultural practices or ideas "belong" to certain people and are "foreign" to others. For example, it is really quite a strange concept to think of a religion like Christianity as being foreign to anyone, since everyone who came to be a believer had to be either acculturated or converted at some point in their lives.

As you may well have noticed, one of the key themes of this text is that there is no fixed "African" culture, but rather the continent, like every other part of the world, has constantly undergone a process of cultural change, exchange, and development.

The Notion of Wild Africa

This photo, of a sign at the Cincinnati Zoo, offers a classic representation of "Wild" Africa. Indeed, it is very common for game parks, in this case the Serengeti National Park in Tanzania, to be used to represent the African landscape, even though they comprise only a tiny percentage of the continent's land area. When the popular "Survivor" television series was set in Africa, a game park was used as the setting, to ensure that the contestants were in an appropriately "wild" location.

In this particular image, tourists on safari photograph giraffe, elephants, and zebra, while a few Masai (identified as "once fierce warriors") go about the business of being "an indigenous people."

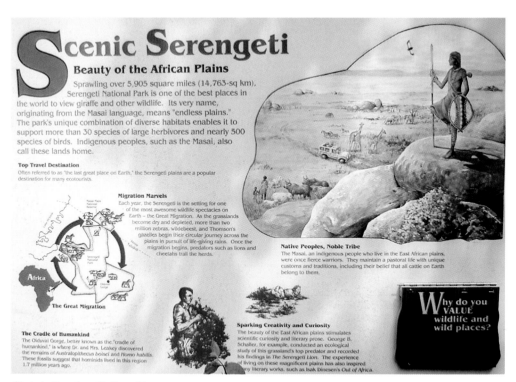

Photo by Jonathan T. Reynolds

Photo by Jonathan T. Reynolds

Contrary to the popular image of "Wild" Africa, roughly 40% of Africans call one city or another home. Indeed, Africa is home to a number of the world's fastest-growing cities, including Lagos, Nigeria, pictured here. Lagos, as the second-largest city in Africa (it is second only to Cairo), is home to some 14 million people. Lagos is often used as an example of uncontrolled urban growth. For example, the city is notorious for its traffic jams (known locally as "go slows") and for frequent electrical outages caused by a demand for power which consistently outstrips supply.

Yet, despite such bottlenecks in infrastructure, the city is also home to Nigeria's thriving film industry and serves as headquarters for most major businesses operating in the country. Internet cafés have, in recent years, grown so common as to be found on almost every street. For Nigerians, living in Lagos holds a similar cachet as does calling New York or Los Angeles home in the United States.

Photo by Patricia Jordan/Peter Arnold, Inc.

The Notion of Exotic Africa

Photos of Africans are certainly not hard to come by in the United States. or Europe. Whether it be on the pages of various "coffee table books" of photographs or on travel brochures for study-abroad programs at colleges and universities, images of Africans are not particularly hard to find. Most of the images found in such sources, however, represent African ethnic groups who have a flair for dress and personal adornment that Americans or Europeans find exotic. As mentioned in the Preface, the Masai are certainly the most popular group used to represent "Exotic Africa." Notably, the Masai number less than 1 million people, meaning they make up less than .35% of the African population.

However, the Mursi people of Ethiopia, in no small part thanks to lip plates such as that sported by the woman pictured, have likely managed an even more disproportionate presence in the Western imagination. Despite a total population of less than 5,000, their photographs have made it into thousands of books, magazines, and Web sites.

Perhaps most notable in their absence are photographs of Africans in styles of dress and in settings that Americans and Europeans might find familiar. Despite this, millions of Africans, including these two women pictured working in a Nigerian Internet café, go about their daily business dressed in suits, blue jeans, and even t-shirts. Perhaps more remarkable than the scarcity of such images is the fact that many observers might dismiss such styles of dress as "un-African"—implying that individuals dressing in such clothes are somehow "less African" than those dressed in more "traditional" fashions. Such a perspective better reflects how those outside the continent define what it means to be African than how most Africans choose to define their own identities.

Photo by Jonathan T. Reynolds

The Notion of Broken Africa

Perhaps due in no small part to the extreme optimism voiced by African nationalists in the era immediately before and following independence, in recent years there has been something of a "backlash" of what is often called "Afro-Pessimism." This perspective dwells almost completely on the failings of African states and societies, often to the point of arguing that Africa is "hopeless" and that any and all efforts to bring stability or prosperity will come to naught.

This perspective on "Broken" Africa is often accompanied by images that evoke social chaos, such as this photo of child soldiers from Sierra Leone. Other common images might be photographs of refugees, casualties of communal violence, or victims of famine.

Photo by Sebestian Bolesch/Peter Arnold, Inc.

Certainly, it is critical for scholars and students of Africa to recognize the reality of poverty and conflict on the continent. Yet, it is similarly important for all observers of Africa to recognize that such factors do not define life for all Africans.

The case of Ghana provides an excellent case study of the triumph over pessimism. Once among the wealthiest of African states, Ghana's economy collapsed in the 1970s, and the country suffered under a series of notoriously corrupt governments (military and civilian). However, by the 1990s, Ghana was undergoing first an economic and later a political revival, as this photo of national elections held in 2000 highlights.

Agence France Press/Getty Images, Inc.

Just as some place the blame for African political, social, and economic troubles squarely on the shoulders of Africans themselves, some also consider the continent's environmental woes to be a direct result of African misuse of land and animal resources. For example, many experts have argued that the growth of the Sahara (and other African deserts) in terms of overgrazing of livestock, the overuse of fragile lands, and deforestation.

Certainly, Africans have had a considerable impact upon the African environment, much of which has been negative. This said, it is important to note that this is true for every region of the world where humans live (which doesn't leave much). Further, it is important to note that the process of "desertification" in Africa has been ongoing for thousands of years, and as such is likely an example of the way the global environment changes in part on its own—and demands adaptations on the part of human populations. Alternately, one must also consider the possibility that current environmental change in Africa is a result of human actions elsewhere, with the extensive production of "greenhouse gases" in the industrial world being a likely culprit. In the event that this is the case, then people elsewhere bear at least some of the guilt for abusing the African environment.

Photo by Thierry Rannon/Getty Images, Inc.

Whatever the source of Africa's environmental troubles, it is clear that Africans will have to play a primary role in developing both the technology and cultural practices to deal with an ever-changing and challenging African environment.

Luckily, African history offers myriad examples of Africans' willingness to develop and adopt new tools and practices in order to adapt to changing environmental conditions and make the most of their continent's environmental potential. In this vein, Kenyan activist Wangari Maathai, pictured here, was awarded the Nobel Peace Prize in 2004 for her leadership in the Kenyan Green Belt Movement, which seeks to reverse environmental destruction through sustainable agricultural practices and reforestation.

Photo by Micheline Pelletier/Corbis/Bettmann

Envisioning Africa

Quite apart from the various negative "notions" of Africa is a perspective toward the continent and its inhabitants that stresses positive aspects of culture and history over all others. Indeed, Africa is quite unique in that it is the only *continent* that is used to represent conceptions of historical and cultural unity. Hence, the very shape of Africa is often used in the form of pendants or as a symbol in artwork to represent a particular sense of identity. In being so used, the shape and culture of Africa are treated in much the same way as the mythologies of identity used to foster nationalism in many countries. Not surprisingly, many of those who pursue such ends are known as "African Nationalists." The celebration of Kwanzaa, a holiday created by the African-American activist and scholar Maulana Karenga in 1966, is an example of this dynamic. The celebration draws upon African (KiSwahili) terms and a variety of symbols chosen to represent the importance of African cultural practices to those of African descent living in the Americas and elsewhere.

Photo by Pierre Burnaugh/PhotoEdit, Inc.

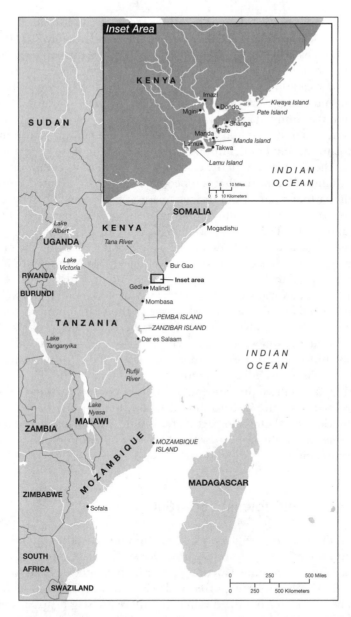

Map 7-1: The Swahili Coast to 1500 (with modern states identified)

Archaeology paints a different picture. Excavations of the Swahili town of Shanga suggest, based on the presence of Muslim burials and a mosque, that Islam arrived in the eighth century, only 150 years after the death of Muhammad. The original mosque at Shanga is small. There was probably room for no more than six worshippers at a time, so clearly the majority of Shangans were not Muslims. This first mosque was a simple building made of wood, but over time it was replaced by steadily larger and more substantial buildings made of coral stone. By 1000, Islam was firmly embedded in Shanga. Other sites on the coast, notably Ras Mkumbuu on the island of Pemba and Unguja Ukuu on the island of Zanzibar, show evidence of large mosques in the early tenth century. Other sites, some as far south as Mozambique, contain what appear to be Muslim burials in the tenth century. Interestingly, Shanga shows no evidence of pre-Islamic religion, and its excavator, Mark Horton, believes that it was founded as a Muslim town.

This religious transition took place in a context of cultural continuity. Pottery styles (a favorite barometer of cultural change) stayed the same. There is simply no evidence that the Islamization of the coast was the result of its colonization by Arabs or Perisans. Rather, it appears that the people of the coast adopted the religion of their trading partners and in the process made it their own. They developed, for instance, their own style of mosque building, distinct from that used in the Islamic heartland, and retained earlier, pre-Islamic ideas about kingship. At the same time, Islam became a crucial division between the people of the coast and the non-Muslims in the interior. For reasons that are not entirely clear, Islam and Swahili civilization did not spread past the coast until the nineteenth century. This is surprising because the evidence suggests that there were many commercial and political links between the Swahili and the peoples who lived in the coastal hinterland.

The arrival of Islam also coincided with the increasing urbanization of the coast. Cities, which along with Islam form the core elements of Swahili identity, emerged on the coast at the same time that Islam did. In the ninth and tenth centuries the scale of Swahili settlements became much larger. They ceased to be villages and became cities, quite distinct from their counterparts in the hinterland. Another distinctive feature of Swahili civilization, the minting of small coins with Arabic inscriptions on them, also began at this time. In short, a new and distinctive civilization emerged in the last centuries of the first millennium. It was urban, Muslim, and cosmopolitan.

Life in the Early Swahili Towns: 750–1000

The towns of this period were deeply involved in trade. In addition to locally made pottery, significant amounts of pottery from the Middle East appear in the archaeological record during this time. Documentary evidence indicates that ivory as well as gold, slaves, and amber were exported to India and the Middle East. Indian merchants also bought iron from the Swahili, and there are slag heaps at some Swahili sites that suggest that there was once a large iron industry in these towns. In exchange they obtained imported pottery and textiles, most of which were purchased for local use rather than for trade with the hinterland.

Ivory and the other trade goods sought by visiting merchants were obtained through trade with the hinterland. Local weaving and ironmaking industries provided the goods needed for trade with the interior. The cities of the coast also maintained alliances with the non-Swahili groups of the interior, relying on them to act as loyal trade partners and as a military buffer that protected the cities from invasion from the land.

Kings generally ruled the cities, but it is not clear how great the power of these kings was. In later times the kings were more *primus inter pares* (first among equals) than absolute rulers, and there were several towns that had no kings. Even towns with the institution of kingship often went without kings for long periods when a suitable king could not be found. One suggestion is that the purpose of the kings, whose office was often as much magical as administrative, was to provide a point of contact with the non-Muslim population in the hinterland. Kings could serve as objects of loyalty for the non-Muslims with whom the cities forged alliances.

Though the social structures of these cities are difficult to determine, evidence tentatively suggests that the cities were divided along clan lines and by social status. Many cities have traditions that they were founded or inhabited by a certain number of clans. Interestingly, in some of the cities the ritual center of the city was walled off, and the number of gates in the wall corresponds with the traditional number of clans in the city. Thus, the clan division of the cities may be quite ancient. Some of the cities are also divided, either by a wall or main street, into two sections. This may represent a divide between those citizens of patrician (elite) status and those of common status. Later Swahili towns were divided this way, and archaeology suggests that this may also have been the case in earlier times. This divide between the patricians and commoners would become one of the defining characteristics of Swahili society and a major point of contention within it.

The High Point of Swahili Civilization: 1000–1500

During the 500 years before the arrival of the Portuguese in the Indian Ocean, the Swahili world reached its peak. It did so while participating in a steadily expanding Indian Ocean trade. When Portuguese sailors arrived on the Swahili coast in 1498, they were amazed by the large stone-built towns and the harbors crowded with ships. So amazed were they, in fact, that they resolved to conquer the coast and did so in the first half of the sixteenth century. In the period between 1000 and 1500, the Swahili coast enjoyed tremendous prosperity that was used to construct both public buildings and lavish homes for the wealthy patricians.

The economic boom was due to two things. First and foremost, it was a case of general regionwide prosperity. In this period the Indian Ocean became a commercial highway stretching from the Red Sea to China. Trade across this ocean became so intense that many port cities came to rely on it for basic needs. Trading ports such as Aden in South Arabia and Melaka in Southeast Asia acted as emporia for goods from India and China. Indian, Arab, Jewish, and Armenian trade diasporas stretched from China to the Mediterranean. This was an age when long-distance trade was sufficiently commonplace that staples like rice and timber began to enter the trading networks, whereas before only luxury goods were traded over long distances. We are accustomed to thinking of these types of trade networks as "modern," but the pre-modern world foreshadowed the globalized trade networks we are now accustomed to. Thus, in 1400 a Swahili patrician might decorate his house with Chinese pottery and wear Chinese silk, a Persian merchant might make a living from trade with East Africa and eat rice imported from India out of bowls made in

China, and Indian textile workers produced cloth that Indian merchants sold as far afield as East Africa and Southeast Asia. In the context of this trade, the Swahili found ready markets for luxury goods such as ivory, slaves, and gold, and also for more mundane products such as timber.

The second major economic development that occurred at this time was the opening of new gold fields in South-Central Africa. Swahili merchants became critical middlemen buying gold that came overland from Zimbabwe to the Swahili trade town of Sofala and then carrying that gold in their ships to more northerly Swahili towns, where it was sold to Arab traders. The result was a critical new source of wealth for the Swahili and trade connections that ran deeper into Central Africa than ever before.

This wealth also attracted migrants, and for the first time modest numbers of Arab and possibly some Persian migrants began to arrive in East Africa. Some of these migrants were from **Sharifian** families (families that claim descent from the prophet Muhammad, a source of great religious prestige); others were wealthy merchants who managed to found ruling dynasties in the towns they adopted. These immigrants were always few enough in number that it was they who assimilated to Swahili society, rather than the other way around, though they did cause changes in the way Islam was practiced on the coast.

Urban Transformation

Until the middle of the fourteenth century, it appears that the majority of the Swahili cities were built of wood. The wooden buildings sometimes had coral stone foundations, and sometimes the wood was covered with a plaster facing. Public buildings like the Friday Mosque (the mosque where the whole city gathered for Friday noon prayers) and the king's palace were made of cut coral stone or broken coral stone (usually called "coral rag") held together with mud. But in the middle of the fourteenth century, fueled by rising prosperity and probably increasing social stability, Swahili patricians began to build their houses in a new way. They used coral rag that was held together and plastered with mortar made with lime (itself a coral product, too). The resulting buildings were sturdy enough that they could be roofed with mangrove pole rafters and another layer of plaster to make a flat stone roof (rather than a thatched roof) or the floor for a second story.

These houses came to symbolize patrician status and the trade connections that made the patricians who they were. The houses of the patricians took on a standard form that included parts of the house that were intended for semipublic display and parts that were intended for the sole use of the patricians' families. The outside of a patrician's house looked quite plain. It offered no grand façade, not even windows. Upon entering, one would find a small reception area where guests would be received. Farther in was an open courtyard where some members of the household might have done craftwork. Just off the courtyard would be an apartment with its own toilet. This would serve as a guest room for visiting foreign merchants. Usually, patrician merchants had one or two Arab or Indian trading partners who would

Voices from African History: The Shanga Lion

"In the 1980s, archaeologists excavating the Swahili city of Shanga made an intriguing discovery. It was a statue of a lion, cast in bronze. It is small, only a bit more than 5 centimeters high, and it shows a male lion with his tongue hanging out, his right forefoot raised, and his tail curled into a closed loop. It dates from 1100 and was found in the ruins of a building adjacent to the town's congregational mosque, which may have been the king's residence.

Nothing similar has been found on the Swahili coast, and stylistically the lion resembles statues that were produced in north-central India for use in Hindu religious ritual. What a Muslim king would be doing with a Hindu ritual object is a bit of a mystery. One possibility is that Indian Hindus who were residents of Shanga used the lion statue for religious ritual. But there is almost no other evidence of an Indian presence at that time in East Africa. Mark Horton, the archaeologist who has supervised most of the work on Shanga, thinks that the lion was used by the Swahili themselves rather than by Indian immigrants. The lion's tail loop is worn in such a way that Horton believes it was suspended by the loop. He guesses that it was used either as a weight for measuring large quantities of the tiny coins minted by Swahili towns or as a part of the King's regalia. Both of these possibilities are credible. The Akan-speaking people of West Africa have long used animal figurines as weights for measuring gold, and kings everywhere have always felt a certain kinship to the king of beasts.

So it is possible that this lion was made in India and then exported to East Africa as a luxury item. But its story is more complicated than this. Interestingly, the artist who made the lion seems to have used an African lion as the model. African lions have longer, shaggier manes than their Asian counterparts, and the manes extend from their necks onto their chests and backs. Indian lion statues have tidy Asian lion manes. The Shanga Lion has a big shaggy African lion mane. This suggests that the artist who made it was either an Indian working where he could look at an African lion (i.e., in East Africa) or an African who was familiar with Indian artistic conventions.

Even more intriguing is the material from which the lion was cast. Bronze is an alloy of copper and tin. The copper in the Shanga lion seems not to derive directly from either East Africa or India. Instead, the copper in the statue appears to be recycled copper coins from China. China exported huge quantities of copper coins—so-called copper cash—during this period, and much of this coinage was melted down and recast in other parts of the Indian Ocean world. So where is the Shanga Lion from? Horton concludes that it 'must not therefore be called 'Indian' or 'African' but 'Indian Ocean' in attribution.'[1]

Nothing could be more representative of the cosmopolitan nature of Swahili society. Here is an art object that depicts an African lion using Indian artistic conventions, that was almost certainly used by Muslim Africans for different purposes than would have been the case in India, and that was made from Chinese copper. It is a product, both physically and conceptually, of the far-flung trade networks that linked the Swahili to a broader world of commerce and ideas that stretched from Sofala to Hangzhou."

[1]M. C. Horton and T. R. Blurton, "'Indian' Metalwork in East Africa: The Bronze Lion Statuette from Shanga," *Antiquity* 62(1988): p. 22.

trade exclusively through them and who would reside with them during their monsoon-enforced stay. The guest apartment allowed the visiting merchants to live comfortably with their host families while preserving the privacy of the patricians' families. The rest of the house would be for the exclusive use of the patrician family.

An interesting feature of the patrician house is the *zidaka*. These are elaborately carved plaster niches on the walls of patrician houses. They were used as decoration and as a place to display luxury items, most often Chinese porcelain. Thus, they had not only an aesthetic purpose, but also a commercial one. The valuable trade commodities displayed in them were symbols of the patricians' links to the broader trading networks of the Indian Ocean. But the goods on display there, like the marble walls at a modern bank, were also meant to demonstrate the creditworthiness of the house's owner. The other items that were sometimes stored in *zidaka* were books. These would either have been Qur'ans, other works of Muslim scholarship, or locally produced histories or poetry. One of the diversions of the Swahili patrician class was scholarship. They read and they wrote, producing works first in Arabic and later in Swahili written with Arabic script. Some towns even had minor manuscript copying industries.

Obviously, most Swahili were not patricians with the money to build grand houses nor the leisure time for scholarship. But like the patricians, the average Swahili person's life was shaped by the Swahili world's trade connections. Swahili commoners lived both in the cities and in what were called country towns. The cities all had, in addition to the houses of the patricians, large areas covered by the simpler homes of the average citizens. The country towns were inhabited exclusively by commoners, who built houses much like those of their city-dwelling counterparts. These houses were often made of sun-dried mud with thatched roofs, sometimes on a foundation of coral stone. They had a different plan than a patrician house and were much smaller. In the front of these houses was something called a *baraza*, a sort of bench incorporated into the structure of the house. These were (and are) used to sit and receive guests and are often the regular meeting places of groups of friends who get together to discuss and debate on a daily basis. In the quieter hours of the mornings, the *barazas* of a country town were given over to Qur'an reading and coffee sellers. The *baraza* is perhaps a perfect symbol of the essential urbanity of the Swahili. Even the rural country towns were densely settled and full of the types of intense face-to-face interactions among people that we think of as an essential element of urban life. So even the commoners, who maybe lacked the urbanity of the patricians, were nonetheless urban.

The commoners were also Muslims, and although their homes were built of sun-dried mud, their towns still contained mosques and tombs made of stone. Their towns, like the cities, were divided along clan lines and often into competing moieties (kinship groups that each constitute half of a community). The country towns were closely linked economically to the cities and produced much of the food that was consumed there. Country people most often made their living from farming or fishing. Country towns were also craftwork centers, producing cotton cloth and, most importantly, boats. Most of the major boat-building centers seem to have been country towns rather than the cities. Locally built boats were used for fishing, for cutting and transporting mangrove wood, and for coastal trading voyages. In modern times most of the sailors and ship captains have come from the country towns rather than from the cities, perhaps because fishing is such a good training ground for sailors. So the country towns and their commoner inhabitants were as closely linked to the coastal trading economy as the patrician residents of the cities.

Economic Transformation

The money to pay for these cities came from a trading economy. The Swahili were intermediaries in a segment of the Indian Ocean economy. Phillip Curtin has dubbed such people "cross-cultural brokers." Cross-cultural brokers are people who are able to act as intermediaries between trading people of vastly different cultures. The people of the coastal hinterland and the Arab merchants who ultimately purchased each others' goods did not have much in common. The Swahili had Islam in common with the Arabs and were the neighbors and often the political allies of the people of the coastal hinterland. They were in a perfect position to facilitate the trade between these two different groups.

But that is not the whole story. As the trading economy of the coast became more and more elaborate, so too did the Swahili economy. Swahili merchants began to act as consolidators, gathering goods from various regions and concentrating them in a few ports for the convenience of the monsoon visitors. But they were also producers. They made iron, cotton cloth, and boats and harvested and processed timber. In more recent centuries the Swahili coast produced grain that was exported to the Middle East, though it is by no means certain that this happened earlier. So there was much more to the Swahili economy than just acting as an intermediary between the Arabs and people of the coastal hinterland.

The best known of the Swahili coast's trade commodities, and the thing that caught the eye of the Portuguese, was gold. Before the opening of the New World's mineral resources, Africa was one of the world's major sources of gold. As was the case in West Africa, the people who produced the gold were too geographically distant from their customers to sell directly to them. Instead, intermediaries obtained the gold and moved it to places where the Arab merchants who brought it to the Eurasian economy could purchase it more easily. In the case of the Swahili coast, the source of the gold was hundreds of miles up the Zambezi and Limpopo rivers. A number of states emerged in this region partly because of the gold trade. Trade often has the effect of triggering state formation, though in this area the wealth generated by cattle keeping may have been as significant as the gold trade.

The most famous of the states associated with this trade is Great Zimbabwe. At Great Zimbabwe a huge stone enclosure bespeaks a powerful centralized state that was able to recruit large amounts of labor to build public or royal buildings. Great Zimbabwe is so large and impressive that when its ruins were first noticed by Europeans in the nineteenth century, they concluded that it must have been the work of someone other than Africans. Phoenicians, Jews, lost Roman legions, and Arabs were all proposed as the possible builders. In fact, the builders of Great Zimbabwe and other similar but smaller sites were in all likelihood Shona-speaking cattle keepers. Great Zimbabwe's peak coincided with the peak of the Swahili gold trade between

1250 and 1350; as a result, most scholars think that long-distance trade played a role in creating Great Zimbabwe. Curiously, there is little archaeological evidence of this trade. Great Zimbabwe shows only minor quantities of trade goods, and what is there is most often found in hoards, suggesting that it was uncommon and highly valued rather than a relatively commonplace component of a major trading system. There are a few possible explanations for this. The gold trade may have been a minor part of the economy. Gold may have been exported but exchanged with neighbors for goods that did not come from the Indian Ocean trading economy. A final possibility is that some evidence of the trade may have been removed when the site was looted of its gold by nineteenth-century treasure seekers. It seems unlikely, though, that they would have removed or disturbed economically valueless things like pottery shards.

Other less-well-known and less visually dramatic sites offer more evidence of long-distance trade between the Swahili coast and the southern African interior. The state of Torwa in modern Zimbabwe contains Chinese pottery and glass trade beads. A site dating from the fifteenth century on the Zambezi River, 500 miles from the sea, contains beads, wire, and other trade goods. So even if the trade networks did not reach to Great Zimbabwe, they did reach 500 miles inland. This suggests that the Swahili and the Indian Ocean economy they represented reached well past the coast and affected the economy and politics of the interior.

Ivory and slaves could be obtained closer to the coast, and the Swahili often had close relationships with the peoples who provided these commodities. Foragers and herders who lived just inland from the Swahili towns probably provided ivory and rhino horn, which the Swahili then sold into the Indian Ocean economy. The groups that provided these goods seem to have had close ties with the Swahili towns. Some towns had political and military alliances with herding and farming groups, and in many instances they relied on these allies to protect them from attack from the land.

The nature and importance of the slave trade are hard to judge. In later times the slave trade was a major component of the Swahili economy, and slaves were obtained as far afield as the Congo basin. We know that before the coastal civilization reached its height there was a significant slave trade from East Africa to the Persian Gulf. In the ninth century, huge gangs of African slaves worked in the swamps of southern Iraq. Slave labor drained the swamps and then worked the agricultural land created by the reclamation effort. That vast numbers of slaves were involved, and that the conditions under which they worked were appalling, are evidenced by the scale and violence of the rebellion they mounted in the late ninth century. This slave revolt, known as the **Zanj** (Persian for "black") **revolt,** lasted nearly twenty years and probably contributed to the decline of the Abbasid Caliphate. In the wake of this violent and protracted rebellion, the Islamic world soured on the use of large-scale slave labor in agriculture. After the Zanj revolt, there is little evidence of the use of African slaves in Middle Eastern agriculture.

But there were other types of slaves. Slaves were used as domestic servants, as soldiers, as sailors, as pearl divers, and as concubines. Africa was by no means the only source of slaves for the Middle East, but it was probably a significant source. Some of those slaves came from the Red Sea area and some came across the desert from West Africa, but some also came from the Swahili coast. Because the slave trade does not leave obvious archaeological evidence, it is difficult to judge its volume and economic significance for the Swahili. Documentary evidence makes reference to the Swahili towns waging jihad, or Muslim holy war, against their non-Muslim neighbors, and the purpose behind this may have been the acquisition of slaves. Some scholars have suggested that one reason Islam did not spread past the coast is that the Swahili purposely kept a monopoly on Islam, because the *sharia* prohibits the enslavement of Muslims. Had the people of the interior converted, it would have limited the supply of slaves. This is, of course, just speculation, and no one knows for certain why Islam did not spread past the coast until the nineteenth century. It is also worth noting that there is no archaeological evidence for a large-scale slave trade from the Swahili coast at the height of its prosperity. No slave baracoons or other evidence of places intended for the confinement of slaves has been found.

Slaves, gold, and ivory represent the luxurious, attention-grabbing side of the Swahili trading economy, but other, more mundane commodities were also there. Timber may be the most important of these. The Middle East is poor in trees, whereas East Africa has them in abundance. Several early documents refer to a trade in wood between East Africa and the lands of the Arabian Peninsula. It is not clear exactly what woods are meant; it could be that the wood referred to is mangrove wood. Mangroves grow in the muddy areas where fresh water mixes with seawater at river and stream mouths. They produce long, straight trunks that when stripped of their branches make excellent poles. These poles are used for making houses, roofs, temporary sheds, boats, and more. In the nineteenth and twentieth centuries they were the rough equivalent of the two-by-four in western Indian Ocean construction. Mangrove poles were used widely in both Arabia and East Africa in the nineteenth and twentieth centuries, and archaeological evidence suggests that they were used extensively before the modern period as well.

What makes the mangrove trade so interesting is that it was an intercontinental trade in a staple rather than a luxury item. It was also something that the Swahili obtained, not through trade, but through their own production. Cutting and processing mangrove wood was hard work that carried little prestige and, at least in recent centuries, was done by the poorer inhabitants of villages and country towns. The mangrove trade is emblematic of the depth of Swahili involvement in Indian Ocean trade. It was not just the patricians living in their cities and stone houses that lived by trade; commoners, too, made their living from trade. To be Swahili was to be somehow involved in Indian Ocean trade.

Kilwa: A Case Study

The Swahili city of **Kilwa** exemplifies the trend and patterns we have discussed. Kilwa is now uninhabited (another town still bears the name "Kilwa," but the original site was abandoned), so it has been thoroughly gone over by archaeologists. It was a wealthy and powerful city that drew the attention of outsiders, so there are reports by Arab travelers of their journeys to Kilwa and reports by the Portuguese of their encounter with and conquest of Kilwa in the early sixteenth century. And most interestingly of all, there is both a written Arabic history of Kilwa, composed by an anonymous Kilwa resident, that dates from early sixteenth century and a nineteenth-century Swahili oral history of Kilwa that was collected by a German scholar. Virtually every type of evidence that African historians use is available for Kilwa.

According to the Arabic history, an immigrant from the city of Shiraz founded Kilwa. Shiraz is a city in the interior of Persia (modern-day Iran), and it is highly unlikely that Shirazis founded Kilwa. Historians believe it is more likely that the founders and ruling families of Kilwa and other towns sought to increase their status by associating themselves with one of the richest and best-known commercial cities of their time. All along the coast there are traditions of Shirazi settlement, and today many coastal people who wish to distinguish themselves as having ancient roots on the coast, as opposed to the more recently arrived Arabs, call themselves Shirazi. It is possible that these "Shirazi" settlers came from somewhere in the northern part of the Swahili world. Of course, it is also possible that there were some settlers from Persia and even a few from Shiraz.

According to the Arabic history of Kilwa, when the founders arrived by boat, they disembarked on the island of Kilwa and found that there was already a Muslim living there. This Muslim, Muriri wa Bari, was presumably not the only Muslim inhabitant because there was already a mosque on the island. However, the island was ruled by a non-Mulsim. The Shirazi decided they liked the island and asked the ruler if they could purchase it from him. He agreed, and the price was enough colored cloth to encircle the island. (The Swahili oral history says that the price was enough cloth to create a sort of carpet for the departing king to walk onto the mainland.) The king then vacated the island and left it to the Shirazi, but plotted to return and take it

The ruins of the Great Mosque at Kilwa. In its time this was the largest enclosed space in sub-Saharan Africa.

back. Muriri wa Bari warned the Shirazi of this threat, and they dug out the channel between the island and the mainland to prevent the king from crossing. According to the Swahili history, this was done not by digging but by Islamic magic: the Shirazi read out passages of the Qur'an that prevented the king from crossing to the island.

Obviously, we are dealing with a mythic history here. As historians, we would be wise to see this as a myth that tells how the authors of the histories saw their place in the world, rather than an authentic account of the foundation of the city of Kilwa. At the same time, it would be unwise to totally dismiss the historicity of these accounts, because the existence of many of the sultans of Kilwa mentioned in the histories is verified by coins that they minted. So archaeological evidence backs up some of the written evidence.

What does this mean? First, it suggests that the Swahili saw themselves as part of a bigger world than just the East African coast. They claim, justifiably or not, that their kings originated elsewhere. They came in boats. They brought trade goods and established their land holdings because they had access to imported cloth. They were Muslims, and Islam was what separated them (literally in the case of using the Qur'an to create the channel) from the non-Muslims of the mainland. However, the Shirazi were not the first Muslims; Muriri wa Bari was already there, as was a mosque. Furthermore, the Swahili history also mentions that the leader of the Shirazi married one of the non-Muslim king's daughters. So the "founders," though separated from the mainland by a channel, were linked to the mainland (and non-Muslim) peoples there, by the sort of alliance created by a royal marriage.

The Arabic history goes on to name numerous sultans and the patricians who held office during their reigns. The existence and reign dates for some of these sultans can be confirmed from coins. Others either did not exist or minted no coins. Most of the sultans mentioned in the Arabic history are said to have performed the hajj (the Muslim pilgrimage to Mecca), and some were involved in political intrigue as far away as Yemen. So even if the Arabic history does not give us a perfect reconstruction of the city's political history, it does provide evidence of the links between the Swahili and the broader Indian Ocean world.

The Arabic history, like most pre-modern histories, is silent on economic matters. But archaeology tells us that Kilwa not only participated in the general prosperity of the period between 1200 and 1500, but it was also one of the leading Swahili cities of the time. It contained several buildings that were unprecedentedly large by Swahili standards. Its Friday mosque was probably the largest fully enclosed structure in sub-Saharan Africa. It was probably domed and had a ceiling made of barrel vaults supported by pillars. In addition to the mosque, there was a huge structure called the Husuni Kubwa that was probably a royal palace. It was a vast structure that dominated a whole section of the city. It included a royal living area and what appears to be a collection of apartments where visiting merchants could stay. The Husuni Kubwa seems to have been a sort of palatial version of the patrician's house. Like the patrician's house, it was meant to allow its owner to entertain and hence monopolize the trade of visiting merchants. If a patrician might aspire to host one or two merchants, the king of Kilwa had bigger things in mind. The Husuni Kubwa had room for eight to ten merchants and storage for their goods. Clearly, the kings of Kilwa were merchant princes.

The source of this wealth seems to have been gold. Merchants from Kilwa took control of the city of Sofala in the early fourteenth century. Sofala was the port city from which the gold that came overland from South-Central Africa was exported. However, Sofala, which is in modern-day Mozambique, is so far south that it would take ships coming from Arabia more than one monsoon season to get there. As a result, Arab and Indian merchants rarely visited Sofala, and Swahili cities farther north acted as intermediaries for Sofala gold. Originally, the city of Mogadishu had controlled this trade, but Kilwa, which was much closer to Sofala, was able to take over.

Ibn Battuta, the Arab traveler, visited Kilwa in 1331. He reported that the city "is one of the most beautiful and well-constructed towns in the world." Next he says that the town is built of wood, though some scholars have suggested that a minor change in the Arabic would yield "elegantly built" instead, which makes more sense in light of the archaeological record. However, it is possible that most of the stone buildings appeared in Kilwa shortly after Ibn Battuta's visit.

Ibn Battuta was impressed by the sultan's generosity both to himself (an amazingly large portion of his travelogue is devoted to either praising or disparaging the generosity of rulers all over the world, depending on whether he liked the gifts they gave him) and to a beggar who accosted the sultan while he was speaking to Ibn Battuta. The beggar asked for a gift, and the sultan gave him the shirt off his back right there in the street. The beggar was an Arab from Yemen. Ibn Battuta says nothing about the ethnicity of the sultan, though he notes that the majority of Kilwans are "Zanj of very black complexion."

The beggar was not the only person in Kilwa from the Arab world. Ibn Battuta mentions that the sultan was in the habit of raiding the non-Muslims of the mainland. A fifth of the proceeds from this raiding was reserved for the descendants of the prophet (sharifs). When these sharifs visited, they were given a share of the stored booty. Ibn Battuta mentioned that in Kilwa he met sharifs from the Hijaz, Iraq, and other parts of the Middle East. So clearly, Kilwa drew its share of visitors from the Arab world.

Our next window on Kilwa comes from the Portuguese. In the last years of the fifteenth century, Portuguese navigators succeeded in opening a sea route between Europe and India. On the way they encountered, much to their surprise, the Swahili city-states. Judging from their descriptions, the Portuguese must have arrived at the peak of Kilwa's prosperity. They judged that the town held 12,000 people. It was surrounded by

> Trees and gardens of all sort of vegetables, citron, lemons, and the best sweet oranges that were ever seen, sugar-canes, figs, pomegranates, and a great abundance of flocks, especially sheep. . . . The streets of the city are very narrow, as the houses are very high, of three and four stories, and one can run along the tops of them upon the terraces, as the houses are very close together: and in the port there were many ships.

Earlier the author of the preceding passage had noted that the houses of Kilwa were made of stone and mortar, so clearly some serious building had been going on since Ibn Battuta's visit.

Other Portuguese writers observed that the trade between Kilwa and the gold-producing regions to the south was intense. The first few Portuguese fleets to enter the Indian Ocean intercepted several ships coming north from Sofala to Kilwa bearing gold, and Portuguese sources even claim that the sultans of Kilwa ruled Sofala and several other southern towns. Portuguese accounts also claim that merchants from Kilwa traveled as far as Melaka, which is near modern-day Singapore. So it may be that in the early sixteenth century Swahili merchants were expanding their trade beyond the East African coast out into the eastern reaches of the Indian Ocean. Whatever trajectory toward economic greatness Kilwa was on in the early sixteenth century was interrupted by the arrival of the Portuguese. Soon after their arrival, they appointed their own puppet ruler in Kilwa, seized Sofala, and eventually sacked Kilwa. Over the next few centuries Kilwa went into decline, the original city was abandoned, and a lesser town with the same name grew up on the mainland.

Kilwa was unable to survive the arrival of the Portuguese, but other Swahili towns did. Malindi, Mombasa, Lamu, Pate, and others suffered at the hands of the Portuguese but carried on in their capacity as intermediaries and participants in the trading world of the Indian Ocean. Despite the incursions of the Portuguese, Omani Arabs, and British over the next 500 years, the Swahili coast continued to thrive. The natural cycle of growth and decline of cities continued. Kilwa fell into ruin, but other cities grew in importance. One of the greatest Swahili poems, *Al-Inkishafi* (c.1650), takes as its subject the fall of once-great cities into ruin. Clearly, decline was a topic that was on the minds of the Swahili elite in the half millennium after the arrival of the Portuguese. But for every city that declined, another rose to take its place. As we shall see in Chapter 11, the 500 years after the arrival of the Portuguese saw an increase in trade, urbanism, immigration, and prosperity on the Swahili coast, though for the Swahili patrician class, many of these developments were out of their control, and for them it was a difficult time.

The Swahili Coast in Global Perspective

The history of the Swahili coast offers us a number of interesting comparative questions and global perspectives. Why were there no comparable cities on the West African coast? Why did Swahili towns become city-states rather than large empires? What was the role of the Swahili in the trading world of the Indian Ocean? Were there other people in the Indian Ocean world who were in a position similar to that of the Swahili?

One of the reasons that the Portuguese were so surprised by the Swahili cities is that they found nothing comparable in West Africa. They encountered a few states as they made their way along the coast—Benin and Kongo come to mind—but these were substantially different than the Swahili states. Neither was a maritime power; in fact, Benin was well inland, and Kongo was near the sea, but clearly not of the sea. Swahili men made ship models in their spare time; the BaKongo did not. The West African coast faces out into a sort of watery desert. There is no coral on the West African coast—in fact, the western edges of continents never have coral reefs—so unlike East Africa, the West African coast does not have the complex systems of islands and reefs that make it possible for ships to find shelter from the sea. Where East Africa has hundreds of little natural harbors, bays, inlets, and coves, the West

African coast is mostly open beach with shallow lagoons behind it. It appears that the sheltered water of the lagoons saw a significant canoe traffic that moved a variety of goods for short distances. But there was no oceanic trade to speak of.

Even if West Africans had acquired the maritime skills to master the open sea without first serving an apprenticeship on the sheltered waters behind reefs, like East Africans did, there would not have been anywhere for them to go. East Africans had the busy, monsoon-facilitated trade of the Indian Ocean to tap into; the south Atlantic was vast and basically empty. As a result, the West African coast remained basically empty, too.

Once the Portuguese and other Europeans opened up the sea trade to West Africa, trading cities with many of the same qualities as the Swahili cities appeared. Elmina, Cape Coast, Whydah, and St. Louis all sprang up around the Atlantic sea trade. The inhabitants of these towns, like the Swahili, were cross-cultural brokers. They acted as intermediaries between the foreign merchants who came in their ships and the trading states of the interior. Like the Swahili, the merchant families of these West African trading towns often traced their origins to a settler from the same place as their foreign trading partners. Where the Swahili claimed Shirazi or Arab origins, these West African families claimed (legitimately) to have European founders. The Brews, the Caulkers, the Da Souzas, and others chose to emphasize one ancestor at the expense of others and thus were able to claim a special connection to the Europeans with whom they traded. Their foreign origins were no more or less real than those of the Swahili, but like the Swahili's foreign origins, they were as much a social and economic statement as a genealogical one.

Why the Swahili coast was never unified into a single large empire is difficult to say. Other sea-trading peoples—the Venetians and Genoese, the ancient Greeks, the trading states of India's western coast, and the Hanseatic towns of the Baltic Sea—have all favored the city-state model over the land-based empire. It may be that a sharp focus on sea trade, always a merchant's affair, precludes significant territorial ambitions.

The role of the Swahili in Indian Ocean trade was clearly peripheral. They were physically located on the edge of the Indian Ocean world, and their commercial contribution was mostly—though not entirely—limited to providing raw materials in exchange for manufactured goods. East African ships may have made the occasional voyage to Arabia, India, or even Melaka, but clearly most of the carrying trade to and from East Africa was in the hands of the Arabs. The situation of the Swahili is highly reminiscent of that of insular Southeast Asians. The Bugis and other sea traders of the islands of Southeast Asia were like the Swahili in many respects. Like the Swahili, they were on the physical periphery of the Indian Ocean. Beginning in the early centuries of the Common Era, sea trade to China and India triggered the formation of the states there. These states owed their existence to their ability to concentrate commodities in places that were convenient for monsoon-driven shipping. Like the Swahili, Southeast Asians had their own boats, which they used in local trade, but they conceded most of the long-distance trade to the Chinese, Arabs, and Indians.

Over the course of the centuries, Southeast Asians associated with the long-distance trade adopted first Hinduism and Buddhism, then Islam and Christianity.

These world religions remained almost exclusively associated with the commercial states; people not directly involved with commerce retained their traditional religions. Islam came later to Southeast Asia than to the Swahili world, but it had similar effects. Malay, a widespread Southeast Asian language, was analogous to Swahili in many respects. Although its grammar has deep local roots, the vocabulary has borrowed much from Arabic, and it was written in Arabic script. Like the Swahili, the Muslims of Southeast Asia welcomed learned visitors from the Muslim heartland. Arabs and Indians, some with religious credentials and others who were primarily merchants, settled among them, but cannot be said to have colonized Southeast Asia. In both Southeast Asia and the Swahili coast, popular Islam has included an emphasis on the veneration of holy men. For many poorer Muslims, visiting the tombs of these holy men has been a substitute for performing the hajj.

Perhaps the most salient difference between the Swahili coast and insular Southeast Asia is that the Swahili coast lacked a great emporium like Melaka. Melaka was one of the great trading ports of the pre-modern world. It sat astride the Straits of Melaka, which is a narrow passage between the Malay Peninsula and the island of Sumatra through which almost all the sea traffic between the Indian Ocean and the South China Sea had to pass. The result was a port city that could tap into both the regional trade of Southeast Asia and the trade between China and the Indian Ocean. No port in East Africa could claim so strategic a location, and as a result the cities of the Swahili coast never attained the magnitude of Melaka.

Useful Works on This Chapter Topic

Probably the best single work on the world of the Swahili is *The Swahili,* by Mark Horton and John Middleton (2000). Horton is one of East Africa's leading archaeologists and helped to trigger a rethinking of the Swahili origins question in the 1990s. His co-author, John Middleton, is the *éminence grise* of coastal anthropolgy. Together they bring an interesting perspective to the world of the Swahili. *The Rise and Fall of Swahili City States,* by Chapurukha Kusimba (1999), is another book by an archaeologist that is readable and informative. *Port Cities and Intruders,* by Michael Pearson (1998), offers the perpective of someone originally trained in Indian history. Pearson's reading of Portuguese sources suggests that ties between the Swahili coast and the interior were stronger than most scholars of the coast have believed them to be. For primary sources in English, the best choice is *The East African Coast: Selected Documents from the First to the Earlier Nineteenth Century,* by G. S. P. Freeman-Grenville (1962).

PART 2

Africa Since 1500 C.E.

Over the course of the fifteenth century, the world went through radical changes. It became both larger and smaller at the same time. European voyages of exploration revealed, for the first time, just how big the world actually was. Whole continents that had previously existed in "different worlds" now were increasingly linked by economic, environmental, and cultural exchange. Thus, the world became bigger. But advances in human knowledge and transportation technology also allowed groups who had previously interacted only through intermediaries and networks of long-distance trade to now meet face-to-face with ever-increasing ease. Thus, the world also became much smaller, as previously "separate" worlds and regional systems of trade were incorporated into a developing "world system." Most world historians use the date of 1500 C.E. to mark the point in time where this transformation into a single world was complete intellectually—if not economically or politically. Notably, this process began not with the "New World" of the Americas, but with Africa—for it was in Africa that the transformation wrought by European exploration and expansion first began.

Different regions of Africa experienced this changing world in very different ways. European contact along the Atlantic coast would redirect and perhaps redefine the nature of the West African and West-Central African economies. For this region, the rise of the trans-Atlantic slave trade would permeate relations with the wider world for hundreds of years. For Central and southern Africa, a long period of relative isolation from distant world regions would be brought to an end, and expanding European migration, particularly in southern Africa and along the highlands of the Rift Valley, would radically change the human landscape. Northern and eastern Africans, who had long been linked to much wider regional networks via Islam, Christianity, and the Indian Ocean trade, would quickly find themselves in a struggle to maintain control over their relationship to the wider world as Ottoman, European, and Omani forces contested for authority in these regions. Across the whole of Africa, new crops, technologies, and economies would have sweeping effects on economic, cultural, and political life.

If you take a careful look at the organization of Chapters 13 through 18, you will notice that the framework of organization changes radically from previous chapters. In Chapter 13 (which begins, of all places, in China), we switch to a pan-African level of analysis. This is because the nineteenth-century European conquest of Africa created a common historical context that allows us to treat Africa as a whole. Thus, rather than stressing the different regional themes of African history, as had been done in the first twelve chapters, now the key themes of African history are unified by a common experience with European hegemony. This does not mean that the experience of all parts of Africa with European colonialism was identical, but simply that it is similar enough to merit comparison within the context of a single chapter. These chapters are organized thematically to allow an examination of the different aspects of the African experience in the nineteenth and twentieth centuries. Notably, we divide the examination of African political history into two chapters in recognition of the watershed of African independence from colonialism in the 1950s and thereafter. As we have stressed before, however, no such thematic boundaries are perfect, and you will notice many instances in which cultural issues creep into our discussion of politics or economics creep into our discussions of culture. We hope such instances will help highlight the richness and complexity of modern African history.

Finally, there is another rationale for our shift to a pan-African framework in the latter part of this text. For all its deprivations and brutality, the European conquest and colonization of Africa also set into motion the creation (or perhaps simply accelerated the growth) of an African identity. Thus, the common experience of Africans as a colonized people, combined with new forms of transportation and communication, allowed and encouraged Africans increasingly to think and act as one for the first time in history. Therefore, the final chapters of this text present not only a shared historical experience, but a growing notion of being African as well.

MASTER TIMELINE: AFRICAN HISTORY SINCE 1500 C.E.

1500—Portuguese claim Brazil

1505—Portuguese sack Kilwa

1511—Sa'adi dynasty established in Morocco, begins to drive Portuguese from ports

1516—State of Benin bans trade in slaves

1517—Ottoman conquest of Egypt

1557—Ottomans capture Massawa from Portuguese

1578—"Battle of Three Kings" in Morocco

1591—Moroccan invasion of Songhai

1600–1650—Ottomans drive Spanish from North African ports

1618—Nzinga becomes ruler of Ndongo

1620—"Maroon" state of Palmares established in Brazil

1671—Rise of Alawi dynasty in Morocco

1698—Omanis seize Fort Jesus and Mombasa from Portuguese

1701—Osei Tutu leads Akan people against Denkyera; origins of state of Asante

1730—Oyo Empire defeats state of Dahomey; Jihad in Futa Jalon

1760—Jihad in Futa Toro

1798—Napoleon leads French invasion of Egypt

1804—Sokoto Jihad

1805—Muhammad Ali named Pasha of Egypt

1807—British unilaterally outlaw Atlantic slave trade

1817—Shaka becomes head of Zulu clan

1820—Liberia founded as settlement for free African Americans by the American Colonization Society

1824—Defeat of British army by Asante

1825—Mzilikazi becomes head of Ndebele

1828—Shaka assassinated by half-brother, Dingane

1830—French invade Algeria

1832—Laird expedition uses steamers to travel up Niger River

1835—First British war against Xhosa

1838—Battle of Blood River; Voortreker defeat of Zulu under Dingane

1839—Omani Sultan moves capital to Zanzibar

1847—Liberia declares independence; prophylactic use of quinine

1852—Jihad of al-Hajj Umar Tal

1854—Transvaal and Orange Free State declare independence

1855—Tewodros II reunifies Ethiopia

1860s—Breech-loading rifles come into common use by European armies

1867—Diamonds discovered in Orange Free State

1869—Suez Canal opened

1874—British sack Asante capital of Kumasi

1881—Muhammad Ahmad declares self Mahdi in Sudan

1884–1885—Conference of Berlin divides Africa among European colonial powers

1885—Mahdist forces break through British defenses at Khartoum; General "Chinese" Gordon killed in the battle

1890—Cocoa introduced to Gold Coast

1896—Ethiopians defeat Italians at Battle of Adwa

1897—Ndebele revolt against British in southern Africa

1898—British victory over Mahdists at Omdurman

1899–1902—South African ("Boer") War

1903—British defeat of Sokoto Caliphate

1904—Creation of "French West African Confederation"; French establish Indiginat code of law for subject Africans; genocide against Herero and Nama begins in German Southwest Africa

1905—Maji-Maji revolt in German East Africa

1912—African National Congress formed in South Africa

1919—W.E.B. Du Bois holds first Pan-African Congress in Paris

1929—Aba "Women's War" in Nigeria

1935—Fascist Italian troops invade Ethiopia

1944–1950s—Formation of African nationalist political parties

1940s–1950s—Mau Mau revolt in Kenya

1948—Nationalist party gains power in South Africa and implements policy of apartheid

1955—ANC and allies release "Freedom Charter" in South Africa

1956—Suez crises

1957—Gold Coast gains independence and renames self as Ghana

1958—Ghana hosts "All African People's Congress"

1960—"Year for Africa"—17 African countries gain independence

1960–1963—"Congo Crisis"

1961—Sharpsville Massacre in South Africa; W.E.B. Du Bois immigrates to Ghana

1963—Organization of African Unity created

1965—Unilateral Declaration of Independence by white minority in Rhodesia

1966—Military coup overthrows Nkrumah in Ghana

1966–1969—Civil war in Nigeria

1975—End of Portuguese rule in Africa

1980—Nonracial constitution ends war in Rhodesia; country renamed Zimbabwe

1990—First "National Conference" held in Benin

1991—Collapse of centralized government in Somalia

1992—"Operation Restore Hope" in Somalia

1994—Anti-Tutsi genocide in Rwanda; Nelson Mandela elected President in South Africa

1997—Mobutu flees Zaire

1998—Multicountry "African World War" in Democratic Republic of the Congo

1999—End to 17 years of military rule in Nigeria

2002—New "African Union" formed

2003—Conflict begins in Darfur, Soudan

2006—Ellen Johnson-Sirleaf elected President of Sierra Leone

CHAPTER 8

Slavery and the Creation of the Atlantic World

The Institution of Slavery before the Rise of the Atlantic Trade

In 1444 the Portuguese navigator Lancarote de Lagos sailed into the mouth of the Senegal River. There on some islands in the river, he and his men captured a group of Africans and carried them off into slavery. In some respects this slaving expedition was a new development. It was one of the first attempts by Europeans to obtain slaves south of **Cape Bojador,** the traditional limit of navigation for European sailors. As such it marked a new development in the lives of the people of the West African coast. In other ways it was not such a novelty. Portuguese, Norman, and Castilian sailors had been taking the Guanche, an olive-skinned people who lived in the Canary Islands, as slaves for nearly a century. They sold their slaves, whether Guanche or African, into a Mediterranean slave market that had existed since classical times. For the Africans involved, the arrival of European ships in the Senegal was a new development, but neither the idea of slavery nor the slave trade was. Though the institution of slavery predated the arrival of the Portuguese, most African societies probably had small numbers of slaves. The long-distance trading of slaves was nothing new either. A steady trickle of slaves had been crossing the Sahara north to the Mediterranean for centuries. Nonetheless, Lancarote de Lagos' raid was a harbinger of a new Atlantic economy that 250 years later would stretch from West Africa to the Americas to Europe. But the new always builds on the old, and it would be well for us to look at the foundations on which this Atlantic economy was built.

Slavery in the Mediterranean and Europe

In classical times slavery was a fundamental part of the economy. Slaves were essential to the large-scale farming that became increasingly common in the waning years of the Roman Empire, to say nothing of their role as domestic servants, craft workers, and even imperial bureaucrats. With the decline of the Western Roman

Empire in the sixth century, slavery became an increasingly marginal institution in northern Europe, where it was replaced by another type of servility—serfdom. But in southern Europe and North Africa, slavery continued to play a modest role in the economy. Slaves did some domestic work, some agricultural work, and some craft work. These slaves came from a variety of sources. At different times they might be captives from Viking raids, Christian Crusaders captured by Muslims, or Muslims captured by Crusaders. But the most common source was the northern coast of the Black Sea, where Italian merchants bought large numbers of Slavs for sale into the Mediterranean markets. Indeed, Slavs were so central to the slave trade that our word "slave" and many other European languages' words for slave derives from "Slav." A small number of these slaves were of African origin. In the early fifteenth century the Spanish city of Barcelona had a large enough African population to support an association of black Christian freedmen. Even earlier, in 859, there is evidence of a small number of Africans arriving as slaves in Ireland where they were known as "Blue men." Africans formed a minor part of the relatively minor institution of slavery in medieval Europe.

On the other side of the Mediterranean, in Islamic North Africa, slavery was part of the texture of daily life. Slaves worked as servants and served as concubines in the homes of the wealthy. But like Europe at this time, slaves were not central to the economy. There were no specific tasks that were performed only by slaves, and the collapse of the slave trade would have been inconvenient but not economically disastrous. Slaves might best be thought of as a luxury good for the convenience of the rich. North African slaves came from two sources. They might be non-Muslim war captives from Europe or Asia (Muslims are not supposed to enslave fellow Muslims) or they might be Africans obtained through the trans-Saharan trade.

As discussed in Chapter 6, trade across the Sahara was well established by the ninth century. One of the commodities traded across the desert was slaves. Historians estimate that roughly 5,500 slaves crossed the desert each year between 1100 and 1400. Although such numbers are somewhat suspect, they reflect the general consensus among historians that the volume of slaves that crossed the desert to North Africa was more a steady trickle than a flood. The trans-Saharan trade was never large enough to have a significant demographic effect on West Africa or on the North African societies that acquired the slaves. It is worth noting that these slaves were rarely, if ever, obtained by Arab raiders swooping out of the desert to kidnap hapless Africans. Rather, they were more often purchased by North African merchants who bought them from African merchants in the trading towns of the Savannah and Sahel. The slaves then walked across the desert, in what must have been a truly perilous journey. Ibn Battuta visited the Sahelian state of Mali during the fourteenth century. When he returned to North Africa he crossed the desert on a camel. But the 600 female slaves who accompanied his caravan walked. Once in North Africa slaves might be sold locally or be transferred east to Egypt, then to the markets of the Middle East. A few—the "Blue men" perhaps—ended up in Europe. It is worth noting that in neither Europe nor the Islamic world at this time was there any strong association between race and slavery. Slaves came from a variety of places and had equally varied appearances.

Slavery in Africa

West Africans did not just trade slaves. They also practiced slavery. When Ibn Battuta visited Mali, the large number of slave girls who served the sultan's meals shocked him. He was not, however, shocked by the presence of slaves or by the numbers of slaves he saw; rather, it was their nakedness that horrified him. But how numerous were slaves in Africa before the Atlantic trade? How important were they to African economies? These are difficult questions and are at the root of a major debate among historians.

One school of thought, championed by the late Guyanese scholar Walter Rodney, argues that African societies rarely held slaves. When they did—as in the case of slavery in Mali—it was a result of their connection to the slave trade. When one looks at societies that were isolated from the slave trade, this school argues, one sees some workers who are not entirely free, but these were not true slaves. And to the extent that true slaves were present, they were few, were likely to cease to be slaves within their lifetimes, and were economically marginal. This school of historians then points to the large number of slaves that were clearly present in African societies after the Atlantic slave trade was established and attributes their presence to the trade. In short, Rodney argued that the widespread use of slaves in African societies in the eighteenth and nineteenth centuries is a corruption of the traditional African social fabric that resulted from the slave trade. By extension, Rodney argued that the slave trade fundamentally transformed the African continent—for the worse.

Another school of thought on this issue was originally championed by the Englishman John Fage. Recently, an American, John Thornton, has refined and elaborated Fage's case for a significant slave presence in Africa before the Atlantic slave trade. Thornton argued that in most parts of sub-Saharan Africa, land was abundant and labor scarce. As a result, control over labor rather than land ownership was the ultimate determinant of wealth. A wealthy person was one who could mobilize the labor to clear and farm land that was, within limits, there for the taking. To be sure, there were many ways of obtaining that labor. But we should remember that wage labor as we know it was uncommon in the pre-modern world, especially in economies that relied more on barter than currency. What to us seems like the most obvious course of action to someone in need of labor—to pay wages for it—was less available to African farmers. The option of buying the laborers themselves was available (a single large purchase through barter is simpler than lots of smaller transactions). Thornton maintains that because of this, slave ownership was widespread and a fundamental feature of African economic life. Thornton and his supporters see the Atlantic slave trade as an unambiguously bad thing. But they also see African states' participation in the trade as voluntary and uncoerced. To them, the slave trade was a natural extension of the way African economies worked, and if the slave trade changed African economies and societies, it did so by amplifying and extending preexisting institutions. We will discuss the dynamics and debates about the slave trade in Africa in greater detail in Chapter 9.

Resolving the differences between these two schools is not easy, and both camps can point to examples and evidence that support their positions. Part of the explanation for these differences comes from the different regions each school uses for evidence. Rodney's work is based on his study of the Upper Guinea Coast, a region that was relatively isolated and had a less complex economy than some other regions of the continent. Thornton's evidence comes from regions with larger trading states, the Kongo and **Asante** kingdoms, for example. In the end it boils down to what one considers a representative African society. Are small, less-developed societies what Africa is all about, or are the bigger, more centralized states, with their more complex economies, the real Africa? We can offer no definitive answer here. As we have said before, history is all about controversy.

The Institution of Slavery

One last and very important thing before we can move on to the story of the Atlantic slave trade. What is a slave? Americans typically have a set of assumptions about slavery that are often valid for the institution of slavery in the Americas, but are not necessarily universal. Americans tend to assume that slaves ought to be primarily agricultural workers, who are completely the property of their owners, who live and work under more or less constant supervision, and who expect that they and their offspring will be slaves for life. We call this type of slavery, which was common in the New World, **chattel slavery.** Chattel slavery has been described as "social death." It is as if the person of the slave were dead—with all the loss of rights and social connections that entails—but the slave's body lived on and was property. Chattel slaves were a sort of dehumanized property. In theory they had no rights. Their owners could employ almost any type of violence they wished to enforce their will on their slaves. Slaves could be bought and sold on their owner's whim. Everything they acquired or earned belonged to their owners. They had no right to control their own sexuality. In practice, most slaves were able to force some concessions out of their owners, but those concessions were few and hard won. Some slaves in Africa lived their lives under these sorts of conditions, but in most places the rules and conditions of slavery were different.

In many African societies the status of a slave might change over time. When first acquired, a slave's position might not be too different from the American model. But over time, as the slave learned the language and customs of the society around him, he would be absorbed into his owner's lineage. He would most likely be a junior member of the lineage, but his status in society would be quite different than when he first arrived there. Furthermore, his children might not inherit his slave status. In many, if not most, African societies, freedom and slavery are not the binary opposites that they are in the West. Rather, it might be better to think of a continuum of degrees of freedom and servitude. One might start out as a chattel slave, but later find oneself neither absolutely free nor absolutely slave. Indeed, the sheer variety of types and degrees of slavery found in African societies makes some scholars wonder about the applicability of the rather obtuse word "slave" to the broad spectrum of relationships of dependency and servitude found in Africa.

The matter is further complicated by two widespread institutions—clientship and pawnship—that resemble slavery but with some fundamental differences. A client is someone who voluntarily becomes a dependent of another person. Someone might do this in time of famine or other catastrophe to avoid death or as a way of escaping poverty. A client is different than a slave in that a client can choose to leave the relationship. A pawn is a person given as collateral on a loan. A person who needed to borrow seed or livestock would offer as a guarantee on the loan a child or other dependent. When the loan was repaid, the pawned person would be returned. In the meantime, the labor provided by the pawn would serve as a sort of interest on the loan. It's not slavery in the classic sense, but it is similar and something that an outside observer might easily confuse with slavery. These issues complicate the debate over the prevalence of slaves and slavery before the Atlantic slave trade. Not only does the answer to the question depend on what one sees as a representative African society; it also depends on what types of institutions one chooses to call slavery.

The Birth of the Plantation Complex

That something as evil and gruesome as the Atlantic slave trade was set in motion largely to produce something as apparently benign as sugar is hard to understand. Nonetheless, sugar and Europe's ever-growing sweet tooth were the driving force in the development of the Atlantic world. We justifiably take sugar for granted. It's so cheap and commonplace that keeping sugar out of your diet is hard. But sugar has only become the stuff of mass consumption in the last 200 years. Only a thousand years ago sugar was the sort of thing that people mentioned in their wills. The plantation economy that absorbed most of the slaves that Europeans obtained in Africa existed primarily to produce sugar. The majority of the more than 10 million Africans who crossed the Atlantic went to work on sugar plantations in the Caribbean and Brazil. North Americans tend to assume that the southern United States was the ultimate destination of most African slaves. In reality the cotton, rice, and tobacco plantations of the Old South were little more than a sideshow in the bigger picture of the Atlantic trade. Less than 5 percent of the Atlantic trade was directed toward the United States. The bulk of the trade fed the sugar industry's voracious appetite for labor.

Sugar is produced from the juice of the sugarcane plant. Originally domesticated in New Guinea, sugarcane diffused to India, where the Arabs encountered it during the early stages of Muslim expansion into India. The Arabs introduced sugarcane to the Levant (the coastal eastern Mediterranean), where it caught the eye of Christian invaders during the Crusades. European Crusaders, who, to put it politely, "lacked polish," learned a great deal from their encounter with the Islamic world. Living for several centuries in the Crusader states they established in the Levant, they acquired a taste for a variety of luxury goods—most prominently silks, spices, and sugar. Indeed, some began to cultivate sugarcane on their estates.

Around 1200 most of the Crusaders were evicted by Muslim armies under the leadership of Salah al-Din (know in the West as Saladin). Many of the Crusaders withdrew not to their ancestral places of origin in Europe, but to islands in the eastern Mediterranean—most prominently to Malta and Cyprus. On Cyprus, Norman nobles continued to grow sugar for export to Europe. And it is on Cyprus that the roots of the Atlantic plantation system, with its peculiar mix of agriculture and industry, feudalism and capitalism, were first set down.

Sugar planters on Cyprus faced several challenges. Cyprus is drier than sugarcane would prefer. New Guinea, the plant's home, is one of the wettest places on the planet. To create comparable conditions in Cyprus meant irrigation. And irrigation called for money, something the feudal nobility lacked. Sugar production was not simply an agricultural undertaking. Growing the cane was only the first step. Then one needs to process the cane's juice into sugar. This calls for sugar milling equipment and evaporating equipment, and because the cane rapidly loses sugar content after it has been cut, each plantation had to have its own processing equipment. In effect, each plantation was part farm and part factory. That, too, costs money.

The third challenge facing sugar planters was labor. It took roughly one laborer per acre of sugarcane to do both the farming and manufacturing that sugar called for. There were people on Cyprus who might have done the work, but working on a sugar plantation was unpleasant and dangerous work. During the harvest the mills ran around the clock, and exhausted workers were frequently injured. The work in the field was often brutally hard. The local peasants were not likely to sign up for the job, and their feudal overlords could not compel them to provide more labor than was dictated by feudal custom. Like their counterparts in West Africa, landowners seldom hired workers, because wage labor was virtually unknown at the time. Slaves were the sugar planters' only answer. They could be compelled to do any work, their labor could be supervised and directed in ways that feudal serfs would not tolerate, and unlike serfs they did not pack up and go home when their twenty days of corvée labor were over. The only catch was that slaves cost money. With little capital of their own to put into sugar production, the Normans were not able to produce much sugar.

Enter the Italians. Italians dominated the commercial world of Europe, and unlike the Normans in Cyprus, they had capital of their own and access to Europe's nascent banking industry. In Cyprus, Italian merchants put their money and their business skills to work managing and later buying sugar plantations from the Norman nobility. The Italians had the money to bring in the latest sugar-processing technology, to build elaborate irrigation systems, and to buy as many slaves as were needed to work the land efficiently. They took their merchants' business sense and applied it to both the farming and the industrial sides of the sugar industry. In doing so, they were able to reach new levels of productivity and to produce more sugar than their Norman predecessors had ever dreamed of. Part of their "secret" was their ability to control and manage their labor force, an option that few European employers had at the time. Because their slave laborers had none of the rights of guild workers or feudal serfs, they could be exploited in entirely novel and brutal ways. On the island of Cyprus, the European economy was experiencing the beginning of a major change. Money and skill acquired in commerce were being shifted into agriculture and industry for the first time. One of the opening acts in the emergence of capitalism occurred in the early days of the plantation system. That the capitalist revolution in Europe and the plantation system grew up side by side is hardly a coincidence. Each fed off the other as money from one reinforced production in the other. It is sufficient to note here that one of the first attempts by merchants to shift their capital into production happened just as the curtain was rising on the opening of the plantation system. The result, of course, was a better-capitalized and economically rationalized sugar industry. The price was a huge increase in human suffering because an increasing demand for sugar was translated into an increasing demand for slaves.

The slaves who worked the sugar plantations of Cyprus, and later in the western Mediterranean as the plantation system spread to southern Italy, Spain, and Portugal, were mostly Slavs and Arabs. Then in the middle of the fifteenth century two unrelated new developments occurred almost simultaneously. In 1453 the Ottoman Turks captured Constantinople, the Byzantine capital. If you take a quick look at a map you will see that Constantinople sits right on the straits that connect the Black Sea to the Mediterranean. The Turks immediately closed the straits to the Italians. In doing so, they cut off the plantation complex from its labor supply. The Slavs were no longer available to the Italian slave merchants. By unhappy coincidence, Portuguese mariners had, about a decade earlier, learned how to sail down the West African coast—which was easy enough—and get back—which was a bit more tricky.

New Sea Routes

Portuguese sailors had been poking around in the Atlantic since the fourteenth century looking first for fish and later for a sea route around Africa to India. They were also interested in getting access to the source of the gold that they knew came across the desert to North Africa. In the process they discovered several sets of islands, first the Canaries and Madeira, and later the Azores. On the Canaries they encountered the Guanche, whom they traded with sometimes and enslaved at other times. Some Guanche slaves went to Lisbon, but many went to the previously uninhabited island of Madeira, where they worked growing sugar. The plantation system had moved into the Atlantic, as Madeira rapidly became the single biggest sugar producer in the world.

Despite their early success in the Canaries and Madeira, the Portuguese hope of finding a sea route to India and access to the African coast south of the Canaries was hindered by the problems of wind and current. The current sweeps southward along the West African coast, as does the wind. This is all well and good if you want to sail southward, but scary for sailors who would like to be able to come home and would rather not claw their way back against wind and current. For several decades Cape Bojador was the farthest south Portuguese sailors would attempt to go. Then in 1434, Gil Eannes managed to double Cape Bojador. He did this by allowing the wind to carry him past the cape, and then instead of turning into the teeth of the wind, he sailed out to sea toward the Canaries, where he was able to pick up the trade winds that took him home. Eannes learned that the fastest way back to Portugal from the African coast was to go way out into the Atlantic and then turn for home. It was a major discovery about the Atlantic wind system, with profound implications for African history. A decade later, using Eannes' discovery, Lancarote de Lagos would be hunting slaves on the Senegal River. Sixty years later Columbus would make a longer version of Eannes' voyage by looping south of the Canaries to make his westward passage and then returning north of the Canaries on the same trade winds that brought Eannes home.

With the supply of Slavic slaves cut off by the Turks and a potential supply suddenly available on the West African coast, the Portuguese became the leading suppliers of slaves to the plantation system. They quickly stopped raiding for slaves, not by choice (as their preference for raiding in the Canaries would seem to indicate), but because the African societies they encountered would not tolerate it. A trading ship that entered the Senegal River a few years after de Lagos' raid was attacked and nearly driven off before the owner was able to make clear that his mission was commercial, not military. As the fifteenth century wore on, the Portuguese developed trading relationships with various African societies on the coast and in 1482 built a trading castle in modern-day Ghana. Significantly, they called this castle El Mina— the mine. El Mina now has the sort of iconic quality for the slave trade that Auschwitz has for the Holocaust. Its brooding mass has become the standard image for television documentaries on the slave trade, and it is often the focus of the heritage tours that African Americans take to West Africa. This is entirely appropriate

Condemned prisoner's cell, El Mina.

The view from El Mina, looking inland at Fort
Conradsburg (Fort St. Jago).

because eventually El Mina became an important feature of the slave trade. But originally it was "the mine"—the place where the Portuguese bought the gold that was one
of their original goals when they first sought to go to West Africa. The Portuguese may
have been the leading suppliers of slaves to the Atlantic slave trade in the fifteenth century, but the trade was small then. The value of the gold and other products the Portuguese sought in West Africa far outweighed that of the slaves they obtained there.
And this would remain the case until the eighteenth century, and even then when
European merchants began to purchase huge numbers of slaves, they also bought
other goods, too. It was never the case that Africa had nothing to sell but slaves.

We have been telling you that the Portuguese bought this and they bought
that, but we have not said how they paid for it. Commerce is always a two-way street.
If you want to buy something, you have to have something to sell. This was a problem for the Portuguese. The societies they encountered in West Africa already produced or could obtain by trade almost anything the Portuguese had to offer.
Indeed, one of the great myths about the slave trade is that a few drunken chiefs
traded away their people for worthless baubles and trinkets. In reality, the Portuguese had to scramble to find sufficiently enticing goods for Africans to be willing
to part with any of the things that the Portuguese wanted. The one thing the Portuguese had to offer was their ships. Their ships and seamanship were among the
finest in the world. So the Portuguese put their ships to work hauling trade goods
from one place to another. They carried cloth from the kingdom of Benin (in modern Nigeria) to modern Ghana, where they traded it for gold. Likewise, they carried
slaves from the kingdom of Kongo to modern Ghana, where the slaves were traded
for gold. So from the very start, Africa had more to contribute to the emerging
Atlantic economy than slaves. A short list of African goods traded in the early
Atlantic world would include cloth (some of which eventually went all the way to
the Caribbean), ivory carvings, gold, hides, and a spice called Malagueta pepper. As
the Atlantic system became more established, the number and variety of goods
Africans contributed increased proportionally.

In 1485 a group of Portuguese settled on the uninhabited island of São Tomé off the West African coast. That they chose an uninhabited island is significant; they were in no position to seize land on the mainland. The Portuguese came to São Tomé in search of land on which to grow sugar. At the time their island of Madeira was the world's leading producer of sugar, but Madeira was not ideal for sugar. It was too dry. São Tomé was right on the equator and wet enough to grow sugar in wild abundance. Better still was its proximity to the kingdom of Kongo, an African state newly allied with the Portuguese and so a potential source of slaves. Within 50 years sugar was flourishing on São Tomé, and levels of production were roughly equal to those of Madeira. São Tomé is a landmark in the history of the Atlantic for a couple of reasons. First, it convincingly demonstrated that sugar could be grown profitably far from the places it was consumed. Never before had Europeans attempted to produce something for their own consumption (or anybody else's either) so far from home. Second, on São Tomé the link between African slave labor and sugar production, which had begun on Madeira, was made firm. When the plantation system moved to the New World, the use of African slaves followed almost unconsciously. And finally, the first documented resistance to slavery in the Atlantic occurred on São Tomé. Slaves on São Tomé could not escape to the mainland but they took to the mountainous interior. From there they mounted attacks on the sugar plantations. Eventually, sugar planters abandoned São Tomé. Slave resistance coupled with competition from Brazil made sugar production on São Tomé unprofitable. It is worth noting that slave resistance, which would be a constant feature of the New World plantation system, was there from the start. Whenever conditions allowed, slaves fought back.

The Plantation System in the New World

Columbus' voyage of 1492 opened up a whole new field of endeavor for sugar planters. But the Spaniards who followed in Columbus' wake were not interested in cultivating sugar. After all, there were empires to conquer in Mexico and Peru and all sorts of loot to occupy them. Growing sugar, or even making someone else grow it for them, seemed like a lot of trouble compared to theft. But farther south, in Brazil, conditions were different, the settlers were different, and soon sugar found a new home there.

In 1500, Pedro Cabral was sailing down the middle of the Atlantic on his way to India. He swung a little farther west than was customary and blundered into Brazil. He claimed it for Portugal and got back on his way to India. In Brazil the Portuguese initially found little to interest them. There were no large empires and no gold. The main commercial attractions were forest products. Compared to West Africa, India, or Spanish America, it seemed uninteresting. A few merchants went there to buy logwood (used for making dyes), but ambitious noblemen went elsewhere. Soon those merchants noticed that western Brazil had some highly favored sugar lands. The area around Bahia with its flat lands adjacent to a large bay became a major sugar-growing area. By 1575, Brazilian sugar planters were producing volumes of sugar that planters on the Atlantic islands could only dream about.

The average production of a Madeira sugar mill was 15 tons a year. By the late sixteenth century the Brazilians were producing as much as 130 tons a year per sugar mill. Total sugar production went up, and demand for slaves went up proportionally. In 1550, when Madeira and São Tomé dominated the sugar trade, annual exports from the Atlantic islands to Europe were estimated at 2,200 tons. In 1600, when Brazil was the dominant force in the industry, annual exports were up to 5,600 tons.

From Brazil the sugar industry spread to the Caribbean basin. One island after another came under cultivation. As the total area under sugar cultivation grew, demand for slaves grew apace. It was not just the newly opened land that called for new slaves. Sugar production was a brutal business, and the life expectancy of slaves was short. The planters usually preferred to replace dying slaves than to establish self-sustaining slave communities. The result was a constant demand for more slaves to feed into the sugar industry. The price of sugar was a steady trade in slaves across the Atlantic.

Race and Slavery in the New World

Why exactly was it that Africans came to provide the bulk of the unfree labor in the New World's burgeoning plantations, mines, and settler economies? Strangely enough, it is a question that is rarely asked. Perhaps because so many of us, particularly Americans, have been raised with racialized images of slavery (black slaves and white slave owners), we don't even stop to think of alternatives. Also, because of the legacy of racism and racial conflict that has characterized much of American history since the rise of the Atlantic economy, many students assume that it was racism that led Europeans to enslave Africans. But as we have seen from previous chapters, relations between Africans (particularly sub-Saharan Africans) and Europeans were remarkably good prior to the advent of Atlantic slavery. If it was conflict and animosity that fueled slavery, then the logical choice for slaves would have been other Europeans or Muslims from North Africa and the Middle East. Although some slaves did indeed come from these regions, the bulk of those enslaved were at first Native Americans and, soon afterwards, sub-Saharan Africans.

Why Indians?

As noted at the beginning of this chapter, the word "slave" covers a wide range of meanings and conditions. But slavery in the New World highlighted one particular aspect of slavery—the drive to create profit. The owners and managers of plantations and mines had a very particular set of needs in mind when they sought a supply of labor that would make their ventures as profitable as possible. At first, Native Americans seemed a perfect source of such labor. First and foremost (to state the obvious), Native Americans were already right there where the labor was needed. Second, the absence of ironworking technology in the Americas gave Europeans a substantial technological and military advantage over local populations. This gave Europeans the ability to enslave Native Americans if they so chose. And choose they did. Further, because the Amerindians were not Christians, their subjugation could easily be justified on the grounds that the imposition of European rule would lead to their conversion to Christianity. Given a worldview that did not value diversity in the form of cultural and religious differences, such a perspective was a perfectly logical way of viewing different societies and of justifying the horrors of slavery.

Why Not Indians?

Native Americans, though, did not prove well suited to the institution of slavery as established by the European colonizers of the Americas. Within a few decades Europeans were seeking other sources of labor for the plantations and mines in the New World. This was true for a variety of reasons.

Some have suggested that Native Americans made poor slaves because they were "too proud." This, however, seems to suggest that other folks were somehow willing to become slaves. More significant was the issue of disease. Long out of contact with the disease environment of the Old World, Native Americans' immune systems had no resistance to the great variety of infectious and parasitic diseases that had long plagued Africans, Europeans, and Asians. Smallpox, measles, whooping cough, chicken pox, and the mumps, just to name a few, were diseases that swept through Native American communities with devastating effect. Native populations throughout the Americas plummeted in the decades following European contact. Smallpox first struck the Caribbean in 1518. Combined with the harsh labor regime of the mines and plantations, population losses were catastrophic. By the 1540s, the Taino population had dropped from perhaps several million to a few thousand. Similar losses struck elsewhere in the New World. Aside from a few clerics, who seem to have genuinely cared for the native populations whom they sought to convert to Christianity (such as Poma de Ayala, who protested to the Spanish crown regarding the brutality of Pizarro among the Inca), the main concern for most Europeans was the impact of such losses on the labor supply. Susceptibility to disease made Native Americans "bad" slaves. Indeed, the life expectancy of Native Americans on plantations and in mines was often less than a year.

Native Americans had other disadvantages as slaves. Even though they were well acquainted with the soils of their native land, they were unfamiliar with many of the crops grown in the new plantation economy. Although familiar with cocoa and tobacco, which would later become important cash crops, others such as sugar, indigo, coffee, rice, hemp, and sisal were unfamiliar to the inhabitants of the Americas. Plantation owners could little afford to invest the time to train Native American slaves when life expectancy was so short.

Amerindians also possessed what might be considered a "home court advantage" in their resistance to slavery. Knowledge of local geography aided slaves who wished to escape and return to their homes (though European slave owners sometimes shipped Native Americans long distances to make escape more difficult). Those who did escape from forced labor on plantations or in mines also had the advantage that there was a large free population in which to immerse themselves. This made recapture unlikely for Native Americans who did succeed in liberating themselves from slavery. Large populations of free Native Americans also acted to discourage slave raiding by Europeans, because local populations were liable to retaliate. Even if Europeans held a military and technological advantage, continuous conflict with local Amerindians was both dangerous and bad for business.

Taken together, all of these factors came together to help make Native Americans undesirable and unprofitable as slaves. This does not mean that slavery stopped for Native Americans in the Americas; it simply means that the European settlers would continue to seek out other forms of forced labor.

Why Europeans?

It should not come as a surprise that many Europeans came to the New World as unfree labor. Certainly, many students are aware of the institution of indentured servitude, but many may not realize just how harsh this institution could be. Indentured servants were often lured into contracts by tales of wealth and ease in the New World, only to be faced by the harsh reality that they had no choice about what sort of labor they performed once they arrived in the New World. Families were often separated, never to see one another again. Plantation owners often sought to extract as much labor as possible from indentured servants during their terms of service. And, if indentured servants died before their contractual obligations were filled, the plantation owner was then spared from the common obligation of providing the servant with land on which to settle.

Some Europeans found themselves in much harsher terms of service—without even the limited legal protections offered to those who signed indentures. Prisons in Europe, generally filled with people whose only crime was debt, were occasionally emptied to provide laborers for New World plantations. Similarly, other groups deemed "undesirables" by European norms of the time, such as the Roma (gypsies) and Jews, were often deported as unfree labor. In a time when European militaries simply "pressed" free persons into military service, it does not seem ridiculous that people could be forced into other forms of unfree labor when demand was high. Even if religious and cultural differences did not exist to justify such harsh treatment, the extreme divisions of class during the period helped aristocratic plantation owners to "dehumanize" the lower-class populations. The value of a peasant or laborer's life was not to be equated with that of the lives of the gentry. In the end, a large portion of Europeans who traveled to the New World prior to the nineteenth century came as indentured servants, and perhaps as many as 50,000 came as outright slaves.

Why Not Europeans?

For the plantations and mines that provided the bulk of the wealth created by the New World economy, Europeans, whether slaves or indentured servants, proved undesirable as laborers. Europeans were familiar with neither the soils of the New World (especially in the tropical regions where plantations flourished) nor the cash crops associated with the new economy. Further, protected by contracts, indentured servants could undertake legal action to protect their rights and demand redress of grievances (though colonial governments, themselves staffed by aristocrats, proved unsympathetic to such claims). Those who fled their service—either to escape harsh treatment or simply to escape their obligations—could hope to be lost in the ever-expanding population of free Europeans. Also, as the enslavement of Native Americans (and later Africans) came to be defined in religious and racial terms, European laborers could increasingly lay claim to Christian and "white" identity as grounds for exemption from harsh terms of service. Finally, and perhaps most importantly, there was the issue of disease. Though Europeans were resistant to many infectious diseases brought from the Old World, they were highly susceptible to the tropical diseases that were rife in the regions where the most important cash crops grew. Of particular danger were diseases such as yellow fever and malaria, which took a staggering toll on Europeans—especially those laboring under harsh conditions. Like Native Americans, European laborers on plantations often had life expectancies of less than one year. Again, such factors added up to make them "bad" slaves.

Why Africans?

In the end, it was Africans who proved to have particular characteristics that made them suitable for forced labor in the New World. Ironically, it was knowledge and disease resistance that helped to doom millions of Africans to servitude in the Americas. Strengths, in the unique setting of the Atlantic system, became curses, not advantages.

Unlike Native Americans and Europeans, Africans were familiar with both tropical environments and soils—there are many similarities between the land and environment of Latin America and West and Central Africa. Further, Africans were

Enslaved Africans harvesting sugarcane.

well acquainted with many of the crops important to the plantation economy. Many African societies had experience growing indigo and rice, for example. Indeed, even the European planters themselves often lacked the skills to cultivate these crops. With a long tradition of gold mining, Africans became a primary source of the technical skill required to find and extract precious ores from the soil of the Americas. Africans even provided much of the knowledge necessary to establish cattle ranching as a profitable enterprise in the Caribbean and South America.

In addition to providing the agricultural and mining technology that helped make the New World economy profitable, Africans also possessed a degree of disease resistance that made them well suited for life in the Americas. As participants in long-distance trade systems linking Africa, Europe, Asia, and the Indian Ocean, African populations, like Europeans, had long since developed some degree of resistance to the infectious diseases that so ravaged Native American populations. Owing to the tropical environment of sub-Saharan Africa, inhabitants from this region also possessed a degree of resistance to diseases such as malaria and yellow fever. Africans were not immune, but they were far less likely to die from such diseases than Europeans or Native Americans. Given such disease resistance, Africans were better prepared to survive the rigors of plantation and mine labor in the Americas. Still, their experience was brutal. Even with such strengths, African slaves were faced with terribly high mortality rates. On Caribbean islands such as Barbados, life expectancies were as low as seven years for enslaved Africans. Still, such life expectancies were far greater than those of Amerindians or Europeans, and this longer life was reflected in the value of African slaves, whose price was generally ten times as much as a Native American.

Why Not Africans?

If Africans possessed the necessary knowledge and disease resistance to "succeed" as slaves in the New World, why then were they effectively the last to be used to provide labor? In part this might be explained by the relative ease of acquiring Native Americans and Europeans as slaves or forced labor. The fact is that Africans had to be both captured and transported to the New World—factors that made their acquisition both dangerous and expensive. Unlike Native Americans, Africans in the sixteenth century were not at a substantial technological or military disadvantage to European forces who attempted to acquire slaves via raids. When the Portuguese attempted such raids in the fifteenth century, they quickly realized that they could not afford the defeats they often suffered at the hands of African forces. Similarly, the unfriendly disease environment of Africa severely limited the ability of Europeans to penetrate beyond the relative safety of coastal waters. European slavers quickly realized that it was wiser to purchase slaves from African rulers and merchants than it was to capture Africans themselves. Such purchases, combined with the expense of outfitting voyages to Africa and the New World, meant that enslaved Africans would be staggeringly expensive once they arrived in the New World. It is both a testimony to and a condemnation of the profits generated by the new Atlantic economy that Africans could be purchased in such large numbers. Further, it is worth noting that the very expense of African slaves might have made them more desirable to some participants in the Atlantic system. Shipping companies such as the Royal Africa Company could take advantage of the demand for and expense of African slaves in a way they could not for slaves captured in the Americas. Similarly, colonial governments could gain revenue from taxes on the slave trade, thus gaining an additional source of indirect wealth from the New World economy. Many individuals in Europe, Africa, and the Americas grew very rich from the Atlantic slave trade. Societies and economies were transformed. The cost in human suffering to those who became the victims of this trade, and to the societies that have inherited the legacy of anger and guilt from it, though, are likely to be far greater than the gains in wealth could ever amount to.

The Nature of the Slave Trade

It is difficult to truly describe, much less comprehend, the horror of the transatlantic slave trade. The degree of physical and psychological torment endured by the captives of the trade is frightening, even placed against the world's history of wars and genocides. In the course of the trade, slave dealers sought to transform human beings into commodities for eventual sale to slave owners, who themselves sought to transform them into tools (reflect on our discussion of the meaning of chattel slavery from earlier in this chapter). Both dealers and owners had the same ultimate goal—profit. To justify their actions, they also had to take an intermediate step—to deny the ultimate humanity of their captives. For us to think of enslaved individuals and groups simply as passive and helpless victims, however, is to deny them their humanity in a different way. It is important to realize that these individuals resisted the denial of their personhood through a variety of overt and covert means. Escape, violent resistance, community, spirituality, and even death itself were only a few of the forms of resistance by which the enslaved sought to maintain their humanity, despite the efforts of their "legal" owners to deny it.

The process of transport to the New World is generally referred to as the **middle passage.** Before being loaded on slave ships, slaves had to be captured and transported to the coast, a journey that was also cruel and often deadly. This subject will be dealt with in Chapter 9. One might consider the middle passage beginning with the arrival of a slave ship at the port, town, or outpost where the enslaved awaited transport to the Americas. Such slave depots were often referred to as factories by those who took part in the trade. Upon arriving at such a location, representatives from the ship would often contact the local rulers and offer gifts as a means of showing their intention of entering into serious trading. In some regions, as was the case along much of the "slave coast," the European traders who resided in the permanent trading fortresses such as El Mina or Cape Coast acted as intermediaries in such exchanges. They often kept large numbers of slaves captive, ready to transport whenever ships of their own nationality arrived.

Once initial terms had been reached, slaves would be brought before the European traders for inspection. These examinations were thorough in the extreme. Traders and ship's surgeons sought to determine the physical health of the captives, not only because healthier slaves brought more money, but also

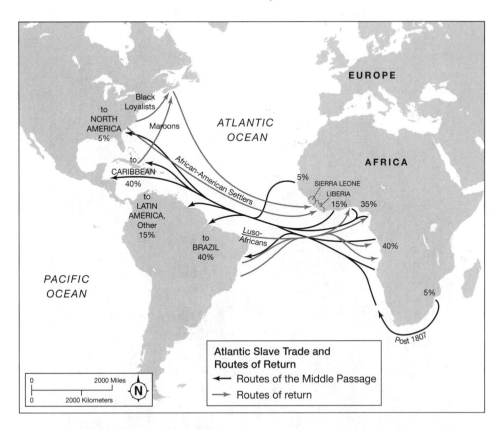

Map 8-1: The Atlantic slave trade and routes of return

because of the fear of illness that could threaten the lives of other captives (and thus profit) and also the lives of the ship's crew. For such inspections, slaves were stripped naked (if they possessed any clothing at all), inspected in the closest detail, and forced to perform various physical activities to display their vigor and health. Slave buyers were well aware that slave sellers often sought to hide the infirmities of sick or injured slaves via a wide variety of techniques. Slaves purchased at this point were generally branded with a mark that identified the buyer. Again, it is difficult to imagine the anger, pain, and humiliation that this process caused those who had been enslaved. It is an important question whether such torture was simply an unfortunate side effect of the necessities of the trade, or whether it was part and parcel of the attempt of slave traders and owners to break the will of the slaves and force them to more passively accept their fate.

If enough slaves were available to provide the ship with a full cargo, then preparations for loading could take place. Often, however, ships had to wait at slave ports for some months before a full load could be acquired, during which time the slaves remained in the factory. Occasionally, slave ships chose to cruise from one port to another seeking available slaves, though this was rare.

Engraving of African and European slave traders conducting "business."

Voices from African History: Equiano's Description of the Middle Passage

"At last, when the ship we were in had got in all her cargo, they made ready with many fearful noises, and we were all put under deck, so that we could not see how they managed the vessel. The stench of the hold while we were on the coast was so intolerably loathsome, that it was dangerous to remain there for any time. . . . Some of us had been permitted to stay on the deck for the fresh air. But now that the whole ship's cargo were confined together, it became absolutely pestilential. The closeness of the place and the heat of the climate, added to the number in the ship, which was so crowded that each had scarcely room to turn himself, almost suffocated us.

This produced copious perspirations so that the air became unfit for respiration from a variety of loathsome smells, and brought on a sickness among the slaves, of which many died—thus falling victims of the improvident avarice, as I may call it, of their purchasers. This wretched situation was again aggravated by the galling of the chains, which now became insupportable, and the filth of the necessary tubs [toilets] into which the children often fell and were almost suffocated. The shrieks of the women and the groans of the dying rendered the whole a scene of horror almost inconceivable.

Happily perhaps for myself, I was soon reduced so low that it was necessary to keep me almost always on deck and from my extreme youth I was not put into fetters. In this situation I expected every hour to share the fate of my companions, some of whom were almost daily brought upon the deck at the point of death, which I began to hope would soon put an end to my miseries. Every circumstance I met with, served only to render my state more painful and heightened my apprehensions and my opinion of the cruelty of the whites.

One day, when we had a smooth sea and moderate wind, two of my wearied countrymen who were chained together (I was near them at the time), preferring death to such a life of misery, somehow made through the nettings and jumped into the sea. Immediately another quite dejected fellow, who on account of his illness was suffered to be out of irons, followed their example. I believe many more would very soon have done the same if they had not been prevented by the ship's crew, who were instantly alarmed. Those of us that were the most active were in a moment put down under the deck, and there was such a noise and confusion among the people of the ship as I never heard before to stop her and get the boat out to go after the slaves. However, two of the wretches were drowned, but they got the other and afterwards flogged him unmercifully for thus attempting to prefer death to slavery."

Source: The Interesting Narrative of the Life of Olaudah Equiano or Gustavus Vassa the African (London, 1789).

Prior to loading, slaves were once again inspected for signs of disease or infirmity. Often, slaves were shaved head to toe and bathed to prevent the spread of lice to the ship. Heavily bound in chains and under close guard, slaves were then transported to the slave ship. Again, one can only imagine the shock and fear that such an unfamiliar setting created (please see the account by Olaudah Equiano).

Shipboard Conditions

From here commenced what was almost certainly the most terrible, if not the most deadly, aspect of the Atlantic slave trade, the sea voyage to the Americas. As many slaves as possible were kept below decks. Chained together (sometimes even hand-to-foot as a means of limiting the ability to move as a group), slaves were placed in the hold. With shelves built overhead to maximize the number of people who could be transported, there was often not enough room to even sit up. There were no facilities for the removal of human waste, except perhaps low tubs that could be passed around. No doubt seasickness struck large numbers in the dark, enclosed space. Certainly the holds were often awash in vomit, urine, and feces. The heat below decks in the tropics sent temperatures to well over the 100°F/38°C mark. Unable to escape, the captives were trapped in an atmosphere so fetid that slavers often remarked that candles could not burn below decks. Slave ships were so foul that some observers claimed you could smell them before they could be seen.

Forced to lie on the wooden decks without padding and unable to easily shift positions, many of the captives no doubt suffered from open sores from the rough decks and constant contact with their shackles as the ships rolled with the seas. In such an environment, disease could spread easily from one person to the next. Infectious diseases traveled quickly through human waste, physical contact, or the hot, damp air. In particular, a variety of intestinal disorders, often referred to simply as the "white flux" or the "bloody flux" by crew members, were common among slave ship captives.

On many ships, the poor nature of the provisions offered to the captives contributed considerably to the hardship faced by those trapped on board. Slaves were often fed no more than a gruel or porridge of rough-ground grains, supplemented occasionally by vegetable oil or dried meat and fish. Water, too, was often in short supply. Stores of food could be expensive, and both food and water were bulky commodities that vied for space with the human cargo below decks. Slavers seeking to maximize potential profits often opted to carry more people and less food or water. Although some ship captains recommended as much as one gallon of water per day for the captives, others provided as little as a pint. Ships might also limit rations of food and water out of fear that unfriendly currents, storms, or winds could stretch the length of the voyage, and a ship that ran out of food was guaranteed to suffer considerable financial losses from starvation. Finally, by keeping the captives hungry and thirsty, the slavers could perhaps foster conflict among the captives and also weaken the slaves temporarily—both steps that could make revolt less likely.

The crews of slave ships did make some effort to deal with the horror belowdecks. Slaves were occasionally brought up for fresh air, exercise, and bathing. Sometimes female slaves and children, considered less of a threat, were kept on deck when the weather allowed. Some ships provided slaves with small quantities of tobacco or alcohol while on deck as a means of "improving morale and health." In the later years of the trade, when the threats of disease were better understood, some ships made the effort to flush the decks with seawater or even scrub the holds with vinegar or lime juice. Such actions not only decreased the rate of mortality among the captives, but also among the crew, who also suffered from the risk of infection brought on by the terrible conditions aboard the ships.

The Human Toll

Not surprisingly, the mortality rate on slave ships could be terribly high. In the early era of the slave trade (roughly up to 1700), death rates on slave ships averaged just over 20 percent (for both captives and crew). In the latter years of the trade, with improved feeding of captives and better ship hygiene, as well as restrictions on the number of individuals who could be carried by ships of varying sizes, death rates were significantly reduced. Yet the average mortality rate for nineteenth-century slaving voyages was still nearly 10 percent. Many factors could decrease the likelihood of one's surviving the middle passage. The region of origin could be influential. During the early eighteenth century, for example, the mortality rate of ships departing from the Bight of Biafra was over 40 percent. The exact cause of this particularly catastrophic rate of mortality is not yet understood.

A key factor influencing mortality was the outbreak of disease. As previously mentioned, slavers made every effort to avoid taking sick captives on board. When disease did break out, the ship's crew would try to cure the ill, but they did not hesitate to throw sick slaves overboard if they thought this might halt the spread of disease among the rest of the ship's captives and crew. Common infectious diseases that threatened slave ships included typhoid, dysentery, and smallpox. Ships struck by such diseases could suffer losses of over 50 percent of the captives and crew in short order. Even less deadly forms of illness such as common colds or chicken pox could threaten the lives of captives given the extreme physical stress of their environment.

The length of the voyage also played a critical role in determining the number of individuals who might survive the Atlantic crossing. The farther east in Africa the voyage originated, roughly, the higher mortality was likely to be. But even voyages beginning from regions such as the Senegambia (on Africa's western tip) could be extended by bad weather or unfriendly winds. Captives on becalmed ships could fall prey to malnutrition or even die of thirst if ships were immobile for extended periods. Storms, always a threat to the vessels of the day, were especially dangerous for the captives of slave ships. These ships carried lifeboats only for the crew, and if weather (or any other such mishap, such as fire or grounding) forced the ship to be abandoned, then those chained below were certainly doomed. In 1738, for example, the Dutch slaver *Leuden* was run aground by a storm. The crew abandoned the ship and left behind 702 slaves to drown as the ship broke apart and sank.

Fear and depression took their toll on those trapped aboard the ships. In 1790, a British ship's surgeon stated that two-thirds of the deaths on slave voyages were due to "banzo"—what he defined as "involuntary suicide brought on by extreme melancholy." The slaves, he said, were so depressed that they simply lost all will to live. Olaudah Equiano reported that he became so despondent on being loaded on the slave ship that he could not eat. Only when beaten by the crew did he take food. Other captives were more active in their resistance to the terrible conditions aboard ship. Many went on hunger strikes as a form of protest. So common was this practice that every ship carried a device known as the speculum oris, which served to pry apart the slave's teeth so that a funnel could be used to force-feed the individual. Other slaves, rendered desperate by the conditions on board, took more direct paths to ending their suffering. Some chose to drown themselves by leaping overboard. For this reason, many slave ships not only kept slaves in irons when on deck, but also strung nets along the sides of the ship to keep those enslaved from drowning themselves (and thus depriving the slavers of the profit of their trade). Even death was a form of resistance.

Those who found themselves trapped aboard slave ships sought to combat such desperation both for themselves and for their fellow captives. As mentioned previously, it is important not to think of those enslaved as captives who simply suffered helplessly at the hands of the slave traders, but rather as human beings who strove to survive and overcome even the greatest of hardships. Below the decks of slave ships, human beings suffered and many died, but most endured. Amidst the horror, these individuals certainly offered one another support and kindness with the only item they possessed—their humanity. For most, even in such a terrible setting, the ultimate human resource, hope, managed to survive. Perhaps with stories, songs, references to religious beliefs, or simply through compassion and empathy, these victims of the slave trade helped one another survive.

Not all resistance was passive. For the crew, the most feared form of resistance was the revolt. No crew was foolish enough to believe that if given the opportunity, the ship's captives would not choose to fight for a chance at freedom. Indeed, roughly a quarter of all slave voyages experienced some sort of attempted group uprising. A far greater percentage faced acts of violence against members of the crew by individual captives. Crews used the harshest forms of punishment to make examples of those who rebelled in hopes of deterring similar acts by others. Well-known cases such as those of the *Amistad* and the *Antelope* offer us some insight into the ferocity of slave ship revolts. Other successful revolts no doubt remain unrecorded, because such ships were likely lost at sea, never to be heard from again.

Justifications for the Slave Trade

From our contemporary viewpoint, it is often hard to imagine how one group of people could so brutalize another. We have examined the Atlantic economy's need for skilled labor that could survive the harsh conditions of New World plantations, but we have also highlighted the fact that slavery, especially chattel slavery, demands some sort of legitimization to explain why one group of people was being so terribly treated. Very few supporters of the Atlantic slave trade were willing to express their motives simply in economic terms. Rather, especially as slavery became institutionalized in the New World, those involved in the trade sought to present their actions in a light that suggested that they were in fact benevolent. Religious justifications were often paramount. By enslaving Africans, such arguments went, the Africans were actually being spared from the eternal damnation that awaited all non-Christians. Such arguments, of course, ignored the reality that some enslaved Africans (particularly those from the Kongo) were already Christians. Further, this argument ignored that avenues of proselytization other than slavery existed. Finally, the use of Christianity as a justification for enslavement also left open the question of what one did with slaves who converted—a dilemma to be faced by the slave owners of the New World. Nonetheless, the use of Christianity to justify slavery existed throughout the era of the slave trade and was used by those who defended the trade against the forces of abolition. Ending the trade, argued James Boswell in the late 1770s, would "shut the gates of mercy on mankind." Indeed, not until 1995 did the Southern Baptist Church of the United States officially recognize that slavery in the Americas had been wrong.

Over the course of the institutionalization of slavery in the Americas, another justification of the trade took root—one that sought to redefine the very nature and character of Africans. This line of reasoning increasingly argued that African blacks were inferior to European whites (blackness and whiteness being fairly novel forms of identity) on the grounds of lack of both intelligence and morality. Africans were incapable of caring for themselves and instead needed the guidance of whites to survive in anything other than the most base of conditions. Slavery, thus, was once again defined as benevolent, because the living conditions that resulted were claimed to be better than what Africans were capable of on their own. Slave owners often sought to characterize themselves as the parents and the slaves as the children in a form of hegemony know as paternalism. Here we see the roots of many of the most painful elements of modern racism. Africans were defined as mentally incapable of undertaking anything but manual labor and too immoral to be trusted not to steal, lie, or commit crimes of violence and passion. Further, only extreme punishments and the denial of basic freedoms to the Africans and their descendants could provide any hope for security in the slave-owning society. According to such a way of thinking, the harshness of slavery was not a result of the greed of slave owners, but rather the only way black Africans could be controlled and made productive members of society. For the United States in particular, which sought to establish a state founded on inalienable rights, the denial of the most basic rights to such a large element of the populace was especially hypocritical.

Such religious and racial justifications of slavery are all the more surprising when one recalls the images of Africans prevalent in Europe prior to the era of the slave trade. As we saw in previous chapters, prior to the slave trade, Europeans sought to find Christian Africans, and when Prester John proved elusive, they sought to promote peaceful conversion. Similarly, the political and economic worlds of Europe and Africa were not so vastly different in the early age of maritime contact, a fact commented on by many a European explorer. Yet, the potential profits of slavery in the New World necessitated a new view of Africa and Africans. By the later years of the slave trade, Africa had become redefined as a barbaric land of witchcraft, cannibalism, and primitive Stone Age tribes—the barbaric foil to civilized European civilization. To this day, our popular vision of Africa is tainted by this overtly racist legacy.

Counting the Cost

Discussions of the nature of the middle passage often lead to a further question: How many people were forced from their homes in Africa to come to the New World as slaves? Estimates have varied widely. The lowest numbers were probably advanced by a group of historians known as the "Redeemers"—historians of the American South who generally sought to portray slavery as a benevolent institution. These estimates placed the total number of slaves brought to the New World at around two million. On the opposite end of the spectrum is the Nation of Islam, an African-American religious organization that has often turned white racism on its head by identifying whites as inherently evil. In the 1990s the Nation of Islam claimed that some 600 million Africans had been brought to the Americas as slaves—a number nearly equal to the contemporary population of all of Africa. Clearly, the real number lies somewhere between these deeply biased numbers—but where?

In 1861, Edward Dunbar published estimates of the number of Africans brought to the New World that placed the total at just under 14 million. In the 1890s, W.E.B. Du Bois estimated the total at about 100 million. In 1936, R. R. Kuczynski reached an estimate of just over 14.5 million. Until the late 1960s, much of the discussion surrounding the question revolved around which set of numbers—the 14 million or the 100 million range—was more accurate. In 1969, though, Philip Curtin challenged previous numbers by estimating that the total number of slaves transported to the Americas was around nine million. Curtin's estimates were released in the form of a book, *The Atlantic Slave Trade: A Census.* Curtin was soon challenged by the Nigerian historian J. E. Inikori and the West Indian scholar Walter Rodney. Both accused Curtin of underestimating the number. Inikori claimed Curtin had missed the true number by nearly 50 percent, stating that 15 million would be a more realistic appraisal. Rodney did not provide an alternative figure. In 1999 a team of researchers led by David Eltis released a CD-ROM database based on the W.E.B. Du Bois dataset at Harvard University. Including searchable data from over 26,000 slaving voyages, this disc is a powerful tool for researchers and students alike. Notably, Eltis and his fellow researchers estimate that the total number of enslaved Africans involved in the trans-Atlantic trade was around 11 million.

Certainly, the exact number of Africans forcibly brought to the New World will never be known—especially given the fact that many of the voyages that took place in the nineteenth century were illegal and were not necessarily part of the public record (we will discuss the abolition of the slave trade shortly). Still, ongoing research into the issue of the size of the Atlantic slave trade has helped provide us with considerable information regarding the demographics of the slave trade, that is, where in Africa did the captives come from and where in the New World did they go? For example, the regions of what are now southern Nigeria and western Angola seem to have borne a particularly heavy brunt during the era of the trade, supplying around four and three million captives, respectively. Similarly, Brazil and the Caribbean seem to have been the primary consumers of slaves, receiving roughly 80 percent of the total exports of human cargo. Today, ongoing research is trying to trace the relative numbers of different African ethnic groups brought to the New World. By so doing, we will be better able to understand the cultural legacy that these groups brought with them to the Americas.

African Culture in Diaspora

Not so long ago, many scholars argued that Africans had played no role in influencing the cultural development of the Americas. The Africans brought to the New World, argued scholars such as Stanley M. Elkins, were so traumatized by the experience of the middle passage that they had become "blank slates" awaiting the imprint of European and "slave" culture. Others have suggested that although Africans may have brought some sort of culture with them, it was quickly destroyed by the hostility of slave owners to all things African. More recent research, however, suggests that Africans were far more successful in carrying their culture to the Americas and have indeed had a most significant impact on the development of the settler societies of the New World. As stressed previously, the human spirit is a difficult thing to break, and no matter how torturous the middle passage was, Africans brought with them a complex set of social, economic, and political ideas that they sought to implement in the Americas.

Perhaps one simple way to look at the potential cultural impact of Africans in the Americas is simply to take another look at the numbers of Africans who came to the New World and when. By 1750, for example, some 6.5 million people had come to the Americas from the Old World. Of this total, somewhere around 80 percent were Africans. In many parts of the Americas, then, the majority of the settler population was African, not European. Even in the United States, where African Americans now comprise less than 15 percent of the total population, the average African-American bloodline has been in North America for over 200 years, whereas the average European-American's family history is roughly 100 years old.

Just what sort of cultural influence did Africans have in the New World? So much that we can only scratch the surface in the context of a textbook. This influence ranges from the foods eaten in the Americas to the music now popular throughout the globe to the way populations throughout the Americas conceive of the divine. Crops brought from Africa and popularized in the Americas include rice, okra (itself an Igbo word), and bananas. Stews such as gumbo and dishes known as "greens" also have their roots in African cuisine. With Africans serving as cooks in plantations, restaurants, and private homes throughout the Americas, it is hardly a surprise that they combined elements of African cooking with European (and Native American) fare.

African musical forms had a significant impact in the Americas. The dance known as the Samba is likely derived from an Angolan wedding dance known as the Quizomba, for example. There can be little doubt that African conceptions of rhythm had a substantial influence on European musical forms, bringing to the fore a beat that propels and guides the melody rather than simply keeping time. African music, though, goes far beyond drums and rhythm. The West African minor pentatonic scale (as opposed to the chromatic octave of "doe-ray-me . . ." found in European music) became the root of blues and jazz, which themselves greatly influenced the development of country music, rock and roll, and hip-hop. African-American gospel has deeply influenced spiritual music in the United States and other regions of the world.

African Religion in the New World

Religion is perhaps the cultural sphere in which Africans had the greatest impact in the New World. Despite the fact that the slave trade was often justified on the grounds that it converted many Africans to Christianity, an unexpected outcome was the degree to which Africans influenced the practice of Christianity or established their own religions in the Americas. It is important to remember that despite the great variety of African religions and the apparent differences between Christianity and pantheistic African religions, Africans and Europeans in the era of the slave trade actually occupied a very similar spiritual universe—one in which spirits (good and malevolent) were a reality and where humans could influence the outcome of events via manipulation of ritual practices and magic charms. Thus, it should be no surprise that the Puritans in the Massachusetts Bay Colony saw Tituba, a slave from the West Indies, as a potential manipulator of evil spirits during the famous Salem Witch Trials. Indeed, the acceptance by many European slave owners of the spiritual power of their slaves was a means by which Africans could influence and even occasionally control their owners. Witness the myriad folk beliefs of juju, hoodoo, mojo, and conjuring in the culture of the southern United States. Further, African systems of worship, which stress the role of possession by (benevolent) spirits and the active participation of the audience of worshipers have had a powerful influence on the very practice of religion in the Americas.

Africans did not only influence the practice of Christianity in the New World, though. Often they sought to transplant their own religious systems. The religions known as **Santeria** (Cuba), **Macumba, Candomble** (Brazil), and Voudou (Haiti and the southern United States) are all African religions that managed to survive in the Americas. They did so, by and large, by assuming a veil of Catholicism, wherein Catholic saints took on the characteristics of African deities. This is a process often referred to as syncretism—a combining of two or more cultural or religious traditions. It is interesting to note that in predominantly Protestant areas African religions did not fare so well—perhaps evidence of both the hostility of Protestantism to perceived "heresies" and also to the wider structural difference between Protestant Christianity and African religions. It is worth noting that religions such as Santeria are today spreading rapidly in the Americas, finding adherents among both African- and European-descended populations.

Independent African Communities in the New World

When conditions were right, Africans tried to do far more than simply reestablish elements of their cultures in the New World; they tried to establish independent communities. Often referred to as **maroons,** these communities of escaped (or perhaps self-liberated) slaves sought to create societies that were independent of European domination. Far more common than was often thought (or taught), these communities were founded throughout the Americas. No doubt they faced a number of difficulties. To be relatively safe from European raids, they often had to be established in economically marginal areas—deep in forests or high in mountains. Further, the members of such communities often had diverse backgrounds of their own, making it very unlikely that they could reestablish a society that mirrored those of Africa (though some did indeed come close). Also, most maroon communities were faced with the constant threat of European attack. **Palmares,** in northeastern Brazil, is perhaps the most famous of these independent settlements. Founded in the early 1600s and with a population that may have reached over 20,000, Palmares successfully fought off Portuguese and Dutch attacks until late in the seventeenth century. The maroons in Jamaica also were successful in holding off the British and living on their own terms for several decades. Some of these societies mixed with large numbers of Native Americans. The Seminoles in Florida, for example, were perhaps as much African as Indian. During the Seminole War of 1812–1818, one American officer wrote, "What we are facing here is really a Negro war." Occasionally, these communities were successful in gaining recognition of their independence from the European authorities. This was particularly common in Spanish holdings, such as in the case of the village San Lourenzo de Los Negros in Mexico in the eighteenth century. Perhaps the most remarkable incident was the successful revolution of the slaves of St. Dominique, who after more than a decade of rebellion, accommodation, and struggle succeeded in establishing the independent state of **Haiti** in the Caribbean, having defeated both French and British armies sent to quash the rebellion.

Diasporic Africans Back in Africa—Routes of Return

Anyone who takes a tour of one of the slave castles along the West African coast will no doubt be shown a "door of no return"—the doorway through which captives passed before being loaded onto the waiting slave ship. Although it was true that the great majority of slaves never returned to Africa, it is important to note that some did indeed survive to make it home. Most of these fortunate souls came from Brazil, where manumission was somewhat more common than elsewhere in the Americas. Also, the close trade links between Brazil and West and West-Central Africa made the return journey less expensive. Known as **Luso-Africans,** these individuals often established profitable trade links between Africa and Brazil. They were so numerous that their homes, characterized by what is known as Brazilian-style architecture, can still be seen in many port cities along the African coast. These individuals helped strengthen the cultural ties between African communities on both sides of the Atlantic.

Not all Africans made it back within a single generation, but some were able to return to the land of their ancestors. North American slaves who had gained their freedom by fighting for the British in the American Revolutionary War (something rarely taught in American history classes) were settled with deported Jamaican Maroons, first in Nova Scotia (where many froze to death or starved owing to the harsh climate) and later in Sierra Leone in West Africa, having made one of the more remarkable journeys in modern history. Similarly, during the antebellum era in the American South, free African Americans were transported to Liberia in West Africa. Sadly, in both cases, relations between these returned Africans (known as **Krio** in Sierra Leone and Americo-Liberians in Liberia) and local African populations have been poor, an animosity that has helped fuel conflicts even in the present day. Nonetheless, both Krios and Liberians played a significant role in carrying Western culture to West Africa—both in the form of education and in the spread of Christianity.

The Atlantic System and Economic Change

As we saw earlier, the Atlantic slave trade created a culturally connected world on both sides of the Atlantic. It is perhaps more obvious that it created an economically connected world, too. Who among us got out of high school without seeing a map of the "triangular trade"? These maps described a system wherein cloth from England was traded for slaves in Africa. The slaves were then sold in the Caribbean where the ships took on molasses or sugar, which they sold in the cloth-producing countries of the North Atlantic. It's all neat, tidy, and accurate to a degree, but it grossly understates the complexity of Atlantic trade. A more accurate map would be a tangle of arrows going in many directions. Africans, as we said earlier, had more to sell than just slaves—it was not until the eighteenth century that the value of the slaves exported from Africa exceeded the value of nonslave goods. Europe had more to sell than just cloth, and the Americas did far more than just import slaves and export sugar and tobacco. By the eighteenth century the Atlantic was the home to what was arguably the most dynamic economic system in the world. Goods and people traversed the Atlantic—some voluntarily, others not—in every imaginable direction. We now imagine that globalization is something new, that the fact that our sneakers all come from Asia, our beef from Brazil, our cars from Japan, and so on is something entirely novel. But a smaller-scale version of this type of globalization went on during the seventeenth and eighteenth centuries on the Atlantic. Some Africans dressed in cloth made in Europe. The workers who made that cloth got a significant portion of their daily calories from sugar grown in the Americas with African slave labor. The list could go on and on. It was a brutal system, but it was far more productive than any economy that had preceded it.

It has not escaped the notice of historians, though, that some parts of the Atlantic system fared better than did others. Most historians would accept the idea that when Africa and Europe began their encounter in the fifteenth century, they were in a state of relative economic parity. But clearly, by 1800 they were not. Europe was in the early stages of the industrial revolution, an economic transformation that would lead what is really a small peninsula of Asia to global dominance. African economies also grew, but at nowhere near the rate at which European economies grew. The sugar-producing regions of the Americas also slipped into poverty relative to Europe. What, one has to wonder, has the Atlantic system to do with the industrial transformation of Europe and the relative impoverishment of Africa?

As you may have already guessed, the answers to these questions are hotly debated, and unfortunately, we cannot offer a simple answer. Let us divide the question into two parts. First, what, if any, role did the Atlantic system play in the creation of industrial capitalism in Europe? And second, what role, if any, did the Atlantic system play in the impoverishment of Africa?

The Atlantic System and the Industrial Revolution

In 1944, Trinidadian historian Eric Williams proposed an interpretation of the Atlantic slave trade that is now known as the Williams thesis. Looking primarily at data from the Caribbean and England, Williams argued that high profits from the slave trade and the use of slaves in the plantation system created the capital that paid for the industrial revolution. In turn, the new capitalist industrial economy of the nineteenth century made the plantation system less profitable, and ultimately the owners of the factories that made the industrial revolution possible, who had an ideological as well as a practical commitment to free labor, led the effort to abolish slavery. The Williams thesis has been attacked from every imaginable direction, but still refuses to go away. It remains the starting point for any discussion of slavery and the rise of capitalism. Critics of the Williams thesis have pointed out that profits from the slave trade and the plantation system were not out of line with profits from other types of commercial or agricultural ventures. It is hard, then, to see the Atlantic system as the source of some sort of windfall that of itself triggered the growth of industrial capitalism in Europe. It is also argued that the second part of the Williams thesis is flawed, in that slavery and the plantation system continued to be profitable well into the nineteenth century and that the abolitionist movement was not led or directed by industrialists. Nonetheless, the timing is suspicious. That the industrial revolution happened first in England, a country deeply involved in the Atlantic world, would seem to require some sort of explanation.

One way that supporters of the Williams thesis have sought to reformulate his position is to focus on productivity instead of profits. And any way you look at it, the Atlantic system was productive. Sugarcane produces more calories per acre than any other crop. Under ideal conditions, an acre of sugar can produce eight million calories of food. That's a lot of chow, especially considering that it would take over four times as much land to produce the same number of calories with potatoes. Significantly, the places with the earliest industrial growth—England—for instance, also were the world's leading consumers of sugar. And sugar was consumed disproportionately by the industrial working class. As the industrial revolution took hold in England, the rate of sugar consumption went up. By the end of the nineteenth century, when Britain was the world's leading industrial power, Britain was the world's largest consumer of sugar, and sugar accounted for a sixth of the calories consumed by that nation's working class. Of course, none of that sugar was grown in England. It was all grown in the tropics, and even if it was not grown by slave labor in the late nineteenth century, slave laborers grew it during the years in which sugar made the transition from luxury product to common necessity. If coal was the fuel of the machines of the industrial revolution, then sugar was the ever-cheaper fuel of the workers in the industrial revolution—and slave labor played a role in creating that fuel.

Slave labor built other things—buildings, roads, canals, irrigation systems—all of which contributed to the wealth of the Atlantic and hence, probably, to the rise of industrial capitalism. But a direct link between money derived from the slave trade and the plantation system and the rise of capitalism remains elusive. Yet clearly, the Atlantic system was part of the context in which capitalism was born.

The Atlantic System and African Poverty

Walter Rodney, mentioned earlier in this chapter, argued that one of the reasons Africa is poor—much poorer than any other continent and certainly poorer than any other major player in the Atlantic system—is the damage done by the slave trade. Rodney and others contend that the loss of population due to the slave trade and the warfare that accompanied it, the harm done to local industries by the cheap imports that Europeans used to buy their slaves, and the reshaping of African economies to serve the slave trade set Africa on a course toward poverty from which it has not yet escaped.

Patrick Manning has refined this argument by using demographic modeling to try to judge the effect of removing 11 million people from the continent. His conclusion is that the population level stagnated and even dropped between 1750 and 1850 as a result of the Atlantic trade and only began to recover in the later nineteenth century. We now worry about excessive population growth, but for most of human history a growing population has been both a symptom and a cause of economic prosperity. For Africa to be stagnating or even losing population at a time when other parts of the world were growing rapidly—1750 is the usual date for the beginning of the modern population explosion—can only be a sign that the slave trade was economically harmful to Africa.

Not surprisingly, there is a counterargument. Critics are fond of pointing out that the British Isles lost 19 million people in the nineteenth century alone to migration. To be sure, it was voluntary migration rather than involuntary, but no one has argued that Britain was economically crippled by the loss of so many people in a single century. (Remember that the entire 500 years of the Atlantic slave trade probably took "only" 11 to 15 million people from Africa.) John Thornton, always reluctant to see Africans as helpless victims, argues that Africans were never compelled to trade in slaves. Rather, they did so for reasons that were rational and served their purposes. Working on the assumption that Africans would not do anything economically harmful to themselves, one might conclude that the slave trade cannot be blamed for African poverty. Others have countered with the argument that the slave trade was like an addiction; that even if Africans were cognizant of its harmful effects, participants in the trade were unable to stop themselves from seeking the short-term benefits the trade offered them as individuals.

And so the debate continues. Once again, we can offer no definitive answers, only a quick tour of the debate. It remains only at this point to take a look at the end of the slave trade and the effects of abolition on Africa and the Atlantic system.

Abolition of the Slave Trade

It's hard to believe, but the idea that there is something fundamentally wrong with slavery is surprisingly new. Slaves have resisted being slaves for as long as there has been slavery. But until the middle of the eighteenth century the one or two rare voices calling for an end to the institution went mostly unheard and entirely unheeded. Even former slaves, the very people whom we might expect to oppose the institution, often sought to improve their lot in the world by purchasing slaves. In ancient Rome, it was not unknown for slaves to own slaves. In the antebellum United States some freedmen owned slaves. The maroons, who resisted slavery by escaping to the forests to build their own states, raided the plantations for slaves to work their own lands. At Palmares, one of the largest maroon states in Brazil, the rule was that any slave who could capture a replacement for himself would be freed. The Luso-Africans, who returned to West Africa after gaining their freedom in

Brazil, were there as often as not to deal in slaves. In short, everyone objected to being a slave himself or herself, but slavery was so ingrained an institution for both Europeans and Africans that a world without slavery seemed unimaginable.

But then, in the middle of eighteenth century, all that began to change, not all at once and not in any one place. The first practical manifestation of this sea of change came in 1760 in Jamaica in the Coromantyn slave revolt. For the first time, slaves revolted explicitly against the institution of slavery. Thirty years later, after a bloody war of Byzantine complexity, the slaves on the island of St. Dominique finally prevailed against the whites and mulattos, and formed the state we know as Haiti. Significantly, the victors in the first successful slave revolt in the Western Hemisphere abolished the institution of slavery.

Some raise the objection, "What about the Quakers and Voltaire and all that?" It is true that before the Coromantyn revolt, John Woolman, a Quaker, published a now-famous letter in which he concluded that no Quaker could own slaves without jeopardizing his own salvation. Eventually, this became the standard doctrine of the Quakers, and it spread from them to other nonconformist faiths; Quakers would become prominent among the abolitionists. But it is a long way, almost 50 years, from objecting to slavery because it might pose an insurmountable moral challenge to the slave owner to finding the entire institution morally unacceptable because of what it does to the slaves. The Coromantyns and Haitians were not worried about their owners' spiritual well-being; they were out to put a stop to slavery—we will give them credit as the first practical abolitionists.

Their idea proved to be one with a future. Religious leaders, freed slaves, and wage labor advocates all embraced the idea. By 1787, the Society of Friends had founded an antislavery society, and soon thereafter William Wilberforce's Abolition Society founded the city of Freetown, in Sierra Leone, as a place for the repatriation of former slaves. By 1803, Denmark became the first nation in the world to outlaw the slave trade. This might seem like a bit of a hollow gesture, but the Danes—a maritime people—were involved in the trade and even controlled a few trade castles in West Africa. Great Britain and the United States outlawed the trade in 1807—the institution of slavery had been effectively illegal in Britain since 1772, though slavery remained legal in British colonies and the southern United States for decades to come.

By 1820, Britain's Royal Navy was treating most slave ships as pirates, and a huge antislave trade squadron operated out of Sierra Leone. When ships were captured with slaves on board or with equipment associated with the trade, the ship and its cargo were seized. The ship was sold and the proceeds divided among the crew. The slaves were taken to Sierra Leone, where they were put in the care of various missions that came there to attend to the needs of freed captives. The crews of the navy's antislave squadrons were paid a bounty for any slaves they recaptured and freed. Interestingly, naval officers referred to their work as slave hunting, rather than slaver hunting.

Britain also used the first decades of the nineteenth century to pressure more reluctant nations into agreeing that the slave trade was a bad thing. Sierra Leone, Britain's first West African colony, was taken as a base of operations for the antislave trade effort. Thereafter, the most common excuse for taking colonies was that it was all part of the effort to suppress the slave trade. On the surface, the abolitionist movement seems entirely noble—and slavery is indeed something one ought to oppose—but this noble cause was often used as a justification for less-than-noble causes.

There were several side effects of the British efforts to put a stop to the trade. First, it made slave running a risky business. Slave prices went up in the New World as purchasers began to pay a premium to compensate the crews of the slave ships for the risks that they accepted in running the British blockade. Slave ships no longer went from port to port seeking a few slaves here and a few there. Instead, they would pay high prices for large groups of slaves that were ready to be loaded promptly. The slavers wanted to be on their way as soon as possible.

Closing the slave trade also caused a crisis for African slave-trading states. States that had been deeply involved in selling slaves found that one of their biggest sources of revenue had dried up and that they suddenly had more slaves than they knew what to do with. Some African states adapted well to this situation; others failed to do so. In all West African states, the end of the slave trade caused political and economic upheavals, as a centuries-old trade ground to a halt—more about this in Chapter 9.

On the American side of the Atlantic, increasingly, short supplies of slaves drove up slave prices and encouraged slave owners to allow their slaves to begin to form families. This was not the result of some newfound benevolence. Rather, it reflected the need to create a self-sustaining slave population in the New World. At the same time, the number of former slaves returning to Africa increased. Sierra Leone and Liberia became centers of the abolitionist movement, but also the point of entrée for Atlantic culture in West Africa. Sierra Leoneans and Liberians created West Africa's first newspapers and secondary schools. They were also active missionaries. The first bishop of Nigeria, for instance, was **Samuel Crowther,** a Sierra Leonean.

The End of the Atlantic World

By 1850, the slave trade era was basically over. A few slave ships still slipped into Brazil and Cuba, but as a practical matter, the slave trade was done. In some ways, the Atlantic system was coming apart, too. Ever-cheaper transportation and the opening of first the Suez Canal and then the Panama Canal made goods from outside the Atlantic cheaper and more widely available. Although commerce between the countries of the Atlantic world continued to grow, the significance of that commerce was diluted by the increasing prominence of trade from outside the Atlantic. American sugar continued to come to Europe, and even now Africans come to the North America and Europe as economic migrants—a sort of semivoluntary migration.

The world that emerged from the crucible of the Atlantic in 1850 was a very different one than that of 1450. In 1450, Europe and Africa were at relative economic parity. The Americas were unknown to either Africans or Europeans. By 1850, there were huge numbers of Africans and Europeans living in the Americas, and the continent had been transformed by Old World plants, animals, and farming practices. Africa was now much poorer and less developed than Europe and was ripe for colonization. Within 50 years, most of Africa was under direct European rule.

The Atlantic Slave Trade in Global Perspective

The Atlantic slave trade has no real historical parallels. There were other slave trades from Africa, notably the trans-Saharan and Indian Ocean trades. These both lasted longer than the Atlantic trade, and at least some scholars think that more people left sub-Saharan Africa by the trans-Saharan route than by the Atlantic route. But neither of these trades removed as many people in as short a time as did the Atlantic trade. More than half of the 11 to 15 million victims of the Atlantic trade were removed from the continent in just over a century; the attendant social and demographic effects were all the more wrenching for it. By contrast, the effects of the trans-Saharan and Indian Ocean trades were spread over much longer stretches of time, and their effects, although not negligible, were less dramatic than the Atlantic trade. Furthermore, the Atlantic plantation economy was uniquely dependent on slave labor. And those laborers were exploited perhaps no more brutally than other slaves in other places, but certainly in a more profit-oriented, rationalized way than ever before.

There were other slave trades in Eurasia, though never on the scale of the Atlantic slave trade. Slave trading was common in precolonial Southeast Asia. Prisoners of war were usually enslaved, and often the purpose of war was to obtain captives. And Southeast Asia might easily have become a major source of slaves for someone, had there been a ready market for slaves nearby. But China and India have not been short of labor in their modern histories, and the Pacific is just too big to allow for convenient slave trading to the Americas. A few slaves from Southeast Asia ended up in the Cape Colony in South Africa, a rare instance of slaves being imported to Africa. In the nineteenth century there was a trade in "indentured servants" from New Guinea to northern Australia to work in the sugar industry there. Although these indentured servants were recruited in ways that seem more reminiscent of slavery than anything else, the scale of this trade was tiny by comparison to the Atlantic. In short, the Atlantic slave trade is the single largest forced-labor migration in modern history, and its social and political effects were correspondingly unique.

Useful Works on This Chapter Topic

There is a vast literature on slavery and the slave trade. For general overviews, see: *Captives as Commodities* by Lisa Lindsay (2006). *The Slave Trade: The Story of the Atlantic Slave Trade: 1440–1870,* by Hugh Thomas (1999); *The Atlantic Slave Trade* (New Approaches to the Americas), by Herbert S. Klein (1999); and *The Atlantic Slave Trade* (Problems in World History), by David Northrup (2002). For an African in the Americas see, *The African Diaspora,* by Joseph E. Harris et al. (1996); *Africanisms in American Culture* (Blacks in the Diaspora), by Joseph E. Holloway (ed.) (1991); and *Africans in the Americas: A History of the Black Diaspora,* by Michael L. Conniff and Thomas J. Davis (1993). For a very recent look at the disapora, see *Reversing Sail: A History of the African Diaspora,* by Micheal Gomez (2004). For a nuanced examination of the role of Africans in shaping the Atlantic world, see *Africa and Africans in the Making of the Atlantic World, 1400–1680,* 2nd ed., by John Thornton (1998). Two classic works on slavery and the slave trade in an Atlantic context are: *Way of Death: Merchant Capitalism and the Angolan Slave Trade 1730–1830,* by Joseph C. Miller (1996) and *The Rise and Fall of the Atlantic Plantation Complex,* by Philip Curtin (1990). Robert Harms' book *The Diligent* (2003) examines a single voyage by a slave ship in incredible detail, offering in the process a look at the financing and organization of the middle passage of the slave trade.

Chapter 9

West and West-Central Africa: 1500–1880

As discussed in the previous chapter, enslaved Africans played an important role in constructing a new Atlantic world during the period after 1500. Our examination of the transatlantic slave trade, however, has so far left some very important issues unaddressed. In particular, what was the nature of the slave trade in Africa? How important was it to the early African understanding of Europeans (and vice versa)? How did it change over time? Exactly what sort of involvement did Africans have, and why? To what degree was African involvement in the trade voluntary, or to what extent was it coerced by Europeans? What were the long-term effects of this trade on Africa in terms of the economic, political, and social development of African societies? As you might guess, the answers to these questions are highly contentious, with historians taking very different positions on the various topics. In order to shed light on these issues, this chapter will examine the setting of West and West-Central Africa at the advent of contact with Europeans and discuss the nature of that contact. Then it will examine a number of the key issues and themes in the study of the role of Africans in the transatlantic slave trade. Finally, we will focus on a number of case studies from different parts of the region as a means of providing context for these issues and themes.

The Setting: West and West-Central Africa Prior to European Contact

In the middle of the fifteenth century, when Portuguese mariners were first making their way along the coast of West and West-Central Africa, these regions were relatively sparsely populated. This is because the regions near the coast were not, at the time, terribly well suited to supporting large populations. Dense rain forests dominate much of the coastline from modern Guinea-Bissau to the Democratic Republic of the Congo. Here, heavy rain, poor soils, and dense forest canopies (which prevent sunlight from reaching the ground) all conspired to make difficult the sort of agriculture that could support large populations. As one moves inland from the coast, the rain forests give way to drier but still heavily forested regions, before eventually making the transition to more open savannah several hundred miles inland. This is not to say that it was impossible to live in the region, but it was hard work. The kinds of grains, such as millet and sorghum, that allowed populations to thrive in the savannahs did not grow well in wetter regions. Root crops, such as yams, or tree crops, such as oil palm, did, but they produced fewer calories per acre planted and produced crops that were more difficult to transport or store than grain. Innovative farmers, perhaps originally from the Niger River region, learned to cultivate rice in the tidal lowlands of modern Guinea and Sierra Leone. As discussed in Chapter 3, the spread of ironworking technology into the region over the first millennium C.E. greatly facilitated the clearing of forests for planting, but the labor required was still considerable. Hundreds or even thousands of tons of trees and undergrowth had to be cut, cleared, or burned to open a single acre to agriculture. Thin and fragile soils also prevented repeated plantings in a single location, forcing new lands to be opened up every few years. Further, the prevalence of tsetse flies in much of the forest region meant that most livestock (aside from pygmy goats and chickens) could not be kept either for food or muscle power.

All these difficulties did not make it impossible for state-level societies to survive in the forest—just very difficult. At **Igbo-Ukwu** in the region of modern southeastern Nigeria, for example, a state developed in the tenth and eleventh centuries C.E. Trade goods found at the site suggest trade links that reached not only the savannah, but even North Africa. The state of Benin developed just to the west, and survived until well into the nineteenth century. Igbo-Ukwu and Benin, however, were exceptions to the rule of states being difficult to establish in the forests prior to the sixteenth century. Indeed, they are tributes to humanity's ability to survive and thrive in difficult environments.

The forests, however, did have some redeeming factors. Certain products, such as valuable hardwoods, kola nuts, palm oil, seafood, and salt, could be had from the forests or coasts. These commodities were not only useful to those who lived there, but were also much in demand in the savannah regions to the interior. Also, particularly in West Africa, the forest regions held one of humanity's most prized items—gold. Long-distance trade flowed between the ecologically distinct regions of the forests and the savannahs, just as it did across the Sahara and along the Indian Ocean Coast. Traders from the Niger River region, often known as the Dyula (or Juula), were instrumental in establishing networks to move gold and kola from the forests to the savannahs in return for salt, copper, and other valuable trade items. Notably, African populations along the Atlantic were not nearly as linked to the ocean as were populations on the Indian Ocean coast. Unlike the "sailor's ocean" character of the Indian Ocean, the Atlantic off the African coast was and is very unfriendly. Harsh tides, unfavorable winds, and a near-total absence of natural ports all conspired to keep West and Central African populations from venturing far into the sea. Some craft went out to fish, but moving beyond sight of land was generally an accident. As a result, islands such as Fernando Pó, Príncipe, and São Tomé remained uninhabited until the coming of European ships. Local African populations did, however, develop a coastal trade that followed the complex system of lagoons along much of the West African coast, allowing for a significant local water-borne trade.

The period of the second millennium saw a general tendency toward the creation of states. In addition to Benin, a state-level society also developed in Kongo (at the mouth of the Zaire River). These populations were aided by the continuing influence of ironworking and also ongoing innovations in agriculture. Further, as populations expanded, more labor was available to clear ever-wider tracts of forest. Once the virgin forest had been cleared, subsequent use of the land was greatly facilitated, because land left fallow for a period of years was much easier to clear a second or third time around. Thus, human environmental modification of the forest regions was steadily expanding in both pace and scope.

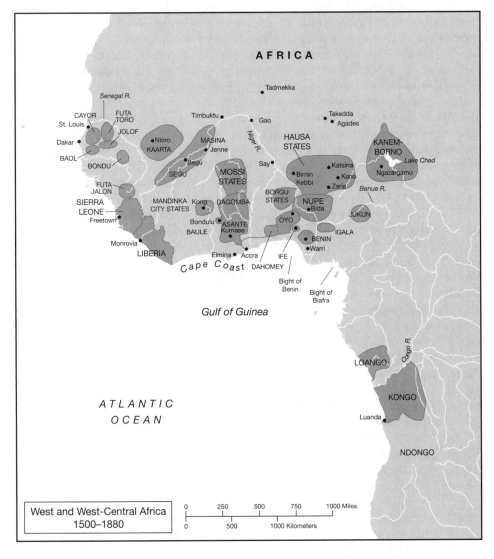

Map 9-1: West and West-Central Africa, 1500–1880

First Impressions

In the latter fifteenth century, new technologies and sea routes brought together populations that had previously interacted only through intermediaries and long-distance trade. West African gold had long made its way to Europe, but the Portuguese voyages to West and Central Africa were the first time regular person-to-person contact was established between coastal West Africans and Europeans. How exactly did these groups see and conceive of one another? Contrary to popular mythologies of "modern" or "civilized" Europeans meeting "primitive" or "barbaric" Africans, the initial contacts between Portuguese sailors and African populations were, by and large, relatively diplomatic and peaceful. Early attempts at slave raiding by the Portuguese in the Senegambia created considerable ill will, but as the Portuguese shifted to less violent methods of trade (in no small part due to the losses they suffered at the hands of African military forces), relations became more civil. Notably absent were modern notions of "race." Although the Portuguese and the various African groups with which they interacted were not oblivious to physical differences, they did not seem to put too great a value on such distinctions. Although many on both sides initially saw the others as not terribly attractive, they also soon overcame these impressions, as evidenced by numerous marriages between the groups—a time-honored approach to creating economic and political connections between far-flung peoples. Only rarely did Africans and Europeans define one another in terms of "whiteness" or "blackness," and even then the distinction held no clear implication of superiority or inferiority. Africans often defined Europeans in terms of religion—simply calling them "Christians." Along the Central West African coast, Europeans were (and still are) often referred to as mindele, which is the KiKongo/Kimbundu word for whale—a reference to the fact Europeans all arrived in whale-like ships. Other names were often quite funny. In the Yoruba-speaking region of West Africa (modern southwestern Nigeria), Europeans were dubbed oyinbo, after the white inner peel of oranges. Europeans' whiteness was thus explained in terms of their having been "peeled." In East Africa, Europeans were dubbed Mzungu (restless people) possibly because they tended to come and go incessantly, without ever settling down to stay. Interestingly, some Africans did identify European visitors in terms of class. In 1482, when a Gold Coast monarch identified as Caramansa by the Europeans (perhaps Kwamenah Ansah) received a group of expensively dressed and bejeweled Portuguese dignitaries, he stated that he was pleased to learn that not all Portuguese were as "ill dressed and foul" as those with whom he had previously interacted.

For their own part, the Portuguese were quick to define African populations in terms of local identities and political systems, seeing the populations of Benin and Kongo, for example, as just as distinct as themselves and the English. By and large, both sides simply saw the others as people. Such a perspective should not be surprising, because the state-level African societies that Europeans found it easiest to deal with had much in common with their European contemporaries. Aside from the Europeans' naval and firearms technology, there was a general technological parity between the two sides—both were preindustrial ironworking societies in which the family served as the primary economic unit. African and European states also shared similar views on political organization. Both tended toward monarchy and saw the sovereign as a representative of divine authority. Moreover, although West and West-Central African populations

This Benin bronze from the seventeenth century gives some sense of how the artist viewed the Portuguese.

were not Christian, they shared a similar spiritual universe with Europeans of the time. Africans tended to be pantheistic (believing in many aspects of the divine); this did not necessarily clash with Catholicism's emphasis on the Trinity and the spiritual role of multiple saints. Both groups believed that spirits populated the physical world and could influence human lives for good or ill and that certain humans, generally called "witches," could influence such spirits. Thus, Africans and Europeans might have seen each others' religions as different, but they were not altogether unfamiliar.

Early Relations—Religion, Trade, and Politics

What, exactly, did Europeans and Africans seek to gain from interaction with one another in the early era of contact? As one might guess, both saw opportunities for wealth and political power that might provide an advantage over their competitors or enemies. In addition, the Portuguese also had a broader cultural agenda, the expansion of Christianity.

One of the motivations of the Portuguese quest for a sea route along Africa was to outflank the Muslim states of North Africa and the Middle East, not only to gain direct access to African gold and Asian spices, but also to find the mythical kingdom of Prester John—believed to be a rich and powerful African Christian king. Since the Crusades, European Christians had hoped that an alliance with Prester John (who apparently was very long lived) would provide the Christian world with the ability to defeat the Muslims. As the Portuguese worked their way around the African coast, they searched for evidence of Prester John and his kingdom. Not finding him, they took the alternative approach of seeking to convert African populations to Christianity. In 1484, Diogo Cao left four Franciscan monks in the Kongo kingdom and also took four Kongo nobles, including the royal prince, Kasuta, back to Lisbon. They returned to Kongo in 1487, having spent three years in the Lisbon court where they studied both Portuguese and Christian theology. The Kongo ruler, Manikongo **Nzinga** a Nkuwu, then sent another delegation to Lisbon and requested that the Portuguese send specialists to train his people in Christianity and European technology. In 1491 the Portuguese sent three ships loaded with carpenters, masons, and tools to build churches in Kongo's capital.

Why did King Nzinga show such an interest in Christianity? Perhaps he was moved by Christian theology, but it seems odd that a ruler would be willing to take such steps hastily, because they threatened to disrupt the cultural equilibrium of his own society and even the legitimacy of his rule. Perhaps he sought to gain favor with the Portuguese or saw showing interest in Christianity as a way of encouraging the Portuguese to establish friendly terms of trade. Notably, the Portuguese followed a papal injunction not to trade firearms to non-Christians, so there were certain advantages to adopting Christianity. It is also possible that he thought showing an interest in Christianity would encourage the Portuguese to support Kongo against its enemies. Evidence does seem to bear out this latter possibility. In 1491, a rebellion broke out in the north of Kongo, and at King Nzinga's request, Portuguese troops joined Kongo forces to put down the revolt. Marching behind a banner of the cross, the Portuguese troops helped soundly defeat the rebels. Whether Nzinga was more impressed by the advantages of having Portuguese allies or by the power of the Christian god is not clear, but on Christmas day after the battle, he, the queen, the prince, and several other Kongo nobles converted to Christianity and took Christian names, becoming King Joao, Queen Eleanor, and Prince Afonso. Such a move was not without costs, however. When King Joao died in 1506, a civil war broke out between those who sought to limit Portuguese influence and those who embraced it. The isolationists were defeated by the forces of Afonso, who established himself as king and sought to strengthen ties to Portugal, sending his son Henrique to Lisbon and Rome. Henrique returned in 1521 as sub-Saharan Africa's first Catholic bishop. The royal family of Kongo had cast their lot in favor of international trade and Christianity. As we shall later see, however, such choices did not guarantee peace or stability.

The case of Kongo is in many ways unique. Although the Portuguese often sought to establish missions where they founded trading posts, they were generally unsuccessful in converting the locals to Christianity. The port town of Warri, in southern Nigeria, saw a similar process of conversion of the local nobility, but it was

King Afonso of Kongo receiving a European delegation.

a single town and of limited political influence in the region. The oba of Benin showed some interest in Christianity, but appears largely to have been trying to curry Portuguese favor, because he never converted. In general, European attempts to convert Africans were unsuccessful and would remain that way until the nineteenth century.

If the Portuguese were unsuccessful in spreading Christianity, they were somewhat more successful when it came to trade. Initially, the Portugese found themselves at a disadvantage in that they had little to sell that was in demand along the African coast—a problem they would also encounter when they finally reached India and China. European textiles, generally made of wool, were not terribly attractive to African buyers, who preferred cloth made of raffia, cotton, or silk. Europeans could offer iron or copper in trade, but the former was often inferior to the high-grade iron and even steel being produced by African smelters and smiths. For example, a British trader attempting to find a market for his iron on the Gambia River in 1620 remarked, "Whereas we thought our iron would have been greedily desired, we found it not so." Initially, Europeans had little of their own to offer in return for the gold, ivory, and spices they sought. As we shall later see, by the latter eighteenth century European iron and trade goods were much in demand in Africa, and the question of why this situation changed is central to our understanding of the period and the impact of the slave trade in Africa.

There were some things that Africans desired. Europeans found good markets for distilled alcohol, and many Africans sought access to firearms, a trade that would grow substantially in importance during the seventeenth and eighteenth centuries.

Textiles from India and cowrie shells (used by many West African states as currency) from the Maldive Islands in the Indian Ocean were also very much in demand, though the long voyages necessary to acquire such goods meant that prices were high, and Portuguese profits for these items relatively low. As a result, the Portuguese found themselves trading between African markets rather than trading directly with Africans. That is, the Portuguese took advantage of their maritime technology to transport goods between African states and reaped the profits of buying low and selling high. The Portuguese were the truck drivers of the early long-distance trade between West and West-Central Africa. In particular, the Portuguese transported slaves and cloth from Kongo and Benin and traded them for gold in the Akan-speaking region that came to be known as the Gold Coast, where slave labor was crucial to clearing land for farming and to gold mining. Interestingly, Akan custom forbade free persons to mine gold, either because of the danger involved or because restricting the process to slave labor meant that only the wealthy could invest in the process. The demand was such that from 1510 to 1540, the Portuguese kept four ships in service just to transport slaves from Kongo to the Gold Coast (often by way of their own newly established sugar plantations on São Tomé). So important was the new gold trade that the Portuguese built the first permanent European trading post in West Africa in 1482 and dubbed it "El Mina"—the mine.

The first century or so of European contact with West and West-Central Africa had a significant impact on African history. For the first time, Europeans had a real influence over the flow and nature of trade. In particular, rather than flowing north across the Sahara, gold increasingly moved south to new trade centers such as El Mina. For gold producers in the West African forest, this meant higher prices for their product, because transport to the coast was easier and involved fewer intermediaries. Such a shift, however, was a huge blow to the wealth of savannah states such as Songhai and was advantageous to states such as Jolof in the Senegambia, which were closer to the coast and the gold-producing regions. The Dyula, who had likely helped develop the gold trade, now had to travel to the coast to bargain for gold—and had to do so in competition with Europeans who threatened to cut them out of the loop. Such was the increasingly competitive nature of trade in this newly global era.

African and European interaction during the first century of contact also led to the creation of a new ethnic population along the African coastal regions—Afro-Europeans. Despite initial notions that the "other folks" were not terribly attractive, Europeans and Africans apparently overcame (or came to appreciate) such differences and in many cases settled down to establish families. For example, in 1571 the Portuguese sent 600 troops to help Kongo repulse an invasion by the Jaga from the east. After helping defeat the invaders, most of the Portuguese troops chose to remain in Kongo, where they married into Kongo families and established themselves as traders. Similar marriages took place (usually on a smaller scale) between Portuguese, English, French, and Dutch traders and Africans elsewhere along the coast. In many cases, the resulting Afro-European families became wealthy and important traders who benefitted from their position as cultural and economic intermediaries and who shared in, but were also slightly distant from, each culture.

Another important change was that the European trade in slaves to the forest region not only facilitated the mining of gold, but also provided labor to help clear land and open it for agriculture—thus expanding the ability of the forests to support larger populations. This was particularly important in combination with the introduction of New World crops to West and West-Central Africa. From Brazil, the Portuguese introduced two crops that would radically change the course of African history—manioc and maize. **Manioc** (also known as cassava) is a large root crop from South America. It grows well in forest soils and requires little light to thrive. Manioc can be left in the ground until needed, making it a flexible crop in terms of harvest and labor demands. Although not particularly nutritious, it produces a remarkable number of calories per acre. The similarity of growing techniques to native yams helped manioc to be adopted by forest populations, although they first had to learn techniques for removing the root's lethal content of prussic acid before eating. Today, you can hardly shake a stick without hitting manioc in West and West-Central Africa. Like potatoes in much of Europe, it was a foreign crop that eventually became a staple of life and culture. Maize (corn) also had a significant impact. Although not quite as easy to grow in the forest, maize grows very quickly and can produce considerable amounts of food per acre. Together, manioc and maize revolutionized food production in the forest zones. Such an explosion in food production was closely followed by a growth in population and, in many places, the rise of state-level political systems. Now there was more than enough food to take away from people to feed a ruling class. As we shall see, the period from the seventeenth century onward saw the rise of numerous state systems in the forest region. For good or ill, the forests of West and West-Central Africa, which had previously struggled to support large populations, were now open to human conquest.

Africa Transformed? Africa and the Atlantic Slave Trade

By the advent of the seventeenth century, the nature of European trade in Africa was beginning to change. Less and less were commodities such as textiles, spices, and precious gold being traded out of Africa, and increasingly Europeans sought a single commodity—human beings. During the 1600s, up to around 10,000 people per year were transported to the Americas as slaves. By the early eighteenth century, the volume of the trade was expanding, and within the first three decades of the 1700s it grew by more than 400 percent. By the latter 1700s and early 1800s, the trade had peaked at around 100,000 individuals per year. As seen in the previous chapter, this new trade fed the labor demand created by the rise of a plantation economy in the New World, and Africans possessed the knowledge and disease resistance that unfortunately made them the most successful population for this harsh system of production. Behind the transport of 11 million or more Africans from the continent over the period from 1600 to 1850 lies one of the most contentious issues in African studies: What exactly was the role that African states and traders played as suppliers to the Atlantic slave trade, and to what extent was their role voluntary? After examining this issue, the chapter will also examine the structure of the slave trade in Africa and the possible long-term impact of that trade.

The answers to the preceding questions vary widely, depending on who you ask. Some parties deny that Africans were involved in the slave trade except as captives and victims. On the opposite extreme are those who say that some Africans were willing and even enthusiastic participants in the trade. In between lie perspectives that stress, to varying degrees, the coercive nature of the new global economy and the slave trade itself, which made it very difficult for anyone—European or African—to seek inclusion in the new Atlantic economy without in some way being affiliated with it. As we shall see, the African side of the Atlantic slave trade was a combination of economic, political, and cultural forces that ebbed and flowed over time in a complex system of interactions that defies easy classification or moralizing.

For many, particularly those of the Afrocentric perspective, the idea of Africans being willing participants in the slave trade is unthinkable. Indeed, rather than "slave trade," these observers described the process of enslavement in Africa as the "slave raid." From this point of view, because of a shared racial and cultural identity, Africans would never willingly force other Africans into slavery. Rather, the entire process of enslavement was undertaken by heavily armed Europeans who utilized their technological superiority to capture their African victims. Images, such as the famous scene of Kunta Kinte's capture by Europeans in the miniseries *Roots* have reinforced this popular belief. Those familiar with the actual historical record, however, find this notion deeply flawed in terms of its assumptions of both African unity and helplessness. The general absence of racial identity on the part of African and European traders also meant a relative absence of African identity. In such a setting, there was as yet little or no idea of "being African." Rather, inhabitants of Africa identified themselves in terms of local ethnic, political, or religious groups and saw themselves as more or less distinct from "other" African populations—just as European ethnic and national groups were more than capable of defining themselves as distinct from other white or European populations. As has previously been argued, it is very important not to project our modern notions of race and identity back onto historical populations and circumstances. Thus, Kongolese leaders were more than willing to take Portuguese allies against fellow African rebels or invaders and sell those captured into slavery elsewhere in Africa.

Similarly, some stress that it was European technology that defined the "slave raid." This notion suggests that superior technology in the form of firearms and artillery gave Europeans free rein to seek out and capture slaves in Africa. Proponents of this theory often point to the heavily fortified trading castles of the Gold Coast as an example of how Europeans used military might to dominate and enslave African populations. Again, however, the historical evidence does not bear out this argument. There can be no doubt that in the early days of contact with West Africa, Europeans did attempt to raid for slaves. Lancarote de Lagos did nothing for the reputation of Europeans when, as one of the first Western sailors to reach the Senegal River in 1444, he and his crew promptly captured a group of locals and enslaved them. In the fifteenth and early sixteenth centuries, there were many such raids. But Europeans soon found such actions to be not only dangerous, but also counterproductive to their (then) long-term goals of establishing trade and gaining converts to Christianity. Slave raids often met disaster. For example, in 1446 a Portuguese ship landed a party of slave raiders, only to be promptly attacked by locals who drove them off with heavy losses. Another Portuguese ship lost most of its crew during a slave raid near the island of **Goree** in 1447. Otherwise peaceful trading voyages suffered from the bad reputation created by Europeans who raided for slaves. In 1455, an Italian sailor named Cadamosto on a Portuguese ship described being attacked as they sailed up the Gambia River. The local population had heard of Portuguese slave raids and was clearly taking no chances. Only after considerable effort was the ship's crew able to prove their peaceful intentions. African vessels may not have been suited to the high seas, but on inland waters they were far quicker and more maneuverable than European ships. As for the European trading forts, they tended to be limited to the region of the Gold Coast—with the specific goal of protecting the gold trade from other European competitors. In fact, these castles were designed to defend against attack from the sea much more than from the land, because European traders were aware that the success of such trading posts depended on local African support. Africans always had the option to boycott or even move away from such a trading post if they so desired. Finally, Africans proved their ability to storm such fortresses when they so desired. For example, the Ga overwhelmed the Portuguese castle at Accra in 1578.

Such events stress that Europeans had no overwhelming advantage over local populations. Firearms and cannons were certainly more dangerous than the weapons common to most African combatants at the time, but their effectiveness was limited by fairly short range, poor accuracy, low rates of fire, and the fact that in the sixteenth century, matchlock-style firearms were nearly useless in the rain. Indeed, in the fifteenth and sixteenth centuries, most Portuguese soldiers carried crossbows and javelins rather than firearms. Similarly, European raiders who attempted to launch raids on their own were almost certain to be outnumbered and have a very poor command of local geography. In the nineteenth century, Europeans would eventually gain the sort of technological advantage that would give them a free hand in competition against most African adversaries (see Chapter 13). Such was most certainly not the case prior to the mid-1800s. Further, the disease environment in West and West-Central Africa was very unfriendly to Europeans who bore little or no natural resistance to malaria and yellow fever. Death rates for Europeans who settled in Africa during the period were well over 60 percent per year. Aside from a few sturdy (or perhaps lucky) souls, most Europeans preferred to remain offshore.

If the historical evidence identifies many African traders and states as participants who enslaved and sold human beings, the question remains of exactly why Africans would be involved in such a thing. There is an all-too-common tendency for those who learn of African involvement in the trade to react either with a certain amount of satisfaction (a sort of "Aha! I knew Europeans weren't the only ones!" response) or even disgust and resentment (more of a "How could they?" reaction). Here, perhaps, it is best to reflect on the fact that Africans, just like anyone else, were subject to a great range of human desires—whether for wealth, status, power, or vengeance. In different settings, each of these motivations could encourage participation in the slave trade. For some African historians, this aspect of "African agency" is key to understanding the Atlantic slave trade. Rather than Africans being victims, this perspective argues that many simply saw the trade in slaves as a way to enrich, empower, or even defend themselves.

Voices from African History: **An Account of the Slave Trade in Africa**

"They then came to us in the reeds, and the very first salute I had from them was a violent blow on the back part of the head with the fore part of a gun, and at the same time a grasp round the neck. I then had a rope put about my neck, as had all the women in the thicket with me, and we were immediately led to my father, who was likewise pinioned and haltered for leading. In this condition we were all led to the camp. The women and myself being pretty submissive, had tolerable treatment from the enemy, while my father was closely interrogated respecting his money which they knew he must have. But as he gave them no account of it, he was instantly cut and pounded on his body with great inhumanity, that he might be induced by the torture he suffered to make the discovery. I saw him while he was thus tortured to death. The shocking scene is to this day fresh in my mind, and I have often been overcome while thinking on it. . . .

The army of the enemy was large, I should suppose consisting of about six thousand men. The enemy had remarkable success in destroying the country wherever they went. For as far as they had penetrated, they laid the habitations waste and captured the people. The distance they had now brought me was about four hundred miles. All the march I had very hard tasks imposed on me, which I must perform on pain of punishment. I was obliged to carry on my head a large flat stone used for grinding our corn, weighing as I should suppose, as much as twenty-five pounds; besides victuals, mat and cooking utensils.

They then went on to the next district which was contiguous to the sea, called in Africa, Anamaboo. The enemies provisions were then almost spent, as well as their strength. The inhabitants knowing what conduct they had pursued, and what were their present intentions, improve the favorable opportunity, attacked them, and took enemy, prisoners, flocks and all their effects. I was then taken a second time. All of us were then put into the castle [a European slave trading post], and kept for market. On a certain time I and other prisoners were put on board a canoe, under our master, and rowed away to a vessel belonging to Rhode Island. While we were going to the vessel, our master told us all to appear to the best possible advantage for sale. I was bought on board by one Robert Mumford, steward of said vessel, for four gallons of rum, and a piece of calico, and called Venture, on account of his having purchased me with his own private venture. Thus I came by my name. All the slaves that were bought for that vessel's cargo were two hundred and sixty."

Venture Smith, *A Narrative of the Life and Adventures of Venture, A Native of Africa* (New London, CT, 1798; expanded ed., Hamden, CT, 1896)

Critical to this particular argument are some underlying assumptions. First, slavery was already well known in Africa. Thus, mechanisms for creating slaves (whether through warfare, debt, or using slavery as a punishment for certain crimes) were already in place, as were systems for transporting and selling slaves. Many scholars point out that most African societies practiced slavery to some degree (although as discussed in the last chapter, slavery in Africa tended to be far less harsh than that practiced in the Americas). Many parts of Africa, particularly West Africa, also sold slaves into the trans-Saharan slave trade—with perhaps five to seven thousand individuals being forced to make the perilous desert crossing each year. According to this argument, Africans and Europeans were not doing anything particularly new in capturing, trading, and transporting slaves; they were simply changing the flow of that trade. As we saw in Chapter 8, likely the strongest exponent of this theory is John Thornton, whose book *Africa and Africans in the Making of the Atlantic World* argues that rather than being victimized in the transatlantic slave trade, many Africans were active participants in shaping the way the trade developed. Thornton cites that African traders and rulers were often able to dictate not only the price of slaves, but often where and how the transactions took place. Some may see this perspective as empowering Africans by showing that African elites were in control of their own destiny (if not also in control of the destiny of those they helped enslave). Others, such as the late Walter Rodney, saw such arguments as an attempt to shift the blame for the slave trade to the victims themselves.

Taking, for the moment at least, the idea that some or even many Africans were willing participants in the transatlantic slave trade, what exactly was it that they sought to gain? Clearly, part of the answer is wealth. As Europeans expanded their role as agents of global trade, they were able to offer more and more of what potential buyers wanted. Among the most popular trade goods exchanged for enslaved persons in Africa were cloth (initially from India, North Africa, and China), distilled spirits such as rum, iron and copper bars, beads, cowrie shells, and guns. Previously, many observers chose to argue that Africans were duped into trading slaves for baubles and low-quality goods. More careful examination of the evidence, however, suggests that Africans very quickly came to develop a keen eye for what goods were valuable and what were not—or even to define the very nature of value itself. Cowrie shells, for example, accounted for nearly one-third of the value of imports into West Africa from the mid-seventeenth to the early eighteenth century. At first, this might seem to have been a great deal for the Europeans, who got to trade a bunch of shells for their human cargos. It may be surprising to readers that Europeans hated having to deal in cowries, which had to come all the way from the Maldive Islands in the Indian Ocean (a considerable departure from the oversimplified model of "triangular trade" so often taught in schools) and thus were not terribly profitable. Firearms, too, represented a comparatively low-value trade item for Europeans, offering a profit of around 130 percent, as opposed to textiles, which averaged a profit of around 220 percent. African demand thus meant that Europeans who wished to trade successfully had to trade in firearms, a fact lamented by a Dutch trader named Bosman, who around 1700 complained that the trade in firearms was undercutting what military advantage Europeans held over Africans. He concluded, however, that African demand and competition between Europeans made it impossible to regulate the trade in firearms.

The goods gained from the trade in slaves could obviously be resold by traders and rulers as a means of gaining further profit, but they appear to have had other uses as well. Goods garnered through international trade were scarcer and thus often more prestigious, making them all the more valuable as a means of rewarding or attracting loyal followers. Many African political systems demanded that those in power (patrons) reward their followers (clients) with gifts or access to wealth via trade. The clients, in turn, supplied labor or political support to the patron. For political elites, then, the slave trade was a means by which they could increase their legitimacy among supporters or even expand that base of political support. Thus, it was not merely greed for material wealth, as might be expected in a capitalist society, but rather the role of material goods in securing political influence that made participation in the slave trade desirable or even necessary for African rulers.

Some scholars challenge the idea that African participation in the export slave trade was purely economic, that is, being undertaken only because slaves were a source of wealth or power. These scholars stress that the export of slaves was itself a political act. The enslaved, then, were being deported, rather than simply exported. According to this argument, following a war or internal power struggle, victors were faced with how to incorporate the vanquished parties into their society. For example, the obas (kings) of Benin, who generally followed a policy of refusing to take part in the slave trade, occasionally required that European traders purchase groups of political prisoners as a precondition to trade in other goods. Notably, such a motivation had important gender implications. Women and children could be incorporated into lineage structures as wives and new family members via marriage—made all the more possible by African systems of polygyny. Indeed, some scholars argue that such a dynamic not only built on but ultimately reinforced the institution of polygamy in many African societies. Powerful men could thus have many wives and more potential supporters from the expanded family group. Men, however, posed a greater problem because there was no easy way to incorporate them as subservient members of lineage groups. Thus, these potentially troublesome former adversaries were conveniently disposed of in the transatlantic trade. According to this argument, the heavy bias toward males in the Atlantic slave trade was as much a matter of African as it was European preference.

Firearms represent a particularly complex aspect of the slave trade and highlight the tricky nature of historical causation. Guns could certainly be resold as a valuable trade good or distributed to followers as a reward, but also had value in their role as weapons of deadly force. Rulers or traders who gained access to large quantities of firearms (especially as technological advances such as the flintlock made firearms more effective) could expand their power based not only on their ability to command support, but also via their ability to use the threat or reality of the new technology to command submission from others. Interestingly, some African states, such as Dahomey and Asante, forbade the export of guns from their territories. Clearly the rulers of these states realized that by monopolizing the trade in firearms, they were gaining an advantage over those neighbors who had fewer or who lacked such weapons altogether.

The role of firearms lies at the crux of one of the critical debates over the nature of African involvement in the transatlantic slave trade. Although scholars such as Thornton see African agency as defining the character of the slave trade out of Africa, others argue European influence ultimately created the trade and also defined the nature of the trade even in Africa itself. First, such scholars stress that it was Europeans who created the demand. Africans may have had a slave trade and slaves, but not to the degree that was created by the transatlantic slave trade. These scholars, such as Paul Lovejoy, argue that the Atlantic market for slaves had such a profound impact that it transformed Africa economically, politically, and socially. Critical to this debate is the issue of the role of guns in Africa. Did access to firearms simply allow African states to expand their militaries as they also expanded their economic power? Or did the introduction of some 20 million guns as trade items into Africa between 1600 and 1850 create political chaos, which itself led to higher rates of enslavement? Notably, the proponents of the "gun-slave cycle," as it is often known, do not necessarily see Europeans as dumping guns on Africa to create slavery. As we have already seen, Europeans often preferred other more profitable trade goods. Nonetheless, these scholars believe that the trade in firearms both created conflict and undermined the authority of African rulers—either by giving challengers a means of unseating legitimate heads of state or by tempting rulers to use force as a means of maintaining power, rather than seeking to maintain the goodwill of their subjects. Critical to this argument is the assertion that the only reliable way to acquire firearms was through the slave trade. Groups or states that embraced the slave trade gained power via access to firearms. Those who did not or could not engage in the slave trade, whether for moral or structural reasons, were soon at a military disadvantage and were all the more likely to wind up as slaves themselves. From this perspective, the very nature of the slave trade created a catch-22 for Africans. Participation in the slave trade was thus essential, even if the ultimate goal was simply to acquire firearms to defend yourself against conquest and potential enslavement.

Some scholars challenge the notion of a gun-slave cycle. Thornton, for example, sees the firearms of the sixteenth through eighteenth centuries as too inaccurate and unreliable to have any real impact. Indeed, Thornton attacks the idea that the introduction of guns in any way destabilized the balance of power among African groups and states. Other scholars, such as Davidson, Lovejoy, and Inikori, see a very different impact. For them, the introduction of firearms, especially from the latter seventeenth century onward, increasingly destabilized regions in which the slave trade was prevalent. Even if the firearms of the era were less lethal than those to come, they were effective in terms of being easy to learn to use, and they had a powerful psychological impact due to the noise and the fright of being harmed from a distance. Davidson suggests a cycle wherein firearms were introduced, slave trading became increasingly rife, and wide-scale wars broke out. Some suggest that a balance of power tended to reassert itself once guns became common enough that everyone had them, but that the frontier of slaving and conflict then simply moved deeper into the African hinterland, beginning the cycle anew. Some academics see such conflict as leading to state creation and consolidation under a new political class whose legitimacy was primarily based on military prowess, either in terms of successfully carrying out conquests or being able to defend against attack. An increasing reliance on heavily fortified towns in some regions reflects this insecurity. Although perhaps leading to a certain form of stability, the trend toward militarization was a move away from political systems in which legitimacy was based on mass support. Lovejoy paints an even more dismal picture, arguing that one cannot even claim that true states were being created during the peak of the slave trade in the latter eighteenth century, seeing instead a spread of "warlordism."

Scholars who see the era of the slave trade in terms of dislocation and chaos also stress that the very means of acquiring slaves were destabilizing to societies. Whether through warfare, kidnaping, or the use of the enslavement as a punishment for crimes, all these elements came together to create an environment in which populations were overwhelmed by insecurity. Perhaps this perspective is best summed up by the Asante proverb, "If you have no master, someone will catch you and sell you for what you are worth." Security in such a time meant being attached to someone who could protect you, but such a centralization of authority did not make for benevolent political and social relations. Reactions to such insecurity could take many forms. A political response could take the form of centralizing power around those who could offer protection. Other scholars have identified increased fears of witchcraft and the need for spiritual (as well as military) protection as a natural outcome of such a period of insecurity. Such an outcome would be similar to the witchcraft panics that swept Europe during the social upheavals and conflicts of the Reformation. Other social changes could take place at the structural level. As discussed before, for either political or economic reasons, men were far more likely to be deported/exported into the transatlantic slave trade, yet women and children could be incorporated into lineage structures as wives and new family members via marriage. This meant that many slave-trading regions experienced the development of considerable gender imbalances, with women in some cases outnumbering men by 2:1. Similarly, such conditions might have encouraged earlier marriage, rather than having individuals wait until their later twenties or even thirties. Other scholars have stressed that such a shift in gender demographics may also have radically changed women's roles within some regions, requiring women to provide the bulk of labor in such areas as agriculture and even retail trade.

Regional Developments in the Era of the Slave Trade

So far, the discussion has largely focused on the broad thematic issues of the transatlantic slave trade in African history. To help place these themes in somewhat more specific context, some case studies of different regions will be considered. A number of these states or subregions have already been identified, but will be examined in greater detail at this point.

This chapter has already touched briefly on the subject of the Kongo kingdom as a rare example of the spread of Christianity in sub-Saharan Africa in the fifteenth and sixteenth centuries. There is much more to the kingdom of Kongo and the history of Central Africa, however. Kongo's origins extend back to the late fourteenth century, when a series of treaties and conquests among the local Kikongo-speaking population carved out a state near the mouth of the Congo River. By the latter fifteenth century, Kongo had taken advantage of its trade position on the river to expand and control some 250 miles of coastline and a similar distance into the interior. Its population is estimated to have reached nearly half a million, no small achievement for a forest state during that period. Kongo had a common currency in the form of Nzimbu shells (being impossible to counterfeit, shells actually make excellent standards of currency), and a comprehensive system of rotating regional markets that facilitated trade within the kingdom. Rival coastal states such as Loango to the north and Ndongo to the south and the inland state of Tio along the Congo River to the northeast were in competition with Kongo for local trade and influence.

In this situation, the Kongo decision to form an alliance with the Portuguese makes a certain amount of sense. Kongo found an outlet for trade in textiles, copper, ivory, and slaves and gained access to goods imported by the Portuguese, such as European spirits and textiles from Asia. As we have seen, the Portuguese also threw their military influence behind their new allies in Kongo, first against rebels in the north and later, in the mid-sixteenth century, against the forces of the "Jaga" who invaded from the east, threatening the very survival of the Kongo state. Only with considerable difficulty was the Kongo–Portuguese alliance able to hold off the Jaga, who grew in importance in controlling the trade to Central Africa's interior, along with other groups such as the Lunda.

While advantageous for much of the early sixteenth century, the Kongo investment in the new international system came at some cost. Competition with Loango and Ndongo led to expanded conflict for slaves and even the enslavement of many Kongolese subjects, a fact lamented by King Afonso to the Portuguese in 1526. Further, as time passed, the economies of the region increasingly came to be focused on the slave trade. In addition to warfare against neighbors, Central African states often turned to acquiring slaves through internal taxation and as a form of punishment (known as judicial enslavement) to meet the demands of the Atlantic trade in this generally sparsely populated region. Trade routes from the interior increasingly transported slaves, with complex systems of depots and slave caravans bringing the captives from as far as 2,500 miles to the interior. The system of slave caravans was likely every bit as torturous as the middle passage across the Atlantic. Moving across difficult territory, bound together with rough and heavy shackles, the enslaved often marched miles per day and passed their nights exposed to the elements for months at a time before reaching the coast. Worse, they were often required to carry their own provisions and perhaps secondary trade goods such as copper or ivory for the greater profit of the traders. Less well known than the middle passage, this "**continental passage**" no doubt accounted for a great deal of human suffering and death.

The Portuguese did not limit their interaction to Kongo, however. Around 1580, they invaded the Ndongo state to the south (in modern Angola). Though their attempts to penetrate beyond the coast met with failure (from a combination of military defeats and sickness), they were able to establish a small coastal colony at Luanda. Through an alliance with the interior Kasanje state, the Portuguese were able to undermine Ndongo. In 1618, the king of Ndongo died and was succeeded in power by the Princess **Njinga.** Interestingly, the Ndongo had no tradition of female sovereigns, and Njinga dressed as a male while serving as king—often surrounded by male "consorts" dressed as women. No pacifist, Njinga invaded and conquered the nearby kingdom of Matamba in the 1620s. Matamba itself had a tradition of female rule, and Njinga settled easily into the role. Indeed, Njinga is a fine example of pragmatism in a time of increasing political complexity and insecurity. In 1641, she sided with the Dutch when they invaded Angola and challenged the Portuguese position there. With the defeat of the Dutch (largely thanks to Portuguese troops from Brazil), however, Njinga signed a treaty with the Portuguese and allowed the introduction of missionaries into her kingdom. Involved in the slave trade, her state utilized Lunda traders to export captives to the coast. Relying on military savvy as well as careful diplomatic maneuvers, Njinga maintained her position and her state's independence until her death in 1663. Njinga is a fine example of the complexity of the era's historical legacy. For some she is an early African "nationalist" who resisted European encroachment. Some see her as a protofeminist, and still others see her as an opportunist who willingly involved her state in the slave trade as a means of gaining power. Some may even see her as all three.

Njinga fared better than her neighbors and rivals in Kongo. In 1665, the Portuguese turned on their former allies and invaded Kongo. As in Angola, however, their initial successes were short lived, and they were ultimately defeated. The Kongolese king was killed, however, at the battle of Ambuila, and this set off a dynastic dispute that developed into civil war. No single claimant to the throne was able to consolidate power, and by 1710 the Kongo state had disintegrated. The only victors in the conflict were slave traders (European and African), who benefited from the strife in the form of a boost in local slave exports during the struggle. Through the early nineteenth century, the Central African region would remain one of the main providers of slaves for the growing Atlantic economy. Joe Miller, in his book *Way of Death: Merchant Capital and the Angolan Slave Trade,* uses the metaphor of a tidal wave to describe the influence of the Atlantic trade on the region during the latter era of the slave trade:

> By the middle third of the nineteenth century, the wave had tumbled populations all the way to the center of the continent. There it rose to towering heights of chaos. . . . Behind it, toward the Atlantic to the west, the turbulence subsided into relatively still demographic pools where quiet-flowing currents of reproduction and debt carried off most of the people sent into slavery, and where only eddies of periodic succession struggles and banditry from the distant sweeping tide continued to disturb the calm surface of politics.

West Africa's experience with the slave trade is both similar to and distinct from the case of Central Africa. With a longer coastline and a larger interior population, no single part of West Africa, save perhaps the Bights of Benin and Biafra, would suffer such a high per capita incidence of enslavement. Also, although the human trade out of Central Africa grew over the course of the centuries of the Atlantic slave trade, the trade from West Africa tended to shift from region to region as the supply and demand of slaves shifted according to local political conditions. For example, the Senegambia, which supplied a relatively large number of slaves in the sixteenth and early seventeenth centuries, declined in importance as a slave provider over time. The Gold Coast was a net importer of slaves until the mid-1600s, and did not become a major supplier until the mid-1700s, when the Bight of Biafra also became a major supplier. Only the Bight of Benin region was a consistent supplier of slaves from the seventeenth through the early nineteenth centuries.

Though it is clear populations in the West African forest grew considerably in the era after 1500, little is really known about the origins of the region's societies and states. Populations appear to have originally moved in from the savannah regions in a series of migrations at different places and points in time. Oral histories of the region generally fail to provide precise information about origins, though they do often point to relationships between groups. For example, both the Kingdom of Oyo and the Kingdom of Benin claim to have been founded by Oranmiyan, a son of the "first human," **Oduduwa.** Thus, even though Ife is Yoruba-speaking and Benin Edo-speaking, it is clear that both regions at one point interacted or shared a similar point of origin.

As previously noted, the early interactions between West African populations and Europeans occurred prior to the advent of the transatlantic slave trade. In Warri and Benin, in the southern region of what is now Nigeria, the Portuguese sought to establish multifaceted trade and encouraged the adoption of Christianity by these African polities—meeting far more success in Warri than in Benin. Farther west, the Portuguese established the trade fort of El Mina in the region that would become known as the "Gold Coast," trading slaves and cloth from Kongo and Benin for gold. Interestingly, Benin withdrew from the trade in slaves in 1516 when the ruling oba (king) banned the trade. Why would the oba make such a decision when other rulers, such as Afonso of Kongo, saw it as a source of advantage? Like so many things in history, the absolute truth is hard to determine. The origins of the state extend back to the Ogosi dynasty and the centralization of power undertaken by Oba Ewedo in the latter thirteenth century. By the fifteenth century, Benin was a very stable and wealthy kingdom. Perhaps nothing expresses the grandeur and power of Benin quite like royal sponsorship for the manufacture of outstanding works of art in the form of the Benin bronzes. Cast using a sophisticated "lost wax" system, these substantial artworks were made with copper imported all the way from the Sahara desert, a fact that reflects Benin's integration into Africa's preexisting long-distance trade networks. Further, at the time Benin had few real competitors for power in the region, perhaps making the oba less desperate for Portuguese allies or firearms. A substantial manufacturing industry in cloth (controlled by female weavers), along with additional trade in ivory, beads, and pepper, provided a diverse line of products very much in demand from European traders. Such options initially provided Benin merchants with considerable leverage in dealings with European traders. Indeed, Benin saw a general period of economic and military growth in the latter fifteenth and sixteenth centuries. By the end of the 1600s, however, Benin's products were less in demand, as Europeans found other producers for products or, in the case of pepper, increasingly produced it for themselves on American plantations. Similarly, other neighboring states such as Oyo and Nupe were rising in power. In the 1700s, Benin reopened the trade in slaves, though it never became a major supplier in the market.

To the west of Benin, three states represent very different responses to the reality of the slave trade. These states are **Dahomey,** Oyo, and **Asante.** In particular, both Dahomey and Oyo are often used as examples of African states that willingly took part in, and profited from, the transatlantic slave trade. Both were initially located to the north of the rain forest region, with Dahomey in the forest edge and Oyo more oriented to the open savannah. Beginning in the early 1600s, each took advantage of the demand for slaves to expand military power. Interestingly, they took two different approaches to this common goal. Dahomey used the profits from the slave trade to invest in firearms. Access to these new weapons not only expanded the power of Dahomey in the region, but also reputedly let the obas of Dahomey centralize their authority at the expense of traditional heads of lineages within the state. Not known for their gentle nature, the obas of Dahomey undertook annual human sacrifices to ensure divine favor for their rule—a fact that some see as an example of the cheapening value of human life in the context of the slave trade. Dahomey's expanded power allowed it to defeat the coastal port states of Popo and Whydah in the early 1700s, thus allowing them to sell slaves, ivory, and other goods directly to European traders rather than sharing profits with coastal middlemen. Dahomey increasingly acted as a middleman itself and reduced its own reliance on the capture of slaves via conquest.

To the northeast of Dahomey, however, Oyo was growing in power. Oyo's power was centered around the king, or alaafin, though his absolute command was tempered by seven "kingmakers," each of whom represented a powerful family lineage in the kingdom. Rather than investing in firearms like Dahomey, Oyo chose to build its military power around horse-based cavalry. Based in the savannah, Oyo was relatively free from the scourge of the tsetse fly, and could purchase horses from other savannah states or even from the trans-Saharan trade. The power of the horse-based military was such that Oyo was able to defeat its neighboring Yoruba city-states, at least those north of the forest belt. Interestingly, a quirk of geography aided the expansion of Oyo's authority to the Atlantic coast. There is a break in the rain forest where the savannah extends to the coastline. This corridor allowed Oyo to move its cavalry south and challenge Dahomey's control of the region. A series of wars pitted the fast-moving Oyo cavalry against the Dahomey's musket-armed troops from 1720 to 1730. Oyo eventually emerged victorious, an outcome that underlines the limited advantage of the firearms of the time against other forms of military organization. Dahomey did not lose its independence altogether, but was forced to pay considerable tribute to Oyo, joining the fate of Nupe, Borgu, and Allada as Oyo's power increased. Dahomey's control over the slave trade to the coast was thus short lived. Notably, however, Oyo and Dahomey did not sell all the slaves they captured into the Atlantic slave trade. In addition to assimilating large numbers of female slaves into the wider lineage structure of the societies, elite elements of both states also utilized slave plantations, mainly to grow food to feed each state's large professional army. Slave plantations, it seems, were not unique to the Americas. Such a situation only highlights how complex the impact of the transatlantic slave trade was and why it is important not to oversimplify the roles played by participants on each side of the trade. Oyo was to remain the dominant power in the region until into the late eighteenth century. In attempting to centralize his authority, the Alaafin Abiodun sparked a series of revolts that led to the breakaway of many subject regions. In 1835, Oyo's capital was overrun by the similarly cavalry-based forces of the expanding Sokoto Caliphate, with aid from the previously subjected Yoruba state of Ogodo. The collapse of Oyo heralded a period of widespread conflict within the Yoruba-speaking region, as numerous city-states vied to fill the vacuum left by Oyo's demise. Although some of these states, such as Osogbo and Ibadan, developed some degree of power, there was not to be another state to rival the scope of Oyo. As in Central Africa, the collapse of central authority and rise of widespread conflict was to see an expansion in rates of enslavement for the local population.

West of Dahomey, the societies of the Gold Coast developed somewhat differently from those to the east. Initially sparsely populated, prior to 1500 there were few states of any real size. Towns and a few cities developed in the Akan-speaking region after the ninth century, mainly to facilitate the mining of gold and trade in forest products such as kola. Perhaps the earliest was the city-state of Begho, which grew up along the Black Volta River around 1000 C.E. Another state, Bono, grew to dominate the gold trade from a location along the forest edge around 1400. Demonstrating the region's close ties to the savannah region, the state of Gonja was reputedly founded by a cavalry commander from Mali in the early 1500s. Many scholars also credit Muslim traders from the savannah known as the "Dyula" for encouraging and organizing the mining of gold in the region. As we have seen already, however, the building of trade fortresses along the coast, combined with the introduction of additional slave labor from Central Africa and crops from the New World, helped to transform the region. By the seventeenth century, states such as Akwamu and Fante (on the coast) and Denkyera (on the southern edge of the forest's gold-producing region) were developing as they vied for control of the flow of gold to the European posts on the coast. Many of these states sought to centralize authority and take advantage of the military technology represented by firearms—replacing traditional elite military units with more of a militia-style military, built around the idea of the "asafo" companies, in which each town organized one or more units of troops under their own immediate commanders.

By far the most successful of the Gold Coast states, however, was Asante. Beginning as a tributary state of Denkyera, Asante grew out of a confederation of Akan-speaking groups under the leadership of **Osei Tutu,** the first "**Asantehene**" or king of Asante. Using the town of Kumasi as his power base and with an alliance with Akwamu that allowed access to the coastal trade, Osei Tutu challenged the power of Denkyera and eventually emerged victorious in 1701. More than a military leader, Osei Tutu understood the need for a system of political integration that created a sense of identity for the new Asante state. He used an organization of Akan groups known as the Kotoko Council to form a consultative body and centralized authority by expanding the judicial wing of the government. As Asante expanded, incorporated areas were allowed to join the union or were maintained as semi-independent tributary states. Perhaps most interesting, however, was the creation of the "**Golden Stool.**" Drawing on the Akan custom of having a stool in each home that symbolized the authority of the family elder and unity of the family, Osei Tutu, aided by his chief spiritual advisor, Okomfo Anokye, miraculously produced the Golden Stool (reputedly it appeared from heaven, heralded by lightening and thunder), which was to become the ultimate symbol of Asante identity and unity. Each division of the Asante state had its own ceremonial stool, but each was subservient to the Golden Stool. Because of the complex and integrative nature of the Asante political organization and the strong sense of identity that the new state sought to create, some scholars see it as the first modern "nation" to be formed in Africa.

Asante's success was long lived. Osui Tutu's successor, Opoku Ware, ruled from 1718 to 1748 and led a series of military campaigns that considerably expanded the area under Asante's control. At its peak Asante controlled much of the region of modern Ghana, comprising perhaps 100,000 square miles and a population of as much as three million, no small achievement for a state that developed in a region long remarkable for its low population density. With such expansion came a greater control over the region's wealth, especially as Asante grew to dominate the coastal region. It was during the course of these wars of expansion, however, that the wealth of Asante increasingly came from a trade in slaves rather than from gold. Many other slaves were acquired as a form of tax from tributary states. Asante did not export all of its captives. Many were retained in Asante, to work in the gold mines, work on plantations to grow food, or even be incorporated into family lineages. The Asante proverb, "Obi nkyere obi ase" (no one should disclose the origins of another person) highlights the desire for the eventual integration of those of slave heritage into wider Asante society—an advantage of settings in which slavery was not based on race. Not all slaves had such a hope in Asante, where many levels of servitude existed. The range extended from slaves with no rights whatsoever, to those whose person was to some degree protected and whose subservient status was likely temporary. Some scholars chafe at even calling these persons "slaves," preferring to stress the distinction between their status and that of those enslaved in the Americas.

As Asante expanded and grew in power, the state sought to take advantage of and maintain its new status. Under Asantehenes Osei Kwadwo (1764–1777) and Osei Bonsu (1801–1824), the state sought to integrate subject areas into the Asante state more effectively, no doubt in response to rebellions by subject areas such as Akim and a brief civil war faced by Asantehene Kusi Obodum. More emphasis was placed on meritocracy within the administration. Nonetheless, a bias toward privilege for those of Akan ethnicity undercut attempts at integration. The state also invested in infrastructure, building and maintaining the roads that ran north and south from Kumasi. By the nineteenth century, Asante was faced with the growing coastal influence of the British, who supported the coastal **Fante** confederation as a counterweight to Asante influence. In a series of wars between the British and Asante, the two powers vied for control over the coast and thus the valuable trade centered there. The first head-to-head battle between the Asante and British took place in 1824. Though the battle was something of a draw in terms of military objectives, the British governor of the Cape Coast colony, Sir Charles MacCarthy, was killed. This made the battle a political victory for Asante. Such an outcome reflects the military balance that continued to exist between African and European states even in the early nineteenth century. After the military innovations of the middle nineteenth century, however, the British found themselves with a considerable military advantage over the Asante and other African opponents. In 1874, for example, the British not only defeated Asante, but burned and sacked the capital of Kumasi for good measure. Asante resistance to British conquest is discussed in greater detail in Chapter 13.

On each side of the state-dominated regions of the Gold Coast and the Bight of Benin were regions that were characterized either by stateless societies or by what might be termed microstates. These regions were the Windward Coast to the west (in the modern region of Liberia and Cote d'Ivoire) and the Bight of Biafra to the east (in the region of southeastern Nigeria). In the absence of overarching and expanding states as seen elsewhere, the slave trade in these regions tended to develop along different terms. Along the Windward Coast, the general absence of even marginal ports (with the exception of what would become Freetown in Sierra Leone) and the resulting absence of European trading stations meant that there was little organization to the trade. Ships would often cruise the coast hoping to be signaled by potential traders (of slaves or otherwise). The ships then relied on local surf boats to transport their cargos from the shore. Such conditions did little to encourage large-scale trade of the sort found at highly developed slaving ports such as Cape Coast, Whydah, Bonny, or Luanda. Certain areas did become short-term focuses of intensive slave trading, but that was usually as a result of local conflicts and did not lead to sustained commerce.

Quite to the contrary, the region of the Bight of Biafra was to become one of the most active regions of slave trading in the latter era of the trade. Prior to around 1725, this region was a relatively minor supplier of slaves, but after that date the numbers of individuals exported radically increased until the region became the top exporter of slaves in the 1760s. Remarkably, this revolution in slave export took place without state centralization or a large-scale war. Rather, it appears that local trading companies organized to compete in the slave trade—a free-market instead of state-controlled approach to the slave trade. Local "canoe houses" controlled the transport of slaves to ports along the Niger Delta. Interestingly, many of those enslaved came from the region's dominant Igbo and Ibibio ethnic groups. Rather than the situation found in regions of state-controlled trade, where states generally waged war on "foreigners" to gain slaves, within the stateless region of the Bight of Biafra, enslavement was largely internal, with relatively local raids and kidnaping providing a large number of the captives for the trade. The famous case of Olaudah Equiano's kidnaping from his family's yard is a case in point. Notably, the Niger Delta region was notorious for the high mortality rate experienced by slave ships embarking from the ports of the area, even in the latter eighteenth century. Whether the haphazard nature of enslavement had any impact on the chance of survival of those sent from the region is, of course, difficult to gauge.

The End of the Slave Trade and the Rise of Legitimate Trade

As discussed in the previous chapter, gradual social and economic changes in European societies eventually resulted in the British unilateral ban on the transatlantic slave trade in 1807. Though certainly not resulting in an immediate cessation of the export of captives from West and West-Central Africa (the Portuguese were particularly unhappy with the ban), the number of people who suffered through the middle passage had dropped off considerably by about 1840. During the same period the demands on African producers shifted to new products. The transition away from slave-based agriculture as a source of wealth in the New World and Europe, and North America's growing industrial output, reduced the demand for a steady supply of slave labor. Rather, products that would support the new industrial process of manufacture were needed. Chief among these was **palm oil,** produced mainly along the coastline of what is now Nigeria, which served as a crucial machine lubricant prior to the discovery of means to refine mineral oil. Other important products included palm kernels (for making soap), **gum arabic** (a dye fixer made from the resin of the acacia tree) and peanuts (both from the savannah region and largely exported via the Gambia and Senegal rivers), **latex** (from West Central Africa), and more traditional trade items such as gold, ivory, and peppers. Notably, an environment of slave raiding was deemed unfriendly to such new "legitimate" commerce, and British attempts to ban the slave trade may reflect in part a desire to create a climate in which more peaceful trade in nonhuman commodities could flourish.

Indeed, the nineteenth century saw a remarkable period of reorganization in African export economies. As the external demand for slaves declined, African traders and states scrambled to produce the goods now in demand. Production and export of goods such as palm oil skyrocketed in a very short period of time—a fine example of the remarkable initiative of African economic actors. A less positive appraisal of the situation, however, would highlight the fact that there was no real change in the distribution of wealth in Africa. Indeed, the very people who benefitted from the slave trade were generally well placed to reorient their efforts to controlling the new "legitimate" commerce. Worse, the end of the transatlantic slave trade did not end slavery in Africa itself. Quite possibly, the need for labor to produce the agricultural products demanded for the new export economy resulted in expanded rates of domestic enslavement, although in some regions much of the production was taken over by free persons acting on their own initiatives. Also, the inability to harness animal power in much of the coastal regions to provide transport of goods meant that human porters or rowers were essential to the transport of goods. As noted before, the often ambiguous nature of servitude in Africa meant that many of those providing coerced labor were not slaves in the sense of those found on the plantations of the New World. Nonetheless, the legitimate trade, like the slave trade before it, likely resulted in a movement of population toward the new economic locus of the coasts.

Perhaps one of the most remarkable outcomes of the era of legitimate commerce was the foundation of the **Krio** (Creole) society in Sierra Leone. This British-administered colony grew up around the port city of Freetown, where "recaptives" from intercepted slave ships were released. As a result, Freetown became the home of one of Africa's first pan-African communities, as recaptives from around West, Central, and even East Africa were set ashore to start new lives (as noted in Chapter 8, Africans in the Americas had been forging such communities for centuries). Notably, a very large percentage of the population were Yoruba who had been enslaved in the wars that had followed the collapse of Oyo. Many took advantage of education and religious instruction provided by missionaries based in Freetown. Together, the recaptives created a new culture and even language that was a mixture of African and European elements. Given their firsthand experience with the wider world and also given the remarkable store of knowledge represented by a community made up of individuals from all along the African coast, the Krio became very active as intermediaries in the new trade. Some Krio entrepreneurs even bought captured slave ships at auction and used them for trade along the African coast. Some also became the first truly successful agents of Christianity since the long-past era of Portuguese missionary activity. Imbued with both a sense of Christian mission and a desire to help provide their home communities with the tools by which to compete with European economic power, many of the recaptives returned to their homes as missionaries. Perhaps among the most famous of all these is **Samuel Ajayi Crowther,** who returned to his native Yoruba-speaking home and became the first Anglican Bishop of West Africa. A talented linguist, he created the first comprehensive Yoruba-English dictionary and helped translate the Bible into Yoruba as well. Where European missionaries had generally failed to convert Africans to Christianity, Africans such as Crowther, who could translate between and find a middle ground for African and Christian spirituality, met with considerable success. It was to be the advent of a new age for African Christianity at much the same time as Islam was undergoing a revival in the savannahs (as shall be discussed in Chapter 10).

Just to the east of Sierra Leone, another new state was created in **Liberia.** Here, beginning in the 1820s, the American Colonization Society funded the settlement of free African Americans from the United States. Over the course of the next few decades, some 15,000 emigres from the United States were "recolonized" to Liberia. In 1847, Liberia declared its independence and was recognized as a sovereign nation. Notably, Liberia was quite different from Sierra Leone. By and large Liberia's new population was generations removed from Africa and had few, if any, links to the surrounding regions. Indeed, they possessed both an identity and a culture that separated them from the local African populations. With U.S. support, this small group soon grew to become an aristocracy that gradually expanded its control over local African groups. Unlike Sierra Leone, Liberia would play little role in influencing cultural change in West Africa.

West and West-Central Africa 1500–1880, in Global Perspective

The coming of European contact to West and West-Central Africa is a textbook case of the advent of an integrated global economic system. Most societies in West and West-Central Africa had been relatively isolated from direct contact with global trade, and the study of their integration into the wider world economy is very instructive in terms of helping scholars determine exactly how societies understand and deal with forces of economic, cultural, and political change. The differing reactions of Kongo, Benin, Dahomey, Asante, and various stateless regions to European contact and to the challenges (moral, economic, and military) of the slave trade provide us with a virtual manual for examining the incorporation of relatively isolated societies into the global system.

On a more specific level, the diverse conclusions by various scholars regarding African agency in the slave trade and the ultimate effect of that trade in Africa tell us much about the factual and political challenges to doing history. For example, perhaps an underlying assumption behind the very different perspectives on the impact of the slave trade is the notion of African "fragility." Do arguments such as those made by Rodney or Inikori suggest that African societies and economies were somehow more subject to disruption than others? Does this create an image of Africans as helpless victims? Or were the ramifications of the slave trade simply so terrible that it could disrupt an entire continent? Conversely, although scholars such as Thornton or Northrup do not exactly sugarcoat the slave trade and its impact, they instead see African societies as "rolling with the punches" and ultimately resilient. Thus, for the "Adaptive Africa" school of scholarship, the slave trade was harsh, but it was not something that could not be overcome as societies reacted to new conditions at the trade's close, so perhaps Africans deserve admiration for so successfully meeting the challenge created by the transatlantic slave trade.

Useful Works on This Chapter Topic

Works on early European and Africa contact include David Northrup, *Africa's Discovery of Europe: 1450–1850* (2002); John Blake, *Europeans in West Africa*, 1450–1560 (1942); John Vogt, *Portuguese Rule on the Gold Coast, 1469–1682* (1979); and David Birmingham, *Portugal and Africa* (1999).

A number of works specifically address the impact of the transatlantic slave trade on African states and societies. These include Walter Hawthorne, *Planting Rice and Harvesting Slaves: Transformations along the Guinea-Bissau Coast, 1400–1900* (2003); John Thornton, *Africa and Africans in the Making of the Atlantic World*, 1400–1800 (1998); Paul Lovejoy, *Transformations in Slavery: A History of Slavery in Africa* (2000); Joe Miller, *Way of Death: Merchant Capitalism and the Angolan Slave Trade*, 1730–1830 (1988); and the beginning sections of Walter Rodney, *How Europe Underdeveloped Africa* (1981). *The Atlantic Slave Trade,* by David Northrup (2001), also includes a brief overview of the issue of how trade influenced African development.

For information on individual African states and regions, the reader might examine the following sources: Anne Hilton, *The Kingdom of Kongo* (1992); Paula Girshik Ben-Amos, *Art, Innovation and Politics in 18th Century Benin* (1999); T. C. McCaskie, *State and Society in Pre-Colonial Ashanti* (1995); Akintola J. G. Wyse, *The Krio of Sierra Leone: An Interpretive History* (1989); Boubacar Barry, *Senegambia and the Atlantic Slave Trade* (1998); and Christopher R. Decorse (ed.), *West Africa During the Atlantic Slave Trade: Archaeological Perspectives* (2002).

CHAPTER 10

North Africa and the Soudan: 1500–1880

As we have seen previously, particularly in Chapters 4, 5 and 6, the fate of North Africa has often been closely connected with that of the Middle East and southern Europe. Tied by land and increasingly by religion, language, and culture to the east, the Islamic states of North Africa, particularly the Fatimids, Ayyubids, and Mamluks of Egypt, were deeply involved with the politics and economics of the Middle East. Though increasingly separated from Europe by religion and culture, North African states and traders nonetheless carried on trade (sometimes clandestinely) with Europeans. During the late fifteenth and early sixteenth centuries, the expanding state of Spain took advantage of the political fragmentation of North Africa to seize a number of ports along the North African coast, including such important towns as Melilla, Mers el-Kebir, Tunis, and Tripoli. On the Atlantic coast of Morocco, the Portuguese took coastal cities such as Ceuta, Tangier, Safi, and Agadir by force of arms, providing the small Iberian state with access to trade with the interior and valuable launching points for further exploration to the south. Such ports were critical to the Portuguese doubling of Cape Bojador, eventual passage into the Indian Ocean, and expansion into the Atlantic, which we examined in Chapter 8. Yet, from the sixteenth century forward, the expansion of the **Ottoman Empire** increasingly set the tone for North African politics and economics, as the Ottomans first drove out European forces and then established their own systems of administration and exchange. As we shall see in this chapter, however, North Africa's fate was not determined by external forces. Rather, North African populations, themselves diverse, at times actively collaborated with populations from the Middle East and Europe when they saw economic, political, or cultural advantage in doing so. At other times, they maneuvered for increased independence or fought for self-determination.

To the south of the Sahara lies a vast swath of savannah that runs from the Senegambia to the upper Nile area. These regions have, in the past, been referred to as the Soudan (for which, obviously, the modern Sudan is named). As discussed in Chapter 6, Islam gradually spread into these regions over the course of the ninth through the fifteenth centuries. Beginning in the eighteenth century, these regions saw a remarkable expansion of Islamic consciousness and political activism, eventually leading to the establishment of several new Islamic states. This movement would alter the cultural face of the region and influence the region's development in the coming centuries.

The Ottomans in Egypt

The Ottoman Empire began its process of expansion in the thirteenth century, first growing to dominate Anatolia (home of modern Turkey). The inhabitants of the region were largely pastoralists, many of whom were descendants of steppe horseman originally from Mongolia and central Asia. By the twelfth century, most had converted to Islam. In 1280 a local noble named Osman began to extend the realms under his control, taking advantage of the collapse of the Seljuk Turks in the east and the ongoing decline of Byzantium in the west. In the fourteenth century the Ottomans captured the Balkans, introducing Islam to Eastern Europe, and in 1453 they succeeded in capturing Constantinople, which had successfully repulsed occasional Islamic attacks since the eighth century. In this latter achievement the Ottomans were aided by their embracing of gunpowder technology, which allowed them to breach Constantinople's walls. Renamed Istanbul, the city became the Ottoman capital.

In the early sixteenth century, under the Sultan Selim the Inexorable, the Ottomans turned their attention to the Middle East and North Africa. With their use of firearms and the training of their infantry to work as a unit via close-order drill, the Ottoman forces made short work of the Safavids in 1514, giving them control over the Holy Land of the Hejaz. In 1516, Ottoman forces defeated the Egyptian Mamluks at the battle of Mardj Dubik in Syria and occupied Egypt the following year. Notably, the Mamluk military, like that of the Safavids, had largely rejected gunpowder technology as cowardly and undignified. As a result, many a brave Mamluk was killed. Further, the Mamluks had been weakened by Portuguese expansion into the Indian Ocean, which had seriously inhibited the flow of trade through the Red Sea to Egypt.

Despite having defeated the Mamluks militarily and having placed some of the elite Janissary slave troops (most originally from the Balkans in Eastern Europe) in Cairo, the Ottomans did not completely restructure the administrative system of Egypt. Khayr Bey, originally a Mamluk governor in Syria who had defected to the Ottomans in 1516, was named as **pasha** or vice-regent. Although the pasha was named by the Ottoman government and thus owed his power to Istanbul, he retained considerable authority in Egypt and was also responsible for protecting the Red Sea and administering the pilgrimage to Mecca in the Hejaz. Such important duties highlight the importance of the pasha—and Egypt—within the Ottoman Empire. Nor were the rest of the Mamluks removed from prominence within Egyptian society. Khayr Bey continued to run the Egyptian administration along largely Mamluk lines, and many of the more wealthy and well-connected Mamluks continued to hold positions of power within the administration. Indeed, although Khayr

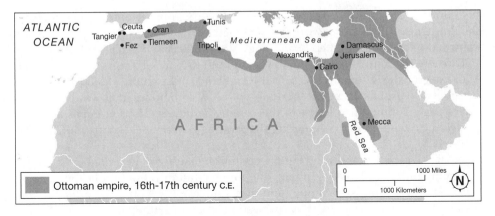

Map 10-1: The Ottoman Empire in Africa

Bey paid tribute to Istanbul and recognized the ultimate authority of the sultan, little changed within the structure of the Egyptian government.

The early years of Ottoman administration were not trouble free. When Khayr Bey died in 1522, the new rulers of Egypt were faced with revolts. In 1524 the vice-regent, Ahmad Pasha, broke with the Ottoman Empire and declared himself "Sultan of Egypt"—even minting his own coinage before being overthrown by some of his original supporters. When the Ottomans reasserted their authority, they implemented a somewhat more centralized system of administration that gave the new pasha greater control over the government, although the Mamluks continued to wield considerable economic and regional authority. Interestingly, many of the Janissaries stationed in Egypt began to adopt Mamluk manners and even move into sections of the economy and administration previously controlled by the Mamluks. Over time, they would even take the same title. Sadly, they and the rest of the Ottoman administration treated the Egyptian peasants no better than had the Mamluks. Taxation remained high because the profits of labor and trade were either paid out in tribute or went to support a small ruling class. By the latter sixteenth century, power in Egypt was increasingly split between an urban class with ties to Istanbul and the more rural Mamluks, many of whom came to be known as **beys** (a Turkish term meaning "chieftan").

The Ottomans were not interested only in the lower Nile region of Egypt. They were quite aware that the growing presence of the Portuguese in the Indian Ocean was a barrier to Ottoman access to that ocean's lucrative trade (see Chapter 11 for more on this). In the late 1530s, the vice-regent, Sulayman Pasha, was tasked with driving the Portuguese from Diu, near the mouth of the Red Sea. Although he was unsuccessful he did secure Aden on the southern coast of the Arabian Peninsula, itself a very important trade center. Sulayman Pasha also seized the upper Nile in Nubia, reaching south to Wadi Halfa. In the middle of the sixteenth century, the Ottomans sent another expedition into Nubia and left garrisons in the upper Nile, establishing a province named Berberistan. Interestingly, the troops posted here were originally from Bosnia—a fine example of how empires such as the Ottoman help move people around. In 1557, Ozdemir Pasha's troops captured Massawa from the Portuguese (in modern Eritrea). Combined with Aden, this gave them complete control over access to the Red Sea, though they would not be able to challenge the Portuguese for control of the Indian Ocean until the early 1600s (see Chapter 11). Massawa gave the Ottomans access to the highlands of Ethiopia, which resulted in a considerable expansion in the trade in coffee, a commodity that was to become increasingly important to Egypt in the coming centuries. The Ottomans also supported the Sultan of Adal, countering the growing Portuguese support for Christian Ethiopia.

By the early seventeenth century, centralized authority in Ottoman Egypt was becoming unstable. This was in part due to the administration's policy of keeping various military groups in competition over sources of revenue. For example, one group of Janissaries, the Odjak party, was in charge of setting grain prices. Such a policy did tend to limit local groups from growing in power at the expense of the Ottoman administration. It did not, however, make for stable local government. As trade declined and inflation sapped profits, the various groups fought among themselves in attempts to gain access to scarce sources of income. In 1631 a group of Mamluks known as the Sandjak beys ousted the vice-regent, Musa Pasha, who had attempted to restrict the right of the military to directly tax the peasants. He was replaced by Ridwan Bey al-Fakari, himself a Sandjak bey, who was approved as pasha by the Ottoman administration in Istanbul.

The Ottoman central government, however, had problems of its own closer to home and was increasingly distracted from the affairs of the North African provinces. In Istanbul, the Ottomans suffered under a series of weak sultans. Ibrahim, who ruled from 1640 to 1648, for example, was more than a bit insane—evidenced by the fact that he drowned some 280 of his concubines in the Bosporus. During the mid-seventeenth century, the Ottomans fought a number of costly wars against the Venetians in the Mediterranean and against the Hapsburgs in Eastern Europe. In 1683 a Polish force broke the Ottoman siege of Vienna and reversed the trend of Ottoman expansion into Europe. Given such a situation, the growing threat from European states such as Russia was more a concern to the Ottomans than the resurgence of Mamluk authority in Egypt.

In 1710, a surge in coffee prices in Egypt (driven in part by expanding European demand) helped fan infighting for control of the coffee trade. Civil war broke out in 1711, and the Mamluks defeated the local Ottoman garrison. Although the office of the pasha was not eliminated, his power was seriously curtailed. Indeed, the vice-regent often remained in power only by playing the increasingly powerful Mamluk beys against one another. One unfortunate vice-regent, Ridwan Kahya, was killed in a Janissary revolt in 1754 when he attempted to put a tax on coffee. Following a period of fierce infighting, 'Ali Bey al-Ghazzawi came to power as pasha. A ruthless leader (his nickname was "the demon"), 'Ali Bey cut a deal with the powers in Istanbul that he would pay off the considerable Egyptian debt to the central government if he were allowed to keep the land of those he had defeated. The Sublime Porte (as the Ottoman government was often known) granted his wish, and with ruthless efficiency (and great hardship on the part of the peasant farmers), he began to pay off the huge debt over a period of some two decades. His tactics were so harsh that in 1766 he was driven out of Egypt and into exile in Syria, but was returned to power with Ottoman support (the central authorities seem to have liked having the debt paid off). 'Ali Bey was no tool of the sultan, however. He replaced the Ottoman vice-regent in Mecca with one of his own followers, and in the 1770s he took advantage of an Ottoman defeat at sea by Russia and captured Damascus. Internal strife in Egypt prevented him from capitalizing on such territorial gains. Perhaps having had enough of the independent-minded Mamluks, the Ottomans sent troops into Egypt in 1786 and drove many of the Mamluks south into Upper Egypt. The new ruler, Hasan Pasha, named new beys, though they still came from Mamluk families. The resurgence of Ottoman authority in Egypt was to be temporary, however, as discussed later in this chapter.

The Ottomans in the Maghreb

The coastal region of North Africa was fiercely contested by local, Ottoman, and European forces in the sixteenth and seventeenth centuries. Indeed, this contestation was nothing new. We saw such tensions between Carthage and Rome in Chapter 4, in Chapter 5 with the invasion of Christian North Africa by the Vandals, and in Chapter 6 with the invasion of Spain by North African Muslims. This theme continued up to the time period covered by our current chapter. The Fatimid dynasty (based in Egypt) controlled Sicily in the twelfth century, and the Sicilians returned the favor by seizing the Tunisian coast a few decades later.

The period of the 1500s and 1600s was a difficult time in North Africa. Expanding Iberian trade with West Africa and the New World was limiting both the value and the quantity of gold being traded across the Sahara into the Maghreb. Worse, numerous epidemics had wracked the densely settled coast, shrinking the population and weakening political and economic structures. **Leo Africanus,** a Moroccan living in Italy, wrote that farmers in the coastal region were so susceptible to raids that they were forced to grow crops within walled enclosures. Weak states such as the Zayyanids at Tlemcen and the Hafsids at Tunis were barely viable. Given such a situation, there is little surprise that both the Spanish and Ottomans saw an opportunity to expand their authority in the North African region.

These two expanding empires clashed along the North African coast in the first half of the sixteenth century. Initially, the Spanish were successful in conquering a few important coastal towns such as Oran and Tripoli. At times they enjoyed the support of the Zayyanids and Hafsids, but for the most part local political leaders saw greater advantage in allying with the Ottomans. If they were to lose their independence, they seemed to prefer to be ruled by other Muslims rather than by Christians, still fervent from the reconquista of Spain. Particularly notable in the resistance to Spanish encroachment were the corsairs. Very much like the privateers later used by the Dutch and British to raid Spanish ships in the Atlantic, these corsairs preyed on European commerce in the Mediterranean with the official blessing of the Ottomans. Most famous were the Barbarossa brothers, known for their red beards. Thus, private enterprise, local interest, and international politics worked hand in hand to oppose the Spanish in the region. With the aid of Ottoman troops and naval power (supported from their new base in Egypt), the Spanish were gradually driven from their coastal enclaves in the latter 1500s, with the exception of Oran, which they were able to hold until 1791. Otherwise victorious, the Ottomans had established themselves as the masters of the Maghreb as far west as still-independent Morocco and could turn to consolidating their authority in the region.

Perhaps because the Maghreb was not so vital to Ottoman interests as was Egypt, which had both a substantial population and an agricultural base, the Ottomans chose to administer the regions to the west with a somewhat lighter hand. The surviving Barbarossa, Khair ad Din, was named as **beylerbey,** the Ottoman authority in the region. Based in Algiers, Khair ad Din and his successors oversaw a very loose Ottoman administration that was divided into the three provinces of Algiers, Tripoli, and Tunis. Although the Ottomans wielded considerable authority in the towns via their administrative, economic, and military influence, their hold over the hinterland to the south was limited. Rather than attempting direct control over the pastoralist and oasis communities of the desert, the Ottomans took a much more pragmatic approach, preferring to operate via informal relationships with the heads of local religious brotherhoods and through family alliances. Although occasional tensions and conflicts erupted between the coast and interior, the Ottoman approach was nonetheless fairly successful.

Ottoman Culture in North Africa

Much of our discussion so far has focused on political and economic history. It is important to note, however, that the expansion of Ottoman authority over much of North Africa also brought cultural change as well. Particularly in the cities, where the Ottoman presence was the strongest, many elements of Turkish culture took root. Turkish dress, for example, became common. Administrative and religious buildings constructed by the Ottomans reflected strong Turkish themes and still stand to this day. An expansion of the use of Turkish among the elite eclipsed Arabic as the language of administration and scholarship (although Arabic, of course, remained the language of religious instruction) for some time. The Ottoman rejection of the printing press (largely due to lobbying by religious scribes who earned their livelihoods copying religious books) considerably limited the potential for the influence of Turkish as a language of empire. Nonetheless, the use of Turkish by elites temporarily undermined the influence of local scholars and institutions such as Al-Azhar University in Cairo. Many powerful families, particularly in Egypt, chose to send their sons to Istanbul for education. Ottoman-style guilds became common among commercial groups. The development of an elite culture that drew on external roots served to further divide the populations of the region. The populous cities of the coastal region were far more influenced by cosmopolitan Ottoman culture, just as they had previously been by Arab culture. As we have seen, this mixing was genetic, as well as cultural. Such developments further separated urban populations from the largely Berber-speaking population of the oases and deserts to the south.

Perhaps one of the more profound influences of the period of Ottoman influence in North Africa was the introduction of many **Sufi** orders, often referred to as "brotherhoods" or Turuq (sing. Tariqa, which means path). Sufism is a mystical expression of Islam. It stresses personal knowledge of God via techniques such as self-discipline, meditation, and physical deprivation, rather than the more legalistic, works-based approach of orthodox Sunni Islam. Thus, although Orthodox Sunnism stresses obeying God's laws (the Shari'a) as a means of achieving salvation after death, Sufis stress God's love and nearness in this life. Sufism has its roots in the earliest centuries of Islam, but it grew in influence after the doctrines of al-Ghazali gained prominence in the twelfth century. Sufism was very popular with Turkish converts to Islam, and as a result, it gained political support with the ascendancy of the Ottomans in the fourteenth and fifteenth centuries. Sufism thus gained sanction from elites in North Africa during Ottoman rule, which accelerated its spread in the region. Groups such as the Qadiriyya (based in Iraq) and "dervish" orders spread first into cities and later into rural areas. The veneration of Sufis who attained union with God, known as **Walis** (friends of God), helped provide local links to what might otherwise seem a distant religion. Further, Sufi Brotherhoods provided a wider sense of community. Thus, although economics and politics served to divide North African populations, Sufism for some became a common cultural element. Also, the Sufis' common use of poetry for devotion helped spread literacy among rural and pastoralist populations. As we shall see later in this chapter, these Sufi orders were to have a considerable impact on North and West African history.

The Rise of Morocco

Hopefully, some of the more geographically aware readers have been asking, "What about Morocco?" Indeed, no discussion of North Africa in the period from 1500 to 1850 would be complete without a discussion of the remarkable developments that took place in Morocco—events that both share in and diverge from historical themes operating at the same time elsewhere in North Africa.

In the fifteenth century, Morocco, like its neighbors to the east, was faced with expanding European power. As mentioned in the introduction to this chapter, it was the Portuguese who were seeking to establish a foothold in Morocco. Not only did the coastal towns such as Tangier, Asilah and Larachi, Safi, and Agadir provide the Portuguese with valuable strategic footholds that helped them work their way down the coast of Africa, but they also allowed for the control (and hence taxing) of the export of sugar from farms and plantations in Morocco itself. Thus, the control of Morocco's coastline was a major factor in Portugal's expanding power in the fifteenth and sixteenth centuries.

Unlike in other parts of North Africa, however, the Ottomans were not to aid in the expulsion of Europeans from Morocco. Indeed, the Moroccans were not terribly interested in having the Ottomans establish themselves as the overlords of their homeland, even if their rule was to be mostly symbolic. The Moroccans viewed both the Portuguese and Ottomans as hostile powers. Remarkably, they were to be fairly successful against both.

It is important to note that in the fifteenth century there was little in the way of a centralized state in the region we call Morocco. The Almohad state, which had once controlled much of North-West Africa (see Chapter 6), had largely deteriorated by this time. Power was diffused among a number of local family groups and Sufi brotherhoods. Such a lack of central authority was one of the key reasons why the Portuguese were able to seize control of so many important port cities. Necessity is often the mother of invention, however, and the challenge from both the sea and the east helped spur a new wave of political organization in Morocco. The early sixteenth century saw the rise of the Sa'adi dynasty, who called for driving out the invaders and who bolstered their political and religious legitimacy by claiming to be *shurafa*—descendants of the Prophet Muhammad. The Sa'adis grew in power quickly and were astoundingly successful, given that they effectively had to fight a war on three fronts. They were able to retake the port towns of Agadir, Safi, and Azemmur from the Portuguese by 1542. Notably, Moroccan use of artillery was critical to retaking these cities. It is important to keep in mind that at this point in time, European armies had little or no technological advantage over African states such as the Moroccans, especially on land. In 1550, the Sa'adis sent troops east to seize the Mediterranean port of Tlemcen to head off Ottoman expansion. The port city traded hands several times over the next few years (with, interestingly, Spanish troops entering on the Moroccan side and European converts to Islam supporting the Ottomans), but in the end the Ottomans gave up on their efforts to expand farther west, though they did later send an assassin to murder the Moroccan leader, al-Shaykh. In 1554 the Sa'adis defeated the last remnants of the competing Wattasid dynasty, securing their power in Morocco.

The sultan, al-Ghalib Billah, set about capitalizing on the Sa'adis' new centralized authority. They found support with the locally based Jazuli Sufi brotherhood, which they supported at the expense of the Qadiriyya, which had strong ties to the Ottomans. They also sought to expand sugar production and increase trade with Europe. A dynastic struggle, however, disrupted the new state's peaceful development—a problem common to almost all dynasties. When the sultan died in 1574, his eldest son, al-Mutawakkil, became sultan. Many in the extended family, however, felt that the position should have gone to al-Malik, the eldest of the family's princes, who was highly respected both in Morocco and abroad. Well educated, he is reputed to have spoken Arabic, Spanish, Italian, and Armenian. Al-Malik fled to Algiers and then to Istanbul, from whence he gained fame fighting for the Ottoman army in Tunis. The Ottomans, no doubt seeing an opportunity for political success in Morocco where outright military conquest had failed, outfitted al-Malik with an army, which he used to invade Morocco. Invading Fez in 1576, al-Malik received considerable local support. His cousin, al-Mutawakkil, was eventually forced to flee to the Portuguese for protection. The Portuguese king, Don Sebastian, saw much the same opportunity as had his Ottoman counterpart. Outfitting an army (filled out by large components of German and Italian mercenaries), he made preparations to invade Morocco with the pretext of returning the "rightful" sultan to his throne. In so doing he was not only seeking influence for Portugal in Morocco, but was also seeking to undermine potentially expanding Ottoman influence in the region. Clearly, politics in North Africa were becoming considerably more complex as outside states and empires vied for influence in the region.

In 1578, Don Sebastian and al-Mutawakkil invaded Morocco, despite correspondence from al-Malik requesting that Don Sebastian not intervene in Moroccan politics. Sultan al-Malik advanced with his army from Marakesh and met the Portuguese force at al-Kasr al-Kebir. What ensued is known as "the Battle of Three Kings." In the battle, each of the "three kings" was killed. The forces of al-Malik, in the end, carried the day. Some 14,000 European troops were taken captive. Many, particularly those whose families were too poor to ransom them, converted to Islam rather than face enslavement. The Portuguese defeat toppled the home government, resulting in the kingdom of Portugal passing to the control of King Phillip of Spain. A new sultan, al-Mansur, came to power and used the momentum of the victory to retake several more coastal towns from Portuguese forces. The considerable decline of Portuguese influence over the next several decades allowed Morocco to expand its influence over the sugar trade, and a period of general growth and prosperity followed. Al-Mansur was no small thinker. Indeed, it was under his rule that Morocco invaded Songhai in 1591, as we saw in Chapter 6.

Al-Mansur's death in 1603, however, led to another round of dynastic struggles and another opportunity for European powers to seize Moroccan port cities. It was not until the rise of the 'Awalite dynasty, founded by Mawlay Rashid in 1671, that the Moroccans were once again able to challenge European forces for control of the coasts. His successor, Mawlay Isma'il, retook al-Mahdiyya from the Spanish in 1681 and Tangiers from the British in 1684, for example. Isma'il attempted to improve the security of the state by relying less on troops raised by local rulers and instead establishing a centralized army, known as the **Bawakhir,** consisting largely of slaves captured from the savannah to the south. This move, however, resulted in considerable debate between the king and religious scholars over whether or not populations from the south, particularly those from the region of Songhai, could legitimately be enslaved because many were known to be Muslims. Isma'il eventually "solved" the problem by stating that he would give freedom to all the soldiers, though they would nonetheless be required to serve for their entire lives. Another wave of internal disputes weakened the Moroccans after Isma'il's death in 1727. Ironically, for the next three decades the "Royal Guard," largely consisting of slaves, controlled who was named as sultan. In the 1760s, Sidi Muhammad ibn Abdallah restored central authority and expelled the Portuguese from ports such as Mazagan. Sidi Muhammad is important in that he was influenced by a very conservative brand of Islam known as **Wahhabism,** which was becoming influential in Arabia at the time. Wahhabism was particularly hostile to Sufism, and the new Sultan undertook a number of measures to weaken the hold of Sufi brotherhoods in Morocco. Sidi Muhammad is also important to the history of the United States: he was the first head of state to recognize the United States as a sovereign nation.

Invasion and Reform in Egypt

As discussed earlier in the chapter, the Ottomans sought to reassert their authority by sending troops to Egypt in 1786 and driving many of the Mamluks to the south. In 1798, however, a French army commanded by none other than the young general

Napoleon Bonaparte invaded Egypt. The French had several motivations. First, surrounded by adversaries in Europe and having mobilized a large element of the French population for war, France was short on food. Egypt, long an exporter of grain, held the potential to help stave off food shortages or even famine in France. Further, Egypt was a major producer of cotton, which could help France develop a textile industry to compete with Britain. Finally, still stinging from the loss of influence in India after a defeat by the British in the Seven Years' War of 1756 to 1763, the leaders of revolutionary France hoped to use Egypt as a base from which to expand eastward, threatening the British in India. The French troops, supported by a naval squadron and with supplies provided (ironically) by the semi-autonomous bey of Algiers, quickly seized Alexandria and Cairo. Interestingly, Napoleon attempted to present himself and his troops as the liberators of Egypt, claiming not only that he had come to free the Egyptians from Ottoman domination, but that he himself was a Muslim. Although many Egyptians, particularly the peasants, had no great love for the Ottomans, they did not seem to be taken with the French, either. Local revolts were put down in 1798 and 1800. By and large, the French seemed just another in a long line of outside powers seeking the wealth created by the Nile and Egypt's population.

The French occupation of Egypt saw the beginnings of "Egyptology"—the careful archaeological examination of ancient Egypt's remains. Many excavations were begun during the occupation, and perhaps one of the most significant outcomes was the discovery of the Rosetta Stone. Because this artifact presented a single text in three different scripts (ancient Greek, Egyptian hieroglyphics, and Egyptian Demotic), it allowed the translation of the ancient Egyptian language. This event allowed modern scholars a whole new window into understanding ancient Egyptian history and life.

The French occupation of Egypt was to be short lived. A British fleet destroyed the supporting French squadron at the Battle of the Nile in 1798, cutting the French troops off from supplies and reinforcements. In 1799, Napoleon abandoned his troops, who surrendered themselves to a combined Ottoman and British force in 1801. The French conquest of Egypt and the necessity of relying on the British to reclaim this important province, however, alerted the Ottomans to the need to reform their own military and political systems. The reality of Ottoman weakness was also not lost on one Muhammad Ali, an Albanian officer who commanded some of the troops who drove out the French in 1801. After a period of political maneuvering and with the backing of Egyptian Ulama (religious scholars), Muhammad Ali was able to have himself named pasha in 1805.

Unlike most vice-regents before him, Muhammad Ali was not content to enjoy power only in Egypt. Rather, he set out on a campaign of military and economic reform that he hoped would give him the ability to not only challenge the Europeans, but also the Ottoman Empire itself (where a similar campaign of reform was cut short by a revolt of the Janissaries). In 1811 he massacred all but a few of the Mamluk beys, thus largely eliminating the local aristocracy's influence and seizing their land. Muhammad Ali also brought the heads of the Sufi brotherhoods under his control to further centralize his authority. He was not concerned at having removed the Mamluk aristocracy of Egypt because he sought to replace them with a

Portrait of Muhammad Ali.

modern peasant army and with a civil service of bureaucrats trained in the Western style. Armed with the latest weapons and trained in European-style tactics, the army quickly became the most powerful in the region. From 1813 to 1819 this army proved itself in Arabia, where Wahabbi revolts had threatened Ottoman control of the holy land of the Hejaz. In the early 1820s, Muhammad Ali turned his attention south, expanding control over the upper Nile. Here he seized slaves with which to expand his army and workforce and brought new areas into cultivation for cotton. Cotton was critical, for it was first a source of income to pay for his new army and also held the potential for establishing an industrial base in the production of textiles. Sensitive, however, to the dangers of relying on a single crop, Muhammad Ali also encouraged the planting of other cash crops such as sugar, indigo, and tobacco. He also invested heavily in new roads, infrastructure, and sanitation. Notably, such efforts made Muhammad Ali even less popular with the Egyptian masses than the Mamluks and the French had been. His military expansion placed heavy demands on families to provide sons for conquest, and his economic policies relied on heavy taxation and forced labor. In 1820, for example, he brutally put down a peasant revolt. Some have tried to present Muhammad Ali as an anti-European crusader or even as an early Arab nationalist. The evidence doesn't very well support either notion (especially the latter because Muhammad Ali wasn't even Arab). Rather, he was an ambitious leader who sought to expand his power by whatever means best served his goals. Much like the French, he was an outsider using Egypt for his own purposes.

For a while it appeared as if Muhammad Ali would expand his authority over the entire Ottoman Empire. In 1825 he occupied Crete, and by 1832 he had seized much of the Middle East. In the early 1830s his armies, led by his son Ibrahim, were threatening Istanbul. The defection of the Ottoman navy to Muhammad Ali's side in 1839 made things look grim indeed for the new 16-year-old Ottoman sultan. However, European powers were not pleased with Muhammad Ali's success, and they demanded withdrawal. When Muhammad Ali refused, a British-Austrian fleet landed troops at Beirut, threatening to split Muhammad Ali's forces in two. Knowing that he could not beat the European powers (particularly the British), Muhammad Ali withdrew his forces and settled for control over Egypt.

It is in some ways ironic that European powers helped protect the Ottoman Empire from Muhammad Ali. In the course of reforming the Egyptian military, Muhammad Ali had purchased his arms from European states, often with cash earned by selling them cotton. Muhammad Ali thus provided Europe with exactly what it wanted, unfinished raw materials and a market for manufactured goods. His use of Western teachers to educate civil servants was a means by which Egypt could be "Europeanized." His use of slavery and his exploitation of peasants were hardly novel for the time, either. Rather, preferring a weak Ottoman state to a potentially rejuvenated one under Muhammad Ali, the European powers acted to stifle his reforms, however "Western" they might have seemed. His ambitions for wider power and conquest broken, Muhammad Ali went into a rapid physical and mental decline, dying in 1847.

After a period of relatively pro-Ottoman reaction, rule in Egypt passed to Muhammad Ali's grandsons Said and Isma'il. Both continued their grandfather's policy of internal reform, but abandoned plans for military expansion. Rather, they embarked on a program of reform that focused on embracing many aspects of Western culture and economic development funded by exports and loans. First Said, and then to an even greater extent Isma'il (who took power in 1863) were encouraged by the high cotton prices created by the American Civil War to spend lavishly on infrastructure and Western education. Most ambitious was the acceptance of a French plan to build a canal between Suez (on the Mediterranean coast) and the Red Sea. But with the end of the American conflict, the price of cotton dropped precipitously, and Isma'il was forced to borrow heavily from European sources to maintain his levels of spending. By the time the canal opened, Egypt was more than 11 million pounds in debt (nearly 10 percent of which had been spent on a lavish international party to celebrate the opening). The canal revolutionized global commerce, but its construction had bankrupted the semi-independent Egyptian state and had also thrust Egypt into a precarious position created by the canal's economic and strategic significance. In 1876 Egypt defaulted on its loans. As a result, Isma'il was forced by the British and French (now co-owners of the canal and the main holders of Egypt's debt) to accept dual control of Egypt's fiscal affairs and international relations. A similar process had led to the effective end of Tunisian independence in 1869. A revolt by Egyptian military leader Ahmad Urabi in 1882 provided the British with an excuse to occupy Egypt militarily. For all practical purposes, Egypt had lost the independence gained by Muhammad Ali and had traded Ottoman suzerainty for British control. An attempt to modernize with European assistance had led to Egypt's colonization.

French Invasion in Algeria

Roughly at the same time that Muhammad Ali was challenging the Ottomans militarily, the French were moving against the semi-independent Ottoman province of Algiers. Relations between the various French governments and the authorities in Algiers had been strained since the French invasion of Egypt, in particular because the French had never paid for grain supplied by the Algerians. Relations deteriorated in the 1820s as the French took advantage of declining Ottoman naval power to enforce increasingly harsh terms of trade on the North African region. A diplomatic incident in 1830 led France first to break ties with Algiers and then to invade. The French troops had quickly overwhelmed the forces of the local ruler, Husayn Dey, who was promptly sent into exile. Although the French had little or no trouble seizing the coast, they soon faced stubborn resistance in the interior. In the mountains, a former opponent of Husayn Dey rallied the escaped Janissaries and put up strong resistance. In the west, a religious scholar named **'Abd al-Qadir** organized the interior's largely pastoralist and Berber-speaking population to resist the French. He called for a jihad and drew on the region's Sufi brotherhoods to organize and unify the forces. The French attempted to co-opt al-Qadir by offering him the position of "Governor of Western Algeria," but he only took advantage of the position to consolidate his base of power and garner support from the Moroccans. A skilled commander, he dealt the French forces a series of painful defeats.

In 1837 the French were able to break resistance in the east and turn their full energies against 'Abd al-Qadir in the west. Al-Qadir's forces fought valiantly, relying on surprise and knowledge of the local terrain to counteract the French command of large-force tactics and technological advantage. The French responded with a scorched-earth approach, destroying crops, livestock, and even towns to force the local population into submission. It was an early and deadly example of the nature of guerrilla warfare, with numerous atrocities committed by both sides. In 1843, al-Qadir fled to Morocco, but the French attacked the Moroccans and forced them to abandon support for the Algerian resistance. In 1847, al-Qadir surrendered to the French. Less-organized resistance, however, was to continue for much of the nineteenth century. Only in 1879 could the French claim that they had "pacified" Algeria. In the conflict the French had created a great deal of ill will on the part of the Algerian populace, an antagonism that was only exacerbated by the arrival of hundreds of thousands of settlers from France and elsewhere in Europe. These settlers took the best lands, almost all found along the coast, and used the advantage of social position as victors to dominate politics and trade. Further, the dogged resistance of Algerian Sufis helped convince French administrators that Islam in general and Sufism in particular were a threat to colonial rule, a theme that would greatly influence the development of French colonial policy in West Africa (a subject that will be examined in Chapter 15).

Religious Change in the Soudan to the 1880s

Stretching from the region of the Senegambia across West Africa to the modern country of the Sudan is a band of savannah and Sahel. Collectively, this region has often been referred to as the "Soudan"—a term taken from the Arabic Bilad al-Soudan, or "Land of the Blacks." As seen in previous chapters, this region has been home to a number of important states, ranging from ancient Meröe in the Sudan to Ghana, Mali, and Songhai in West Africa. The Moroccan invasion of Songhai in 1591, however, was the beginning of a long period of decline for large-scale states in the savannah. With the establishment of European trading posts along the West African coast, much of the trans-Saharan trade was diverted, and some traders from the savannah were forced to move south to continue their livelihoods. This movement is often referred to as the "**Dyula** Diaspora."

Trade and states certainly did not die out in savannah with the decline in the trans-Saharan trade. Cities such as Jenne and Timbuktu survived, but their heyday had passed. States also existed, but they tended to be fairly small compared to their predecessors in the region. The theme of state decline, however, began to reverse in the early eighteenth century. Central to this revival was a new Islamic movement. In contrast to the previous era when Islam had been a predominantly urban phenomenon, most of the new revivals were organized by predominantly rural and pastoralist populations. Often, a group called the **Fulani** (alternately spelled Fulbe or Puel) was at the forefront. In part, the expansion of Sufism was responsible for the spread of Islam to more rural communities. Perhaps Sufism's strong emphasis on community and its more mystical expression of Islam made it more palatable to African populations beyond the cosmopolitan cities of the savannah. These revivalist movements were often fostered by local scholar–warriors. These leaders called attention to the failure of the local authorities to adhere to Islamic standards of governance and behavior. A particularly common complaint was that Muslims were being captured and sold into slavery. In such a situation, the creation of Islamic states offered the hope of establishing security in the face of the chaos engendered by the trade in slaves. Also significant is that these movements were defined as Jihads of the Sword by their participants. Such events show not only a growing Muslim consciousness, but also a growing awareness of Islam as a political and social, as well as religious, system.

The first of the West African jihads took place in Futa Jalon (a hilly region in the north of modern Guinea). Beginning around 1730, Fulani pastoralists waged a running conflict with the region's ruling Jalonke. Two key leaders of the campaign, Ibrahima Sori and Karamoko Alfa Barry, shared power, and authority in Futa Jalon shifted back and forth between their descendants (though not without occasional conflict). The new state of Futa Jalon became known for the high levels of scholarship practiced by the local Fulani, in part because the new ruling class benefited from the region's wealth (some of it drawn from the slave trade) and had the free time to devote to learning. Aspiring students of Islam from across West Africa traveled to study in Futa Jalon.

The second jihad took place in the Futa Toro region (in the middle valley of the Senegal river) in the 1760s. A group calling themselves the **Torodbe** (seekers)

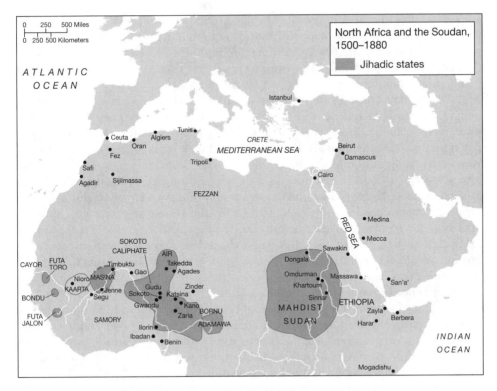

Map 10-2: North Africa and the Soudan, 1500–1880

began to criticize the local Denyanke dynasty for not protecting Muslims from enslavement. Conflict soon broke out not only with the Denyanke, but also with the Bani-Hassan, a new group of Arabic-speaking migrants who were backed by Morocco. A leader named Abdul Qadir Kan organized much of the campaign and was successful in defeating the Denyanke and holding the Bani-Hassan to the north bank of the Senegal River. Notably, he also organized the establishment of mosques, schools, and Islamic courts in the region's towns and villages. In 1786 he negotiated a trade agreement with the French that provided them access to the region as long as they guaranteed Muslims would not be sold into slavery. Abdul was killed in battle with the neighboring state of Kaarta in 1807, however, and the new state of Futa Toro fell into decline. The legacy of Islam that he had helped establish, however, survived.

The next jihadic movement took place far to the east in the region that is now northern Nigeria and southern Niger. Interestingly, the leader of this movement, **Usman dan Fodio,** was from a Fulani family that had, generations before, migrated east from the Futa Toro region. In his early life dan Fodio distinguished himself as a devout scholar even among his family of scholars. His knowledge and piety attracted a growing number of students until he was surrounded by a small community. Such fame brought him into conflict with Na Fata, the local ruler of the state of Gobir. Na Fata attempted to force dan Fodio to stop preaching, but his attempts were futile. In 1804 conflict broke out between dan Fodio's followers and Na Fata's successor, Yunfa. Reputedly, word came to dan Fodio's community that a slave caravan was passing nearby, and that among the enslaved were Muslims. After the caravan was attacked and the Muslims freed, war broke out between Gobir and dan Fodio's community.

Usman dan Fodio's campaign was a sophisticated affair not only in terms of military strategy, but also because he was careful to present his actions and motives in terms of Islamic political ideology. For example, he carefully modeled his campaign on that of Muhammad in his war against the Meccans. Faced by the power of Yunfa's army, he announced a hijra (flight) from Gobir and then regrouped his forces to wage a Jihad of the Sword—a direct reference to Muhammad's hijra to Medina. Notably, Usman dan Fodio was also deeply influenced by **al-Maghili's** instructions on proper Islamic governance, written for the Hausa King of Kano, Muhammad Rumfa, roughly 300 years before. Dan Fodio wrote extensive tracts carefully justifying his war against Gobir. In this he was aided by his family, particularly his brother Abdullahi, son Muhammad Bello, and daughter **Nana Asma'u.** In these tracts dan Fodio and his supporters argued that Yunfa had failed to uphold the proper practice of Islam and had allowed local culture to corrupt the religion. Further, it was argued that the state did not offer proper protection to Muslims, as evidenced in particular by enslavement. To gain further support, dan Fodio also very carefully drew on growing local loyalties to the Qadiriyya Sufi brotherhood, claiming, for example, that Abd al-Qadir al-Jilani (the eleventh-century Iraqi founder of the brotherhood) had appeared to him in a vision years before. By 1808, Gobir had been defeated, and dan Fodio and his followers were able to establish a new state with its capital at Sokoto. Soon, dan Fodio's fame had spread so much that others came seeking his blessing for their own campaigns against corrupt rulers. He responded by handing out flags to those whose cause he thought just. These flags became a powerful symbol of legitimate jihad. By 1814 almost all of the region's Hausa city-states had been overthrown by Islamic campaigns organized largely by local Fulani, though they were often supported by local Hausa who also thought their rulers corrupt.

The result of this coordinated series of campaigns (generally recognized as a single Jihad of the Sword) was the formation of what was perhaps the largest African state of the time. Known as the Sokoto Caliphate, this new state was a confederation of semi-autonomous city-states, each ruled by an emir (**sarki** in Hausa) who owed ultimate allegiance to the Sultan of Sokoto. Notably, Usman dan Fodio did not seek to become sultan, but rather divided administrative duties between his brother and son. It was his son, Muhammad Bello, who eventually came to hold central authority. Even after victory, dan Fodio and his supporters continued to seek the expansion of Islam within the new state's borders. Perhaps none were more influential in this than his daughter Nana Asma'u, whose poetry and essays were aimed primarily at the region's women, with the specific goal of replacing the region's syncretistic blend of African traditional religion and Islam known as **Bori.** Because it was women who oversaw the education of children, the extension of more orthodox Islamic practices to the female population had a particularly powerful impact not only on the then-current generation, but also those that followed.

Voices from African History: **Clapperton in the Sokoto Caliphate**

In 1824, the British traveler Captain Hugh Clapperton journeyed across the Sahara and reached the Sokoto Caliphate, where he met with the Sultan Muhammad Bello. On a second visit in 1826, this time traveling north from the West African coast, he visited the commercial center of Kano. In April of 1827, Clapperton died of a fever and was buried near Sokoto city. Following are excerpts from his accounts.

Arrival in Sokoto and meeting with the Sultan:

"At noon we arrived at Sokoto, where a great multitude of people was assembled to look at me, and I entered the city amid the hearty welcomes of young and old. I was conducted to the house of the vizier, where apartments were provided for me and my servants. . . .

After breakfast the sultan sent for me; his residence was at no great distance. In front of it there is a large quadrangle, into which several of the principal streets of the city lead. We passed through three guardhouses . . . and were immediately ushered into the presence of Bello, the second sultan of the [Fulani]. . . . The Sultan bade me many hearty welcomes. . . . He asked me a great many questions about Europe, and our religious distinctions. He was acquainted with the names of some of the more ancient sects, and asked whether we were Nestorians or Socinians. To extricate myself from the embarrassment occasioned by this question, I bluntly replied we were called Protestants. 'What are Protestants?' says he. I attempted to explain to him as well as I was able. . . . He continued to ask several other theological questions, until I was obliged to confess myself not sufficiently versed in religious subtleties to resolve these knotty points, having always left that task to others more learned than myself. . . ."

From Thomas Hodgkin, *Nigerian Perspectives* (London: University Press, 1960)

Tour of the Kano Market:

"The soug, or market, is well supplied with every necessary luxury in request among the people of the interior . . . [and] is numerously frequented as well by strangers as inhabitants: indeed, there is no market in Africa so well regulated. The sheikh of the soug lets the stalls at so much a month, and the rent forms a part of the revenues of the governor.

I may here notice the great convenience of the cowrie, which no forgery can imitate; and which, by the dexterity of the natives in reckoning the largest sums, forms a ready medium of exchange in all transactions, from the lowest to the highest. Particular quarters are appropriated to distinct articles; the smaller wares being set out in booths in the middle, and cattle and bulky commodities being exposed to sale in the outskirts of the marketplace. Wood, dried grass, bean straw for provender, beans, Guinea corn, Indian corn, wheat, etc. are in one quarter, goats, sheep, asses, bullocks, horses, and camels in another; earthen ware and indigo in a third; vegetables and fruit of all descriptions, such as yams, sweet potatoes, water and musk melons, pappaw fruit, limes, cashew nuts, plums, mangoes, shaddocks, dates, etc. in a fourth, and so on. Wheaten flower is baked into bread of three different kinds; one like muffins, another like our twists, and the third a light puffy cake, with honey and melted butter poured over it. Rice is also made into little cakes. . . . Near the shambles there is a number of cook-shops in the open air; each consisting merely of a wood fire, stuck round with wooden skewers, on which small bits of fat and lean meat . . . are roasting. Everything looks very clean and comfortable; and a woman does the honours of the table, with a mat dish-cover placed on her knees from which she serves her guests, who are squatted around her. Ground [sugar-cane] water is

(Continued)

retailed at hand, to those who can afford this beverage at their repast.

The interior of the market is filled with stalls of bamboos laid out in regular streets; where the most costly wares are sold, and articles of dress, and other little matters of use or ornament are made and repaired. Bands of musicians paraded up and down to attract purchasers to particular booths. Here are displayed coarse writing paper, of French manufacture, brought from Barbary; scissors and knives, of native workmanship; crude antimony and tin, both products of the country; unwrought silk of red colour, which they make into belts and slings, or weave in stripes into the finest cotton robes; armlets and bracelets of brass; beads of glass, coral and amber; finder rings of pewter and a few silver trinkets, but none of gold, robes, turkadees, and turban shawls; coarse woollen cloths of all colours;

coarse calico; Moorish dresses; the cast-off gaudy garbs of the Mamelukes of Barbary; pieces of Egyptian linen, checked or striped with gold; sword blades from Malta, etc.

The market is regulated with the greatest fairness, and the regulations are strictly and impartially enforced. If a robe or a turkadee, purchased here, is carried to Bornu or any other distant place, without being opened, and is there discovered to be inferior quality, it is immediately sent back, as a matter of course,—the name of the dylala, or broker, being written inside every parcel. In this case the dylala must find out the seller, who, by the laws of Kano, is forthwith obliged to refund the purchase money."

Adapted from Hugh Clapperton, *Journal of the Second Expedition into the Interior of Africa from the Bight of Benin to Soccatoo* (1829)

The Sokoto Caliphate continued to grow even after the initial wave of jihad. After the conquest of the region's Hausa city-states, the caliphate's forces continued to expand in every direction except north. Ironically, this expansion seemed to dilute the ideals of the caliphate itself. Slavery became a major source of income for the new state—both via capture for sale and also because the new rulers developed a plantation system that relied on extensive slave labor. Most of those enslaved were pagans from the southern borders of the caliphate. However, this was not always the case in practice. For example, Muhammad Bello received letters from the **Shehu** of Bornu, who ruled an Islamic state to the east near Lake Chad, complaining that the Caliphate's forces were raiding his lands and enslaving his (Islamic) subjects.

> Tell us why you are fighting us and enslaving our free people. If you say that you have done this to us because of our "paganism," then I say that we are innocent of paganism, and it is far from our compound. If praying and the giving of alms, knowledge of God, fasting in Ramadan and the building of mosques is paganism, what is Islam?
>
> Thomas Hodgkin, *Nigerian Perspectives* (London: University Press, 1960)

Bello replied that although the Shehu was perhaps a good Muslim, many of his subjects were not, and thus they were open to capture and enslavement under Islamic law. Thus, as the demands of power and wealth grew, the ideals of dan Fodio seemed increasingly relegated to the sidelines.

The Sokoto Jihad was to directly influence two following campaigns. Just as the Sokoto Caliphate was consolidating its control over the former Hausa states, Seku Ahmadu Bari, a scholar and teacher from the area along the Niger River in the modern country of Mali, contacted Muhammad Bello and received a flag of legitimation for his war against the pagan rulers of Segu and the "corrupt" Islam practiced by those living in the city of Jenne. In 1818, Bari emerged victorious and established a state, often referred to as Massina, and a new capital at Hamdullahi (meaning "thanks be to God"). Bari's administration made heavy use of local representation, ruling in cooperation with an immediate council of about two dozen advisers and also a larger council of around 100 local representatives.

Ahmadu Bari certainly seems to have had plans for expansion. He organized the settlement of Fulani pastoralists around the state's "frontier" as a means of expanding the region under his authority. Further, although his initial request for a flag from Sokoto suggested that he would submit to the authority of Sultan Bello, Ahmadu broke ties with Sokoto and declared himself the "Twelfth Caliph," sending letters announcing his ultimate authority to Islamic leaders throughout the region. Few, however, recognized his authority, and on his death in 1845, he was succeeded by his son, who took the title Ahmadu II.

The last of the jihadic movements in West Africa was taken by al-Hajj **Umar Tal.** The life and exploits of Umar Tal tie together many of the themes of the wider jihadic movements. He was born in Futa Toro and studied in Futa Jalon. As such, he was clearly steeped in the jihad tradition established in those regions. From 1828 to 1830 he made the Hajj to Mecca and Medina, showing that West Africa had become very much a part of the Dar al-Islam, where even those outside the ruling class could undertake the pilgrimage. During his stay in Mecca, he was reputedly tasked with spreading the Tijaniyya Sufi Brotherhood in the savannahs (the Tijani Brotherhood has its origins in Morocco). While en route home from the Middle East, Umar spent a period of several years residing both in Sokoto and in Hamdullahi, where he clearly was impressed by the achievements of these new Islamic states. Upon returning to Futa Jalon in the 1840s, he began teaching and soon developed a considerable following. In 1852 he launched a jihad first against the king of Tamba. After skirmishes with the French, he turned east and launched campaigns first against the state of Kaarta and then against pagan Segu (which had previously lost territory to Ahmadu) and captured that state's capital in 1861. However, after this success Umar launched a major campaign against Ahmadu II and captured the town of Massina only after a long and costly siege. Thus, despite his dedication to Islam, Umar Tal was willing to challenge a fellow Islamic ruler. Some attribute this fact to his dedication to Tijaniyya Sufism rather than the Qadiriyya form practiced by most other Muslims in the region. It is quite possible that economics were also a factor because Massina was a very important trading center. Umar died in 1863 and was succeeded by his son, Ahmadu Seku, who struggled to maintain the unity of the new state—a task made particularly difficult by the fact that Umar had done little to establish a framework of administration during his process of conquest. Ahmadu Seku was faced with numerous internal revolts and also growing pressure from the French to the west.

Umar Tal's jihad was not to be the last of the Islamic revivalist movements in the Soudan, however. Far to the east in the region of the modern Sudan, another

movement was to take place. For some time, this region had been loosely administered by administrators from Ottoman Egypt and even the Mamluks, who had
sought to escape Ottoman authority. Muhammad Ali had invaded the region in
hopes of expanding the production of cotton and also in search of slaves with which
to expand his military forces. When the British asserted their authority in Egypt in
the 1870s, they also sought to gain greater control over the region of the upper
Nile—appointing the famous General "Chinese" Gordon as governor of the Sudan.
None of these administrations had done much to engender the love of the populations of the region. Clearly, there was fuel for a popular revolt.

Muhammad Ahmad was to provide the spark for revolution in the Sudan. In
1881 he declared himself to be the **Mahdi,** a character in popular Islamic belief who
will herald the Second Coming of Christ, the defeat of the Anti-Christ, and the usher-
ing in of a new era of peace and prosperity. Ahmad preached extensively on the
need to drive the "Turks" (a general term for foreigners) from the land and soon
drew to himself a huge following. In 1881 his forces defeated an Anglo-Egyptian
army sent to arrest him and disperse his followers, and also succeeded in capturing
a number of garrisons in the region. Busied with revolts in Egypt in 1882, the
British were not able to send another army against the Mahdists until 1883, and this
force, numbering some 10,000 Egyptian troops, was also defeated. Indeed, with
each victory, Ahmad's claims to be the "appointed one" seemed to be strengthened.
In 1884, Gordon was sent to Khartoum to oversee the city's evacuation. Gordon,
however, disobeyed orders and decided to make a stand. Surrounded by the
Mahdi's troops, the city was starved and eventually stormed in January 1885, dealing
the British one of the most famous defeats in colonial history. Though Ahmad died
shortly after taking Khartoum, his state would survive under the leadership of
Abdullah Ibn Muhammad until the British reconquest of the Sudan in 1898. The
legacy of Mahdism, however, would be a source of fear for colonial governments
throughout the Sudan and West Africa for decades to come.

North Africa and the Soudan, 1500–1880, in Global Perspective

The topics and events outlined in this chapter highlight a number of important
global themes. In particular, this chapter focuses on the three-way conflict over control of North Africa. Europeans and Ottomans both sought to extend their authority over the fertile and strategically important North African coast. Local populations,
often including assimilated Europeans and Ottomans, used a variety of tactics to
expand their own degree of independence. Sometimes they utilized military
force, which was particularly successful for the Moroccans. Other times they
sought to play the contending Turkish and European forces against one another. And
sometimes they simply worked within the dominant system to make a way for themselves as best they could. By and large, however, the period examined in this chapter saw a fairly steady trend toward expanded European power at the expense of
both the Ottomans and the North African states. Here we can see how the relative parity in power between Europeans and Africans in the sixteenth, seventeenth, and eighteenth centuries gave way to a rise of European dominance in the nineteenth

century. Indeed, the events in North Africa during the early 1800s, particularly in Egypt and Algeria, were foreshadowing for the coming of colonialism elsewhere in Africa.

Notably, the relatively minor cultural impact of Ottoman rule in North Africa during the period, compared to the considerable influence of European colonialism in the nineteenth and twentieth centuries, points up the very different nature of these two eras of empire. Though the Ottomans were culturally different from North African populations in many ways, their rule often rested fairly lightly on the region's inhabitants. Even in the case of Egypt, Ottoman rule was at least no worse than that of the Mamluks. The Ottomans did not seek to force cultural change on their North African subjects, preferring instead a fairly limited economic and political subjugation. Perhaps the common bond of the populations as Muslims helped downplay what differences did exist, or at least provided something of a common framework for social interaction and exchange. European colonizers, however, brought with them not only occasional historic biases against Muslims, but also a growing sense of racial superiority that was fueled by the economic and political developments of the scientific and industrial revolutions and the development of the notion of race itself. New technologies (see Chapter 13) and new ideas such as scientific racism and social Darwinism would make the coming wave of European colonialism something very new in the world.

In respect to the West African Savannah, the jihadic movements show the intersection of a number of important themes. First, these movements show that the "weight" of Islam in the region had finally shifted to that of being the dominant spiritual force, rather than existing simply as a religion of outsiders or urban elites. In some ways these seemingly sudden movements highlight how centuries of gradual cultural change can suddenly yield remarkable and sweeping political results. Clearly, by the nineteenth century, a very large number of West Africans saw themselves as a part of the Dar al-Islam. Further, these jihadic movements left a legacy of political Islam, which influences governance in the Savannah regions to this very day. Indeed, it was only the expansion of colonial rule during the "scramble for Africa" in the 1880s and 1890s that would bring the downfall of the Islamic states established by the era of jihad. The French were to expand up the Senegal and Niger river valleys, defeating states such as that of Ahmadu Seku and Ahmadu III of Massina over the period. In the east, the British were to defeat the Mahdists in 1898 and the Sokoto Caliphate in 1903. Although the expansion of colonialism was to bring to a halt the era of Islamic state-building in West Africa, it would, ironically, help advance the spread of Islam itself. This theme will be addressed in Chapter 16.

Useful Works on This Chapter Topic

Remarkably, few texts cover the subject of Ottoman rule in North Africa. See Michael Winter, *Egyptian Society under Ottoman Rule, 1517–1798* (1992); Andre Raymond, *Arab Cities in the Ottoman Period: Cairo, Syria and the Maghreb* (2002). *A History of the Maghrib in the Islamic Period*, by Jamil M. Abun-Nasr (ed.) (1987) also includes some useful information, as does Julia Clancy-Smith (ed.), *North Africa, Islam and the Mediterranean World: From the Almoravids to the Algerian War* (2001). For a more general study of the Ottoman Empire, see *History of the Ottoman Empire and Modern Turkey: Volume 1, Empire of the Gazis: The Rise and Decline of the Ottoman Empire 1280–1808*, by Stanford J. Shaw.

For material specifically relating to the jihadic movements in West Africa, see Mervyn Hiskett, *The Sword of Truth* (1985); David Robinson, *The Holy War of Umar Tal: The Western Sudan in the Mid-Nineteenth Century* (1992); and Ibraheem Sulaiman, *The Islamic State and the Challenge of History: Ideals, Policies, and Operation of the Sokoto Caliphate* (1987).

Several chapters from Nehemia Levtzion and Randal Pouwels (eds.), *The History of Islam in Africa* (2000), and Nehemia Levtzion, *Islam in West Africa: Religion, Society and Politics to 1800* (1994), offer excellent surveys of the material discussed in this chapter.

CHAPTER 11

East Africa, 1500–1850

In 1490, coastal East Africa was thriving. In addition to controlling the trade between the East African interior and the lands of the western Indian Ocean rim, the Swahili city-states were centers of manufacturing and scholarship. Their trade reached into the interior as far as the goldfields of Great Zimbabwe. A common Islamic culture gave the cities a religious and cultural unity that contrasted with their fiercely independent politics and commercial rivalries. Although one city might dominate others either politically or commercially, no city or group of cities had attempted to create a coastal empire. In the 350 years that this chapter covers, that situation would change. Several waves of invaders would arrive on the East African coast with the intention of reshaping the politics and trade of the Swahili cities in unprecedented ways. First came the Portuguese. They first raided and demanded tribute but eventually began to build forts and attempted to build East Africa's first coastal empire. Their success at empire building was limited, but they left in their wake a trail of destruction that permanently altered the life of the coast. Next came Arabs from Oman, who came first as liberators driving out the hated Portuguese, but then stayed to create an empire of their own. On the heels of the Omanis came the British, who did not create a formal empire before 1850. Instead, the British undermined and co-opted Omani sovereignty on the coast, in the process setting the stage for a formal empire in the second half of the nineteenth century.

It is tempting to see this time of abrupt and violent transition in stark, black-and-white terms. Some historians have seen this time as the downfall of the Swahili world, a time when the commercial and cultural world created by the Swahili ceased to exist. To be sure, the Swahili elite saw their power and cultural prestige undermined, but this era of rapid change created opportunities for new players to emerge in the realm of commerce, it greatly increased connections between the coast and the interior, and it brought waves of migrants from the western Indian Ocean rim who landed on the East African coast and ultimately moved into the interior.

At the same time, there was indeed a darker side to this era. Many East Africans entered the commercial world of the Indian Ocean, not as merchants but as slaves. The rise of plantation agriculture on the coast and an increase in the demand for slaves in Arabia and on the sugar-producing islands of the Indian Ocean led to a steady increase in the demand for slaves from East Africa. The result was that by the mid-nineteenth century much of East-Central Africa was in a state of upheaval as new types of states and new social formations emerged in response to the increasing tempo of the trade in slaves.

At the same time that the demand for East African slaves was increasing, so, too, was the demand for other East African commodities. As Europe and North America began to industrialize, they created a growing demand for raw materials. Some of these, such as ivory, gum copal (a tree resin used to make varnishes), coconut copra (used to make food oils and soaps), coconut coir (used to make rope), and hides, were available in East Africa. The trade networks and systems of production that were created to provide these goods profoundly reshaped East African life. In the case of the ivory trade, the ecological effects of the large-scale slaughter of elephants may have changed settlement patterns of farming communities.

The Arrival of the Portuguese

The Portuguese exploration of the Atlantic in the early fifteenth century was a sort of nautical extension of the reconquista—the military effort to take the Iberian Peninsula from the Muslims who ruled it. The reconquista was a crusade of a sort. It mixed religion, politics, and warfare. By the early fifteenth century there were only a few Muslim rulers holding out in Iberia (the last holdout would fall in 1492), and the Portuguese were looking for new territory in which to pursue their crusading urge. This resulted in attacks on North African ports—most famously at Ceuta, which is still a colonial outpost belonging to Spain—and an effort to outflank the Muslims of North Africa by sailing down the West African coast in search of gold and Christian allies. The Portuguese also hoped that a sea route to Asia might be found that would undermine the monopoly that the Venetians and Egyptians enjoyed on trade through the Red Sea. This, of course, was the same sea route that Christopher Columbus hoped to find when he set out across the Atlantic. The Portuguese effort to find this sea route to the wealth of Asia was shaped by its crusading origins, so everywhere they went, the Portuguese were on the lookout for Christians to form alliances with and Muslims to attack. Their explorations of the West African coast yielded few Muslims or Christians, but once they entered the Indian Ocean, they found themselves in a world dominated by Muslims. This they set out to change.

The first Portuguese sailor to get around the southern tip of Africa and into the Indian Ocean was **Bartolomeo Diaz.** In 1485, Diaz was sailing south along the coast of what is now Namibia and was caught in a storm that blew him far out to sea. When the storm abated, land was nowhere in sight. Diaz knew that he could raise land by sailing north. When he finally sighted land, it was on his left, rather than on his right where he expected to find it. He had been blown into the Indian Ocean. Diaz apparently wanted to follow through and go all the way to India. His crew, however, had had enough and demanded that they go home. Diaz landed on the South African coast on Christmas Day, named the place Natal (Christmas in Portuguese), and erected a pillar to leave tangible evidence of his achievement. Diaz stopped too far south to encounter the world of the Swahili, so when the subsequent Portuguese navigators followed up on his discovery, they were surprised to find the Swahili cities.

The first Portuguese to follow Diaz's route was Vasco da Gama. In 1497, da Gama led a small fleet of vessels around the Cape and up the East African coast on their way to India. They were thoroughly surprised to find thriving stone-built cities on the East African coast—something they had not found in West Africa where the major urban centers were on the "coast" of the Sahara, not the sea—and they were shocked to find that the people of these towns were Muslims.

The commercial world of the Indian Ocean was a fairly tolerant place. Although people often preferred to do business with their coreligionists, there is ample evidence of trade and business partnerships that crossed religious and ethnic lines. Hindu, Muslim, Jewish, Zoroastrian, and the occasional Christian merchants in the western Indian Ocean seem to have been more interested in profits than prophets. Similarly, the various states that were involved in trade preferred to lure merchants to their ports through incentives rather than coercion. To the extent that trade in the western Indian Ocean was militarized, it was to keep pirates at bay rather than to force merchants to use or not use certain ports.

The world the Portuguese came from could not be more different. Trading states in the Mediterranean regularly used military force to prevent others from trading where they did. The Venetians, whose trade monopoly the Portuguese were trying to undermine, used their powerful navy and maritime empire to maintain their monopoly on trade with Egypt. The Portuguese themselves made every effort to keep "interlopers" out of the West African trade. As for religious tolerance, we need only remember that their voyages were part of a broader effort that they saw as a crusade. Thus, the Portuguese encounter with the Indian Ocean had all the ingredients for conflict, and nowhere was the conflict as destructive as it was in East Africa.

Da Gama called at several Swahili towns during his first voyage, most famously at Malindi, where he found an ally. Malindi was at war with nearby Mombasa, and the sultan of Malindi saw in the Portuguese and their warships an opportunity. In exchange for an alliance and for providing da Gama with a pilot to guide his ships to India, he would get Portuguese assistance in his war with Mombasa. With the help of the pilot, da Gama made it to the Indian port of Calicut, where he was able to acquire a cargo of pepper. Da Gama's voyage was followed by many other Portuguese fleets, which managed to take control of several port cities. In India the Portuguese took control of Goa, which they made the capital of their Asian empire, and the lesser port of Diu. They plundered and then seized the East African cities of Sofala, Mombasa, and Kilwa and maintained their alliance with Malindi. They also established themselves in minor East African ports like Zanzibar. By 1600, they had constructed forts in many of these places, the grandest of which was Fort Jesus in Mombasa. Fort Jesus has the distinction of being the first European-style fortress built outside Europe that was designed to withstand cannon fire. They also built a string of churches from which they conducted a mostly futile effort to convert the Swahili to Christianity.

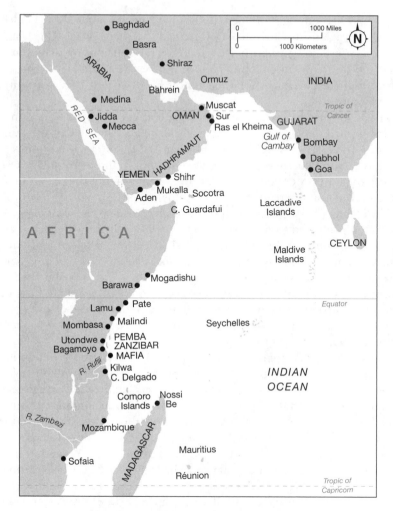

Map 11-1: East Africa and the Indian Ocean

These efforts in East Africa were part of a broader and largely unsuccessful effort to take control of western Indian Ocean trade. Using Goa as a base, the Portuguese set out to control the trade bottlenecks of the Indian Ocean. They sent ships to take the port city of Aden, which lies next to the entrance to the Red Sea. (Taxi drivers in Aden like to show visitors the place where the Portuguese are believed to have come ashore—it's right next to the Pizza Hut.) When this effort failed, they tried to blockade the entrance to the Red Sea using just their ships; this, too, failed due to the difficulty of keeping the ships supplied with food and water. They were able to take Hormuz at the entrance to the Persian Gulf and Malacca, which lies where the Bay of Bengal meets the South China Sea. They then imposed restrictions on trade by requiring that ships that wished to trade buy passes called **cartaz,** which could only be obtained at certain Portuguese-controlled ports. This

Fort Jesus, constructed by the Portuguese in 1593 in the Swahili city of Mombasa, remains the most tangible evidence of the Portuguese presence on the Swahili coast.

forced trade to pass through Portuguese ports where it could be taxed, it generated income through the sale of cartaz, and it gave Portuguese sea captains the "right" to plunder ships they found at sea without a cartaz.

It was a wildly ambitious plan. And the Portuguese were just ruthless enough that they nearly carried it off, but ultimately they failed to take control of the Indian Ocean or its trade. That a tiny place like Portugal would even consider such an audacious imperial venture so far from home is remarkable, but given the challenges the Portuguese faced, it is hardly surprising that their impact was limited. Although they did succeed in taking a few ports, it is worth noting that these were but pinpricks in the larger scheme of things. The Mughal Empire of India hardly noticed the Portuguese presence. Merchants in India and Africa soon found ways of dealing with the Portuguese. There were not enough Portuguese ships to patrol the whole Indian Ocean, so many ships traveled without cartaz, and for many merchants the cartaz was just another business expense. But more importantly, the Portuguese had a limited effect on commerce because they had nothing to sell. Portugal, and for the most part sixteenth-century Europe in general, made nothing that Africans or Asians wanted to buy. The Portuguese had to content themselves with trading in goods that were produced in the world of the Indian Ocean. This meant that they had to make deals, make alliances, and even borrow money from Asian and African merchants. It also meant that Portuguese governors called "captains" had to take into account the wishes and advice of Asian and African merchants if they wanted their territories to thrive. It would be wrong to say that the Portuguese dominated Asian trade, conquered Asia or East Africa, or anything like that. To be sure, they caused change, but it would be a gross overstatement to see them as having fundamentally changed the trading world of the Indian Ocean. Historians of Asia have long since concluded that the Portuguese were little more than a new wrinkle in the story of Indian Ocean trade. Historians of Africa, however, see them in a different light, and it is worth considering the possibility that the Portuguese caused more profound change in East Africa than they did in other parts of the Indian Ocean.

In East Africa the Portuguese were able to move away from the seacoasts in ways that they did not in Asia. In India their only territorial possessions were coastal cities and enclaves. In East Africa they were able to follow the **Zambezi** River several hundred miles into the interior. Unlike the rivers of India (and most African rivers, for that matter) the Zambezi was navigable by oceangoing ships for almost 400 miles. This allowed the Portuguese to establish huge privately owned estates there that they called **prazos.** The **prazeros** that governed these vast estates used them not only to produce agricultural products, but also to control the trade in two of the three goods that the Portuguese sought most—ivory and slaves. The other was gold. The prazeros maintained private slave armies that they used to strong-arm the villages within their territories into paying tribute, to hunt ivory, and to obtain slaves. The slaves might be exported or employed on the prazos.

That the Portuguese did "better" in Africa than they did in Asia may have to do with the commodities they sought in each place. In Asia they were attempting take control of a trade in manufactured goods, cloth in particular. The complex system of credit, labor, and agricultural and industrial production that made Indian cloth was something far outside the experience of Portuguese soldiers and even merchants. By contrast, the system that produced ivory and slaves in southeastern Africa was something the Portuguese were intimately familiar with—it was the economics of plunder.

In the area of southeastern Africa that was to become the modern nation of Mozambique, the Portuguese established a presence that would last until 1975, when they were eventually thrown out. At Sofala and the island city of Mozambique (from which the modern nation takes its name), they seized trading cities that controlled the wealth that came from the slave and ivory operations on the Zambezi and from the trickle of gold that still came from the central highlands. In the eighteenth century people called the Yao pioneered new trade routes to areas near Lake Malawi. Yao traders brought slaves and ivory from the lakes to the coast where they exchanged them for cloth and other trade goods the Portuguese obtained in India. By the eighteenth century, there were also increasing numbers of merchants from India who came to Portuguese Mozambique to participate in the trade.

Farther north, from Kilwa to the Lamu archipelago—the Swahili "heartland"—the Portuguese were more destructive. Cloth production and iron production, both of which seem to have thrived in pre-Portuguese Kilwa and Mombasa, become less prominent in the record once the Portuguese arrive. The authority of local patrician families was undermined as the Portuguese installed puppet rulers in most towns. In the hinterlands new groups of people appeared called the **Mijikenda**. The Mijikenda lived in fortified hilltop settlements called **kayas** and used these as bases from which to raid the coastal cities. The Mijikenda speak languages that are so similar to Swahili that it is clear they are closely related to the Swahili. Until recently, it was thought that the rise of the Mijikenda was a result of upheaval in the interior and that these upheavals probably weakened the Swahili cities, making them more vulnerable to the Portuguese. Recently, another explanation has been proposed. This theory, advanced by the archaeologist Chapuruka Kusimba, suggests that the Mijikenda were not refugees from upheaval and strife in the interior but rather former residents of the coastal cities who took to the hills rather than submit to the Portuguese. He sees the Mijikenda not as desperate refugees turned to raiding but as former city dwellers trying to drive the Portuguese and their lackeys from their former homes. Whatever the origins of the Mijikenda, they are part of a broader trend of movement in East Africa during this period. The Portuguese records are full of references to attacks on the coastal cities by migrating people from the interior. From the north the Somali began to press southward looking for new pastures; the Masai raided as far east as the coast, also looking for fresh pasture. From the south came other groups that were apparently fleeing drought. Many Swahili cities were abandoned during the Portuguese era, probably because of the combined effects of Portuguese abuses, drought, and raiding.

But as troublesome as the Portuguese were, their control over the coast, especially north of Sofala, was limited. With the exception of the prazos and trading posts on the Zambezi, the Portuguese rarely ventured inland. Their fortresses allowed them to control the coastal cities, but even these were often manned by little more than a skeleton crew desperately awaiting relief from the next Portuguese ship to arrive. By no means were the Portuguese invulnerable. The first intimations of their weakness came in the early seventeenth century when a Turkish corsair named Ali Bey arrived on the coast. Ali Bey had only one leaky ship and about 50 followers, but he claimed to be vanguard of a major Ottoman fleet. The Portuguese believed this and abandoned many of their northern posts. They had a healthy respect for Ottoman power and clearly realized their weakness in relation to the Turks. A few years later Ali Bey again showed up, this time with a slightly more substantial fleet, and raided merrily on the north coast with little opposition from the cowed Portuguese. The ease with which Ali Bey was able to carry off these feats exposed the weakness of the Portuguese and made Ali Bey a Turkish folk hero. By the end of the seventeenth century another Muslim power would capitalize on the weakness and drive the Portuguese south to their stronghold in Mozambique.

While they were in Mozambique the influence of the Portuguese was substantial, north of Sofala their legacy is remarkably small. Fort Jesus still looms over Mombasa, but it is as much a symbol of Arab power as it is of Portuguese power. The Portuguese may have built it, but the Arabs controlled it longer than the Portuguese did. Other Swahili towns often have a ruin or two that are locally and often erroneously attributed to the Portuguese. A small church and its cemetery survive in Malindi that is claimed to be the burial site of some of da Gama's crew. The Swahili language has a few Portuguese-derived words in it. Interestingly, these are the words for jail, one of the words for brothel, and the names of playing cards, which tells you something about the sort of people who were sent out into the Portuguese empire.

The Omani Empire in East Africa

Oman lies just on the Indian Ocean side of the entrance to the Persian Gulf. Its mountains and its location allow it to capture a little bit of annual monsoon rainfall and so allow some regions of Oman to have what passes for agricultural abundance in the Arabian Peninsula. For our purposes the most important Omani crop was dates. Date palms tolerate very dry conditions and produce huge quantities of calorically dense food. Dates keep well and are easy to transport, and so were a major item of trade. Dates were sold as feed for camels, they were eaten by people as a sweet, and they are the traditional food with which Muslims break their daily fast during Ramadan. Dates were so much a staple of sea trade that the standard way of measuring the size of Arab ships in the nineteenth century was by the number of bags of dates they could carry. Oman's location and its date production made it a nation of seafarers. The Omani ports of Muscat and Salala have long been loci of long-distance trade.

The other distinctive feature of the Omanis is their approach to Islam and how that affects politics in Oman. The Omanis practice the **Ibadi** form of Islam. As discussed in earlier chapters, there are two main branches of the Muslim faith: the Sunni and the Shia. The Ibadis are neither; instead, they derive from an earlier group of Muslims called Kharijites. The Ibadis believe that the Imams (in the sense of leaders of the Muslim community rather than prayer leaders) need not come from a particular family nor need there always be an Imam. Instead, whenever someone with piety and skills to take the office comes along, he should be elected to that post. That the Omanis are Ibadis is important because it made them the enemies of Sunni reformers called Wahabis, which encouraged the British to ally themselves with the rulers of Oman, and also because their relatively minor religious differences with the Shafi (a branch of the Sunni) Swahili served to keep the Omanis slightly distinct from the larger East African Muslim population when they began to settle there in large numbers in the eighteenth and nineteenth centuries.

Oman was united in the seventeenth century under the **Yarubi dynasty.** The Yarubis had sufficient religious prestige that some of them were considered Imams. Under the Yarubis, Oman went through a poorly understood invigoration of its naval power. The Yarubis first drove the Portuguese out of their fort at Muscat, then from the Persian Gulf, and then began to raid Portuguese settlements in India and East Africa. They became among the most feared sea fighters in the Indian Ocean, and there is some speculation that they learned the use of the cannon at sea from the Portuguese.

Once it became apparent that the Portuguese were weakening and that Omani power was on the rise, the Swahili towns invited the Omanis to rid them of the Portuguese. The invitation came from the citizens of Mombasa who asked the Omanis to throw out the puppet king who ruled Mombasa and Malindi for the Portuguese. The Omanis were only too happy to oblige. In 1696 they laid siege to Fort Jesus. Two years later the fort, and with it Mombasa, was theirs. Portuguese power quickly collapsed north of Sofala. Nearly 200 years of Portuguese rule was over.

But things did not change that much. Having run off the Portuguese, the Omanis settled quite comfortably into the role of imperial master. They moved

Swahili Family from Lamu—an engraving made in the mid-nineteenth century.

right into Fort Jesus and other Portuguese forts and eventually constructed others in places the Portuguese had never fully controlled. The Swahili had thrown off one yoke for another. This time their new rulers, who were at least fellow Muslims, were easier to deal with, but they were still bent on controlling the trade of East Africa and making it suit their own purposes.

The Busaids

By the middle of the eighteenth century the Yarubis were replaced by a new ruling family in Oman—the **Busaids.** The Busaids were less pious than the Yarubis and never took the title "Imam." Instead, they might be described as merchant-princes much like the so-called grocer-kings of Portugal. For the Busaids, trade, war, and foreign policy were all of a piece. The Busaids' interest in trade would have profound consequences for East Africa because they controlled huge date palm plantations in Oman. For them, East Africa represented a potential market in which to sell dates and at the same time a source of slave labor for their date plantations. The other effect of the Busaid interest in trade was that Muscat, their capital in Oman, became home to many Indian merchants. The Busaids welcomed and protected Indian merchants—Hindu as well as Muslim—in Muscat because they had access to the goods and more importantly the sophisticated financial markets of India. Muscat served as a sort of bridgehead between India and East Africa, and Indian dominance of East African trade—which continues in the present—can be said to have begun in Busaid-controlled Muscat.

In the second half of the eighteenth century, the Busaids encouraged migration from Oman to East Africa and established their headquarters in the island port of Zanzibar. When the Omanis took over, Zanzibar was a fairly minor port. It had once been home to a small Portuguese trading post, but was otherwise a commercial backwater. This is surprising because Zanzibar is one of East Africa's finest natural harbors. The Omanis apparently liked the security of being twenty miles offshore where they could defend themselves with their ships, while still being close enough to the coast for small coasting vessels to easily make the voyage from the coast to the island's port.

The Busaids made Zanzibar the main collection point for trade on the East African coast by requiring that all long-distance traders buy their goods at Zanzibar. Foreigners were not allowed to trade directly on the coast, and even Omani merchants had to pass through Zanzibar before clearing for ports outside East Africa. At Zanzibar merchants paid a 5 percent tax on the value of their goods, a major source of revenue to the Omani state. The principal collection point on the coast for goods to be brought to Zanzibar was Kilwa. Kilwa, which had been abandoned during the Portuguese period, was revived and rebuilt on a nearby site during the eighteenth century as Yao trade routes moved away from Portuguese territory in the south toward Omani territory in the north. Kilwa had an Omani governor and a trading community of Arabs, Indians, and older Swahili families. Many of the latter found their fortunes improving under the Omanis, in part because they could intermarry with the Muslim Omanis, something that had not been an option with the Christian Portuguese. It appears (and scholars debate this vociferously) that during this time many of the Swahili patrician families began to claim Arab or Persian origins and even descent from the Prophet Muhammad.

The Omani leader whose life best reflects the changes that occurred under the Omanis in East Africa was **Seyyid Said.** Although Said's own initiative clearly helped to shape events, there were larger forces at work. We might think of Said as a surfer riding the historical groundswell of industrial capitalism. He might choose to turn this way or that way on the wave, but his speed and the overall direction of his choices are dictated by the wave. Seyyid Said made many critical changes in Omani policy toward East Africa, but he made all those choices with the specter of British military and commercial power looming over him.

Perhaps Said's most revolutionary act was to decide that East Africa was economically more important to him than Oman. He began to visit East Africa as early as 1827. He soon began to build palaces for himself and his family in Zanzibar, and in 1839 he moved the seat of Omani power to Zanzibar. For twenty years, Oman was governed from Zanzibar rather than the other way around. When Seyyid Said moved to Zanzibar, he brought his family and retainers and all the people and paraphernalia that surround a ruler. He also brought with him an Englishman named Atkins Hamerton. Hamerton was an agent of the East India Company (EIC), who represented the company's interests to Seyyid Said. In addition to being a commercial enterprise, the EIC ruled most of India. It had its own army and a small navy and pursued its own foreign policy in consultation with the British government.

The EIC became interested in Oman in the early nineteenth century when it became involved in the suppression of piracy (though it's worth noting that the British had a habit of labeling their commercial rivals as pirates) in the Persian Gulf. The sultans of Oman saw in the British a source of support against the Wahabi religious reformers who threatened them, and they pragmatically allied themselves with the British.

Britain and the Suppression of the Indian Ocean Slave Trade

But British support came at a price. As discussed in Chapter 8, the early nineteenth century was the time when Britain outlawed the slave trade and began to attempt its suppression in the Atlantic. Though it was less of a priority, they also sought to end the slave trade in the Indian Ocean. The volume of the Indian Ocean slave trade is hotly debated and no certain numbers have emerged yet, but it is clear that the slave trade was increasing in volume in the early nineteenth century and that the Omanis, with their control over the East African coast, were in the thick of it. In the early part of the nineteenth century the British were not in a position to force a complete end to the slave trade, so they settled for limiting it. In 1822 they created the Moresby line—an imaginary line from Mozambique to what is now Pakistan. West of the Moresby line the slave trade was legal; east of it the slave trade was illegal. Thus, the Omanis could legally transport slaves from East Africa to Oman and to the slave markets in other parts of the Persian Gulf, but not to British-ruled India. Shortly after the Moresby line was drawn, the British began to pressure Said to place further limits on the slave trade. He resisted, claiming that while he, of course, agreed with the British and wished to abolish the slave trade, his subjects would not stand for it. But Said seems to have seen the handwriting on the wall. Realizing that the slave trade could not be relied on as a permanent source of income, he encouraged diversification. If industrializing Britain did not want slaves, he would find other products more palatable to the British.

One of these he had ready to hand. Ivory had been exported from East Africa from time immemorial, going mostly to India. But in the nineteenth century in Europe and North America, a growing middle class began to buy ivory combs, billiard balls, and pianos with ivory keys. As a result American merchants began calling at Zanzibar in the 1820s, and by the 1830s several American merchant houses had offices in Zanzibar. These firms bought a variety of goods, but the staple of their trade was ivory. By the 1840s there were German, French, and British merchants in Zanzibar, all buying ivory. Omani rules prevented them from trading directly on the coast, so they worked through intermediaries, some of whom were Arabs, but most of whom were Indians. These Indian merchants, the most famous of whom was Jairam Sewji, traded in their own ships to India and other parts of the Indian Ocean and got access to the North Atlantic economy through the American and European merchant houses in Zanzibar. It is worth noting that for the most part it was the Indians who held the upper hand in this relationship. Indian commercial firms typically provided the capital that made the system work, often advancing goods to the Americans and Europeans on credit.

Voices from African History: A French Slaver in East Africa: Captain Dallons

While there is no doubt that there was an extensive slave trade between the East African coast and the ports of the Persian Gulf and South Arabia, much of the slave trading revival of the eighteenth and nineteenth centuries was related to the expansion of the sugar economy in the French Mascarenes, especially the island of Mauritius. In the following document we find a Captain P. Dallons' 1804 description of the slave trade in East Africa. Note that this description dates from shortly before Seyyid Said moved his capital to Zanzibar. It is apparent from Dallons' account that European slave traders in East Africa faced many of the same challenges as their counterparts in West Africa.

"Zanzibar is governed by the Prince of Muscat [Seyyid Said]. It suffers constant changes because of the fear the Sultan has of a governor becoming too strong and taking the lordship from him. This has happened at Pemba, Mombasa, and Pate. The choice of commander becomes daily more difficult, and nowadays he only appoints eunuchs, and even divides powers between them . . .

When we were going to trade in this island, we at first promised ourselves a good and advantageous treaty, but we were soon disappointed of our hopes. On our arrival the government gave us an interpreter on whom, under the appearance of the greatest liberty, we had entirely to depend. We brought them trade goods, such as cloves, sugar, iron, and so on. The government only asked from us a first option at the same price [as others were paying], and made us an immediate offer, but without telling us that it had forbidden the people of the country to trade with us concurrently. By their use of such means, the French are always made to submit to the price fixed by the government, and, by a payment of the Governor, to suffer a further loss of thirty percent by his atrocious underhandedness.

Before engaging in trade the French are made to giv1e very costly presents to the government and to the interpreter, a subtle and pliant man on whom all success depends. If his eager cupidity is not satisfied, he finds every means to deflect them from their object."

The other and much more innovative choice that Said made was to encourage the creation of clove plantations in Zanzibar. Cloves are native to Southeast Asia, and most of the world's clove production was in the hands of the Dutch, who controlled the islands where cloves were grown. It's not clear how the first clove tree seedlings made it to East Africa, but by the 1830s, Seyyid Said was appropriating land on Zanzibar and Pemba and giving it to his family, friends, and supporters to plant clove trees.

Clove production is extremely labor intensive. Land has to be cleared to plant the trees, then the area around the trees needs to be weeded, and finally, once the trees have matured, there is a twice-annual harvest of the tiny flower buds that are then dried to make the spice we call cloves. All of this requires lots of people, but the harvest in particular requires many people because the buds must be harvested before they bloom. Once they have blossomed, they are useless, so time is of the essence during the harvest.

To meet these labor needs, it was a simple matter to redirect the flow of slaves formerly headed for the Gulf and Oman to the clove plantations. As the extent of the land planted in cloves increased in Zanzibar and Pemba, the need for slaves there went up, too. Soon the plantations on the islands and the coast (these produced grain and coconut rather than cloves) became more important markets for slaves than the markets of Oman and the Gulf. Not that these distant markets ceased to be important, but they declined in importance relative to the markets created by the rise of the plantations in East Africa.

Interestingly, the British had no problem with the exportation of goods produced by slaves and were happy to have Zanzibari cloves sold in India. Indeed, cloves eventually came to be modestly important to European industry, where oil extracted from them was used to make vanilla and dentifrices. Here again Europeans had no difficulty buying products made by slave labor. So Seyyid Said had hit on a clever solution to the British opposition to the slave trade. By redirecting slaves into production in East Africa, he was able to participate in both the slave trade and the emerging industrial economy.

Links to the Interior

Two new, interrelated developments occurred related to the continued growth of the slave and ivory trades. First, a new group of long-distance overland traders emerged to rival the Yao. These were the **Nyamwezi** of central Tanzania. The Nyamwezi opened trade routes that linked Lakes Tanganyika and Victoria to the coast. Nyamwezi caravans brought ivory and slaves hundreds of miles overland to the coast. Second, people from the coast began to move up the trade routes into the interior. This process seems to have begun in the early nineteenth century. By 1848, when the British traveler Richard Burton reached the Nyamwezi capital at Tabora, he found a community of coastal Muslims living there. This community included—to the extent that one can really make distinctions between them— Swahilis, Arabs, and Indians. In the next few decades coastal people would end up crossing to the Congo basin, where they established commercial empires devoted to the collection of slaves and ivory.

In the eighteenth century the Nyamwezi seem to have been primarily farmers, but early in the nineteenth century, as the demand for ivory began to increase on the coast, the ivory frontier pushed west into their territory. The Nyamwezi adapted to this new opportunity with remarkable alacrity. In many East African societies young people are expected to go through some sort of coming-of-age experience to mark their transition to adulthood. This might mean withdrawing from society for a month or two while being taught the duties of adulthood or participating in a military campaign or any number of other challenging experiences. For the Nyamwezi, joining a caravan and traveling to the coast became the rite of passage that separated the men from the boys. A journey to the coast might take as much as a year, and when the porters came back they had earned enough money that they could afford to get married.

One of the myths spread by nineteenth-century abolitionists was that the ivory sold on the coast was carried there by slaves, who were then sold also. While in some regions slaves were used as caravan porters and there was some synergy between the slave and ivory trades, the majority of such porters were free professionals, and many of these were Nyamwezi. Carrying elephant tusks is not an easy task. They are heavy and lack natural "handles." Thus, it took someone who was being paid for his

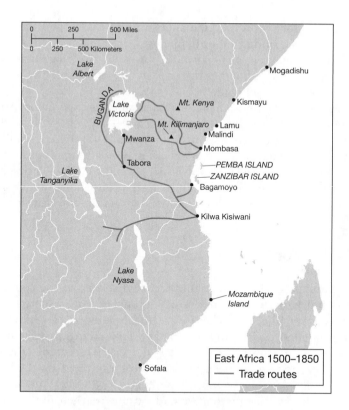

Map 11-2: Nineteenth century trade routes

trouble to carry such awkward loads for hundreds of miles. When they reached the coast, the ivory was sold, and the returning caravans carried trade beads and cloth. The standard cloth in this trade was merikani, which means "American." American merchants were prominent among the ivory buyers in Zanzibar, and New England textile mills provided cotton cloth that was so standard a part of the East African caravan trade that it was the standard unit of value for trade goods.

These caravans were usually financed by coastal merchants and led by their agents. Thus, many coastal merchants began to pass up and down the caravan routes into central Tanzania, creating communities in Tabora and other towns in the interior. These communities grew in size and importance as the century wore on and the tempo of trade increased. By the 1860s there were even boats built in the fashion of Indian Ocean trading vessels plying the waters of the East African Great Lakes, and the coastal merchants were playing an ever greater role in organizing the capture of slaves.

It is worth stopping for a minute to look at all these changes in perspective. If one were to drop into central Tanzania in 1750, one would certainly find evidence of long-distance trade. Archeologists have found Chinese porcelain in Uganda dating as far back as the middle of the eighteenth century. Goods like these were traded from person to person through a long chain from the coast into the interior. Furthermore, the goods in question were rare prestige items, probably used by the

Men displaying ivory in Zanzibar. Ivory was one of the principal
commodities in East African trade in the nineteenth century.

elite to emphasize their social status. Although a visitor in 1750 might find trade
goods from the coast, he would be hard-pressed to find anyone in central Tanzania
who had ever seen the sea or met a Muslim.

By contrast, a visitor to Tabora in 1850 would find it considerably changed.
Tabora was teeming with porters for hire and with caravans readying themselves for
the journey east to the coast or west to the lakes. Caravan leaders could hire as many
as several hundred porters at a time—all from the pool of labor available in Tabora.
One could also buy provisions for a caravan. That all these porters were working in
jobs outside agriculture for at least part of the year—and many worked for a full
year or more—implies that someone else was growing food to feed them. Farmers,
who in 1750 would have been growing food mostly for their own families, were in
1850 growing food for sale. They were at least in a limited way cash croppers rather
than subsistence farmers. And it was not just local people entering into this market.
At least a few of the coastal people who had settled in Tabora were getting involved
in producing food for sale. Burton mentions that he encountered an Arab in Tabora who was using slave labor to grow rice for sale to the caravans. Our imaginary
visitor would also have seen people wearing imported cloth. Although the Nyamwezi

elite seem to have preferred cloth from India, many common people were starting to wear merikani. Our visitor would also have seen beads, most made in Europe, being used to make personal decoration.

What was the force behind these changes? Ultimately, it lay in the industrial transformation that was sweeping through northwestern Europe and North America. The industries on either side of the Atlantic were creating enough wealth that a growing number of people could afford things such as pianos with ivory keys or billiard tables with ivory balls or combs made of ivory. The industries themselves sought raw materials such as clove and coconut products and produced things such as cheap cloth to pay for them. A place like central Tanzania, which had only the slenderest thread of a connection to the world economy in 1750, was deeply involved in that economy in 1850. The Nyamwezi's world revolved around trading in goods that the industrial West wanted. They marched hundreds of miles to the coast carrying ivory so that Americans could "tickle the ivories" of their pianos. They marched hundreds of miles back so that their fellow Nyamwezi might wear merikani. Those Nyamwezi who stayed home found their world transformed, too, as imported goods, a growing Muslim community in their midst, and the possibilities of cash cropping entered their world, courtesy of the caravan trade.

The industrial West also helped indirectly to support the demand for slaves. Cloves and other plantation crops were among the raw materials that European and American industries needed. Most of these goods were produced by slave labor in coastal plantations. That coastal merchants were pressing farther and farther into central Africa to supply those plantations with slaves was in part because of the steady demand for plant fiber and oils to feed into the maw of industry. If the Omani empire in East Africa looks remarkably different than the Portuguese empire did, it is in large part because the Omani efforts there took place in the shadow of the industrial revolution. Seyyid Said made some shrewd choices about how to surf the wave of industrial capitalism, but the Portuguese never had that option.

Living in the age of industrial capitalism had some benefits for the Omanis, but there were also costs. Foremost among these was the power that it gave the representatives of industrial capitalism. The British used their wealth and power to subvert Omani sovereignty in East Africa. As the Omanis became increasingly dependent on trade with British India and the West, the British began to flex their muscles more and more. Atkins Hamerton, the EIC agent who had followed Seyyid Said from Muscat to Zanzibar, declared that all Indians in the Omani territories in East Africa were British subjects and hence subject to British law, of which he was the official representative. This was an extremely dubious claim because many of the Indians in East Africa had been living in Muscat, not India, before they came to East Africa. Second, many of those who had emigrated there from India came from Cutch, which was not directly ruled by the British. Nonetheless, Hamerton was able to claim them as British subjects and require that they refer their legal affairs to his offices. He was also able to prevent them from trading in or owning slaves because both the slave trade and the status of slavery had been outlawed in the British Empire.

His actions on this front had several effects. First, it made Indians focus on the ivory trade and on money lending because without access to slave labor they could not participate in the clove industry. Thus, they ended up in the unlikely position of holding mortgages on clove plantations that they could not really foreclose on because they could not operate the plantations themselves. Second, Hamerton's actions helped to strengthen the group identity of the Indians. Where before the Muslim Indians mixed quite freely with other Muslims on the coast (less true of Hindu Indians, of course) their status as something separate and different from other coastal Muslims was reinforced by Hamerton's definition of them as a legally discrete group. This would have long-term implications for Indians in East Africa, who still constitute a discrete group and are subject to a certain amount of hostility as a result.

Hamerton's other major intervention in Zanzibar's affairs was to force on Seyyid Said a new treaty further limiting the extent of the legal slave trade. The Moresby line had allowed the legal slave trade to extend north to Oman and the Persian Gulf. The Hamerton line of 1848 ended the northern trade. The legal slave trade was limited to Omani dominions in East Africa. Slaves could be transported along the coast or from the coast to the islands of Zanzibar and Pemba, but no farther. The legal trade to the Gulf and South Arabia was over, at least in theory. Just like the Atlantic slave trade, the Indian Ocean slave trade refused to die just because it had been outlawed. Despite the Hamerton line, an illegal slave trade flourished between East Africa and the Arabian Peninsula. It was one thing for the British to force a treaty on Seyyid Said; it was another matter entirely to enforce the new treaty.

It is not clear whether Seyyid Said made a good faith effort to end the long-distance slave trade, but it is near certain that he lacked the means to enforce the ban. The East

Slaves captured by the HMS "Undine" during the British antislavery effort in the western Indian Ocean. The crews were paid a bounty for each slave taken on patrol. The slaves were usually turned over to Christian missions where they became apprentice workers.

African coast had thousands of boats on it and miles of mangrove swamps and other isolated places where slaves could be quietly loaded on boats for the voyage to the Gulf. Furthermore, the presence of many slaves of African origin in the crews of ships made it difficult to distinguish between slaves being transported for sale (which was illegal) and slaves who were crew members (which was legal). Even if Seyyid Said and his successors had wanted to end the slave trade, it might well have been beyond their capacity to do so.

Even the wealthy British Empire proved unequal to the task of controlling the newly illegal slave trade. Initially the antislavery patrolling was entrusted to the Bombay Marine—the EIC's navy. But the Bombay Marine's pay structure was set up in such a way that the commanders of their ships usually lost money if they captured a slaver. Each captured ship had to be brought to a court of adjudication, and while the case was in court, the ships' captains were considered to be off duty and so put on half pay. So when they saw a potential slaver, most turned a blind eye. Thus, the immediate effects of the new treaty were few. Slaves continued to flow into the plantations on the coast legally, and many also went north, albeit illegally. Coastal merchants continued to press farther and farther into Central Africa in search of slaves and ivory to meet the demands of the global economy. What had changed was that now the British had an issue to press against Seyyid Said. They had a treaty with him that clearly was being violated. This became an ever bigger bone of contention between Britain and the Omani Empire in East Africa, and eventually it became one of the major rationales for the British establishment of a protectorate in Zanzibar.

By 1850 the British were becoming more and more assertive in Zanzibar. When Seyyid Said died, the British Consul in Zanzibar helped to choose his successor. The British then forced a split in the Omani Empire, putting Zanzibar and Muscat under the control of different branches of the Busaid family. Then in the later part of the 1850s they set out to clamp down on the slave trade. Antislave trade duties were shifted from the Bombay Marine to the Royal Navy, and the captains and crews were given all sorts of financial incentives to capture slavers. They were awarded prize money for every ship they took and for each slave they liberated. As a result, Royal Navy captains pursued their work with a gusto not seen in the Bombay Marine. They stopped any ship they could find on the high seas that looked like it might be a slaver—any ship, that is, that flew an Arab flag. Ships flying the flags of most European nations were usually exempted from search and seizure. So despite the fact that there was a lively illegal trade in slaves to the French-controlled sugar islands in the Indian Ocean and even a trade in slaves destined for the Americas, the Royal Navy's efforts focused on the politically more vulnerable Arab ships.

The result was that the trade in just about anything between East Africa and Arabia became much more difficult. Royal Navy ships stopped any Arab-flagged vessels they could. Their judgment skewed by the financial incentives at stake, they concluded that most of these were slavers—often on the flimsiest of evidence. Although doubtless many slaves were freed and many real slave ships were captured, there was also much harassment of perfectly legitimate trade by the Royal Navy. A second effect of the antislave trade effort was to build a permanent British naval presence in Zanzibar. Warships on patrol were sometimes based out of Zanzibar, and eventually the Royal Navy moved its administrative offices there to oversee the antislave trade patrolling. This meant that there was always a ship on hand that could turn its guns on the city of Zanzibar, and marines and sailors on board the ships who could intervene at the British consul's behest. The noose was closing on Zanzibar.

A formal protectorate would not be declared in Zanzibar until 1890. In many respects, however, the last vestige of Omani sovereignty in Zanzibar disappeared in 1872 when the British forced a new treaty on Zanzibar, this time outlawing the slave trade entirely. Slaves could not be moved from the coast to the islands nor could slaves be transported from one island to another. This was in part a response to the work of David Livingstone. Livingstone was a Scottish physician and missionary who traveled widely in East-Central Africa. Though he made few converts, the books he wrote describing his travels were wildly popular in Britain. His books painted a picture of a land ravaged by the slave trade, and caused an outcry in Britain against the East African slave trade and the Arabs who were depicted as its perpetrators. The result was the 1872 treaty that outlawed the slave trade. In a sign of the changing times, John Kirk, the British consul in Zanzibar, did not even bother to carry on the pretense of negotiating the treaty. He dictated it. And with British warships in the harbor, Seyyid Bargash—one of Seyyid Said's sons and Sultan of Zanzibar—signed.

The Omani period in East Africa left a considerable legacy. Many people on the coast still identify themselves as Omani Arabs, and there are many Ibadi mosques found in the cities of the coast, though few coastal Muslims would care whether they prayed in an Ibadi or Shafi mosque. Perhaps their greatest legacy is the spread of the Swahili language away from the coast. Swahili is currently the most widely spoken African language. Although as a first language it is used almost exclusively by coastal people, it is used as a trade language and lingua franca in Kenya, Tanzania, Uganda, Rwanda, Burundi, and eastern parts of Democratic Republic of Congo. Later German and British colonial policies about languages played a role in this dispersion, but the trade routes and commercial settlements that were carved out by coastal people in the nineteenth century were also critical to the process. Unlike West Africa, where European languages or local patois based on French or English are the standard means of cross-cultural communication, East Africans often choose to communicate across language barriers in Swahili.

There is also a darker legacy of the Omani period in East Africa. In much of the interior of East Africa, the people of the coast are remembered primarily for their role in the slave trade. The picture that David Livingstone painted of the horrors of the slave trade and the effects that slave raiding had on East-Central Africa was at least partly correct. There is still resentment on this score in modern East African nations, especially Kenya. In Kenya, where the government is largely in the hands of the people from the interior, most of whom are Christians, coastal Muslims feel that they have been intentionally marginalized and neglected by the government. They contend that the government shortchanges them on development money and that schemes to resettle people from central Kenya to the coast are meant to "dilute" the Muslim culture of the coast. By way of example, in 1997 the government of Kenya decided to celebrate the five hundredth anniversary of the arrival of Vasco da Gama on the East African coast. They thought this might help attract tourists to the Portuguese monuments on the coast, Fort Jesus in particular.

A dhow in the colonial era port in Zanzibar.

From the perspective of coastal Muslims, this was at best a thoughtless suggestion and at worst a calculated insult. Why celebrate the end of Swahili autonomy? Why celebrate the arrival of "crusaders" in a Muslim land? Even in Tanzania, where government policy has always sought to downplay ethnic identities and minimize interethnic tension, the rise of a political party, which the government believes is attempting to revive Arab dominance on the coast, has led to brutal repression on the islands of Zanzibar and Pemba. Although these tensions are mostly the result of colonial-era divide-and-rule policy, they clearly have their roots in the Omani-led expansion of the coastal world into the interior of East Africa.

Portuguese and Omani Dominance in Global Perspective

East Africans' experience with the Portuguese was not that different from that of other people around the Indian Ocean rim. As was the case with India or the Persian Gulf, the Portuguese used their naval power to carve out coastal enclaves from which they attempted, with only partial success, to seize control of the trade that passed through their ports. As noted before, the main difference between Asia and Africa was that in a few places in Africa the Portuguese were able to control and occupy much more land than they ever did in Asia. The Portuguese prazos have no real analogue in Asia. In many ways they more resemble the sugar estates the Portuguese created in Brazil than any Portuguese territory in Asia. That this only happened on the

Zambezi is telling. In the core areas of the Swahili world, the Portuguese had less success. It is also worth noting that the Zambezi let the prazeros have at least some access to the sea, which would not have been possible farther north on the Swahili coast.

The Omani Empire's rise in East Africa and usurpation by the British has some parallels in other parts of Africa. Perhaps the most pertinent is the rise of the Boer Republics in southern Africa. In this instance, the descendants of Dutch settlers, called "Afrikaners," in the Cape of Good Hope region of South Africa set out in the early nineteenth century to establish states beyond the control of the British. This meant seizing lands north and east of British control in South Africa. Like the Omanis, the Afrikaners acted for their own reasons but were constantly under the shadow of the British Empire. Like the Omani–British relations, Afrikaner–British relations soured over the issue of slavery, which the Afrikaners practiced despite British disapproval. When the British finally took over the states that Afrikaners had created, it was a far bloodier process than had been the case in East Africa, but in both instances the British were able to take over a sort of ready-made empire.

Perhaps the most interesting parallels to be found in this era are with Southeast Asia. At approximately the same time that the British were working to stamp out the slave trade in East Africa, they were trying to suppress piracy in Borneo. In both cases the "villains" were whomever the British chose to define as villains. If just about any boat encountered at sea in the Indian Ocean could be slaver if a Royal Navy captain said so, so too in Borneo could any local leader who crossed the British be defined as a pirate. In one of the stranger moments in the history of the British Empire, an Englishman named James Brooke managed to establish himself as the "White Rajah of Borneo" as a result of his private efforts to suppress "piracy" there. In both places, imperialism arrived cloaked as law and order.

Useful Works on This Chapter Topic

M. N. Pearson, *Port Cities and Intruders* (1998) is a good source for the Portuguese period in East Africa. For the Omani conquest and administration, see Norman Bennett, *Arab versus European* (1986). For the economics of East African trade and the loss of Zanzibar's sovereignty, see Abdul Sheriff's classic work, *Slaves, Spices and Ivory in Zanzibar* (1987). Stephan Rockel's new book, *Carriers of Culture* (2006), is the first serious study of the caravan trade. On the lives of slaves in East Africa, see Frederick Cooper, *Plantation Slavery on the East Coast of Africa* (1977). For the slave trade at sea and its suppression by the Royal Navy, see Erik Gilbert, *Dhows and the Colonial Economy of Zanzibar* (2004).

CHAPTER 12

Southern Africa, 1500–1870

The history of the southern portion of the African continent is different in many respects from that of other regions of sub-Saharan Africa. It was one of the last places on the continent where there were significant numbers of foragers. It was the first region of the continent to see large-scale European settlement and the only part of the continent in which there are still significant numbers of European settlers. It is the richest area of the continent. The Republic of South Africa's gross domestic product exceeds that of the rest of sub-Saharan Africa put together. South Africa was also the last place on the continent to have white minority rule, was home to some of the most protracted and bitter anticolonial struggles on the continent, and perhaps most infamously, was the birthplace of the white supremacist ideology called **apartheid.** Apartheid was an ideology, expressed through the laws of the white minority government of South Africa, that called for the legal separation of the races and ethnic groups in education, housing, employment, marriage, and just about anything else. It was not formally adopted in South Africa until the Nationalist Party came to power in 1948, but its roots go back much further. Obviously, 1948 falls outside the chronological scope of this chapter, but apartheid casts its shadow over the historical record. Much of the early writing of South African history took place within the context of apartheid in South Africa, and as such was intended as justification for white rule. Thus, more than anywhere else on the continent, history and myth are so closely intertwined that they are almost impossible to separate. As we go through the centuries that preceded the rise of apartheid, we will make frequent reference to the ways in which apartheid has shaped the interpretation of South African history.

Terrain, Climate, and Settlement

As you will remember from Chapter 2, southern Africa is home to a broad variety of climates. At one end of the spectrum are the Namib Desert and its neighbor, the Kalahari. The Namib is one of the driest places on the planet and is basically uninhabitable by humans. The Kalahari is less dry and can support foragers and, in some places, pastoralists. To the east, the climate grows wetter as one approaches the Indian Ocean. The area called Natal is quite wet—wet enough to support intensive farming as well as cattle. In the south, around the Cape of Good Hope, there is a Mediterranean climate. This means winter rains, temperate weather, and conditions reminiscent of Southern California. In the Cape one can grow grapes for wine, wheat, apples, and other Eurasian crops. The tropical diseases that made most of sub-Saharan Africa such a challenging environment did not flourish in the Cape. As a result, Europeans were able to occupy the Cape long before they moved into most other regions of the continent. Furthermore, the Cape was in a strategic location. Until the construction of the Suez Canal in 1869, the Cape sat astride the main route from the Atlantic Ocean to the Indian Ocean. In the seventeenth century the Dutch East India Company (usually known by its Dutch initials as the **"VOC"**) came to be the dominant European player in Indian Ocean trade. This began to spark Dutch interest in the area, and in 1652 the VOC established an outpost at the Cape. Originally intended as little more than a place for VOC ships to resupply themselves on the way to and from India, this outpost eventually became the city of Cape Town.

When Jan van Riebeeck founded Cape Town, neither he nor the Heren XVII (the Seventeen Gentlemen, as the board of directors of the VOC was called) expected that they would be creating anything more than a trading post. Their hope was that van Riebeeck would be able to buy on the local markets the foodstuffs that Dutch East Indiamen needed to finish their journeys to Asia. This turned out to be a serious

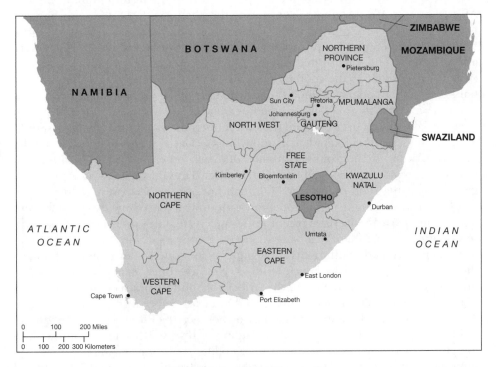

Map 12-1: Southern Africa today

miscalculation. The inhabitants of the Cape region did not farm. Rather, some of them were foragers and others were pastoralists, but neither of the two major groups of indigenous peoples in the Cape farmed. Furthermore, they were not always willing or able to sell cattle to the Dutch in the quantities that the latter desired. So, shortly after their arrival, the Dutch began to move out of their trading post to farm and keep livestock themselves. Conflict with the herders whose grazing lands they took immediately ensued.

The people whom the Dutch initially encountered in South Africa are now called the Khoikhoi and the San (sometimes grouped together as the Khoisan in recognition of the fuzzy line between the two groups). The Khoikhoi, whom the Dutch disparagingly called **"Hottentots,"** were cattle keepers. They practiced what is called transhument pastoralism, which means that they moved in a regular cycle from winter to summer pastures, in a sort of systematic nomadism. They lived in small, decentralized chiefdoms rather than large states. The San, whose languages were probably related to those of the Khoikhoi, were foragers who occupied the mountains and lands that were too dry to support pastoralists. They lived in small bands that were even more politically decentralized than the chiefdoms of the Khoikhoi. They were more mobile than the Khoikhoi because they could move from place to place without the need to bring herds of cattle with them. Despite the primitive appearance of their material and political culture, the flexibility of their society and their ability to live in the mountains allowed them to mount a formidable resistance to Dutch expansion.

It is worth noting that the line between the Khoikhoi and the San cannot be drawn too sharply. There is a tendency, particularly in the historiography of South Africa, to treat African ethnic groups as if they had always existed and the lines between them were sharply defined. Furthermore, the assumption was that those sharply defined ethnic groups—what the older literature would call "tribes"—were always at odds with each other, waging bloody wars that owed more to atavistic "tribal" hatreds than to the good rational reasons that Westerners have fought their wars. Part of this tendency is due to apartheid. One of the premises of apartheid was that not only were there differences between blacks and whites, but there were also irreconcilable differences between the different ethnic groups that made up South Africa. Just as apartheid kept blacks and whites separate, it also sought to keep the various African ethnic groups separate from each other, ostensibly because they were distinct and, of course, all hated each other. Thus, historians who were apologists for apartheid and others who, although not overtly racist, were influenced by this line of reasoning, sought to demonstrate that these ethnic differences were ancient and permanent. More recent work suggests that this assessment is wrong in several ways. Ethnic identity in southern Africa appears to have been quite fluid, with people regularly shifting their allegiances from one leader to another and in the process adopting new ethnic identities. New identities seem to have emerged on a regular basis. In fact, most of the "tribes" of South Africa seem to be creations of the nineteenth century and probably did not exist before then.

In all likelihood this meant that the line between the Khoikhoi and the San was fluid. Khoikhoi who lost their cattle to raiding or disease became San and took to foraging. San who acquired cattle became Khoikhoi. So as the Dutch moved into the hinterlands of the Cape, they encountered a mixed bag of herders and foragers, and indeed by raiding for cattle they probably increased the numbers of San foragers.

One final point before we return to a discussion of the Dutch and their expansion into the interior of southern Africa. Why didn't the Khoikhoi and the San farm? After all, people had been farming in various parts of southern Africa for at least 1,000 years when the Dutch arrived, and the Dutch were able to farm quite successfully on at least some of the land that the Khoikhoi had used just for grazing. The answer seems to lie in the isolated nature of the southern tip of Africa and in the unusual climate of the Cape. The Cape, as we have said, has a Mediterranean climate. The only other part of the continent to have this sort of climate is in North Africa. Crops such as grapes and wheat, which thrive in North Africa, also thrive in the Cape. But they do very poorly in the roughly 6,000 miles between the Mediterranean and the Cape. Thus, although the Khoikhoi might have been able to get their hands on crops suitable in nearby, but quite different, climates, they did not have access to the types of crops that would thrive in the Cape. The area of the Cape that is suitable for rain-fed farming is also rather small. Once one moves a couple of hundred miles into the interior, it becomes dry enough that farming does not work well. Instead, extensive grazing—what the Khoikhoi were doing and the Dutch soon learned to do—worked much better.

As the Dutch moved out of Cape Town and into the interior, they needed labor for their farms. To get this labor, they made indentured servants of the Khoikhoi and to a lesser extent the San. They also imported slaves from Madagascar and occasionally Indonesia. There evolved a system whereby Dutch settlers, with their privileged access to firearms, horses, and markets at Cape Town, came to control big pieces of land that they used to produce wheat, wine, and meat for sale in Cape Town. The populations of these farms included Khoikhoi laborers, and over time came to include many people of mixed Dutch and Khoikhoi ancestry. These people have gone by a variety of names, depending on where and when they were living. In the Cape they came to be called Coloureds, which was recognized as a distinct racial category by the laws of the apartheid system. People of mixed Dutch and Khoikhoi descent that moved out beyond the boundaries of Cape Colony called themselves "Bastards," in reference to their mixed ancestry, a name that horrified British missionaries convinced them to change to **Griqua.** The name Griqua is a reference to a fictional ancestor and represents just the sort of ethnic formation that was so common in nineteenth-century South Africa. Here a group created by the arrival of the Dutch, with no prior existence in southern Africa, that often welcomed new members—and often obtained them by raiding—suddenly went from being a more or less amorphous group of transfrontiersmen to a "tribe" with the requisite ancient ancestor.

The Coloureds and Griqua spoke Dutch and were members of the Dutch Reformed Church. Basically, they were like the Dutch in every respect except for skin color. And even then they were not always that different. Some of the wealthy and prominent members of Cape society were white primarily because to be wealthy and prominent in effect made one white. In Brazil they say that "money whitens" (i.e., to be rich makes one white). So it is not just among the tribes that ethnicity and race were slippery and negotiable categories. The same was true of Dutch identity.

Cape Town's ethnic complexity was amplified by the importation of slaves from other parts of the Dutch empire. Malays were brought from Batavia (the center of Dutch administration in Indonesia), creating a population known to the apartheid system as "Cape Malay." Slaves were also obtained from Madagascar, and these were often lumped in with the Malays. The Malays introduced Islam to the Cape and played a curious role (which will be discussed later) in the creation of the South African dialect of Dutch called Afrikaans.

As the Dutch moved into the interior, they fairly quickly occupied the land suitable for settled, rain-fed agriculture. As they moved into the drier lands of the Karoo, they adopted, with some critical modifications, the pastoralist habits of the Khoikhoi. Like their Khoikhoi predecessors, they could not keep their herds in one place year-round. Instead, they moved seasonally as the various pasturelands came into season. Some might have a home base from which they launched these migrations; others basically lived out of their ox wagons. These people were called Trekboers, and they and their herds, families, and slaves trekked about in search of pasture, much as the Khoikhoi had done. However, the Trekboers had several things that the Khoikhoi had not had. They had firearms, horses, and wagons. In general pastoralists are warlike. They must be ready to defend their herds from human and animal predators, and they usually have few qualms about raiding other peoples' herds. The Trekboers were no exception. With their guns and horses they developed a military formation they called the commando. A commando would approach its enemies on horseback, fire off a volley, then ride out of range of its enemies to reload, and begin the process all over again. As long as the Trekboers retained their monopoly on firearms and horses, they were able to appropriate land and cattle more or less at will. They also learned to use their wagons as a sort of mobile fort called a "laager." When faced with a numerous enemy, the Trekboers circled their wagons into a laager and used it to fight a defensive battle.

The Trekboers, with their covered wagons, horses, slouch hats, and bonnets, present a spectacle reminiscent of a Disney movie about American pioneers. And they have figured as prominently in the myth-history of the Afrikaners (as the Dutch settlers in South Africa came to call themselves) as the pioneers and the movement west have played in the American self-imagining. So it is worth noting that many settlers were not Trekboers, that many of the Trekboers became sedentary farmers when they were able to get land, and that the Griqua were often basically Trekboers—only they had the "wrong" skin color from the perspective of later Afrikaner Nationalist thought. The Griqua, however, were often at the forefront of the expansion of gun-wielding, horse-riding settlers out of the Cape and into new territory farther to the north. During the eighteenth century these two groups rapidly filled in the territory south of the Orange River and west of the Fish River. By one estimate, their population doubled almost every generation, as did the amount of land they occupied. One might almost compare their rapid occupation of this land to what happens when an alien plant or animal species is unleashed into an environment where it thrives at the expense of native species—rabbits in Australia or kudzu in the American south come to mind. One result of this was the disappearance of the Khoikhoi as an independent people. With their lands taken over, they either died or ended up as servants or slaves to the Dutch or Griqua. By the end of the eighteenth century, the first stage of the Dutch expansion into southern Africa was drawing to a close. The second stage would be marked by two new factors. One was the arrival of the British at the Cape in 1805. The other was the new types of African people and states they encountered as they moved across the Orange and Fish rivers.

The British took control of the Cape in 1805. They acquired it during the Napoleonic wars and did so primarily because they were interested in controlling the sea route to India, which is why the colony was founded in the first place. They were not terribly interested in the territorial expansion of the colony, at least when they first took it over. But they did feel that it was their duty to protect people within the Cape Colony from raids and attack from beyond its borders. On the other hand, the British also realized that one of the reasons that there were attacks across the borders was that Trekboer and Griqua land seekers were pushing beyond the frontiers in search of cattle and sometimes land. Thus, they found themselves trying both to protect their colonists and to prevent them from antagonizing their neighbors.

The other thing we must know about the British is that they took over the Cape just at the time that the antislavery movement was taking off in Britain. This eventually brought them into conflict with **Boer** slave owners who, like British slave owners in the West Indies, were put out when told first that they could no longer buy slaves and then that they had to free their slaves. The extent of the friction between the Dutch and English elements of South African society in the early nineteenth century is debated, as is the role of British abolitionism in alienating the Boers. Traditionally, the movement of the Boers out of the Cape and into new lands to the northeast has been blamed on discontent among Boers who wished to be able to own slaves. However, recent scholarship downplays the role of the abolition of slavery as a motive for Boers to leave the Cape Colony and has suggested that probably land hunger had more to do with it than a "principled" objection to the end of slavery.

By the late eighteenth century, however, the Boers were bumping up against the **Xhosa** in the east, and the Griqua were encountering Sotho, Tswana, and Herero in the north. For both the Boers and the Griqua, this was a new type of challenge. Unlike the Khoikhoi, the Xhosa, Sotho, Tswana, and Herero were farmers who spoke languages of the Bantu family. They represented the southernmost extent of the Bantu expansion and thus made iron tools and weapons, and lived in much more densely settled and politically centralized states than the Khoikhoi. Some of these states were highly militarized. In short, they were much more formidable opponents than the Khoikhoi.

These Bantu-speaking farmers grew millet and sorghum and, beginning in the eighteenth century, maize. They also kept cattle. Indeed, cattle were essential to their way of life. Cattle provided insurance against crop failure, they were the currency used to pay bridewealth, and above all, they were symbolic of royal wealth and power. In the 1830s, **Dingane,** ruler of the Zulu, put on a parade with the intention of overawing a visiting delegation of Boers. The march included 6,000 fighting men. They were followed by thousands of cattle paraded past in regiments of uniform color. Kings might own tens of thousands of cattle, which they loaned out to followers. The followers usually got to keep the milk and some of the calves. The kings got the herding services and loyalty of their followers. Thus, a successful cattle raider might go from relative nobody to great man or king as a result of his expanding herds. Mzilikazi, the ruler of a group of people that has come to be called the **Ndebele,** began life as a minor chief, but his success as a raider and then as a leader made him a king. One effect of this was to make the purpose of warfare in southern Africa the capture of cattle. Although the Boer invaders also placed a high value on their herds and were themselves adept cattle raiders, their vision of warfare was a more European one that sought to kill people and to obtain land. Thus, several military encounters between the Boers and the Mzilikazi's forces seemed to be victories to both sides. The Boers themselves survived, and they killed many of Mzilikazi's soldiers—a victory. For Mzilikazi's men the fact that they went home with thousands of their enemy's cattle made it a victory for them.

Perhaps the main difference between the second-stage Boer expansion into southern Africa and the first stage was that the Africans whom they encountered in the second stage lived in large and highly militarized states, quite different from those of the Khoikhoi. There is some debate about the antiquity of these states. The older view is that they were new at the time that Boers encountered them. Big states were said to be a response to any number of things including drought and chronic insecurity caused by things ranging from Griqua raiding to the slave trade, "tribal" hatreds, and the discovery of a new way of organizing fighting men. Recent scholarship suggests that the novelty of these states may be exaggerated. It now appears that there were large states present in southern Africa in the eighteenth century if not before, and these either served as models for the newer states that emerged in the nineteenth century or in some cases were actually ancestral to them. Furthermore, what have long been seen as military innovations of the nineteenth century seem to have been around for some time.

The social institution of the age grade shaped the military organization of these states. An age grade is a group of young men who are initiated into a group that is expected to all make various social transitions together. Thus, an age grade might all be initiated into adulthood together, serve as warriors together, and then make the transition to elders together. There were also age grades for women, but these were not closely linked to the military side of the state. Usually an age grade would not be allowed to marry until they had completed their military service. These armies were not citizens' militias. Although the members of the age grade who were doing military service at any given time might also herd cattle, they were professional soldiers. They drilled, they had formal chains of command, and they were capable of marching long distances, supplying themselves with the milk from the herds they brought with them or from cattle they acquired in the course of their campaigning. These armies fought on foot using both throwing spears and shorter stabbing spears.

Several great leaders emerged during this time who used armies on this model to carve out states. We will focus here on three of them: Shaka, a leader of the Zulu; Moshoeshoe, founder of what eventually became the nation of Lesotho; and Mzilikazi, founder of the Ndebele. Again, let us emphasize the fluidity of these ethnic designations. Mzilikazi called his people **"Zulu,"** and "Ndebele" is a made-up word that in all likelihood Mzilikazi never uttered in his life. Zulu is just the name of a clan that was transferred to a state when that state came under the control of people from the Zulu clan. Furthermore, people might become Zulu either because they were conquered by the Zulu state or simply sought to join up as the prestige and power of the Zulu state grew.

Shaka and the Rise of the Zulu State

Of all the people that figure in the history of southern Africa in the early nineteenth century, few loom larger than Shaka. He has been celebrated as a great general and military genius, vilified as psychopathic killer, held up as an example of a great leader and state builder, and accused of genocide. He has been featured in a TV miniseries and even cropped up in a series of Budweiser ads devoted to the "Great Kings of Africa." What to make of him?

Shaka built a state on the foundations of another state built by a man named Dingiswayo. Dingiswayo was the ruler of a group called the Mthethwa. Shaka, who came from a minor branch of the then-obscure Zulu clan that was part of Dingiswayo's chiefdom, gained Dingiswayo's attention through his courage and leadership on the battlefield. When the leader of the Zulu clan died, Dingiswayo supported Shaka's bid to assume leadership of the clan. In 1817, Dingiswayo fought a climactic battle with his enemy Zwide. During the battle he was captured and ultimately killed by Zwide's men. The Mthethwa army and state immediately began to unravel. Shaka and his followers had not yet arrived on the battlefield when the rout began, and so while the rest of

CHAKA KING OF THE ZOOLUS.

London. Published by E. Churton, 26 Holles St.

A nineteenth-century depiction of Shaka. It is typical of its genre in that it depicts him as heroic and perhaps as a worthy enemy.

Dingiswayo's followers were dispersed, he kept his followers together and quickly began to fill the power vacuum left by Dingiswayo's death.

The Zulu state created by Shaka was forged in crisis. Dingiswayo's enemies were still out there, and others, sensing opportunity, decided to try to assert their control over the remnants of Dingiswayo's followers. Shaka, using an army that was more highly drilled and disciplined than others, repelled these initial threats and then set out on his own campaigns of conquest, acquiring in the process many new followers and cattle. His soldiers were forbidden to use throwing spears and relied exclusively on stabbing spears and shields made from cowhides.

The main thrust of his campaigns was toward the north, and in addition to conquering new lands, his campaigns forced some peoples to flee before him as refugees. The ripple effects of his campaigns seem to have reached as far north as modern Tanzania, where "Nguni" kingdoms were founded in the middle of the nineteenth century. This violent upheaval is sometimes called the **Mfecane** or, when it occurred farther to the west, the Difecane. Just as Shaka has been mythologized, so have his campaigns. The Mfecane is usually translated as the "crushing" or more prosaically as "unlimited warfare." And just as some of the names of ethnic groups in southern Africa have been made up by Europeans, so, too, have some of the "African"-sounding terms used to describe the events of this period. There is no evidence that the Zulu or their enemies used this word to describe these events. Instead, the term was first employed by European observers and historians. And its use was highly politicized. The Mfecane was originally cited as evidence of the innate savagery of Africans. By the 1840s, British authors were reporting that over a million people had died as a result of Shaka's campaigns. Where they got the figure no one knows, but it was repeated enough that it became a "fact." Further, these authors argued that the Mfecane had effectively depopulated most of the northwestern parts of the modern country of South Africa, leaving the land empty and hence open to settlement by whites. Thus, they claimed, the settlers who moved into these areas were not taking anyone's land. Rather, they were just arriving in the aftermath of a severe bout of African savagery. It was merely their good fortune to step into an "empty land."

Not surprisingly, more recent scholarship has questioned this story. First, no one really knows how many people died as a result of violence during this period. The one million figure seems to have been conjured out of thin air. Second, many things other than "innate savagery" have been proposed to explain this outburst of violence. There were severe droughts during the period, and these may have been exacerbated by the introduction of maize. Maize, which is more productive than the millet and sorghum traditionally grown in the area, may have caused an increase in the population density. This may have made the effects of drought more severe and thus triggered more violent contests over scarce resources in times of hardship. Another possibility is that pressure from Griqua and Boer raiders from the west coupled with an upsurge in slave exports from the Indian Ocean port of De la Goa Bay may have triggered violence, though this explanation seems to have lost credibility. Finally, the historian Norman Etherington has proposed that there really was not a Mfecane at all. The scale of Shaka's wars may not have been that much greater than previous wars in the area. If the Boers found what appeared to be an empty land when they entered the grasslands of the high veldt, that was because these lands had always been sparsely and seasonally populated. State builders preferred the mix of forest and grass found at lower altitudes so the high veldt had never been a core part of their territories. In the end, it is hard to say how critical Shaka's wars were in creating an opening that Boer settlers could exploit. What can be said with more certainty is that Shaka created a state that was able to resist encroachment from European settlers for a long time and that has survived as a recognizable political force in South Africa.

Shaka did not live to see his state fight off the Boers. His campaigning took a toll on his own followers, and despite his efforts to eliminate potential rivals within the Zulu state, in 1828, Shaka was murdered by his brother, **Dingane.** The years just before Shaka's death had been trying for the Zulu state. The period of military service expected of young men stretched until men well into their thirties were still enrolled in the regiments and forbidden to marry. This is thought to have caused grumbling in the ranks. Shaka also became increasingly dubious of the loyalty of some of his followers; there were mass executions of regiments that he suspected of treachery. Much has also been made of the year of national mourning Shaka ordered after his mother's death, the suggestion being that a whole year of mourning might be a sign that Shaka had crossed the line into madness. Recent scholarship suggests that extravagant mourning of the death of queen mothers was not out of the ordinary in southern African states. Certainly, a "mad Shaka" scenario dovetails conveniently with the vision of the Mfecane as an irrational outburst of violence. So it may be that Dingane was motivated more by ambition than by a desire to save the Zulu from Shaka. In any case, Dingane proved to be an able ruler, and it was he who confronted the movement of Boer trekers into what is now KwaZulu-Natal.

 Controveries in African History: **Shaka and the Media**

If someone is trying to depict a stereotypical traditional or primitive Africa, one of the preferred choices for this, if no pictures of the Masai are handy, is to use a picture of Zulu warriors. Somehow, over the last two centuries, the Zulu have become one of the standard names and images associated with tribal Africa. Further, it is not just the white, Western public that has come to see the Zulu and especially Shaka as a standard image of traditional Africa. Shaka and the Zulu have also been embraced by many communities of the African Diaspora as a "great" African leader and society, respectively. In India, when Sidis (Indians of African descent) do "traditional" dances they dress in Zulu-like costumes, despite the fact that few if any of their forebears were Zulu. On the island of Mauritius, the site formerly occupied by a

unit of the King's African Rifles (a British military unit from Kenya) is called the Camp des Zulus.

Shaka and the Zulu have had a mythic quality almost from the start. The first popular depictions of Shaka's world come from the writings of Nathanial Isaacs and Henry Francis Fynn, both of whom were slightly disreputable nineteenth-century characters who visited Shaka's court. Their depictions of the Zulu under Shaka describe horrific executions and horrible violence as everyday aspects of Zulu life. Their accounts are now mostly discredited, but were wildly popular in their time. The book that has done the most to shape popular conceptions of Shaka is E. A. Ritter's historical novel *Shaka Zulu* (1955), which again leaned heavily on the violent imagery of Isaacs and Fynn's works.

In North America the big moment for Shaka came when the Anheuser-Busch Corporation decided in the mid-1970s to reach out to potential African-American beer buyers by promoting African history. The result was the commissioning of a series of paintings of African kings and queens by African-American artists. The series was referred to as the "Great Kings and Queens of Africa" and the portraits were used in magazine ads, in posters, and bar mirrors. Each was accompanied by a short and highly laudatory biography of the leader in question. The historical advisor to the series was the Afrocentrist scholar John Henrik Clarke, who presumably wrote or at least approved the mini-histories that accompanied the paintings. Many of these paintings and their accompanying histories are heavily influenced by the Afrocentrist notion that all "real" Africans are black. Thus, for example, the Carthaginian general Hannibal looks more like a West African than a Phoenician. Such highly mythologized representations of historical individuals are hardly unusual. Nobody knows exactly what Columbus looked like, for example, but almost every Western civilization textbook features a portrait of him anyway.

Shaka's turn came in 1976 when artist Paul Collins painted his portrait. The mini-history that accompanied the picture ends by saying that he unified all African tribes against colonialism, which, given that he never fought the British or the Afrikaners, seems a bit of a stretch. Nonetheless, these images have an enduring popularity among some African Americans. Thus, we have a curious situation in which a beer company has played a significant role in shaping how a segment of the American public sees Shaka and other African leaders. There are numerous Afrocentrist Web sites that have reproduced both the Budweiser paintings and the histories of their subjects. Anheuser-Busch still has all these images on the Web at AfricanAmericanBud.com.

Shaka has also had his fair share of exposure on the silver screen. The best known of these was a miniseries produced by the South African Broadcasting Corporation (SABC) in 1985 called *Shaka Zulu*. In 1985, South Africa was ruled by a hard-line white supremacist government, and although the SABC was partially independent, the miniseries served to support the government's apartheid ideology. Based on a screenplay by novelist John Sinclair, the series proved popular both in South Africa and in the West. It was shown on American television (as well as in Britain and Australia). While both black and white critics of the film in South Africa denounced it as historically inaccurate and demeaning, Zulu nationalists liked it. At a time when Zulu leaders were asserting a militant version of Zulu identity, the film's depiction of a strong though violent Shaka struck a cord. Chief Buthelezi, leader of the Inkatha Party (a Zulu nationalist group), began to point out his genealogical links to Shaka. The miniseries was popular enough that it was rebroadcast in South Africa in 2001, by a post-apartheid SABC.

John Sinclair, troubled by the links between the SABC and the South African government, distanced himself from this SABC miniseries before it was shown, but has since written and directed another miniseries called *Shaka Zulu: The Citadel*. This one has the same actor, Henry Cele, who played Shaka in the original miniseries, but also includes such luminaries as Grace Jones (as Shaka's mother Nandi), Omar Sharif (as an Arab Sheik), and David Hasselhoff (sans Speedo, as a slave trader). This was then edited into a 90-minute movie that is apparently even worse than the miniseries itself.

Few Africans have been embraced by as many different constituencies. Remarkably, Shaka seems to be beloved by white supremacists (who use him to exemplify supposed African tendencies toward atavistic violence), by Afrocentrists (for whom he embodies personal greatness, ambition, and leadership), by Zulu nationalists (who use him as a model for Zulu identity and greatness), and by makers of b-grade movies (for whom he is a source of dramatic material and profit.)

Mzilikazi and the "Ndebele"

The second of our profiles looks at Mzilikazi, who was a rival of Dingane and whose followers became one of the major tribes of southern Africa. Mzilikazi's story illustrates several things about the period. First, it shows the extent to which talented and ambitious leaders could rise from obscurity to become major state builders and great kings. Second, it reinforces our previous assertions about the fluidity of ethnic identity in nineteenth-century southern Africa and the newness of some of the major ethnic groups.

Mzilikazi first appears with clarity in the historical record in 1825. Prior to that it is difficult to track his career. His father was a chief under the king Zwide and was apparently put to death for disloyalty. Mzilikazi took over the chiefdom after his father's death. According to some accounts, Mzilikazi then switched his allegiance to Shaka. According to this version of the story, Mzilikazi had a falling out with Shaka, and he and a couple of hundred followers fled from Shaka's lands and settled to the northwest on the high veldt. Shortly after this, they may or may not have fought a battle against people called the Pedi that resulted in the death of the Pedi king.

By 1825, Mzilikazi was no longer the leader of a band of refugees but a king, albeit of an itinerant state. In the aftermath of a great drought, which broke in 1825, he began creating a state with himself as king. To people whose lives had been disrupted by the drought, his state offered security and order. He organized a system of military outposts meant to protect his people and cattle against raids by the Griqua from the west and the Zulu state to the east. He, like every other king of the time, also organized cattle raids, often with the neighboring Tswana as the victims. The order he provided and the relative benevolence of his rule attracted followers, who often came voluntarily under Mzilikazi's protection. Others came to be incorporated into Mzilikazi's state as a result of military conquest. All were expected to become Zulu.

For many, that meant learning to speak Nguni, the language of the Zulu. It meant learning to dress Zulu, though for some peoples this required wearing less clothing than either the weather or their ingrained notions of modesty would seem to require. It meant learning to do Zulu dances and sing Zulu songs. In short, whatever you were when you came to Mzilikazi's state, you were expected to adopt a new Zulu identity. All of this is a bit surprising because Mzilikazi's followers were known to their Tswana-speaking neighbors as "Matabele," which is their word for anyone who speaks Nguni. If one were to take the name Matabele and transform it into an Nguni word, it would become "Ndebele." This eventually became the name of a large group of people who live in what is now Zimbabwe. But Mzilikazi called himself and his people Zulu. Despite a common name and a common language, Mzilikazi and Dingane, leader of the other Zulus, were archenemies.

Mzilikazi's state was open to talent, no matter its ethnic origin. Many of his commanders and regional governors had non-Zulu origins; some were even of Griqua origin. Whole regiments were made up of people incorporated into the state from other places. In short, Mzilikazi's state provides a stark refutation of the idea that the violence of this period was motivated by "tribal" hatreds. Mzilikazi's people came from a number of backgrounds and were all in effect becoming Zulu together. At the same time some of their worst enemies were "fellow" Zulus. It is hard to see in this any evidence of deep-seated ethnic hatred.

By the 1830s, Mzilikazi's state was in trouble. Pressed hard by Dingane from the east and facing increasing pressure from the Boers and Griqua in the west, Mzilikazi eventually went north and settled what remained of his followers in the southern part of modern-day Zimbabwe where they are called the Ndebele. Thus was a "tribe" created.

Moshoeshoe

Moshoeshoe's real name was Lepoqo, and he seems to have been born in 1786. His nickname, Moshoeshoe, is an onomatopoeic reference to the sound a razor makes. Moshoeshoe was the "razor of cattle." In other words, when he passed through an area, it was scraped clean of cattle. Much like Shaka or Mzilikazi, Moshoeshoe was the son of a minor chief who rose through leadership and charisma to become the founder of a state—in this case a state that has survived and currently exists as Lesotho.

Moshoeshoe took over his father's chiefdom in the Celadon Valley while his father was still alive, apparently through sheer force of personality. His father's chiefdom had at its heart a flat-topped mountain called Butha Buthe. During a battle early in his career, Moshoeshoe was able to save his army from disaster by retreating to the top of Butha Buthe. This experience made him realize both the value of

Moshoeshoe, the founder of the state that eventually became the modern state of Lesotho.

a natural fortress and that he would not be able to withstand a long siege on top of Butha Buthe. He then set out to find a better natural fortress. About 80 miles away was another flat-topped mountain called Thaba Bosiu. Thaba Bosiu's flat top was completely surrounded by cliffs, with only a few narrow breaks that allowed access to the top. These were easily defended from above, making the mountaintop impregnable to armies not equipped with powerful modern artillery. Moshoeshoe led his people on a dangerous trek to the new mountain, where he established what was to be the core of a new BaSotho state.

Like Mzilikazi, Moshoeshoe offered people a haven in a time of political and military upheaval. His military exploits and cattle raiding were tempered by a willingness to accommodate people into his state, regardless of their origins. Although he was BaSotho, many Nguni speakers were incorporated into his state and became Sotho speakers over time, just as Mizilikazi's subjects learned Nguni. Moshoeshoe's most distinctive quality was his ability to engage Europeans diplomatically.

Both Shaka and Mzilikazi had made overtures to various groups of Europeans. Shaka befriended a group of British merchants who operated out of Natal, from whom he tried, mostly without success, to obtain firearms. Mzilikazi was able to attract British missionaries to his capital, but never got much from them in terms of either material or diplomatic support. In contrast, Moshoeshoe not only attracted missionaries to his capital, he also used them to obtain trade goods, including weapons and blankets. Moshoeshoe was able to obtain horses and guns, the essential weapons of the commando style of warfare. The blankets he and his people obtained through trade might at first glance seem inconsequential, but they kept people warm in the cold mountains where Moshoeshoe built his state. In effect, they let people occupy an environment that previously would have been difficult to inhabit. He also so charmed his resident missionaries that, although he never converted to Christianity, they thought highly of him, and their high opinion eventually translated into support from the British government. The British government's support for Moshoeshoe was never complete and without reservation, but it was sufficient that during the upheavals triggered by the arrival of new waves of Boer trekkers in the late 1830s, his state survived while others collapsed.

The "Voortrekkers"

By the 1830s, British control of the Cape had begun to create divisions within the white settler community. As Britain became increasingly opposed to the slave trade, and to the institution of slavery, the authorities initially placed limits on the authority of slave owners and ultimately abolished slavery without fully compensating slave owners. The abolition of slavery in the Cape coincides with the beginning of a movement by Boers beyond the frontiers of the Cape Colony to seek new lands in the areas beyond the Orange and Vaal rivers. Later Afrikaner Nationalists have seen in these events the birth of a national consciousness among the Boers—the birth of an Afrikaner nation. And there may be something to this. Just as Zulu, Ndbele, and Sotho identities were being forged by the events and leaders of the 1820s and 1830s, it seems plausible that the Boers may also have been defining themselves as a people at the same time. But precisely because of the importance of the Great Trek (as it is called sometimes), it has been highly mythologized. Note that calling something a "myth" is not to say that it is pure fabrication or falsehood. Rather, it means that it is a story that has taken on an important explanatory meaning, which means that it is also subject to distortion and manipulation when the events themselves are overshadowed by their meaning.

The short version of the mythic story is that the British administered the Cape in a high-handed and anti-Boer way. They meddled in the affairs of farmers, especially in the relationship between the farmers and their households of slaves and retainers. In addition to having a long tradition of slave owning, the Boers believed that their ownership of slaves was religiously justified. Thus, oppressed by the British, they decided that the only answer was flight beyond the reach of British authority. They set out in groups of hundreds of families with their wagons and their herds, seeking a new life and new lands. After terrible hardship; the massacre of their leaders by Dingane, leader of the Zulu; and ultimately a tremendous victory, itself a clear sign of God's favor; they occupied the territories beyond the Orange and the Vaal rivers and created the independent Boer Republics of the Transvaal and the Orange Free State. The Boers had a covenant with God, not unlike that of the Israelites, and until the collapse of apartheid the Day of the Covenant was the high holy day of Afrikaner nationalism.

Much of this story really happened; some aspects of it, such as the covenant with God, are difficult to prove one way or the other; and some of it appears to be after-the-fact reinterpretation of the events to make them suit later purposes. Historians now question many aspects of this story, from its beginnings in the Cape Colony to its purposefulness, to its claims to land by right of conquest. Let us begin in the Cape. Modern historians question the assertion that there was significant tension between the Dutch- and English-speaking populations in the Cape. They note that one of the Trek's main opponents was a Boer who had been appointed as the vice-governor of the Cape. One of the Trek's biggest supporters was an English newspaper editor. Further, those Boers who had the most reason to be aggrieved over the slavery issue—the big landowners who owned most of the slaves—did not take part in the Trek. They stayed home and made a fairly smooth transition to using legally coerced "free labor" rather than slave labor. The bulk of the participants in this movement seem to have been relatively poor Boers with a bad case of land hunger. Thus, the Trek probably resulted as much from social and class divisions within the Cape Colony as it did from ethnic tension between the Dutch and the English.

The initial leaders of the trekking movement were poor, uneducated Boer farmers. They were eventually replaced by a much more sophisticated leader named **Piet Retief.** Retief had made and lost several fortunes through land speculation and holding contracts to supply the British government and military—an unlikely occupation for a hero of Afrikaner nationalism. Retief was also legally knowledgeable and managed to cast most of his public pronouncements in ways calculated not to alarm the British. He was especially careful not to say anything that might suggest to the British that the trekkers were taking slaves outside the boundaries of the Cape Colony. The British had hunted down and executed the leader of an early group of trekkers who had made public his intention to take his slaves outside the Cape rather than allow them to be freed.

In 1836 groups of **Voortrekkers,** as these migrants were called, began to head off into the area around the Vaal River. Initially, many local leaders were unsure how to treat the newcomers. Some offered them land either for free or on lease. Others seem to have had a clearer idea that this group was too large and powerful to be incorporated into existing political structures the way other landless migrants and refugees might. Mzilikazi seems to have come to the latter conclusion. Seeing the Voortrekkers in much the same light as he might Griqua raiders, Mzilikazi sent his forces after them.

Mzilikazi's men caught a major Boer encampment at a time when most of the men were away on a reconnaissance mission. When Hendrik Potgeiter, leader of the reconnaissance mission, returned, he found the wreckage of the camp, littered with bodies and with most of their cattle taken. The shock of this caused most of the trekkers to withdraw to the south. Another party went north toward the Vaal, where they hunkered down hoping to escape Mzilikazi's notice. They failed, and Mzilikazi sent 5,000 men to attack a party of 45 wagons at a place the Boers called Vegkop. This time Mzilikazi's men came without the advantage of surprise. The Boers had formed their wagons into a laager and filled the spaces between the wagons with thorn bushes. They had built an inner circle of wagons to further protect their children. Mzilikazi's soldiers made repeated charges at the laager, but were unable to get inside. The withering gunfire produced by the laager's defenders killed hundreds of the attackers, whereas only two of the defenders were killed. Fewer than 40 Boer families and their guns had defeated an army of 5,000. Mzilikazi's men made off with most of the Boers' livestock, which, numbering in the thousands, could not fit inside the laager. By the standards of South African warfare, it was a draw. The Boers had shown they could defend their lives and take the lives of many of their attackers. Mzilikazi's men had, however, taken their wealth and livelihoods from them. Until they could get their cattle back, the Boers were little more than impoverished, though heavily armed, refugees.

In order to replenish their herds, the Boers made a series of alliances with Mzilikazi's enemies, and together they raided his herds. Eventually, Mzilikazi concluded that his position was untenable, and he withdrew to the north into what is now Zimbabwe. At this point the Voortrekkers split up, with some of them pressing north onto the high veldt, and others, under the leadership of Piet Retief, taking a more southern route toward lands with higher rainfall. Retief's group soon came into conflict with Dingane and the Zulu. Dingane was deeply concerned with the large number of trekkers pouring into his lands. He was also concerned that the Boers were raiding for cattle in his territory. Apparently, groups of Boers raiding cattle from Mzilikazi had taken cattle from Zulu raiding parties, whom the Boers had encountered in Mzilikazi's land.

Retief went to Dingane to seek a land grant for his followers. Dingane refused to even discuss such a thing until the cattle taken from his territory were returned. Retief said that his people had not taken the cattle; rather, he said, the followers of a man called Sekonyela had taken them. Retief arranged for a raid on Sekonyela and then brought the cattle from this raid to Dingane. Apparently this gesture did little to assure Dingane. On February 6, 1838, Dingane invited Retief to a celebratory dance, where Retief and about 70 of his followers were put to death. At the same time, Dingane's soldiers attacked the main party of the Voortrekkers. Taking them by surprise, the soldiers were able to take their cattle and kill many of them.

After Retief's death and the assault on the main party of Voortrekkers, the trekkers were in disarray. Potgieter and others organized commandos to try to recover their livestock, but the mantle of leadership fell to Andries Pretorius. Pretorius arrived in November 1838 leading a group of trekkers fresh from the Cape. His party was well armed and had cannons in addition to the usual guns and horses. On December 9, the trekkers, facing an imminent battle with Dingane, vowed that if God would grant them victory, they would keep that day sacred in perpetuity. A few days later, on the fifteenth, they met Dingane's army at what came to be called the Battle of Blood River. The Boers' horses, guns, and cannons turned the battle into a massacre, and the river ran red with the blood that gave it its name. Dingane, who had been just at the point of staving off Boer advances into his territory, was put to flight and eventually killed. With both Mzilikazi and Dingane removed from power, the way was open for Europeans to assert control over much, though not all, of this territory.

The British Expansion and the Formation of the Boer Republics

As the power of the Zulu diminished and the Ndebele withdrew, the trekkers were able to occupy some of the lands formerly dominated by these states. In some places they settled and began to farm or raise sheep; in others they preferred to collect rents from the Africans who already lived on the lands. During this time the extent and scope of British power increased steadily. As the trekkers pushed out the frontier of white settlement, the British followed along behind, swallowing up territory in fits and starts. Although the various wars, agreements, and treaties that made all this possible are outside the scope of this chapter, it is worth looking at a few of the events along the way.

One of the events that helped trigger the movement of trekkers into the territories beyond the Orange River was the Xhosa war of 1835. The Xhosa were the Cape Colony's nearest neighbor to the east. The Xhosa war of 1835 had been a victory for the British and their Afrikaner allies, but after the war the British allowed less white settlement in Xhosa lands than many Afrikaners had hoped. One result was that land-hungry trekkers looked elsewhere, but another was the survival of the Xhosa as a political force. In the years after the war, the Xhosa became increasingly involved in the life of the Cape Colony. Many Xhosa worked on farms in the Cape, beginning a process of labor migration in southern Africa that persists even today.

In 1846, the military escort accompanying a criminal accused of stealing an axe was attacked and killed. The culprits fled into Xhosa territory, and Xhosa chiefs refused to extradite them. The result was the War of the Axe. The Xhosa were initially quite successful in this conflict. They had obtained firearms and employed African deserters from the British Army to use them. They had fewer firearms than the British, but they used them well and were able to seize land in the Cape Colony. Eventually, though, the greater resources available to the British prevailed, and the Xhosa were defeated. This time the British decided not to allow the Xhosa to survive as a political entity and annexed their land. They designated this area as the colony of British Kaffraria. Soon Xhosa lands were open to white settlers, and the Xhosa's situation became increasingly difficult.

The Xhosa's response to this situation was as desperate as the situation itself. In the mid-1850s, a young girl named Nongqawuse received a revelation that appears to be at least partly influenced by Christian teaching. Two gods, Sifuba-Sibanza and Napakade, would bring about an apocalyptic change for the Xhosa. If the Xhosa would kill off their herds, destroy all their grain, and smash their pots, a new era would dawn. The two gods would replenish the Xhosa herds, their pots would come back bursting with grain, their ancestors would return, and the whites would be driven into the sea. That the Xhosa were willing to try this speaks eloquently to the extremity of their situation.

In 1857 they began to kill off their herds and destroy their grain stocks. The ancestors, however, did not return, their herds did not miraculously return, and the whites remained stubbornly in place. Simultaneously, an epidemic of lung sickness swept the region, killing any cattle that had avoided slaughter. A terrible famine ensued. Thousands died, and many thousands more were forced to find work in the Cape Colony as migrant workers. The Xhosa Cattle Killing played perfectly into the hands of the British. It simultaneously broke what remained of Xhosa power and provided much-needed labor in the Cape.

At about the same time that the British were creating a colony in the lands of the Xhosa, they set out to take control of the lands seized by the trekkers. To this end, they declared the Orange River Sovereignty, which was a colony that included most of the lands south of the Vaal River that had been occupied by the Boers and the Griqua. Soon, however, the British concluded that taking responsibility for the behavior and protection of the settlers in the lands beyond the Orange River was more than they had bargained for. The farming settlements in these areas were so dispersed and so far from British centers of power that protecting them was almost impossible. Furthermore, the bellicose behavior of the settlers, who were seizing land that belonged to other people and who were getting back into the habit of slave ownership, meant that there were constant flare-ups of violence. So by 1854, the British recognized two independent Afrikaner republics. One was the Orange Free State, and the other was the South African Republic in the Transvaal. Of the two, the Orange Free State had the larger white population and the sounder economy. It had a fairly vibrant agricultural economy and maintained close economic links with the Cape Colony. The Transvaal had fewer settlers and was more isolated. There were several attempts to unite the two into a single, large Afrikaner state, but all failed, in part because many Afrikaners feared that unifying the republics would result in British intervention. Thus, although independent, the republics lived in the shadow of the British Empire.

In the republics a new vision of an Afrikaner identity emerged. Although Dutch-speaking white South Africans had always seen themselves as distinct from

English-speaking South Africans, there is little evidence of real antipathy between the two groups in the Cape. In the republics, though, a much more nationalistic vision of Afrikaner identity emerged. Nationalists began to promote the use of Afrikaans, the dialect of Dutch that had developed in the complex cultural mix of the Cape. They pointed out that the Afrikaners were a people distinct from the Dutch in Europe, distinct from the British in Africa, and distinct from the black-skinned peoples of southern Africa, too. According to nineteenth-century national-ist ideology, a "nation" was defined by common origins, common language, a common "race," a common religion, and a territorial homeland. Afrikaners increas-ingly saw themselves as a nation defined by the Great Trek, the Afrikaans language, the Dutch Reformed Church, and their territorial homelands in the republics. Although it would take decades for this ideology to be fully formed and almost a century for its ideological handmaiden—apartheid—to be fully articulated, the process began in the new independent republics. In the republics the Afrikaners increasingly saw themselves as being at odds not just with the Africans whose lands they had appropriated, but also with the British. Those concerns were ultimately projected on the story of the Great Trek, which became the foundation myth of the republics and of Afrikaner nationalism. The Trek became not a movement of land-hungry farmers, but a flight from British oppression. Their victories in battle became a sign of God's favor and His sanction for their conquests. The Afrikaans language, which owes its origins to the Cape Coloured population from whom the nationalists were quick to distance themselves, became a symbol of their identity. Interestingly, the first published works in Afrikaans were Qur'anic commentaries written using Arabic script by Cape Malay Muslims. Nonetheless, Afrikaners used this language as one of the touchstones of their identity. In the twentieth century, one of the most hated aspects of apartheid was the requirement that Afrikaans be taught in all the schools.

National identity is always built on myths and half-truths, and Afrikaner nationalism is not alone in its refashioning of the past to help create a national identity. Like the Zulu and the Ndebele and many other groups in South Africa in the nineteenth century, the Afrikaners became a people as a result of a complex process of migration, warfare, and conscious identity creation. Like the Zulu and the Ndebele, this newly created identity would survive into the twentieth century, with serious repercussions for the politics and race relations of recent years.

For a brief time the British left the republics to their own devices. The Afrikaners created a world that mixed limited democracy with white supremacist politics. To be fair, the Afrikaners were not alone in their racism. The British-controlled Cape Colony and Natal also placed political and legal restrictions on nonwhites, but the republics were worse. However, in 1867 everything changed with the discovery of diamonds in the Orange Free State and then gold in the 1880s in the Transvaal. Soon there was a diamond rush in progress, bringing mostly English-speaking Uit-landers (outlanders) to the republics. Not only did these people not speak Afrikaans, they were not Dutch Reformed Church members—indeed most were of the dance hall and brothel school of secularism—and they did not share the Afrikaner interest in farming. Soon the British began to covet the lands that they had once been willing to write off as giant pastures populated by troublesome

Afrikaners. Once it was clear that the pastures covered a tremendous mineral wealth, the British began to see the republics in a different light. And because the governments of the republics limited the political rights of the Uitlanders, the British were able to claim that they needed to protect the rights of their citizens. The Afrikaner myth of a nation founded by British oppression was turning into a self-fulfilling prophecy.

South Africa in Global Perspective, 1500–1870

The most obvious comparison to South Africa's history is that of the United States. Northern European settlers arrived at approximately the same time in both North America and South Africa. In both cases they encountered people who already lived there. Conflict ensued. In both places settlers were able to introduce European crops and livestock and to create what we have described as "neo-Europes," a term coined by Alfred Crosby. In their neo-Europes they were able to live a life recognizably similar to the lives they might have lived in Europe. They lived in European-style towns and cities, grew and ate European foods, and brought with them familiar European microbes.

In both places there was a frontier, there was a nationalist revolt against the British, and both societies created white supremacist ideologies that justified their dominance and their right to keep slaves and, once those slaves were freed, to deny political rights to nonwhites. Today South Africa is governed by its original inhabitants, and European settlers are a shrinking minority. In North America the original owners of the land are mostly gone, and the surviving few are politically marginal; the descendants of immigrants from various parts of the Old World are the vast majority of the population. Why the different outcomes?

Probably the most critical factor has to do with disease. In the New World, introduced Old World diseases ravaged the Indians. The European conquest of North America was greatly facilitated by this massive die-off. In South Africa, this did not happen, at least not on the disastrous scale of the Americas. For European settlers in southern Africa, each new conquest involved facing enemies whose worlds had not been devastated by epidemic disease. Thus, the contest was a much more equal one, and in every conquered territory Africans continued to constitute the majority of the population. Although the apartheid ideology proclaimed that South Africa was a "white" land, in practice it was not. Whites were always a minority of the population.

Perhaps the other critical difference is that in North America, before 1870, most of the immigrants came either from northern Europe or Africa. In South Africa, there were northern Europeans, Malays, Indians, and Chinese. The northern Europeans were divided between the British and the Dutch, and the contest between the two, coupled with their desire to ensure that political rights were denied to everybody else, made the settlers internally divided to a much greater extent than in North America. Thus, a South African leader like Moshoeshoe could play off the British against the Afrikaners in a way that no Native American leaders could. Despite the superficial similarities between the European settlement of North America and South Africa, the results were different in telling ways.

Useful Works on This Chapter Topic

A recent and very compelling book about this period is Norman Etheringtons, *The Great Treks* (2001). Etherington makes an effort to present both Boer and African movements as "treks" rather than seeing Africans as static and the Boers in motion. For a survey of the Xhosa, who get less attention than the Zulu, see Jeff Peires, *The House of Phalo: A History of the Xhosa People in Their Days of Independence* (1981). Robert Ross' *A Concise History of South Africa* (2000) is a good general survey of the region. Leroy Vail's *The Creation of Tribalism in Southern Africa* (1989) is the classic work on the formation of tribes in southern Africa and a template for similar work on other parts of the continent. For a recent overview of the religion's history, see Aran MacKinnon, *The Making of South Africa, Culture and Politics* (2004).

CHAPTER 13

Colonialism and African Resistance

In November of 1840 a steamship called the *Nemesis* reached the South China port of Macao. She arrived in the midst of a simmering conflict between imperial China and Britain over the latter's "right" to sell opium, a potent narcotic, to the Chinese public. Although Britain's Royal Navy was vastly superior to any force the Chinese could send to sea, its ability to carry the war to the Chinese was limited by the difficulties of handling seagoing warships in the rivers that served as highways into the heart of China. China's government was willing to concede the sea to Britain and to allow British merchants access to a few treaty ports because China saw itself as a land power, not a sea power. The important parts of China were the inland bits, and these were beyond the control of the British or any other European power. In 1792, for example, the Ch'ien Lung Emperor responded to a British request for expanded trading rights in a letter to King George III. His answer was "no," and he closed the letter by admonishing the King thusly:

> Should your vessels touch the shore, your merchants will assuredly never be permitted to land or to reside there, but will be subject to instant expulsion. In that event your barbarian merchants will have had a long journey for nothing. Do not say that you were not warned in due time! Tremblingly obey and show no negligence!

George III could do nothing about this except to tremble. But 48 years later, the aptly named *Nemesis* would change all that.

In 1841, shortly after the *Nemesis'* arrival, the British renewed their attack on the forts that guarded the mouth of the Yangtze River. *Nemesis* and several other steamers were used to tow the big sail-powered ships of the line up the river. The combined firepower of these warships overcame the forts and a fleet of Chinese war junks sent to oppose them. *Nemesis* then pursued the fleeing Chinese fleet through shallow river channels that had hitherto been inaccessible to European warships. Eventually, *Nemesis* and other similar river steamers allowed the British to take the port city of Canton and then to press their way upriver toward Nanjing and the strategically important Grand Canal. By July of 1842 the presence of British gunboats deep in the interior waterways of China forced the emperor to sign a peace treaty with Britain. China had resisted with little difficulty all previous European efforts to gain entry to the interior of China; *Nemesis* let a relatively small British force strike at China's all-important canal system.

What has this to do with Africa? Britain's victory in the First Opium War and the role of steam-powered ships in the victory was a harbinger of a shift in the global balance of power, a shift with profound implications for Africa and Africans. The nineteenth century began with Europeans clinging to a few coastal outposts in Africa as in China. A private company, the East India Company, ruled parts of India through a convoluted series of treaties with local political powers. A relative political and economic parity between Europe and the major powers of the Old World prevented European empires from dominating Asia and Africa. By the middle decades of the nineteenth century that parity had disappeared, and Europe was poised to intervene in the affairs of the world in an unprecedented way. The "New Imperialism," as this development is called, was felt worldwide, but in many ways it was Africa that bore the brunt of this onslaught. China's *Nemesis* was also Africa's nemesis.

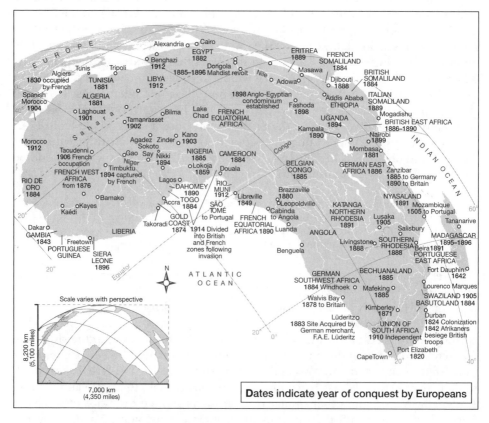

Map 13-1: African territory controlled by Europeans in 1914

Europe's Industrial Transformation and Africa

The *Nemesis* is a perfect example of the forces at work in this shift in the global balance of power. She was 184 feet long and 29 feet wide, with a draft (the depth of water needed to float a boat) of only 5 feet. Her hull was not vee-shaped, like that of a sailing ship, but flat with a retractable keel. This was possible because her main source of power was a pair of 60-horsepower steam engines and because her hull was made of iron. The iron hull made possible the hull's radical shape and also allowed the ship to be divided into multiple watertight compartments. As a result, water entering because of damage to the hull—always a concern in the shallows of rivers—was confined to only a few of the compartments. *Nemesis* was bristling with guns, but most of her armament would have been familiar to any naval officer a hundred years earlier. What was radical was her iron hull and her steam engines. And these were both the result of the industrial revolution.

The precise causes of the industrial revolution and the ticklish question of why it first emerged in northwestern Europe are outside the scope of this book. What is important from the African perspective is that it happened first in Europe and not elsewhere. From the last decades of the eighteenth century well into the twentieth century, European industry made quantum leaps, not just in how much it could produce, but also in the sophistication of the products it produced. First water and then steam power were harnessed to permit fewer people to do more work. Producers (i.e., the people who owned the factories) took more and more control over how their workers worked and lived. Engineers and scientists, many of whom increasingly worked for industry, developed ever more efficient means of production and ever more clever things to produce. Steamers like the *Nemesis* were made of industrially produced iron, were fitted with steam engines that had been painstakingly refined and miniaturized until they would fit in a boat, and were produced in shipyards that used the latest in production techniques.

Other tools and weapons that would contribute to this sweeping change in the global balance of power came out of the burgeoning factories of Europe. Firearms that were not only more lethal, but also cheaper than their precursors had been, were issued to soldiers on their way to wars of colonial conquest in Africa. Those same soldiers, and later on administrators and settlers, were able to survive unfamiliar—to them—tropical diseases because they were medicated with drugs produced by industry. In short, the industrial revolution opened the door to a new phase in Africa's relationship with Europe.

The steamers that were to follow in the *Nemesis'* wake would eventually open to Europeans the vast river and lake systems of the African interior. The Niger, the Congo, the Zambezi, and the equatorial parts of the Nile had mostly been closed to Europeans. The complex deltas and rapids that characterized the lower reaches of the rivers were major obstacles in the age of sail. But the flat-bottomed iron, and later steel- and aluminum-hulled, steamer made these waterways into highways.

First they opened the way to exploration. In 1832, Macgregor Laird led an expedition to the Niger River. The expedition managed to ascend the Niger past its confluence with the Benue. This feat opened up the possibility—later exploited by the Lairds—that a commercial steam service might be opened on the Niger and that European merchants might be able to trade directly with the interior and bypass the African merchants who then dominated trade on the Niger.

Other explorers also exploited the possibilities of the river steamer. David Livingstone, a prominent opponent of the slave trade and one of the first Europeans to travel into Central Africa from the East Coast, used a steamer to ascend the Zambezi in 1858. He later had a steamer carried in pieces to Lake Nyassa. As shipwrights learned to build steel hulls in sections, explorers frequently used steamers they could take apart, have carried around an obstacle, and then reassemble. Henry Morton Stanley (1877) and Savorgnan de Brazza (1880) both did this on the Congo. Once around the rapids and falls that make the first 200 miles of the Congo impassable, Stanley and Brazza were able to steam deep into the interior on hundreds of miles of easily navigable river. Where explorers showed that steamers could go, commercial steam traffic was never too far behind. But commercial exploitation of Africa's rivers by Europeans, usually accompanied by or followed shortly by a colonial seizure of the same rivers, would require a few new developments.

Quinine and Colonialism

When Macgregor Laird returned in triumph from his 1832 ascent of the Niger, that triumph was tainted by the appalling loss of life among his fellow expeditionaries. Of the 48 Europeans who set out in 1832, only 9 returned. Most of those 39 deaths were caused by disease. The West African disease environment was discussed in Chapter 8, but a few points are worthy of reiteration. Two diseases, malaria and yellow fever—both endemic in West Africa—were most likely responsible for the deaths on Laird's expedition. A mosquito-borne virus causes yellow fever; a mosquito-borne protozoan causes malaria. For most Africans yellow fever is a childhood disease that passes unnoticed and confers lifetime immunity. For Europeans, who arrived without prior exposure to the disease, it was much more severe and often fatal. Conversely, malaria is if anything harder on children than it is on adults, and one never gains immunity to the disease. However, if one survives multiple attacks as a child, the severity of the attacks one suffers as an adult are reduced and less likely to be fatal. Again, for Europeans arriving as adults with no prior experience of the strains of malaria present in tropical Africa, malaria was often fatal.

Until the middle of the nineteenth century, Europeans in Africa had no option but to live, or more often die, with these conditions. West Africa was known as the "white man's grave." In the years between 1695 and 1722, of every ten European employees sent to West Africa by the Royal Africa Company, "six died in the first year, two died in the second through seventh years, and only one lived to be discharged in Britain." With odds like these, most European merchants were more than happy to let African merchants dominate trade between the interior and the coast. They brought their ships to trade ports, bought their goods, and cleared out as fast as they could. So even though Laird had shown that steamers could operate on the Niger, no one was enthusiastic about the prospect of risking the disease costs of following through on his discovery.

A drug that could be used to treat malaria—cinchona bark—had been available in Europe since the seventeenth century. However, it was often in short supply. In the early part of the nineteenth century, chemists isolated **quinine,** the active ingredient in cinchona bark. In 1847 a breakthrough came as an English physician published an article indicating that quinine could be used prophylactically (taken to prevent rather than to cure) against malaria. By the 1850s and 1860s, the great age of European exploration in Africa, quinine was an essential part of any traveler's equipment. Quinine, which was soon being produced on a lavish scale, reduced but did not eliminate the disease costs for Europeans trying to trade with, travel in, or conquer Africa. There remained one innovation that would fully tip the scales in favor of European conquerors—the repeating rifle.

Weapons and Colonialism

In his book, *How I Found Livingstone* (1872), Henry Morton Stanley included a section of advice for "the young traveler." He recommends a good tent and a few other creature comforts, and then moves on to the important things—guns. After a few suggestions about hunting weapons he comments that

> for a fighting weapon, I maintain that the best yet invented is the American Winchester repeating rifle, or the "sixteen shooter" as it is called, supplied with the London Eley's ammunition. If I suggest as a fighting weapon the American Winchester, I do not mean that the traveller need take it for the purpose of offence, but as the best means of efficient defense.

Offense, of course, was precisely how Stanley and others employed their repeating rifles. And it was rifles like these that let relatively small groups of Europeans first venture into the interior and then claim it as their own.

When the nineteenth century began, European armies enjoyed only very limited technological advantages over their African counterparts. Indeed, parts of the African continent were awash in guns. In West Africa, where European-made firearms were frequently exchanged for slaves and gold, guns were part of the fabric of life. By the middle of the eighteenth century most West African states had acquired large stocks of guns and had changed their military tactics to accommodate the new weapons. By way of example, in 1742 a Dutch observer reported that in the kingdom of Asante there was a 5,000-man unit of musketeers. A few years earlier a single ship delivered a cargo to the Gold Coast that included 55,135 pounds of gunpowder and 2,243 muskets. In 1829, the British sold 52,540 guns and almost 2 million pounds of gunpower in West Africa. West African states clearly had a taste for guns, and the various European nations were willing to satisfy it. By at least the end of the nineteenth century, African blacksmiths were learning to repair and sometimes even build their own firearms. There is also evidence that some states were making their own gunpowder, but by then it was too late.

It is significant that the guns were made in Europe and that many of them were made specifically for export to Africa. There are two reasons for this. The first was to cater to the particular tastes and preferences of African buyers. In certain regions and times, for instance, longer barrels were preferred over shorter ones; at other times and in other places the opposite was true. But the other reason was that the guns sold into the African trade were often of inferior quality. In Asante gun barrels were often wrapped with cord to prevent them from bursting. At times the preferred varieties of gunpowder were relatively weak—they were less likely to damage inferior but precious guns. So the guns West Africans had were generally inferior to those used by European armies. However, they were not that different. Like the muskets that virtually all European armies used in the early nineteenth century, the guns West Africans had were smooth-bored muzzle loaders that were inaccurate and slow to load.

If European armies had a significant advantage, it was in their bureaucratic structures and the discipline inculcated in soldiers by drill. But those counted for little when soldiers were dropping dead left and right from disease or when European troops encountered African armies with their own tradition of drill. As a result, where European garrisons were present in Africa at the turn of the nineteenth century, they were usually confined to a few coastal enclaves that a few sick soldiers defended with courage born of desperation.

By the mid-nineteenth century, a host of innovations in the design of guns dramatically changed the fortunes of European military ventures in Africa. The flintlock musket was smooth bored, which meant that the ball it fired more or less skittered off in the direction of the last bounce it made on its way up the barrel. Such weapons had a useful range of about 75 yards and to be effective had to be used by well-drilled infantry that fired them in mass volleys. Europeans had no monopoly on drill, and several African states trained their soldiers to fire their muskets in organized volleys. Rifles are much more accurate because grooves carved into the barrel spin the bullet. Rifles had been known since the sixteenth century, but their use was largely confined to sport because forcing a bullet down a rifled barrel required the use of greased patches and much effort. Their accuracy did not offset their slow rate of fire, and most military officers avoided them like the plague. Myths about American frontiersmen using their hunting rifles and guile to defeat British redcoats, whose muskets forced them to stand in the open to deliver mass volleys, are just that—myths.

The first major innovation of the nineteenth century was the percussion cap. This was a brass cap that fit over a nipple on the breech of the gun, and when struck by the gun's hammer, it detonated the charge in the barrel. It took less time to use percussion caps than it did to use the flint-and-steel ignitions of flintlocks, they worked better in the rain, and by igniting the charge over a shorter period of time they drove the ball harder and faster. Next came bullets that when exposed to the force of the exploding charge expanded to fit the rifled barrel. Such a bullet could slip down a rifled barrel as easily as a musket ball went down the barrel of a smooth-bored musket. So rifles that used these bullets could fire at the same rate as a musket, but were far more accurate. The next step was to produce rifles that loaded from the breech rather than the muzzle. Breechloaders could be loaded more quickly than muzzle loaders. They used brass cartridges that held the bullet, the powder, and the primer (the aforementioned percussion cap inserted into the base of the brass cartridge) in a convenient watertight container, so ammunition for these weapons could be transported through almost any amount of wetness and still function. A breechloader can also be reloaded without standing up, something virtually impossible with a muzzle loader. A soldier equipped with such a rifle could lie on the ground and fire his weapon at a distant enemy without exposing himself to return fire and without pausing more than a second or two to reload. Soldiers who at the beginning of the century had to fire massed volleys at ranges that were at times closer than 50 yards could now spread themselves out, fire aimed shots at individuals, and do so while lying on the ground. Furthermore, they could shoot much faster. Even the best-trained infantry could get off only three rounds a minute with a musket. Almost anyone could fire a shot every five to ten seconds with a breechloader. In short, the military potential of a single soldier had increased markedly, especially if his opponent was not equipped with similar weapons.

European armies began to adopt breechloaders in the 1840s. They were not in widespread use until the late 1860s, by which time the French and British had fully converted to breechloaders. African military forces, which had acquired and used muskets—especially the famed "Dane guns" manufactured specifically for the African trade—suddenly found themselves outgunned. Europeans carefully restricted the supply of the new weapons. The Brussels Convention of 1890 forbade Europeans to sell modern firearms in Africa. Some African leaders did manage to purchase a few modern weapons, but these (with a few notable exceptions) were too little and came too late. Unlike muskets, which could be furnished with locally produced ammunition and repaired—occasionally even built—by local craftsmen, repeating rifles required imported ammunition, and once broken they could not be repaired, much less manufactured, locally. The balance of power was now firmly in the hands of Europeans. They could now send soldiers, missionaries, and merchants to tropical Africa without the devastating losses to disease they once suffered. They could now ply the inland waterways of the continent wrapped in the steel cocoons of their steamboats. A few Europeans or Africans equipped and trained in the use of European weapons could now defeat numerically superior African forces. Conquest could now be conducted on the cheap.

This is not to say that Africans did not fight back. They did and did so valiantly. But the cards were stacked against them. When African states directly resisted European encroachments, the costs were high. The most appalling example of this was the Battle of Omdurman (1898). At Omdurman, a small but well-armed Anglo-Egyptian army confronted a Sudanese army of 40,000. The Sudanese launched wave after wave of cavalry and infantry into a storm of machine-gun, rifle, and artillery fire. When it was all over, 40 members of the Anglo-Egyptian army were dead, and 11,000 Sudanese had perished. Courage was no match for modern weapons.

African societies that were less politically "developed," which is to say societies that lacked the structures of a large-scale state, ironically often provided a more effective resistance to European invasions. Stateless societies such as the Tiv and Igbo in Nigeria were more difficult to conquer than larger entities such as the Sokoto Caliphate in Nigeria or the Mahdist State in Sudan. Because colonial invaders had to deal with each village separately, it took far more time and effort to "pacify" these politically fragmented peoples. Smaller societies also sometimes

The Battle of Omdurman in 1898 as depicted in a British magazine. Note the inability of the Mahdist troops to approach the British lines. Modern weapons made this one of the most lopsided battles in history.

mounted fierce military resistance. Modern-day Tanzania had no large-scale states in the nineteenth century except for the Arab state of Zanzibar. When the Germans began their conquest, the Zanzibari-controlled areas of the coast were taken relatively easily. There was resistance, but it came mostly from private citizens who organized resistance when the state could not or would not. Away from the coast, some Tanzanian societies chose to accommodate the Germans; others fought them ferociously. The Hehe fought for most of a decade against the Germans, only succumbing after the death of their leader Mkwawa in 1898. But succumb they did. Military resistance was futile when the odds were so uneven.

The Great Transformation

Fifty years before Mkwawa's death, Europeans were a minor military and political force on most of the continent. Outside the few coastal enclaves and the temperate parts of southern Africa, Europeans were noticed, when they were noticed at all, as an economic force. Between 1850 and 1900 what had been a stable balance of power between Europe and the rest of the world was upset. Gunboats appeared on Chinese canals. India came under the direct control of the British government. The French and the Dutch conquered Southeast Asia. In the American West, this same period saw the final demise of independent Indian nations. And Africa, which had previously been less affected than any of these other places by Europeans, suddenly came to be carved up by Britain, France, Germany, and Belgium.

We would be wrong, then, to assume that Europe has dominated Africa for a long time. In fact, direct European political domination of the African continent lasted about a human lifetime. Europeans did not conquer Africa because of any inherent superiority they enjoyed. Rather, they did so because for a time they were the only ones who had access to the tools and weapons created by industry. Once their monopoly on industrial weapons was broken, colonialism was abandoned. And it was not just Africans who fell behind technologically and so suffered the humiliations of conquest. A Vietnamese official, who took his own life in 1862 rather than submit to the French, wrote that

> The French have huge battleships, full of soldiers and armed with powerful cannons. Nobody can resist them. . . . And I said to myself: It would be as senseless for you to assail your enemy as for a fawn to attack the tiger. You would only draw suffering upon the people whom Heaven has entrusted to your care. I therefore wrote to all civilian and military officials to lay down their arms.

> Quoted from Anthony Reid, *Last Stand of Asian Autonomies* (New York: St. Martin's, 1997)

In less than a century the Vietnamese and their counterparts in Africa would take up their arms again. But in the first half of the twentieth century Europe held the upper hand.

The Limits of Resistance

The military imbalance between Africans and Europeans was not the only reason that Europeans were able to control most of the continent for the better part of a century. The other was that there was never a unified "African" response to colonialism. We would do well to remember that a broader notion of African identity did not emerge until the twentieth century. Thus, at the time that all these places were being colonized, it was up to particular states, societies, and individuals to determine their reactions to the European presence. In some cases this meant a vigorous military reaction. In others cases the European presence was seen as an opportunity. European merchants brought desirable goods, mission stations offered education and medical care, and the emerging colonial governments provided new employment opportunities. What might be a threat to a state could be an opportunity to an ambitious individual. There was no standard response to European interventions.

It is also worth noting the role of African troops in the process of colonial conquest. The Germans in East Africa relied heavily on locally recruited soldiers, as did the Belgians in the Congo, and the British and French in their colonies. While from the present perspective we might wonder how African soldiers felt about participating in the subjugation of their fellow Africans, we should remember that these soldiers did not think of themselves or their opponents as either African or fellows. We might just as well ask how French and German soldiers of the First World War felt about fighting their fellow Europeans. Clearly they had few qualms.

Although military conquest paved the way for the emergence of the colonial state, it was just the beginning of the process of colonization. For the colonial state to really assert control it had to establish itself politically and economically and this process opened up a host of opportunities for colonized people to either cooperate with or resist the colonial state, or to do a bit of both. That aspect of the colonial project will be the subject of the next two chapters.

The Colonization of a Continent

In the second half of the nineteenth century, colonial conquest was cheaper and easier for Europeans than ever before (or since). But the process of colonization unfolded differently in different places. In some places, usually those in which European powers had long-standing economic interests, colonization evolved from existing economic interests, often in gradual and unplanned ways. In other instances, colonial conquest was the result of a few ambitious individuals deciding that a region of the continent was ripe for colonization and then setting out to acquire the territory with the expectation that commercial or strategic gain would follow. In Senegal and the Gold Coast, for example, French and British colonial conquest evolved from over a century of prior commercial activity. By contrast, in the Belgian Congo and German East Africa, the Belgians and Germans had few prior economic interests and set out on a conscious program of conquest and colonization. In Kenya and South Africa, colonization followed a different pattern, in part because of the presence of large numbers of European settlers. Of course, these few examples do not exhaust all the possibilities. Some colonies—Liberia and Sierra Leone—were created for and settled by former slaves from the Americas. And Ethiopia, a place that seems to consistently be the exception to every rule, avoided colonization except for a few years in the 1930s. Although the process of colonization was highly variable—both from the perspective of the people being colonized and from the perspective of the colonizer—we have chosen to look at a few case studies that will give you a good sense of the larger process.

The Expansion of the Gold Coast Colony

The coastal regions of Gold Coast (now the modern country of Ghana) had been deeply involved with Europeans for centuries before the area was colonized. The Portuguese had built the first European fortress south of the Sahara at El Mina. There they had bought gold and slaves. Later they were driven from El Mina by the Dutch, who were joined on the coast by the British and the Danes. The British built a trade fort at Cape Coast, and the Danes used the nearby Christianbourg Castle. By the early nineteenth century all three groups of Europeans were still present, but the power of the British was waxing steadily, while the Dutch and Danes found their power to be waning. Still, their presence is an important part of the story because it meant that African states could always seek another European trading nation if one tried to cut them out of the trade.

On the African side of this trade system were the Asante empire and a loose confederation of Fante states. The Asante, as discussed in Chapter 9, had carved out an empire in the eighteenth century from a collection of Akan-speaking states.

Initially a sort of confederation, it had gradually come to be dominated by the city of Kumasi, whose rulers called themselves the Asantehene. Asante had been deeply involved in the slave and gold trades, selling both commodities into the Saharan and Atlantic trades. The Asante state was directly involved in trade and drew much of its revenue from trade. Kumasi, the Asante capital, was inland, over 100 miles from the coast. Between Asante and the trade forts was the Fante confederation. The Fante states lacked Asante's political centralization, but usually unified when threatened by the Asante. Because the major trade forts were in Fante territory, the Fante were a chronic thorn in Asante's side. Thus, a consistent component of Asante policy was to try to get direct access to the trade forts, either by conquering Fante, overawing the Fante so that they would not hinder trade, or seeking alliances with the European powers.

In the Fante-dominated towns around the trade forts—El Mina and Cape Coast—a class of mixed-race (mulatto in the parlance of the time) merchants and professionals had grown up. Many of these mulattos were the descendants of European merchants who had settled on the coast long before. They had names like Bannerman and Brew and served as cross-cultural intermediaries between the Europeans and the Fante and Asante. Many of them were educated in Europe or in Sierra Leone and so had a foot in both the worlds of Europe and West Africa. Later they would play a role in the administration of the Gold Coast Colony (James Bannerman was the first Attorney General of the Gold Coast) until forced out in the second half of the nineteenth century as Africans were replaced in colonial administrations by whites. Mulattos also played a prominent role in opposing the expansion of British power in the Gold Coast and in the creation of a pan-African consciousness.

One last bit of background: In 1807, Britain outlawed the slave trade. The slave trade did not end immediately, but because the British had been the principal buyers of Asante slaves and they stopped buying slaves, Asante lost an important source of revenue. This may have weakened the Asante state and made it more susceptible to British domination in the second half of the nineteenth century. Certainly the Asante attempted to pressure the British into reopening the slave trade.

In the first half of the nineteenth century, the balance of power in the Gold Coast was fairly even. The Asante were often at odds with the Fante, but could not defeat them decisively. The Fante sought British support in their wars with the Asante, and for their part the Asante usually got some support from the Dutch. The British were not in a position to seize any territory they wanted. Instead they were a powerful but not dominant element in the politics of the Gold Coast. In fact, when the Asante invaded Fante in 1824, the British suffered a major defeat (the governor of Cape Coast was killed in the battle) before the Asante withdrew.

What happened in the subsequent 74 years or so was that the British slowly acquired control over more and more territory. Growth was incremental until 1850, but afterward the pace picked up. Before 1850 the main change was the signing of "bonds" in 1844 that created what the British came to call a protectorate over the Fante states. What resulted was a sort of proto-colony in the southern Gold Coast. The British slowly took more and more administrative power and created courts in the protectorate. But their power was limited by the absence of a real source of revenue. They could not levy customs duties because if they did, local merchants would simply sell their goods to the Danes or the Dutch. In 1850 the Danes departed, but it was not until 1872 that the Dutch pulled out.

In 1863 the Asante invaded the Fante protectorate and were repelled, but with difficulty. At the same time the Fante were growing less and less willing to cooperate with the British. Fante intellectuals and political leaders began to demand greater local control, and a Sierra Leonean physician who was working in the Gold Coast wrote a book that called for the creation of a republic with its capital at Accra. (The physician was Africanus Horton; the book is *West African Countries and Peoples*.) It is interesting that before there was even a fully formed colonial state in Gold Coast, an educated elite was challenging colonialism.

In 1872 the departure of the Dutch opened up a new possibility for the British. They could now charge customs duties, and so had a new source of revenue. They promptly put their new money to work by invading Asante. The Asante had spent much of 1872 invading the southern regions of Gold Coast and trying to reclaim the territory taken from them in 1824. They were remarkably successful. However, the British decided to take decisive action and brought in Sir Garnet Wolsey, a veteran of colonial wars in western Canada. Wolsey brought in troops from Britain, but also used soldiers from other parts of the empire. There were a large group of West Indians and some Nigerians in his force—an example of empire begetting more empire.

Wolsey's troops, armed with Enfield rifles and modern artillery, marched to Kumasi in 1874. After two battles, in which the Asante suffered many casualties and the British suffered few, Kumasi was taken. The British looted the palace and burned it (much of the loot is still on display in art museums in Europe). They then withdrew, demanding that the Asante pay an indemnity and relinquish their claims to their southern territories.

The events following the British withdrawal were, if anything, more damaging to the Asante than the invasion itself had been. Impoverished by the looting of the palace and the indemnity, the Asantehene was forced to take grave goods from the tombs of his ancestors, an offense for which he was dethroned. Emboldened by clear evidence of Asante weakness, most of their subject states revolted. Soon there was little left of the Asante empire except the area immediately around Kumasi. In 1896 the British offered their "protection" to the rump of the Asante empire. When it was refused, they sent an expedition that took the city and took **Prempeh,** the Asantehene, into exile. He was not allowed to return until 1924.

The final indignity occurred in 1900 when the British governor of Gold Coast demanded that the golden stool—the throne of the Asantehenes—be turned over to him. From the Asante perspective, this was rubbing salt in their wounds, and it was too much to bear. Although the odds were clearly against them, they revolted. It took nine months and much blood before the revolt was put down. Even after all these defeats, the Asante never totally abandoned their cause. When Prempeh was allowed to return in 1924, the British required that he live as a "private citizen," not a political one. Soon they relented and allowed him to take the title "Kumasahene" (i.e., the ruler of Kumasi but not Asante). Former parts of the Asante empire began to send him tribute. Eventually, in 1934, the British were forced to allow the creation of an Asante Confederation.

It is worth looking at the timing of these events. In the first half of the century the Asante and the British were on more or less even terms. Had conquering Asante been a major British foreign policy objective, they almost certainly could have found the resources to defeat the Asante. But it never was that important to the British, and so they held their portion of the coastal areas and fought a series of indecisive wars. They won some, they lost some. In the second half of the century, conquering Asante was still not critical to the British, but it was a much cheaper and easier proposition. With modern firearms, quinine, and steamships bringing supplies and troops from other parts of the empire, they could take Kumasi despite the vigorous resistance of the Asante. So they did.

At the same time, we should note that the Asante did not crumble in the face of all this modern weaponry. The British did not try to hold Kumasi after their expedition of 1874. And even once the British occupied Kumasi, the Asante did not give up. They revolted in 1900 and remained a threat into the 1930s. So changing technology set the terms of the encounter between these two empires but was not the sole determinant of the outcome.

Creating the Belgian Congo

The British conquest of the Gold Coast represents one end of a continuum of colonization experiences. The British had been involved with the Gold Coast for a long time before they colonized it, and both the extent of the area under their control and the degree of their control over the area they occupied grew gradually out of their commercial interests. The other salient characteristic of the British conquest of Gold Coast was that they had to wrest control of the country from a larger and highly organized imperial state. The Belgian colonization of the Congo River basin was a very different sort of encounter. First, the Belgians had few pre-conquest commercial interests in the Congo. Indeed, they had no prior interest in Africa or in an empire elsewhere. Second, the Congo had no states of the same scale as the Asante empire. Rather, it comprised many smaller states and chiefdoms. No one of these could put up the sort of resistance that a major state could, but there were an awful lot of these smaller states to either talk or bully into submission.

Another major difference between the world of the Congo basin and that of the Gold Coast was that the Gold Coast had been deeply involved in trade with Europeans and others for centuries before it was incorporated into the British Empire. The dense tropical rain forest that draped the banks of the Congo and the falls that made it impossible for boats to move from the coast into the upper reaches of the river served to isolate this region from the broader world economy until the nineteenth century. To be sure, trade within the region was extensive. Trading canoes plied a river system that served as a watery highway connecting an area roughly the size of Western Europe. Isolation is a relative term. People in the Congo basin partook in trade across a huge area, but that area had few links to either the Atlantic or the Indian Ocean.

But in the nineteenth century that isolation began to break down. As the price of both slaves and ivory went up, Swahili traders began to encroach from the east, and slave traders in the western reaches of the river found they could profitably march slaves to the coast. The Congo's isolation—although beneficial in some ways—came at a price. Unlike West Africa, where trade brought guns, the people in many parts of the Congo had never seen guns until they encountered slave raiders or the leading edge of a growing colonial state.

The first European to bring a report of the Congo was Henry Morton Stanley—the one whose comments on the Winchester rifle we saw earlier. Stanley was a naturalized American who had fought on both sides in the Civil War, run a shop in Arkansas, served in the Merchant Marine, and eventually found his calling as a reporter. He became famous when the *New York Herald* commissioned him to find the missing David Livingstone. His next feat was to cross Africa from east coast to west coast, in which journey he descended the Congo. His reports of a great river system in the interior of the continent failed to excite much interest with the British, but caught the eye of Leopold, King of the Belgians. Leopold, using his own fortune, sent Stanley back to the Congo, not to explore but to obtain treaties with anyone who could be convinced to sign one.

Stanley returned with a fistful of treaties just in time for the **Berlin Conference** of 1884–1945. The Berlin Conference was called to sort out competing European claims to various parts of the African continent and to determine when and how European powers might stake their claims to African territories. No African nation was invited, and indeed the conference's convener, the German Chancellor Otto von Bismarck, was more concerned with the balance of power in Europe than he was with the fate of Africa. For Leopold, it was an opportunity to legitimize his claims to the Congo. Leopold produced Stanley's treaties between Central African rulers and the Congo International Association—an association he controlled—and on the strength of them was able to claim sovereignty over a new entity that he called the Congo Free State.

The Congo Free State was unique among African colonies. It was not the creation of the Belgian nation; it was the personal property of King Leopold. It was his to do with more or less as he pleased. Although his stated intentions were philanthropic—he especially hoped to stamp out the slave trade—he quickly set out to get a return on his investment. At first this meant trying to dominate the ivory business. The Congo Free State brought river steamers onto the Congo to try to control—or at least get a share of, the ivory trade.

The Free State's goals immediately brought conflict with the Swahili merchants/imperialists who were carving out trading empires in the eastern parts of the territories claimed by the Free State. **Tippu Tip,** a Zanzibari in the ivory and slave business who had aided Stanley on his first expedition down the Congo, felt especially betrayed and fought off the Belgians for several years. Curiously, there was little initial resistance to the Belgians on the part of the indigenous populations. But once the Bobangi river traders who had controlled the river trade before the arrival of the Belgians realized the threat the Belgians posed, they struck back by attacking the Free State's trading posts. The Free State retaliated by using its river steamers and guns to destroy whole villages along the river. By 1895 the Free State ruled the river and thus the ivory trade.

But controlling the river was not cheap, and the revenues from ivory were not sufficient to pay the cost of administration. Leopold was forced to take a series

Leopold II, King of the Belgians and ruler of the Kongo Free State.

of loans from the Belgian state to keep the Free State functioning. In 1890 the Free State borrowed 25 million francs, which was supplemented by another 7 million in 1895. Despite these bailouts, the Free State would most likely have collapsed were it not for a new development. In the last decade of the nineteenth century, the demand for rubber took off suddenly in Europe because of the invention of the pneumatic bicycle tire, which was, of course, made of rubber. Several species of plants produce rubber, and one of them, a type of vine, is found growing wild in the forest regions of the Congo. Soon the Free State's interests focused almost entirely on rubber rather than ivory, and it pursued that interest in such a brutal manner that other colonial powers (no slouches themselves when it came to brutality) were shocked.

Step one in the exploitation of the Congo's rubber was to declare that all land that was "unoccupied" was property of the crown. Much of this land was then turned over to private concessionaires whose job was to get the rubber out—by whatever means they saw fit. Step two was to set rubber production quotas that villages had to meet. Step three was to require that all men and women perform 40 hours of work a month for the state. This work was in theory to be compensated by the state.

In the early 1890s the rubber business did not seem particularly onerous to the African subjects of the Free State. The Free State paid for the rubber, and they were happy to provide it. But it soon became clear that the Free State's thirst for rubber could not be slaked by the quantities of rubber that Africans would provide willingly. The Free State's response was not to raise the price they paid for rubber, but to encourage their agents to get more rubber at the same price. The agents used forced labor provisions to require Africans to collect rubber on the state's land. Because the rubber vines were not that common and were spread over vast areas, the agents themselves did not supervise the production of rubber; they simply required as much rubber of the villagers as could be obtained in 40 hours of work. Because the agents received bonuses and commissions based on the amount of rubber their regions produced, their estimates of how much rubber could be obtained in 40 hours—optimistic from the start—increased over time.

At the same time the government agents were demanding more rubber, the work of gathering rubber was getting more difficult. The agents who collected the rubber knew little about the actual business of gathering rubber. They overestimated the number of rubber vines in the forest and also misunderstood how often the vines could be tapped without killing them. As their demands increased, rubber gatherers had to travel farther afield to find untapped vines, or if they were desperate, they would tap the same vines over and over again until the vines died. Soon the amount of work needed to meet the rubber quotas made it virtually impossible for gatherers to do any other work.

Naturally, no one would do this type of work for so little compensation without compulsion. The Free State may have been too cheap to pay market prices for rubber, but it did not skimp on compulsion. The Free State's agents made liberal use of the soldiers under their command to punish villages that were not meeting their quotas. Soldiers killed gatherers or sometimes their families as punishment for not meeting their quotas. To show that they had not stolen or wasted the ammunition they took on these missions, the soldiers were expected to bring back the hands of their victims. Eventually, unable to meet the demands of the Free State and to feed themselves, whole villages fled into the forest. Others fought back by attacking the representatives of the state. There were several major rebellions around the turn of the century, and one of the concessionaires lost 140 sentries in 1905 alone. Africans also resisted by adulterating the rubber they handed over and by destroying vines in the forest in the hopes that if there were no rubber to be had, the Free State might go away.

And where did all this rubber money go? Remember that Leopold had borrowed money from the Belgian government to keep his Free State from foundering under the weight of its debts. He chose to pay Belgium back, but not in the usual cash-with-interest way. Rather, the Free State created a foundation that skimmed off the income from a 250,000-square-kilometer region of the Congo and then used that money to build infrastructure in Belgium. This Fondation de la Couronne ultimately transferred 60 million francs from the Congo to Belgium. There was brutal exploitation in other colonies, but nowhere was imperialism so nakedly and unashamedly exploitative. Leopold's Free State was imperialism in its purest form.

Even by the standards of the time, this was considered beyond the pale. Roger Casement, the British consul in the Congo, and several missionaries sent out a series of reports documenting the abuses being perpetrated in the Congo. Soon there was a London-based Congo Reform Association, and newspapers in Britain and even Belgium were criticizing Leopold and the Congo Free State. In 1908, the Belgian government stepped in and took over the Free State. It was renamed the Belgian Congo, and most of the worst abuses were stopped, though the situation remained—and remains—grim.

As was the case with the conquest of the Asante and the Gold Coast, the relationship between these events and the rise of industrialism in Europe and the United States is interesting. Steamers and modern firearms made Stanley's initial journeys on the Congo possible. The subsequent domination of the river by the Free State's representatives was made possible by the same technologies, abetted later by a rail link between Stanley Pool and the sea. The two commodities that kept the Free State going and indeed drove its conquest of the Congo were ivory and rubber—both of which were key raw materials in the emerging industrial economy of the North Atlantic. Because Americans and Europeans wanted bicycles and pianos, steamers roamed the Congo basin collecting rubber and ivory and leaving corpses and severed hands in their wake.

 Controversies in African History: **Mkwawa: Leader of the Hehe**

Of the Africans who led the resistance to the German occupation of East Africa, few were as successful or dramatic as Mkwawa, leader of the Hehe. The Hehe had been an expansionist power in southwestern Tanganyka since the 1870s and much of this expansion was led by Mkwawa. The Hehe fought their wars with spears at a time when most people in the interior were acquiring firearms. But they fought well. The need to arm and train a large army of spearmen made Hehe society inclusionist rather than aristocratic, and hence internally resilient.

When an impetuous German officer named Zelewski arrived in Uhehe in August of 1891 with artillery, modern rifles, and machine guns, he had every expectation of defeating Mkwawa quickly and easily. Instead, Mkwawa's forces ambushed the Germans as they passed through a narrow valley. Zelewski was killed along with nine other Germans and over 300 African askaris (soldiers who fought for the Germans) and porters who worked for the Germans. A small group managed to escape to the coast.

Mkwawa returned to the Hehe town of Iringa where he had constructed a five-kilometer defensive wall around the city. In 1894 the Germans returned to seek revenge. The Hehe were unfamiliar with artillery and thought their fortification impregnable. The Germans fired their artillery into the fortification and set up their machine guns in trees so as to be able to fire into Iringa. Despite having captured machine guns during their last encounter with the Germans, the Hehe did not know how to operate them. Using only spears, they defended the city, fighting house to house. Mkwawa's soldiers enabled him to escape and he carried on as a fugitive from the Germans. His subjects sacrificed their lives on occasion to give him time to escape German patrols. In 1898, after four years on the run, the Germans ran him to the ground. He shot himself and a companion rather than surrender. Once again raw courage was defeated by superior technology.

Ethiopia: Where European Imperialism Failed

Ethiopia represents a general exception to the larger pattern of imperial conquest in Africa. The Italians came, they saw, and they tried to conquer, but they were sent packing. The story of how Ethiopia managed to avoid European conquest is important in that it shows us that there was nothing inevitable about European domination in Africa. Given the right circumstances, Africans could defeat European armies. Perhaps more importantly, the survival of an independent African state served as an inspiration to Africans throughout the diaspora. People as different as W.E.B. Du Bois and Jamaican Rastafarians (whose name derives from Ras Tafari, the name used by the Ethiopian emperor **Haile Sellassie** before he took his throne name) found a source of pride and validation in Ethiopia.

In many ways Ethiopia was very different from the Gold Coast or the Congo. Its fertile highland soils allowed for intensive plow-based farming, something found nowhere else in sub-Saharan Africa. It had a hereditary nobility, united by an ancient Christian church and an imperial history. The church was run by a literate clergy that played a role in spreading religion and culture into conquered lands. Ethiopia's proximity to Egypt and the Red Sea meant that it was able to participate in the economy and culture of the Middle East, but the highlands acted as a natural fortress keeping out the more dangerous parts of the larger world.

On the other hand, in the years before its encounter with the Italians, Ethiopia had been riven by internal war, as various nobles tried to either revive the long-collapsed empire or to prevent others from doing so. Ethiopia was being squeezed between an expansionist Egyptian government in the process of extending its rule in the Sudan, the Turks who were trying to expand their holdings on the African side of the Red Sea, the English who sent the occasional punitive expedition into Ethiopia, and the Italians who were gobbling up what is now Eritrea. At the same time, the church was deeply and at times violently divided over the question of the number of Jesus' births. One school of thought (*sost lidot*) held that Jesus had been born once in eternity, once in utero, and finally in the usual physical sense. The other camp (the *Ewostathians*) rejected this because it suggested that Christ had multiple natures—an idea at odds with Monophysite thought. In any case, these competing theologies divided the church and the main provinces from each other. In short, if there was nothing foreordained about European conquest in Africa, neither was there any obvious reason why it should not succeed in Ethiopia. That it did not was the result of several factors: the leadership of three extraordinary men (Tewodros II, Menelik II, and Haile Sallassie), the willingness of Ethiopians to unify behind the imperial idea at crucial times, and finally the fact that the Italians were not skilled in imperialism.

The century before **Tewodros II** (1855) reunified Ethiopia under a single emperor is known as the **Zamana Masafent,** or the age of princes. It was a time when even the fiction of imperial unity had disappeared, and various kings and warlords ruled the former provinces of the empire. Before his conquest of Ethiopia, Tewodros (actually called Kassa before he became emperor) had been the prince of a territory on the border between Ethiopia and the Sudan. During that time he fought a battle against an Egyptian force that had encroached on

Ethiopian territory. The Egyptians, who were equipped with modern arms and trained in European tactics, soundly defeated Tewodros and his men. The lesson was not lost on Tewodros, and henceforth he diligently worked to acquire modern arms and training in their use for his men. He even managed to acquire the equipment and the technicians needed to make his own artillery. Subsequent Ethiopian emperors, Menelik in particular, understood the importance of modern weaponry and regularly played one European power against the other to obtain weapons and expertise.

Tewodros' ability to acquire modern weapons—mostly from the French, but at times from the British—combined with tremendous ambition enabled him to reunite Ethiopia under his imperial leadership. Sadly, the later years of his reign were marked by internal strife. Uprisings within the empire led to civil war, and over time Tewodros seems to have suffered some sort of breakdown. He became intensely suspicious of his own followers and ordered several mass executions of military units he considered disloyal. The final straw came when he detained several British emissaries. Britain organized a punitive expedition in 1868 under the leadership of Robert Napier. Napier's men moved swiftly into Ethiopia and defeated Tewodros' army. Tewodros, rather than suffer the humiliation of surrender, took his own life. Napier withdrew, having achieved his goals of freeing the Britons held hostage and humbling Tewodros.

In the following years another emperor emerged, but his control over Ethiopia was tenuous compared with Tewodros' at the height of his power. Yohannes II had two chronic sources of irritation to deal with: the Italians, and the Ras (Duke) of Shewa, Menelik. Menelik had formally submitted to Yohannes, but always kept an eye out for opportunity. While the Italians were encroaching on Ethiopia's Red Sea coast, they were anxious to obtain allies in the highlands. To this end they courted Menelik by trading with him and selling him weapons. Menelik also sought out trade and weapons from the French, and over time his province of Shewa became increasingly powerful, richer and better armed than any other part of Ethiopia. When Yohannes was killed in a battle on the frontiers with Sudan in 1889, Menelik had himself crowned emperor.

The decade of the 1890s saw increasing pressure from the Italians. A newly unified Italy was eager to take its place in the community of European nations, and one way of doing this was to acquire an empire. One of the few places left to be colonized was Ethiopia, so the pressure was on. In 1889, Italian officials in Eritrea signed a treaty with Menelik that recognized his rule over Ethiopia. However, there were two texts of the treaty, one in Amharic and the other in Italian. Menelik and his advisors were forced to rely on the Italians to translate the Italian version, because none of them could read Italian. As it turned out, there was a significant difference between the two texts. The Italian version required that all relations between Ethiopia and the rest of the world take place through Italian intermediaries. In effect, it made Ethiopia a protectorate. Once it became apparent what had happened, Menelik prepared to take action. He conceded Eritrea to the Italians. No one is sure why he did so. He did, however, allow the Rases who commanded the border regions to raid into Eritrea. The Italians, at little cost to themselves, defeated several of these raiding forces. Lulled by a false sense of optimism, they moved into Ethiopia proper with a force of about 10,000 men.

Menelik was able to seize the moral high ground—it was his territory being invaded and not the other way around—and so received intense popular and elite support. He was able to pull together an army of 100,000 men, many of whom were equipped with repeating rifles obtained from the French. The Italians had occupied a group of mountaintops, and had they had the patience to wait there, they might have defeated Menelik. He was unwilling to try to drive the Italians out of their mountain redoubts and was forced to wait. Soon food shortages and disease began to weaken his army. He was on the brink of withdrawing when the Italian commander, whose superiors had accused him of cowardice, came down out of the mountains to engage Menelik. In February 1896 at Adwa the two armies came to grips. When it was all over, the Italians had lost 70 percent of their men to capture, wounds, or death. By contrast, the Ethiopians lost roughly 10 percent of their much larger army. The surviving Italians retreated to Eritrea, and the highlands were safe from further colonialist adventures until the rise of the Fascists in Italy, who took another and still basically unsuccessful crack at conquering Ethiopia during the reign of Haile Sallassie.

African Colonization in Global Perspective

The nineteenth century—the second half of it especially—was a busy time for imperialists. At the beginning of the century Europeans controlled just a few coastal territories and the Cape region of South Africa. By 1900 virtually the entire continent had been conquered or was on the verge of succumbing to European control. One can question the depth of that control; as we will see in the next two chapters, European rulers often had to tread lightly for fear of provoking their "subjects." One can also point out that the era of European dominance was rather brief—in most cases it was clear by 1955 that independence was just a matter of time in most colonies. But without a doubt, there was an upheaval in the global balance of power in the nineteenth century.

That upheaval was not limited to Africa. The steamboats that plied the Congo and the Niger also appeared on the Irrawaddy River in Burma and in the many rivers of Sarawak. Dutch soldiers used their repeating firearms to conquer Indonesia. The French did likewise in Indo-China. The Germans, Dutch, and British seized parts of New Guinea, and European settlers poured into New Zealand and Australia.

The parallels between the European colonization of Africa and their colonization of Asia are revealing. In some instances (the Dutch colonization of Indonesia, for example), the late-nineteenth-century land grab came after years of trade and creeping imperialism—much like the British colonization of the Gold Coast. In other cases (the Germans in New Guinea, for example), the pattern was more akin to that of the Congo Free State. The Germans decided they wanted a colony and grabbed what seemed available. In New Zealand, roughly paralleling Kenya or South Africa, British settlers moved in and created what Alfred Crosby has dubbed a "neo-Europe." Interestingly, New Zealand worked far better (for the settlers, worse from the Maori perspective) as a settler colony than Kenya. Perhaps the most interesting parallel is between Thailand and Ethiopia; both managed to avoid being colonized while their neighbors were gobbled up.

Indonesia

The Dutch presence in Indonesia began in the seventeenth century with the creation of the Dutch East India Company. Originally involved mostly in the spice trade, the Company slowly acquired territorial interests in Java and a few smaller islands. But its rule there did not result in fundamental change. They did not attempt to impose Dutch law, culture, or ideas. All they sought was to skim off tax revenues, much as previous regimes had done. Then between 1870 and 1910 there was an explosion of Dutch territorial acquisition. Parts of Java that had been "ruled" by the Dutch through treaties with local rulers came under direct Dutch control. Islands other than the main islands of Java and Sumatra—of which there are thousands—also came under Dutch control.

Unlike the old imperialism of the previous centuries, the late nineteenth century saw a burst of new imperialism. Dutch-owned steamship lines plied the waters between the islands and the Netherlands. The Dutch built railways, established courts, imported a large corps of Dutch civil servants, and established plantations of various sorts. The Dutch also brought Christianity to a few parts of Indonesia.

Like Africans, the Indonesians resisted the Dutch in a variety of ways. The Ache region of Sumatra fought a 15-year war to preserve its independence. Bali, the small island off the coast of Java known as one of the few places that Hinduism has survived in Indonesia and as a tourist destination, fought hard against Dutch encroachment. But kris knives and courage were no match for repeating rifles.

As with Africa, the imperialism of the late nineteenth century was not just imperialism on a larger scale, it was a qualitatively different type of imperialism. After 1870 the Dutch had different aims and sought much greater control over the places they governed. They were no longer content to just collect a share of the tax receipts; they wanted to govern. This provoked resistance, which was put down with modern weapons. In short, until the Japanese expelled the Dutch in 1939, Indonesia was every bit as colonized as any part of Africa.

That the Indonesian colonial experience was similar to that of sub-Saharan Africa is telling. Indonesia, like Africa south of the Sahara, had been in limited contact with the Eurasian landmass for centuries. Like sub-Saharan Africa, trade with Eurasia brought Indonesia first Hinduism and Buddhism, then Islam, and later Christianity. Trade shaped the rise of kingdoms that controlled access to river trade. But as was the case with Africa, geography placed limits on Eurasian influences, which in turn limited the spread of technology. As a result, Indonesian societies remained less economically and technologically sophisticated than their Eurasian counterparts. As was the case with Africa before the middle of the nineteenth century, these differences in economic and technological development were not so great that Europeans could easily conquer Indonesia. But by the second half of the nineteenth century, there was a sufficiently large gulf between the technology available to the Indonesians and Europeans that the latter were able to conquer the former—swiftly, if briefly.

Thailand: An Asian Ethiopia?

While the French, the British, and the Dutch were colonizing other parts of Southeast Asia, Thailand managed to maintain its independence. It did so by many of the same means that Ethiopia used. In Thailand, like in Ethiopia, a strong and resourceful King Mongkut (r. 1851–68) (and later his son and successor Chulanlongkorn) sought out European advisors and technical experts. They both were adept at playing the French against the British and knew when to make minor concessions so as not to have to give up the whole show. By conceding minor amounts of territory—like Menelik, who let the Italians have Eritrea—Thailand was able to maintain its territorial integrity. The Thai kings also allowed European powers to have trading privileges and granted foreign merchants the same sort of extraterritorial rights they had in China and the Ottoman Empire. If there is a critical difference between Ethiopia and Thailand, it is that the Thais never had to face a European army in the field. Instead of defeating Europeans on the field of battle, they outmaneuvered them in diplomacy.

The nineteenth century saw a major shift in the global balance of power. That shift had different effects in different places. In some places indigenous cultures were devastated and replaced by transplanted Europeans; in others, Europeans ruled but did not settle; and in a few, local rulers were forced to make trade concessions and other compromises but managed to avoid European rule. Africa's experience during this period was roughly comparable to that of other similar parts of the world. If Africa figures large in the Western imagination when imperialism is mentioned, it is more because of the vast size of the continent than because Africa was uniquely or especially vulnerable.

Useful Works on This Chapter Topic

Tools of Empire, by Daniel Headrick (1982) is a great place to begin an examination on the growth of European empires in the nineteenth century. The authors wish to acknowledge a particular debt to this book. Headrick's argument about the role of technology in shaping nineteenth-century imperialism inspired the central thesis of this chapter, and several of our examples are drawn from this thought-provoking book. For a history of Ethiopia that considers in detail the Ethiopian defeat of the Italians, see *The History of Ethiopia*, by Harold Marcus (1994). For a world historical take on the British Empire, see *The British Imperial Century, 1815–1914: A World History Perspective*, by Timothy Parsons (1999). For a controversial look at these events, consider *Conquests and Cultures: An International History*, by Thomas Sowell (1998).

CHAPTER 14

Economic Change in Modern Africa: Forced Integration into the World System

Africa, like the rest of the world, has gone through dramatic economic change in the last 130 years. As the technology needed to create an integrated global economy has become available, places that were once almost immune to world market forces have become part of a global economy. An array of technologies from the telegraph to the fax machine and the steamship to the shipping container has made this degree of economic integration possible. Today farm subsidies in Europe and North America affect African farmers, who sometimes cannot compete against imported foods in their local markets. A global market for light manufacturing labor has made the island of Mauritius a center of clothing production. Nigeria produces large amounts of oil, most of which is sold to the industrialized countries of the West. Copper from the Congo, gold from South Africa, fresh cut flowers from Kenya, and tropical aquarium fish from the lakes of East-Central Africa all are fed into a global economy. At the same time, many Africans wear imported clothes, eat imported food, drive imported cars, and burn imported fuel. The economies of most African nations are utterly dependent on trade.

Trade is nothing new in Africa, nor is trade across continental boundaries a major innovation of recent times. Rather, trade has grown more or less steadily in importance for Africa, and over time Africa's incorporation in the world economy has increased. The advent of colonial rule in the last decades of the nineteenth century accelerated a process that had been going on for centuries. Prior to the advent of colonial rule in Africa, there were any number of means by which Africans participated in long-distance trade. West African gold had been exported across the Sahara for centuries in exchange for North African cloth. Salt, smoked fish, and kola nuts were traded over long distances within the continent. The East African coast traded cereals, ivory, and slaves for things as valuable as Chinese porcelain and as mundane as dried shark. Some West African states were deeply involved in an Atlantic trading system that included cloth, slaves, plant oils, gold, and other commodities. Trading canoes plied the waters of the Niger River carrying goods from the dry Sahel to the wet forest country of the West African coast. Bobangi canoeists likewise traded up and down the length of the Congo River, while Douala traders did likewise on the rivers of Cameroun. The Zambezi saw gold, grain, slaves, and ivory move along its waters. In short, Africans were producing and consuming trade goods long before the colonial period began and continued to do so after the colonial era came to an end. However, the advent of colonialism marks, in a rough way, the onset of a period of intensification of Africa's incorporation into the world economy. This chapter will consider how these changes affected farmers, merchants, wage laborers, slaves, and ultimately the leaders of independent African nations.

The Cash Crop Revolution

In 1800, most Africans were subsistence farmers. Subsistence farmers typically strive to grow all of the food they need to support themselves and their families. They are in effect their own main customers. Thus, they would grow a mix of staples, such as sorghum, maize, yams, and vegetables. They might also keep animals and grow fiber crops as well. Of course, it is virtually impossible to produce locally everything that a family might need. It is also standard practice among subsistence farmers to grow more food than a single family requires. This is in part a safety measure. It is always better to have a surplus of food—even if some is wasted—than to go hungry. Furthermore, there are always a few things—salt, pottery, cloth, fish—that either limitations of environment or labor prevent being produced within the household. So the surplus that is normally generated by subsistence farmers rarely goes to waste. Instead, it is exchanged for essentials or luxuries that the household cannot produce.

By contrast, farmers who are cash croppers usually focus on a single crop that they then exchange for all the other things they need. For example, a cash cropper might grow nothing but cotton. The cotton would then be sold and the proceeds of the sale would be used to buy food, clothing, and whatever else one might need. For cash cropping to work, a number of other institutions and economic structures are needed. For example, there must be someone willing to buy the farmers' crops, and there must be some means of paying for them. Often there are systems of credit involved that allow farmers to buy supplies and to meet expenses before the harvest is sold. There must be a system for storing and transporting the cash crops, and a way of bringing food to the farmers who grow cash crops. And all of this must work smoothly and reliably or farmers will not be willing to grow cash crops. If for some reason one of these institutions fails, a farmer could end up stuck with more cotton than he could ever hope to wear and nothing but cotton to eat. In short, cash cropping can only take place in the presence of a developed and integrated economy.

From the perspective of a state, cash crops have some big advantages over subsistence farming. Cash crops are almost always sold for money at some point. Money transactions are much easier to document and hence to tax than barter transactions. A state composed entirely of busy and prosperous subsistence farmers would not have much of a tax base because the majority of its citizens would live outside the money economy. Cash crops also appeal to states because they can be exchanged for commodities that elites find desirable, or in the case of colonial governments, cash crops may be desirable because they are needed by industry in the colonial metropolis. Thus, colonial states often encouraged cash crop production because the home markets needed cotton or palm oil or whatever. Independent African states find cash crops equally desirable because they can be exchanged for the hard currency needed to import necessities such as fuel, medicine, and food or luxuries.

The history of cash cropping in Africa is one of cautious innovation on the part of farmers and wildly overoptimistic enthusiasm on the part of states. States have encouraged and even coerced African farmers to produce for world markets, often before the economic institutions that would permit them to succeed were in place. African farmers have usually wisely rejected cash cropping in the absence of suitable transportation networks and markets and enthusiastically embraced cash cropping when the necessary economic structures were in place. Interestingly, the most successful instances of cash cropping have occurred where farmers rather than states took the initiative to introduce cash cropping or where farmers have used infrastructure provided by the state in unanticipated ways.

It is also worth noting that cash cropping did not begin with colonialism. Where water provided cheap transport, cash cropping thrived. Along the Senegal River farmers had been growing groundnuts (peanuts to Americans) for export

Harvesting sisal, a fiber crop used to make twine. Note the light gauge rail cars used to transport the sisal within the plantation.

since the late eighteenth century. Farmers on the East African coast produced grain for export to South Arabia from at least the early nineteenth century and probably long before. Plantation owners on the islands of Zanzibar and Pemba, where water transport is easily available, produced cloves for export for more than 50 years before the British seized their islands. **Palm oil** was produced all along the rivers and lagoons of West Africa. Thus, where there was suitable transportation Africans were enthusiastic cash croppers. We should not assume that it was an irrational resistance to change that made farmers sometimes reluctant to become cash croppers. Rather, it was usually a keen awareness of the risks involved.

Colonial Transportation Networks

If colonial governments caused a major shift in African farming habits, it was in part because they provided new types of transportation. Colonial states built these transportation networks for two reasons. The first was that they hoped that improved transportation would enable their colonies to yield enough revenue to support the cost of government. The second was an ideological commitment to "modernization" that was often expressed through the construction of modern forms of transportation. Obviously, these two motivations are related to each other, but it is worth examining each of them separately.

European powers acquired colonies in Africa for almost as many reasons as there were colonies. And once they had acquired colonies, European colonial states had an equally varied approach to governing their new possessions. But whatever reasons they had for acquiring colonies or methods of government they chose, colonial governments were all expected to meet the costs of administration locally. The French or British public might be willing to meet the cost of conquest and the occasional public works project, but colonial governments were expected to find enough revenue to pay government salaries and the cost of administration. Faced in many instances with colonies mostly populated by subsistence farmers whose involvement with the money economy was limited, colonial governments had to find ways of getting their subjects into the cash economy and then taxing them. To this end, most colonial states sought to compel people to enter the money economy through the imposition of taxes that were payable only with money. With the stick of taxation in place, they then provided the carrot of either wage labor on European-owned mines and farms, or support for cash cropping. On most of the continent European investment in farms and mines was limited, though in some places like southern Africa it was significant, so for most Africans paying taxes meant becoming cash croppers.

Taxation took many forms, some of them rather creative. One of the more common early means of taxing Africans was the hut tax. Tax collectors would visit a town or village, count roofs, and present the community with a tax bill based on the number of houses. This was quickly countered by building fewer but larger houses, so authorities switched to other types of taxes, such as the poll tax (a per capita tax)

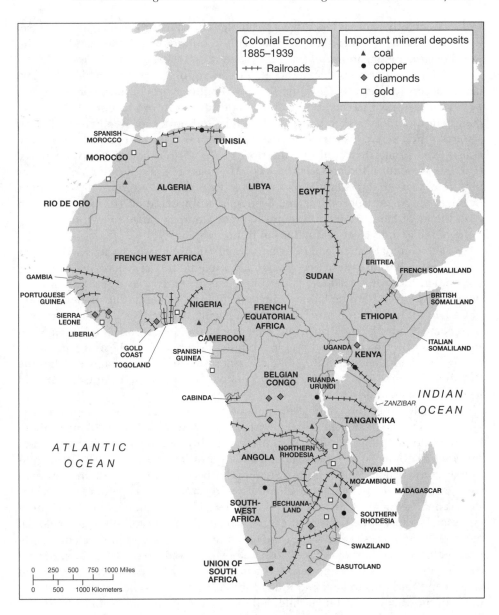

Map 14-1: Colonial economy, 1885–1939

and taxes on other things less subject to changes in scale. In Zanzibar, for instance, there was a canoe tax, meant to draw the fishing communities of the islands into the world of cash and taxation.

Colonial authorities were aware that cash cropping was impossible if farmers lacked access to markets. Thus, the first post-conquest acts of most colonial states were public works projects meant to facilitate cash crop production. All over the continent there was a spate of railway building and port improvements. Rail lines, some of which were constructed at great expense and at the cost of many lives, were constructed primarily to link the interiors of the various colonies to their ports. One line linked the Indian Ocean port of Mombasa to Lake Victoria, another was built to bypass the rapids in the lower Congo River and allow goods to be brought by rail to the Atlantic port of Matadi. Even on the tiny island of Zanzibar the British built the mellifluously named Bububu Railway, a narrow-gauge railway that linked some of the island's clove plantations to its port.

Each colonial nation had its own national rail gauge, which they used in their own colonies. Because there were few attempts to link the rail systems in one colony to another, this rarely made any difference, but in some cases it resulted in independent nations inheriting bizarrely incompatible rail systems. The modern nation of Cameroun has the dubious distinction of having first belonged to the Germans, then being divided by the British and the French, and then at independence having some of the British-controlled regions reunited with the French-controlled areas. As a result, the independent Republic of Cameroun came into existence with some British-built railways, some French-built railways, and a few surviving German-built lines, all incompatible.

Virtually all of the colonial-era railways terminated at a port. Their purpose after all was not to facilitate exchange within the colony or between colonies, but to link the colonies to the world market, preferably through the domestic economy of the colonial power. So port construction and improvement was as much a priority as railway construction. Where ports or natural harbors already existed, dredges were soon at work deepening the channels and creating deepwater berths for steamships. Colonial states constructed new piers, built warehouses, and brought in cranes, all to speed the passage of cargo through the ports and off to the colonial metropoles. In places where there were no natural harbors, ambitious colonial officials built artificial harbors. The British colony the Gold Coast (later the independent nation of Ghana) had, despite its long history of oceanic trade, relied on canoes and surfboats to load and unload the steamers that called at its port at Secondi. In the 1920s the colonial state built, at great expense, an artificial harbor at Takoradi. In this case, local revenues paid for the construction at Takoradi, but in general these types of projects, whether rail or port, were funded either with loans or grants from the metropolitan governments. These always came with the expectation that increased tax revenues and increased trade between the colony and the metropole would ultimately justify the expense.

On one level, this investment by European nations in infrastructure in Africa was meant to improve the economies of the colonies. And for many Africans, work on the railroads or in the ports provided economic opportunity. For many others, the opportunity to sell their crops in exchange for imported goods was also beneficial. In some colonies, farmers who produced certain cash crops—most notably cocoa—came to form a prosperous middle class. The fact that the Gold Coast could pay for its own artificial harbor was due to the revenues from cocoa. But there was another, less benevolent side to all of this investment. First, it usually took the economic interests of the metropole as the starting point for any development scheme. Thus, when the French began to encourage cotton production in their colonies, it was because they felt the French industry needed a safe supply of cotton. Most colonial regimes at one point or another in their history used neomercantilist schemes meant to use tax incentives to favor trade between the metropole and its colonies rather than trade with other nations. Thus, the British tried to encourage trade within their empire, whereas the Portuguese and French did likewise within their own imperial systems. The other complaint one might make about this apparently benevolent investment in infrastructure was that it was often meant to supplant preexisting transportation systems that were outside the control of the colonial state. So railroads were sometimes justified as a way of ending head porterage, whereas investment in modern ports and steamships in East Africa was seen by the colonial state as a means for undermining the local sailing ships called **dhows**.

This brings us to the ideological element of the colonial state's commitment to transportation technology. In addition to being a practical means of encouraging cash crop production, transportation technology was meant to bring modernity to Africa. Many of the features of late-nineteenth-century African life that the colonial state disapproved of were related in some way to transportation technology. Slaves were associated with the caravan trade where it was believed that they formed the majority of the porters, so colonial states built railways along the traditional caravan routes. The **canoe houses** of the Niger Delta transported palm oil, but they also transported slaves and indeed were comprised mostly of slaves; river steamers replaced them. The dhows of the East African coast were associated with the slave trade, so colonial governments went to great lengths to introduce and subsidize steamship service.

The clearest articulation of this ideology comes from the **Brussels Treaty** of 1890. This treaty is best known for helping to justify the Belgian King Leopold's exploitation of his Congo Free State by casting his efforts there as an antislavery effort. But there is another element to the Brussels Treaty, and this was a call for other colonial powers to help to stamp out slavery and the slave trade in Africa by introducing river steamers and railroads and carefully tracking the movements of dhows. Thus these technologies, which were symbols of modernity as much as they were practical means of transportation, were often built in places where they were inappropriate to the scale of the economy. An excellent example of this comes from Zanzibar where the colonial government decided that steamships should supplant dhows on the short, 50-mile run between Zanzibar and her sister island of Pemba. This in turn required the construction of three ports on the 50-mile-long island of Pemba and major port improvements in Zanzibar. Despite all this investment, local merchants continued to use dhows because they better fit the needs and scale of the local cash crop economy. So although one may occasionally read disparaging reports about independent African governments doing apparently irrational things such as constructing eight-lane highways to nowhere, you should know that they were not alone in this habit. Colonial governments showed an almost superstitious belief in the power of modern technology to modernize other aspects of the colonial economy.

Cocoa Farming in Ghana

The move from subsistence farming to cash cropping took place many times in different parts of the continent, and the nature of that transition was highly variable, so there is no way to look exhaustively at all the permutations. The rise of cocoa farming in Ghana makes as instructive case study. Cocoa farming was a tremendous success in Ghana, and many of the reasons it succeeded help to explain the failure of imposed cash cropping schemes in other parts of the continent. The success of cocoa farming also brought great social strains, as farmers sought to get access to the labor and capital needed to grow the new crop. Foremost among these social strains were struggles to define the extent to which married women were obligated to provide labor to their husbands' cocoa farming ventures.

Cocoa, the plant from which chocolate is made, is not native to the African continent. Rather, it is one of the American crops that only became available in the Eastern Hemisphere as a result of the Columbian Exchange. However, unlike many New World crops, cocoa was only slowly adopted outside its homeland. It is a tree crop that thrives in tropical forest environments. Because it is a tree crop, it takes several years to reach maturity. The earliest a cocoa farmer can hope to see his, or often her, first harvest is three to four years after planting. Even then the trees are not at full productivity for several more years. The beans also require processing once they are harvested, so cocoa farming is a capital-intensive form of farming. One must have the capital to clear land, buy seedlings, plant them, keep the field weeded for three or four years until the trees shade out all the weeds, and finally to harvest and process the beans. A cocoa farmer needs lots of cash to start up the business and then does not get any income for at least three or four years. An aspiring cocoa farmer also needs some means of recruiting the labor needed to perform all of these tasks. Thus, cocoa farming requires a complex set of social and financial institutions for it to succeed in a new place.

In the nineteenth century the Spanish introduced cocoa to the island of Fernando Po (now renamed Bioko), which lies just off the coast of Cameroun. How cocoa arrived in Ghana is uncertain, and it looks as though three separate groups may have introduced cocoa almost simultaneously in the 1890s. One was the British colonial governor, another was a group of missionaries, and the third was an African blacksmith. The governor oversaw the opening of the Aburi Botanical Gardens, which in addition to being a scientific research station was also a cocoa nursery. But Teten Quashie, the blacksmith, also opened a nursery and it is he who seems to have done the most to sell the cocoa seedlings to local farmers.

Indeed, the most interesting thing about cocoa farming in Ghana is that the local farmers always seem to have been a step ahead of the British. Whereas in other parts of Africa, colonial governments tried to push Africans into cash cropping, in

Ghana the British mostly found themselves supporting and encouraging initiatives already begun locally. Governor Sir William Griffith's nursery at Aburi, for example, probably provided fewer than 10 percent of the seedlings planted in the 1920s, the decade when cocoa farming went through its most dramatic expansion; the other 90 percent were provided by Ghanaian entrepreneurs. Likewise, the expansion of cocoa farming preceded the creation of a railway system in Ghana. In most cases colonial states built railways hoping that their existence would stimulate the transition to cash cropping; in Ghana the opposite happened. Ghanaian farmers started growing cocoa, so the British decided to build a rail system that linked the cocoa farming regions to the ports.

The enthusiastic adoption of cocoa by Ghanaian farmers was most likely the result of a prior history of cash cropping in the region. Ever since the abolition of the slave trade, West Africans had been producing more and more palm oil as a way of staying involved in Atlantic trade. Thus, farmers in southern Ghana had a tradition of growing oil palm as a cash crop. By the early twentieth century the price of palm oil was declining, and farmers were looking for other crops. Cocoa came along at just the right time to fill this need. Cocoa farming also benefitted from a prior history of kola nut farming in the region. Many of the skills and tools used in kola nut farming could be applied to cocoa farming, so although the cocoa tree was alien to Africa, it was a near-perfect fit for Ghanaian farmers.

Cocoa farming spread like wildfire in Ghana. By 1911, Ghana was the world's leading producer of cocoa. By the 1920s there was a full-scale boom in effect. Cocoa prices were high, new land was still being brought into production, and labor was

Cocoa drying in the colonial Gold Coast. This was a seven-to-ten-day-process, during which the beans had to be stirred hourly by hand.

becoming scarce. Though slavery was outlawed in Ghana in 1874, the British had, at the same time they outlawed slavery, passed a law called the Masters and Servants Ordinance. This was a fairly common way for colonial governments to formally end slavery without totally upsetting the social and economic conditions that had prevailed when slavery was legal. Masters and Servants Ordinances usually required former slaves to accept labor contracts with their former owners or someone else. These contracts placed great power in the hands of employers, and the courts usually leaned toward the employers when enforcing these contracts. Thus, in the early years of cocoa growing, even though slavery had ceased to exist as a legal institution, many of the workers involved in the cocoa industry were either former slaves or wage laborers whose contracts made them easily controlled by the growers. Family labor was also used. There was, however, much crossover between former slaves and family members. When slavery was legal, it was common for men in southern Ghana to take slave wives. After slavery was abolished, it was still acceptable to have pawns as wives. (Pawns were people given as collateral and interest on a loan; see Chapter 8 for more detail.) Not surprisingly, wives who were former slaves had many fewer rights than free wives. Free wives could, for instance, keep any property they brought to a marriage separate from their husbands' property. Any income they earned from their property was likewise theirs to keep. They were expected to provide their husbands with farm labor, in exchange for which they expected to be provided with "subsistence" by their husbands. Note the use of the word "expect" in the last sentence. As demands for labor grew in the 1920s, a period of what historian Jean Allman has called "social chaos" ensued. Both men and women began to try to redefine the expectations of marriage.

By the 1920s male cocoa farmers seem to have been trying to use marriage as a means of obtaining labor. They would marry women, insist that they work on their farms, and often not provide the subsistence that had previously been part of the deal. Women resisted this by either using the failure of their husbands to feed them as a reason to avoid working on their husbands' farms and putting more effort into their own farms, getting into cocoa farming themselves, or avoiding marriage altogether. This latter strategy became so common that local courts, dominated, as you might expect, by men with an interest in cocoa farming, in some places ordered all unmarried women to be rounded up and placed in custody until someone could be found who was willing to marry them. When a potential husband arrived, he paid a fee to the court that was comparable to normal bridewealth and took home his bride. If the woman refused to marry the man, she had to pay him the amount he had paid the court.

In effect, these courts were trying to force women into providing labor through the institution of coerced marriage. Women used many strategies to circumvent these roundups, such as getting a male friend to come and claim them as a wife or paying their own bridewealth. Such was the social upheaval of the 1920s that bedrock social institutions like marriage were being challenged and manipulated during this time. Although the Akan farmers of southern Ghana adopted cocoa of their own accord and profited more from it than most other cash croppers in colonial Africa, the new crop brought great social strain.

Cotton and Groundnuts in Nigeria

British colonial authorities in Nigeria were just as anxious as colonial authorities in Ghana to have a taxable cash crop industry. In Nigeria the situation was made even more urgent because unlike Ghana—which had some mineral wealth in the form of gold—Nigeria was totally dependent on agriculture. That situation has changed with the discovery of oil in southern Nigeria, but those deposits were unknown in the early colonial period. In southwestern Nigeria the British successfully introduced cocoa. But in the north they saw the potential for the production of a crop dear to the heart of British industry—cotton.

Cotton has been cultivated in the Sahelian regions of West Africa for centuries. The northern Nigerian city of Kano is famous for dye pits where locally produced cotton cloth was dyed dark blue and then pounded to a smooth and shiny finish. That cotton cloth was traded in the Sahel, and some was sold into the transSaharan trade to North Africa. The climate and soil of northern Nigeria is well suited to cotton production, and the British reasonably concluded that large-scale cash cropping of cotton would be a sure hit in northern Nigeria.

In 1912 the railway to Kano was opened. Its principle purpose was to facilitate cotton production in the area around Kano. At the time the railway opened, the British Cotton Growers' Association (BCGA), a **marketing board,** had already laid the groundwork for increased cotton production. Marketing boards were devised originally in Europe, where their purpose was to set a price floor for agricultural commodities. The idea was to stabilize farm prices so that farmers would know in advance of planting that they would get at least the marketing board's price for their crops. Marketing boards were often a bit more coercive in the colonies. They not only set price floors, they sometimes required that farmers sell them their crops at a price—usually a low one—set by the board. Marketing boards were a standard feature of colonial economies and remain a part of the African economic landscape today.

The BCGA went to work in northern Nigeria, setting up ginneries (the factories where cotton is processed) and distributing seeds and fertilizer. In 1912, with the railroad opened and the BCGA ready and waiting for the cotton to come rolling in, they were disappointed. Most of the cotton grown in the region was sold locally just like it always had been. The BCGA was not offering better prices than the region's own merchants, so farmers did not sell to the BCGA. Over the next couple of years there was an increase in cash crop production in northern Nigeria, but it was not cotton. Rather, groundnuts became the cash crop of choice. Groundnut prices were higher than cotton prices, and if there were crop failures or other disasters, farmers could eat the groundnuts. In 1912 there was a major famine in northern Nigeria that killed almost 30,000 people. In the following years, farmers, chastened by their experience in the famine, planted more and more groundnuts and less cotton. So the railway the British built to stimulate one kind of cash cropping resulted in a major export industry in a different crop. The railcars went south heavily loaded not with cotton, but with groundnuts. This is not to say that cotton was not produced in northern Nigeria. Cotton was and is widely grown in northern Nigeria and the rest of Sahelian region. However, the colonial state failed to capture this sector of the economy.

The French also sought to capture the cotton industry in their Sahelian colonies. For the French, the drive to take charge of the cotton industry in the colonies was driven partly by the need to create a tax base, but also by the concerns of French industry. France had a textile industry, but it lacked a secure cotton supply. British industry could depend on cotton from India and Egypt in addition to cotton from the American South. The French were much more dependent on American cotton and wanted the sorts of secure cotton supplies the British had. Indeed, access to the raw materials needed for industry was one of the major justifications for colonialism. So in their West African colonies the French saw a tremendous opportunity to acquire a safe and dependable cotton supply.

They tried every possible approach, and nothing worked. They attempted to create large-scale, irrigated plantations. These had trouble getting the labor needed to make them work, so they tried to encourage small producers to grow cotton and then to sell it to the French. Small-scale producers were only too happy to grow cotton, but they typically sold it to local merchants who sold into a regional cloth market. In the end the French failed to take control of the cotton economy in their colonies. The regional cotton industry that had existed when they took over grew during this period, but it also remained outside state control.

What all of this demonstrates is that there was nothing certain or predictable about colonial efforts to shape and control the transformation of African economies. The availability of new markets and new crops caused all sorts of changes. Sometimes the colonial state was able to control those transitions. In Uganda the British introduced cotton through the BCGA. Although the BCGA had been singularly unsuccessful in northern Nigeria, it worked well in Uganda. There an all-new cotton industry was created, and most of the cotton was sold through BCGA. In other places, such as Ghana, African farmers took the initiative in adopting cash crops, and the colonial state just followed along. In many instances, though, colonial governments tried to force change on unwilling farmers, and they mostly refused to cooperate. Thus, we should remember that although colonial governments could be quite brutal, they had limited resources and could only enforce their will up to a point.

Africans as Wage Laborers

If there was a limit to the extent to which the colonial state could enforce its wishes in the vast world of farming, it could be much more coercive when it came to labor recruitment. Colonial governments got involved in labor recruitment for a variety of reasons. In some cases they needed the labor for their own projects. For instance, much of the early road and railway building was done with forced labor. Most colonial governments at some time in their history used forced labor of some sort, which says much about the colonial state. When colonial governments first arrived in many parts of the continent, wage labor was almost unknown. In the absence of money, it was difficult, though not impossible, to recruit voluntary labor. In some places labor was paid with post-harvest beer parties, in much the same way that you might buy pizza and beer for the people who help you paint your apartment or move. Big farmers might do this to recruit extra labor for the harvest, but as a means of permanently supporting a group of employees, it would not work. To get around this, African farmers relied on labor drawn from kinship groups and slaves. Neither of these options was open to the colonial state. States had no kin, and even if colonial governments did not rush to outlaw slavery, they were not willing to formally purchase slaves. So getting labor for projects like building a road or a bridge was often accomplished by requiring local people to work on the bridge. In some cases this would be done informally by low-level colonial officials who simply made demands of local chiefs or villages. In other places, there were formal systems of forced labor in which the state required of every man a certain amount of labor per year.

Another approach that colonial states might use to obtain necessary labor was to pay wages. This only worked, though, if people either needed the money or wanted it. Here, taxation could play a role just as it had with the transition to cash cropping. If colonized people had no use for the money issued by the state, collecting taxes in cash rather than in kind could compel people to work for wages. Bear in mind that in many places there was nothing to buy with money in the very early part of the colonial period. In East and Central Africa at the turn of the century, for instance, there were neither sufficient tax collectors nor enough of a retail market for anyone to want cash. So when the British built the Uganda Railway (1902) (the backdrop against which the movie *Ghost in the Darkness* takes place), which linked Uganda to the port of Mombasa, they had to bring in workers from India. They could neither entice nor coerce local labor. Interestingly, many of the Indians who came to work on the railways stayed on rather than going back to India when their contracts were finished. Some of these Indians then became small-scale retailers, opening shops in places where there had been no shops before. In so doing, they helped to create a reason for people to want cash. Their role as pioneers in the retail trade helped to monetize the East African economy and stimulate an interest in cash crops and wage labor. It is worth noting that this was not part of the plan when the British brought in Indian labor. Rather, it was an unintended consequence.

The other, and in many ways more important, source of demand for labor was European-owned business. In places where there were significant numbers of European settlers, colonial states were faced with the task of providing labor for their farms and businesses. Although almost every colony had some European business and farms, a few places stand out as centers of this type of activity. In the Kenya highlands there was a large population of mostly British settlers. Most were engaged in growing coffee or sisal (a fiber crop). In Zimbabwe (then Rhodesia) settler farmers grew maize and tobacco. In the southern part of the Congo there were huge copper mines that required lots of labor—and skilled labor at that. In South Africa the gold mines of the Rand needed labor, as did the area's farms. In other parts of the colonial world, African farmers also needed labor, such as West African cocoa farmers and Zanzibari clove planters, who sought the help of the colonial state. In these regions colonial governments found themselves engaged in a sometimes frantic hunt for labor that often spilled across the colonial frontiers.

This scramble to find labor was complicated by the abolition of slavery. One of the ways that colonialism in Africa was justified to dubious voting publics in Europe was that imperialism was needed to stamp out the evils of slavery. However sincere this objective might have been, once in power colonial regimes were reluctant to abruptly end slavery. Colonial officials relied on the cooperation of African elites to rule their colonies. In many cases, they also depended on tax revenue from farms staffed by slaves. So despite the frequent demands of home-country public opinion, the people in charge in the colonies did not rush into abolition and when they finally got around to it, they tried to minimize the economic and social upheaval associated with abolition.

Slavery and Labor in Zanzibar

When the British took over Zanzibar in 1890, they decided to rule through the pre-existing structures of government. They left the sultan's government more or less intact and used its institutions for their own purposes. They did this partly out of habit—this was how most of British India was governed—but also because Zanzibar was a "protectorate," and they felt some need to keep a protected government in place. Because Arabs politically dominated the state they took over, the British usually took the interests and perspective of Arabs into account when making policy. Thus, because the main source of income for the Arab elite was clove growing and the state's main source of tax revenue was a tax on clove exports, the colonial state did nothing that might jeopardize the clove planters' labor supply. It was not until 1907 that slavery was formally abolished in Zanzibar, a full seventeen years after the British took over.

When they did get around to abolishing slavery, they still made every effort to keep former slaves under control and linked to their former owners and to keep up a supply of new labor. Most of the former slaves became "squatters" on the land of their former owners. They lived and farmed on that land, and as rent for their land they harvested cloves. They got to keep a small portion of the cloves they harvested as payment. A critical difference between this and slavery was that the squatters could not be forced to weed the plantations. Laborers recruited from the colonies on the mainland did the work of weeding the plantations. Most came from Tanganyika or Nyasaland (now Malawi) and from precisely the same areas that most of the slaves came from. These "Nyamwezi," as they were called, were recruited by colonial officers in the rural areas on the mainland and brought to Zanzibar at a reduced fare on the Zanzibar government's steamships.

Colonial states worked to provide labor to African farmers as well as European farmers. When critical income from cash cropping was threatened by a labor shortage, they took action regardless of the ethnicity of the planters. Colonial states sometimes seemed to work harder on behalf of white farmers and industrialists. This usually did not reflect the preferences of colonial officials, who often found settlers to be a troublesome bunch. Instead it reflected the much stronger political voice that white settlers had. When European settler farmers or industrialists felt that governments were not doing enough on their behalf, they could make themselves heard in ways that no African planter could.

Controversies in African History: Coltan Mining

Not all of Africa's mining operations function on the scale of the Union Minère pit mines in Congo or the deep shaft mines of the South African Rand. Some mining takes place in areas so war-torn and unstable that no sane mining company executive would risk an investment there. Deep in the forests of eastern Congo, in an area where as many as four million people may have perished since 1994 because of a war that has provoked what is arguably the least publicized humanitarian disaster of the late twentieth century, free-lance miners dig up coltan.

Coltan is an earth that is rich in tantalum. Tantalum is valued in the manufacture of capacitors. It is especially useful because it helps make electrical components smaller. That it is now possible for us to carry devices like cell phones and laptops with us on a regular basis is due in part to the miniaturization that is possible because of the labor of coltan miners. We tend to think of the tech industry as a "clean" industry in that it does not involve smokestacks belching soot, but it does rely on some products that have messy origins in one of the most troubled regions of the world.

Though much of the world's coltan comes from big commercial mining operations in places other than Africa, the high-tech explosion of late 1990s and early 2000s drove demand up to the point that coltan miners in Congo were getting $80 a kilo for coltan. Considering that a diligent miner could dig a kilo a day and that most people in eastern Congo get by on less than $1 a day, coltan mining was the best job in eastern Congo (other than warlord).

Under these conditions it should not come as a surprise that people began mining coltan in earnest. Unlike copper mining, where it takes tons of ore to make a day's work profitable, or diamond mining where the shafts run hundreds or thousands of feet underground, coltan can be profitable on a very small scale. Coltan miners need little more than a shovel and bucket to go into business. The coltan is usually near the surface and mixed in with other material of lesser or no value. The muck that is dug out of the ground is mixed with water and panned like gold. The coltan is denser than the dirt so it eventually settles out. Thus, coltan mining can be done on a sort of artisanal level, with minimal capital investment and without much technical expertise.

All this led to classic gold-rush-like conditions. Prices for anything the miners required, from shovels to beer, were wildly inflated and paid for in coltan. Prostitutes flocked to the area. One *New York Times* reporter noted the surreal quality of following trails to the coltan diggings deep in the forests, miles from the nearest road of any sort, and encountering groups of giggling young women dressed in their best dresses and high heels, headed for the mining camps. Naturally, this wealth coming out of the ground attracted the attention, as it always does, of the guys with the guns. Soldiers from the various armies that had invaded eastern Congo charged the miners "protection fees." Some of the militias in the region funded themselves by controlling the coltan trade.

For coltan miners the opportunity to make a living outweighed the nuisances of paying inflated prices and protection money. But the effect on the region's wildlife was disastrous. Much of the coltan mining was done in areas designated as reserves or National Parks. The Congolese state has not been strong enough to really protect these places for a long time and the war has been hard on Congo's wildlife, but coltan mining has been a major disaster. To feed the miners, who have money to spend on luxuries like meat, hunters killed lots of bush meat. The region's lowland gorilla population, hunted as food, has been reduced to the point where it is in danger of disappearing altogether. The Pygmy population of the reserves has also been threatened by coltan mining. The Pygmies rely partly on game in the reserves for their food and competition from market hunters for that game, as well as the presence of extra people in the forest, puts them at risk of murder and exploitation, something that has been common during Congo's civil war.

In 2002 the UN issued a report on coltan in Congo and suggested that not only was coltan mining environmentally destructive and the source of exploitation of miners, sex workers, and children; it mostly benefitted the nations to Congo's east through whose territories most of the coltan is illegally exported. These countries have the governmental capacity to tax these exports, a capacity the nearly powerless Congolese government lacks. The result is that though Congo suffers the hardships associated with coltan mining, the benefits mostly accrue to the neighbors. A number of organizations have launched boycotts against Congo coltan, though these are difficult to enforce because it is nearly impossible for consumers to look at a cell phone or DVD player and determine the origins of the coltan in it. Meanwhile, most Congolese—and not just coltan miners—are scandalized that people in the West would hinder the efforts of people trying to make a living in one of the most desperately poor corners of the one of the world's poorest nations.

The situation has been further complicated by the Iraq war, which has increased military demand for tech products and hence for coltan. Then, only a year after the U.S. invasion of Iraq, the Sons of Gwalia, an Australian company that mines coltan and is one of the world's major coltan ore processors, went through an Enron-like accounting scandal that drove it into bankruptcy. The fates of Central Africa's artisanal miners and of the lowland gorilla remains up in the air.

Settlers in the Kenya Highlands

The Kenya Highlands became a major locus of white settlement in the first decades of the twentieth century. The mountains of central Kenya are just high enough that temperatures are cool year-round. Thus, many of the tropical diseases that inhibited white settlement in other parts of Africa are less prevalent there. It also means that some European crops and livestock survive there. It was and is a perfect place to grow coffee, which thrives in tropical highlands. The most valuable varieties need to be grown at altitudes over 6,000 feet. European settlers could grow coffee to support themselves while also producing grain and dairy products that were familiar to them. They could keep horses, which was important to their sense of upper-class dignity. (This was oddly important to colonial self-esteem. In Nigeria, it was considered much better to work in the north where one could keep a horse than in the south where horses did not survive long.)

Settlers began to move into the Highlands in large numbers only after the Uganda Railway was finished in 1902. Once there, they took over land that had previously belonged to the Kikuyu and Kamba, farming people who lived in the Highlands. Kikuyu and Kamba land was taken in a series of land alienations, on the grounds that it was not being used to its full potential. It was then sold at nominal prices to settlers. Some of the Kikuyu and Kamba were relegated to "Native Reserves," and some remained on the land that had once been theirs as "squatters." Squatters were expected to work for the new landowners in lieu of paying a cash rent. People living on the Native Reserves were also expected to work for settlers, though in their case, they were wage workers who initially worked primarily to satisfy government-imposed taxes. Later they worked to feed themselves as the Reserves became overcrowded and it became nearly impossible to make a living on them.

Settler farmers typically grew their crops on large and labor-hungry plantations. Their search for labor was complicated by a number of erroneous beliefs they held about African workers. One was that Africans, coming from an environment that supported them with little effort on their part, were naturally disinclined to hard work. Thus, their labor was worth little, and their pay should be correspondingly low. If, in their sloth, they failed to be attracted to low-wage work, means other than raising wages should be used to get them to work. Frequently, settlers simply demanded that the colonial government make the Africans work. Although the settlers' belief that Africans were naturally conditioned to laziness by their environment was the purest of nonsense, another settler belief about African work habits had more merit, at least in the early decades of the colonial period. This was the belief that Africans were "target workers." That is to say that they did wage work with an earnings target in mind, and when they had achieved that target they stopped working. From the perspective of people who are only doing wage labor because the state has informed them that they must pay taxes in cash but who otherwise have little use for money, working after you have satisfied your tax obligations made little sense. So if you were taxed 5 shillings, you worked until you had earned 5 shillings, then you went home and lived off farming like you did before someone demanded that you pay taxes. As long as the subsistence economy survived alongside the cash economy, workers could move back and forth between them, earning money when they needed to and living off their farms the rest of the time. According to this logic, if settlers raised their workers' wages, the workers would just reach their earnings targets sooner, and their workers would disappear.

So coercion rather than attractive wages was the order of the day. A Masters and Servants Ordinance gave employers a variety of powers over their employees. Employees could be jailed for leaving before their contract expired, for breaking tools, for being drunk on the job, and even for being disrespectful to their employers. To ensure that there were enough employees available, government-appointed chiefs were told they had quotas of workers that they must furnish. Workers were coerced into entering into wage labor and coerced into staying at least for the length of their contracts. To be fair to the colonial state, many colonial officers in Kenya made some modest efforts to ensure that workers were not mistreated. The government also required that employers feed their laborers and that they be provided with blankets and housing. However, they more often turned a blind eye to employer negligence than they did to worker negligence.

Perhaps the most significant way in which the colonial state favored settler farmers in the Kenya Highlands was to prevent African farmers from competing with them. Whereas Kenyans often had to be forced to work on coffee plantations, many Kikuyu and Kamba farmers found growing coffee themselves to be much more appealing. The colonial state quickly stepped in to ensure that local people did not grow cash crops, lest they should cease to need work from white farmers. In some places the colonial state was doing everything in its power to coerce African farmers to grow cash crops, but in other places it feared that cash cropping might hinder the labor supply needed by white commercial farmers. There was no single approach that colonial states took toward agriculture. In some places, such as Ghana, they were mostly content to let African farmers choose their own crops. In others, like Mozambique, the colonial state went to destructive lengths to force cash crops on unwilling farmers. In still other instances, Kenya and Rhodesia for example, the colonial state tried to stamp out cash cropping and supported white commercial farmers instead. As both Rhodesia and Kenya approached independence in the 1960s, the majority of the best land was in the hands of a white minority, and most Africans were either employed by white farmers or eking out a meager living on subsistence farms on overcrowded reserves.

Perhaps the biggest user of African labor was the mining industry. Mines in the Congolese Copper Belt and the South African Rand had a voracious appetite for labor. In both instances, the mining companies' access to labor was complicated by politics and geography. The Copper Belt had a relatively low population density, so there were few people available locally to work in the mines. Much of the labor that was available was found in other colonies ruled by other European powers. Thus, the Belgian companies that ran the mines in a Belgian colony found themselves looking for labor in British and even Portuguese colonies. In the Rand, the mining companies had to work with the prevailing racial ideology of South Africa. One of the premises of apartheid was that most of South Africa was to be inhabited by whites. If any Africans or Asians were there, they were visitors, not permanent residents. Thus, the mines were allowed to bring in workers as long as the workers were there only temporarily. The mining companies not only learned to live with this ideology, they embraced it as a means of controlling their labor force.

In 1911, the Union Minère, the company that ran the biggest mines in the Copper Belt, was competing with the railways and other employers for labor. The government's response to this was to create the Bourse du Travail du Katanga (Katanga Labor Exchange), a body that was meant to recruit labor and then see that it was equally shared among the labor-hungry employers of the region. The Union Minère, like most mining companies, sought to put its employees on short-term contracts and to prevent them from bringing their families to live with them. The idea was that miners who were there on contracts of a year or less could always be sent home if they did something like organize a union, and if their families were elsewhere the mines could claim that the miners' wages were meant to pay only for their labor and not to support their families. The presumption was that the miners' families would support themselves by farming and that when the miners themselves were away from the mines, they too could live off the income of these farms. The subsistence economy was supposed to support the majority of the population and provide a labor surplus that could be used by the mines, but the mines were not going to pay for anything beyond the actual labor of the miners. In economics jargon, the mines sought to externalize the costs of reproduction of the labor force.

Although mining companies in South Africa succeeded at externalizing these costs—at a great social cost—the scheme failed in the Copper Belt. This was partly due to the nature of the work in the copper mines. These mines required more skilled than unskilled labor, so the short-term contracts that the Union Minère hoped to impose on miners turned out to be counterproductive. Rather, it made more sense to keep skilled workers once they had been trained. In the 1920s, physicians working for the mining companies pointed out that if the miners were allowed to live with their families, there would be fewer prostitutes around the mines and hence less venereal disease among the miners. So in the late twenties, the mines in the Copper Belt started to build housing for the miners and allowed their families to join them. Ultimately, miners in the Copper Belt came to enjoy some of the best living standards of workers anywhere in Africa. They had schools, clinics, homes, and decent wages. Miners were recruited, though as conditions improved they were often volunteers, from places as diverse as Northern Rhodesia (later Zambia) and Mozambique. Authorities in these colonies often sought to send people to the mines in the Copper Belt in the hopes that they would repatriate some of their income.

On the mines of the Rand (one is said to work "on the mines" in South Africa rather than "in the mines"), labor conditions could not have been more different. There the short-term contract was the norm for Africans. White miners demanded that the best jobs be reserved for them and that they should get long-term employment while African miners got short-term contracts. African miners, who were considered temporary visitors to white South Africa, were compelled to live in hostels. The hostels were more or less all-male barracks, often fenced with barbed wire. The workers were herded from the hostel to the mine and back each day. Workers were also expected to return home to their families periodically to ensure that they did not put down roots near the mines.

The result was a system of often brutal exploitation wherein black miners made a fraction of the wages earned by their white counterparts. They often traveled long distances to get to the mines—some coming from as far away as Mozambique or Rhodesia. They were then forced to live in the harsh world of the hostels. This system was possible because there was less skilled work to be done on the mines of the Rand, and what skilled work there was, was reserved for white miners, so the companies could treat workers as disposable.

The mines of the Rand set up a pattern of labor migration that was unique to southern Africa. It has sometimes been described as "oscillating migration" because workers went back and forth across the subcontinent going between their homes and the mines. They lived part of the year on the mines and part of the year at home. The result was the movement of all sorts of things from religious ideas to germs between the mines and the rural hinterlands of southern Africa. Mine workers from Rhodesia/Zimbabwe brought home with them knowledge of the teachings of the Zion Church. This was an independent church that was popular in South Africa. Miners returning from South Africa in the 1940s and 1950s set themselves up as leaders of the church in Rhodesia. The Zion Church still exists and is a major religious force in modern Zimbabwe.

A miners' hostel in South Africa. African miners were required to live in the hostels. Their short term labor contracts did not permit them to live in the communities in which they worked.

Another thing that followed miners home was disease. The conditions in the hostels favored the spread of tuberculosis and sexually transmitted disease. These were then spread into rural areas by miners. This remains a problem today in southern Africa. Today in Mozambique, miners returning from South Africa often bring HIV infection with them, which then spreads to their sex partners. Thus, seemingly isolated parts of rural Mozambique have been plugged into labor migration networks for decades and are as exposed to the global HIV pandemic as people in the world's major cities.

The Cities of Africa

Although there have been cities in Africa for centuries, one of the notable features of the colonial period was the creation and rapid growth of cities. Colonial authorities had to compel Africans to work in mines or grow cash crops, but they had no trouble getting them to come to cities. In fact, colonial governments were more often concerned with discouraging migration to the cities than the opposite. There was economic and social opportunity in the new cities and people flocked to them to take advantage of it.

Some of the great colonial cities grew out of preexisting cities. Lagos in Nigeria, Dakar in Senegal, and Mombasa in Kenya were cities that had existed prior to the advent of colonialism but grew rapidly once they became centers of colonial government or commerce. Others were created ex nihilo. Leopoldville (later Kinshasa) was a creation of the Congo Free State. Nairobi was little more than a watering hole for cattle when the Uganda Railway opened, but quickly grew into one of the major cities of East Africa. Dar es Salaam, the capital city of Tanzania, was the site of the sultan of Zanzibar's summer residence when the Germans selected it as their capital. It is now a sprawling, multiethnic city of over one million people. The creation of these cities and the location of major employers there such as the railways meant that there was work of every sort to be done. There was work for educated people. Typically, Europeans occupied only the top rungs of the colonial administration. Africans, and in East Africa Arabs and Indians, occupied all the lower rungs. Any colonial office would have had an abundance of clerks. By the end of the colonial era, as independence became imminent and more Africans obtained university educations, Africans began to occupy more responsible positions as well. Educated workers along with skilled railway men and port workers became a sort of urban African elite, thus the cities became home to an emerging African middle class. They were also home to people whose employment options were more humble but perhaps more varied and less subject to state control.

The cities needed construction workers, street sweepers, domestic servants, and more. These positions were mostly taken by men, most of whom came to the cities without their families. These men worked long hours at grim and often humiliating jobs. The absence of families created the opportunity for a huge, mostly informal, service industry to meet workers' need for food, shelter, and clothing as well as entertainment, comfort, and respect. Women dominated much of this industry. Entrepreneurial women prepared and sold hot food. They brewed and sold beer. Through prostitution, they offered men temporary access to what Luise White has termed "the comforts of home," even when home was hundreds of miles away.

Women and Work in Colonial Africa

White has done a fascinating study of prostitution in colonial Nairobi and argues that while some women became prostitutes out of economic desperation, for others it was a path to economic independence as well as social respectability. There were many forms of prostitution in colonial Nairobi, ranging from streetwalking to situations where women owned the buildings out of which they ran their business. These women were selling much more than sex. They offered bath water, food, clean sheets, conversation, and respect—comfort for those who could pay for it.

There were several ways in which the profits from prostitution were used. Many women came to the city to work as prostitutes with the intention of seeing their families through some sort of economic crisis. For these women, their profits were mostly returned to the countryside and the prostitutes' families. Urban prostitution in this instance was a sort of safety net for the rural areas. When rural areas became impoverished as a result of colonial taxation, misguided efforts to effect a transition to cash cropping, or drought, income earned through prostitution in the cities often kept families on the land. Thus, says White, prostitution in this instance was an expression not of moral decay, but of strong family values.

Other prostitutes had more capitalistic visions of how to invest their income. They carefully saved their income and used it to invest in real estate. In the 1940s many of these women built houses for themselves and to use as rental properties. One Nairobi prostitute used her income to purchase automobiles with which she got into the taxi business. White notes that perhaps the most interesting aspect of the entrepreneurial success of Nairobi's women is that they successfully evaded state interference in their business. The state may have succeeded in controlling the rural economy, but the urban economy remained more elusive.

This roughly parallels events in West Africa where women parleyed income from petty trade in food into a major share of the trucking business. By the 1960s much of the commerce of West Africa moved in "mammy wagons," trucks owned by female entrepreneurs. Women, though, had been an economic and hence political force in urban West Africa long before the 1960s. Perhaps the most famous instance of this is the **Aba Women's War** of 1929. Aba is a district in southern Nigeria, where palm oil production was the main source of income. Women and a few men traded palm oil in small quantities in local markets. In the twenties the British were in the process of imposing a system of direct taxation on southern Nigeria. Men were required to pay a poll tax, and in 1929 government chiefs were ordered to count women in their districts so that they, too, might be taxed. When women observed that they were to be taxed they revolted, apparently fearing that the small margins in their business would not support a tax.

They held a meeting where they decided that they would bide their time until they knew for sure that they were to be taxed. Within a few days, a scuffle broke out between a woman and a man sent by the local chief to count heads in her village. Other women rushed to her aid, and they detained the man. Soon the rebellion spread, and thousands of women were in the streets carrying palm branches and smearing their faces with charcoal—a local symbol of war. The conflict came to a head when a crowd of women thought to be in the thousands surrounded the district officer's compound in Opobo. He allowed a delegation inside to talk to him, but things took a turn for the worse when the delegation left and the crowd surged through the fence and began to beat the district officer with sticks. A police lieutenant then shot the women's leader in the head with his revolver, and his men fired on the crowd. Thirty-two women were killed, and thirty-one were wounded. For the next month there were attacks on Native Courts—one of the most visible and hated signs of the colonial state—and most of these were destroyed in a 6,000-square-mile area. So women were not just an economic force during the colonial era; their economic interests involved them in politics.

The Movement to Independence and Modernization

By the 1950s it was clear throughout the colonized world that colonialism's days were numbered. The European powers had been so weakened and their subjects so emboldened by the Second World War that although Africans and Europeans had different timetables in mind, most people could see that colonialism would soon end. In some places, such as Rhodesia, white settlers unwilling to face a future in a majority-ruled state declared independence from Britain and kept the reins of power carefully in their own hands. For the Portuguese, whose colonies served as a critical safety valve for the home countries' economic problems, the prospect of relinquishing power in their African colonies was so unsettling that they chose to resist it at all costs. But in Britain and France, a more sober approach prevailed.

The British and the French used the second half of the 1950s to prepare their colonies for independence. One can make a convincing case that this was partly a delaying tactic. By taking a decade or two to lay the groundwork for independence the colonial powers were also delaying the granting of independence. But to be fair, there were some genuine efforts to prepare the colonies for independence. Most of these efforts were political rather than economic, but some elements of the "preparation" process had economic implications, too. One was the establishment of universities where there had been none before. Between 1948 and 1953 the British founded universities in Nigeria, Ghana, Uganda, and Sudan. The French built their first university in Senegal in 1957. There were no universities in Belgian or Portuguese Africa until quite late, and places with politically dominant white minorities like South Africa and Rhodesia founded universities but excluded Africans from them. In these places, it was seen as politically unwise to educate Africans, who might then think that they were capable of managing their own affairs.

Prior to the Second World War the few Africans who were able to obtain university educations did so in the United States or in Europe. University education was the privilege of a tiny few. The creation of universities on the continent made it significantly easier for Africans to obtain university educations, though doing so was of course still a rare privilege. It is also worth noting that in some ways the elites that these schools created assimilated certain beliefs and prejudices of their colonial rulers. The British had convinced themselves that the key educational element in the creation of an empire was their superior knowledge of Latin grammar and the character-building qualities of rugby, cricket, and rowing. Specialized knowledge, such as knowing how to be an accountant or knowing how to build a bridge, was fine for those who needed to do such things, but a gentleman could always let someone else handle such mundane matters. Furthermore, gentlemen favored military or government service over business. So as the British and the French groomed Africans to replace them, they were mostly concerned to create a class of educated and able administrators for the government offices they would be vacating. They were much less concerned with creating a class of business leaders who might improve the economic standing of the colonies. This was in part because they expected that in areas outside the agricultural sector, power would remain in the hands of European- or Asian-owned business. Thus, although Africans were educated to prepare them to manage the affairs of government and then had the reins of government handed over to them at the end of the colonial period, the same was not true for the high ground of the economy. Big business—mining, oil production, and what manufacturing there was—remained firmly in European hands. Africans were neither trained for nor invited into this type of work, except as laborers.

Non-European immigrant groups most often controlled the economies' middle ground. In West Africa, immigrants from Lebanon and Syria were deeply involved in retail trade and food processing. In East Africa and Central Africa this segment of the economy was in the hands of Asians. These Asian immigrants most often came from the Indian subcontinent, though a few Chinese were to be found as well. Their ancestors had mostly come to East Africa in the early nineteenth century, though some also arrived in the late nineteenth century to work on the railroads. Thus, most of them are no more alien in Africa than the majority of Americans are in the United States. Like some groups of immigrants in the United States, Asians in East Africa retained strong group identities. Although many of them adopted Swahili as their first language after a generation or two, religious and cultural beliefs about marrying people from one's own community served to keep both the Muslim and Hindu Asians from marrying outside their communities.

Immigrant groups like the Asians and Lebanese often brought with them business skills that few Africans had. They came from places where bookkeeping was an ancient skill and where credit markets were highly developed. They had access to capital and could use a variety of financial instruments to move that capital over long distances. They enjoyed great advantages over Africans who attempted to compete with them, and were willing to take risks and live under conditions that few Europeans would willingly endure. Thus, these ethnic groups came to dominate the retail, wholesale, and import/export business of East and West Africa. When independence came, they continued to dominate this sector of the economy.

So when independence arrived, African leaders were better prepared to run the government than to run their nations' businesses. To generalize a bit, they preferred to use government to shape and direct the economy than to directly get into business themselves. The result was a situation in which the preferred career path for educated and ambitious men was government service rather private-sector business. And when these new elites did enter the world of commerce or manufacturing, they did so as representatives of the state. Therefore, the early years of independence in Africa were marked by a major expansion of the state's role in the economy.

This resulted from more than the educational practices of the late colonial period. The colonial state had also been heavily involved in the management of the economy. Marketing boards, labor recruitment, and large centrally planned development schemes had all been part of the economic landscape of the colonial era. Independent governments merely took these ideas and ran with them. In other cases, state direction of the economy was a conscious choice made by African elites who wished to reject the capitalist economic ideology that colonial regimes had espoused.

In the 1960s and 1970s, leaders of what was coming to be called the Third World were growing increasingly disillusioned with the global economic order and with the economic ideology they inherited from their colonial rulers. In the 1960s, when most African nations got their independence, they were primarily producers of agricultural commodities. Only white-ruled South Africa had any sort of industrial base. African nations, like the new nations of Asia and many of the nations of Latin America, were dependent on the West and Japan for manufactured goods. To pay for these goods, they needed to sell their agricultural produce into the world market. But market prices for tropical agricultural products were highly variable and have generally been dropping since the late 1970s. People looking at this situation came to the conclusion that the way out of this bind was for African nations to "modernize" their economies. By this they meant creating an industrial sector that would allow them to be less dependent on imports and hence less dependent on the world market prices for agricultural goods. Up to this point there was nearly universal agreement. But as to how one would achieve this there were several different schools of thought.

The first of these schools of thought was associated with American and European economic experts who sought to help African nations to develop their economies. These experts, the Americans among them especially, did their work in the context of Cold War conflict with the Soviet Union. For them, improving the economic life of Africans was, at least in part, a means of limiting the appeal of socialism and Soviet-style communism. Economic growth was seen as the best means of preventing the type of unrest that plagued Indo-China in the aftermath of independence from French rule there. These experts, who are sometimes called "modernization theorists," sought to transform African nations by introducing not just modern industry but also modern forms of social organization. They felt that the real obstacles to economic development in Africa were social institutions such as communal land ownership and the use of kinship networks to recruit labor and to distribute income. For modernity to work in Africa, it would be necessary for land to be owned by individuals who could buy and sell it, improve it, and not have to share the proceeds of the sale with their relatives. Africans, in short, would have to become more like Europeans and Americans if they wanted to enjoy the type of prosperity that people in the West enjoyed. So although it was all well and good to try to set up new industries, those industries were meant to effect social as well as economic change. They were to help Africans break out of their "traditional" way of life.

Another school of thought saw African poverty not as the result of the persistence of "traditional" social structure, but as a result of colonial and "neocolonial" exploitation by the capitalist West. They argued that if Africans were dependent on income from agriculture to buy manufactured goods, it was because that was how the colonial powers had constructed their economies. Britain and France, they argued, had used Africa as a source of raw materials and as a market for their own industries. Indeed, a fundamental belief about capitalism was that it extracted wealth from the periphery—Africa, Asia, and Latin America—and concentrated it in Europe and North America. This school, known as the "dependency theorists," argued that maintaining this relationship of dependency was precisely what the West hoped to do, so listening to their "development experts" was the worst possible choice one could make. For them, economic progress would come not by trying to gain admission to the charmed circle of wealthy nations by copying their ways, but by realizing that those places were wealthy because they excluded and exploited other nations. Because the system would fail if there were no poor nations left to exploit, it was unreasonable to think that wealthy nations would admit others to their privileged club, no matter how modern they became. Instead, the future lay with a socialist economy that did not rely on the exploitation of others.

Although some countries adopted one or the other of these strategies, most found themselves saddled with a combination of both. In Kenya, the government ended the legal status of communal land tenure and went to a European-style system of individual ownership. At the same time, the state sector was allowed to grow tremendously, and some of the large, white-owned farms were taken over by Africans with strong ties to government. In Tanzania, President **Julius Nyerere** tried to marry what he saw as traditional African ideas about communal ownership with European ideas about socialism. The result was the philosophy called **Ujamaa,** which derives from the Swahili word for family. In the cities his government nationalized some businesses and most rental housing. In the countryside he sought to steer a middle path between the private landownership that was being implemented in Kenya and the large state-owned farms of the Soviet block. Nyerere oversaw the creation of Ujamaa villages, which were to be a sort of Africanized socialist village. The villagers would cooperatively work the land and engage in small-scale manufacturing. Each village would have a clinic and a school, as well as a group of educated administrators who would run the cooperative. It all sounds rather idyllic, and European socialists were enthralled by Nyerere's vision. The Swedes and Norwegians poured huge amounts of money into Tanzania to support the implementation of his ideas.

However, Nyerere's economic vision was a failure (his political legacy was much more successful). State-owned industries proved to be inefficient and produced little, but had huge payrolls. In one instance, a bicycle factory donated by China never produced a single bicycle, but still had a staff of hundreds. State-owned housing soon began to crumble. In the countryside, people had to be forced onto the Ujamaa villages (collective farms), and in some places there were revolts when authorities tried to move people onto the collectives. Once there, the villagers began to call the government administrators who ran their villages "wakoloni," the same term that was used to describe British colonial authorities. Farmers who did not live on collectivized villages still had to sell their crops through government marketing boards—usually called para-statals in the postcolonial era—at prices so low that they either resorted to smuggling their crops out of the country or simply left the cash economy and became subsistence farmers again.

Tanzania is an extreme case, but it is an example of how a well-meaning and reasonably honest government could take a country from poor to poorer. All across the continent the initial euphoria that followed independence and the relative prosperity that resulted from high commodity prices yielded to disappointment as producer prices fell and real economic growth rates either stagnated or fell in the 1980s and 1990s. Even countries like Kenya and the Ivory Coast, which had encouraged private farmers and light industry with some success, found themselves in trouble by the 1980s.

Perhaps the single biggest element in this post-independence economic crisis has been debt. Both modernization theorists and dependency theorists had one

Photo Essay II: Crossing the Borders
of African and World History

In this, the second of our photo essays, we attempt to illustrate (literally) what we see as some of the most interesting examples of Africa's interaction with other parts of the world. One of our major contentions is that there is nothing so simple as a single "African history" or "African culture," but rather that the various regions and eras of African history are sometimes also defined by their connections to other parts of the world. Similarly, other parts of the world have been defined by their contacts with Africans.

What we see in these images are examples of African participation in broader global trends and processes, and also examples of Africa's connections with wider commercial and cultural areas such as the Indian Ocean, Atlantic, and Mediterranean worlds. These connections throw into question the very meaning of "African." In addition to being defined simply by their continent of birth, many of the continent's peoples are also members of transcontinental networks and systems of identity. From such a perspective, a person living today might be African, Muslim, Tunisian, Arab, Mediterranean, and French, all at the same time. Further, any one of these aspects of that person's identity might be paramount at a given moment, depending upon the situation in which the individual found himself or herself.

When the Sahara was Wet

Located in what is now an Algerian national park, the rock art of Tassili was created some time between 6000 and 2000 B.C.E., a time when the Sahara was wet. The people depicted here are harvesting grass seeds of some type. It is not clear whether this is wild grass or a domesticated grain or some transitional form between the two. Notably, some scholars believe that the central Sahara was where people first began to gather wild grasses, and that this foraging strategy spread from there into the Middle East, bringing with it the Afro-Asiatic languages. Note that the grain gatherers appear to be women, while the hunter depicted above appears to be a man, supporting the general notion that in foraging societies men hunt and women gather.

Henri Lhote Collection. Musee de l'Homme, Paris, France. © Photograph by Erich Lessing/ Art Resource, NY

A Multiethnic Egypt?

The two frescoes below depict subject peoples bringing tribute to Egypt. New Kingdom Egypt's imperial forays into Nubia and the Levant brought them into contact with a broad variety of people from other parts of the Mediterranean and Africa, a process which greatly expanded and accelerated Egypt's interactions with peoples living outside of the lower Nile Valley. The two figures in the upper fresco are probably sub-Saharan Africans, likely from the upper Nile states of Nubia. The four men in the lower fresco appear to be almost caricatures of Greeks or Phoenicians. Though often harsh for those subjugated by military conquest, empires such as that of the Egyptian New Kingdom have often created new and expanded systems of cultural and economic exchange. These systems serve not only to export the imperial culture to those conquered, but also to foster the flow of "subjugated" cultures back to the empire.

Copyright The British Museum

Copyright The British Museum

Rome in Africa and Africa in the Roman World

Different parts of the African continent have participated in different regional systems at different times. North Africa has often had more immediate connections to the Mediterranean than to sub-Saharan Africa. This photo, taken in the modern nation of Morocco, depicts a triumphal arch from the Roman colonial city of Volubilis. Constructed in 40 B.C.E., Volubilis was the administrative capital of part of Roman North Africa and itself was constructed on the site of an old Carthaginian city. Although direct Roman rule in North Africa faded in the third century C.E., Roman culture was so deeply embedded that Volubilis remained a functioning city and Latin survived as the local language until the Islamic conquest of the region in the seventh century.

Photo by Jonathan T. Reynolds

Here we see the Mosque of Abu'l Haggag, named for a local Sufi saint from the Egyptian city of Luxor. Interestingly, the mosque was constructed in the ruins of the ancient Egyptian temple of Luxor. When the temple was first excavated in the nineteenth century the excavators attempted to remove the mosque as part of the restoration project, but the local outcry was so great that it was left in place. Muslims were not the first to try to redefine the sanctity of this location. When the Romans ruled Egypt they built shrines to their emperors on the site, which were in turn replaced by a church in the sixth century. The current mosque was constructed in the mid-nineteenth century.

Robert Harding World Imagery

Africa and the Indian Ocean World

If the previous images show North Africa's links to the Mediterranean world, this photo, taken in the 1980s in the dhow harbor of the port of Zanzibar, shows East Africa's links to the Indian Ocean world. This modern ship, called a *jahazi*, descends from the dhows that once came to Zanzibar and other East African ports from Arabia and India. This trade created cultural and economic connections between the lands of the Indian Ocean rim comparable to those of the Mediterranean. Today these vessels mostly move goods between the ports of East Africa, though occasionally one will make the voyage to South Arabia.

Photo by Erik Gilbert

The Early Atlantic Encounter

This is a salt cellar (the sphere with the boat on it holds the salt) made of ivory in the fifteenth century in the West African city of Benin for a Portuguese customer. As such it is an interesting example of the encounter between West Africans and the Portuguese. Presumably, the artist who made this depicted the Portuguese as he thought they would like to be depicted, and in so doing surrounded them with images of things he associated with them. The men in the sculpture look intimidating with their scowls, beards, and swords. We also see crosses and a highly stylized ship complete with ratlines, cannon ports, and a crow's nest. The capital of Benin lay over 100 miles from the Atlantic coast, and while it is possible that the sculptor had seen the Portuguese himself, he was likely working from secondhand descriptions in his rendition of the boat. These carved ivories, which were quite popular with wealthy Portuguese, inaugurated a tradition of African artists creating work meant to appeal to the tastes of visitors. These sculptures are an early example of the emergence of an Atlantic world.

Africans in the New World

This colorful image from colonial Brazil shows another side of the Atlantic world that was created by Africa's encounter with Europe and the Americas. Here enslaved Africans are shown carrying what appear to be baskets of charcoal, eating sugar cane, and roasting ears of maize. Sugar cane is native to Southeast Asia and was introduced to the Americas by the Portuguese and the Spanish. It was primarily to provide labor for the sugar industry that Africans were brought to the Americas. For Africans in the New World, maize, a highly productive crop native to the Americas, was often the staple on which they lived. While this painting likely represents a somewhat idealized image of the lives of enslaved Africans, it nonetheless reflects the unique Atlantic culture that was being created in the Americas, and the influence of Africans upon that new cultural system.

Photo by Dagli Orti/Picture Desk, Inc./Kobal Collection

Africa and Global Environmental Exchange

Peter Arnold, Inc

At the same time that Eurasian and African crops were being introduced to the Americas, American crops, such as maize, were arriving in Africa. Maize is reported as early as 1540 in West Africa and seems to have spread rapidly. As long as it gets enough rainfall, maize is highly productive and some scholars think that it played a role in sustaining Africa's population during the slave trade era, a time when labor was often in short supply and food was in high demand. In the last 200 years maize has steadily displaced millet and sorghum, two indigenous African grains. Indeed, Africa, especially southern Africa, has come to depend upon maize as a staple in ways that no other part of the Old World does. In so doing, Africans have taken a New World crop and made it very much their own.

Here we see a South African woman roasting green maize ears. Interestingly, the means of preparing the maize, roasting it over an open fire, is similar to that seen in the previous image set in Brazil.

Africa and the Global Cash-Crop Economy

Cocoa was also introduced from the Americas, but unlike maize, very little of the cocoa crop has served to feed African appetites. Instead, cocoa has been one of Africa's most successful cash crops. At one time the West African nation of Ghana was the world's leading producer of cocoa, a title it lost to Brazil in the 1980s. The wealth that derived from cocoa created middle classes in cocoa-producing colonies, and in the Gold Coast (the colonial name for Ghana) cocoa wealth paid for the development of much of the colony's transport infrastructure. Nonetheless, as an example of the structure of the global economy, the profits made from processing cocoa into chocolate, a process undertaken largely in Europe and the United States, are greater than the profits made from growing the crop.

The basic unit of cocoa production in Ghana was generally the family, and it was not unheard of for Ghanaian cocoa farms to be owned by women. This photo likely shows a woman working with her children to prepare harvested cocoa for curing.

British Information Services

Africa and the Cold War

China's involvement with Africa is quite ancient but mostly fleeting. During the Cold War, however, China became deeply involved in African political and economic affairs. Here we see an African, dressed in a sort of generic traditional garb, with recently severed chains still hanging from his wrist, joining an international anti-imperialist movement that probably existed more as a Chinese propaganda fantasy than anything else. Today the Chinese involvement in Africa has more to do with their desperate need to secure access to Africa's natural resources. The Chinese involvement with Africa is an example of a type of interaction that takes place in a global rather than regional context. China's engagement with Africa takes place not in the context of an ocean or desert trade route, but through geopolitics and world trade.

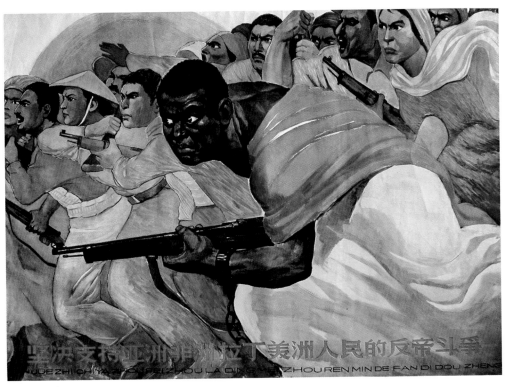

Courtesy of www.maopost.com

The Political Economy of International Relations

Photo by Jonathan T. Reynolds

The direct engagement of Africans with the global economy is well represented by the predominance of money-changing centers in most cities. One of the ways that Africa now finds itself engaged, and sometimes snared, in the global economy is through its dependence on so-called "hard currencies" to pay for imports. In general, African currencies, save for the South African Rand, are not accepted or are heavily discounted outside of the countries where they are issued. Thus, every African merchant is also a currency trader, constantly trying to find enough dollars or pounds to pay for the next round of imports he or she needs. African national governments are engaged in the same struggle to get the currency needed to pay for energy imports and other goods (medical supplies, vehicles, textbooks, etc.) that can only be paid for with hard currency.

Interestingly, a major source of hard currency for African states now comes from wire transfers from African immigrants living abroad, who regularly send funds to their families in Africa.

Oil and African Economies

A few African nations do not have to import their oil; they produce and export it themselves. This is sometimes as much a curse as a blessing. Africa's oil-producing nations are among the most corrupt on the continent, and often oil is pumped and transported with scant regard for the health and well-being of people who live near the oil fields. Spills and fires like this one are often caused by people trying to tap into pipelines to steal oil. This is sometimes the work of criminal gangs, but it is often simply very poor people trying to gain access to the wealth they see flowing out of their land. As oil-consuming nations try to diversify their sources of oil, African oil is increasingly drawing the interest of Western and Asian investors and diplomats.

Copyright Reuters NewMedia, Inc./CORBIS

Africans and Global Peacekeeping

Since independence, various African nations have been active participants in international organizations. Here we see Kenyan soldiers wearing the blue beret of the United Nations on a peacekeeping mission in the West African nation of Sierra Leone. In 2000, seven Kenyan soldiers were killed while serving in Sierra Leone and in the last 50 years 41 Kenyans have lost their lives while serving as UN peacekeepers. Kenyans have also served in UN peacekeeping missions in Namibia, Eritrea, Ivory Coast, East Timor, and Croatia, making Kenya a significant contributor to the peacekeeping process, and putting African states into a global community of nations.

Photo by Brennan Linsley/AP Wide World Photos

The Globalized African Family

Here we see three generations of a middle class Nigerian family gathered for a photograph in a Lagos apartment. In many ways their lives reflect the transformations and tumult Nigeria has seen in the twentieth century. The family is descended from a prosperous Warrant Chief who was appointed by the British. Displaced during the Nigerian Civil War, the family nonetheless prospered during the "oil boom" of the 1970s. When the oil economy collapsed in the 1980s, the family was nearly bankrupted, but recovered as one member (the woman on the center-right) founded a successful office-service company in Lagos. Another daughter of the family immigrated to the United States in the 1990s, went on to complete a graduate education in computer science, and founded a software company. Together, the two have subsidized university educations for most of their siblings and cousins. Along the way, family members have intermarried with British, Irish, Japanese, and American families.

Photo by Ivy Omeife

Of Mosques and Pop Stars

The Jenne mosque, seen in the background here, is emblematic of Sahelean Africa's engagement with the broader Islamic world. This style of mosque was devised in the fourteenth century by an Andalusian architect (a Muslim from Spain) who adapted his knowledge to West African building materials. The resulting style is seen in mosques across the West African desert edge. These mosques are also popular in documentaries and on postcards, where they often appear as timeless symbols of the African past. Obviously, the coexistence of the ancient mosque and the global pop star belie the notion that Jenne is somehow a place outside of the modern world. If one photo could be said to sum up the central idea of our book, this would be it. Africa's past and present are not about isolation. Africa is part of the world's history and vice versa.

Photo by Chris Brown/Stock Boston

thing in common. They thought that massive influxes of capital into the manufacturing sector were needed for African nations to make the transition to modernity—though, of course, they differed as to what that modernity should be like. Initially, the consensus was that this capital should come from the agricultural sector. So surplus income generated by the sale of agricultural goods would be plowed back into manufacturing to break the cycle of dependence on imports. At first it worked. Though the usually centrally planned industrial sector remained torpid, there was enough income generated from agriculture to support it. Then in the mid-1970s came the oil crisis, and fuel prices went up sixfold. At the same time, prices for both agricultural and mineral exports fell. So the only way to keep capital flowing into manufacturing was to borrow.

By the 1990s, Africa's debt burden had grown to the point where it exceeded the annual gross domestic product (GDP). Debt service payments exceeded the value of aid money and loan money that was coming in. In effect, loans were being used to pay loans. By 1990 the total debt load had exceeded $135 billion, and often it was the richest nations that had the biggest debt burdens. Sovereign nations can default on their debts in a way that individuals cannot. If individuals default on a loan, their creditors can usually seize their property. But the banks that loan a nation money cannot foreclose on that nation if it defaults. However, banks are loath to loan money to a country that has defaulted, so for countries that need to borrow to get fuel, food, and medicine, default is usually not an option. To do so is to make a commitment to living without imports.

Thus, many countries ended up on a sort of treadmill in the 1980s and 1990s. They borrowed to buy imports and pay their debts and sold what commodities they could in an effort to slow the rate of increase in their debt. This made banks all the more leery about putting more and more money into economies that were so burdened with debt. So the International Monetary Fund (IMF) and the World Bank got into the business of putting together loan programs for cash-strapped countries, but these came with conditions. In exchange for IMF or World Bank loan packages African nations had to accept **Structural Adjustment Programs**. These were meant to transform the loan recipients' economies so that they would eventually be able to repay the loans.

Structural Adjustment Programs usually required countries to devalue their currencies so that their exports would be cheaper, shift more resources into cash crop production to generate more income, cut public-sector employment, and cut social services and food subsidies. Proponents of these programs claim that the root causes of poverty in Africa have to do with state-directed economies and the ways in which they distort market forces. By forcing African governments to abandon food subsidies, fire government employees, and stop overvaluing their currencies, Structural Adjustment is, despite the pain it causes in the near term, actually benefiting the countries that are subjected to it. Detractors point out that the shift to cash crops sometimes comes at the expense of food crops. Lowering exchange rates makes imports cheaper for rich-country consumers while lowering incomes for poor-country producers. Cutting social services and public-sector employment may help banks to collect their debts, but it harms people in poor countries.

Africans often point to the debt crisis and Structural Adjustment as an example of how limited their independence is. They may have achieved political independence in the 1960s and 1970s, but economic independence remains elusive. In the late 1990s most of the continent experienced negative GDP growth per capita. Most of the time, this was due to war or drought, but even in countries at peace, poverty has remained a serious problem.

African Economic History in Global Perspective

Ralph Austen, a prominent student of Africa's economic history, has observed that one of the long-term trends in Africa's relationship with the world economy has been increasing involvement, but increasing marginality at the same time. Arguably, Africa was less involved in the world economy in 1700 than it is now, but the labor and gold it exported were more important to the world economy than anything it now produces. Likewise, in the 1920s and 1930s African oil crops and fiber crops were essential to industry in the developed world. Now many of these crops have petroleum-based synthetic substitutes. Africa is probably now more dependent on trade than it has ever been. Most Africans wear imported clothes and ride in imported vehicles, which burn imported fuels. If they live in cities, they probably eat imported food. If they live in the countryside, they probably grow something for export.

Meanwhile, Africa has become less important than ever to the world economy. There are alternative sources for most of the crops and minerals the continent produces. With the Cold War over, less aid money goes to Africa because the wealthy countries of the world are less inclined to try to buy friends than they were when they needed political allies. Direct foreign investment, a critical ingredient in the growth of many Asian economies, has been virtually nonexistent. Many people hoped that the collapse of apartheid in South Africa would allow that country to emerge as a continental economic powerhouse that would at least drive economic expansion in southern Africa. Some South African companies have indeed expanded into other countries, but any advantage from this has been more than offset by foreign capital flight triggered by political unrest in Zimbabwe.

A new development in Africa's relationship with the world economy is the growing importance of China. China's emergence as an economic power has been accompanied by a surge in China's thirst for oil and other natural resources. China became a net importer of oil in 1993 and by 2010, Chinese oil imports are expected to reach four million barrels a day. Curently, most Chinese imports come from the Middle East, but like other importing nations it is seeking alternative sources in less volatile places. Chinese oil companies, usually partly owned by the Chinese government, have been scouring the continent looking for new oil fields to explore and develop. This has proven a boon to some of the continent's dodgier regimes. Sudan, which many consider an international pariah because of its human rights record, sells more than half of its rapidly growing oil exports to China. China recently invested heavily in the construction of a refinery in Sudan and has "peace keeping" troops on the ground to protect Sudan's pipelines. The Chinese have shown a strong interest in Central African copper. China also exports manufactured goods to Africa and, as Chinese merchants set up shop in African cities, small Chinatowns have begun to spring up. China has given nearly a billion dollars in aid, usually with few of the strings that are attached to aid from the West, and has offered even more in loans. China is now Africa's third-largest trade partner, after the United States and France, and Chinese trade and investment in Africa are growing fast.

Africa has become the world's poorest continent. Even regions with worse debt burdens, South America for instance, have done better in the 40 years since African countries began to get their independence. And some parts of the world, notably in Asia, have come to enjoy standards of living comparable to those of Europe and North America. Perhaps the next 40 years will be kinder to Africa than were the previous 100.

Useful Works on This Chapter Topic

The best survey of the entire continent's economic history remains Ralph Austen's *African Economic History* (1987). For an examination of the failure of colonial economic policy in West Africa, see Richard Roberts, *Two Worlds of Cotton* (1996). For a magisterial overview of the question of poverty in Africa, John Iliffe's *The African Poor* (1987) is the book to read. Polly Hill's *Studies in Rural Capitalism* (1970) on cash cropping in West Africa is dated, but still provides a useful overview. For other types of entrepreneurship, see Sara Berry, *Fathers Work for their Sons* (1985). Luise White's *The Comforts of Home* (1990) presents prostitution in an unconventional light and provides a fascinating window or life in a colonial city.

CHAPTER 15

Political Change in the Time of Colonialism

With the "Scramble for Africa" largely completed by the early years of the twentieth century, the nature of European activity in Africa began to change. Colonial powers shifted their efforts from conquest to governance as they sought to consolidate the territories that had been added to their dominion. As we have already seen in Chapter 14, one of the key goals of colonialism was to control the economic output of Africa to ensure maximum benefit for the colonial powers. To exploit Africans economically, it was necessary to establish systems of colonial administration that would, one way or another, guarantee economic benefits for the colonizing states. The steps taken to achieve this ultimate goal of economic gain might be thought of as "colonial imperatives," in that all colonial governments had common needs and goals. These shared imperatives took several forms. First, colonial governments needed to create functioning bureaucracies and systems of authority to regulate state–society relations. Systems of hierarchy had to be established that determined who told whom what to do. Not surprisingly, such systems placed Europeans at the top of the chain of command. Also critical to colonial authority was the maintenance of peace. Empires generally disapprove of conflict in regions under their control, and the new colonial rulers of Africa were no different. They sought to establish peace within their regions of administration not so much out of altruism, but rather because conflict, whether aimed at the colonial rulers or between subject groups, was bad for business. A *Pax Colonial* was to be established. To this end, Africans, as individuals and groups, were to be disarmed, and deadly force was concentrated in the hands of the new colonial governments.

Further, colonial governments needed to legitimize their activities. Even if their ultimate goals were economic exploitation and a desire to show racial or cultural superiority, colonial administrations were generally not willing to say, "We are in it for the money and the power." Rather, they sought to justify colonialism in terms of altruism. Indeed, the British notion of "the white man's burden," and the French concept of the *Mission Civilitrice* both represent the ways in which colonial powers sought to create an image of themselves as benevolent agents of civilization— selflessly toiling to bring the benefits of Western culture and technology to the "backward" races of the world. There were two audiences for these images of colonialism. First, there were the populations of the home countries, who had to be convinced to supply troops to establish colonial rule and money to invest in future returns. By and large, simple promises of economic return were not enough to encourage Europeans to support colonialism, and hence calls for campaigns against slavery or promises to spread Christianity were essential to "selling" colonialism to these populations. Other claims of benevolence centered around the spread of Western education and technology, medicine, and economic development. The second audience was, of course, the Africans themselves. Though colonialism was established through force of arms (as we saw in Chapter 13), most colonial powers preferred not to maintain it solely through the threat of violence, which was both expensive and dangerous. Thus, colonial administrations sought to "sell" colonialism to Africans as well, promising to Africans that the benefits of European tutelage would more than offset the loss of self-determination. As we shall see, some Africans did indeed see advantages in things European, but at the same time, many chafed at European notions of superiority and paternalism.

From such a macrolevel, all colonial governments might seem very similar. Yet, the various colonial powers took different paths to attain these common goals. These different approaches to colonial administration resulted in very different colonial cultures and legacies.

Varieties of Colonial Administration

Charter Companies

Charter companies were a common means by which colonial powers (though less so France) sought to establish colonial rule with a minimal amount of public investment and state oversight. Companies such as the British Royal Niger Company, British South Africa Company, Leopold's Congo Free State, and the German East Africa Company played critical roles in expanding the areas under colonial domination. This is not surprising, really, because charter companies had, for centuries, been a tool of European expansion. The British East India Company had been established in 1600 to help establish a British commercial presence in India. Similarly, the Virginia Company was chartered in 1606 to facilitate the first permanent European colony in North America. In the long run, however, these companies proved either unsuccessful or undesirable as tools of colonial exploitation in Africa. First, these companies often did poorly in their attempts to wage military campaigns against African states and societies. For example, it took over a decade for the Royal Niger Company to expand just over 100 miles inland from the Nigerian coast. By 1897 the company had conquered much of the Yoruba-speaking region and had defeated and sacked the centuries-old Kingdom of Benin, but had failed to expand farther north. It had also been repeatedly thwarted by the largely stateless Igbo and Ibibio societies in the east. Such progress was too slow for the British government, who feared that the French (who largely relied on state-funded armies for

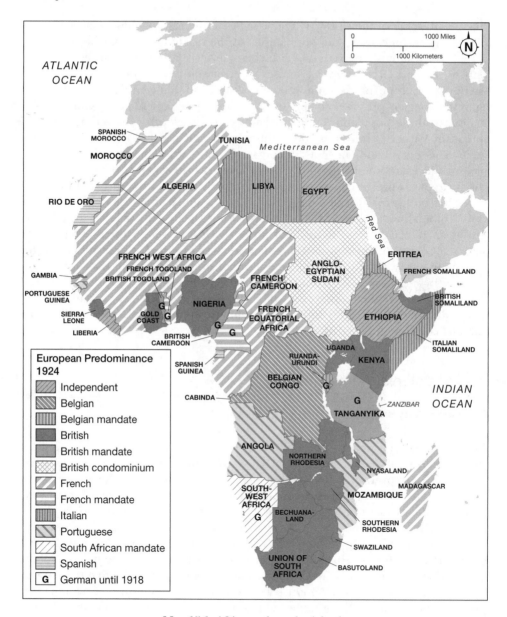

Map 15-1: Africa under colonial rule

conquest) would beat them to the valuable population centers of the Sokoto Caliphate deep in the interior to the north. In 1900 the British handed responsibility for the region's conquest to General Lugard, who was placed in command of the West African Frontier Force (WAFF). In only three years, he had successfully conquered the Sokoto Caliphate. The stateless societies of the east held out until around 1910—largely because their decentralized systems of authority rendered them difficult to defeat in a single blow.

Charter companies also acquired a well-earned reputation for brutality. Perhaps there is no better example of this than the atrocities committed by Leopold's Congo Free State (already examined in Chapter 13). The Belgians were not alone in committing such crimes. Driven first and foremost by financial concerns and often interested in short-term rather than long-term gains, charter companies representing all the colonial powers were often heartless toward the people under their administration. Like in the Congo, it was not unheard of for such companies to burn villages, take hostages, or use torture to force local populations to meet quotas for the production of export products. Such brutality, however, often led to uprisings, such as the revolt of the Ndebele against the British South Africa Company in 1897. Similarly, brutality undercut the altruistic justifications of colonialism, and many colonial powers preferred to avoid the kind of bad press received by Belgium as a result of the Congo scandal. Even when local populations did not take up arms, they often simply "voted with their feet" and left the regions under the control of the Charter Companies—denying the companies the labor and markets that were critical to profitable business. By the early 1900s, it was clear to most colonial powers (although less so to the Portuguese) that charter companies were an imperfect tool for African colonization.

As charter companies were "phased out" by most colonial powers in the early 1900s, they were usually replaced first by military-style administrations and later by somewhat more bureaucratic civil service–style administrations. The European architects of colonial rule, however, were faced with a number of critical issues—and chief among these was to be the degree to which Africans and African forms of administration would be utilized within the colonial governments. Most colonial states, for various reasons, chose to minimize the degree of African participation in colonial administrations. Most scholars refer to the resulting form of administration as "direct rule," which was used to varying degrees by the French, Belgians, Germans, Italians, Spanish, and Portuguese. Quite to the contrary, the British developed a system of colonial administration that relied heavily on African participation and administrative structures—a system known as indirect rule. Further, distinct from colonies which were primarily administrative in nature, many colonial powers also ruled over areas that came to have large populations of permanent European settlers. These "settler states" tended to have unique characteristics all their own.

Direct Rule

Direct rule offered a variety of advantages to the colonial powers who sought to so establish their administrations. By imposing a new and centralized system of administration, there would be a clear chain of command, and rules and regulations would be consistent across the entire colonial dominion. Colonial officers would be in charge of all aspects of administration. African participation in such bureaucracies would largely be limited to employment as functionaries—police constables, clerks, translators, and the like, who reported directly to the colonial administrators who oversaw their work. Direct rule had its disadvantages, as well. In particular, it demanded a relatively high investment in manpower. If Europeans were to oversee all aspects of administration from the regional to the local level, then they needed a fair number of colonial officers. The colonial powers often had a hard time finding personnel to fill such positions, particularly in more rural settings where an individual could be quite isolated from other Europeans for extended periods of time. In the late 1800s, many colonial powers made do with military administrations—hardly a surprise, given that most regions had been acquired via military conquest. Military officers were often not terribly pleased with the bureaucratic routine of administrative duties, however. Further, a number of unsavory characters found their way into colonial administrations because the job often attracted those who had reason to leave their homes or who relished having near absolute power over others. In 1905 the French tried two colonial agents for having used dynamite to blow up a porter while posted in central Africa. Indeed, high-level colonial administrators often lamented the poor quality of their officers, but remarked that they could not be fired because there was no one available to replace them. In 1897 the French established the **École Colonial** to train colonial agents for service in Africa and elsewhere, hoping that such a move would improve the quality of colonial officers both through better training and by attracting a higher class of applicants for the job.

Assimilation and Direct Rule

Critical to the understanding of the system of direct rule, particularly as implemented by the French, is the notion of **assimilation.** For the French, and to a lesser extent also the Portuguese and Belgians, a critical aspect of the "civilizing mission" of the colonizing powers was to replace African cultures with their own. This is a very complex notion deeply rooted in assumptions of European superiority. From this perspective, the reason why Europeans had been able to conquer and subjugate Africa was because European culture was itself superior and gave Europeans the ability to advance technologically and socially. Thus, if Africans were to be "civilized" as a result of colonialism, they had to become more like Europeans. The original architect of this policy for the French was Louis Faidherbe, the military officer largely responsible for French expansion in the Senegambia in the mid-1800s. Faidherbe's concept of assimilation really worked on two levels. First was the idea that new colonial territories would be "assimilated" into existing French administrative systems and would be part and parcel of a "Greater France"—a concept already somewhat established in Algeria. Second, however, was the idea that subject peoples would ultimately become French citizens who were culturally indistinct from their counterparts at "home."

This notion, interestingly enough, was deeply rooted in the political Enlightenment of the eighteenth and early nineteenth centuries and in the French Revolution itself. Critical to the Enlightenment was the principle that all people (if properly educated) were basically rational and had the potential to be responsible for their own actions—and thus sovereignty (the right to make choices) should lie in the individual, not a single ruler or class of elites. As such, the legacy of the

French Revolution had left French "Republicans" with a deep distrust of both inherited aristocratic rulers and of those in religious authority. As we have seen in previous chapters, most African political systems combined religious and political authority in the person of the chief or king. Thus, existing African political systems were largely antithetical to the "enlightened" French concept of legitimate government. For most French, marginalizing or even doing away with existing African systems of authority was doing Africans a favor because it set them on the path to a more secular and egalitarian form of society. Speaking in 1963, the former governor of Cote D'Ivoire, Deschamps, described assimilation as "the Revolution of 1789 sneaking into Africa rather late on tiptoe." Thus, the more Africans (or for that matter Asians) assimilated to French culture in terms of speech, dress, habits, and behavior, the more rights they deserved. More than any other colonial power, the French seemed concerned with spreading their culture as a central goal of their colonial endeavor.

The ultimate example of assimilation's ideal of inclusion was to be found in the four communes of Senegal. The inhabitants of St. Louis and Gorée, for example, were granted French citizenship following the French Revolution of 1848. Rufisque and Dakar's inhabitants gained similar rights in the 1880s. The inhabitants of these regions enjoyed representation in the Chambre des Deputies in Paris, French-style local administration and municipal councils, and access to state-funded standardized French education. Such Africans were defined as **"évolues"** (culturally "evolved," a term also utilized by the Belgians). The Portuguese had a similar status for Africans who took on Portuguese culture and whom they termed *assimilatos.* Notably, Africans lacking such cultural advantages were seen as subjects rather than as citizens. These other Africans, referred to as *indigenes* by the French, enjoyed no such privileges. They were excluded from all political participation and were subject to a special code of law known as the *indiginat.* Established in 1904, but drawing on a body of laws in use in Algeria for several decades, the indiginat allowed colonial officers to try to punish the indigenes without the due process of law owed to French citizens. Fines and punishments could be quite harsh, and the indiginat was a particularly unpopular aspect of French colonial rule.

It should be noted that the ideology of assimilation notwithstanding, there were often barriers to individual Africans receiving the status of évolue. There were no hard-and-fast criteria by which the status could be gained, and thus it was easy for French colonial administrators to raise or lower the bar as they saw fit. By and large, the status became harder to achieve as time went by because granting the status to Africans meant that French colonial administrators had to share both power and prestige with these former subjects. By 1922, barely 100 French West Africans had attained full French citizenship. Given such a situation, very few Africans responded by casting off their existing cultural norms completely. Most, like people throughout history, picked and chose between cultural practices that were deemed useful and those that were found distasteful. In the process, they moved toward creating new cultures that fused elements that were both African and European. As will be discussed in the next chapter, much of this fusion took place in urban areas.

It is important to recognize, however, that not all French policymakers agreed with the goals of assimilation. Many argued that Africans were intellectually incapable of either appreciating or applying the complexities of European culture. Such opponents of assimilation were thus deeply influenced by the scientific racism of the day, which argued that a clear racial hierarchy of intelligence existed, with Europeans being at the top and other "races" falling below them. In 1889, for example, Gustave LeBon attacked the idea of participation by non-Europeans in government with the following statement: ". . . a Negro or a Japanese can accumulate all the diplomas possible without ever arriving at the level of on ordinary European." There thus existed within French colonial ideology a tension between idealists who felt that replacing African culture with French culture would uplift Africans and a contrary belief that Africans were inherently inferior and incapable of understanding or benefitting from European culture. Clearly, both groups believed that Africans were, nonetheless, in need of European guidance if they were to function in the "modern" world.

Other practitioners of direct rule were less concerned with the issue of cultural rewards from colonialism. By and large the Portuguese, Germans, and Belgians simply tolerated rather than rewarded Africans who assimilated to European culture. The Belgians tended to favor a much more comprehensive and paternalistic administration that isolated Africans from any sort of incorporation into the administrative process except as functionaries. The heavy Belgian reliance on missionaries for education tended to result in a more rapid expansion of Christianity in the region of the Congo.

This photo, which presents a scene from the Belgian Congo in the mid-twentieth century, provides some sense of the haughtiness that often characterized colonial administration.

Portuguese administration was perhaps the least sophisticated of all the colonial powers. Portugal was easily one of the least-developed Western European states in the nineteenth and twentieth centuries, with little or no industry and very low standards of living for most of the population. Indeed, having colonies was really Portugal's only remaining claim to fame since having lost its once considerable hold on global commerce. Even more strapped for cash and capable administrators than other colonial powers, Portugal never quite broke completely with the charter company model of colonial administration. As a result, large tracts of Angola and Mozambique were leased out to commercial concerns for agricultural and mining purposes. Not surprisingly, these companies tended to be quite harsh in their labor practices. Revolts, such as one that lasted from 1917 to 1921 in the Zambezi River Valley of Mozambique, as well as other forms of resistance undertaken by local populations, tended to be dealt with very harshly by company and Portuguese colonial administrators. The Portuguese did little or nothing to invest in education or health care for the Africans under their dominion. Only a tiny number of *assimilatos* and **mestizos** (people of mixed African and European heritage) received any rights or privileges. In 1914 the Portuguese implemented the *Indignato* code of law, which, like its French counterpart, sharply curtailed the rights of the vast majority of Africans. Notably, the Portuguese were unique among colonial powers in that they made no effort whatsoever to take African custom or values into account in their colonial legal system. Force, rather than even a superficial attempt at ideological legitimation, defined Portuguese colonialism. As a response to the harshness of Portuguese colonial rule, hundreds of thousands of Africans fled into neighboring territories administered by French, Belgian, and British administrations. In part, perhaps, to deal with such labor losses, Portuguese colonial administrations encouraged immigration by native Portuguese, a theme to be discussed in more detail later in this chapter.

The Germans, too, developed a reputation for dealing very harshly with any challenge to the authority of the colonial administrators. Perhaps the most frightening example of colonial brutality took place in German Southwest Africa in 1904. Here, frustrated and desperate from having lost cattle to a rinderpest epidemic and also being driven off their lands by German and Afrikaner settlers, the Herero, a largely pastoralist people, took up arms against colonial administrators and settlers, killing around 100 and largely reclaiming the central Namibian lands from which they had been driven. In response, the German general, Lothar von Trotha, issued his infamous "extermination order."

> The Herero nation must leave the country. If it does not do so I shall compel them by force. . . . Inside German territory every Herero tribesman, armed or unarmed, with or without cattle, will be shot. No women and children will be allowed in the territory: they will be driven back to their people or fired on. These are the last words to the great Herero nation from me, the great General of the mighty German Emperor.

When many Herero fled into the desert, the German forces poisoned the water holes. By the end of the campaign around 60,000 Herero were killed, leaving less than 20,000 alive. Worse still, many of the survivors were placed in work camps and became the subjects of medical experiments and examinations—the results of which would later become fodder for Nazi notions of racial superiority. When the Nama joined the Herero in rebellion in 1905, they received similar treatment. The near-extermination of the Herero and Nama was perhaps the first genocide of the twentieth century. Similarly, in 1905, a revivalist cult known as **Maji Maji** (spirit water) took hold in German East Africa. Driven by a belief that the magic water rendered them invulnerable to firearms, a coalition of local ethnic groups attacked Germans and other foreigners in the region. Surprise and fervor earned them some early victories, but the German forces soon regrouped and were reinforced by troops from Somalia and New Guinea (having access to international reservoirs of manpower was always a colonial advantage). So strengthened, the Germans launched a massive "scorched earth" campaign that succeeded in retaking lost territories and rooting the rebels out of the highlands by 1906. Such was the dislocation and destruction wrought by the revolt and scorched earth campaign that perhaps as many as 50,000 Africans died from a resulting famine that year. The campaigns in southwestern and eastern Africa left the German administrators of the region with an almost unequaled reputation for ruthlessness in dealing with revolts.

British Indirect Rule

Quite in contrast to their fellow colonial powers, the British in Africa developed a system known as **indirect rule.** As the name implies, the British sought not to displace African systems of authority and administration, but rather to rule through them whenever possible. The system of indirect rule built on British colonial experience elsewhere in the world, particularly India. Credit for the codification of indirect rule itself goes to F. D. Lugard, who served as a colonial officer in Uganda and later in Nigeria. Indeed, it was his experience in Northern Nigeria that led him to formulate his perspective on indirect rule. In 1922 he published a book, *Dual Mandate in Tropical Africa,* which outlined his ideas for colonial administration in considerable detail. The text quickly became a statement of policy for British colonial rule in Africa. Thus, unlike the French policy of assimilation (or, as we shall see, association), which tended to have a variety of meanings at given places and times, indirect rule developed around a fairly consistent set of assumptions and goals. As Lugard stated:

> The British Empire . . . has only one mission—for liberty and self-development on no standardized lines, so that all may feel that their interests and religion are safe under the British flag. Such liberty and self-development can be best secured to the native populations by leaving them free to manage their own affairs through their own rulers, proportionately to their degree of advancement, under the guidance of the British staff, and subject to the laws and policy of the administration.

As designed, indirect rule offered a number of advantages to the British. First and foremost, because the system utilized, wherever possible, African structures of administration, the British colonial system demanded a considerably smaller investment in personnel. For example, rather than having British judges present to hear cases in court, existing African judicial systems would be utilized. Of course, this did not mean that British colonial officers were not ultimately in charge. Nonetheless, the ideology of indirect rule stressed that they were tasked with overseeing and helping to educate local authorities, not with commanding. Again, to quote Lugard:

> . . . the primary duty and object of the political officer will be to educate [the native chiefs] in the duties of the rulers according to a civilized standard; to convince them that the oppression of the people is not a sound policy, or to the eventual benefit of the rulers; to bring home to their intelligence as far as may be, the evils attendant on a system which holds the lower classes in a state of slavery or serfdom, and so destroys individual responsibility.

With less administrative overhead, ideally, also came less cost. Indirect rule offered the promise of colonialism with minimal investment. A further advantage, and one that was certainly not lost on the British, was that indirect rule, with its promise of not threatening local cultural norms, would rest more easily on the shoulders of the colonized. Thus, the British legitimated their colonial rule, in part, with the promise that theirs was not a mission of cultural conquest, but rather an attempt to help the colonized find their own cultural path toward modernity. Both the colonizer and colonized would benefit—which was the very nature of the "dual mandate." Quite contrary to the goal of assimilation that underlaid French colonial policy, the British stressed what might be termed "change within tradition." Some aspects of African culture might be outlawed, such as the continuing practice of slavery or certain religious practices that the British deemed "uncivilized." The British could be quite squeamish about certain forms of dance, for example. There is a reason that "Victorian" has become synonymous with being a bit on the prudish side. But, by and large, the British stressed tolerance for things local. For example, British colonial officers were required to learn to speak local languages, and extensive ethnographies were undertaken to better understand local social and legal customs. Such a situation was in stark contrast to the more common direct rule tendency to impose the colonial language as the official language of administration and the practice of establishing new Western-based legal codes.

For the most part, populations living under indirect rule did indeed seem to find the British style of administration less onerous. Hausa-speaking populations in West Africa that had been divided by colonial rule recognized the difference by describing French administration in Niger as *mulkin zafi* (painful rule), while in Nigeria they referred to British administration as *mulkin sauki* (easy rule). Further, the British often enjoyed considerable degrees of support from existing African rulers, who often found their positions strengthened by their incorporation into the wider British system of administration (and ultimately backed up by British firepower). An example from the Sokoto Caliphate is instructive here, particularly in that Sokoto served as both the inspiration and model for Lugard's system of indirect rule. In 1906 the village of Satiru in Nigeria's northwest rose in revolt against the British. Led by Malam Isa, who claimed to represent the Mahdi (the Islamic second coming), inhabitants of the village marched toward the regional capital of Sokoto with the goal of driving the British "infidels" from the region. The WAFF, the sole British military unit in the region, was mobilized and sent to deal with the revolt. Perhaps overconfident, the WAFF was ambushed in a ravine where their maxim guns and rifles were rendered largely useless. The force was completely destroyed.

A still from the film *Saunders of the River,* which was set in Nigeria and celebrated British colonialism. Such films played an important role in legitimizing colonial rule to home audiences. As an interesting note, the "native" on the right is none other than Jomo Kenyatta, then a student of Anthropology in London. He would later go on to become the first President of Kenya.

Thus, only three years after the successful conquest of the Sokoto Caliphate, the British colonial administration in Northern Nigeria was left almost completely defenseless. Remarkably, the British colonial administration was saved by the local political class of the *Masu Sarauta* (the possessors of governance), who mobilized the Sokoto cavalry and hemmed in the Satiru rebels until new troops could be brought in and the revolt crushed. Afterward, the town of Satiru was razed, and the sultan of Sokoto formally cursed the town and its inhabitants. Such an outcome is all the more remarkable when one takes into account the fact that only three years before the British had defeated the Sokoto Caliphate by force of arms and killed the previous sultan in battle. The Masu Sarauta, perhaps for reasons best understood by themselves, had clearly decided that their lot was best cast with the British.

As already mentioned, the Sokoto Caliphate served as Lugard's inspiration and model for the system of indirect rule. There are a number or reasons why this is the case, not the least of which is that the Caliphate, as one of the largest precolonial states in Africa, already had a sophisticated system of administration and ideology in place. There was a clear hierarchy of authority that subordinated local emirs to the sultan of Sokoto. Further, each emir was based in an urban center and held authority over a local civil service. Established principles of Islamic law regulated aspects of local criminal, civil, and political law. In such a system, it only made sense for the British to use the preexisting structures, rather than try to impose their own. In other cases where large states were in place, such as the regions under the control of the Asante in the Gold Coast or the Buganda in Uganda, the system of indirect rule also worked fairly well. The problem came, rather, when the British attempted to apply the model in regions where no clear centralized authority existed. This happened first when Lugard amalgamated Northern and Southern Nigeria into a single colony in 1914. In the Yoruba-speaking area of southwestern Nigeria, which had been torn by civil wars for much of the nineteenth century, the British struggled to create a centralized system of authority that placed the alaafin of Oyo at the head of a local elite, but found little support for the alaafin's authority that was analogous to that enjoyed by the sultan of Sokoto. In particular, the British found themselves at a loss when dealing with stateless societies. How were they to establish indirect rule through local leaders when there was no chief or king? Ruling through the complex systems of lineage and consensus that provided authority in such societies seemed far too foreign or problematic to the British, who instead opted to simply create local rulers where none had previously existed. Known as **warrant chiefs,** these new local rulers were generally distrusted and disliked by communities that had long chosen not to concentrate political power in the hands of individuals.

What exactly might have led to the British support for (and even creation of) African systems of authority? On the one hand, one should note that the British had never rejected monarchy and social hierarchy in quite the same way as had the French. To the contrary, the British, especially the upper-class elites who filled most positions in the colonial service, had a great respect for inherited authority and a belief that each society had a class of "natural rulers" who were simply superior to the common folk. Another factor for the British was the underlying notion of African stasis and inferiority that underpinned the philosophy of indirect rule. Influenced by the same concepts of scientific racism and social Darwinism that led many French to challenge the idea of assimilation, Lugard advocated the use of existing African political systems in no small part because he believed the complexity of European culture was simply unsuitable for the "African mind." Notably, this underlying assumption had the remarkable effect of defining Africans who assimilated to European culture as "bad Africans" in most British colonies. In the eyes of many British, such Africans could only develop a veneer of Western culture and were doomed to tragic ends if they attempted to think, act, and live as would a true European. The tragic death of the English-speaking-and-dressing African character Mr. Johnson in the Joyce Cary novel of the same name is a case in point.

Such a belief in the inability of Africans to adopt Western culture often put British colonial officers at odds with Christian missionaries. Missionaries were inherently assimilationist in their desire to bring Western Christianity and related notions of behavior to Africans. British colonial administrators often saw Christianity as "too complex" for Africans. Further, because indirect rule depended on maintaining African systems of authority, many of which were underpinned by traditional religious or Islamic legitimacy, the introduction of new systems of religion threatened political stability as well. particularly in Nigeria, the British colonial office sought to restrict the spread of Christianity and support the spread of Islam, which according to Lugard was "a religion incapable of the highest development, but its limitations clearly suit the limitations of the people." British colonial administrators were thus in a catch-22. They had to allow missionaries to operate in British colonies because such activity was essential to legitimizing colonialism to the home audience. Yet, the missionaries themselves held a perspective on African culture that was contrary to that of indirect rule. The religious implications of colonial rule will be discussed in more detail in the next chapter.

A further disadvantage of indirect rule was the fact that reliance on local systems of authority and administration rendered impossible any attempt to routinize or regularize colonial policy. Each recognized "tribe" under the British system could conceivably have its own system of political authority and code of law. Indeed, rather than breaking down systems of local ethnicity, as was sought by the French, the institutionalization of such distinctions within the system of indirect rule may inadvertently have strengthened such identities. Where notions of ethnicity and identity may once have been flexible, their incorporation into indirect rule potentially made them more fixed and more "real." Further, individual British colonial officers often developed rather bizarre notions regarding which ethnic groups were "best" in terms of notions of sophistication or their support for colonial rule. Such beliefs were often played out in terms of favoritism and even competition between colonial officers for the support of their preferred groups. Thus, some contemporary scholars see ethnic conflict in former British colonies to be a legacy of the system of indirect rule itself.

On a broader level, the decentralized nature of British colonial rule also meant that there was little or no coordination from colony to colony. As a result, individual colonial governors could set very different paths for the areas under their administration, resulting in different and even contradictory policies. For example, while the Nigerian colonial government, for both economic and political reasons, sought to restrict the outmigration of agricultural labor to the Sudan, the administration there actively encouraged it. As already mentioned, in Nigeria the colonial administration sought to restrict the spread of Christianity and encourage the spread of Islam, but in the Gold Coast, Christian missions were generally welcomed and supported. Ironically, despite the fact that British indirect rule was built on a clearer set of goals and assumptions than French assimilation, its actual application resulted in a much more varied and complex system of colonial administration.

Association: Assimilation Reconsidered

It is important to note that French assimilation policy was challenged as the colonial era progressed. In 1910, Jules Harmand first advanced the notion of association in the text *Domination et Colonisation*. Harmand defined association as "scrupulous respect for the manners, customs and religion of the natives" and advocated that the system of assimilation be dropped in favor of association, which he saw as more closely modeled along the British system of indirect rule. Over the course of the next several years, the idea of association gained increasing favor within the French colonial service, and some scholars have even gone so far as to suggest that it effectively led to the repudiation of the philosophy of assimilation. In particular, association and the effort to utilize existing African administrative systems was most effectively applied by the French in Morocco. Not completely subjugated by the

French until 1912, and with a long-standing and large-scale administration built around Islamic precepts, the Moroccan Sultanate, like the Sokoto Caliphate in Nigeria, was well suited to a more "indirect" approach to administration. Here, the French administrator Lyautey stated that he would "maintain as much as possible their entirely native governmental machinery, institutions and customs." This policy seems to have worked fairly well in Morocco. Elsewhere, however, evidence suggests that the new policy of association often had little effect on the already entrenched notions of the superiority of French culture held by many French colonial officers. For example, the language of administration and education remained French. By and large, the existing system of direct rule continued unchanged, and this meant that the structure of French colonialism continued to subordinate and marginalize African authorities and culture.

Thus, in the contrasting systems of administration adopted by the two dominant colonial powers, one sees competing notions of the role of the West in the colonized world. French assimilationists, even under the revised system of accommodation, saw themselves as bringing the universal benefits of the Enlightenment to a world as yet unenlightened. The British saw themselves as helping inferior people to a somewhat higher standard of living through benevolent yet paternalistic patronage. Both, however, shared a common notion of African inferiority. For most French, this inferiority was cultural, whereas for most British this inferiority was genetic. Both perspectives on Africans were clearly racist.

Settler States

Most of the colonial systems we have examined so far fall under a broad rubric that might be described as "administrative colonies." Here, a relatively small number of European colonial officers, perhaps no more than a few hundred in an entire colony, oversaw the affairs of the administration. Quite in contrast to this situation were those parts of Africa that saw considerable European settlement. In colonies such as Algeria, Kenya, Southern Rhodesia, Angola, Mozambique, and South Africa, large numbers of Europeans came to permanently settle. The political atmosphere of such colonies was radically different from that found in administrative colonies.

Why exactly would large numbers of Europeans move to these parts of Africa? It is important to keep in mind that the late nineteenth and early twentieth centuries were periods of considerable outmigration from Europe, which was already one of the world's most densely populated regions. Immigration, whether to the United States, Argentina, or Kenya, offered the hope of a better life for many settlers. Notably, many of those who decided to move to Africa were seeking a particular commodity that had long been in short supply in Western Europe: land. Because of the exploitative dynamics of colonial rule, it was relatively easy for settlers to demand access to the best land to be found in African colonies. In some cases it was argued that this land was "vacant" in that recent colonial conquest or famine/epidemics had left the land sparsely populated. Such was the case, for example, in Namibia, where rinderpest epidemics had wiped out local cattle populations owned by the Herero. This situation gave colonial authorities the excuse to cede land to

German and Afrikaner settlers. In other cases, it was simply argued that Africans didn't know how to make adequate use of the land, and Europeans would do a better job, which would improve everyone's quality of life in the long run. Thus, Europeans would provide the knowledge and Africans the (cheap) labor to make the land profitable.

In truth, there were relatively few parts of Africa that were seen as desirable by settlers. In most places, the physical and disease environment was unfriendly enough to Europeans to make immigration to such locations undesirable. Further, in much of Africa the unfamiliar soils and climate rendered European-style farming disastrous. Attempts at plow-based intensive agriculture in the savannah or forest region soon produced lovely little plots of desert. A few regions of Africa, however, were suitable to European sensibilities and agriculture. In the Mediterranean climatic zones along the North African coastline and in South Africa, climates were mild, malaria was rare, and the soils were friendly to European-style farming. As such, French settlers flooded into the coastal region of Algeria, claiming the best lands and setting up extensive farms to grow wheat, grapes (for wine), and olives. Northern Algeria and southern France just aren't really all that different, environmentally. In South Africa, Afrikaner farmers found that in addition to raising cattle, the region was well suited to cultivating wheat and corn. As we saw in Chapter 12, the Afrikaners expanded across southern Africa at the expense of a number of African groups who had long inhabited the region. Despite the reality of the long-standing African presence in the region, however, the Afrikaners developed a mythology of the land having been "empty" on their arrival. Similar mythologies were developed by European settlers in the Americas and Australia. On top of Afrikaner agricultural settlement, the mineral revolution that occurred with the discovery of diamonds and gold led to a whole new wave of European immigration into the region. Indeed, as will be discussed in greater detail shortly, South Africa was to become the ultimate "settler colony" in Africa.

Settlers also found fertile ground for their desires along the highlands of the East African Rift Valley. As we saw in Chapter 14, the highlands of Kenya, Uganda, and Southern Rhodesia (now Zimbabwe) were well suited to European habitation and agriculture. The high elevations of these regions, often well over 5,000 feet, mean that the weather is mild and that the mosquitos that carry malaria and yellow fever are not present. Further, unlike the nutrient-poor lateritic soils found in most of Africa, these highlands, by virtue of their volcanic origins, were home to some of the finest soils in the world. Here crops could be sowed repeatedly without any inputs whatsoever. The climate was also perfectly suited for the growing of some of the most valuable cash crops—coffee and tea in particular. Such a combination of factors, combined with the political power afforded Europeans by the imposition of colonial rule, made the displacement of Africans from these lands largely inevitable.

The Portuguese colonies of Angola and Mozambique are somewhat unique in the establishment of settler colonies. In neither case were conditions particularly conducive to European agriculture. Nor was the disease environment particularly welcoming. Rather, given that the economic situation in Portugal was so poor, many Portuguese nonetheless found hope in immigrating to these colonies. Also important is the fact that in 1917 the United States placed restrictions on the ability of "illiterate" immigrants to come there. This new policy largely shut out the great bulk of Portuguese from the United States, and would-be migrants chose the path of least resistance by simply moving to areas under Portuguese colonial rule. Further, rather than being "outsiders" in such colonies, they immediately became part of a ruling colonial elite. Thus, Portugal's relative poverty was a major factor in defining the tone of Portuguese colonialism in Africa.

The presence of tens of thousands (or, in Algeria and South Africa, millions) of Europeans radically changed the dynamics of colonial administration. Settlers, both as citizens of "legitimate" states and simply as "whites," demanded a say in the administration of the areas in which they lived. Thus, administrators in settler regions could not act with the impunity they enjoyed elsewhere. Further, settlers in French and British colonies demanded the right to form their own representative bodies that would advise or even outrank the colonial administrations. Indeed, rather than getting to act as local rulers, colonial officers often found themselves being treated as civil servants. As such, tensions often developed between colonial administrators and settler communities. Notably, settlers often demanded special economic treatment that placed Africans at an even greater disadvantage than elsewhere in colonial Africa. In most colonies administrators sought to encourage or even demand the growing of certain crops for export, and African producers could at least hope to profit from expanding their production and taking advantage of the new economic structures created by colonial rule. In settler colonies, however, African producers were potential competition for the settlers, who demanded and generally received monopoly protections for the production of cash crops. For example, in Kenya it was illegal for African farmers to produce either tea or arabica coffee, the most profitable crops. Rather, the only place for Africans in this new economy was as labor—and often low-paid and seasonal labor at that. By and large, most settler states created landed aristocracies, and such aristocracies tend to be very unfriendly toward the extension of political rights to their laborers. In order to restrict the rights of their African labor supply, such colonies generally passed legal codes that sought to control where Africans could live, what jobs they could hold, and how they could move between the two.

Perhaps the ultimate example of the potential complexities of the settler colony is South Africa. By the late 1800s, the independent Afrikaner republics of the Orange Free State and the Transvaal were struggling with how to control the massive influx of immigrants (mostly British) that were flocking to the region as a result of the diamond and gold booms. By and large, the Afrikaner citizens of these republics lacked the capital to become influential in these mining industries. Kruger, the president of the Transvaal, sought to extract maximum profit from the foreign-owned mining concerns through high rates of taxation. Such efforts were resented by those who ran the mining concerns, in particular by Cecil Rhodes, who was both governor of the Cape Colony and head of the DeBeers mining company, which had come to dominate diamond mining in the region. Further, Rhodes, who had bankrolled the creation of colonies (the Rhodesias) to the northeast, saw the Afrikaner republics as a barrier to his dream of a "Cape-to-Cairo" British Africa.

In 1895, Rhodes organized an invasion of the Transvaal that he hoped would result in a widespread revolt by non-Afrikaners. The raid was a dismal failure and resulted in Rhodes being forced to step down from the governorship. Tensions did not abate between the Boer republics and the British in southern Africa. Convinced that another attempted invasion was imminent, in 1899, Kruger declared war and invaded the Cape Colony and Natal. The resulting **South African War** (often called the Boer War) was remarkable for its brutality.

Although eventually successful in beating the Afrikaner armies in large-scale engagements, the British were unable to control the countryside once the Afrikaner combatants shifted to guerrilla hit-and-run tactics. The Afrikaners would act as civilian noncombatants by day and as raiders by night. As elsewhere in Africa, the British were able to defeat such tactics only by importing large numbers of troops and resorting to scorched earth tactics. To deny local support to the commandos, the British forced civilian populations into concentration camps and laid waste to surrounding farms and towns. Conditions in the camps were truly horrible, and perhaps as many as 10 percent of those interned died of starvation and disease. Such tactics are about the only way to win a guerrilla war, however, and by 1902 the ability of the Afrikaners to carry on the campaign had been broken. The campaign also wrought considerable suffering for the local African populations, who found themselves caught between the contending Afrikaners and British. No doubt tens of thousands died as "collateral damage" from the British scorched earth tactics.

The South African War is in some ways evidence that the conquest of Africa by Europeans was not simply about race. The British were perfectly willing to slaughter Afrikaners to achieve colonial objectives in the region. Interestingly, the Afrikaners saw themselves as having been colonized by the British. Despite their own heritage as colonists and settlers, they felt that they had been illegitimately dispossessed of their land and rights by an invading foreign power. Such is the irony of history. Notably, however, the Afrikaners were better treated by the British than were most defeated African states. Given that British interests in the region were largely in mineral resources, farmland was largely left to the Afrikaners. After the war, Afrikaners' rights were better respected than those of local African populations. The brutality of the war had been no small scandal in Britain, and the new South African administration had little will to continue harsh policies toward the Afrikaners. Rather, the general policy undertaken sought reconciliation, though Afrikaner populations were generally resentful of the British and did all they could to avoid being assimilated by the now dominant British administration and ever-growing English-speaking population. In 1910 the Union of South Africa was formed with Afrikaner and English-speaking communities ostensibly sharing equal rights of citizenship.

If there was anything that the British and Afrikaners could agree on, it was the need to control the new country's vast African majority. Despite considerable immigration from Europe, Africans still represented more than 85 percent of the region's population in the early twentieth century. Further, both Afrikaner agriculture and British mining relied on cheap African labor to ensure profitability. Over the course of the early part of the twentieth century, a number of laws were put into place to guarantee the control of the white minority over the region's African and "Coloured" populations. In 1911 the Mines and Works Act established a "color bar" that limited all administrative and skilled or semiskilled industrial jobs to whites. This law guaranteed that even if Afrikaners had lost political control over mining, they could at least benefit by having a lock on the best-paying jobs in the industry. In 1913, the Native Land Act set aside some 93 percent of South Africa's land for whites—despite the fact that whites represented only about 13 percent of the population. The land area available to native Africans would be expanded to a whopping 13 percent in 1936. These steps guaranteed white control over the ultimate source of wealth, the land itself. In 1920 the Native Affairs Act created Tribal Councils for the black "reserves," which sought to legitimize the reserves by giving African elites some degree of local authority. In effect, however, Africans were being herded into marginal areas so that they would become dependent on migrant labor to the "white country" of South Africa. To help control this movement of labor, the Native (Urban Areas) Act of 1923 established a pass system that was used to determine where "foreign" Africans were allowed to be, when. Only Africans who attained employment with white companies could leave the reserves, and then they could only reside in isolated townships or company barracks during their periods of employment. When their term of employment was finished, they were required to return to the reserves.

Apartheid-era billboard from South Africa.

This system of laws would lay the basis for the policy which would, in the 1950s, come to be known as *apartheid* (separateness). Notably, many view apartheid as a creation of the Afrikaner-dominated Nationalist party. Although this is in part true, it is important to recognize that much of the underpinning ideology of apartheid was closely related to the same notions that legitimized British indirect rule. Just as the British stressed the inability of Africans to understand and adopt Western culture, the system of apartheid was justified on grounds that African culture needed to be protected by "isolating" it from European influence through the creation of the reserves and the minimizing of contact between the "races." Similarly, the reserves were divided up according to the "tribes," allegedly on the grounds that each group's culture should be preserved. The side effect, of course, was that by treating the various African ethnicities as separate nations, they could be discouraged from cooperating in resistance to the government's expanding policy of white supremacy. A parallel system might also be found in the United States, where remaining Native American populations were restricted to ever-shrinking and economically marginal "reservations." The key difference between the experience of native peoples in South Africa, as opposed to the United States, however, is that native South Africans were spared the near eradication experienced by Native Americans. Africans remained a majority in South Africa and in other African settler colonies. As will be discussed in later chapters, this reality would have a profound effect on the future of these states.

World War I and Colonial Rule

As might be expected, World War I had a significant effect on Africa and on the nature of colonialism on the continent.

World War I got its name because it was the first truly global conflict, and it was so largely because Europe's colonial empire was drawn unwillingly into the war. As a new part of this imperial system, Africa was no exception. Hundreds of thousands of Africans were mobilized to serve as combat and support troops for campaigns outside Africa. Tens of thousands served on European battlefields. In Africa, European powers launched campaigns designed to seize one another's territories. German Togo, which suffered the profound strategic disadvantage of being surrounded by British and French colonies, was quickly overrun. German Kamerun, however, was the site of a bloody two-year campaign before it fell to Allied troops. In the south, an invasion from the Union of South Africa in 1915 led to the overthrow of German Southwest Africa. There, with the extermination of the Herero and Nama still very much a part of local memory, African populations cheered the invading South Africans as liberators. East Africa was the scene of the largest and bloodiest campaign of the war in Africa. Here, British troops from West Africa and South African troops converged on German East Africa. In response, troops under the command of the Germans undertook a sweeping invasion of Portuguese and British colonies in the region, attacking through Mozambique, Nyasaland, and Rhodesia in a move to tie down Allied troops and disrupt the region's important mining industries. In the course of the fighting, both sides utilized scorched earth tactics to deny supplies to enemy troops. Caught in the middle were local African populations, tens of thousands of whom likely died as a result of the destruction of food supplies. Ironically, the *Pax Colonial* may have ended conflicts between Africans for African reasons, but it certainly did not prevent Africans from being drawn into even larger and bloodier conflicts waged for European reasons.

The end of the war ushered in a new era of colonial consolidation. The Allied powers now had no real external competition for control of Africa. The period between World War I and World War II is often referred to as the "high tide" of colonialism. However, economic depression in Europe squeezed colonial economies in the 1930s, and World War II, with the renewed threat of European conflict for the continent, would soon appear on the horizon. In the meantime, however, the key political theme would be the increasing African demand for political incorporation in colonial systems and even a changing notion of what it meant to be "African."

Colonialism and African "Elites"

Despite the reality of European domination that characterized colonial rule, African populations were neither meek nor powerless in the face of colonial administrations. Although violent resistance to colonialism proved unsuccessful in the early twentieth century, changing economic and social conditions provided many Africans with the tools they needed to demand political influence in the face of colonial rule. Indeed, thanks to economic, educational, and cultural accomplishments, a growing class of Africans were able to exert pressure for change on colonial administrations from within the new colonial system. These groups are often referred to by scholars as the "African Elite." Some have seen these individuals and the organizations that they founded as "collaborators," in that they often pressed for greater inclusion for Africans within European administrations and greater inclusion by Africans in European society and culture. Other observers, however, see these individuals as the first African "Nationalists" and as the first to truly challenge the European hold on power in Africa in the twentieth century.

It is important to note that these elites were already an important force in African history even before the advent of colonial rule. African traders who had done well in the era of the slave trade and legitimate trade often sought European education and adopted aspects of European culture as a means of enhancing their position vis-à-vis European traders. Many were of Euro-African heritage, which helped them serve as cultural mediators—a familiar theme in the history of long-distance trade. Long present in European coastal enclaves such as St. Louis, Freetown, Accra, Lagos, Luanda, and Cape Town, these Africans were quick to push for recognition and incorporation in new colonial governments. As already discussed, within the British system of indirect rule, preexisting African authorities often found continued influence. The new environments created by colonial rule also provided opportunities for new elites to be created. The expanding cash economy and rapid development of transportation infrastructures allowed some farmers and traders to amass considerable fortunes. The fact that the imposition of colonialism was designed to benefit the colonial powers did not mean that some Africans were not able to exploit the new setting to their advantage.

The new class of elites was quick to take steps to improve their position within the colonial administration and society. In 1897 a group calling itself the **Aboriginal Rights Protection Society** (ARPS) was formed in the Gold Coast. Made up of both local chiefs and Western-educated elites, the ARPS organized to protest a move to declare large tracts of land in the region as "uninhabited." If the proposal had gone through, the lands would have become the property of the colonial government. The ARPS, however, sent a delegation of representatives to London to protest the proposed action and succeeded in having it stopped. During the early twentieth century, other colonies in Africa saw similar groups being organized. The Gremio Africano (African Union) was formed in Angola in 1908. In 1912 the African Native National Congress (later renamed the African National Congress) was formed in South Africa to protest the ongoing marginalization of African rights as the state moved towards a formal policy of white supremacy. In 1914 the ANNC, too, sent a delegation to London to protest the 1913 Land Act. In no small part due to the influence of South Africa's white population, the act went through despite the delegation's efforts. A number of individuals came to prominence as political activists in the early twentieth century. In 1914, **Blaise Diagne** was elected to the French Parliament as a representative from the Communes of Senegal. In Nigeria, Herbert Macaulay founded the Nigerian National Democratic Party. Harry Thuku, of Kenya, founded the Young Kikuyu Association in 1921. Such activists were instrumental in acquiring limited representation for elite Africans in colonial administrations, often through the organization of consultative bodies. Although these assemblies had neither the power to make nor veto legislation, they did establish the critical precedent of making Africans a formal part of colonial governments.

 Voices from African History: **The ANNC Protests the Land Act of 1913**

The signatories of this Appeal have been sent to this country by The South African Native National Congress, an organization for focusing native opinion, and consisting of paramount chiefs, headmen, councillors, educated native leaders, and representatives of the various native tribes and races within the Union of South Africa.

This Congress, gravely disturbed at the menace to native rights under the Natives' Land Act, passed a strong resolution against the Bill. Furthermore the following Religious Conferences of South Africa have passed resolutions against the passing of the Bill: Anglican, Wesleyan, Congregational, Baptist and Presbyterians. But in spite of these resolutions the Bill was hurriedly passed through Parliament.

The Act

The Land Act which the Governor-General of the Union of South Africa signed on June 16th, 1913, declares in its first clause:

"Except with the approval of the Governor-General-

"(a) A Native shall not enter into any agreement or transaction for the purchase, hire, or other acquisition from a person other than a native, of any such land, or of any right thereto, interest therein, or servitude thereover, and "(b) A person other than a native shall not enter into any agreement or transaction for the purchase, hire, or other acquisition from a native of any such land, or of any right thereto, interest therein, or servitude thereover."

It may be said that according to this Sub-Section, Europeans are restricted as well as Natives. But this is a restriction on paper only, as the Natives have no land to sell; besides, no European would think of settling in the scheduled native areas, already crowded, except for trading purposes. Consequently, the provisions of the Act really operate only against the Natives.

The Effect

Out of thousands of cases which might be cited we give a few, indicative of the severe hardships inflicted by the Act.

In the Cape Colony, where we are repeatedly told that the Act is not in force, the Magistrates of East London, King Williams Town and Alice prohibited native tenants from re-ploughing their old hired lands last October, and also ordered them to remove their stock from grazing farms.

About 9 months ago, application was made on behalf of 400 natives by Mr. Wilcox, of the Weenen Division, in Natal, to purchase a farm between two native holdings. The Governor-General's permission was not granted, and the farm has now passed into the hands of a white man, who forthwith demanded annually from the old occupiers of the farm six months' unpaid labour.

At a meeting held at Thaba Nchu, on Sept. 12th, 1913, attended by some thousand natives amongst whom were several evicted tenants seeking such permission of the Governor-General, through Mr. Dower, Secretary for Native Affairs, who addressed them, Mr. Dower said, inter alia: "The Act does not allow for any special cases in the Free State being submitted to the Governor-General under the First Section of the Act, so my best advice to you is to sell your stock and go into service."

Only last mail (June 23rd) we received news of great unrest amongst the Natives in these Districts. In the Districts of Peters, Waschbank, Colworth and Weenen (Natal), 522 families are under notice to leave at the end of this month (June).

These are but typical of the evictions that have been taking place, almost weekly, in the four provinces of the Union, namely, Transvaal, Orange Free State, Natal and the Cape since the Act came into force last June.

We would like to point out that one of the reasons which led to the coming of the present deputation to England, was, if possible, to avert the danger of our people being forced to commit acts of violence.

Objections to the Act

The Native races most strenuously and earnestly object to the provisions of the Act, where they differentiate against them, because

1. They exclude the Native from the free purchase of and dealing in land, a right never challenged hitherto.
2. With regard to Natives on the farms of the White people, they interfere with rights the Natives have exercised for generations. In particular they interfere with the right the Natives have as British Subjects of bargaining with the owners of these farms. In effect this produces a condition of slavery. This is due to a provision which encourages the farmer to exact unpaid service from the native tenants. In the event of eviction the tenant is unable to settle upon any other farm, except as a farm servant, and therefore is forced to accept almost any conditions the farmer likes to impose upon him. This we claim is slavery.
3. In point of fact the avowed object of the new law is that of forcing the Native to labour, by making it the only condition of his living on a White man's farm.
4. Under the new Law also no native may occupy or own any land in the Orange Free State.

The natives of South Africa are loyal subjects of His Majesty the King, but they have no voice in the Legislative Councils of the country in which they live (except to a limited degree in the Cape Province), and their appeal was first made through us to His Majesty's Representatives in South Africa. This having failed to secure redress we then approached the adviser of His Majesty the King in this Country on Colonial affairs (The Rt. Hon. Lewis Harcourt), but without avail. Among the natives of South Africa His Majesty is looked upon as their natural protector, and it is their faith in His Majesty's sense of justice that has impelled them to send us here. We append herewith our memorandum to the Rt. Hon. Lewis Harcourt and a letter from the Anti-Slavery and Aborigines Protection Society, and we are confident that these documents, together with the foregoing statement, establish the reasonableness of our appeal, and the urgent necessity of some public action on the part of the Parliament and people of the United Kingdom.

From the online archives of the African National Congress, South Africa. *http://www.anc.org.za.*

As mentioned previously, some have dismissed these early African political activists as conservatives and collaborators in that they sought to work within colonial structures and to utilize European ideologies rather than seek an immediate end to colonialism or rely on African values and norms. It is important to note, however, that these individuals and groups were very often disliked and feared by the colonial administrators. The Nigerian Herbert Macauley may have used British legal and political principles in his demands for greater incorporation of Africans into British colonial administration, but he also sought restitution for traditional African leaders such as the Eleko of Lagos, who had been denied a pension by the British. Macauley was himself repeatedly jailed by the British for his activities. Elites such as Macauley may well have been "Westernized," but they had not lost their concern for their fellow Africans. Further, their familiarity with Western legal and moral systems meant that they could utilize the very rhetoric of "civilization" against the colonial powers themselves. As any good debater or politician knows, there is no argument more powerful against your opponent than your opponent's own argument.

World War II and the Twilight of Colonial Rule

Although most history texts teach students that World War II started with Germany's invasion of Poland, the expansion of the Fascist powers actually began years earlier in Africa. In 1935, Mussolini's troops invaded Ethiopia. Ethiopia was important to the Italians not only for strategic and economic reasons, but also as a symbol of the rebirth of Italian power under the Fascists. Mussolini, as the founder of Fascism, believed that only obedience to the state could bring countries out of "decadence" and that the proof of a nation's greatness was its ability to conquer and subjugate weaker societies. For the Italian Fascists, the fact that Italy had been soundly defeated by the Ethiopians at the battle of Adwa in 1896 was thus proof of their former weakness. To invade and defeat Ethiopia would prove that the country was reborn. National, as well as racial, pride was at stake for the Italians.

L'ITALIA A.O
HA FINALMENTE
IL SUO IMPERO

Poster celebrating that "Italy Finally Has Its Empire." For Italian fascists such as Mussolini, the successful conquest of parts of Africa was seen as proof that the nation had been redeemed from weakness and had once again proven its martial merits.

Not taking any risks, well over 100,000 troops poured into Ethiopia from Italian Somaliland and Eritrea. Unlike the situation in 1896, the Italians now had a considerable technological advantage due to developments in motor transport and aviation. Further, in utter disregard for international law, the Italians made use of poison gas against the Ethiopian troops. The Ethiopians put up a determined defense, but were ultimately unable to stop the Italian advance. Haile Selassie, the Ethiopian emperor, traveled to the League of Nations in Geneva and in May 1936 made an impassioned plea for aid from this new "government of governments." Although the League condemned the Italian invasion, they were not willing to take any action. The invasion of Ethiopia, however, became an important rallying point for Pan-Africanists and Nationalists. **Jomo Kenyatta** published an editorial entitled "Hands off Abyssinia" in 1935, and **Kwame Nkrumah** (first president of independent Ghana) later remarked that the event was a turning point in his own growing African identity. "Ethiopian Defense Funds" were founded in a number of parts of Africa. Colonized Africans donated money to help keep Ethiopians from suffering a similar fate. The plight of Ethiopia also became a concern for African Americans. Not only did African-American communities donate money to support Ethiopia and organize protests in response to the League of Nations' inaction, but some volunteered to serve with the Ethiopian forces fighting the Italians. John C. Robinson, an African-American pilot nicknamed the "Brown Condor," even became the commander of the fledgling Ethiopian Air Force.

The Allied policy of "appeasement" toward the Italians in Ethiopia and the Germans in Czechoslovakia was ultimately unsuccessful. With Germany's lightning invasions of Poland and France in 1939 and 1940, it seemed that the Allied victory in World War I would soon be overturned and that the old colonial order would be replaced by a new colonial order. Eager to reclaim colonies in Africa, the Germans and their Italian allies turned their attentions south. The Italians launched a campaign in North Africa that sought to seize the Suez Canal and cut off British access to the oil fields of the Middle East and colonies in Asia (where Italy's Axis ally, Japan, was moving against British and American territories). When their campaign faltered, the Germans sent reinforcements, which soon overmatched British forces in the region.

Further, when the French surrendered to the Germans in 1940, a new French government was established in Vichy. Ostensibly independent, this government was in reality a German puppet and had no choice but to follow German whims. France's West African colonies allied themselves with Vichy—further strengthening the hand of the Fascist powers in West and North Africa. Remarkably, in French Equatorial Africa, the governor of Chad, **Felix Eboue,** refused to pledge loyalty to Vichy and declared his support for General Charles de Gaulle's "Free French" government-in-exile. Notably, Eboue was himself a West Indian of African descent. Other governors in the region followed Eboue's brave lead, and Brazzaville in the French Congo actually became the capital for the Free French government. For a short time, the only remaining legitimate French government was in Africa.

The year 1943 is often seen as the time when the tide of war turned against the Axis powers. In Africa the tide had already begun to turn. In 1941, Ethiopian "Patriots" fighting alongside forces from British, Belgian, and French Equitorial Africa defeated the Italians in Ethiopia, and Haile Selassie reclaimed his throne. In 1942 the German advance in North Africa was finally halted in Egypt. An Allied invasion of North Africa then drove the Germans from the region. By May 1943, when General Rommel surrendered in North Africa, the shooting war in Africa was over.

Like World War I before, World War II brought significant changes to Africa. Wartime production soared to meet demands for raw materials and food-stuffs. Many colonies saw substantial development of infrastructure to help facilitate the extraction and transport of critical war materials. Also, hundreds of thousands of African troops saw service and combat not only in Africa, but also in Europe and Asia. Another generation was thus introduced to a wider world and would return home at war's end with very different perspectives than when they left. Demobilized troops are always a powerful political force at the end of a conflict, and this was certainly to be the case in Africa, as will be seen in Chapter 17. Further, the anti-Fascist and pro-democracy propaganda utilized to garner African support for the war was not lost on Africans. If democracy was worth fighting for in Europe, then why not fight for it in Africa, too? A new era of African nationalism was at hand.

Colonial Rule in Africa in Global Perspective

Africa's experience with colonial rule was, in some ways, fairly brief. If you were an African born in 1900, you had a fair shot at outliving colonialism and seeing the move to independence that would come in the postwar era. As a result, it is often argued that it is important not to "privilege" colonialism as having too much of an impact on African history. This perspective argues that African political culture was sturdy enough to survive being displaced by colonialism and was able to reassert itself as colonialism waned.

A different argument sees the political impact of colonialism as quite profound. Africa was colonized as Europe neared the zenith of its global power and influence. If Africa's experience with colonialism was not particularly deep in terms of time, it was nonetheless intense in terms of the degree of power wielded by colonial administrations. Colonialism brought a temporary end to African sovereignty. Most colonial powers replaced African systems of authority and administration with European systems of governance. In others, particularly those under British indirect rule, African structures were subjugated to European authority. In the view of many, the impact of such foreign dominance could not help but be profound.

The twentieth century was a time of monumental change across the globe, and colonialism was a major force in shaping the modern world. As such, the colonial experience is something that Africans share with peoples in Asia, the Middle East, and much of Austronesia. This shared experience with European domination helped create a common sense of identity not only among Africans, but among all "colonized peoples" as well. Colonialism helped create identities that stretched even beyond the borders of Africa. The legacy of colonial rule in influencing African perspectives on the world will be examined in more detail in Chapters 16 and 17.

Useful Works on This Chapter Topic

There is a vast literature on the topic of colonialism in Africa. General studies include Volume VII of the UNESCO General History of Africa, *Africa under Colonial Domination 1880–1935*, edited by A. Adu Boahen (1990); Gregory Maddox (ed.), *The Colonial Epoch in Africa* (1993); and Crawford Young's *The African Colonial State in Comparative Perspective* (1994). Patrick Manning's *Francophone Sub-Saharan Africa: 1880–1985* (1988) offers a quick introduction to French colonial rule. Bruce Fetter's edited volume, *Colonial Rule in Africa: Readings from Primary Resources,* provides some excellent insights into the workings of colonial administrations. A. Adu Boahen's *African Perspectives on Colonialism* (1987) provides a specifically African viewpoint. Rudolf Von Albertini's *European Colonial Rule, 1880–1940: The Impact of the West on India, Southeast Asia, and Africa* (1982) offers a wider comparative context.

CHAPTER 16

African Culture in the Modern World

Culture is a challenging concept. It is the stock-in-trade of cultural anthropologists, but they still fight bitterly about what it is. Indeed, many anthropologists now avoid the term altogether, favoring the adjective "cultural" tagged to a noun like change or habits. Some people use the word "culture" in the sense associated with the nineteenth-century Englishman Matthew Arnold, who used it to distinguish between the mundane aspects of human life, such as getting enough food to stay among the living, and the more refined, artistic side of human life. For Arnold, culture was reserved for a few people, not the mass of humanity. It is this sense of the word that people have in mind when they say that someone is "deeply cultured." By contrast, anthropologists see culture (to generalize grossly) as the sum of human beliefs, habits, and ideas—something that any human has, some parts of which are universally human and others particular to them and the people with whom they share their social world. We will use the term in both senses, looking at modern Africans through the lens of anthropology and at the influence of African scholars and artists. Perhaps the best place to begin is not with Africans but with that exotic and little-understood tribe—the anthropologists.

Africa and Anthropology

A bad joke:

> **Q:** What's the difference between anthropology and sociology?
> **A:** Sociologists study people who wear pants; anthropologists study people who don't.

Although anthropologists have been working hard for the last thirty years to render this rather tasteless joke obsolete, it does capture the intentions of early anthropologists. Anthropology's original charge was the study of the exotic and alien, whereas sociologists studied the habits of familiar people (i.e., their own societies).

The rise of anthropology as a professional discipline more or less parallels the rise of European imperialism. As Europe conquered more of the world, nineteenth-century Europeans became increasingly interested in the lives and habits of the people they encountered. At the same time, they were growing increasingly curious about the structure and nature of their own societies. This curiosity was reflected in the rise of sociology. Sociologists like Weber and Durkhiem set out to explain their own world, though both occasionally thought in comparative terms—contrasting Europe with other parts of the world.

Anthropologists made the collection of this comparative material their main goal. They did their work in an intellectual world that was profoundly influenced by Darwinian thought. Many early anthropologists used a sort of rethought Darwinism that sought to apply evolutionary thought not just to biological change, as Darwin had done, but to social or cultural change. This type of thought has been labeled social Darwinism. The term is now used as a denunciation of views that one disagrees with and wishes to dismiss out of hand. Anthropologists almost universally reject this line of reasoning now, but it was considered perfectly plausible 150 years ago. This system of thought organized societies by their level of cultural development with Europe on top, China next, on down to peoples who were outside of history, living (they assumed) much as people had lived in the Paleolithic. It was the people at the bottom of the heap that intrigued anthropologists. They sought out societies that appeared to be untouched by history as a window on the universal aspects of human nature. For them, Africa and the islands of Oceania were a natural laboratory where they could see into the early days of human societies and record the fundamentals of human culture.

Another force drew anthropologists to Africa. This was the need of colonial governments to understand the people they ruled. This was especially a concern in places where colonial governments sought to rule through indigenous political institutions. If you were going to use native chiefs or kings or whomever to rule for you, you had to know who these people were and what their customary powers were. Anthropologists, accompanied by their tents and notebooks, began to pop up all over the sub-Saharan landscape in the 1920s and 1930s, seeking to explain the natives to the colonial state and primitive man to the scholarly audience back home.

In doing this, anthropology proceeded from some deeply flawed premises. For example, anthropologists studied "tribes," which were defined as a group related by blood, language, and culture. Tribes were bounded entities, which is to say that they had clearly discernable edges. A person who was a member of tribe X could not be confused with a member of tribe Y. If such a confusing person appeared, he or she could be ignored because his or her existence was the result of change introduced by the arrival of Europeans who had brought history to the unchanging world of the tribe. Tribes were timeless; their purpose was to preserve an ancient, unchanging culture. By looking past the historical changes that had already occurred by the time the anthropologists got there, usually by finding older people to interview, one could learn what the original, unchanging Ur culture of the tribe was.

This was, of course, the purest of nonsense. As we have seen earlier, many tribal identities are the products of history, not the result of its absence. The Zulu, the Ndebele, and the BaSotho became tribes precisely because of history; they were not timeless transmitters of an unchanging culture. In fact, even the seemingly most primitive African societies, the foragers of the Kalahari and the equatorial forests, are not immune to history; they live with change and are in contact with the broader world. San hunters make their arrowheads from barbed wire and Pygmy, or (Twa) foragers use crossbows that ultimately derive from China, and both exchange goods with the farmers and herders who are their neighbors. Neither they nor anyone else can serve as an unobstructed window on the life of Paleolithic humans.

These anthropologists reflected the prejudices of their times—as any sort of scholarship does—but they also served to reinforce some of these ideas. Anthropology became one of the most important ways in which Africa and Africans were represented in the West. Anthropology represented Africans as primitive, exotic, and alien. As such, it helped to justify colonialism and the European sense of racial superiority. Perhaps the most shocking example of this came in the 1904 World's Fair in St. Loius, Missouri, when a Pygmy man named Ota Benga was displayed like any other object of scientific inquiry might be put on display. He was later transferred to the Bronx Zoo, where he was displayed in a cage in the primate section on weekends. He eventually ended up at a seminary in Virginia, where he killed himself in 1916.

African intellectuals soon found themselves confronted by this ideology. The Nigerian author **Chinua Achebe** has written that it came as quite a revelation to realize that he was one of the savages he read about in books on Africa. It galvanized him to write books intended to undermine this representation of Africa. His novel, *Things Fall Apart*, was in part a refutation of this primitivist view of African life. Jomo Kenyatta, the man who would ultimately lead Kenya to independence, wrote *Facing Mount Kenya* as a sort of insider ethnography of his own people. Although Kenyatta accepted many of the anthropological principles of his time— he presents the Kikuyu as just as much of a discrete, bounded entity as a European anthropologist would—he used his book to undermine the notion that the Kikuyu were primitives or that their world was savage or irrational.

Kenyatta, Achebe, and many other intellectuals were products of mission schools. Long before the colonial governments built their first schools, missionaries were educating converts and potential converts. It was this group of people who were in the best position to present alternative views of what African culture was like in the anthropological sense of the word and to create a new African high culture in the Arnoldian sense of the word.

Christianity and Colonialism

As you will recall from Chapter 5, European missionaries in the nineteenth century were not the first to introduce Christianity to the African continent. Egypt, Ethiopia, and the Sudan had ancient traditions of monophysite Christianity, and the Portuguese had introduced the Roman Church to Kongo in the fifteenth century. But the nineteenth and twentieth centuries saw a huge expansion of scale and intensity of missionary efforts in sub-Saharan Africa. In most instances, missionaries preceded the flag. That is to say that their work often took them beyond the frontiers of colonial control, and as a result one of the more popular excuses for the extension of colonial boundaries was to protect missionaries who had gotten into trouble or caused trouble. Frederick Lugard was sent to Uganda in part to put a stop to a civil war being fought between the converts of competing Christian missions.

Christian missions took many forms, from David Livingstone's solo journey across East-Central Africa to Albert Schwitzer's hospital at Lambarene to the many more conventional efforts at evangelization. From the beginning, Africans were involved in these efforts. Livingstone's "solo" journey was done in the company of two African converts who continued the journey after his death. The first Anglican Bishop of Nigeria, Samuel Ajayi Crowther, was a Sierra Leonean. If you have read Achebe's *Things Fall Apart,* you will remember that most of the missionaries who came to the village of Umofia were not Europeans, but Africans. So from the start, the missions were catalysts for cultural change, and Africans were often deeply involved in this process of cultural creation.

The missions, especially those run by Protestant sects, placed a high value on the reading of scripture and hence on literacy. Teaching converts to read and write in English or French was considered the core purpose of mission schools. And for those who first learned these esoteric skills, new worlds and new possibilities were

A mission church in colonial Northern Rhodesia.

opened. The mission-educated had privileged access to the colonial state. They could work in its offices, read its laws, write letters of protest, and in general claim more of its attention than people who were less able to meet the state on its own, literate terms. The same mission-educated people often found that their status had changed in their own societies. People of indifferent social status could be propelled to prominence through education. A new elite emerged during the colonial era, characterized by mission education and access to the broader world that came with literacy.

Literacy was put to many different uses. Sometimes these were political and sometimes social or cultural—though of course there are no firm lines between these categories. The literate elite formed social organizations ranging from debate societies to sporting organizations. In some regions these organizations were organized because Africans were barred from taking part in European-only clubs and societies. Self-help and philanthropic unions also provided economic aid to group members and others in need in the absence of any sort of state welfare system. Also very important was the founding of independent African newspapers. A number, including the *Sierra Leone Weekly,* the *Lagos Weekly Record,* and the *Gold Coast Independent,* were established in the later nineteenth century. The twentieth century saw a growing number of African papers. Interestingly, newspapers were particularly common in British colonies, where censorship tended to be less strict. Although social organizations, churches, and newspapers were not necessarily political in focus, they are all important building blocks of what is often called "civil society." In creating such institutions, Africans were developing the tools and skills essential to influencing, competing with, or providing alternatives to colonial administrations.

Among the most important developments of the early twentieth century was a radical shift in the nature of African identity itself. Prior to the colonial era, it is very difficult to speak of an "African identity." Few, if any, of the inhabitants of Africa thought of themselves as a single group that shared common goals, interests, or culture. Identity during the precolonial period was largely based on linguistic and religious identities rather than on continental or racial perspectives. Expanded contacts with other Africans and with the world beyond Africa, however, greatly accelerated in the twentieth century, and like in other parts of the world, this helped lead to the creation of a broader sense of identity—a notion of being African. Participation by hundreds of thousands of Africans in World War I, for example, gave them a much broader experience with other regions of Africa and also with Europe. New transportation systems based on rail, steamships, and motor transport also made it much more possible for Africans to travel long distances—further breaking down geographical divisions between African regions. As we have seen in previous chapters, Africans had long engaged in long-distance trade, but never before had so many Africans covered so much distance so quickly or so frequently.

Perhaps the most notable effect of the increasing contact between the various parts of Africa and the diaspora was the development of a global African identity. Members of the African diaspora in the Americas had long since developed such notions of African identity, and colonialism provided the framework for expanded cooperation between Africans and their counterparts in the diaspora. In 1912,

Booker T. Washington's "International Conference on the Negro" was held at his Tuskegee Institute in Alabama, and it was attended by several delegations from Anglophone Africa, Rwanda, and Mozambique. In 1919, W. E. B. DuBois organized the First Pan-African Congress, which was held in Paris. Subsequent congresses were held in 1921 and 1923 and drew increasingly large attendance from Africa. Drawing on the rhetoric of "self-determination" utilized by the League of Nations, the Pan-African congresses demanded an end to colonialism and independence for Africa. Also very influential was Marcus Garvey's United Negro Improvement Association (UNIA), which advocated the repatriation of all blacks in the Americas to Africa. The UNIA's newspaper, *The Negro World,* was popular reading in many parts of Africa, despite the fact it was universally banned by colonial governments. Copies were nonetheless smuggled in. Black merchant seamen from the West Indies were a major source of this smuggling and in the spread of the UNIA to port cities in Africa. In *Facing Mount Kenya,* Jomo Kenyatta describes how once a copy of *The Negro World* was acquired, people would memorize whole stories so as to spread the news orally to an even wider audience.

Perhaps nothing represents the developing consciousness of African identity better than the concept of **Negritude.** Largely an intellectual and literary movement, Negritude had its origins among Francophone African and Caribbean students living and studying in Paris in the 1930s. Here young scholars such as **Leopold Senghor** (who would later become the first president of Senegal) and Leon Damas began to develop a philosophy of "blackness," which stressed the shared culture of all those of African descent. In contrast to the European ideas of racial and cultural superiority, Negritude celebrated African culture and achievements. Senghor argued that African sensibilities and sensitivities, rooted in emotion, were actually superior to the cold empiricism of Europe's scientifically and technologically driven society. Thus, unlike some new African elites who accepted and utilized the tools of Western political thought, Senghor and the advocates of Negritude actually proposed an alternative construction of what was truly civilized.

Independent Churches

Although the new African elite embraced the orthodox version of Christianity, other Africans found other uses for Christianity. Rather than accepting Christianity as it was taught by Europeans in its entirety, they sought to modify and adapt Christianity to local conditions and concerns. The rise of what are called Independent Churches began shortly after the arrival of the missions. These were created virtually everywhere missionaries went, but they are most prominent in West and southern Africa and least prominent in East Africa.

In West Africa the best-known manifestation of the Independent Churches are the Aladura Churches. These are churches that on some levels represent a reconciliation of Yoruba religious thought and Christian religious thought. One of the founders of the movement was a young Anglican woman named **Abiodun Akinsowon,** who was attending the procession of the Corpus Christi in 1925 and was followed home from the procession by an angel. From the angel she received a revelation. The gist of the message was that God was unhappy about the continuing practice of Yoruba religion and wanted it to stop. She was instructed to create a new religious society called the Cherubim and Seraphim Society (both are types of angels). Initially the society remained affiliated with the Anglican Church—the established church in England. In 1928 the society broke with the Anglicans and became independent. The Aladura Churches offered a form of Christianity that filled many of the spiritual needs that Yoruba religion satisfied but mission Christianity did not. Aladura leaders received frequent revelations from angels that kept their followers informed about their spiritual missteps, just as Yoruba priests used divination to determine whether a person had offended a god or ancestor. Aladura Churches also offered protection from witchcraft, a major preoccupation of Yoruba religion. In contrast to the mission churches, which saw witchcraft as superstition rather than a genuine threat, the Aladura Churches offered the protection of angels whose function was to lead the church against witches. The Aladura Churches also placed a great emphasis on prayer; indeed "Aladura" derives from the Yoruba word for prayer. Estimates of the number of adherents to the Aladura movement in modern Nigeria run as high as 1.1 million.

In South Africa the **Zion Church,** which was initiated by American missionaries from Illinois but quickly took on a life of its own, has grown to the point where its followers number in the hundreds of thousands. The Zion Church has its own scripture, its own prophetic leaders, its own sites of annual pilgrimage, and even its own imitators. An Afrikaner named P. L. Le Roux, who split with the Dutch Reformed Church when he became interested in faith healing and other charismatic aspects of Christian practice, founded the Zionist Apostolic Church. He came under the influence of missionaries from Zion, Illinois; hence the name of the church. Most of his followers were black South Africans, and in 1908 the church came under the leadership of Daniel Nkonyane, the first of a long line of African church leaders. The Zionist Churches stress faith healing, speaking in tongues, and baptism in open water. Their adherents often wear white robes, carry special staffs, and observe certain food taboos. Like the Aladura Churches, the Zionist Churches offer protection from witches and witchcraft, a crucial function of many indigenous religions in southern Africa.

This religion spread out of South Africa into neighboring countries. Migrant mineworkers returning to Rhodesia in the 1950s brought the Zion Church with them. But instead of accepting the hierarchy of the church in South Africa they set themselves up as church leaders and created a body of scripture in Shona. They, too, stress faith healing and have incorporated many of the outward manifestations of Western medicine into their religious ritual. In Rhodesia/Zimbabwe, Zionist faith healers use injections with hypodermic needles as part of their ritual, appropriating modern medical imagery for their own purposes.

Independent churches spread not only within the continent, but have followed African migrant workers wherever they go. There are African Independent Churches all over Europe, most of which are affiliated with churches in Africa. They generally make extensive use of the Internet to attract new followers and to keep geographically dispersed churches in touch with each other. African Independent Churches are found even in Israel. Tel Aviv has forty different independent churches represented, though they keep a low profile. Many of the members of these churches are in Israel illegally, and they also try to keep a low profile.

What the rise of these churches shows is how culturally dynamic the modern world is. Here we have a variety of global influences appearing in Africa: Christianity, colonialism, modern medicine, and international mining companies, and an equally varied response to those influences. For some Africans this encounter made for a degree of assimilation to European culture. Leopold Senghor became a Catholic and a leading French poet and intellectual. For others, this encounter was a stimulus for the creation of equally new cultural practices grounded in local experience. The Aladura Churches and the Zion Church and the dozens of other new religious movements that sprang up during the colonial era were among the many sites where the global met the local.

Islam as a Globalizing Force

Even in predominantly Muslim colonies, the mission-educated played a disproportionate role in public life. Leopold Senghor, who led Senegal to independence, was a Christian in a country where the vast majority was Muslim. For the Senegalese, his ability to meet the French on their own terms, to say nothing of his extremely tolerant religious views, outweighed his embrace of Christianity. Still, for most Muslims, mission education was not a possibility. Islam forbids apostasy, so colonial governments often tried to prevent missionaries from attempting to convert Muslims, fearing the social strife that would result. Thus, much of the West African Savannah was insulated from the types of changes triggered by the arrival of Christian missionaries and their schools.

This did not mean isolation from larger global trends; rather it was the intellectual upheavals going on in the twentieth-century Muslim world that shaped the debates and cultural discourses of the savannah and the Swahili world. This is not to say that either of these regions was previously isolated from the rest of the Muslim world or that the Westernizing influences of colonialism were not a factor here; it is only to point out that the ease of movement and the proliferation of communication technology in the twentieth century has created much more direct and intimate connections between the various parts of the Islamic world than ever existed before. Thus, just as Christianity became a point of contact between the global and the local, Islam also has its global forms and local forms. The tension between these two forms of Islam became much more pronounced in the twentieth century, as communication between sub-Saharan Africans and other Muslims became easier.

West Africa's encounter with twentieth-century Islamic orthodoxy is intriguing. At some levels of society, Muslims have been anxious to embrace the reformist branch of Islam espoused by Wahabis and Salafis, among others. Perhaps the critical source of contact with these ideas has been the hajj—the Muslim pilgrimage to Mecca. The hajj has brought Muslims from West Africa—and to a lesser extent East Africa—to the Islamic heartland in ever-increasing numbers in the last century. When the British and French first took over in West Africa, they intentionally limited the numbers of people allowed to go on the hajj. They did so because they feared that West African hajjis would pick up dangerous ideas in Mecca, so they especially worried about the Muslim political elite participating in the pilgrimage. After the Second World War, the colonial powers began to relent and opened up the hajj to more people. They even used it as a reward for the Muslims who had served in the Allied military forces during the war.

Perhaps the leading voice for Islamic orthodoxy in colonial Nigeria was Amadu Bello, who was a prominent politician and the Sardauna (head of the Emir's bodyguard) of Sokoto—the former capital of the Sokoto Caliphate. Bello was involved in the politics of decolonization and sought to strengthen his hand by forging ties with Islamic nations outside Africa—especially Saudi Arabia. The Saudi government championed *izlah*—the modern reformist vision of Islam that sought to purge Islam of those elements that entered the religion after the Prophet's death. Thus, they opposed Sufism, the veneration of Sufi saints, and any sort of spirit possession cult. Bello made his first hajj in 1955 and many others after that. In 1956 he appointed a young scholar named Abubakr Gumi as his representative in Jeddah with a charge to look after Nigerian pilgrims. Soon Gumi began to report that the behavior of Nigerian hajjis was becoming a source of embarrassment. This was not because they were carrying on in an immoral fashion, but rather that they did not know how to carry out the rituals of the hajj in the usual way. Gumi arranged for a sort of selection process to ensure that persons going on the hajj would have at least a rudimentary knowledge of orthodox Islamic practice. The state also began to crack down on certain Sufi orders, forbidding their adherents from participating in the hajj.

In this instance, increasing contact with the Islamic heartland caused an increasing interest in Islamic orthodoxy. Muslim elites embraced the global form of the religion and tried to educate and coerce others to follow their lead. But that was not the whole story. Just as the rise of the African Independent Churches was partly a response to European control of the mainstream churches, some Muslims in West Africa seem to have reacted against the efforts to universalize Islamic practice there.

Indeed, the inroads made by global, reformist Islam in West Africa seem to have also strengthened the local practices deemed un-Islamic by the reformers. Specifically, the practice of **Bori**—a spirit possession cult—has shown no signs of fading in importance, and its practitioners have put the hajj to their own uses. Bori practitioners heal people who are vexed by spirits—people whose illnesses do not respond to modern medical treatment. They also help women unable to conceive children, unmarried women seeking marriage, and people seeking wealth. Some Bori practitioners also put on public performances where they are possessed by spirits and then perform extraordinary feats.

Bori enjoys an uneasy coexistence with orthodox Islam in the Hausa regions of northern Nigeria and southern Niger. Regularly denounced as contrary to Islam, Bori refuses to go away. Bori seems to answer some powerful need both for those who practice it and for those who seek the services of the practitioners. Practitioners are often people who have survived a bout of illness caused by spirit possession. They are disproportionately female. Homosexual or effeminate men are also frequently involved in Bori. For these two groups, whose role in mainstream public life is limited, Bori offers a realm of both social and economic endeavor. Female Bori practitioners are often wealthy and independent of their husbands in ways that few other Hausa women are. For people seeking the services of Bori practitioners, their ability to deal with or at least try to deal with critical social and medical problems keeps them in demand. Nigeria's economic woes seem to have increased both the demand for Bori services and the numbers of practitioners.

The historian Susan O'Brien has argued that the hajj plays a critical role in the lives of many Bori practitioners. For Bori practitioners, the hajj presents all kinds of opportunity. Bori practitioners see themselves as Muslims, even if some Muslims see their practices as un-Islamic. So for them the hajj fulfills the same religious duties as it does for other Muslims. It also confers a number of additional benefits on them. First, having gone on the hajj confers religious prestige on the pilgrim. So despite the suspicion with which Islamic reformers view Bori, practitioners who can call themselves hajji or hajjia can claim solid Muslim credentials. Second, there is money to be made from bringing trade goods back from Saudi Arabia. Pilgrims often return with radios, TVs, clothes, and other consumer goods that they can either sell back home or, in the case of Bori practitioners, distribute to their followers and apprentices, thereby strengthening their social ties to their followers. This aspect of the hajj is perhaps most important to women. For men who have the resources, traveling for commercial reasons is common. For unaccompanied women, there are few opportunities to travel abroad for any purpose. The hajj, which is a duty for all Muslims male or female, is the exception. Third, and perhaps most intriguing, there is a market for Bori services in Saudi Arabia. Bori practitioners often overstay their visas and remain in Saudi Arabia after their pilgrimages to provide surreptitious Bori services to wealthy Saudis. This is exactly the opposite of the effect the hajj is supposed to have. The hajj is usually thought to help increase the orthodoxy of the Islamic periphery by bringing it in contact with the Islamic heartland. Instead, O'Brien argues, the hajj seems to be reinforcing the status of Bori practitioners in Nigeria and spreading Bori to Saudi Arabia. Thus, the increased contact between Nigerian Muslims and Middle Eastern Muslims is not causing a homogenization of Muslim practice. Instead, it has led if anything to greater diversity both in Nigeria and in Saudi Arabia. It also shows that Africans are not passive recipients of global culture. They are just as involved in changing other people's worlds as they are in absorbing and modifying what they get from the rest of the world.

Migrants and Mobility

Perhaps the biggest change that has occurred in nineteenth- and twentieth-century Africa is the dramatic increase in mobility within and without the continent. Of course, Africans moved around before the nineteenth and twentieth centuries—witness the 11 million people who involuntarily crossed the Atlantic and the many others who were displaced within the continent because of the slave trade. But the nineteenth and twentieth centuries opened up new possibilities. Now there are Indian communities in East Africa, Lebanese and Syrian communities in West Africa, and growing African communities in North America, Europe, and even

Japan. Within the continent there are migrant laborers who come to the cocoa plantations of Ivory Coast from Ivory Coast's poorer neighbors. There are Hausa trading communities in Senegal and other places far from the Hausa homeland. There are Swahili communities in parts of Central Africa, and the Swahili language, once spoken exclusively on the East African coast, is now a lingua franca employed in Tanzania, Kenya, Rwanda, Burundi, Uganda, and parts of the Democratic Republic of Congo. There are now Somali communities all over East Africa and the world. There is even a relatively coherent—they have a list serve and Web site—community of East African Asians who now live in Europe, North America, and Australia.

Of course, diaspora, exile, and migration are nothing new. But what is new about these communities is that since the 1960s they have often been able to maintain connections with the places they have left. They have their feet in two worlds—their place of residence and their former homes. Let us look at some examples.

The Lebanese have been coming to West Africa since the early twentieth century. For a variety of reasons having to do with the presence of a religious group called the Maronite Christians in Lebanon and the protection extended to them by the French in the nineteenth century, France and Lebanon have had a long-standing and close relationship. Would-be Lebanese migrants to the Americas often found themselves in the French port of Marseilles unable to afford the fare to the New World, but with just enough money to make it to French West Africa. Thus, there was a sizable movement of Lebanese migrants into West Africa, where they engaged in retail trade, manufacturing, and the buying of cash crops. The Lebanese proved so successful at this that they often drove out the so-called *petits blancs* (little whites)—the French settlers of modest means who also tried to occupy this part of the colonial economy.

These early settlers kept a sort of fleeting contact with their homes in Lebanon. But slow mails and the vast distances involved hindered regular communication. As a result, they often married African women and had stronger ties with their fellow Lebanese in West Africa than with their fellow Lebanese in Lebanon. Since the 1960s, changes in transportation and communication technologies have created a new type of community that exists simultaneously in West Africa and Lebanon. Cheap airfares, e-mail, videos, cassette tapes, and satellite television all allow the Lebanese to have a social world that easily spans the thousands of miles that separate Abidjian, the commercial capital of Ivory Coast, and their "homes" in Lebanon.

Lebanese who live in West Africa are still considered members of their home village in Lebanon. Despite having rarely or even never visited, most consider "home" to be not just Lebanon but a particular village in Lebanon. Some who have never been there before go there to get married or to find a spouse. For those who do not make the journey, weddings in both places are videotaped and sent to relatives at the other end. Funerals likewise are videotaped and shared. During Lebanon's civil war (1975–1990) and the 1982 Israeli incursion into Lebanon, videotape allowed Lebanese in West Africa to see what was happening in their other homes, and more recently satellite television means that they often watch the same television news as their relatives in Lebanon. In fact, sometimes people in West Africa find out what is going on at home before their relatives there do. For those

Lebanese villages with a history of migration, even people who never leave have strong connections to West Africa. Their houses are often decorated with West African art and cloth brought as gifts by visiting migrants. Their villages are full of houses built by residents of West Africa who often use them only a few weeks each year. They attend memorial services for people who, though members of the village, have lived and died in West Africa. Modern technology allows Africa to exist in Lebanon and Lebanon in Africa.

In East Africa, the social and economic niche occupied by the Lebanese in West Africa is occupied by Indians, or Asians as they are often called. Their migration to East Africa predates the rise of European empires in East Africa and mostly stopped by the 1920s. Indians came to East Africa in the nineteenth century as merchants. In the early twentieth century many Indian contract laborers came to work on the railways, and some remained in East Africa. Economic migrants continued to trickle in as late as the 1930s, but by the Second World War the migration was over. Asians in East Africa do everything from car repair to teaching in universities to construction to retail trade. Unlike the Lebanese in West Africa, they have few and often no ties to their former homes. All are citizens of the countries in which they live, and few could tell you, except in vague generalities, what part of India their ancestors came from. In part because caste rules often require Hindu Indians to only marry within their castes, they have remained a discrete group (groups, really).

Since the 1960s, when most East African colonies became independent nations, Asians have been more welcome in some places than others. In Tanzania, their lot has been fairly good. There are several Asians who have occupied prominent places in government. In the early days of independence, when most forms of private enterprise were considered suspect, Asians involved in commerce came under a cloud, but since then Asians in Tanzania have generally done well. In Kenya and Uganda things have been more difficult. In the 1970s, Idi Amin expelled all Asians from Uganda. Most went to Britain or North America. This expulsion is the subject of the movie *Mississippi Masala,* which looks at the family of an Asian lawyer who is expelled from Uganda and ends up running a motel in Mississippi.

This created a sort of diaspora within a diaspora. East African Asians living in the West have created a community that has connections that stretch across the globe, linking Australia, Canada, the United Kingdom, and the United States to Kenya, Uganda, and Tanzania. Whereas in East Africa Asians are divided into many communities defined by religion and caste, in the secondary diaspora in the West their common connection to East Africa overrides religious and communal differences. The postcolonial situation has created East African Asians who now see themselves as defined by their African origins. In East Africa it is their position as "non-Africans" that defines Asians. In the West it is their African-ness that defines them, making them different from immigrants who come directly from South Asia. So just as imperialism helped to create a common African identity for indigenous Africans, imperialism's aftermath has had a similar effect on some parts of the East African Asian community.

Other African communities have also been affected by the new levels of global mobility. Many of the poorer nations of West Africa send migrant workers to the

Indian contract workers on a sugar plantation in Natal, South Africa.

more prosperous nations of the region. Cocoa farmers in Ivory Coast rely on workers from Burkina Faso. These workers are often recruited by specialist labor
recruiters who arrange for them to get their papers and find employers for them.
The recruiters then take a cut of their wages or get a lump-sum payment from the
employer. Although on some level these migrants come voluntarily, there are some
aspects of this system that are eerily reminiscent of slavery. Workers are often at the
mercy of their employers, who can easily arrange to have them deported, and it is
difficult for the migrants to force their employers to pay them the amount they are
promised at the beginning of their employment. The presence of large numbers of
labor migrants has caused tensions in Ivory Coast. When the economy was booming, no one much cared about them. As the cocoa industry went into decline in the
1990s, their presence became a much more contentious issue. In 2003 there was a
civil war in the Ivory Coast. Government troops fought army mutineers, who were
demanding, among other things, that there be new elections and that immigrants
be given a larger voice in the political process. There was mob violence directed at
immigrants, and the Ivorian government maintained that Burkina Faso—the country from which many of the immigrants come—provided material support to the
rebels. Since then, an uneasy truce has been achieved, but there are still tensions
between immigrants and those who see themselves as natives. So, just as the forces
of globalization have strengthened local elements of religious practice in Northern
Nigeria, they also seem to be strengthening localism, nationalism, and even xeno-
phobia in the Ivory Coast.

Other Africans have migrated out of the continent in search of economic opportunity. The suburbs of Paris are crowded with immigrants from former French colonies, who do jobs ranging from driving taxis to working in restaurants to being musicians. Paris is also home to most of the stars of the Congolese music industry. Soucous, a style of music that derives from the Congo, is popular throughout East and Central Africa, but most of the big stars live, record, and shoot their videos in Paris. What is interesting about these migrants is the extent to which they are able to stay in touch with their homes in West and Central Africa and their mobility in general. Many are men who return to their homes, whether cities or villages, on a regular basis. They repatriate part of their incomes, usually supporting relatives at home. Like the Lebanese, they remain part of the community at home while spending most of their time away. Also like the Lebanese, many of these migrants remain intimately connected to their former homes by modern technology. When being courted by a migrant worker, women often expect to be given cell phones and phone cards so that they can call their suitors while they are in Europe. Indeed, phone cards have become an expected part of bridewealth payments (payment the groom's family makes to the bride's) in some parts of West Africa.

The African migrants in Paris and London are mostly unskilled workers. In the United States, the situation is rather different. African immigrants in the United States have the highest level of educational attainment of any ethnic group recognized by the census. They also hold more Ph.D.'s per capita than any other group of people in the United States. African immigrants to the United States, although sometimes poor and unskilled, more often represent the educated elite of their home countries. Physicians, university professors, software engineers, and so on all find that they can make so much more money in the United States than they can at home, that the move is almost irresistible. By way of example, in the early 1990s professors at the University of Dar es Salaam in Tanzania were often making less than $300 a month. To be sure, that would go farther in Tanzania than it would in the United States, but the pay increase from coming to the West is significant. This trend is sometimes described as a brain drain. It takes the most talented and educated people out of countries where their skills are often desperately needed. It also shows the extent to which globalization is not just about the West affecting the poorer regions of the world. Globalization also means that Americans may take a computer science class from a Liberian or be treated by a Ghanaian in the emergency room.

Soccer on the Global Stage

The colonial era brought many things to Africa, but soccer balls and electric guitars have to number among the most important. The British in particular have always believed in the edifying qualities of sport. Wherever the British went, they built golf courses, tennis courts, polo grounds, cricket pitches, and soccer fields. The French did likewise, though without the obsessiveness of the British. Most of these sports required too much expensive equipment for the majority of Africans to be able to participate, and many, such as tennis, golf, and polo, were played entirely at clubs that barred nonwhites. In East Africa some Asians took up cricket and field hockey (a men's sport outside the United States). In Nigeria and the Sudan wealthy army officers and other members of the elite play polo. Bicycle racing is popular in Burkina Faso. But far and away the most popular sport on the continent is soccer. All that is needed are a ball and a bit of flat ground, and you are in business. And the ball need not be a regulation ball. Soccer games are played with tennis balls, cans, and even balls made of banana tree fiber held together with twine.

Soccer teams and clubs helped to promote social cohesiveness in colonial cities. Often men coming to the cities from disparate rural backgrounds found a sort of social anchor in the soccer clubs they joined or supported as fans. Sometimes soccer allowed people at the bottom of the social hierarchy to challenge people above them. In Zanzibar some soccer teams were associated with the elite neighborhoods in the Stone Town and others with the poorer area called N'gambo. When a N'gambo team played a Stone Town team the latter's claims to superiority were often undermined when they were defeated by their social inferiors. The same dynamic was present when local teams played against French or British teams. The "superiority" of the colonial power was challenged when they were beaten, literally, at their own game.

As independence approached, soccer became the medium through which political rivalries between African politicians were expressed. In Kenya, there were teams associated with Jomo Kenyatta and his KANU party and other teams associated

Soccer began its reign as Africa's favorite sport during the colonial era.

with his rival, Tom Mboya. In contemporary Zanzibar at least one wealthy business-man with political ambitions launched his political career by buying and promoting a soccer team. Winnie Mandela, ex-wife of former South African president Nelson Mandela, had a soccer club that served her as bodyguards and enforcers. The abuses committed by this club while in her service contributed to Nelson Mandela's decision to distance himself personally and politically from his wife.

In recent years African national teams have done well in international competition. In 2002 the Senegalese beat their former colonial rulers, the French, in the world cup. One of the authors of this book (Reynolds) was in Dakar, the capital of Senegal, when the winning goal went in. He reports a citywide collective yell of shocking volume. In the 2006 World Cup, Ghana dominated the United States. For a continent that seems lately to have had little to boast about, successes like these are cherished. African soccer players are also found on the professional teams in Europe. Until his retirement in 2006, France's greatest player was a Franco-Algerian named Zinedine Zidane. So national pride and for that matter regional and continental pride often find an outlet in soccer.

 Voices from African History: **Siti binti Saad—The Voice of Taarab**

"Taarab was originally performed in the palace of Seyyid Bargash, who ruled Zanzibar from 1870 to 1888. As a young man Bargash had traveled widely in the western Indian Ocean and had lived at various times in India and Arabia. One of the ways that rulers in this region demonstrated their authority to their subjects was through the patronage of the arts, especially music. Elaborate musical performances were central to the life of royal courts. When Bargash returned to Zanzibar as sultan, he initiated performances in his palace that were modeled on the musical performances he had seen during his travels. These performances used instruments drawn from around the western Indian Ocean rim, including the zither, the udh (a sort of Arab lute), tambourine, flute, drums, and the violin. The lyrics at these proto-Taarab performances were sung in Arabic.

Only a small number of elite Zanzibaris understood Arabic, which indicates who the intended audience for these performances was. In fact, Bargash punished people who lurked around the palace trying to hear music that was not intended for the ears of the common people. Originally, Taarab was a musical form intended to amuse the elite and to help define the boundaries between the rulers and the ruled.

In 1890 what had once been fairly clear-cut boundaries between rulers and ruled were confused by the British declaring a protectorate in Zanzibar, at least partly undermining the authority of the Omani elite. The situation was further clouded by the abolition of slavery in 1897. These twin political and social upheavals triggered an upheaval in the world of culture. The emergence of Taarab as a popular musical form, and one that often voiced the concerns of common people, was part of that upheaval. At the forefront of this transformation was Siti binti Saad.

Siti binti Saad was born a slave; indeed her name was originally Mtumwa, which means 'slave.' When she arrived in Zanzibar Town shortly after the First World War she made her living as a potter. By this time, Taarab was no longer performed solely in the palace. Several Taarab bands played publicly and a number of dance associations had incorporated elements of Taarab into their performances. Siti binti Saad, once she began her musical career, brought to this a voice of rare beauty. But she also broke with Taarab tradition and sang in Swahili as well as Arabic. The use of Swahili lyrics opened the style to a wider audience, but also meant that her band could write songs that dealt with local issues.

A good example of such a song is 'Wala Hapana Hasara' (There is no loss). It was written after a local man, who worked for the colonial government and was seen by poor Zanzibaris as particularly corrupt, was convicted of embezzlement and sentenced to hard labor. The song calls on the powerful not to steal from the poor and especially not to abuse their literacy:

> You men should stop oppressing and stealing from the poor,
> Especially those who are said to be the stupidest of the stupid.
> Forever their pen is ink upon the thumb,
> Ink upon the thumb . . .[1]

This particular song became very popular, both because of its message and because of its catchy tune. Songs like these served to warn the powerful about their excesses and gave voice to popular discontent.

What is interesting about Siti binti Saad is that even though her songs were often critical of the elite—albeit usually in discreet ways—she and her music were as popular with the elite as they were with the urban poor. No society wedding was complete without an appearance from her band. In fact, the man who is the subject of Wala Hapana Hasara had used his authority in the government to force her band to appear at his daughter's wedding not long before his downfall.

Not only did Siti binti Saad ride the popularity of Taarab out of slavery and into the home and weddings of Zanzibar's elite; she gave shape to a musical form that spread out of East Africa and into the Persian Gulf. In her time, she made several trips abroad, usually to recording studios. Since the 1970s Taarab bands have been traveling extensively in the Gulf, enjoying the patronage of the new elites of the western Indian Ocean world. Taarab has returned to its Arab roots, but now with a strong Swahili inflection."

[1]Song lyrics from Laura Fair, *Pastimes and Politics* (Athens, OH: Ohio University Press, 2001), 191. This book also served as the main source for this sidebar. The other major work on Taarab is Kelly Askew, *Performing the Nation* (Chicago: University of Chicago Press, 2002).

Movies and Music

African popular music is beginning to make an impression on the American side of the Atlantic, but it is popular in Europe, and a few styles of African music are increasingly becoming popular throughout the continent. The birth of some of the better-known strains of African music is intimately connected to the history of the Atlantic world. You will remember from Chapter 8 that the Atlantic slave trade created a huge flow of ideas and culture across the Atlantic. Some of those ideas were musical ideas that came from various parts of Africa to the New World, where they contributed to the creation of new musical forms like jazz and the blues. In Cuba, the encounter between West African rhythms and Iberian instruments yielded "rumba." The Atlantic was not and is not a one-way street, and by the 1930s Cuban rumba recordings were being sold in West and Central Africa.

The encounter between rumba and local musical traditions seems to have been a fruitful one. Two of the most long-lasting and popular musical styles to appear in twentieth-century Africa resulted from the combination of rumba with local musical ideas. In Ghana, a style called *highlife* dated from this encounter, and in the Congo, the birth of *soukous* dates from the period. Soukous, more than any other African music, has transcended local and national tastes and is popular throughout the continent and in Europe. You can hear soukous in Paris, in Kinshasa, or in Nairobi. There are soukous "cover bands" that play in the style of the big Congolese bands even in provincial East African cities.

The first recording studio in Kinshasa opened in 1948, when a Greek merchant saw an opportunity to record local bands. Soon there were dozens of studios, and soukous was on its way to becoming a national music for the Congolese. When a delegation went to Brussels in 1960 to demand the Belgians grant Congo independence, the nation's most popular soukous band went along with them. After independence, the major soukous stars moved to Paris, which is now the center of soukous recording and distribution. Since the end of the Mobutu regime in the Democratic Republic of the Congo, some soukous bands have moved back, but for most the attractions of Paris are hard to overcome. Ongoing unrest and the general danger associated with being known to be rich have deterred most soukous stars from returning to Kinshasa. Thus, soukous is on its way to becoming the premier African international music, but it is doing so from a base of operations in Paris.

It is, of course, hard to describe what music sounds like, but soukous is dance music played by bands that feature multiple electric guitars. The guitars play an intricate, repetitive, fugue-like melody with subtle variations in the repetitions. There are usually lyrics, and these are usually sung in Lingala, which is the Congo's lingua franca.

A different sort of musical synthesis created one of East Africa's more popular musical forms—**Taarab.** Taarab was born out of an Indian Ocean synthesis rather than an Atlantic one, such as soukous. Taarab originated on the island of Zanzibar. There, in the late nineteenth century, bands that performed music that combined the styles of various western Indian Ocean regions with Arab instruments entertained the sultan's court. In the 1920s a new twist was added to this by a Zanzibari woman of slave origin named **Siti binti Saad,** who formed a band. Her innovation was to sing in Swahili rather than Arabic and to perform for nonelite audiences. Her music addressed issues of concern to women and to those Zanzibaris who were at the bottom of the new post-slavery social hierarchy. Eventually, the elite also became interested in her music, and she performed for the sultan. Siti binti Saad created the modern popular form of Taarab, which is still popular in coastal East Africa.

Like soukous, Taarab also has an international audience. The connections between the East African coast and the Persian Gulf are sufficiently strong that there is a major audience for Taarab in the Gulf. It is not uncommon for the more popular Taarab bands to spend most of their year in the Gulf, where they can earn more. Now much of the recording is done on the Gulf also. So a musical style that has its origins in Arab music, but went through an indigenizing process in East Africa, is now popular with Gulf Arabs. Like soukous, it is an African cultural export.

In an example of cultural "round-tripping" a West African drummer wears a tee shirt featuring Elvis, a white American musician famous for his embrace of African-American musical styles.

African filmmakers have been active since the 1970s, but until recently most of their work was made with Western art film audiences in mind. With a few exceptions, like the Camerounian comedy *Pous-pous,* few of them attracted much in the way of an African popular audience. The average moviegoer was more likey to prefer either American action films or Bollywood dramas with the ocasional Kung Fu movie thrown in for variety. The reason for these preferences has to do with language. Even in countries where the national language is French or English, many people have limited commands of these languages. In places like Tanzania where Swahili is the national language, or in Portuguese-speaking countries, the average person can only follow a bit of the dialogue in an English movie. As a result people prefer movies that they can enjoy without understanding the dialogue. Bollywood movies, which are mostly in Hindi but cater to the multilingual audiences of the subcontinent, are done in ways that allow an audience that does not understand Hindi to still follow the plot and enjoy the movie. The bad guys look like bad guys, the good guys look like good guys, the actors over-act so that it's easy to guess what they are saying. As a bonus the movies are long and also feature lots of song and dance. Hollywood action movies and Kung Fu movies are likewise fun even for an audience that does not speak a word of English or Cantonese. Sylvester Stalone's grunting in the Rambo movies is as meaningful/less to non-English speakers as it is to English speakers.

The dominance of these genres has been challenged by the rise of a movie industry in Nigeria that caters specifically to Nigerian audiences, but has proven popular outside of Nigeria as well. The industry was born in 1992, when a Nigerian business man was stuck with a surplus of videocassettes, and decided to make a movie and sell the videos with a pre-recorded movie. This first movie, called *Living in Bondage,* was a huge success. Its success demonstrated the huge demand for movies that actually dealt with African themes and issues, and local entrepreneurs quickly jumped on the bandwagon. The Nigerian film industry, refered to as Nollywood, now cranks out roughly 2,000 titles a year and is the the nation's biggest employer after agriculture. Nollywood films are released directly to video or DVD and are usually very low budget. Nonetheless they have proven sufficently popular outside of Nigeria that there is a cable channel in South Africa that shows nothing else. Nigerians in the diaspora also enjoy Nollywood movies and they are available in the United States. There is an online merchant based in Atlanta called the Nigeria Store that offers a number of titles, including a selection of Nigerian porn. Not all Nigerians are happy about the rise of Nollywood. Some members of the Nigerian government are troubled by the routine use of magic and witchcraft in the plots of Nollywood movies. The Nigerian public, and presumably the non-Nigerian audience for Nollywood too, seem to enjoy these plots. The huge demand for these films has made Nollywood the world's biggest film industry in terms of titles produced each year.

Modern African Culture in Global Perspective

Just as the African continent has had its economy and politics reshaped by its encounter with colonialism and the global economy in the twentieth century, its cultures have also experienced a transformative encounter in the last century. Africans have been exposed to new forms of and approaches to religion, new types of education, new sports, and new musical ideas. These encounters have rarely led to passive borrowing. Instead, Africans have usually adapted these cultural novelties to local conditions and concerns. In so doing, they have often created new cultural forms that are in turn used as a sort of global cultural currency. African musicians, athletes, professors, Bori practitioners, and others all find that there are Africans outside the continent, and non-Africans too, interested in what they do.

The Africa of the late twentieth century has also become more intensely connected to the world than it has ever been before. Migrants who come to the continent or leave it for other places live their lives closely linked to several localities. Television, although not universally available, is surprisingly universal in its offerings when it is available. International satellite programming is usually more popular than local-produced television. Thus, there is a great deal of exposure to just a few news sources. Airplanes, e-mail, mail, telephone, and other means of communication mean that migrants are better connected than ever before.

Of the three forms of encounter we have discussed in this and the preceding two chapters—economic, political, and cultural—perhaps the cultural exchange has been the most equal of the group. To be sure, soukous stars live in Paris, and no French musicians have moved to Kinshasa. But the move to Paris has brought soukous to a bigger and broader audience. Soukous now reaches the French, and non-Congolese Africans, while keeping its traditional Congolese audience. African culture is reaching a world audience in a way that Africans have failed to match on the economic and political fronts.

Useful Works on This Chapter Topic

Two prominent Nigerian writiers have weighed in on the topic of African culture and the world: Chinua Achebe, *Home and Exile* (2000), and Wole Soyinka, Myth, *Literature, and the African World* (1976). For a truly intriguing and unconventional account of African religious practice outside of the continent, see Susan O'Brien, "Pilgrimage, Power, and Identity: The Role of the Hajj in the Lives of Nigerian Hausa Bori Adepts," *Africa Today* 40, no. 3 3(2000). For a look at the life of one the continent's great intellectuals, try Janet Vaillant, *Black, French, and African: A Life of Leopold Senghor* (1990). For many of the topics in this chapter, the best source of information is the Internet. Many of the Independent Churches have strong Web presences, and African music and soccer are well represented on the Web too.

CHAPTER 17

Politics in the Era of Decolonization and Independence

The end of the Second World War heralded a new era of global politics. Exhausted from more than half a decade of total war, European economies were in a shambles. Britain emerged victorious, but the cost to the country had been devastating. The war had necessitated a total effort to produce military weapons and supplies, and it would take years to retool factories to produce consumer goods. On the European mainland, transportation infrastructure, industrial complexes, and even whole cities lay in ruin. Also, European powers had to take a cold, hard look at the policies and ideologies that had led them to such destruction. Western Europe, after centuries of looking outward with an ever-growing sense of superiority, was forced to take a self-critical look inward. At the same time that Western Europe sought to rebuild, two new powers were on the rise. In the West, the capitalist United States emerged from the war largely undamaged and with an industrial and military capacity unmatched elsewhere in the world. In the East, the communist Soviet Union had survived a near catastrophic German invasion and had rallied not only to help defeat the Germans, but also to spread its own dominance over much of Eastern Europe. These two global powers were soon embroiled in an ideological and physical struggle for influence that became known as the Cold War. Although many American history textbooks identify the Cold War as an ideological conflict fought with words and ideas, this global contest often took on a much more deadly aspect in other parts of the world—including several parts of Africa.

Equally significant, the end of World War II signaled the advent of an era of "liberation movements" that would continue for the balance of the twentieth century. Indeed, the war to liberate Europe from Fascism helped embolden and strengthen movements to end colonial and racial domination elsewhere in the world. In less than two decades, much of Africa and Asia had been "decolonized," and dozens of new countries, sometimes referred to as the "Third World" or "Developing World," took their place in a new global community of sovereign nations. In most cases, this process of liberation was relatively peaceful; in others, freedom only came after armed struggle. After the achievement of independence, however, the leaders and citizens of new African states found themselves faced by a whole new set of challenges.

On the global level, the brutal politics of the Cold War meant that African states were faced with ideological minefields, which, all too often, became real as the conflict between the capitalist West and communist East was extended to Africa. Internally, the new states struggled to develop political systems that could bring development and build unity among diverse populations bound together by borders that were largely colonial creations. As a result of all these factors, the history of Africa probably represents the triumphs and tragedies of the tumultuous political history of the latter twentieth century better than any other part of the world.

The Era of Decolonization

At the close of World War II, the European colonial powers seemed to need their colonies more than ever before. With Britain, France, Italy, and Belgium's economies and infrastructures in need of rebuilding, having overseas sources of cheap labor, commodities, and captive markets must have seemed invaluable. This was all the more true in the face of the expanding power of both the United States and the Soviet Union at the time. Balanced against the economic potential of the colonies, however, were the growing ideological disadvantages of colonial rule. If World War II had been fought to stop Fascism on the grounds of its antidemocratic politics and the ideology of Aryan racial superiority, how could colonialism possibly be condoned? Certainly, it seemed more than hypocritical to Africans, who had endured decades of such policies under even the most benevolent colonial powers. Africans had helped defeat the Axis powers in Europe, Asia, and Africa, and they were encouraged to expand their ongoing battle against colonial rule at home.

Working to the advantage of African nationalists in this quest were the new "superpowers" of the United States and the Soviet Union. Both of these states were opposed to colonialism. The United States attacked colonialism on the grounds that it was antithetical to free trade and self-determination—both ideals that the United States had lauded in the Atlantic Charter (1941), a document that outlined the policies and goals that would guide the Allied war effort against Fascism. In particular, point three of the Charter seemed to support decolonization with the admonition that the Allies would ". . . respect the right of all peoples to choose the form of government under which they will live; and they wish to see sovereign rights and self government restored to those who have been forcibly deprived of them." The Soviets opposed colonialism because Lenin and other Marxist thinkers had defined it as the "highest stage of capitalism." Despite their support for decolonization, however, the influences and activities of the superpowers would be far from benevolent as independent Africa became an arena of Cold War conflict.

At the close of World War II, Britain and France seemed to hope that a "middle-ground" approach to colonial policy might maintain for them the economic benefits of colonialism while offsetting the ideological disadvantages. Also significant was a postwar political shift in Britain and France that strengthend the hand of the more "leftward" leaning Labor and Socialist parties. As a result, both Britain and France sought to replace force with increasing (but still limited) African participation in the administrative process. This was defined as being the first step to eventual decolonization—a goal that the British and French nonetheless saw as taking place in the distant future. This kinder, gentler colonialism, it was hoped, would offset both external criticism from the superpowers and also quiet African Nationalists by providing the small class of elites with a greater say in colonial administration. In 1944 at a conference held in Brazzaville, in Central Africa, the French announced their plans to expand African participation in "local affairs"—a major step given the generally top-down nature of French direct rule. Further, in 1946, the French repealed both the much-hated *Indiginat* legal code and the *Corvee* system of forced labor. In an effort to show French good faith in integrating the colonies into a "greater France," the government also added ten seats for African representatives to the French National Assembly. It was a step forward, no doubt, but it should be noted that this system offered Africans representation at a tiny fraction of that accorded to full French citizens. In the British colonies of West Africa, a wave of new constitutions in 1946 and 1947 created African majorities in colonial legislative assemblies. With a twist typical of indirect rule, the representatives in these assemblies were largely nominated by traditional rulers or by the colonial administrators themselves. As such, the most radical of African nationalists generally remained outside the reformed system of colonial administration.

Colonial reforms were not limited to political concessions. Britain and France invested increased amounts of capital (scarce in the postwar era) in health care and education. Although minimal by the standards in the home countries, these investments were still substantial improvements over the bare-bones levels of human services offered to the colonies before the war. In particular, new universities were established in some British colonies, such as the Gold Coast and Nigeria. "Development" projects were also established to help boost agricultural productivity. Some were successful, but others, such as the infamous British East African Groundnut Scheme, did far more harm than good. In this particular case, the British sought to utilize war-surplus tanks as tractors to establish a giant peanut farm in central Tanzania. Within a few years the project had created a barren zone of hundreds of thousands of acres destroyed in an attempt to export European-style agriculture to tropical African soils.

As many readers may have already noticed, the postwar reforms mentioned were notably absent in certain parts of Africa. The Belgians, and to an even greater extent the Portuguese, continued on with "business as usual" in their own colonies. Further, in those parts of British and French Africa where significant numbers of white settlers were present, these groups used their political influence to block the extension of greater rights to Africans. As shall be discussed later in the chapter, the resistance to African liberation in these regions would lead to a very different process of decolonization than found elsewhere on the continent.

The Rise of African Nationalist Movements

Few Africans were content with the limited gains offered by the colonial reforms of the 1940s. Significant on the international level was the fact that many Africans were aware of the wave of decolonization already taking place. The end of World War II saw the end of colonial rule in the Middle East (including Egypt) and India.

The replacement of colonialism in these regions by new sovereign states, in large part as a result of local nationalist agitation and peaceful mass resistance to European dominance, served as a great inspiration to nationalists in Africa. Further, a growing political consciousness on the part of Africans themselves was making the continued maintenance of colonial authority more difficult. As more Africans traveled outside the continent, whether for service in the war or for education, they developed an increasing sense of African identity that helped expand their desire for self-determination. Similarly, greater levels of literacy and expanded systems of communication in the form of newspapers and radio also helped create an awareness of anticolonialism and nationalism. Ironically, colonialism was helping to sow the seeds for its own demise. Indeed, the Pan-African Congress of 1945 was held in London, the very nerve center of the British Empire. London was the perfect rallying point for those who sought to end British colonialism. One of the first Pan-African Congresses had been organized by W.E.B. DuBois in Paris in 1919, but the 1945 meeting was the first where the balance of leadership had shifted from Africans in the diaspora to those from Africa. Notably, reflecting divisions along colonial boundaries, no representatives from French, Belgian, or Portuguese Africa were present at the Congress. Even the process of decolonization would at times reflect colonial divisions. Nonetheless, the list of those in attendance reads like a who's who of Anglophone African nationalism, including Kwame Nkrumah, Jomo Kenyatta, and Hastings Banda, each of whom would later become the leader of an independent African state.

Critical to the actual mobilization of African populations for anticolonial agitation, however, was the creation of mass parties in many colonies and regions. They include the National Council of Nigeria and the Cameroons (1944), the **Rassemblement Democratique Africain** (1946), the United Gold Coast Convention (1947), the Kenya African Union (1947), and the National Council of Sierra Leone (1950). Although these organizations built on the efforts and membership of existing African elite organizations, the new parties tended to be less willing to compromise on issues of African participation and the need for rapid movement toward independence. In some cases the division between older and younger generations of activists led to splits. For example, in 1949 Kwame Nkrumah broke with the United Gold Coast Convention and formed his own **Convention People's Party** (CPP), because he felt that the leadership of the UGCC was too willing to accept British gradualism and was not interested in involving the wider population in the process of dissent and reform.

In many ways it was Nkrumah's CPP that set the tone for the process of decolonization in much of Africa. Nkrumah was not only frustrated by what he saw as the "conservatism" of the UGCC's leadership, but he was also radicalized by the February 1948 shootings of a number of former servicemen who had been protesting nonpayment of benefits by the British government. (A similar incident had occurred with former French servicemen in Dakar in 1944.) Nkrumah was not only horrified by the willingness of the British government to turn on those who had recently served in its military, but was also amazed at the strength of the public reaction—riots shook Accra for days after the incident. Nkrumah became convinced that the path to decolonization should be through coordinated mass action, rather than a gradual extension of power to the elite. In reaching this conclusion Nkrumah was likely influenced by both his study of Gandhi's use of mass nonviolent protest in India, and his experience with mass democracy in the United States, where he had been a student. Nkrumah's CPP soon attracted an extensive membership, who were mobilized in what Nkrumah called "Positive Action," which relied on nonviolent protests and strikes to force rapid decolonization. Not much amused, the British arrested Nkrumah and charged him with complicity in the riots following the shootings of 1948. Nonetheless, when elections were held in 1951 for positions in a new system of limited self-government, the CPP won an overwhelming majority. The British, who had hoped for a victory by the more conservative UGCC, had no choice but to release Nkrumah from prison to immediately take the position as "Leader of Government Business." Humorously, Nkrumah made his first appearance after being released wearing a hat with the letters "P.G." on it, standing for "Prison Graduate." Over the next several years Nkrumah and the CPP continued to agitate for rapid decolonization and to win large majorities in subsequent elections. Nkrumah became prime minister in charge of an "autonomous internal government" following elections in 1954, and in 1957 became the first head of state of Ghana, as the Gold Coast was renamed at independence. Despite continued British efforts to slow the process of decolonization and pass independence to political "moderates," Nkrumah's CPP seemed able to force the British hand at every turn. Unwilling to appear openly hostile to democracy, the British had little choice but to hand power to the CPP.

Interestingly, nationalist agitation was often strongest where British indirect rule had been least successful. Indeed, it was often those Africans who were most "Westernized" who were the most anticolonial.

 Voices from African History: **Nnamdi Azikiwe on Imperialism**

"Every sixth man on the Continent of Africa is a Nigerian. Every other person in the British colonial empire is a Nigerian. Add the British Isles to Belgium, Holland, Portugal and the Irish Free State, and then you have an idea of the area of Nigeria. There is gold in Nigeria. Coal, lignite, tin, columbite, tantalite, lead, diatomite, thorium (uranium-233), and tungsten abound in Nigeria. There is palm oil galore. Rubber, cocoa, groundnuts, benniseeds, cotton, palm oil and palm kernels are there in very large quantity. Timber of different kinds is found in many areas of this African fairyland. Yet, in spite of these natural resources which indicated potential wealth, the great majority of Nigerians live in want.

It is our considered opinion that factors of capitalism and imperialism have stultified the normal growth of Nigeria in the community of nations. We are confident that only by the crystalization of democracy in all aspects of our national life and thought—political, economic and social—can we develop *pari passu* with the other progressive nations of the peace-loving world. We are determined that Nigeria should now evolve into a fully democratic and Socialist Commonwealth in order to enable our various nationalities and communities to own and control the essential means of production and distribution and thereby more effectively promote political freedom, economic security, social equality, religious toleration and communal welfare.

For these reasons, we define imperialism as the enforced rule of one nation by another nation. This we hold to be the antithesis of democracy, for the realization of which our sons have shed their blood in two world wars. Therefore, we are compelled to denounce imperialism as a crime against humanity, because it destroys human dignity and is a constant cause of wars. And in doing so, we make the following declarations:

1. That we shall no longer be scared by false alarms sounded by imperialists and their venal press in respect of any ideology which is basically Socialist in its concept.
2. That we shall no longer be prepared to pull the chestnut out of the fire for blundering war-mongers.
3. That we shall no longer be dragooned to act as cannon-fodder in the military juggernaut of hypocrites who dangle before our people misleading slogans in order to involve humanity in carnage and destruction.

4. That we regard imperialism as our primary moral enemy against which should range all the various nationalities and communities of our country.
5. That we assert that we are entitled to be consulted and our consent obtained before we are stampeded into another world war.
6. That in the event of another world war, we reserve the right to adopt an independent attitude and a line of action which would accelerate our national liberation, by casting in our lot with any people whose attitude towards our national struggle for freedom warrants such an alliance.
7. That in the next world war, we shall pitch our tent in any camp which by word or deed satisfies our immediate national aspirations."

From an address at the Second Annual Conference of the Congress of Peoples against Imperialism, London 1949. Quoted from *Zik: Selected Speeches of Nnamdi Azikiwe* (Cambridge University Press, 1961).

Southern Nigeria saw energetic demands for decolonization as early as did the Gold Coast, yet traditional elites in Northern Nigeria (the very place of origin for indirect rule) delayed independence for several years, arguing that they needed time to be able to organize their own party (the Northern Peoples Congress) to "compete" with more Westernized populations in the south. With British support (often covert), these rulers were able to dominate politics in the country when Nigeria became independent in 1960. Notably, the often strong anti-Western and anticolonial rhetoric of the nationalists was nearly or totally absent among the Northern People's Congress leaders. Rather, these leaders spoke of British benevolence and the partnership of colonialism. The British, as you might expect, were most pleased with such an outcome. In other regions where indirect rule had been particularly successful, such as Uganda and Botswana, similarly conservative traditional rulers continued to wield power into independence.

Elsewhere, mass political parties successfully led several other African colonies to independence in the latter 1950s and early 1960s. In doing so, these nationalists were inspired and aided by the newly independent Ghana. In December 1958, Ghana hosted the first All African People's Congress (AAPC), which, even more than the Pan-African Congresses of before, served as a rallying point for anticolonial and nationalist leaders from around the continent. The goals of the AAPC were not only to aid in the movement of colonies to independence, but were also designed to aid in Nkrumah's goal of creating a single unified African state (a topic to which we will return shortly).

This photo, featuring Julius Nyerere and supporters in Tanganyika, reflects some of the heavy exuberance that came with independence.

The process of decolonization in French colonial Africa was somewhat different from that found in Anglophone colonies such as the Gold Coast. As already noted, the French hoped that extending limited representation within the French National Assembly would satisfy nationalists in French West and Central Africa. They were to be sorely disappointed. In October 1946, the new African representatives and many other nationalists defied French attempts to block a gathering and met in Bamako (now capital of Mali). Under the leadership of Felix Houphouet-Boigny, from Côte d'Ivoire, they formed the Rassemblement Democratique Africain (African Democratic Assembly, or RDA), a party that sought to unify nationalists throughout the French African Colonies. The RDA was not welcomed by the French government. It faced considerable pressure, especially in 1947, when the conservative government of France attempted to oust officials belonging to the Communist Party (of which Houphouet-Boigny and several other African representatives were members—in no small part because the communists favored full citizenship for all colonized Africans). Only when Houphouet-Boigny agreed to disassociate the RDA from the communists in 1950 did the French let up pressure on the party. Despite fractures in the group created when nationalists from individual colonies formed their own parties, as did the Senegalese nationalist Leopold Senghor in 1948, the RDA remained a potent force for nationalist agitation in French Africa.

In the early 1950s, the French gradually expanded the representation allowed to Africans in West and Central Africa. This was both in response to pressure from the RDA and also a result of the fact that France was embroiled in brutal colonial wars in Algeria and French Indochina (Vietnam). The French defeat and surrender at Dien Bien Phu in 1954 showed that France could not rely on military force to maintain its colonial territories. The Viet Minh had proven the ability of colonized people to overthrow the once-dominant colonial powers—especially with the military aid made available by the Soviet Union. The French could afford no more such conflicts and sought instead to maintain peaceful ties with its colonies via a system of loose economic and political ties. In 1956 the French passed the *Loi Cadre,* which granted universal suffrage to adult Africans in the colonies, but also dissolved the large regional federations of French West and Central Africa and created twelve smaller colonies. This move was in part because Houphouet-Boigny feared that the poorer regions of French West Africa would drain resources from relatively wealthy colonies such as his own. Other nationalists, Leopold Senghor in particular, decried the move, and argued that it would create states that would be small, poor, and politically impotent.

By 1958, French embarrassments during the Suez Crisis of 1956 and the brutal war in Algeria had brought the French government to the brink of collapse. Charles de Gaulle, the WWII hero, was brought back to power amid promises that he would end the conflict in Algeria and elsewhere in the colonies (an anticolonial rebellion was brewing in Cameroon, for example). In France he proposed a new constitution and for the colonies he delivered something of an ultimatum. A referendum would be held in which each of the twelve African colonies would vote a simple "Oui ou Non" (Yes or No) on continued economic and political relations within a loose global "French Community." Only in Guinea, where the nationalist movement was led by the trade unionist Sekou Toure, did the population vote "non"—a move represented by Toure's statement that they would prefer "poverty in liberty to riches in slavery." France granted Guinea immediate independence, but also took Toure at his word, removing not only critical government documents but also destroying "French" infrastructure for communications and transport. Telephone exchanges were destroyed, and even heavy equipment such as port cranes and railroad switching centers was smashed. The new Guinean government survived only with considerable aid from the Soviet Union (who were happy to gain a Cold War foothold in West Africa) and from the recently independent Ghana.

Independence for the rest of French continental Africa and the island colony of Madagascar followed in 1960. Along with Anglophone colonies such as Nigeria and with the Belgian decolonization of the Congo, seventeen African countries gained their independence in that year—often called "the year for Africa." Many other colonies would follow in the early years of the 1960s. But decolonization elsewhere would require both more time and bloodshed.

Decolonization in the Settler States and Portuguese Africa

Even as most of Africa moved toward peaceful decolonization in the 1950s and early 1960s, tensions began to flare in settler colonies. White settler resistance to expanded sovereignty for Africans in Algeria, Kenya, Rhodesia, and Portuguese

A poster celebrating the expulsion of European colonizers and their influence.

Africa gave Africans little option but to turn to violence as a means of liberation. In each of these cases, repressive legislation aimed at maintaining white control over African populations, African protests, and colonial reprisals led to brutal guerrilla wars and legacies of violence and distrust that continue to complicate national and regional politics to the present day.

As discussed previously in Chapter 10, the French conquest of Algeria and the subsequent settlement of millions of French in the rich farmlands of the coast had been marked by brutal conflict. Only through the use of tens of thousands of troops and brutal scorched earth tactics were the French able to squash Algerian resistance in the nineteenth century. Tensions simmered throughout the early twentieth century, however, and by the end of World War II the pot was threatening to boil over once again. In 1945 a demonstration by Islamic nationalists (who sought independence for Algeria similar to that being granted to Islamic states in the Middle East) was fired on by police. Many were killed in the attack and riots that followed. Attacks on French administrators and settlers (many of whom were now second or third generation) led to colonial reprisals and a worsening cycle of violence. In 1954, the various Algerian resistance groups joined under an umbrella organization called the *Front de Liberation Nationale,* greatly improving the coordination and effectiveness of the revolution. By

1958 the French had over half a million troops under arms in Algeria (many of them Algerians who supported the French administration), but were nonetheless unable to maintain peace. Hundreds of thousands of Algerian and thousands of French lives were lost as the conflict became increasingly brutal, with atrocities and massacres being committed by each side. As mentioned previously, this crisis led to the collapse of the Fourth Republic and the return of de Gaulle to power. De Gaulle traveled to Algeria, hoping to find a compromise. Finding little common ground, de Gaulle eventually granted independence to Algeria in 1962—much to the dismay to the French population of the colony. The use of armed resistance had scored its first victory against settler colonialism in Africa. The cost to Algeria, however, was terrible.

As in Algeria, whites in Kenya had settled in the colony's finest agricultural region—in this case the central highlands. During the 1930s, these settlers had established large and profitable plantations, evicting large numbers of the native Kikuyu from the land. Though numbering only about 60,000 by the 1950s, the settlers wielded considerable political influence in the colony, in no small part because many came from wealthy English families with strong formal and informal ties to the British government. These settlers demanded and received monopoly rights over the production of tea and coffee—restricting the local populations to work as paid laborers. By the 1940s, the indigenous populations increasingly turned to violence as their attempts at political action were rebuffed by settlers who resisted the extension of political concessions to African populations. The violent resistance in Kenya soon came to be known as "Mau Mau" (though the movement often referred to itself as the "Land and People's Party"). The Mau Mau rebels relied on secret oaths to ensure the loyalty of participants. They attacked white settlers when possible (killing nearly 30 during the 1950s), but more often struck against less-well-protected African "collaborators"—killing well over 1,000. The Kenyan colonial government responded by declaring a state of emergency in 1952. Suspected participants and supporters of Mau Mau, including the nationalist Jomo Kenyatta, were arrested, and thousands of Africans were detained in concentration camps to deny the rebels support. Attacks on suspected Mau Mau strongholds left thousands dead. A concerted propaganda campaign was also waged by the British to highlight the barbarity of the Mau Mau, who were represented in the most base of stereotypical "savage" images. The British declared victory over the Mau Mau in 1955, but did not lift the state of emergency until 1960. Despite this "victory," it was clear that the colonial government had lost its will to pursue a violent repression of the rebellion, which it was feared could flare up again at any time. Britain moved to grant independence to Kenya, releasing Kenyatta from house arrest in 1961. Kenya became independent in 1963, with Kenyatta becoming the country's first prime minister.

The British colony of Southern Rhodesia also had a substantial population of white settlers—well over 150,000 by the end of World War II. The adjoining colonies of Northern Rhodesia and Nyasaland also had small but politically influential populations of settlers. Following World War II these settlers clearly saw the writing on the wall in terms of the rise of African nationalism and took steps that they hoped would preempt a move to African majority rule. A "Central African Federation" was proposed that would join the three colonies and give the white populations sovereign authority over revenues created by agriculture and mining (especially the copper mines of Northern

Rhodesia). Protests by the Nyasaland African Congress found sympathetic ears within Britain's Labour government at the time, however, and the Federation was not to become a reality until 1953. The creation of the Federation meant that the extensive restrictions on African rights that existed in Southern Rhodesia would be extended to Nyasaland and Northern Rhodesia as well. In both colonies, African nationalists mobilized protests. In Northern Rhodesia mining strikes organized by the African Mine-Workers Union were a potent tool of resistance. In Nyasaland, Dr. Hastings Banda returned from years of residence overseas and in Ghana to assume the presidency of the Nyasaland African Congress. A strategy of "noncooperation" and protests prompted a state of emergency in Nyasaland in 1959. Crackdowns on the protesters resulted in dozens of deaths and prompted a British investigation, which named the Nyasaland administration as guilty of using excessive force. By the early 1960s it was clear that neither Northern Rhodesia nor Nyasaland could justify the denial of sovereignty to the colonies' vast African majorities. The Central African Federation was dissolved in 1963, and Northern Rhodesia (renamed Zambia) and Nyasaland (renamed Malawi) both moved to independence in 1964.

Progress was not so simple in Southern Rhodesia. Here there was a much larger European population, and the African resistance was hampered by internal feuding between competing nationalist organizations. Joshua Nkomo's Zimbabwe African Peoples Union (ZAPU) favored a nonviolent strategy of resistance, whereas Robert Mugabe and Joshua Sithole's Zimbabwe African National Union (ZANU) advocated "armed struggle." The contest between the two groups became violent in 1963 and 1964, a situation that worked to the advantage of the settlers, who were preparing to declare their own independence. In November 1965, the white Rhodesians issued the Unilateral Declaration of Independence (UDI), announcing that Rhodesia was now an independent state. Britain responded with only superficial verbal protest. One can hardly imagine that any nonsettler colonies would have been allowed to simply declare independence! Taking advantage of the end of ties with Great Britain, Rhodesia quickly moved to establish a South African–style system of white minority rule.

With the UDI in Rhodesia, something of a divide had been established in Africa. On the one hand, by 1965 most of the continent had successfully, and for the most part peacefully, made the transition from colonialism to independence. Yet, a few colonies and states refused to accept the idea of political equality for Africans. These were the Portuguese colonies (Guinea-Bissau, Cape Verde, Angola, and Mozambique), South Africa and its protectorate of South-West Africa (later Namibia), and Rhodesia. Each of these settings pitted a relatively small European minority (South Africa had by far the largest percentage of Europeans at about 15 percent of the total population) against a large African population growing increasingly frustrated with their continued subjugation. With the great bulk of these "settler states" being located in Central and southern Africa, there should be little surprise that the struggle for liberation in each of these colonies became deeply intertwined. The South African, Rhodesian, and Portuguese governments cooperated in their attempts to maintain European power in the region. On the other hand, resistance movements often coordinated efforts and were supported in their quest for sovereignty by newly independent African states and the Soviet Union.

Most African leaders were driven by a genuine desire for complete African libera-tion. Kwame Nkrumah stated that the job of decolonization was not done until all of Africa was free. For their own part, however, the Soviets were largely driven by a desire to expand their influence in the region—a prospect that offered the potential of cutting off the flow of strategic minerals such as copper, titanium, and chromium to the West. The United States, although generally supportive of decolonization, was desperate to maintain the flow of these minerals (you can't make jet or rocket engines without chromium and titanium) and fearful of the socialist rhetoric espoused by many African leaders and revolutionaries in the region. Further, Portu-gal was a member of NATO (the North Atlantic Treaty Alliance) and was hence a United States Cold War ally—limiting the ability of the United States to apply pres-sure to the country. The Cold War was heating up in central and southern Africa.

Although most of Africa spent the decades following World War II moving toward the extension of political rights to Africans, South Africa was moving in the exact opposite direction. Indeed, it was in the late 1940s and 1950s that the policy of apartheid was put into place. The roots of apartheid were as old as European set-tlement in the region, but the policy itself was implemented following the National-ist Party's victory in the 1948 elections and merger with the Afrikaner Party in 1951. With a solid lock on political power, the Nationalists passed a series of laws that came to define the very nature of institutionalized racism in the modern world. All aspects of a person's life in South Africa became segregated and regulated on the basis of how the government defined his or her race. What you did for a living, who you worked with, where you could live, where you could be at certain hours of the day, and who you could date or marry all became a part of legislated "right and wrong." Although such laws regulated everyone's lives, obviously the system placed far more restrictions on nonwhites than on whites. Further, apartheid necessitated a complex framework of racial classification to provide the criteria for separating "Whites, Indians, Coloureds, and Bantu." In South Africa under apartheid it was perfectly legitimate for the government to measure your skin color or check how curly your hair was if your "race" was in question. To make matters even worse, apartheid placed even greater restrictions on the movement of nonwhites with a more comprehensive pass system in 1952; the pass book increasingly became the most hated symbol of apartheid. Efforts at restricting where nonwhites could live centered around moves to legitimize the "Bantustans" as sovereign states and to iso-late the African labor force in mining compounds and squalid "townships." The 1956 Native Relocation Act allowed the government to evict nonwhites from resi-dential areas and resettle whites in the area—often bulldozing entire neighbor-hoods as an intermediate step.

Not surprisingly, protest against apartheid became a fact of life for many South Africans. In 1952 the ANC staged a nonviolent "Defiance Campaign" against the pass law and forced segregation of South African communities, resulting in thousands of arrests. In 1953 the predominantly white Liberal Party was formed in opposition to the Nationalists. In 1955 the ANC came together with Indian leaders and progressive whites to author the "Freedom Charter," a document that called for the end of white privilege and the creation of a nonracial political system in South Africa. The government responded by arresting the leading authors of the charter

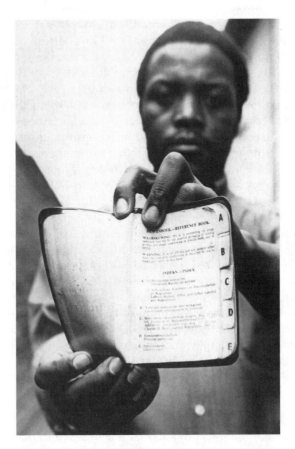

This pass book was a hated symbol of the indignities
apartheid forced upon non-whites in South Africa.

and charging them with treason. The trial lasted until 1961, with all those charged, including the young lawyer **Nelson Mandela,** eventually being declared innocent.

Reflecting the political tenor of the times, the South African government sought to delegitimize those in opposition to apartheid by calling them communists—indeed, the South African government took a particularly novel line by effectively defining communism as "resistance to apartheid." Notably, there were communists in South Africa, and they were significant for their steadfast resistance to the country's system of racial oppression. Certainly, however, opponents of apartheid were not all inspired by communist ideals. Just as in the Civil Rights movement in the United States (which was taking place at much the same time), protests against apartheid brought together people from all walks of life who found the notion of a race-based hierarchy of political and social rights unacceptable.

For South Africa, the 1960s began with a terrible incident. During a protest at a police station on May 21, 1961, the police opened fire on the crowd. Some 180 people were wounded and 69 were killed. The police said they acted in self-defense, but the fact that the vast majority of those killed or injured were shot in the back belied these claims. Horrible as it was, the **Sharpsville Massacre,** as it became known, was a turning point in the history of South Africa. The South African government, fearing organized protests, promptly banned the ANC and the more recently formed Pan-African Congress (which had broken away from the ANC in 1958 in protest over the prominent role played by whites in the organization). Nearly 20,000 South Africans were arrested in a government crackdown on protests following the massacre. A state of emergency was declared, and special reserves of white troops were called up to "maintain order." Increasingly disillusioned by the growing brutality of the government and facing a growing belief that nonviolent resistance was ineffective, the leadership of the ANC ended five decades of nonviolent protest by forming a military wing called *Umkhonto we Sizwe* (the Spear of the Nation). The Pan-African Congress, too, created an armed wing called *Poqo*. The ANC focused on striking only against physical structures such as power stations, specifically seeking to avoid any loss of life, but the more radical PAC specifically targeted government officials and African "collaborators." In response, the government instituted a number of security measures. Individuals could be arrested and "detained" without charges being filed, and such prisoners had no right to counsel or defense. Unless witnesses were present at the arrest, families and friends would often have no word of the whereabouts of those detained. Reports of torture were common, and a number of prisoners died while in jail—officially due to accidents or mysterious circumstances. In trying to maintain apartheid, South Africa was rapidly becoming a police state. Among those arrested included the young lawyer and ANC leader Nelson Mandela, who pled guilty to acts of sabotage. He also made clear, however, that the choice to use violence had been a difficult one forced on the ANC by the actions of the government.

> At the beginning of June 1961, after a long and anxious assessment of the South African situation, I, and some colleagues, came to the conclusion that as violence in this country was inevitable, it would be unrealistic and wrong for African leaders to continue preaching peace and non-violence at a time when the Government met our peaceful demands with force.
>
> This conclusion was not easily arrived at. It was only when all else had failed, when all channels of peaceful protest had been barred to us, that the decision was made to embark on violent forms of political struggle, and to form Umkhonto we Sizwe. We did so not because we desired such a course, but solely because the Government had left us with no other choice.
>
> Nelson Mandela's statement at opening of the Rivona Trial. From the online archives of the African National Congress, South Africa, http://www.anc.org.za

Mandela was sentenced to life in prison.

The harshness and racism of white rule in South Africa increasingly became an international issue in the 1960s. Newly independent African states highlighted the issue and offered stinging condemnations of South Africa in the United Nations, and only repeated vetoes by the United States and Great Britain in the Security Council prevented sanctions from being leveled against the country. Independence for Botswana in 1966 and Lesotho and Swaziland in 1968 encouraged black South Africans in their hope for African sovereignty. Many international businesses, fearing the outbreak of a bloody civil war, began to withdraw from the country. Even some members of the Nationalist Party began to voice concern over the brutality that was

Nelson Mandela meets with women at a rally in 1959.

increasingly necessary to maintain the system of white rule. Calling themselves the *Verligtes* (Enlightened Ones), they dubbed the hard-line membership of the party *Verkramptes* (Cramped Ones). Despite such seeds of hope, repression and atrocities would continue to plague South Africa throughout the 1970s, with the killing of Steven Biko (the student founder of the Black Consciousness Movement) and the massacre of schoolchildren by government troops at Soweto in 1976 being notorious examples. Such events threatened to even further radicalize nonwhite populations in South Africa and make the likelihood of reconciliation in the future seem all the more elusive.

The ruling white minority of Rhodesia was less successful in maintaining its own position in power. Faced with two rebel movements with bases in Zambia to the north and Mozambique to the east, the government of Rhodesia found its resources stretched thin as it tried to control large swaths of territory in the face of highly mobile rebel forces who enjoyed considerable local support. The government launched a propaganda campaign that sought to identify the rebels as "communist terrorists," but the ZANU and ZAPU forces responded with their own popular propaganda of **Chimurenga** songs that promised peace and prosperity after the end of white rule. Further, having "illegally" declared independence in 1965, Rhodesia enjoyed little or no international support aside from that of Portugal and South Africa. International sanctions placed both moral and economic pressure on the state. By 1980 it was clear that the attempt to maintain white minority rule could not be sustained, and the Rhodesian government agreed to hold constitutional talks with the rebels. In 1980 a new nonracial government was formed following the extension of elections based on universal adult suffrage. Renamed Zimbabwe, the new country hoped to serve as a model of racial reconciliation and cooperation. Though whites, who controlled the great bulk of the fertile land and economy, were offered numerous legal protections for their property, many chose to leave the country. Thousands immigrated to South Africa, where they were nicknamed "wheniwees," since they so often made wistful statements about "when we were in Rhodesia . . .".

South Africa and Rhodesia were certainly not alone in their pursuit of continued white rule in Africa. Portugal, governed by the Fascist dictator António de Oliveira Salazar and with no other claim to global influence beyond its remaining colonies, steadfastly refused to consider decolonization. In 1956 the Cape Verdian Amilcar Cabral founded the *Partido Africano da Independencia de Guine e Cabo Verde* (African Party for the Independence of Guinea and Cape Verde). A strike by dockworkers organized by the party in 1959 in Portuguese Guinea was brutally repressed, and dozens were killed. In 1963, Cabral went underground and shifted to the use of guerrilla warfare to end colonial rule in the mainland colony. In Angola, three different revolutionary organizations were founded. The *Movimento Popular de Lieratacao de Angola* (MPLA) was founded in Luanda in 1956, and the *Frente Nacional de Libertacao de Angola* (FNLA) was organized soon afterward in the Bakongo-speaking region of the north. The MPLA, with Soviet backing, began a military campaign against the Portuguese in Angola in 1961. The FNLA, which would later gain U.S. support, began military operations in the north soon afterward. In 1966 they were joined by the *Uniãão Nacional para a Independêência Total de Angola* (UNITA), which established a base of operations in Angola's predominantly Ovimbundu-speaking southern region and was initially supported by the Chinese. In Mozambique, the *Frente de Libertacao de Mozambique* (FRELIMO) was founded in Dar es Salaam (in neighboring Tanganyika) in 1962. FRELIMO, with Soviet support, began a military campaign against the Portuguese in Mozambique in 1964.

The campaigns against the Portuguese made steady progress. A poor country by European standards, Portugal could ill afford to compete with multiple liberation groups on several fronts—especially given the extensive supplies sent to the rebels by the Soviet Union (and to a lesser extent, the United States). Notably, Portugal's membership in NATO provided them with training and armaments that no doubt served to prolong the conflict. Certainly one of the greatest factors working against the Portuguese, however, was the brutal legacy of their own style of colonialism. Unlike the British and French, who could lay claim to at least some moderate degree of support among the African populace, Portugal had little such goodwill to draw on. Rather, populations in the Portuguese colonies offered eager support to the various liberation movements. With the exception of the FNLA (and later UNITA), the harshness of Portuguese rule did much to encourage a decidedly anti-Western political slant among most of the revolutionaries. Speaking of the colonial legacy, the *Partido Africano* leader Amilcar Cabral said:

> We are not interested in the preservation of any of the structures of the colonial state. It is our opinion that it is necessary to totally destroy, to break, to reduce to ash all aspects of the colonial state in our country, to make everything possible for our people.

From Robert O. Collins, *Problems in African History* (1997), p. 163

The harshness of Portuguese rule and lack of social services also made it relatively easy for the rebels to offer real improvements in quality of life wherever they were militarily successful. By providing a relative lack of oppression, lower taxes, and basic education

This Chinese propaganda poster, reading " Get Out of Africa, American Imperialism," reflects the international context of African politics during the Cold War era.

and health care in territories where they gained control, these movements established even greater legitimacy for themselves. By the latter 1960s, the anti-Portuguese forces controlled substantial portions of Portuguese Guinea, Angola, and Mozambique. Only in Cape Verde, where the barren nature of most of the islands made guerrilla strategy difficult, did the rebels fail to make headway. By the 1970s, Portugal was reeling under the expense of the conflict and was also faced by growing international condemnation, even from its NATO allies. In 1974, the Portuguese dictator Salazar was overthrown in a military coup. Indeed, the coup leader, General Spinola, had spent years fighting against the guerrilla forces in Africa and had become increasingly aware of the pointlessness of ongoing war. With Salazar removed, Portuguese Africa quickly moved to independence in 1975.

Sadly, the end of colonial rule did not mean peace for Angola and Mozambique. In Angola, the three main resistance groups (the MPLA, FNLA, and UNITA) initially signed cooperative agreements to share power in a unitary Angolan government. However, Augustino Neto, the leader of the socialist MPLA, soon declared that his party would head a new state named the People's Republic of Angola—a move backed by the arrival of thousands of Cuban troops. The FNLA and UNITA responded by declaring a rival Democratic People's Republic of Angola with a capital at Huamba in the central highland region. Given the recent defeat in Vietnam, the United States was eager to "contain" the expansion of Soviet influence in Central Africa and began offering expanded support to the FNLA and UNITA. Meanwhile, aware that an independent socialist Angola would mean expended support for the SWAPO fighters seeking to end South African administration in the protectorate of South West Africa, the South Africans launched an invasion of Angola in cooperation with the FNLA and UNITA. In heavy fighting the MPLA and Cubans, backed by massive amounts of Soviet military aid, were successful in driving South African forces back into South-West Africa and in limiting the area of operations for the FNLA and UNITA. By the late 1970s, the FNLA was largely defeated, but UNITA continued a guerrilla war against the MPLA. The war led to widespread loss of life and economic decay because a large portion of Angola's considerable oil wealth went to maintain the conflict against UNITA, which by the 1980s was receiving millions of dollars in aid from the United States. In a classic case of Cold War irony, the oil companies operating in Angola were largely American owned, and the revenue produced by the export of oil was used to fight against American-backed rebels. Indeed, the situation eventually became so absurd that Soviet-funded Cuban troops were defending American oil wells from U.S.-backed rebels who sought to deny income to the socialist MPLA government. As the saying goes, "Politics makes strange bedfellows."

In Mozambique, independence also quickly gave way to civil war. Here, the South African government offered funding to a rival group RENAMO (Mozambican National Resistance), who challenged the ruling FRELIMO (Front for the Liberation of Mozambique) for power. Rhodesia also offered support to RENAMO in hopes of restricting the ability of ZAPU and ZANU to utilize Mozambique as a base of operation in their war against the white minority government. As in Angola, the fighting led to extensive human suffering and economic decay. A particularly ugly legacy of both conflicts was the widespread use of land mines, which rendered large tracts of farmland unusable and created a daily threat to life and limb even for non-combatants. Hundreds of thousands of land mines remain in each country.

After Colonialism: Independence . . . or into Dependence?

Across most of Africa, the coming of independence was heralded with great joy and high expectations. Kwame Nkrumah set the tone with his famous phrase, "Seek ye first the Political kingdom, and all things shall be added unto you." Such a perspective certainly seemed to make sense. If the denial of African sovereignty via colonialism had been the root cause of the loss of human rights and economic exploitation, then would the return of African self-determination not herald the return of rights and economic development? In the first years of independence, Africa's new governments sought to prove their worth by showing that they could right the wrongs of colonialism.

Early on there seemed to be great cause for optimism. Across the continent new independent governments moved to substantially expand social services. Education was extended at all levels. Further, some governments "nationalized" missionary schools as a means of centralizing education and showing self-sufficiency. Almost all countries established Western-style universities, allowing university students to study at home rather than seek advanced education abroad. Health care also saw massive expansion as government-funded clinics and hospitals were established in rural and urban areas. With such projects, the newly independent states sought to show their citizens that the rewards of independence were real.

Economic development, as we have already seen in Chapter 14, was also a means by which new states sought to prove their legitimacy. In many colonies substantial development projects were launched with great fanfare. Huge hydroelectric dams were built in Egypt, Ghana, and Nigeria, for example, to provide electricity to power new industries. Along with damming the Volta River (and creating the world's largest man-made reservoir), Ghana invested millions in a giant aluminum-smelting factory to take advantage of the country's bauxite reserves, planning to process the bauxite in-country rather than export it in raw form. Extensive irrigation projects were established in many countries as a means of boosting agricultural production.

Finally, a third central goal of independence was to build new national identities. Sovereign African states were faced with the challenge that they were usually haphazard conglomerations of dozens or even hundreds of different ethnic groups with little historical precedent for shared political cooperation. Worse, some bore historical antagonisms that dated back to the era of the slave trade and that had been exacerbated or created by colonial "divide and rule" policies. Africa's new leaders often decried these subnational identities as "tribalism" and sought to replace tribal identities with allegiance to the new nation. Thus, identities such as Luo and Kikuyu would be replaced with Kenyan, and Hausa and Ibo would be replaced with Nigerian.

The case of Tanganyika (renamed Tanzania after union with Zanzibar in 1964) in the 1960s very much exemplifies the drive of new African states to radically change the course of their development. As we saw in Chapter 14, Tanganyika, as one of the poorest and most sparsely populated of Britain's colonies, faced great challenges in the quest for economic and social development. The country's president, Julius Nyerere (nicknamed Mwalimu—our teacher), stressed the need for Tanganyika/Tanzania to pursue a policy of self-help in which the people would pursue development themselves, rather than relying on large loans from outside the country to finance development schemes. Local populations would thus finance and build their own schools, roads, clinics, and such. In so doing, Nyerere hoped for many things. First, self-help would keep the country out of debt and limit the influence of loaner nations (an important consideration during the Cold War). Next, the energy that had brought about nationalist demands for decolonization could be channeled into economic development in the form of a "war against poverty." Further, and perhaps most importantly, by working locally for national development, individuals from various regions would potentially begin developing a consciousness of their Tanzanian identity. As Nyerere stated, such projects could be "their first contact with the Tanganyikan Nation." Thus, ideally, citizens were not only physically building the nation, they were doing it psychologically as well. Nyerere took the program of self-help even further in 1967 with the "Arusha Declaration," which aimed to strengthen the program of self-help via a policy of "African Socialism," that sought to build on notions of inherent African communalism and kinship. Nyerere's policies gained wide acclaim not only in Africa, but also among Western scholars, who applauded Tanzania's uniquely "African" course and rejection of both Western capitalism and Soviet-style communism.

Pan-Africanism

For some, the building of national consciousness in new African countries was not enough. Kwame Nkrumah, in particular, sought to help build a Pan-African consciousness that would outweigh even the new national identities. Nkrumah had long been an advocate of African unity. No small thinker, he hoped that a unified Africa would provide the political and economic influence necessary to compete globally with the United States and Soviet Union. In 1958, Nkrumah and Egyptian President Gamal Abdel Nasser organized the "Eight States African Conference" of decolonized countries in hopes of laying the groundwork of an organization to link all of Africa in the future. As Nkrumah remarked during the conference, "[We] want to come together to link ourselves in a chain so that no other nation can pull one of us without having to cope with the rest of us." There were repeated calls by Nkrumah and Egypt's Nasser for African leaders to meet and establish the framework for a unified Africa (notably, Nasser was similarly attempting to organize a pan-Arab union in the form of the United Arab Republic). The push for greater African unity, however, soon ran into trouble. By the second half of 1961, there were two competing "blocs" with very different visions of Africa's political future. On the side of a unified Africa was the "Casablanca Group," which included Morocco, Ghana, Egypt (the U.A.R.), Mali, and Guinea. In opposition were the nineteen states of the "Monrovia Group," which included Liberia, Côte d'Ivoire, Nigeria, Madagascar, and others.

The difference between the two groups was largely ideological. The Casablanca Group advocated nonalignment in the Cold War, strenuously protested continued influence on the continent by colonial powers (often referred to as neo-colonialism), and advocated a single African government at the earliest possible date. The Monrovia Group, on the other hand, generally supported continued economic and political ties with their former colonial rulers, which had the effect of also placing them in the Western "camp" in the Cold War (many of the nonaligned states later "drifted" into the Soviet Camp). Although the Monrovia states were not entirely opposed to the concept of African unity, their leaders tended to stress that such a goal was not realistic in the short run. For example, Senegal's Leopold Senghor, who had seen an earlier attempt at union with Mali fail in a matter of months, argued that steps toward union be made first on the basis of "regional and cultural affinities." Further, it cannot be doubted that many new African leaders were hesitant to share power with other rulers—which would require giving up positions as "heads of state" for positions as "representatives of states" in a wider union.

Something of a compromise was reached at the African Summit Conference in May 1963. More than thirty African heads of state attended this meeting in Addis Ababa (the capital of Ethiopia). Many impassioned speeches were delivered. Sekou Toure called for a "fund for national liberation" to bankroll an African military force that could be sent, if necessary, to help end colonialism and white minority rule where it still remained on the continent. Nkrumah unveiled a "unity plan," which called for a "Union of African States" that would include economic union in the form of an African common market, unified currency, and a central African bank. In political terms Nkrumah called for a common African foreign policy, an African defense force, and a single African citizenship. A proposed African flag and national anthem were also circulated by the more ardently pan-African participants of the conference. On May 25 (the fourth day of the conference), the gathered heads of state signed a charter forming the Organization of African Unity. Although the charter called for the member states "to promote the unity and solidarity of the African States," it also stated that the OAU would defend the individual states' "sovereignty, their territorial integrity and independence." Such ideals were, of course, at somewhat cross purposes because they called for the organization to work for unity while also ensuring the sovereignty and independence of individual states. Clearly, the division between the Monrovia and Casablanca blocks was still very real. Nonetheless, the independent African states had shown that they could come together at least for the purpose of laying the groundwork for later unity. Nkrumah's goal of a unified Africa was not to be during his lifetime, but the OAU would provide an important voice in such crises as the Nigerian Civil War and during the struggle against apartheid in South Africa. Detractors, however, would charge that the OAU served mainly as a platform from which African leaders could moralize on international topics while ignoring the deprivations faced by their own citizens. As we shall see in the next chapter, African leaders would seek a new African Union in 2002.

Pan-Africanism was not limited to the continental borders of Africa. The spread of African independence and the hope of a united Africa became an increasingly powerful symbol for members of the African diaspora throughout the world. In the United States participants in the Civil Rights movement and advocates of Black Power were thrilled and encouraged by the successes of African Nationalists. W.E.B. DuBois, one of the first and greatest advocates of pan-Africanism, renounced his U.S. citizenship and moved to Ghana in 1961. Malcolm X traveled in Africa in 1964, meeting with Nkrumah, Nyerere, and other African leaders. Stokely Carmichael, who coined the term "Black Power" in the 1960s, was so impressed by African nationalism that he changed his name to Kwame Toure (in honor of Kwame Nkrumah and Sekou Toure) in 1978. Like DuBois, he immigrated to Africa, finding a new home in Guinea in 1969. Indeed, there was remarkable "feedback" between Africa's move to independence and the Civil Rights movement in the United States. Both sides closely followed the other's progress and were inspired by each step toward political emancipation. Ghanaian newspapers, for example, closely followed the forced integration of schools in Little Rock, Arkansas, in 1959. *The Daily Graphic,* one of Ghana's leading newspapers, even dispatched a reporter to cover the issue. The reporter took time to write of his own dismay at experiencing segregation firsthand. For their own part, many African-American newspapers closely followed the path to African independence. Further, increasingly large numbers of African descendants from throughout the Americas traveled to newly independent Africa in an effort to establish greater emotional and intellectual ties with a continent that in many ways remained a "home" even after generations of separation.

The Challenges of Independence

The period of decolonization and early independence clearly concentrated efforts for African development and saw many achievements. Yet, in all too many African states the period of high hopes and optimism characterized by the years immediately following independence soon gave way to disillusionment. Many scholars have termed this situation the "crises of expectations," in that so much was expected from the new states that there was no way they could possibly deliver in so short a time. As we have previously seen in Chapter 14, the rising expenses faced by independent governments were a particular problem.

Many African states also experienced threats to national unity. As already stated, most of these new countries were artificial conglomerations of preexisting ethnic groups. Some governments sought to share development projects and government jobs as equally as possible, but others tended to favor ethnic groups that supported the ruling party. Also, Cold War meddling by the Soviet Union and United States, as well as the continued influence of former colonial powers, tended to exacerbate forces of division within the new countries. During the 1960s a number of new states were faced by threats of ethnic conflict, secession, and civil war. Riots swept Zanzibar shortly after independence in 1964, as African populations on the island, many of whom had been slaves during the Omani period, sought retribution against Arab colonialism, striking out against the island's once-dominant Arab minority. Religious divisions could also exacerbate tensions. In the early 1950s separatist movements were organized among the largely Muslim population of Eritrea (which had been joined with predominantly Christian Ethiopia in 1952) and in the predominantly Christian and Pagan region of Southern Sudan, which had been joined to the overwhelmingly Muslim north by the British in 1946. In Nigeria, tensions between predominantly Christian Ibos and Muslim Hausa led to anti-Ibo riots in 1966.

With the exception of Tanzania, each of these cases of conflict led to civil war as minority regions sought to break away and establish their own states—arguing their own right to self-determination. As we have already seen in the cases of Angola and Mozambique, Cold War politics also played a substantial role in fueling such conflicts. Not surprisingly, international politics played heavily into the civil conflicts in Eritrea, Sudan, Nigeria, and elsewhere as developed countries sought leverage via aid to belligerent parties. For example, France extended considerable aid to the breakaway Ibo Republic of Biafra during the Nigerian civil war of 1966–1969, hoping both to gain access to the region's considerable oil supplies and also limit the influence of an already large and potentially wealthy Anglophone Nigeria in an otherwise largely Francophone region of Africa.

The Congo Crisis

Perhaps no single event better exemplified the challenges faced by new African states than the "Congo Crisis" of the early 1960s. The Congo (later renamed Zaire and then the Democratic Republic of the Congo [DRC], and not to be confused with the neighboring Republic of the Congo to the west) represents both the huge potential and terrible challenges embodied by new African states. A huge country, the DRC was blessed with a relatively large population and remarkable mineral wealth (concentrated in the south). The country's extensive network of rivers (centered around the Congo River itself) provided an outstanding transportation network. At the point of independence from Belgium in June 1960, Congo was thus viewed as a state rich in potential. Within weeks, however, the new country was spiraling into chaos as the army mutinied, provinces seceded, and the UN was called in to "maintain order." Viewed with the benefit of hindsight, it is hardly a surprise that the country collapsed. Belgium, like Portugal, had gone to great lengths to isolate the inhabitants of its colonies from political participation, and at independence practically no one in the government had any experience in administration. The new prime minister, **Patrice Lumumba,** had worked as a postal clerk and brewery manager prior to launching his political career with the foundation of the Mouvement National Congolais (MNC) in 1958. Further, the Belgians had made no arrangements for a transfer of power until pro-independence riots shook major cities in the late 1950s. Suddenly, the Belgians decided to pull out as quickly as possible. In the absence of any centralized planning, some 120 political parties were formed to compete for 137 seats in the proposed parliament. Lumumba's MNC won the greatest number of seats, but was nonetheless forced to rule through a fairly shaky coalition with many smaller parties.

The Congo gained its independence amid much rejoicing on June 30, 1960. But less than a week later, on July 4, the army mutinied against the still largely Belgian officer corp, demanding that officer positions be granted to Congolese immediately and that pay raises be granted to all troops. With no means to control the mutinous troops who were looting stores, threatening government buildings, and attacking Europeans, the Congolese government appealed to the United Nations to help reestablish law and order. Meanwhile, the Belgians had flown in paratroopers to "protect European lives and property"—a terrible blow to the nascent sense of Congolese sovereignty and self-confidence. In desperation, Lumumba initially welcomed the Belgians. Clashes between Belgian and Congolese troops, though, greatly increased tensions. On July 11, just as Lumumba was calling for aid from the UN, Moise Tshombe, governor of the mineral-rich Katanga province, declared that his region was breaking away from the Congo to form an independent state. Soon afterward the diamond-rich region of Kasai also declared its independence.

The Congo, only weeks old, appeared to be disintegrating. By July 15, UN troops were arriving in the Congo, but the Western powers who were bankrolling the operation (particularly the United States) were hesitant to provide the forces with a mandate to do anything more than maintain order. Lumumba hoped that the UN troops would aid him in gaining control over his army and eventually in bringing Katanga and Kasai back into the Congo, by force if necessary. In this desire, Lumumba found a strong advocate in Kwame Nkrumah of Ghana. An ardent pan-Africanist, Nkrumah saw Africa's future in larger, not smaller, political units, and the breakaway of Katanga and Kasai represented a threat to Nkrumah's goal of a unified Africa. Nkrumah repeatedly attacked the UN for not being willing to use military force against Katanga and even called for a combined African military force that would aggressively reestablish the territorial integrity of the Congo. Such a force was beyond the capacity of young African states, however, and Lumumba made overtures to the Soviets for military aid to reestablish his government's authority in the Congo.

Tensions also threatened the new Congolese government internally. On September 4, President Kasavubu "dismissed" Lumumba from the position of prime minister, and Lumumba returned the favor by firing Kasavubu, even though neither one had any such constitutional power. Ten days later, Col. Joseph Mobutu declared that he had seized power in Leopoldville. Although he soon threw his support behind Kasavubu as head of state, the event was a clear foreshadowing of the role Mobutu would play in the country in the years to come. The power struggle between Lumumba and Kasavubu continued. In December, Lumumba was taken into custody by troops under Mobutu's command, even as his followers were setting up a rival government in Lumumba's hometown of Stanleyville. By this point, four separate governments were laying claim to all or part of the Congo. Despite guarantees that Lumumba would be well treated, he and several associates were found dead on February 14. Officially, Lumumba and his companions were reputed to have stolen a car and escaped from military custody, only to be killed by "unknown parties." Predictably, many observers have suspected that Lumumba was instead murdered on Mobutu's orders.

Only after Lumumba's death did the UN take a more active role in bringing Katanga (which was defended largely by Belgian-funded mercenaries) back under

Ghanaian women protest the death of Patrice Lumumba in the Democratic Republic of the Congo.

Congolese control. December 1962 saw a UN invasion of Katanga, and by January 1963, Tshombe was unseated by UN forces. Remarkably, Tshombe became prime minister of the Congo in July of 1964. On November 25 of 1965, however, Mobutu seized power in a military coup, dismissing President Kasavubu from power. Relying on both clever politics and brutal repression, Mobutu would remain as head of state in Congo (renamed Zaire) until his ouster in 1997.

It is important to note that the events in the Congo were not isolated from wider global political currents. Though some observers chose to use the Congo Crisis as proof that Africans were incapable of governing themselves, in fact the Congo had much help in its collapse. In addition to the failure of the Belgians to provide any sort of political preparation for their colony, international pressures were also at work in the new country. Lumumba had threatened to nationalize the mines in the Katanga region, a move that threatened to cost Belgian businesses millions of dollars. Further, Lumumba's socialist leanings led many U.S. policymakers to fear that he would align with the Soviet Union, and thus potentially deprive the United States of access to the strategic minerals (mostly copper) produced in Katanga. Clearly, both Belgium and the United States had motives to either separate Katanga from the Congo or ensure that the Congolese leadership would not switch Cold War camps. Indeed, numerous studies have implicated both countries in supporting the Katanga secession and in the death of Patrice Lumumba. In February 2002, the Belgian government officially acknowledged that it had taken part in planning Lumumba's death and offered a state apology. There can also be little doubt that Mobutu enjoyed considerable support from the United States during the Cold War, despite his reputation as one of Africa's harshest dictators. Mobutu managed to maintain some degree of stability in the Congo during his long reign, but he is also notorious for his government's high degree of corruption and minimal investment in social services, leading some scholars to use it as the model for what has been dubbed "kleptocracy"—government by theft.

Political Change in Independent Africa: Innovation or Regression?

Clearly, the forces arrayed against the survival and success of many new African states were very real. Increasingly, many African leaders pointed to the multiparty political systems inherited from their former colonial rulers as a key source of weakness—or even as the key problem itself. As a result, many African leaders advocated a switch to a one-party system of government. Thus, rather than have one or more opposition parties, all political activity would be contained within a single party. The argument against multiparty government and for one-party rule was based on a number of claims. First, many politicians decried the multiparty system as inherently Western in its "confrontational style," whereas a one-party system would more effectively represent the "natural" African tendency to seek consensus and unity. Similarly, the very nature of having competing parties was seen as at best a waste of time and resources, and at worst a threat to the new nations themselves. Julius Nyerere, a strong advocate of the one-party system, made the following statement:

> There can be only one reason for the formation of [multiple] parties in a country like ours—the desire to imitate the political structure of a totally dissimilar society. What is more, the desire to imitate where conditions are not suitable for imitation can easily lead us into trouble. To try and import the idea of a Parliamentary Opposition into Africa may very likely lead to violence—because the Opposition Parties will tend to be regarded as traitors by the majority of our people—or at best, it will lead to the trivial maneuverings of "opposing" groups whose time is spent in the inflation of artificial differences.
>
> Julius Nyerere, "Democracy and the Party System" (1963), p. 15

Multiparty systems were also seen as enshrining "tribalism" and regionalism—both of which were seen as threats to the building of new national identities. Such was certainly the case in many new African states where political parties often formed largely along ethnic lines. In Nigeria, for example, each of the three dominant parties was built around regionally dominant ethnic groups—the Hausa and Fulani in the north, the Yoruba in the southwest, and the Ibo in the southeast. Certainly, in such a case the threat to national unity posed by ethnic political parties was very real. One-party states would thus ideally help create unity by forcing various ethnic groups to work together in a single political framework.

One-party states were also justified in terms that they could build on the energy of the anticolonial struggle and translate it into efforts to develop the country. Rather than wasting time and resources on competitive and potentially divisive electoral contests, a one-party system would ensure a unity of purpose that would streamline the development process. The success of the Soviet one-party model in rapidly transforming a largely agrarian society into a world leader in technology and manufacturing was very much in the minds of many African leaders. Guinea, led by the trade unionist Sekou Toure, enshrined one-party rule in its first constitution in 1958. For other countries, however, the move to one-party rule was largely de facto. In Tanganyika, for example, Nyerere's Tanganyikan African National Union simply had such wide support that there was soon no party to contest their authority—a development that was touted as a great success for African democracy and consensus. In other locations ruling parties grew as opposition members crossed the carpet—tempted either by offers of positions or simply the desire to be on the inside.

The question, of course, is whether or not a one-party system is inherently antidemocratic and prone to drift toward dictatorship via a squelching of dissent. Defenders of the system, which included many Western academics and policymakers, argued that there was nothing about the one-party system that guaranteed the failure of democracy, as long as free speech and dissent were allowed within the framework of the single party. In the 1960s and 1970s, both Tanzania and Kenya were held up as models of one-party democracy. From the perspective of many opposition parties elsewhere, however, such was not the case. In the quest for unity, many states did crack down on dissent and protest—and the line of division between the ruling party and the state often became blurred. In Ghana, Nkrumah often stated that "the CPP is Ghana and Ghana is the CPP." In such a situation, dissent against the ruling party became analogous to treason. In 1959 the Ghanaian government, dominated by the CPP, allocated itself sweeping powers to restrict dissent, stating that "the Western concept of a two-party system . . . becomes absolutely meaningless if the opposition party devotes itself as a party to conspiracy, boycotts parliament and abandons all but a token interest in the ballot-box." In 1960 a member of the United Party was arrested and sentenced to three months at hard labor for publicly tearing up a picture of Nkrumah. The United Party initially spoke out vociferously against such restrictions, admonishing the government that ". . . mass arrests are a further step in the calculated establishment of a one-party totalitarian state in Ghana by the familiar communist techniques of inventing and planting plots on leaders of the opposition party." By the early 1960s opposition had become effectively impossible in Ghana, and such a situation became increasingly common in other parts of the continent over the decade. By the early 1980s only Botswana could point to having maintained a multi-party system since independence. Notably, however, not all one-party states were socialist in orientation. In Côte d'Ivoire, for example, Houphouet-Boigney's Parti Democratique de Côte d'Ivoire (PDCI) followed a consistently pro-Western and free-market political orientation.

Some states even went beyond the entrenchment of a single party in power and increasingly concentrated political authority in the hands of the head of state. Just as the party became the symbol of national unity, so did the head of the party and head of state (usually the same person) become a national symbol. In Ghana, Nkrumah instituted "Founder's Day" in 1960 to celebrate his own efforts in founding the nation of Ghana. Similarly, by the early 1960s the occasion of Nkrumah's birthday was greeted by state-funded celebrations, and "congratulations" to the head of state in the country's newspapers by companies and organizations became de rigeur. Nkrumah even took the nickname "Osagyefo" (the Redeemer), by which he was increasingly known. The personalization of power in the person of the ruler often took on semi-religious tones. Witness the following statement by the Chairman of the CPP:

> To us, his people, Kwame Nkrumah is our father, teacher, our brother, our friend, indeed our lives, for without him we would no doubt have existed, but we would not have lived, there would have been no hope for a cure for our sick souls, no taste of glorious victory after a lifetime of suffering. What we owe to him is greater even than the air we breathe, for he made us as surely as he made Ghana.

Quoted from Mazrui and Tidy, *Nationalism and New States in Africa* (1989), p. 192

Leaders of one-party states, however, were hardly invulnerable to being removed from power. From the earliest years of independence in the 1950s and 1960s, military coups became a familiar part of the African political landscape. A coup in Egypt in 1952, for example, ended the constitutional monarchy of King Faruk and brought the military to power. Other coups followed in Sudan in 1958, Togo in 1963, and Algeria in 1965. In some cases the military ruled through a council of officers, often in cooperation with existing civilian authorities. Such was the case, for example, during the military administration of Yakabu Gowan in Nigeria (1966–1976). In others, such as in the case of Mobutu in Zaire or Idi Amin in Uganda, a single military ruler concentrated authority in his own hands.

The advent of military rule was often justified in recurring terms. The military would declare that the civilian rulers had failed to live up to their promises and that the military was acting to protect the country from further mismanagement and corruption. Indeed, in many cases the arrival of military rule was greeted with great celebration. In Ghana, newspaper headlines shifted from praising Nkrumah to vilifying him in a single day. The new military governments often argued that the military's discipline and devotion to the nation would guarantee freedom from any abuse of power. Further, military regimes generally promised that their stay would be brief. Once things had been "put back in order," new elections would be held for a return to civilian rule. This was, indeed, the case in some states. Three years after unseating Nkrumah, Ghana's military-led National Liberation Council held elections and handed over power to a new civilian government in 1969. That government, however, was overthrown by another coup in 1972—bringing the National Redemption Council to power. By the 1970s many military rulers had given up any pretense of handing over power. Indeed, in some states the only way to unseat a military regime was to have it replaced by another. In Nigeria in 1966, Yakabu Gowan came to power by ousting Johnson Aguiyi-Ironsi, who had overthrown Nigeria's First Republic a few months before. Gowan ruled until 1975, when he was overthrown by General Murtala Mohammad. Mohammad was then killed in an abortive coup attempt in 1976. General Olusegun Obasanjo then assumed power and oversaw a three-year transition to civilian rule, handing over power to a new elected government in 1979. That government was overthrown by Col. Muhammad Buhari in 1983, and Buhari was unseated by General Ibrahim Babangida in 1985. The comings and goings of the military in Nigeria became so routine that Nigerians, with characteristic humor, coined the phrase "soja come, soja go" to describe the routine.

Military rule, however, did not seem to offer much of an improvement over the deprivations of corrupt one-party states. In states such as Nigeria, Sierra Leone, Uganda, and Zaire, new military governments often proved every bit as capable of theft and corruption as had civilian leaders. Indeed, many fell prey to exactly the same sorts of "cults of personality" as did one-party states. In Zaire and Uganda both Mobutu and Amin, respectively, named lakes after themselves. In the Central African Republic, Lt. Col. Jean-Bedel Bokassa overthrew the president (his cousin) and seized power in January 1966. In 1976 he renamed the country the Central African Empire and named himself Emperor Bokassa I. His enthronement ceremony allegedly cost some $50 million (much reputedly paid for by the French) and involved dozens of brand new cars, over 100 tons of imported wine and champagne, and a custom-made jeweled crown and throne. Such self-aggrandizement may seem absurd and even amusing, but it must be noted that such lavish spending utilized funds that could have expanded services to populations suffering from the absence of even the most basic of health and social services. Some military governments also became notorious for their abuse of human rights and even outright slaughter. Both Bokassa and Amin are reputed to have killed thousands who, one way or another, were deemed as threats to their rule.

By the 1980s and early 1990s, it seemed that some African states had become so fragile that almost anyone could seize power. In 1992 a group of soldiers in Sierra Leone traveled to the capital to protest a lack of support for troops fighting against rebels in the eastern part of the country. Fearing an attack, the bodyguards of President Momo (himself originally a military ruler) fired on the soldiers. After a short battle, the soldiers (all veterans) seized the presidential mansion, and Momo fled the country. Seemingly by accident, the soldiers had overthrown the government. In response, they elected one of their number, the twenty-six-year old Captain

Valentine Strasser, as head of state. For many, this event was symbolic of the breakdown of political order in much of Africa. Across the continent military regimes and strongmen seemed the dominant political force. Wars and famine raged in many parts of the continent. Had Africa's revolution of the 1950s and 1960s failed?

Independent African States in Global Perspective

When judged against the expectations that heralded the coming of African independence, there can be little doubt that African states failed to deliver the great bulk of the hopes and dreams that characterized decolonization. Rather than bringing development, most oversaw a steady decline in terms of real income and general standards of living. Instead of greater freedom, most offered what was at best benign neglect. A few, such as Amin's Uganda, managed to shock the world with oppression—even in the face of the ugly standards of the twentieth century. In the absence of increased unity and purpose, political elites seemed to turn to favoritism and corruption. As a result, chronicling the shortcomings of the African state has become something of an academic industry, with both scholars and popular authors coining terms such as "kleptocracy" and "vampire state" to characterize the failure.

From a more historical perspective, however, it is perhaps unfair to judge the African state so harshly. Indeed, governments are somewhat like small businesses—only a tiny percentage of those established manage to survive and turn a profit. Even the history of a "successful" modern nation such as France offers a litany of revolutions, upheavals, and defeats. With roughly four dozen African states gaining independence within the space of a little over a decade, there should be little surprise that so many failed. Also, as this chapter has sought to stress, the African state faced an unprecedented number of challenges. Despite rhetoric to the contrary, colonial powers did little to create a framework conducive to the formation of a robust civil society and legitimate governance. Indeed, military rule was a more apt reflection of colonialism than was democracy. Further, the artificial boundaries created by colonialism and enshrined by independence meant that the new states of Africa were faced with the hurdle of creating a national identity while also seeking economic development. Finally, the global context of the Cold War meant that these new states were forced to "come of age" in an unusually dangerous period of international politics. Gaining independence during the Cold War was like getting your driver's license in the middle of a demolition derby. Dictatorship, civil war, and corruption were all global hallmarks of the Cold War era because all too many states owed their survival and legitimacy more to the superpowers than to the support of their own populations. Dictatorships, military governments, and one-party states were common not only in Africa, but also in Southeast Asia, the Middle East, and Latin America during the period.

Perhaps no collection of states has ever faced such a frightening set of challenges as did the new states of Africa. In part, the very survival of African states has been something of an achievement. It is also important to note that self-determination is a commodity that many people find far more valuable than wealth. Despite the failure of most African states to deliver on the hopes of independence, very few Africans would prefer

Dates of Independence for African States

Ethiopia: Never successfully colonized
    1847—Liberia
    1910—Union of South Africa
    1922—Egypt gains formal independence from Great Britain. British troops remain until 1947
    1951—Libya
    1956—Morocco, Sudan, and Tunisia
    1957—Ghana
    1958—Guinea
    1960—"Year for Africa"; independence gained by Benin (initially named Dahomey), Burkina Faso (initially named Upper Volta), Cameroon, Central African Republic, Chad, Congo, Côte d'Ivoire, Democratic Republic of the Congo, Gabon, Madagascar, Mali, Mauritania, Niger, Nigeria, Senegal, Somalia, and Togo
    1961—Sierra Leone

    1962—Algeria, Burundi, Rwanda, and Uganda
    1963—Kenya, Tanzania (initially named Tanganyika)
    1964—Malawi, Zambia
    1965—Gambia (Rhodesia—settlers declare independence from Great Britain)
    1966—Botswana, Lesotho
    1968—Equatorial Guinea, Mauritius, and Swaziland
    1974—Guinea Bissau
    1975—Angola, Cape Verde, Comoros, Mozambique, and Sao Tome and Principe
    1976—Seychelles
    1977—Djibouti
    1980—New constitution ends conflict in Rhodesia and creates Zimbabwe
    1990—Namibia
    1993—Eritrea

to return to the era of colonialism. Independence at least offered Africans an opportunity to seek development on their own terms. Indeed, what in the present seems a period of instability may in time come to be seen as an era of experimentation—as a time when African civil society sought to find political formulae that would suit the continent's own unique historical and social setting. Such a perspective does not excuse the abuses and deprivations of power that have taken place, but instead simply seeks to place them in a context that makes the "failure" of the African state seem somewhat less unique. Such is the perspective brought by placing Africa in a wider historical context.

Useful Works on This Chapter Topic

There is a considerable literature on African nationalism. See, for example, Ali Mazrui and Michael Tidy, *Nationalism and New States in Africa* (1989); Toyin Falola, *Nationalism and African Intellectuals* (2001); Gregory Maddox (ed.), *African Nationalism and Revolution* (1993); and David Birmingham and Kwame Nkrumah, *The Father of African Nationalism* (1998). For general perspectives on African decolonization, see Trevor Royle, *Winds of Change: The End of Empire in Africa* (1998); J. D. Hargreaves, *Decolonization in Africa* (1988); and David Birmingham, *The Decolonization of Africa* (1996). For comparative perspectives on nationalism and decolonization, see Robert H. Taylor (ed.), *The Idea of Freedom in Asia and Africa* (2002); and John Springhall, *Decolonization Since 1945: The Collapse of European Overseas Empires* (2001).

    The study of the resistance to apartheid and the "armed struggle" in settler states is almost a field unto itself. Some key works include William Beinart and Saul Dubow (eds.), *Segregation and Apartheid in Twentieth-Century South Africa* (1995); Deborah Posel, *The Making of Apartheid, 1948–1961: Conflict and Compromise* (1997); and Alan Schwerin (ed.), *Apartheid's Landscape and Ideas: A Scorched Soul* (2001). Works on revolution include Bill Sutherland and Matt Meyer, *Guns and Gandhi in Africa* (2000); Irene Staunton (ed.), *Mothers of the Revolution: The War Experiences of Thirty Zimbabwean Women* (1991); David Birmingham, *Portugal and Africa* (1999); and Wunyabari O. Maloba, *Mau Mau and Kenya: An Analysis of a Peasant Revolt* (1998).

Works on the early era of African independence are also plentiful. Works such as Kwame Nkrumah's *Neo-Colonialism: The Last State of Imperialism* (1968) and Samir Amin's *Neo-Colonialism in West Africa* (1973) represent the neocolonial or dependency schools. *African Politics in Post Imperial Times: The Essays of Richard L. Sklar,* edited by Toyin Falola (2001), provides a good survey of political issues in independent Africa. Basil Davidson's *The Black Man's Burden: Africa and the Curse of the Nation State* (1993) offers a sympathetic examination of the difficulties faced by new African nations. *In Africa Betrayed* (1993), George B. N. Ayittey takes Africa's political leadership to task for the failures of the postcolonial era. For an overview of military rule in Africa, see Samuel Decalo, *Coups & Army Rule in Africa: Motivations & Constraints* (1990).

CHAPTER 18

Contemporary Africa

For much of Africa, the final decade of the twentieth century seemed to open with little to cheer about. The 1970s and 1980s had been decades of economic decay and both political and civil hardship. The 1990s opened with a legacy of shrinking incomes and declining quality of life for most Africans, as increasing debt burdens and economic decline led to cuts in social services. As a result, most Africans lost, rather than gained, access to health care and education. One-party states and military governments seemed to dominate the political landscape, and rather than ensuring unity or development, both seemed more inclined to invest their resources in maintaining their own positions. In Kenya, where the monopoly of the Kenyan African National Union had once been hailed as "African democracy," the entrenchment of President Daniel arap Moi in office was, by the late 1980s, clearly a case of power being used to maintain power. Describing the situation, the African scholar Ali Mazrui stated, "While Africans have been quite successful in uniting to achieve national freedom, we have utterly failed to unite for economic development and political stability."

As the 1990s progressed, there seemed reason for hope. The collapse of the Soviet Union and the end of the Cold War (symbolized by the destruction of the Berlin Wall in November of 1989) were followed by a third wave of democratization in Africa and elsewhere in the world. Across the continent, dictatorships, military governments, and one-party states seemed to give way to new multiparty democracies. This fact, combined with the belief that the end of the Cold War would lead to a cessation of hostilities in many superpower-funded conflicts (such as that in Angola), led many to proclaim that a new era was dawning when Africa would at last be allowed to develop free of international manipulation. The collapse of the apartheid state in South Africa and the creation of a nonracial Government of National Unity there seemed to further herald an Africa reborn.

In some parts of Africa, however, the optimism of the early 1990s soon gave way to horror. Quite contrary to the hopes that the end of the Cold War would bring peace, a series of state collapses led to brutal conflicts and resulted in losses of life not seen since Leopold's decimation of the Congo. Further, these conflicts threatened to disrupt entire regions, a dynamic perhaps best represented by the genocide in Rwanda and ensuing conflict in the Democratic Republic of the Congo. Contributing to the crises, the global scourge of AIDS spread with particular ferocity in southern Africa. By the late 1990s it was clear that the epidemic would take a staggering toll in the region and perhaps across the continent, as infection rates in some countries climbed to over 25 percent of the adult population.

Perhaps Nigeria's Nobel Prize–winning author Wole Soyinka best summed up the dichotomy of Africa in the 1990s with his statement, "South Africa is our dream, Rwanda our nightmare." In the early twenty-first century, the continent is a complex combination of hope and horror—representing both the best and worst of which human beings are capable. In this chapter we will examine the complex dynamics of Africa in the 1990s and the implications of these developments for Africa in the next few years.

The End of the Cold War and Political Change in Africa

As was discussed in Chapter 17, the Cold War did little to promote good governance in Africa. Both the United States and the Soviet Union supported unrepresentative governments as long as the rulers in question toed an appropriate ideological line in terms of global politics. This meant that many African rulers owed more of their allegiance to outside powers than to their own people. In 1990 a great majority of U.S. aid to Africa (not counting Egypt) went to support dictatorships by Samuel Doe in Liberia, Mobutu Sese Seko in Zaire, and Muhammad Siad Barre in Somalia. Additional aid went to support the campaign led by Jonas Savimbi against the Soviet-supported MPLA government in Angola. Similarly, the Soviets backed repressive regimes such as FRELIMO in Mozambique and the Mengistu Haile Miriam government in Ethiopia. In the 1980s, only five African countries (Botswana, Gambia, Mauritius, Senegal, and Zimbabwe) held regular elections built around universal adult suffrage. The end of the Cold War and the collapse of the Soviet Union, however, meant that Soviet aid disappeared with the Soviet state and that the United States had less incentive to invest in dictatorships. This opened the door for political activists in African states who had long been demanding greater political freedom.

A particularly striking phenomenon of the process of democratization in the early 1990s was the national conference. The first of these remarkable events took place in Benin. Indeed, Benin in early 1990 was representative of many of the challenges facing the African state. The ruler, Matthew Kerekou, had been in power for sixteen years, during most of which time he had ruled via a one-party state that advocated a decidedly Marxist political agenda. The country was in crisis. The central bank had collapsed, and civil servant and student strikes and demonstrations rendered day-to-day life, especially in the capital, almost impossible. Attempts to use force to quell dissent had simply resulted in larger and more energetic protests. With few alternatives available, the Kerekou government agreed to hold a National Conference of Active Forces of the Nation. Convened in February 1990, the conference was composed of several hundred representatives from opposition parties, civil liberties organizations, professional bodies, and religious organizations—a veritable who's who of Benin's civil society. Remarkably, soon after being convened, the conference body voted themselves to be sovereign—that is, the actual governing and lawmaking authority in the country. They promptly got set to rewrite the country's constitution. Perhaps even more remarkably, Kerekou and his ruling party accepted the sovereignty of the conference and agreed to step down in favor of a newly nominated interim government. When elections followed in March 1991, Kerekou ran against and was soundly defeated by Nicephone Soglo, the interim prime minister. The Benin Conference and the following peaceful transition to multiparty democracy were unprecedented in postcolonial African politics and were dubbed a "civilian coup d'état."

In the three years following the Benin Conference, eleven countries (most of them Francophone) followed the country's example. In several, such as Niger and Mali, the conferences resulted in moves to representative democracy. In others, such as neighboring Togo, the conference's goals were stymied by the ruling elite, who managed to hold onto power. In still others, such as Kenya, rulers simply refused to hold conferences—perhaps all too aware that such proceedings could risk the ruler's hold on power. Elsewhere on the continent, democracy slowly advanced even in the absence of national conferences. In Nigeria, for example, the sudden death of military dictator Sani Abacha paved the way for the eventual return of civilian rule. From the nadir of the 1980s, Africa in 1994 had seen democratic processes spread to over a dozen countries. Many more states, although not fully democratic, expanded the scope of competitive elections on the local and regional levels. Perhaps no single democratic transition, however, meant as much as the dismantling of apartheid and the establishment of a nonracial democracy in South Africa.

The End of Apartheid

As examined in the previous two chapters, the creation and maintenance of a white supremacist government in South Africa was a key point of concern for African leaders and activists the world over. Despite international condemnations, South Africa's ruling Nationalist Party continued its attempt to maintain and legitimize apartheid into the early 1980s. In 1982 and 1983, however, a new policy of "separate development" was announced as a replacement for apartheid—something akin to the famous "separate but equal" ruling of the U.S. Supreme Court in 1896. Also, in an attempt to break the nonwhite anti-apartheid coalition, the government created separate chambers of parliament for Asians and Coloureds. Despite such superficial changes, however, whites continued to hold the reins of power in South Africa, and black Africans were still completely excluded from government outside the ostensibly "sovereign" homelands. Indeed, the moves by the Nationalists seemed only to strengthen the anti-apartheid movement, which formed the United Democratic

Front across racial lines. For example, the replacement of the hated pass books with identity cards in 1986 did little to stop protests.

Significant changes took place when P. W. Botha was replaced by **F. W. de Klerk** as prime minister in 1989. The de Klerk government promptly moved to lift the bans on African political parties such as the ANC and PAC and even on the South African Communist Party (very much a sign that Cold War tensions were receding, even in South Africa). In March 1990, Nelson Mandela was released from jail after nearly three decades of imprisonment. As a result of the new "good faith" measures by the South African government, the ANC declared an end to the use of violence as a political tool. After maintaining a system of race-based rule for nearly a century, the South African government, in cooperation with the ANC and other former protest groups, moved to arrange multiparty and nonracial elections. South Africa quickly moved from a position as an international pariah to a model of progressive spirit and reconciliation.

The path to democracy was still not easy for South Africa. Many groups that had been insiders to power under apartheid suddenly found themselves on the outside, as it became apparent that the ANC would politically dominate a post-apartheid South Africa. Ironically, a number of conservative white groups joined with Chief Mangosuthu Buthelezi's predominantly Zulu Inkatha Freedom Party (which had generally worked with the apartheid system) to form the Freedom Alliance in opposition to the ANC. Sadly, the run-up to elections was marked by violent conflicts between Inkatha and ANC activists, particularly in the Zulu-dominated areas of Natal and KwaZulu. Thousands were killed in these clashes. Nonetheless, in 1994 peaceful elections were held, and the ANC returned a strong majority of the vote. Nelson Mandela was sworn in as the first president of a truly democratic South Africa.

As suggested by the Soyinka quote ("South Africa is our dream"), the creation of a free South Africa became a beacon of hope for the continent. In part this was a result of simple economic realities. Even by global standards, South Africa represents an economic powerhouse. In addition to unparalleled wealth in precious and strategic metals, it is also an industrial giant. South Africa accounts for nearly a third of Africa's total economic output and has a power and transportation infrastructure unequaled on the continent. For many, having South Africa as a partner for African development rather than as a shunned pariah state meant that the huge engine of the South African economy could help to power a development revival across the continent. Indeed, within a few years of the collapse of the Nationalist government, the end of sanctions meant that South African companies were moving into markets elsewhere on the continent. South African Breweries (now SAB Miller) sells beer in many African countries and has even purchased Miller Brewing in the United States to become the world's second-largest brewer. South African cell phone companies now compete for markets in Nigeria and Kenya. South African cable television is available in many regions of the continent.

Like most African countries, however, South Africa also has unique challenges to overcome. Not the least of these is the legacy of violence and the unequal distribution of wealth engendered by colonialism and the system of apartheid. One can hardly expect the great mass of the South African population to simply write off decades of oppression with the attainment of political equality. South Africa, thus, must deal with both a tragic past and a challenging future. Recognizing that the system of apartheid had led to the commission of violence and abuses by all sides, the new South African government instituted a most remarkable plan. The country established a **Truth and Reconciliation Commission,** which offered amnesty to those who would come forward and confess to their crimes. Proceedings were often televised, and transcripts of all sessions were made a part of the public record. By placing the reality of violence in the open, South Africans hoped to establish a climate of forgiveness that would allow the healing of the wounds of apartheid. Many welcomed the commission as a way for the country to move forward as a nation, not as a collection of antagonistic racial and political groups. Of course, such a unique undertaking was not without its opponents. Because of the broad application of the policy of amnesty, many victims and families of victims of violence under apartheid felt that the commission allowed murderers and torturers to go free. For some, honesty was no substitute for justice or retribution.

Economic challenges, too, face the new South Africa. Despite the country's considerable wealth, poverty exists on a brutal scale within some communities—particularly among the indigenous Africans whose economic activities were most restricted and exploited under apartheid. Populations in the former homelands and segregated black townships still lack decent housing, sanitation, and access to social services. Extending social services and creating opportunity for a previously dispossessed population is no easy thing. Simply transferring property or wealth from the (predominantly white) wealthy class to the poor would be politically expedient in the short run, but would certainly disrupt the fragile balance of the industrial economy—perhaps leading to a complete economic crash. Fears of instability initially led to considerable capital flight from South Africa, resulting in years of recession and a devaluation of the Rand (the national currency). Yet, one can hardly expect the impoverished majority of South Africans to continue to accept their poverty (itself an apartheid legacy) passively. A skyrocketing rate of violent crime in South Africa since the end of apartheid reflects the difficulties of extending political, but not economic, opportunity to previously oppressed populations. In contrast to the high hopes and ideals of newly independent African states in the 1960s, South Africans are aware that the attainment of the "political kingdom" does not necessarily lead to wealth. However unfairly, South Africa bears the burden of serving as a test case of whether African leaders have learned from the crises of expectations of the 1960s and can successfully navigate the myriad challenges to African development. For the African state, the stakes are always high—Africans must bear the heavy burden of the past to advance into the future.

Conflict and Collapsed States in the Post–Cold War Era

Although for some countries the early 1990s seemed to herald a new era of political freedom and opportunity, in others the decade seemed to lead in exactly the opposite direction—into state decay and even total collapse. Notably, these cases of collapsed states took place most often in those countries where rulers had most benefitted from Cold War clienthood—Liberia, Somalia, and Zaire. Ironically, the

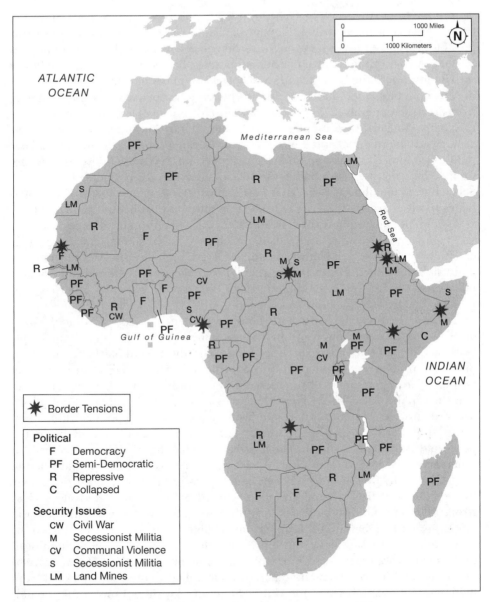

ATLANTIC
OCEAN

Mediterranean Sea

Red Sea

Gulf of Guinea

INDIAN
OCEAN

✸ Border Tensions

Political
F	Democracy
PF	Semi-Democratic
R	Repressive
C	Collapsed

Security Issues
CW	Civil War
M	Secessionist Militia
CV	Communal Violence
S	Secessionist Militia
LM	Land Mines

Map 18-1: Politics and security in contemporary Africa

Cold War was capable of encouraging conflict even by its very absence. Further, in the early 1990s the continent would witness its most appalling genocide since early in the century when the Germans had called for the extermination of the Herero—the massacres of Tutsi and Hutu in Rwanda. By the late 1990s these conflicts would have resulted in the loss of millions of lives and would threaten to destabilize their neighboring states.

If the Cold War could be a contributing factor to conflict in Africa, as in the case of Angola or the Somali–Ethiopian wars, how could the end of the Cold War possibly be a cause for new or even worse violence? The answer lies, at least in part, in the complex dynamics of international politics. As discussed previously, during the Cold War both the United States and Soviet Union backed abusive governments in Africa (and elsewhere in the world) as a means to various strategic ends, ranging from access to minerals (as in the case of Zaire) to control of a strategic location (as in Liberia, Somalia, or Ethiopia). With strong military backing from their super-power patrons, rulers of some of these states became unnaturally insulated from public opinion. This situation all but guaranteed unprecedented levels of corruption. Perhaps no case better highlights this dynamic than Zaire, where Mobutu Sese Seko enjoyed unfailing U.S. backing from the mid-1960s to late 1980s. The United States received access to Zaire's considerable mineral wealth (critical in the Cold War), and Mobutu enjoyed considerable U.S. aid in the form of finances and military equipment, providing him with the means to reward supporters and brutally crack down on dissent. Meanwhile, infrastructure and social services in most of Zaire all but vanished. For example, at independence Zaire possessed some 88,000 miles of all-weather roads. By the mid-1980s only some 1,200 miles of paved road remained passable in the entire country.

As the Cold War drew to a close, however, both the United States and the Soviets withdrew their backing from their client states. The Soviets pulled out simply because they had ceased to exist as a country, and the United States because such dictatorships were no longer politically expedient. Indeed, these client states had become glaring reminders of the ideological compromises the United States had made to win the Cold War. As a result, regimes once backed by superpowers quickly found themselves without support and facing years of pent-up popular discontent. Thus, although in some cases African states made peaceful transitions to the post–Cold War political climate (such as via peaceful change of governments), in others, wars resulted as force of arms became the determinant of political power.

One of the first instances of new conflict was in Liberia. As a former colony for "repatriated" free persons from the United States, Liberia had always had strong economic and political ties with the United States. However, in 1980, the largely Americo-Liberian government of William Tolbert was overthrown by Sergeant Samuel Doe in a wave of unrest that followed a government attempt to increase the price of rice sharply. Despite the summary executions of many ousted politicians and the commission of many atrocities against the country's small population of Americo-Liberians, the United States quickly shifted support to the new government—demonstrating more concern for its strategic interests in the region than anything else. Doe proved to be a harsh dictator, however, and popular resentment grew as he seemed to favor his own Krahn ethnic group over other Liberians. In 1989, an Americo-Liberian, Charles Taylor, with alleged backing from Libya, Côte d'Ivoire, and Burkina Faso, invaded Liberia with a small military force. Taylor's troops received considerable local support and soon controlled a large proportion of Liberian territory. Another power broker soon appeared in the form of Prince Johnson, a former Doe ally, who organized his own army by drawing on support from the regions of the country populated by the Grio and

Mano ethnic groups. Johnson soon gained a reputation for a tactical brilliance matched only by his ruthlessness. By summer 1990, Doe's forces controlled only a small area around the capital of Monrovia. An ensuing stalemate resulted in massive loss of life and a growing refugee crisis as civilians sought to escape the fighting, and shortages of staple foods began to develop. Within a few months, Liberia had imploded.

In August 1990 the Economic Community of West African States (ECOWAS) organized a military force called ECOMOG (Economic Community Monitoring Group). Nigerian troops made up the majority of the force, but they were reinforced by peacekeepers from Ghana, Senegal, and elsewhere in the region. The effort was facilitated by limited U.S. financial backing. The West African forces were dispatched to Monrovia and were soon able to establish a degree of security within the city. ECOMOG troops later lured Doe to their headquarters under a guise of negotiation and turned him over to Prince Johnson's forces. Doe was then tortured and executed—with the event being recorded on video. Following Doe's death, an interim government was formed with representatives of the country's various factions, although flare-ups of violence between regional factions continue to plague the country. Peace talks eventually bore fruit, and elections were held in 1997, awarding the presidency to Charles Taylor. Taylor remained in power until August 2003, when rebel groups and international pressure forced him to step down and accept exile in Nigeria. West African peacekeepers were again dispatched to the country, though they were soon subsumed into a UN force of nearly 15,000 troops, forming one of the UN's largest contemporary peacekeeping operations.

With its economy and infrastructure in shambles, Liberia sought to rebuild. The effort was made more difficult in that diamond exports, which could potentially serve as a much-needed source of income for the country, were embargoed because they had instead come to serve as a source of income for rebel groups. Despite such impediments, however, Liberia has made important strides toward regaining some degree of stability. Indeed, 2006 was a year of milestones for the country. In January, Mrs. Ellen Johnson-Sirleaf was elected president, making her the first female African head of state. Known as "the Iron Lady," she is famous for her hard line against corruption and no-nonsense administrative style. Further, the creation of a Truth and Reconciliation Commission (following the South African model) in February of 2006 has helped Liberians establish some sense of closure with the violence of the past decade.

The conflict in Liberia helped to destabilize neighboring Sierra Leone. This unrest was in part because forces in the Liberian civil war occupied eastern Sierra Leone to use both as a base for incursions into Liberia and as a source of funding. Sierra Leone is rich in diamonds, and access to the mines in the east provided funds essential to purchasing arms and supplies for Liberian belligerents. This "spillover" from Liberia soon led to fighting between the Sierra Leonian military and rebel groups in the east, who were eventually organized under the name of the Revolutionary United Front (RUF). This fighting provided the catalyst for the overthrow of Sierra Leone's government by a group of disaffected troops in 1992. Subsequent coups in 1996 and 1997 added to the country's growing instability, despite UN-brokered elections in 1996. Human rights abuses became rife as the country sank into anarchy. Child troops were utilized by the rebel forces, and atrocities were committed against civilians. The frequent chopping off of hands as punishment for supporting "the enemy" became a symbol of a country in chaos. United Nations troops seemed poorly prepared to operate in Sierra Leone, with hundreds of international peacekeepers being captured and held for ransom by the rebels. Only the intervention of ECOMOG in 1998 allowed for the return of the democratically elected president, Tejan Kabba. ECOMOG troops, however, suffered a number of costly defeats at the hands of the RUF forces and sought to cut short their occupation as soon as possible. The intervention of British troops in 2000 guaranteed the continuation of order in the area around the capital. The British forces were soon reinforced by UN peacekeepers, who, in contrast to their setbacks in the country in the 1990s, were successful in disarming the rebel groups. This was facilitated by the capture (and subsequent death) of Froday Sankoh, the main rebel leader. In 2002, Tejan Kabbah was elected president, returning him to the office he had held briefly in 1997. In 2004, a war-crimes tribunal was established to try those accused of atrocities during the civil war. Most notably, Charles Taylor, the former president of Liberia, was arrested in Nigeria and charged with crimes against humanity for his role in fostering the conflict in Sierra Leone.

Sadly, as conflict seemed to be abating in Liberia and Sierra Leone, it was spreading in Côte d'Ivoire. Long hailed as an "African success story," Côte d'Ivoire had enjoyed considerable peace and prosperity since independence in 1960. Some attributed this situation to the thirty-three-year rule of President Houphouet Boigny and his maintenance of close economic ties to France. Following Boigny's death in 1993, however, politics in the country became increasingly divided, with political parties splitting along religious and ethnic lines, leading to growing tensions between the country's predominantly Muslim north and Christian south. A military coup in 1999 and a divisive election the following year led to growing insecurity. In the election, southerner Laurent Gbagbo was declared victor after his northern opponent, Allasane Ouattara, was disqualified because his mother was allegedly non-Ivoirian. The disqualification was itself based upon a new law requiring that all candidates prove their "pure" Ivoirian heritage—a move seen by many northerners as discrimination against mostly Muslim migrants from Burkina Faso and Mali. Protests following the election turned violent, with many northerners allegedly being killed by police and military forces. During 2001, negotiations between Gbagbo and Ouattara's parties held out some hope of peace, but an army mutiny in 2002 grew into a wide-scale rebellion in the north, with a group calling itself the Patriotic Movement of Côte d'Ivoire seizing control of much of the region.

French-sponsored peace talks between the factions in 2003 led to a short-lived "consensus government" and a cease-fire. French troops were sent to serve as a buffer force between the two factions. However, a harsh government crackdown on an anti-Gbagbo rally in 2004 reignited tensions, and Gbagbo and his supporters began to take an increasingly anti-French position, decrying Ouattara and his supporters as "French Stooges." When planes operated by the southern government bombed a French position and killed nine French soldiers in November of 2004, the French retaliated by destroying much of the Ivoirian Air Force. In response, anti-French riots swept the southern part of the country, particularly the capital of Abidjan, which was home to thousands of French expatriates. Worse, during an evacuation of French nationals from the capital, French forces allegedly fired on protestors, reputedly killing dozens.

In December of 2004, however, the southern parliament removed the "purity" requirement from the constitution, apparently opening the door for reconciliation. Talks in South Africa in 2005 resulted in the northern rebels promising an end to hostilities. But, Gbagbo's delay of elections scheduled for that year, and the outbreak of violent anti-UN riots in the south and the failure of pro-Gbagbo militias to meet disarmament deadlines in June of 2006, led to the delay of elections that had been rescheduled for October of 2006. Further, the UN extended the mandate of the transitional government to run through 2007. As of the writing of these words, the fate of Côte d'Ivoire is very much in the balance, as a confluence of historical and global factors threaten to inflame local and regional identities and interests. However, in what is perhaps a characteristically African twist, the Côte d'Ivoirian soccer team, the Elephants, qualified for the 2006 World Cup and scored victories in the African Cup of Nations. Made up of players from north and south, the team temporarily rallied the country. As one protestor told the BBC, "We stopped so we can watch the Elephants in the Nations Cup. When they get knocked out we will be on the streets again."

Although the conflicts in Liberia, Sierra Leone, and Côte d'Ivoire unfolded in relative obscurity, the collapse of the Somali state and the ensuing famine and conflict made global headlines—largely because the loss of life suffered by U.S. troops during attempts to capture the warlord **Muhammad Aideed** in 1993 was dramatized in the popular movie *Black Hawk Down*. Even prior to these events, the United States had been deeply involved in Somali politics. After the loss of Ethiopia as a client state to a Marxist-inspired coup in 1974, the United States increasingly backed the regime of Siad Barre in Somalia to maintain influence in the strategically important Horn of Africa. Barre's government faced considerable internal opposition, in no small part owing to the country's defeats in conflicts with neighboring Ethiopia. Barre was also accused of favoring his own Marehan clan in terms of government positions and development projects. In 1982 the National Opposition Movement was organized from bases in the northern region of the country. Only harsh crackdowns in the later 1980s allowed Barre to maintain his position in power. Yet by 1990, Barre had lost control over much of the country. Further, with the Cold War drawing to a close, the United States was increasingly unwilling to back Barre. In 1991, Barre fled the country, and the political situation quickly deteriorated as over a half dozen clan-based groups fought for control. Significant stores of weapons in the country were a legacy of years of Cold War military "aid." If you ever wondered where all those guns came from, the answer is quite simple— they are a leftover of the Cold War. None of the groups, however, was able to emerge supreme, and the country was soon the domain of regional warlords. This situation would have been bad enough, but years of drought had also led to critical food shortages. With the advent of a multiparty civil war, food supplies could no longer be effectively distributed because whichever group controlled the airport or port could easily seize food shipments. In times of famine and conflict, hunger is a weapon in and of itself.

As humanitarian groups forecast massive loss of life due to starvation, the United Nations organized a U.S.-led intervention, popularly known as Operation Restore Hope. In 1992 some 30,000 troops landed in the capital of Mogadishu, quickly restored order, and arranged for the distribution of foodstuffs. Many were optimistic that the worst of the famine had been averted—though more than 100,000 had already died. In 1993, however, the UN and U.S. troops attempted to expand their mission from the comparatively simple delivery of food to the disarming of the various "militias" that controlled the country—beginning with the capital and surrounding area. This move led to conflict between peacekeepers and the troops of Muhammad Aideed, a commander in charge of one of the groups in Mogadishu. Aideed's troops soon ambushed and killed a number of Pakistani peacekeepers. The United States and UN then placed a price on Aideed's head and sought to capture him as an example to other regional commanders. Aideed, however, proved too skillful to be caught. In October 1993 a botched U.S. attempt to capture Aideed resulted in two U.S. helicopters being shot down. Eighteen elite U.S. troops were killed and dozens wounded in the resulting attempt to rescue the downed pilots. Although over 1,000 Somali fighters lost their lives in the battle, it was nonetheless seen as a defeat for U.S. forces. Further, the televised display of dead U.S. troops being dragged through the streets of Mogadishu caused a considerable backlash in the United States against the mission in Somalia. Troops from other UN states also experienced losses in local battles. Canada was scandalized when news came out that some of its troops had tortured and murdered Somali civilians—taking "trophy" pictures of the process. The news led to a series of investigations and several resignations within Canada's military leadership. Soon troops from the United States and most other countries had been withdrawn. The UN had abandoned Somalia.

Unlike in Liberia and Sierra Leone, where intervention eventually helped to restore order, Somalia has become the archetype of a "collapsed state." From 1991 to 2006 it existed as a country only in that there is no other name to put on the map. There was no effective central administration. Rather, competing militias vied for control of regions and local resources. Muhammad Aideed, who had so skillfully eluded American forces, was killed in an ambush by local rivals in 1996. Aideed was replaced in power by his son, Hussein Aideed, who, ironically, is an American citizen and former Marine. In the northern region there has been considerable progress toward establishing peace. A judicial system, police force, and elected parliament have all been created by local initiative. This area has sought international recognition as the independent state of Somaliland. No country has yet recognized the fledgling "state," however, and without international recognition, the government cannot receive any form of international aid to rebuild infrastructure or attract investment.

Remarkably, the Somali conflict has not meant an end to economic activity. Indeed, the survival of business in the region is a testimony to human ingenuity and perseverance. Amid the seeming chaos, cell phone businesses operate and offer international calls. Flights of food, manufactured goods, and of course, armaments arrive regularly even as control of the airport changes hands. Exports also continue. Somalia remains a major regional exporter of beef, for example. Notably, there have been environmental costs resulting from the disappearance of the state. Somalia's forests, once protected by the central government, are now being destroyed as charcoal producers, often in the employ of local warlords, have expanded production to meet demands for the product in the Middle East. This certainly doesn't mean that there are not Somalis who are concerned for the environment, but simply that in the absence of the state, there is no means to regulate the extraction of resources.

Hopes for a reassertion of formal sovereignty and state functioning were raised in 2005, when talks between various factions held in Kenya laid the groundwork for the establishment of a new Somali parliament. In February of 2006, the new parliament met for the first time in the Somali city of Baidoa. The new government has the support of both the African Union and the United Nations. Hopes were soon marred by the outbreak of heavy fighting in Mogadishu, where a new group, calling itself the Union of Islamic Courts (UIC) began expanding its area of influence. Notably, the UIC began in the 1990s, when local populations supported the establishment of autonomous Islamic courts in an attempt to deal with the crime wave that came with the collapse of the central government. However, over the intervening years, the courts eventually joined forces and formed their own local militia, which sought to inforce first Islamic codes of social conduct, and later moved to establish more formal political power. For its own part, the group has said that it only seeks to implement Islamic unity and justice in the place of rampant clan-based conflict.

The conflict between the UIC and the provisional government escalated in late 2006, when the Ethiopian government, with the support of the African Union, entered the war. With the aid of several thousand Ethiopian troops, backed by aircraft and armoured vehicles, the provisional government was able to route the UIC fighters from the capital in a matter of days. Driving the UIC from the area was only part of the challenge, however. The new government has faced considerable turmoil since taking Mogadishu, including rampant looting and a resurgence of clan-based fighting. Further, given the history of conflict between Somalia and Ethiopia, much of the Somali population has shown considerable distrust for the Ethiopian forces and their links to the new government.

Africa and the War on Terror

Notably, in response to the growth of the UIC, the United States has reputedly offered aid to the provisional government and the various militias fighting the Islamic group, leading many to see the conflict as an outgrowth of the U.S. conflict with Islamist groups such as *Al Qaeda*. In January of 2007, the United States launched an air attack on alleged *Al Qaeda* operatives in southern Somalia. These developments reflect a growing U.S. military involvement in many parts of Africa as part of the "Global War on Terror." Security experts in the United States have often argued that not only collapsed states such as Somalia, and also weak states elsewhere in the continent, could result in "safe havens" for terrorist groups. The 1998 bombing attacks on the American Embassies in Kenya and Tanzania were seen as examples of how terrorists could strike at U.S. interests in Africa. Fears also arose that terrorist groups could use African settings for the establishment of training camps or the raising of capital so as to pursue attacks on the United States itself. As a result, in policy moves that often echo the policies of the Cold War, the United States has extended military support in the form of training, equipment, and financial aid to countries deemed "allies" in the War on Terror, despite the fact that some of these countries, such as Chad, have weak records of democratic process and often have records of human rights abuses.

The Rwandan Genocide and the "African World War"

The genocide in Rwanda represents one of the most terrible losses of life in contemporary Africa. Tensions between Hutu and Tutsi populations in Rwanda date back to the imposition of colonial rule, when first the Germans and later the Belgians favored the ostensibly "more advanced" Tutsi as "natural" rulers. As a result, Tutsis received greater education and access to positions within the colonial administration and military. However, when the Belgians moved toward decolonization in the late 1950s, tensions began to rise. The Hutu, who made up some 85 percent of the population, were eager for elections because their numbers would guarantee victory in the polls. Tutsi populations, however, feared that democracy would spell an end to their privileged status. Riots in 1959 left thousands dead. Interethnic violence flared again in 1963, and tens of thousands of Tutsis fled to Burundi, Uganda, and Tanzania. Abroad they formed a political and military group called the Rwandan Patriotic Front (RPF). A military coup in 1973 brought Major General Juvenal Habyarimana to power in Rwanda, and he justified his lock on power by stating that he would control the ongoing ethnic conflict. He established a quota system, which ostensibly guaranteed proportional representation for Hutus and Tutsis in all public offices and services. Nonetheless, by the early 1990s, Habyarimana faced growing internal dissent by conservatives because of his move to multiparty elections and negotiations with the RPF.

In April 1994, shortly before UN-sponsored elections were scheduled to take place, Habyarimana's plane was shot down over the capital of Kigali. Witnesses allege that the missiles were fired from a nearby Rwandan army base. Within hours of Habyarimana's death, it was clear that the events were far more than a coup—a carefully planned genocide was taking place. Radio broadcasts called for the mass slaughter of Tutsis in the country, calling them "cockroaches who must be eliminated." Within two months, over half a million people had been killed—not only Tutsis but also key Hutu moderates who had advocated multiethnic government and those who sought to protect their Tutsi neighbors. Images and tales of the slaughter shocked people around the globe. Amazingly, rather than respond to the massacres, the United Nations opted to pull what troops it had in the country out—in part due to the death of ten Belgian peacekeepers at the hands of a Hutu militia group. A small force of some 200 Ghanaian peacekeepers remained in Kigali. Poorly equipped for the situation (they had been stationed as monitors for the upcoming election), they nonetheless saved perhaps thousands of lives—a heroic act for which they received little international acclaim.

Indeed, there was little international response, aside from horror, to the massacres in Rwanda. American and UN teams surveyed the region but declared that poor infrastructure and ongoing conflict rendered relief efforts too difficult to undertake on a large scale. United Nations reports on the conflict studiously avoided the use of the word "genocide," which would have required intervention under international law. Perhaps the recent failure in Somalia was a factor in the hesitancy to become involved in another conflict. In response to the mass slaughter of Tutsis, the RPF launched a major campaign from the north, and by July 1994 had taken control of Kigali and established a new government. The RPF even named a Hutu, Pasteur Bizimungu, as president, though few doubted that real power remained with the RPF leaders, particularly Paul Kagame. Perhaps as many as two million Hutus, fearing reprisals, fled into eastern Zaire. Among these refugees, however, were the very Hutu militias who had perpetrated the massacres. From bases in refugee camps, these militias began to launch raids back into their native Rwanda—allegedly to try and halt trials of Hutu arrested for genocide. By 1996 the new Rwandan government had sent troops into Zaire in an attempt to disrupt and arrest the militias. Here they came into conflict with Zairean troops, whom they defeated with little trouble. The conflict in Rwanda was soon to help set off an even larger conflagration in Central Africa.

In the latter 1990s, Zaire was already tottering on the brink of collapse. Mobutu's dictatorship was in disarray. Attempts at installing a new government via a national conference in the early 1990s had been blocked by Mobutu and the military. At one point there were two competing governments in the capital of Kinshasa. Inflation ran rampant, and the military often looted shops and businesses as a form of "pay." Mobutu, largely abandoned by the United States, was both physically ill and increasingly incapable of maintaining control over the country. Disorder in the capital forced him to rule from a luxury yacht on the Congo River. In the eastern regions of Zaire, the troops of the Rwandan government found an ally in the person of Laurent Kabila, who had been organizing resistance to Mobutu's rule since the 1960s. The precise chronology is hard to determine, but soon Mobutu was arming the Hutu militias, and the Rwandans were supplying arms and troops to Kabila's Alliance of Democratic Forces for the Liberation of Congo-Zaire. The tables quickly turned against Mobutu and the Hutu forces, as Kabila's army (made up largely of Tutsi troops, but also allegedly backed by troops from Uganda) rapidly advanced across Zaire. By May 1997 the ailing Mobutu was forced to flee the country, and Kabila assumed control of the central government, changing the name of the country from Zaire back to the original post-independence name of Democratic Republic of the Congo (DRC).

The ascension of Kabila to power, however, brought neither peace nor stability to the DRC. First, numerous allegations emerged that Kabila and his backers had committed mass atrocities against civilians during their campaign across the country. Attempts to investigate were largely blocked by the new government. Further, citizens of the country began to feel as if Kabila's backers were a foreign army of occupation. In August 1998 tensions between Kabila and his Ugandan and Rwandan supporters turned into open conflict. Desperate for support, Kabila appealed to neighboring countries for military aid. He found backing from Angola and Zimbabwe, in

Women pass a disabled armored vehicle in the DRC. Fighting in the country led to millions of deaths prior to peace accords and elections in 2005 and 2006.

particular, and also from his former Hutu "enemies." By 2000 over half a dozen states and the UNITA rebel movement from Angola were involved in the DRC. Even troops from Chad were allegedly involved. The fighting in the DRC had escalated to a multifront, multination conflict, a situation that led many observers to dub it the "African World War."

Why would so many countries so willingly involve themselves in the conflict in the DRC? The reason is the same as for why there had been conflict in the region during the Congo Crisis—the country's incredible mineral wealth. In the eastern DRC, Ugandan and Rwandan troops took over gold mines and also leased "concessions" for the mining of tantalum—a critical component in the manufacture of miniaturized electronics such as cell phones. Kabila's new allies received concessions for access to the DRC's wealth. Zimbabwe gained access to diamond mines, and the Angolan government signed an agreement to create a jointly owned oil company with the DRC. The UNITA rebel group, which was suffering from an end of U.S. aid at the end of the Cold War, sought haven in the DRC from attacks by the Angolan government and also gained access to diamond resources with which to continue operations. Such divisions of spoils made the conflict a profitable venture for the various countries involved. Even without Cold War aid from the United States and Soviet Union, war was perfectly possible. In 2001, Kabila was assassinated by one of his own bodyguards. He was succeeded as president by his son, Joseph Kabila.

The conflict in the DRC took a massive toll on the region's civilian population. Hundreds of thousands, if not millions, have been displaced as refugees. With the region divided between warring states, even local economies and networks of distribution have been disrupted. Perhaps some 350,000 have been killed in the fighting, and an estimated three million have died as a result of hunger, disease, and exposure. Remarkably, this catastrophic loss of human life has largely occurred "below the radar" of international awareness. The ongoing conflict remains "back page" and "late night" news for media groups. As such, the inaction of the UN has received little attention or condemnation. Similarly, because the ruling elites within the DRC and other regional governments are profiting from the conflict, there has been little or no call for intervention from Africa itself. Ironically, although Africa seemed to suffer from too much international intervention during colonialism and the Cold War, for a time, it seems perhaps to have suffered from too little.

There have been, however, at least some signs of hope. In July 2002 the DRC and Rwanda signed an accord aimed at ending their conflict. Rwanda has agreed to withdraw troops from the country, and the DRC has promised to disarm the Hutu militias using the region as a base of operations. A similar pact involved Uganda in the peace process in September of that year. In the years since, Rwanda, Uganda, and Zimbabwe have withdrawn their troops from the DRC. In 2003, a French-led UN force was established to keep the peace, though its small size and the vastness of the DRC rendered its mission difficult. Over the course of 2005, the interim government drafted a new constitution which was approved by a national referendum. During this same period, the UN forces undertook a campaign to disarm local militias. The resulting clashes between UN and militia troops led thousands to flee the northeast region of the country. By the summer of 2006, the country was ready for national elections, which were held on August 1. Run-off elections between Joseph Kabila and Jean-Pierre Bemba were held in October, though the polls were marred when forces loyal to the two candidates clashed in the capital. In November, Joseph Kabila was declared president. Kabila's government faces numerous challenges, ranging from an infrastrcuture and economy shattered by years of corruption and conflict, and also numerous independent militias and warlords who still control large swaths of the country.

Genocide in Sudan?

Sudan has, all too often, served as an example of what has gone wrong with African states. Formed when the British amalgamated two different colonial regions in 1946, the country experienced civil war between the predominantly Muslim north and predominantly traditional and Christian south from 1962 to 1972 and from 1983 to 2002. These wars cost the lives of perhaps 1.5 million people, inflamed tensions between regional populations, and left much of the southern region's infrastructure in ruins. However, the discovery of large oil reserves in the south in 1999, and the 2002 signing in Kenya of the Machakos Protocol ending the civil war and providing relative autonomy to the south, gave Sudanese and observers reasons to hope for peace. Perhaps with an end to fighting, the newfound petroleum reserves would provide the capital necessary to rebuild the country and even pave over ethnic and historical fissures. Indeed, the peace has held between the northern and southern regions since 2002.

However, since 2003, the conflict in Darfur, in the country's western region, has grown in scale, and has attracted a considerable degree of international attention, if not action. The conflict began when a rebel group in the Darfur region attacked government installations, alleging that the government was neglecting the region's "black" farming population while favoring the "Arab" pastoralists. This situation not only highlights the tensions common between farmers and herders, but also just how complex local identities can be. Both the agriculturalists and the pastoralists in Darfur are Muslims. Further, to an American observer, all would appear "black." Nonetheless, cultural and linguistic divisions between the populations are often characterized in oversimplified "black" versus "Arab" terms. Whatever the divisions, the Sudanese government sent troops (many of whom were veterans of the civil war) into the region to root out the rebels. Local and international groups, however, accused the army of attacking civilian populations. By mid-2004, a local "Arab" militia known as the **Janjaweed** was active in the region, and was apparently targeting civilians. A Human Rights Watch report issued that year stated that the Janjaweed were undertaking a program of "ethnic cleansing." Though the Sudanese government denied any links to the Janjaweed, many believed that the government was supporting the militias. In September of 2004, the United States government characterized the situation as a genocide, and called for international intervention. Motions for action by the UN Security Council, however, were blocked by threatened vetoes from China and Russia, both of which are substantial investors in Sudan's new petroleum industry. Further, the Sudanese government flatly refused any sort of UN involvement, and characterized the UN as a "colonial force."

By 2005, however, negotiations had led to the implementation of a small force of African Union peacekeepers. Numbering only a few thousand, poorly supplied, and lacking a mandate beyond that of observing the situation, the group has been able to do little to stop the killing of civilians. As of mid-2006, it is clear that tens of thousands of civilians have lost their lives, and perhaps as many as two million have been displaced, either moving to ill-equiped refugee camps or seeking haven in neighboring Chad. Further, cross-border raids by militia groups on both sides have inflamed tensions with Chad, leading that country to threaten war against Sudan in 2005. Peace talks between two Darfur rebel groups and the Sudanese government have been held in Abuja, Nigeria, though to date little progress has been made toward a peaceful solution to the situation. The UN has still stopped short of calling the situation in Darfur a "genocide" (reminding many observers of the UN's inaction in Rwanda in 1994). However, in 2006 the UN did take the step of calling for war crimes trials of leaders of rebel and militia factions from both sides.

While conflict continues to be a contemporary concern in states such as Sudan and Côte d'Ivoire, and in places such as the Horn of Africa, it is important to emphasize that the past few years have seen at least partial resolutions and significant reductions in violence in previously war-torn regions. Internationally brokered talks and peacekeeping initiatives have not only led to peace accords in Sierra Leone, Liberia, Angola, and the DRC, but have also led to elections in all except Angola. Accords have also been reached with separatist movements in countries such as Uganda and Senegal. Given the brutality of these conflicts, and their destabilizing influence on surrounding countries, these are no small acheivements, and credit must be given where due. Such cases provide crucial counterpoints to the "Afro-Pessimismist" perspective that there is no hope for things African, by showing that conflicts can end, and new beginnings can be forged out of even the most terrible situations. Each of these states must overcome significant difficulties to rebuild

Voices from African History: **Fela Anikulapo Kuti on the Difficulties of Daily Life in Urban Africa.**

"Everyday. . . for house
Everyday. . . for road
Everyday. . . for bus
Everyday. . . for work
My People, My People, My People, My People
This is what happens to we Africans everyday
now which I go tell you now, na secret oh
na confidential matter
don't tell anybody outside
na between me and you, now listen
as I say before, this happen to all of us
everyday, we Africans all over the world
Everyday my people inside bus
Shuffering and Schmiling
49 sitting 99 standing
Shuffering and Schmiling
Them go pack themselves in like sardines
Shuffering and Schmiling
Them go faint they be wake like cock
Shuffering and Schmiling

Them go reaching house water not there
Shuffering and Schmiling
Them go reaching bed power not there
Shuffering and Schmiling
Them go reaching road go slow go come
Shuffering and Schmiling
Them go reaching road police go slap
Shuffering and Schmiling
Them go reaching road army go whip
Shuffering and Schmiling
Them go look pocket money not there
Shuffering and Schmiling
Them go reaching work worry ready
Shuffering and Schmiling
Everyday now the same thing
Everyday now the same thing
Suffer Suffer for world (Amen) enjoy for heaven (Amen)"

From *Shuffering and Schmiling,* Fela Anikulapo Kuti & the Africa 70 (1977)

---

both their economies and their sense of community following these conflicts. But, it is a testimony to the human capacity to make amends and rebuild that progress is being made.

Globalization and Development in Contemporary Africa

At the beginning of the 1990s, many African states were facing dire economic crises. Whereas Africans once had great faith in the ability of their governments to create wealth, by the 1980s that faith had largely vanished. Their own governments seemed to seek only self-enrichment, and international bodies seemed to demand only belt-tightening to squeeze out money to pay debts. For most Africans, plans for development, whether hatched at home or abroad, have generally led to hardship and disillusionment.

During the 1990s, the development "flavor of the decade" had switched to liberalization and globalization. Central to this shift was the success of development strategies in Asia, which had led states such as Indonesia, Malaysia, Thailand, and China to post remarkable rates of economic growth (though this growth slowed considerably following the Asian stock crashes of 1997). Indeed, although African and Asian countries had shared similar standards of living in the 1960s, years of growth in Asia and decline in Africa had led to stark contrasts between these two world regions by the 1990s. By emulating Asian strategies of dropping trade barriers, courting international investment, and privatizing state-run businesses, argued some, African countries could encourage similar levels of economic growth. Indeed, the small East African island country of Mauritius did actively court global trade in the 1980s and 1990s and did post remarkable levels of economic growth.

The potential gains from expanded trade are indeed huge. By 2002, Africa's share of global trade had shrunk to less than 1.5 percent—down from a 4 percent share in 1970. An increase to 2.5 percent would represent a gain of some $70 billion, nearly five times the total foreign aid of $17 billion that Africa received from various sources in 2001.

Although few argue with the fact that expanded trade is a good thing, many fear that the playing field of "globalization" is far from level. Would the dropping of trade barriers by African countries really result in productive investment, or would it simply mean cheaper access to African resources for the already wealthy countries of the world? Further, few countries have ever industrialized without tariffs or price supports—certainly such tactics were used to good effect by the world's industrial states. How could fledgling African industries possibly compete with established high-volume factories in Europe, America, and Asia without some degree of protection?

The sign for the Hard Rock Café, Capetown, incorporates the new South African flag, and reflects South Africa's close involvement with the global economy.

Similarly, detractors of free trade point out that the markets of most developed countries are still far from open. The United States, for example, places considerable restrictions on the importation of African textiles, despite the fact that African fabrics are in high demand and that African factories generally run at a fraction of capacity. For example, the African Growth and Opportunity Act, passed in 2000, doubled the quantity of fabric imports allowed into the United States from Africa. But, this increase still limited the total volume of African fabrics to a minuscule .8 percent of U.S. textile imports.

Similarly, huge price supports provided to American and European farmers allow them to dominate international food markets by selling at prices that undercut even local producers. American rice is cheaper in most African countries than is locally produced grain. Notably, these subsidies have been increased (for example, with the 2002 U.S. Farm Bill), even as African countries are being encouraged to privatize. Thus, in the economic areas in which African states are most prepared to compete—textiles and agriculture—they nonetheless face the most barriers. Further, although most Western states import unprocessed commodities from Africa without obstacle, African attempts to process goods prior to export (and thus build industrial capacity) face barriers. For example, Ghana can export unlimited quantities of unprocessed cocoa beans to Europe, but it faces stiff quotas on the export of (higher value) processed cocoa butter. Many observers find such economic restrictions all too reminiscent of colonialism.

In June of 2005 the world's eight wealthiest countries (known as the G-8) agreed to cancel some $40 billion in debt owed by nineteen countries—fifteen of which are located in Africa. This was by far the most significant act of debt reduction ever announced, and had the effect of eradicating or substantially reducing the national debt of countries such as Tanzania, Zambia, and Mali. It is estimated that this debt forgiveness will free up some $1.5 billion per year that would otherwise have gone to paying interest on the loans in question. This represents a significant amount of capital that could potentially be redirected toward education, health care, and economic development. Ten additional African states, including Chad, the Democratic Republic of the Congo, and Sierra Leone, are likely to receive similar debt relief in the near future. However, other countries, including such regionally influential oil producers as Nigeria and Angola, were denied similar debt reductions on the grounds that they have failed to show adequate progress toward reducing corruption. Meanwhile, in something of a surprise move, Nigeria allocated $6.4 billion in April of 2006 to pay off its debt to other countries (including the G-8), a step made possible by a steep rise in oil revenues resulting from soaring crude oil prices.

The HIV Pandemic and Africa

Since its initial identification in the United States in the 1980s, human immunodeficiency virus (HIV) and the resulting disease of AIDS (autoimmune deficiency syndrome) has grown to become a pandemic—a global epidemic. Rates of infection vary from country to country, city to city, and community to community, but nowhere

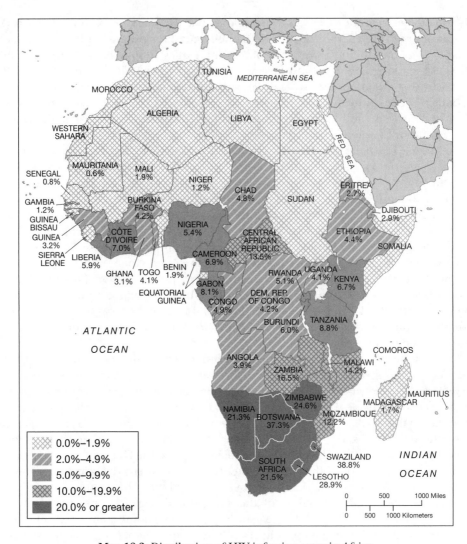

Map 18-2: Distribution of HIV infection rates in Africa

has the disease spread more quickly than in southern Africa. By 2002, Botswana had the world's highest rate of HIV infection, with over 30 percent of adults estimated to be HIV positive. In western and northern Africa, HIV infection rates range to as much as 5 percent of the population, still high by global standards, but nowhere near the levels found in the south. Altogether, nearly 80 percent of global AIDS deaths are currently believed to be in Africa, with as many as 6,000 Africans dying of AIDS each day. Clearly, the HIV/AIDS situation has reached crisis levels, especially in southern Africa. This raises significant questions. Why has HIV spread so much more quickly in parts of Africa than elsewhere in the world? What has been the response of international agencies and African governments? What has been the social impact of the epidemic, and what are the implications of the epidemic for Africa's economic growth? What hope is there for the future?

Africa's high rates of HIV infection are a result of a complex interaction between a variety of factors. Some studies suggest that HIV first became a human disease in Africa and was only later diagnosed when it spread to populations in the United States. Because victims of AIDS actually die from secondary infections such as pneumonia, the diagnosis is difficult to make without the proper testing equipment. Thus, HIV in Africa may have been growing as a problem for some time, allowing the disease to build momentum before being recognized. Conditions of migrant labor are probably also a contributing factor. In much of southern Africa in particular, workers from rural regions often travel long distances to work in mines or factories in urban areas for months at a time before returning to their homes. With prostitution common in many of the mining camps and urban areas, many workers are infected, and in returning to their homes they act as vectors for the transmission of the virus. Low instances of condom use (resulting from expense, as well as cultural or religious beliefs) and relatively high rates of infection for other sexually transmitted diseases (due to low access to health care) also act to increase rates of transmission. Further, a growing social stigmatization of victims of HIV has driven many into silence until the disease reaches its final stages. Claims of various "miracle cures" by local doctors and even the denial of the existence of the disease itself by some local leaders have allowed the virus to continue to spread. In the climate of inadequate health care, education, and communication that exists in some parts of Africa, HIV has thrived.

Sadly, evidence suggests that action could have been taken much sooner to slow or halt the growth of HIV in Africa. In the early 1980s groups as diverse as the CIA and World Health Organization (WHO) were projecting that African infection rates would extend into the tens of millions by 2000. Nonetheless, many saw HIV as less dangerous than "known quantity" killers such as malaria (which is indeed a deadly disease) and failed to act. Staggeringly, some groups even suggested that HIV would be a boon to Africa in that it would reduce "overpopulation." Attempts to spread the use of condoms, one of the most effective barriers to HIV, met with both local cultural resistance and opposition from the Catholic church, which opposes all forms of birth control.

Only as incidences of AIDS deaths have become too high to ignore has the crisis attracted attention and spurred genuine action. And with concerted action there is hope, as the examples of Uganda and Senegal show. In Uganda, thanks in large part to personal action taken by President Museveni, HIV infection rates appear to have dropped from a high of about 15 percent to around 8 percent over the past decade. Museveni has challenged commonly held taboos about openly discussing sexual issues and called for an end to discrimination against those infected. Utilizing a media campaign on TV and radio and grassroots organizations such as religious and community networks, the Ugandan government succeeded in spreading accurate and realistic information. And the public clearly responded. Infection rates are still high in Uganda, but the trend in infection is now downward rather than upward. In countries where rates of infection have remained fairly low, such as Senegal, concerted programs of frank education have helped to keep the virus from expanding as rapidly as was the case in southern Africa. Whether other countries will follow with their own campaigns is yet to be seen, but evidence suggests more and more action is being taken. In South Africa, for example, President Thabo Mbeki has reversed course from having once claimed that there was no connection between HIV and AIDS, to spearheading the successful campaign to legalize the production of cheap generic versions of patented antiviral drugs, putting life-extending AIDS treatments more within reach of cash-strapped African states.

African Solutions

The turnaround in policy of many African states and international organizations on the subject of HIV shows that changes in policy and action are possible. Indeed, the last decade has seen some major shifts in direction from African populations and leadership. One key change has been an increasing tendency to call not only for African solutions, but also greater African responsibility. For most of the time since independence, explanations of failed development or economic decay have centered around notions of neocolonialism and dependency. Over the past decade, however, this focus on external causation has been challenged by a growing demand that African governments take greater responsibility for the lack of development since decolonization. For example, a recent poll of Kenyans identified government corruption as the country's number-one problem. Perhaps the best-known advocate for this perspective is the Ghanaian G. B. N. Ayettey, who has published works such as *Africa Betrayed* and *Africa in Chaos*, which stress that although there can be no discounting the negative influence of colonialism or the lack of a level global economic playing field, African political elites have only made matters worse, rather than having found ways to effect change at home or more effectively interact with a difficult world. Change, argue many advocates of internal reform, must begin within Africa, not from without.

There is ample evidence that change is indeed afoot in terms of how African governments operate and interact. There have been setbacks in countries such as Zimbabwe, where the brutal repression of white farmers and black opponents by Robert Mugabe's ZANU party has been accompanied by an almost unprecedented economic collapse. Inflation fueled by government overprinting of money was so bad by 2006 that backpacks (humorously dubbed "Zimbabwe Wallets") were necessary to carry a single week's wages. Despite such ill developments, representative governments have increasingly taken hold across the continent. Although few African states are free of corruption or are completely transparent in their activities (rare enough anywhere in the world), there is evidence of growing pressure for accountability from African populations. For example, in 2002, President Moi of Kenya stepped down from power and his party (the Kenya African National Union) saw the defeat of its chosen candidate, resulting in KANU losing power for the first time since independence.

In part, improved rates of literacy and an expansion of private media have helped force governments to be more responsive to public opinion. For example, in Nigeria, a return to democracy in 1999 was accompanied by an end to state control over television. Numerous private stations were created and now present myriad opinions and offer open criticism to those in power. When asked if their country will return to military rule, most Nigerians now say no, where once they joked "soja come, soja go." Economically, there is also growing evidence of an African turn-around. Countries as diverse as Guinea, Mozambique, and Uganda have shown strong rates of economic growth over the past several years. Lesotho posted growth rates as high as 10 percent in the late 1990s. Overall, Africa's rate of economic growth has ranged from 3 to 5 percent since the mid-1990s. If such rates of growth continue, the results will be profound indeed.

There seems to be a growing reappraisal of how African states interact, as well. The original Charter of the Organization of African Unity in 1963 stressed policies of noninterference in the affairs of other African states. All too often, this principle of sovereignty seemed to excuse inaction in cases of even the worst disrespect for human rights or life. Indeed, many have faulted the noninterference clause as both an institutionalization of unnatural and illogical colonial boundaries and a division of spoils between ruling elites, who effectively recognized the right of their fellow rulers to exploit their nation's populations without fear of condemnation or action. For all their horror, the interstate conflicts of the 1990s helped spell the end for such policies of nonintervention. The intervention of ECOMOG forces in Liberia and Sierra Leone, for example, established an important precedent that states saw events in neighboring countries as their business. Even such conflicts as that in the DRC have been seen as a sign of potential change. Kenyan scholar Ali Mazrui has suggested that regional wars could finally mean the end for colonial boundaries and allow for a new and more logical political map for Africa.

Perhaps recognizing that the old model of African interaction was no longer appropriate, the leaders of the Organization of African Unity in 2002 scrapped the old OAU charter and reorganized themselves as the "African Union." The new AU is similar in structure to the European Union and empowers the members to legally intervene in one another's states in the event of crises such as the commission of war crimes or genocide. Plans have been laid for the creation of an African Peacekeeping Force to allow greater local agency in controlling conflict—in part perhaps a result of the failure of the UN to intervene in Rwanda and the DRC. On the economic front, the new AU has made plans for the creation of an African central bank as a step toward a unified African currency. The organization also approved the New Partnership for Africa's Development, a plan that changed the course from older, state-centered development strategies and also sought to increasingly connect notions of economic and political reform. This plan has met with support from the European Union and the United States, suggesting that there is at least the potential for greater cooperation on the subject of African development than existed in the past.

Contemporary Africa in Global Perspective—Looking Back, Looking Ahead

At the beginning of the twenty-first century, Africa represents something of a modern paradox. On the one hand the continent and its peoples represent a number of critical contemporary global themes. Like the countries of Latin America and

Southeast Asia, African states were challenged by the new political realities of a post–Cold War world. And, as in these regions, Africans responded by taking part in the third wave of democratization—a process that continues to unfold and influence global politics. Such developments provide evidence of an African willingness to change with the times. Similarly, new governments and organizations such as the AU offer the potential for economic as well as political rebirth.

Yet, for all Africa's participation in current events, the continent still represents something of a "world apart." Even as globalization has increasingly linked the fates of distant regions, years of economic decay have eroded Africa's economic relevance, even in the continent's role as a producer of vital commodities and minerals. The willingness of the rest of the world to stand by as some Africans have been ravaged by war and disease offers a stinging indictment of Africa's perceived irrelevance to the rest of the world.

Part of the problem continues to be the way the world views Africa and Africans. Issues such as corruption, conflict, and HIV in Africa bring up the critical issue of representation. As discussed in the Preface to this text, there is a tendency to oversimplify the notion of Africa into some single characteristic or stereotype. For those so inclined, corruption, conflict, and disease provide all the "evidence" necessary to support the image of Africa as hopeless. Indeed, in May 2000, *The Economist,* a popular and internationally influential British news magazine, ran a cover story that featured an image of a Sierra Leonian armed with a rocket launcher. The picture was cropped in the shape of Africa, and the headline read "The Hopeless Continent"—perhaps the most extreme example of the stereotype of "Broken Africa." Advocates of Africa from the continent and abroad raised a cry of protest to the article. Certainly, it was unfair and misleading to use the crises and chaos of Sierra Leone to so represent a continent in which most people live in peace. One can hardly imagine using the genocides of Bosnia and Albania to represent the whole of Europe, yet such approaches seem to be standard fare for representations of Africa.

There can be no denying that contemporary Africa faces many harsh realities. The collapse of Somalia, ethnic conflict in the Sudan, and the AIDS crisis are all very real, but it is also critical to realize that these factors are not the factors that define Africa, especially not for most Africans. The reality is that even in the face of hardship, Africa is a continent of life and diversity. There is poverty, but there is also wealth—often in the form of family and community, if not in cash and property. In the face of hardship there is also joy and perseverance. Many first-time visitors to Africa are shocked not only by the existence of poverty and hardship, but also by the fact that these conditions do not seem to defeat, but are rather defeated by, the African spirit. For those who have not lived in Africa, it is a difficult paradox to describe, but it is one of the reasons that so few people only go to Africa once—and why so many Africans who leave later return. When one passively observes Africa from the outside, he or she is bombarded with images of death. When one is in Africa, it is the very vitality of life that overwhelms.

History also provides another perspective. Although there may be great hardship in the African present and many challenges to come in the immediate future, the history of Africa and its peoples shows that there is far more to the continent than contemporary struggle. As we have sought to show in this text, Africa has not

Despite negative press, daily life in much of Africa is
characterized by humor and joy, not despair.

been on the sidelines of human history nor has it spent that history as an outcast or
a victim, but rather as a vital participant in a growing and developing world. Africa's
history, far from stagnant or unimportant, is both complex and relevant. To better
understand the history of Africa is to better understand the history of the world.
Like other histories, it chronicles the struggles of a rich and diverse population to
improve their lives and define their own destiny. Here lies the hope that the current
hardship shall be temporary. Perhaps the unofficial motto of Nigeria says it best:
"No Condition is Permanent."

Useful Works on This Chapter Topic

Fredoline Anunobi, *International Dimensions of African Political Economy: Trends, Challenges and
Realities* (1994).

George Ayittey, *Africa in Chaos* (1999).

Edna G. Bay and Donald L. Dunham, *States of Violence: Politics, Youth, and Memory in Contemporary
Africa* (2006).

Michael Bratten and Nicholas van de Walle, *Democratic Experiments in Africa: Regime Transitions in
Comparative Perspective* (1997).

Basil Davidson, *The Black Man's Burden: Africa and the Curse of the Nation State* (1992).

Jeffrey Herbst, *States and Power in Africa* (2000).

Lisa Lindsay and Stephan Miescher, *Men and Masculinities in Modern Africa* (2003).

Gideon Mendel et al., *A Broken Landscape: HIV & AIDS in Africa* (2002).

Martin Meredith, *The Fate of Africa: A History of Fifty Years of Independence* (2006).

William Reno, *Warlord Politics and African States* (1999).

M. A. Mohamed Salih, *African Democracies and African Politics* (2001).

Glossary

A

Aba Women's War Tax revolt by women traders against British colonial authorities in southeastern Nigeria, 1929 C.E.

Aboriginal Rights Protection Society (ARPS) African rights lobbying group founded in Gold Coast in 1897.

'Abd al-Qadir Leader of resistance to French invasion of Algeria in 1830s and 1840s.

Achebe, Chinua Nigerian author and activist.

Acheulean Paleolithic era typified by the use of bifacial and flake stone tools.

Adulis Important port on Red Sea in region of modern Eritrea.

Afrikaans South African language that combines elements of Bantu, Dutch, Khoisan, and Malay languages.

Afro-Asiatic Language family originating in North Africa and extending from West African Coast into Middle East. Includes languages such as Arabic, Amharic, Berber, Hausa, and Hebrew.

Age Grades System of social organization common across Africa. Generations are divided into "age grades" with specific duties and expectations according to their stage of maturation.

Aideed, Muhammad Somali warlord sought by U.S. and UN troops in Somalia in 1992 and 1993.

Akinsowon, Abiodun Nigerian woman whose revelation in 1925 led to the creation of the Cherubim and Seraphim Aladura church.

Aksum (common spellings Axsum/Acksum) State in the highland region of Ethiopia during the period of the first century C.E. to the eleventh century C.E.

al-Inkishafi Seventeenth-century C.E. epic Swahili poem.

al-Kahina "The Soothsayer," woman who led resistance to Islamic expansion in North Africa in the late seventh century C.E.

al-Maghili Algerian scholar who traveled widely in West Africa during fifteenth century. Author of *The Light of Princes* for Sarkin Rumfa of Kano.

Alaafin Title of ruler of Oyo.

Almoravids State established as result of Islamic renewal among the Sahanja Berbers in region of Mauritania during the eleventh century C.E.

Americo-Liberians Liberian population descended from former American slaves who settled in Liberia during nineteenth century C.E.

Amun Egyptian and Nubian Sun God. Particularly important during New Kingdom era.

Ankh Ancient Egyptian symbol of rebirth and eternal life. Very similar to Christian cross in form.

Apartheid *Apartness* in Afrikaans. Policy of racial segregation and oppression begun in South Africa in 1948.

Apedemek Merotic/Nubian Lion God.

Arianism Christian sect named for Arius, a priest living in Alexandria in the latter third century C.E.

Asante (common spelling Ashanti) State in central Ghana during the early eighteenth through late nineteenth centuries.

Asantehene Title of ruler of Asante.

Askiya Mohammad Founder of Askiya dynasty of Songhai in latter fifteenth century C.E.

Assimilation French colonial policy of replacing culture of colonized peoples with French culture.

Austronesian Language family originating in South East Asia. Extends from Madagascar to Hawaii and Easter Island.

Austronesian expansion Spread of Austronesian-speaking peoples throughout Indian and Pacific Ocean worlds.

Awdaghust Trading city in West African savannah during tenth and eleventh centuries C.E. Source of conflict between ancient Ghana and Almoravids.

Ayyubids Dynasty established by Salah al-Din in Egypt in 1171. Lasted until 1252.

B

Bahia Region of Brazil where sugar production and African enslavement were most common.

Bantu Niger-Congo word meaning *the people.*

Bantu expansion/migration Expansion of Niger-Congo–speaking populations from West Africa across Central and Southeastern Africa over period of several thousand years.

Banu Hilal Arabic-speaking nomads who spread into Maghreb during the eleventh century C.E.

Bantustans Name given to Native Reserves in South Africa.

Bawakhir Slave-based state army of Morocco's 'Awalite Dynasty in the latter seventeenth century.

Bayajidda Mythical founder of Hausa City-States

Berber Refers to both the language and Berber-speaking ethnic group that inhabits much of North Africa and the Sahara.

Berlin Conference Conference in 1884–1885 when European colonial powers partitioned Africa.

Bey Title of land-holding nobles in Ottoman Egypt.

Beylerbey Title of Ottoman regent in the Maghreb.

Bilal Bunama first Muezzin of Mecca and companion of Prophet-Mohammad.

Blombos Cave Site in South Africa where decorated ochre blocks and polished spear points have been dated to 70,000 Y.B.P.

Bori Religion in Hausaland that combines elements of both local traditional religious belief and Islam.

Boer Afrikaans word for *farmer.*

Boer War See South African War.

Brazilian style Architectural style introduced to West and West-Central Africa by Luso-Africans returning from Brazil.

Brussels Treaty Treaty calling on European colonial powers to eradicate slavery in Africa.

Busaids Omani dynasty that replaced Yarubis in the mid-seventeenth century C.E.

C

Candomble Religion practiced in Brazil that combines elements of both Yoruba traditional religion and Catholicism.

Canoe houses Trading companies in Niger delta that transported goods between coast and interior.

Cape Bojador Cape in Northwestern Africa. Unfavorable winds and currents meant that wind-powered ships that ventured south of this point could return north only with great effort and luck.

Cape Coloureds Term given to population of mixed Malay, African, and European origin in region of Cape Town.

Cape of Good Hope Southernmost tip of Africa.

Cartaz "Trading Licences" sold in Indian Ocean by Portuguese in sixteenth century C.E.

Carthage Trading state established in region of modern Tunisia by Phonician colonists around 1000 B.C.E.

Cassava Also known as Manioc. Root crop imported from South America to Africa in sixteenth century C.E.

Charter companies Private stock companies utilized by many colonial powers to initiate colonialism at a minimal investment.

Chattel slavery Term used to describe slavery where the slave has no rights whatsoever and has been reduced from a state of person-hood to simply one of property.

Chimurenga Style of music characterized by protest songs against Rhodesian government in 1970s. Form of popular propaganda and protest.

Cocoa Key ingredient of chocolate. Originally from MesoAmerica, it was introduced into Africa via the Gold Coast in the 1890s.

Coltan A mineral found in eastern Congo.

Conference of Berlin See Berlin Conference.

Congo Free State Central African colony that was the private property of King Leopold of Belgium.

Continental passage Passage of slaves from point of capture in Africa to points of export on coast.

Convention Peoples Party (CPP) Mass-based political party founded in Gold Coast by Kwame Nkrumah.

Coptic (1) Language formerly spoken in upper Nile and Ethiopia; (2) Monophysite Church in Egypt and Ethiopia.

Corvee Forced labor or "labor tax" in French colonial Africa.

Crowther, Samuel First Anglican Bishop of Nigeria and historian. Translated Bible into Yoruba.

Cushitic Eastern African subgroup of Afro-Asiatic language family.

D

Dahomey West African state that rose to prominence during the era of the Transatlantic slave trade.

Dane guns Low-quality firearms produced specifically for sale into Africa during the era of the Transatlantic slave trade.

Dar al-Harb Arabic term meaning "The Abode of War." Reference to any region where people do not accept Islam and are thus "at war" with the will of God.

Dar al-Islam Arabic term meaning "The Abode of Peace." Reference to any region where the religion of Islam is accepted and followed.

Darfur "Land of the Fur." A region in western Sudan.

de Klerk, F. W. Nationalist party prime minister of South Africa from 1989 to 1994. Oversaw the loosening of Apartheid restrictions and the transition to nonracial democracy.

Dependency theory School of economic and political thought, common in the 1960s and 1970s, that stressed the efforts of Western states to maintain Africa in a position of economic and political dependency.

Dhow A style of ocean-worthy boats and ships common to Eastern Africa and the Middle East. Characterized by sewn construction, lanteen sails, and shallow draft.

Diagne, Blaise First African representative to French Parliament (1914).

Diaz, Bartolomeo First Portuguese captain to round the Cape of Good Hope (1485).

Didascalia First catechetical school in Christian history. Established in Alexandria around 190 C.E.

Dingane Head of Zulu clan in early 1800s.

Direct rule Style of colonial administration that placed Africans under the direct authority of European administrators.

Donatists Christian sect in North Africa in fourth to seventh centuries C.E. Named for Numidian Bishop Donatus. Rejected the authority of the Roman Christian church.

Dongala Capital of state of Makurra in Nubia in the sixth century C.E. Site of cathedral and defeat of Islamic army in 651 C.E.

Dhimmi Non-Islamic but monotheistic "people of the book" who are under Islamic authority.

DuBois, W. E. B. African-American activist and African Nationalist. Organized the first Pan-African Congress in Paris in 1919. Emigrated to Ghana following independence.

Dyula (Common alternate spelling *Duala*) From the Wangara word for "trader." Generally a reference to Muslim traders in West Africa in the sixteenth to eighteenth centuries C.E.

E

Eboue, Felix Originally from the West Indies, he was French colonial governor of Chad at outbreak of World War II. Eboue refused to recognize the Vichy regime and thus created in French Equatorial Africa a haven for the Free French administration.

Ècole Colonial French institute established in 1897 to provide training to colonial administrators.

ECOMOG Economic Community Monitoring Group. An African-organized and staffed peacekeeping force created to help end the Liberian civil war in 1990.

ECOWAS Economic Community of West African States, founded in 1975.

El Mina Portuguese for "the Mine." First permanent trading post established by Europeans in sub-Saharan Africa. Initially important to the gold trade, it later became a major point for the export of enslaved Africans.

Ensete Sometimes referred to as "false banana." A starchy food crop unique to Ethiopia.

Equiano, Olaudah Enslaved African who in 1789 wrote an autobiography after gaining his freedom. He became an influential abolitionist (and accomplished French horn player).

Evolue French term identifying Africans who had assimilated to French culture and thus "earned" French citizenship.

Ezana King of Aksum during the early fourth century C.E. Converted to Christianity during his reign.

F

Falasha Term used to identify Jewish population in Ethiopia.

Fante Confederation of small African states that controlled the coastal region south of Asante during the nineteenth century C.E.

Fatimid Caliphate Shi'i Islamic state established in Algeria. Moved to Egypt in 969 C.E.

Fezzan Region of Sahara Desert in central modern Libya. Notable for having the largest population of any part of the desert. Contains many archaeological sites featuring ancient cave paintings.

Freetown Port city in Sierra Leone. Established by British in 1787 as a point of release for former slaves from the Americas and later from captured slaving vessels.

Fulani (Common alternate spellings *Fulbe* and *Peul*) Pastoralist group common in West African savannah and sahel. Particularly influential in spreading Islam during the eighteenth and nineteenth centuries C.E.

G

Gao Important commercial city along the Niger River in the eastern region of modern Mali. Was particularly important during the era of the trans-Saharan trade and Songhai empire.

Ge'ez Afro-Asiatic language spoken in Nubia and Ethiopia.

Glaberrima rice Species of rice developed and cultivated in West Africa, probably first in the region of the Niger inland delta.

Glottochronology Linguistic technique used to "age" languages based on an analysis of rate of change to other related languages.

Gnosticism Early variant of Christianity common in Egypt. Gnostics believed that all matter was evil and that salvation depended on access to "secret" knowledge.

Golden stool The "throne" of the Asantehene and the symbol of the Asante nation.

Goree Island just off the coast from the modern city of Dakar, Senegal. Was an important entrepot for the transatlantic slave trade.

Great Zimbabwe Impressive stone-walled structure in southeastern Africa. Notable in that the construction technique uses no mortar, a style known as "dry stone" architecture. Was the capital of an important trading state during the fourteenth and fifteenth centuries C.E. Was the source of the name of modern Zimbabwe.

Griqua Name given by missionaries to mixed-race Khoisan/Dutch population in South Africa who had previously been known as "the bastards."

Groundnuts African term for peanuts.

Gum arabic Resin of the acacia tree found in the West African savannah and sahel. A useful dye-fixer, it was an important trade item in the latter nineteenth century C.E.

Gum copal Resin found in East Africa that was used to make varnishes. Important trade item in eighteenth and nineteenth centuries C.E.

H

Habyarimana, Juvenal Rwandan head of state assassinated in April 1994. His murder was part of a premeditated plan to instigate genocide against Tutsis and Hutu moderates in the country.

Haiti Island in the Carribean. Originally named Hispaniola, it was renamed after a successful slave revolution in the late eighteenth century C.E. ended French control of the west end of the island. Most successful slave revolution in history.

Hajj The pilgrimage to Mecca; the fifth "pillar" of Islam.

Hanno Carthaginian sailor who led expedition to explore western coastline of Africa around 500 B.C.E. Some believe he traveled as far south as modern Cameroun.

Hatshepsut Female pharaoh during the New Kingdom phase (fifteenth century B.C.E.). Notable for launching large sea expedition to the "Land of Punt" in East Africa.

Highlife Ghanaian musical style influenced by Central African and Cuban "rhumba" rhythms.

Homo Biological genus meaning *human.*

Horus Egyptian god, son of Isis and Osiris. Often represented as a falcon.

Houphouet-Boigny, Felix Francophone African nationalist and first president of Côte d'Ivoire.

Hottentots Dutch derogatory term for Khoisan speakers in South Africa.

Hyksos Middle Eastern invaders of Egypt during the seventeenth century B.C.E.

I

Ibadi Variety of Islam practiced in Oman. Reflects close ideological connections to Kharijite Islam.

Ibn Battuta Fourteenth century C.E. Moroccan world traveler and chronicler. Traveled extensively in West Africa, East Africa, the Middle East, and Asia.

Ifrikia Roman term for North Africa. Origin of modern name of Africa.

Igbo-Ukwu Archaeological site in southeastern Nigeria. Reveals presence of a state-level society in the region as early as the tenth century C.E. Bronze goods and trade items indicate contact with other regions as far away as North Africa.

Indirect Rule Style of colonial administration that stressed the use of African rulers as intermediaries between European colonizers and common Africans.

ITCZ Inter Tropical Convergence Zone. Also known as the "rain belt." Zone where cool wet air from south Atlantic Ocean meets warm dry air from the Sahara Desert.

J

Janjaweed A general term used to describe a militia group backed by the Sudanese government and notorious for atrocities in Darfur.

Jenne-Jeno Major urban center along the Niger River in the region of both ancient and modern-day Mali. Was occupied from roughly 300 B.C.E. to 1400 C.E. Played a critical role in both the trans-Saharan trade and also trade in food and other products between the savannah and forest region of West Africa.

Jihad Islamic duty to "strive." Includes the internal jihad to behave in a moral fashion (jihad of the heart) and the obligation to spread Islam by peaceful means (jihad of the mouth). If Muslims are prevented from performing these actions, then they are obligated to take up a jihad of the sword to create a political setting where they can properly practice Islam.

Jizya Tax paid by non-Muslims living under Islamic rule.

Johnson-Sirleaf, Ellen. Elected president of Liberia in 2005. She is Africa's first democratically elected head of state.

K

Kebra Negast "The Book of the Glory of Kings." Ethiopian account of meeting and union of the Queen of Sheba and King Solomon. This tale legitimized the rule of Ethiopian Christian kings by allowing them to claim blood ties to Solomon and Sheba.

Kenyatta, Jomo Author of *Facing Mt. Kenya* and Kenyan nationalist leader. First president of independent Kenya.

Kerma Nubian state that prospered in the twenty-sixth to sixteenth centuries B.C.E. Joined Hyksos in invading Egypt at end of the Old Kingdom era.

Kharijites Arabic term meaning *those who leave.* Were the first Islamic group to break away from the wider community on theological grounds. Kharijites stress the absolute equality of all Muslims, but also demand absolute piety from all believers. Many Kharijites settled in North Africa.

Khoisan Linguistic and cultural group that includes both the Khoi and San peoples of Southern Africa.

Kikuyu Ethnic group who inhabited the region of the Kenyan highlands during the nineteenth century. Were dispossessed of their lands by British settlers.

Kilwa An island off the coast of Tanzania. An important Swahili trading port from the eighth century C.E. through the sixteenth century C.E., when it was sacked by the Portuguese. Was visited by Ibn Battuta in 1331.

Klasies River Archaeological site in South Africa where remains of anatomically modern humans have been found dating to 130,000 Y.B.P.

Krio From *creole.* Reference to community and identity formed by Africans from a wide range of ethnicities who were released in Sierra Leone after being rescued from slaving vessels by the British antislaving squadron in the early nineteenth century.

Kulughli Term used to identify those of mixed North African and Ottoman blood.

Kumasi Capital city of Asante empire. Located in modern-day Ghana.

Kush Nubian state that thrived from roughly eleventh century B.C.E. to late sixth century B.C.E. Kush invaded and conquered Egypt during the eighth century B.C.E.

L

Latex Natural rubber acquired by "tapping" the sap of a variety of equatorial trees and vines.

Laterite Soil type common to much of African savannah and forest regions. Characterized by high iron and salt contents and low overall fertility.

Leo Africanus A scholar and traveler, he was born in Muslim Spain in the latter fifteenth century. He was educated in Morocco at Fez. Captured at sea by Europeans, he was presented to the pope, who granted him freedom and encouraged him to convert to Christianity. He wrote extensively of his travels in West Africa.

Liberia Colony for former slaves from the United States, founded in West Africa by the American Colonization Society in the 1820s. Declared independence in 1847.

Loi Cadre Proclamation in 1956 that provided universal adult suffrage to all French African subjects.

Lugard, Frederich (Lord) British colonial administrator who served in both Uganda and Nigeria. He is the author of *Dual Mandate in Tropical Africa* (1922), which is held by many to be the textbook of British indirect rule.

Lumumba, Patrice First prime minister of the Democratic Republic of the Congo. Was assassinated in February of 1961.

Luso-African Term referring to populations of former Brazilian slaves who, on gaining freedom, returned to Africa. Most settled in the coastal towns of West and West-Central Africa.

M

Macaulay, Herbert Early twentieth century Nigerian nationalist and founder of the Nigerian National Democratic Party.

Macumba Brazilian religion that combines elements of both African religion (particularly Yoruba belief) and Catholicism.

Maghreb Arabic word for *the West*. Commonly used as a reference to the coastal region of North Africa.

Mahdi Figure believed in popular Islam to be the second coming of the Prophet Jesus. The Mahdi will herald the coming of a new era of renewal and peace.

Maji-Maji "Spirit Water." This was a revolt against German colonial rule in Tanganyika in 1905 and 1906. Participants believed that the "spirit water" would provide protection against German firearms.

Malaria Parasitic disease spread by mosquitos. It is endemic in most of tropical Africa.

Mamluks Class of slave soldiers imported from Anatolia and Black Sea region to Egypt during the Ayyubid dynasty. In 1252 they overthrew the Ayyubid sultan and established themselves as a ruling class.

Mandela, Nelson South African activist and leader of the African National Congress (ANC). Was jailed from 1963 to 1990 for his resistance to apartheid. In 1994 he was elected president of South Africa.

Manioc See Cassava.

Mansa Musa Fourteenth-century ruler of Mali empire. Famous for his pilgrimage to Mecca in 1324–1325 and support for Islam and education in Mali.

Marketing boards Government organizations common in both colonial and independent Africa in the twentieth century. These boards set prices for the purchase of cash crops such as cocoa, cotton, and coffee and then sold these commodities on the world market.

Maroons Term used to describe escaped slave communities in New World who established free communities beyond control of the slave-owning socieites.

Matriliny System of descent that traces family lines not through the father, but through the mother.

Mau Mau Revolt in Kenya during 1940s and 1950s that sought to drive European settlers and their employees from lands previously held by Africans.

Mauritania Name of Berber state that lay south of Carthage in the fourth through second centuries C.E. Also name of modern West African state.

Meroe Nubian state established after Egyptian invasion around 590 forced the state of Kush to relocate farther to the south, and the resulting state is now known by the name of its apparent capital city. Meroe survived for several centuries, until defeat by neighboring Axum led to its final decline.

Mestizos Portuguese term for people of mixed African/Portuguese descent.

Mfecane "The crushing." Term used to describe a period of intense warfare in southern Africa during the early nineteenth century C.E., ostensibly due to an expansionist Zulu state. Some scholars now believe the phenomenon was largely a British-created myth.

Middle passage Ocean journey of enslaved Africans across Atlantic to New World.

Mijikenda East African group who resisted Portuguese control in sixteenth century C.E.

Millet Grain crop grown extensively in Africa's savannah regions. Highly resistant to drought.

Mission Civlitrice French for *civilizing mission.* This was a key French justification for extending colonial rule to Africa.

Mobutu, Sese Seko Military dictator of the Democratic Republic of the Congo (then named Zaire) from 1965 to 1997.

Monophysite Belief by many Christians that Jesus' divine nature outweighed his human nature. This belief was condemned by the Roman church at the Council of Chalcedon in 451 C.E. As a result, monophysite Christians in Egypt formed their own Coptic church.

Monsoons Prevailing winds in the Indian Ocean, which blow to the southwest from November through April and to the northeast from May to October.

Mugabe, Robert Leader of the Zimbabwe African National Union during the war against white rule in Rhodesia. First and to date only president of Zimbabwe. His seizure of land owned by white Zimbabweans and his repression of political opponents brought international condemnation in 2002 and 2003.

Muhongo Title of female rulers of the central African state of Matamba.

N

Nana Asma'u Daughter of Usman dan Fodio, founder of the Sokoto Caliphate. A noted scholar and poet, she was instrumental in helping reform Islam in the new state during the early nineteenth century C.E.

N'Dama West African cattle breed that is resistant to trypanosomiasis (sleeping sickness).

Ndebele Name given to Mzilikazi's state and people after their migration to region of Zimbabwe in the midnineteenth century C.E.

Ndongo Central African state (south of Kongo) in sixteenth century C.E. Invaded by Portuguese in 1580.

Negritude "Blackness." Intellectual movement in Francophone colonies in Africa and Carribean that stressed the achievements and, superiority of "black" civilization. Leopold Senghor of Senegal was one of the movements' key proponents.

Neocolonialism Term describing the continued influence of former colonial powers even after the coming of independence to African states.

Ngalawa Style of ocean-worthy outrigger canoe common along Swahili coast.

Niger-Congo Family of African languages that extends from the West African forest region southeast to the Indian Ocean coastline. Includes languages as diverse as Fulani and Zulu, as well as the Bantu language subgroup.

Nilo-Saharan Family of African languages found predominantly in the upper Nile of the Sudan. Includes languages such as Dinka and Masai.

Njinga Female ruler of central African states of Ndongo and Matamba from 1624–1663. She successfully balanced threats and alliances with both the Portuguese and neighboring states during the dangerous early years of the slave trade.

Nkrumah, Kwame Nationalist and first president of independent Ghana. Nkrumah was a leading advocate of pan-African unity.

Nok Early state-level society located on the Jos plateau of what is now Nigeria. Flourishing from about 800 B.C.E. to 200 C.E., Nok society created remarkable terra-cotta works of art and undertook considerable amounts of iron smelting.

Nongqawuse Young Xhosa girl who experienced divine revelations calling for the killing of cattle and destruction of grain in the 1850s. She foretold that such action would lead to the exodus of Europeans from the region.

Nubia Name of region of the upper Nile that extends past the sixth cataract and well into modern-day Sudan. Home to many significant states including Kerma, Kush, Meroe, Noba, and Makura.

Numidia Name of Berber state that lay south of Carthage in the fourth through second centuries C.E.

Nyamwezi East Central African trading state that profited from the Indian Ocean market for ivory and slaves in the nineteenth Century C.E.

Nyerere, Julius Nationalist and first president of independent Tanganyika/Tanzania. Nicknamed Mwalimu (our teacher), he gained fame by advocating a path of "self-reliance" and "African socialism" as a means to development.

Nzinga Kongo Monarch who first dealt with Portuguese in late fifteenth century C.E. Converted to Christianity in 1491 and took name King Joao.

O

Oba Title of rulers of the West African state of Benin.

Oduduwa According to Yoruba oral tradition, Oduduwa was the first human.

Ogun Yoruba Orisa and god of iron. Patron of warriors, blacksmiths, and taxi drivers.

Olodumare Yoruba high god who ordered the creation of the world.

Orange Free State Independent Afrikaner state established in South Africa in 1854.

Orisa Yoruba lesser dieties, each with specialized duties.

Osei Tutu Founder of the Asante state in the early eighteenth century C.E. First Asantehene.

Osiris Egyptian god of the dead. Reputedly murdered by the god Seth and brought back to life by his wife, Isis, Osiris was also a symbol of rebirth.

Ottomans Turkish empire that expanded out of Anatolia in the fifteenth century C.E. By the sixteenth century they had expanded to control much of Middle East, North Africa, and the Balkans.

P

Paleolithic Stone Age.

Palm oil Oil from the kernels of the oil palm tree. Long utilized as a food in West and Central Africa, it was also an important export to Europe as an industrial lubricant during the nineteenth century C.E.

Palmares Independent state in northeastern Brazil created by escaped slaves in the early seventeenth century C.E.

Pasha Title of the Ottoman regent in Egypt.

Petits blanks French term for lower-class white traders and skilled laborers who lived in the colonies.

Plasmodium falciparum Parasite that causes cerebral malaria, a particularly virulent form of the disease that is often fatal.

Polygyny Having more than one wife.

Pongid Biological classification (family) to which all "great apes" and their ancestors belong.

Prazos Estates established by Portuguese along Zambezi river in sixteenth century C.E.

Prempeh Asantehene captured and exiled by the British, 1896–1924.

Prester John Mythical Christian king whom medieval Europeans believed lived in Africa.

Ptolemy One of Alexander the Great's generals. Given rule over Egypt in 323 B.C.E., he established the Ptolemaic dynasty, which ended with CleopatraVII in 30 B.C.E.

Punic Culture and language that resulted from the combination of Phoenician and North African populations in Carthage.

Punt Ancient African state believed to have existed in Horn of Africa. Site of trade expedition by Egypt in the sixteenth century B.C.E.

Q

Qadiriyya Sufi brotherhood common in Africa. Originated in Iraq during the eleventh century C.E.

Quinine Drug (an extract of cinchona bark) that provides both a cure for and prophylactic against malaria.

R

Rassamblement Democratique Africain African Democratic Assembly. Political party founded by African nationalists in French Africa in 1946.

Red Rubber Name given to the scandal that developed when the brutal treatment of

Africans in King Leopold's Congo Free State became public.

Retief, Piet Leader of Afrikaner *Voortrekkers* in the 1830s. Was assassinated by Zulu leader Dingane in 1838.

Rhapta Believed to be the most southernly African port in the premodern Indian Ocean trade. Its location is now unknown.

Rhodes, Cecil Founder of the DeBeers mining company and later governor of the Cape Colony in South Africa. Was also a driving force behind the settlement and colonization of the Rhodesias. He aspired to establish a British control "from the Cape to Cairo."

Ribats Fortresses established on the frontier of the expanding Islamic state during the seventh century C.E. Many grew to become important cities.

Rift Valley Geologically active region extending from the Ethiopian highlands south through the great lakes region to Zimbabwe. Characterized by mountains and fertile volcanic soils.

Rinderpest Disease that strikes livestock, particularly cattle. A particularly devastating epidemic swept across Africa in the 1890s.

S

Saad, Sinti-binti East African singer who created the Taarab musical style in the 1920s C.E.

Sabean Term used to identify Southern Arabia populations.

Sahel Arabic word for *coast*. Is used to denote the semiarid southern fringe of the Sahara desert.

Salah al-Din (alternate spelling Saladin) Kurdish military commander who helped defeat Second Crusade in the twelfth century C.E. Also overthrew the Fatimid Caliphate in Egypt and established the Ayyubid dynasty there.

Santeria Syncretistic religion practiced in Cuba, which draws on elements of both West African religions and Catholicism.

Sao Tome Island off the West African coast near Cameroun and Nigeria. Uninhabited until settlement by the Portuguese in 1485. Was a major site of sugar production.

Sarki Hausa word for *King* or *Emir.*

Selassie, Haile Last emperor of Ethiopia. Instrumental in the defeat of Italian invaders during World War II, he was overthrown by a Soviet-backed coup in 1974.

Senghor, Leopold Senegalese poet and nationalist. Was instrumental in the creation of the concept of *negritude.* First president of independent Senegal.

Seyyid Said Omani ruler who moved capital from Oman to Zanzibar in 1839 C.E.

Sharif (alternate spellings Sharifa and Sharufa) Name used to identify a family claiming descent from the Prophet Muhammad.

Sharpsville Massacre Catastrophic attack on unarmed protestors by South African police on 21 May 1961. Sixty nine were killed, and nearly 200 were wounded.

Shehu Title of Ruler of state of Bornu, located near Lake Chad.

Shifting cultivation Agricultural system wherein land is left fallow after repeated plantings, so as to allow it to regain its fertility.

Shi'i (alternate spellings Shi'a and Shi'ite) Islamic sect that identifies the descendants of Muhammad through his dauther Fatima and son-in-law Ali as the only legitimate rulers in Islam. Many Shi'i settled in North and Eastern Africa in the eighth century C.E.

Slave Coast General term of reference for the West African Coast from Ghana to Cameroun during the era of the Atlantic slave trade.

Solomonid dynasty Ethiopian dynasty that came to power in 1270 C.E.

Sonni Ali Ruler of the savannah empire of Songhai, he greatly expanded the state's boundaries in the 1470s and 1480s, C.E. Died in 1492.

Sorghum Grain crop grown in African savannah and sahel regions. Highly resistant to drought.

Soumaoro Ruler of West African state of Sosso in the thirteenth century C.E. Was defeated by Sundiata at the battle of Krina in 1230.

South African War Often referred to as the "Boer War." War between Great Britain and Afrikaans-speaking population of Southern Africa from 1899–1902.

Stanley, Henry Morton American adventurer and newspaperman who mapped much of the Congo River during the latter nineteenth century C.E. Famous for his search for Dr. Livingstone and his aid to King Leopold of Belgium.

Structural Adjustment Program(SAP) Type of economic reform program frequently mandated by the International Monetary Fund and World Bank during the 1980s and 1990s. Generally called for currency devaluation, an expansion of commodity exports, and reductions in social services such as education and health care.

Sublime Porte Term used to refer to the Ottoman central government.

Sudd Vast swamp that lies along the White Nile in the Sudan.

Suez Canal Canal across the Sinai Peninsula that connects the Mediterranean Sea with the Red Sea. Was completed by the French in 1869. Egyptian nationalization of the canal in 1956 resulted in a combined French-British-Israeli invasion and an international crisis.

Sufism Mystical branch of Islam that stresses the ability of believers to achieve union with God in this life. Very common in Africa.

Sundiata (alternate spellings Sundjata, Sunjata, and Son-jara) Founder of the West African savannah empire of Mali in thirteenth century C.E.

Swahili "People of the Coast," from the Arabic *sahel.* Language and ethnic group characterized by a mix of African and Middle-Eastern languages and populations.

T

Taarab East African musical style characterized by a combination of African, Arab, and Persian musical styles.

Tantalum A highly valued element that is widely used in the manufacture of electronics products. Tantalum is extracted from Coltan, which is mined extensively in the Democratic Republic of the Congo, Mozambique, and Nigeria.

Tarika (plural Turuq) Arabic for "path" or "way." Term used to identify different Sufi orders or brotherhoods.

T'eff Grain crop grown in Ethiopia.

Tending Part-time maintenance of scattered crops. Considered to be an incremental step toward sedentary agriculture during the Paleolithic period.

Tewordros II Ethiopian emperor who reunified the state in 1855, bringing to an end the "age of princes."

Thaku, Harry Founder of the Young Kikuyu Association in 1921.

Thebes Dominant city in the upper Nile region of ancient Egypt.

Timbuktu Important trading city along Niger River during the period from 800–1600 C.E. Was home of the famed Sankore University established by Mansa Musa in the thirteenth century C.E. Europeans mythologized it as a "city of gold."

Tip, Tippu Swahili trader in ivory and slaves in central East Africa. Cooperated with Stanley and Leopold.

Torodbe Wolof for "seekers." Grow who organized jihad of the sword in Futa Toro in the 1760s C.E.

Transvaal Independent Afrikaner state established in South Africa in 1854 C.E.

Tribe Anthropological term used to designate a group whose main sense of identity is kinship to a mythological founder and who are under the authority of a chief. Has become a general term of reference to any African ethnic or linguistic group. Used carelessly, it has been known to give African history professors indigestion or even cases of hives.

Trypanosomiasis Medical name for "sleeping sickness."

Tuareg Ethnic group that inhabits much of the southern Saharan and Sahel region of West Africa.

Twa Central African ethnic group, often referred to as "pygmies."

U

Uitlanders Afrikaans word for *outlanders*. Generally used to identify the British and Americans.

Ujama Swahili term for *family*. Used by Nyerere to identify his philosophy of African socialism and self-help in Tanzania.

Ulama Arabic term used to identify a class of religious scholars.

Umma Arabic term identifying the wider Islamic community.

Umar Tal (al-Hajj Umar Tal) Leader of Massinah Jihad in West Africa during the 1850s C.E.

Usman dan Fodio West African scholar and sufi. He led a jihad of the sword against the Sarkin Gobir in 1804 C.E., ultimately leading to the creation of the Sokoto Caliphate.

V

VOC Dutch East India Company.

Voortrekkers Africans term describing Africaners who moved from Cape region of South Africa into the interior during the 1830s and 1840s C.E.

W

Wahhabism Conservative sect of Islam originating in Arabia during the eighteenth century C.E. Vociferously anti-Sufi.

Wali Used to identify a Sufi saint, someone who is a "friend" of God.

War of the Axe War between Xhosa and British in South Africa in 1846 C.E.

Warrant Chiefs Chiefs installed by British in previously "stateless" societies.

Williams thesis Thesis by Trinidadian scholar Eric Williams that the Atlantic slave trade provided Europe with the capital necessary for the industrial revolution.

X

Xhosa Ethnic group in South Africa. Also a large state-level society that resisted the expansion of European power in the nineteenth century C.E.

Y

Yams Group of root crops grown in the West and Central African forest regions. Notably, sweet potatoes are not really yams and are indigenous to South America, not Africa.

Yarubi dynasty This dynasty unified Oman in the seventeenth century C.E. and oversaw a rapid expansion of Omani naval and trading activity in the Indian Ocean.

Yellow fever Mosquito-borne tropical illness.

Z

Zagwe Ethiopian Christian dynasty founded in the tenth century C.E. Overthrown by the Solumnid dynasty in 1270 C.E.

Zamana Masafent "Age of Princes." Period of political division and conflict in Ethiopia during the latter eighteenth and early nineteenth centuries C.E.

Zambezi Major East African river that flows from Zimbabwe through Zambia and to the Indian Ocean. Unlike most African rivers, the Zambezi is navigable from the coast to the interior.

Zanj Revolt Uprising by East African slaves in the agricultural region of Basra on the Persian Gulf in the latter ninth century C.E. Lasting nearly 20 years, the rebellion inflicted repeated defeats on armies sent by the Abbasid Caliphate to end the revolt.

Zanzibar Important island trading port off the coast of Tanzania in East Africa. Merged with Tanganyika in 1964 to create Tanzania.

Zion Church Independent African church that originated in South Africa. Has spread extensively in Southern Africa over the latter twentieth century.

Zulu South African clan group that expanded rapidly in the nineteenth century C.E. to create a powerful state-level society.

Selected Bibliography

Works Focusing on Africa before 1500

Abun-Nasr, Jamil M. *A History of the Maghrib* (1971)

Baines, John, and Jaromir Malek. *Cultural Atlas of Ancient Egypt* (2000)

Beach, D. N. *The Shona and Zimbabwe, 900–1850(1980)*

Bovill, E. W. *The Golden Trade of the Moors* (1985)

Clark, J. D., and S. A. Brandt, eds. *From Hunters to Farmers: The Causes and Consequences of Food Production in Africa* (1984)

Collins, Robert O., James M. Burns, and Erik K. Ching, eds. *Problems in African History: The Precolonial Centuries* (1993)

Connah, Graham. *African Civilizations: An Archaeological Perspective* (2001)

Davies, W. V., and L. Schofield, eds. *Egypt, the Aegean and the Levant, Interconnections in the Second Millennium* (1995)

Diop, Cheikh Anta. *The African Origin of Civilization: Myth or Reality* (1993)

Ehret, Christopher. *The Civilizations of Africa: A History to 1800* (2002)

_____. *An African Classical Age* (1998)

Ehret, Christopher, and Mary Posnansky, eds. *The Archaeological and Linguistic Reconstruction of African History* (1982)

Hall, M. *The Changing Past: Farmers, Kings and Traders in Southern Africa, 200–1860* (1987)

Hamdun, Said, and Noel King, eds. *Ibn Battuta in Black Africa* (1994)

Hoffman, M. A. *Egypt before the Pharaohs* (1990)

Hopkins, J. F. P, and Nehemia Levtzion. *Corpus of Early Arabic Sources for West African History* (2000)

Inskeep, R. R. *The Peopling of Southern Africa* (1978)

Kent, Susan. *Gender in African Prehistory* (1998)

Levtzion, Nehemia. *Ancient Ghana and Mali* (1980)

McIntosh, Susan Keech. *Excavations at Jenne-Jeno, Hambarketolo, and Kaniana: The 1981 Season* (1995)

Monges, Re. *Kush, The Jewel of Nubia: Reconecting the Root System of African Civilization* (1997)

Munro-Hay, Stuart. *Aksum: An African Civilization of Late Antiquity* (1991)

Newman, James. *The Peopling of Africa: A Geographic Interpretation(1997)*

O'Conner, David. *Ancient Nubia: Egypt's Rival in Africa* (1997)

Oliver, Roland, and Brian Fagan. *Africa in the Iron Age: c. 500 BC-1400 AD* (1975)

Parkinson, R. B. *Voices from Ancient Egypt: An Anthology of Middle Kingdom Writings* (1991)

Phillipson, David W. *African Archaeology* (1993)

Schmidt, Peter. *Iron Technology in East Africa: Symbolism, Science and Archaeology* (1997)

Shaw, Ian, ed. *The Oxford History of Ancient Egypt* (2000)

Shaw, Thurston, ed. *Archaeology of Africa: Foods, Metals and Towns* (1993).

Stringer, Christopher, and Rachel McKie. *African Exodus: The Origins of Modern Humans* (1998)

Vansina, Jan. *Paths in the Rain Forest: Towards a History of Political Tradition in Equatorial Africa* (1990)

Vogel, Joseph O., ed. *Encyclopedia of Precolonial Africa: Archaeology, History, Languages, Cultures and Environments* (1997)

_____. *Great Zimbabwe: The Iron Age in South Central Africa* (1994)

Works Focusing on Religion and Culture in Africa

Abun-Nasr, Jamil M. *A History of the Maghrib in the Islamic Period* (1987)

Achebe, Chinua. *Home and Exile* (2000)

Barnes, Sandra T. ed. *Africa's Ogun: Old World and New* (1997)

Brenner, Louis, ed. *Muslim Identity and Social Change in Sub-Saharan Africa* (1993)

Cannuyer, Christian. *Coptic Egypt: The Christians of the Nile* (2001)

Comaroff, Jean, and John L. Comaroff. *Of Revelation and Revolution: Christianity, Colonialism, and Consciousness in South Africa* (1991)

Gifford, Paul. *African Christianity: Its Public Role* (1998)

Hackett, Rosalind I. J. *Art and Religion in Africa* (1999)

Harrison, Christopher. *France and Islam in Africa* (1988)

Hastings, Adrian. *The Church in Africa: 1450-1950* (1996)

Hiskett, Mervyn. *The Course of Islam in Africa* (1994)

_____. *The Sword of Truth* (1985)

Isichei, Elizabeth. *The History of Christianity in Africa: From Antiquity to the Present* (1995)

Laitin, David. *Hegemony and Culture: Politics and Religious Change among the Yoruba* (1986)

Lawson, E. Thomas. *Religions of Africa: Traditions in Transformation* (1998)

Levtzion, Nehemia, and Randall L. Pouwels, eds. *The History of Islam in Africa* (2000)

Mbiti, John S. *African Religions and Philosophy* (1992)

Peel, J. D. Y. *Religious Encounter and the Making of the Yoruba* (2001)

Ray, Benjamin C. *African Religions: Symbol, Ritual and Community* (1999)

Reynolds, Jonathan. *The Time of Politics (Zamanin Siyasa): Islam and the Politics of Legitimacy in Northern Nigeria, 1950-1966* (2001)

Robinson, David. *The Holy War of Umar Tal: The Western Sudan in the Mid-Nineteenth Century* (1992)

_____. *Muslim Societies in African History* (2004)

Rosander, Eva Evers, and David Westerlund. *African Islam and Islam in Africa: Encounters Between Sufis and Islamists* (1997)

Sannah, Lamin. *The Crown and the Turban: Muslims and West African Pluralism* (1997)

Searing, James F. *God Alone Is King: Islam and Emancipation in Senegal: The Wolof Kingdoms of Kajoor and Bawol, 1859-1914* (2001)

Soyinka, Wole. *Myth, Literature, and the African World* (1976)

Tamrat, Taddesse. *Church and State in Ethiopia: 1270-1527* (1972)

Thornton, John. *The Kongolese Saint Anthony: Dona Beatriz Kimpa Vita and the Antonian Movement, 1684-1706* (1998)

Tilley, Maureen A. *The Bible in North Africa: The Donatist World* (1997)

_____. *Donatist Martyr Stories: The Church in Conflict in Roman North Africa* (1998)

Vaillant, Janet. *Black, French, and African: A Life of Leopold Senghor* (1990)

Wilks, Ivor. *Wa and the Wala: Islam and Polity in Northwestern Ghana* (1989)

Works Focusing on Africa from 1500–1880

Alpers, Edward A. *Ivory and Slaves in East Central Africa* (1975)

Crais, Clifton. *White Supremacy and Black Resistance in PreIndustrial South Africa: The Making of the Colonial Order in the Eastern Cape, 1770-1865* (1992)

Curtin, Philip. *The Atlantic Slave Trade: A Census* (1972)

Daaku, Kwame Yeboa. *Trade and Politics on the Gold Coast: 1600-1720* (1970)

Eldredge, Elizabeth. *A South African Kingdom: The Pursuit of Security in Nineteenth-Century Lesotho* (1993)

Eltis, David, Stephen D. Behrendt, David Richardson, and Herbert S. Klein, eds. *The Trans-Atlantic Slave Trade: A Database on CD-Rom* (1999)

Hamilton, Carolyn. *The Mfecane Aftermath: Reconstructive Debates in Southern African History* (1996)

Kriger, Coleen. *Pride of Men: Iron Working in nineteenth century West Central Africa* (1999)

Last, Murray. *The Sokoto Caliphate* (1977)

Law, Robin. *The Slave Coast of West Africa, 1550-1750 (1991)*

Lindsay, Lisa. *Captives as Commodities* (2007)

Lovejoy, Paul. *Transformations in Slavery: A History of Slavery in Africa* (1983)

Manning, Patrick. *Slavery and African Life: Occidental, Oriental, and African Slave Trades* (1990)

Mostret, M. *Frontiers: The Epic of South Africa's Creation and the Tragedy of the Xhosa People* (1992)

Omer-Cooper, John D. *The Zulu Aftermath* (1966)

Miller, Joseph. *Way of Death: Merchant Capitalism and the Angolan Slave Trade, 1730-1830* (1996)

Northrup, David. *The Atlantic Slave Trade* (2001)

Ogot, B. A. *Kenya before 1900, Eight Regional Studies* (1976)

Peires, J. B. *The Dead Will Arise: Nongqawuse and the Great Xhosa Cattle Killing Movement of 1856-7* (1989)

Roberts, Andrew. *A History of the Bemba: Political Growth and Change in Northeastern Zambia before 1900 (1973)*

Rodney, Walter. *How Europe Underdeveloped Africa* (1981)

Shariff, Abdul. *Slaves, Spices and Ivory in Zanzibar* (1987)

Smith, Robert. *Warfare and Diplomacy in Pre-Colonial Africa* (1990)

Thornton, John. *Africa and Africans in the Making of the Atlantic World, 1400-1800* (1998)

Vansina, Jan. *Kingdoms of the Savannah* (1966)

Wilks, Ivor. *Asante in the Nineteenth Century* (1975)

Works Focusing on Africa since 1880

Amin, Samir. *Neo-Colonialism in West Africa* (1973)

Anunobi, Fredoline. *International Dimensions of African Political Economy: Trends, Challenges and Realities* (1994)

Austin, Ralph. *African Economic History: Internal Development and External Dependency* (1987)

Ayittey, George B. N. *Africa in Chaos* (1999)

Beinart, William, and Saul Dubow, eds. *Segregation and Apartheid in Twentieth-Century South Africa* (1995)

Berkeley, Bill. *The Graves Are Not Yet Full: Race, Tribe, and Power in the Heart of Africa* (2002)

Berry, Sara. *Fathers Work for Their Sons: Accumulation, Mobility and Class Formation in an Extended Yoruba Community* (1985)

Birmingham, David. *Portugal and Africa* (1999)

Boahen, A. Adu. *African Perspectives on Colonialism* (1989)

Bratton, Michael, and Nicholas van de Walle. *Democratic Experiments in Africa: Regime Transitions in Comparative Perspective* (1997)

Campbell, Greg. *Blood Diamonds: Tracing the Deadly Path of the World's Most Precious Stones* (2002)

Chazan, Naomi, ed. *Politics and Society in Contemporary Africa* (1992)

Davidson, Basil. *Black Man's Burden: Africa and the Curse of the Nation-State* (1992)

Decalo, Samuel. *Coups & Army Rule in Africa: Motivations & Constraints* (1990)

Falola, Toyin. *Nationalism and African Intellectuals* (2001)

Falola, Toyin, ed. *African Politics in Post Imperial Times: The Essays of Richard L. Sklar* (2001)

Fetter, Bruce, ed. *Colonial Rule in Africa: Readings from Primary Resources* (1999)

Golan, Dafnah. *Inventing Shaka* (1994)

Hargreaves, John. *Decolonization in Africa* (1988)

Herbst, Jeffrey. *States and Power in Africa* (2000)

Hochschild, Adam. *King Leopold's Ghost* (1999).

Iliffe, John. *The African Poor* (1987)

_____. *The African AIDS Epidemic: A History* (2006)

Kennedy, Dane. *Islands of White: Settler Society and Culture in Kenya and Southern Rhodesia, 1890-1939* (1987)

Maddox, Gregory, ed. *The Colonial Epoch in Africa* (1993)

Maloba, Wunyabari O. *Mau Mau and Kenya: An Analysis of a Peasant Revolt* (1998)

Manning, Patrick. *Francophone Sub-Saharan Africa, 1880-1985* (1988)

Mazrui, Ali, and Michael Tidy, *Nationalism and New States in Africa* (1989)

Meredith, Marlin. *The Fate of Africa: A History of Fifty Years of Independence* (2006)

Nkrumah, Kwame. *Neo-Colonialism: The Last Stage of Imperialism* (1965)

O'Collins, Robert, James M. Burns, and Erik K. Ching, (eds). *Historical Problems of Imperial Africa* (1996)

_____. *Historical Problems of Modern Africa* (1996)

Posel, Deborah. *The Making of Apartheid, 1948-1961: Conflict and Compromise* (1997)

Reno, William. *Warlord Politics and African States* (1999)

Royle, Trevor. *Winds of Change: The End of Empire in Africa* (1998)

Salih, M. A. Mohamed. *African Democracies and African Politics* (2001)

Springhall, John *Decolonization Since 1945: The Collapse of European Overseas Empires* (2001)

Sutherland, Bill, and Matt Meyer. *Guns and Gandhi in Africa* (2000)

Vail, Leroy, ed. *The Creation of Tribalism in Southern Africa* (1989)

Von Albertini, Rudolf. *European Colonial Rule, 1880-1940: The Impact of the West on India, Southeast Asia, and Africa* (1982)

Young, Crawford. *The African Colonial State in Comparative Perspective* (1994)

Credits

Bolesch; Peter Arnold, Inc. **Photo 12:** © AFP/COR-BIS. **Photo 13:** Thierry Rannou; Getty Images, Inc.–Liaison. **Photo 14:** Micheline Pelletier; Corbis/Bettmann. **Photo 15:** Pierre Burnaugh; PhotoEdit Inc.

Photo Essay II

Photo 1: Henri Lhote Collection. Musee de l'Homme, Paris, France. © Photograph by Erich Lessing/Art Resource, NY. **Photo 2:** (a,b) © The British Museum. **Photo 3:** Jonathan T. Reynolds. **Photo 4:** Philip Craven; Robert Harding World Imagery. **Photo 5:** Erik Gilbert. **Photo 6:** The Granger Collection, New York. **Photo 7:** Dagli Orti; Picture Desk, Inc./Kobal Collection. **Photo 8:** Robert J. Ross; Peter Arnold, Inc. **Photo 9:** British Information Services. **Photo 10:** © www.maopost.com. **Photo 11:** Jonathan T. Reynolds. **Photo 12:** © Reuters NewMedia Inc./CORBIS. **Photo 13:** Brennan Linsley; AP Wide World Photos. **Photo 14:** Courtesy of Ivy Omeife. **Photo 15:** Chris Brown; Stock Boston.

Inside front cover map: *How Big is Africa's* home site is www.bu.edu/africa/outreach where the map can be purchased and many other resources on Africa can also be found. © Boston University.

Index

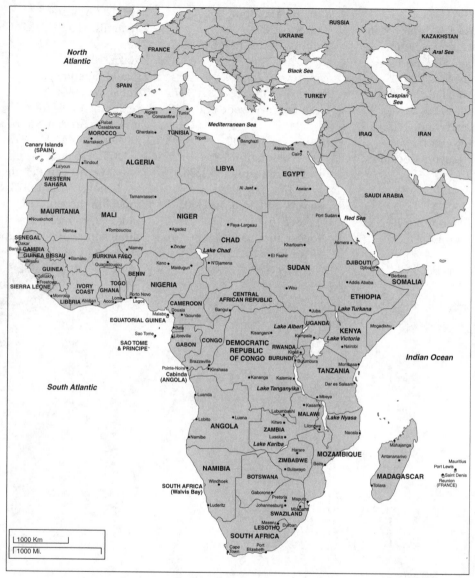

Contemporary Africa